# Forensic Investigations and Miscarriages of Justice

# Forensic Investigations and Miscarriages of Justice

## THE RHETORIC MEETS THE REALITY

BIBI SANGHA
KENT ROACH
ROBERT MOLES

IRWIN LAW

Forensic Investigations and Miscarriages of Justice: The Rhetoric Meets the Reality


Published in 2010 by
Irwin Law Inc.
Suite 206, 14 Duncan Street
Toronto, ON
M5H 3G8
www.irwinlaw.com

ISBN: 978-1-55221-186-1

**Library and Archives Canada Cataloguing in Publication**

Sangha, Bibi
Forensic investigations and miscarriages of justice : the rhetoric meets the reality / Bibi Sangha, Kent Roach, Robert Moles.

Includes bibliographical references and index.
Issued also in electronic format.
ISBN 978-1-55221-186-1

1. Judicial error—Great Britain. 2. Judicial error—Canada. 3. Judicial error—Australia. 4. Forensic sciences—Great Britain. 5. Forensic sciences—Canada. 6. Forensic sciences—Australia. 7. Criminal investigation—Great Britain. 8. Criminal investigation—Canada. 9. Criminal investigation—Australia. I. Roach, Kent, 1961– II. Moles, Robert N III. Title.

K5560.S25 2010 345'.05 C2010-905140-8

The publisher acknowledges the financial support of the Government of Canada through the Book Publishing Industry Development Program (BPIDP) for its publishing activities.

We acknowledge the assistance of the OMDC Book Fund, an initiative of Ontario Media Development Corporation.

Printed and bound in Canada.

2 3 4 5 14 13 12 11 10

*Footnotes and supplementary materials*:
Where available, the legal cases, commission reports, and articles referred to in this book have been set up on or linked to the Networked Knowledge website. There are also links and references to further materials and cases at this address: http://netk.net.au/home.asp.

Kent Roach gratefully acknowledges the financial assistance of Canada's Social Sciences and Humanities Research Council.

# Summary Table of Contents

FOREWORD *xvii*

ACKNOWLEDGMENTS *xxiii*

CHAPTER 1: Overview of the Book *1*

**PART ONE: THE RHETORIC: GUIDING PRINCIPLES** *25*

CHAPTER 2: Prosecutors and Expert Witnesses *27*

CHAPTER 3: Law on Miscarriages of Justice: Britain *55*

CHAPTER 4: Law on Miscarriages of Justice: Canada *91*

CHAPTER 5: Law on Miscarriages of Justice: Australia *133*

CHAPTER 6: Fraud in Criminal Proceedings *169*

**PART TWO: THE REALITY** *189*

CHAPTER 7: Investigations and Prosecutions *191*

CHAPTER 8: Forensic Science Issues *241*

CHAPTER 9: Forensic Pathology Issues *285*

**PART THREE: RESPONSES TO MISCARRIAGES OF JUSTICE** *323*

CHAPTER 10: Error Correction and Systemic Reform *325*

CHAPTER 11: Improving Forensic Science *369*

CHAPTER 12: Recommendations to Bring the Reality Closer to the Rhetoric *403*

TABLE OF CASES *415*

INDEX *425*

ABOUT THE AUTHORS *447*

# Detailed Table of Contents

FOREWORD *xvii*

ACKNOWLEDGMENTS *xxiii*

CHAPTER 1
**OVERVIEW OF THE BOOK** *1*

**A. Part One — The Rhetoric: Guiding Principles** *5*

1) Chapter 2: Prosecutors and Expert Witnesses *5*
2) Chapters 3 to 5: The Law Relating to Miscarriages of Justice *7*
3) Chapter 6: Fraud in Criminal Proceedings *9*

**B. Part Two — The Reality** *10*

1) Chapter 7: Investigations and Prosecutions *11*
   a) The British Experience *11*
   b) The Canadian Experience *13*
   c) The Australian Experience *13*
2) Chapter 8: Forensic Science *14*
   a) The British Experience *15*
   b) The Canadian Experience *15*
   c) The Australian Experience *16*
3) Chapter 9: Forensic Pathology *17*
   a) The British Experience *17*
   b) The Canadian Experience *19*
   c) The Australian Experience *20*

**C. Part Three — Responses to Miscarriages of Justice** *20*

1) Chapter 10: Error Correction and System Reforms *20*
2) Chapter 11 — Scientific Problems *21*
3) Chapter 12 — Recommendations *22*

PART ONE: THE RHETORIC: GUIDING PRINCIPLES 25

CHAPTER 2
PROSECUTORS AND EXPERT WITNESSES 27

A. Prosecutions 29

1) General Principles 29
2) Guidelines 30

B. Expert Witnesses 32

1) General Principles 32
2) Australia and Britain 33
3) Experts to Assist the Jury 35
4) Assessment of Reliability: Facts plus Reasoning Essential 35
5) Speculation Not Permitted: Probative versus Prejudicial Value 43
6) Duty of Disclosure 44

C. UK Law Commission Reforms 47

D. Canada 47

E. Codes of Conduct 50

1) Forensic Scientists and Pathologists 51

F. International Collaboration 53

G. ~~Conclusion~~ 53

CHAPTER 3
LAW ON MISCARRIAGES OF JUSTICE: BRITAIN 55

A. History of Appeals 56

B. Contemporary Appeal Provisions 59

C. The Process of Appeal 60

D. Appellate Discretion to Enter Acquittal or Order a New Trial 62

E. Crown Appeals 63

F. Where Appeals Have Been Exhausted 64

G. Procedural Error: The Right to a Fair Trial 65

H. Fresh Evidence on Appeal 69

I. Deference of Appeal Court to the Jury 72

J. Contemporary Standards 76

K. Meaning of "Beyond Reasonable Doubt" *77*

L. The Role of Defence Lawyers and Ineffective Assistance of Counsel *82*

M. Proper Investigations and the Need for Disclosure *85*

N. Prosecutorial Concessions *88*

O. Conclusion *90*

CHAPTER 4

**LAW ON MISCARRIAGES OF JUSTICE: CANADA** *91*

A. History of Appeals *94*

B. Contemporary Appeal Provisions *96*

C. Appeals by the Dead *99*

D. The Grounds for Appeal *99*

E. Appellate Discretion to Enter an Acquittal or Order a New Trial *106*

F. Prosecutorial Uses of Stays of Proceedings *109*

G. Pardons *110*

H. Crown Appeals *111*

I. Fresh Evidence on Appeal *112*

J. Contemporary Standards *113*

K. Meaning of Guilt beyond a Reasonable Doubt *113*

L. Crown Concessions *114*

M. When Appeals Have Been Exhausted: The Petition Procedure *114*

N. The Hearing of Appeals as a Result of the Petition Procedure *122*

O. The Role of the Prosecutor and Disclosure *123*

P. The Role of Defence Lawyers and Ineffective Assistance of Counsel *127*

Q. Expert Evidence *128*

R. Conclusion *131*

CHAPTER 5

**LAW ON MISCARRIAGES OF JUSTICE: AUSTRALIA** *133*

A. Contemporary Appeal Provisions *134*

B. Reopening an Appeal *138*

1) The Petition Procedure *141*
2) A Pardon Not Sufficient *145*
3) Royal Commissions *146*

**C. The Proviso** *147*

**D. Appellate Discretion to Enter an Acquittal or Order a New Trial** *151*

**E. Crown Appeals** *152*

**F. Importance of the Jury** *152*

**G. Error of Law and Procedural Error** *154*

**H. Fresh Evidence on Appeal** *156*

**I. The Role of the Prosecutor and Disclosure** *158*

**J. "The Prosecution" Includes Police and Others** *160*

**K. Public Confidence in the Trial Process** *161*

**L. The Role of Defence Lawyers and Ineffective Assistance of Counsel** *163*

**M. Fragmented Appellate Structure** *165*

**N. Conclusion** *167*

CHAPTER 6
**FRAUD IN CRIMINAL PROCEEDINGS** *169*

**A. Civil and Criminal Cases** *170*

**B. Reopening an Appeal** *171*

**C. Links from Australian to British Cases** *172*

**D. The Due Administration of Justice** *176*

**E. Public Law—Criminal** *177*

**F. Inherent Power** *185*

**G. Conclusion** *186*

**PART TWO: THE REALITY** *189*

CHAPTER 7
**INVESTIGATIONS AND PROSECUTIONS** *191*

**A. The Police** *193*

1) Investigations *194*

**B. Prosecutions** *195*

**C. The British Experience** *197*

1) IRA Bombing—The Birmingham Six *197*
2) IRA Bombing—The Guildford Four *199*
3) IRA Bombing—The Maguire Seven *199*
4) IRA Bombing—Judith Ward *200*
5) The Runciman Royal Commission on Criminal Justice's Response to Miscarriages of Justice *201*
6) Police Torture and Assault—The Case of Keith Twitchell *202*
7) Police Torture and Assault—The Case of Derek Treadaway *204*
8) Intimidation and False Confessions—The Case of Trevor Campbell *205*
9) Informer Identification Not Disclosed—The Case of Murphy, McMahon, and Cooper *207*
10) Police Notebooks Not Correct—The Case of Maynard, Dudley, Bailey, and Clarke *208*
11) An Odd Fellow—and Little Evidence—The Case of Barry George *210*

**D. The Canadian Experience** *211*

1) Tunnel Vision, Police Misconduct, and Inadequate Disclosure—The Case of Donald Marshall, Jr. *212*
2) Tunnel Vision and Jailhouse Informants—The Case of Guy Paul Morin *215*
3) Use of Science in Investigations, Eyewitness Evidence—The Case of Thomas Sophonow *217*
4) Tunnel Vision—The Cases of Gregory Parsons, Randy Druken, and Ronald Dalton *221*
5) Credibility of Police Witnesses and Non-disclosure—The Case of James Driskell *224*
6) Witnesses Pressured by Police—The Case of David Milgaard *227*

**E. The Australian Experience** *231*

1) Police Behaving Badly—Commissions and Inquiries *231*
2) Intimidation by Police—The Case of Rupert Maxwell Stuart *233*
3) Police Pressure to Obtain False Confession—The Case of John Button *233*
4) Faulty Reasoning by Police—The Case of Edward Splatt *234*
5) Fabricated Evidence—The Case of the Mickelberg Brothers *235*
6) Discredited Informer Evidence—The Case of Tim Anderson *236*
7) Manipulation of Mentally Fragile Person, Inadequate Disclosure—The Case of Andrew Mallard *237*

**F. Conclusion: Individual or Shared Failures?** *240*

CHAPTER 8

## FORENSIC SCIENCE ISSUES 241


A. **The British Experience** 244

1) Preliminary Test Misrepresented—The Case of the Birmingham Six 244
2) Fraudulent Scientific Evidence—The Case of the Maguire Seven 245
3) The Fraud Continued, Independence of Scientists—The Case of Judith Ward 246
4) Recommendations of the Runciman Royal Commission on Criminal Justice 248
5) Non-disclosure of Test Results—The Case of Sally Clark 250
6) Misuse of Probabilities—The Case of Angela Cannings 251
7) Professor Meadow's Discredited Evidence—The Case of Donna Anthony 252
8) Misreading of Bloodstain Pattern Analysis—The Case of Stephen Downing 253
9) Poor Scientific Methodology—The Case of Craig McCreight 254
10) New Forms of Scientific Evidence 254

B. **The Canadian Experience** 255

1) Misuse of Scientific Evidence (Hairs and Fibres)—The Case of Guy Paul Morin 255
2) Discredited Hair and Fibre Evidence—The Case of James Driskell 257
3) Misleading Serology—and DNA—The Case of David Milgaard 258
4) The Nature of Systemic Error 259

C. **The Australian Experience** 260

1) Multiple Scientific Errors—The Case of Edward Splatt 260
2) Scientific Tests False and Confusing—The Case of Lindy Chamberlain 267
   a) Kuhl's Evidence about Blood 269
   b) Professor Cameron's Evidence 271
   c) Professor Chaikin and Sergeant Cocks 272
   d) Summary by the Commissioner 273
3) Bloodstain Pattern Analysis—The Case of Alexander McLeod-Lindsay 275
4) Unreliable Scientific Evidence—The Case of Douglas Harry Rendell 276

D. **The DNA Experience** 277

1) Tunnel Vision—Frank Button: First DNA Exoneration Case in Australia 278
2) "Low-Copy Number" DNA—The Case of Sean Hoey, Northern Ireland 280

E. **Conclusion** 283

CHAPTER 9

FORENSIC PATHOLOGY ISSUES 285

A. The British Experience 287

1) Failure to Disclose Test Results—The Case of Sally Clark 289
2) Autopsy Findings Inadequate and Misleading—The Case of Patrick Nicholls 293
3) Inappropriate Diagnosis of Forcible Asphyxia—The Cases of Kenneth Fraser and Steven Puaca 295
4) Misinterpretation of Time of Death—The Case of Trevor Wickens 297

B. The Canadian Experience 299

1) Stomach Contents and Time of Death—The Case of Steven Truscott 299
2) Pediatric Cases—The Work of Dr. Charles Smith 303
   a) "No Possibility of a Fall"—The Case of Amber 304
   b) "99 Percent Certain of Non-accidental Injuries"—The Case of Nicholas 305
   c) "Sexual Assault by Babysitter"—The Case of Jenna 306
   d) "Stabbed Eighty Times"—The Case of Sharon 306
   e) "Rape and Murder of Four-Year-Old Niece"—The Case of Valin 307
   f) Recommendations by Justice Goudge 310

C. The Australian Experience 313

1) Frits Van Beelen 313
2) The South Australian Baby Deaths 317

D. Conclusion 322

PART THREE: RESPONSES TO MISCARRIAGES OF JUSTICE 323

CHAPTER 10

ERROR CORRECTION AND SYSTEMIC REFORM 325

A. The Move to Establish the Criminal Cases Review Commission 326

B. The Criminal Cases Review Commission 331

1) The Review Process 334
   a) Ways to Assess Possible Cases for Review 335
   b) Ways to Categorize Cases for Review 337
2) Case Review Personnel 339
3) Fresh Evidence 340
4) Deciding Whether to Refer 341
5) Judicial Review of Commission Decisions 342

6) References to and from the CCRC 343
7) The CCRC as "Last Resort" 343
8) Facts and Figures 344

**C. The Reception of Referrals from the CCRC in the Courts** 344

1) Differing Court Judgments 345
2) "Change of Law" Cases 345

**D. The CCRC Compared with the Scottish Criminal Cases Review Commission** 347

**E. Review of CCRC Practices** 347

**F. An Error Correction Commission Limited to Claims of Factual Innocence: The NCIIC** 351

**G. Innocence Projects and the Investigative Media** 356

**H. Striking the Appropriate Balance between Correction and Prevention of Miscarriages of Justice** 357

**I. The Limits of Error Correction Commissions in Achieving Systemic Reform** 358

**J. Systemic Reform Models** 361

1) The Canadian Public Inquiries 362

**K. Conclusion** 366

CHAPTER 11

**IMPROVING FORENSIC SCIENCE** 369

**A. Assessment of the State of the Science: The *NAS Report*** 371

**B. Specific Forensic Disciplines Reviewed by the *NAS Report*** 372

1) DNA 373
2) Controlled Substances 373
3) Fingerprints 374
4) Other Pattern Evidence 375
5) Reference Image Databases 375
6) Hair Evidence 375
7) Other Issues 376

**C. *NAS Report*'s Overall Assessment of the Use of Forensic Science in the Legal Process** 376

**D. Strengthening Oversight of Forensic Practices** 378

1) Accreditation 378

2) Standards and Guidelines *379*
3) Proficiency Testing *379*
4) Individual Certification *380*
5) Linking Funding with Improvements *380*

**E. Recommendations Related to Education and Training** *380*

1) Education and Training *381*
2) Research and Training *381*
3) Education in the Legal System *382*
4) Issues Pertaining to Death Investigators *382*
a) Shortage of Medical Examiners and Forensic Pathologists *383*
b) Difficulties in Implementing Standards and Accreditation *383*
c) Underdevelopment of Forensic Pathology Research *383*

**F. The Move to Evidence-Based and Research-Based Forensic Science** *384*

1) Limits of Relying on Published Research: A Cautionary Tale from Canada *385*
2) The Role of Proper Methodology and Full Disclosure in Promoting Evidence-Based Forensic Science *387*

**G. The Need to Adopt a Unified Vision to Reforming the Forensic Sciences** *387*

1) Central Regulation of the Forensic Sciences *391*
2) Limited Availability of Skilled Persons: The Case of Forensic Pathologists *391*
3) Forensic Science Centres and the Issue of Independence *393*

**H. The Role of the Defence in Challenging Forensic Science Presented by the State** *394*

**I. How Should Uncertainty in the Forensic Sciences Be Expressed?** *395*

**J. The Admissibility of Expert Evidence: The Judicial Gatekeeping Role** *396*

1) Varying Use of the *Daubert* Standards *398*

**K. Conclusion** *402*

CHAPTER 12
## RECOMMENDATIONS TO BRING THE REALITY CLOSER TO THE RHETORIC *403*

**A. Research and Review Developments in Forensic Science** *403*

**B. Audit Cases Involving Suspect Forms of Evidence** *405*

**C. Establish CCRC-type Bodies** *406*

**D. Obtain Better Judicial Control over Expert Evidence** *411*

**E. Impose a New Standard of Demonstrable Reliability** *413*

TABLE OF CASES *415*

INDEX *425*

ABOUT THE AUTHORS *447*

# Foreword

Mistakes sometimes occur. Even in a criminal justice system dedicated to fair trial within an accusatorial methodology and with a facility for appellate review.

Not long before I retired from the High Court of Australia, I had this truth brought home to me in a very personal way. In 2006, a bundle of appeal papers landed on my desk. They related to an appeal by a Western Australian prisoner, Andrew Mallard. He was challenging orders of the Court of Appeal of his state which had rejected his petition for the exercise of the royal prerogative of mercy in respect of his conviction of murder more than a decade earlier.

The written submissions in the case were extremely thorough. As I read them, features of the matter seemed familiar. I then noticed that the case had been before the High Court ten years earlier. Mr. Mallard had then unsuccessfully sought to obtain special leave to appeal from the appellate decision that had originally confirmed his initial conviction. Discreetly, the record and the submissions did not reveal the names of the Justices who had participated in the earlier refusal of leave.

I consulted the published schedules in the *Commonwealth Law Reports*. I found that I had been one of the judges who had so decided. The parties raised no objection to my participating in the second appeal.

Andrew Mallard had always protested his innocence. He gathered up support from his family and from a number of political, community, and media interests. This initiative led to a petition for a review of the case by the Executive. That petition, which followed a statutory procedure common throughout Australia, was referred to the highest appeal court of the state. When it was rejected, Andrew Mallard returned to the High Court. On this occasion, he was successful. Unanimously, the Court found a miscarriage of justice and set aside his conviction.[1] Soon after, he was released from prison. A judicial enquiry has since exonerated him of the murder of which he had been convicted. It is now accepted that he was innocent—just as he had earlier continuously protested.

To cope with the stresses of each day, professionals, such as surgeons and trial lawyers, have to inure themselves against excessive introspection. They need to sleep at night. They cannot continuously speculate on the possibility that they have been party to great mistakes and to wrongs to innocent people. So it was for me. When one case was finished, I moved to the next. I knew that I had given my all, as a lawyer or a judge, to contribute to lawful and just outcomes. I could not tarry in the past.

But when it is objectively demonstrated, and repeatedly affirmed, that an earlier trial which one had the power and responsibility to review has miscarried, it is natural that those involved should be haunted by the discovery. It is, as Justice Cory of the Supreme Court of Canada said in conducting a commission of enquiry into a suggested wrongful conviction, "the nightmare of all free people" to impose imprisonment wrongfully on an innocent person, let alone capital punishment which is now happily repealed in Australia as in most civilized countries. As Justice Cory declared: "It cannot be accepted or tolerated."

The authors of the book have examined the responses that have been adopted to the problem of miscarriages of justice in the United Kingdom, Canada, and Australia. A number of models have been enacted, partly because of the discovery (sometimes in old capital cases) that innocent people have been convicted and even executed, leaving a burden of guilt on those involved and on society. That burden can only be expiated partly by the adoption of techniques and institutions that will reduce the risk.

As the authors explain, the responses to miscarriages in criminal convictions include the following:

1) The ordinary facility of appeal against the conviction;
2) The opportunity to petition the Minister or the Governor (as Mr. Mallard did), normally with the result of a reference of the case back for *ab initio* review by the judiciary;

---

1 *Mallard v. The Queen* (2005), 224 C.L.R. 125.

3) The creation of *ad hoc* enquiries or royal commissions to revisit the circumstances of the case and the conviction, and to derive any lessons that should be drawn to improve the system of justice itself; and
4) The establishment of a new and specialised institution, independent of the Executive and of the courts, with power to receive complaints of alleged miscarriages and to reach conclusions and make recommendations.

The foremost models of this last kind are the Criminal Cases Review Commissions in the United Kingdom, one based in Birmingham, which deals with references from England, Wales, and Northern Ireland; and the other in Edinburgh, which deals with Scottish references. The authors strongly support the creation of such a review commission or commissions in Canada and in Australia. They point to many defects in the current institutional arrangements in each of those countries. They explain the advantages that a permanent body, such as a commission, would bring.

As one who has participated in many criminal appeals in a State Court of Criminal Appeal in Australia, I can attest to the serious-minded devotion of the judges in such reviews and to their shared appreciation of the solemn responsibility that the task involves. However, there are weaknesses in the appellate system, at least standing by itself. Mr. Mallard's earlier appeals are testimony of this.

A lot depends on the talent and discernment of the advocates presenting the challenge. There is a natural resistance to reopening a jury verdict, given that the jury is the constitutional tribunal of fact-finding and a traditional defender of the liberties of accused persons. As well, the growing jurisprudence of the High Court of Australia on the "proviso" will sometimes effectively deprive the accused of a lawful trial by jury and substitute a trial on the facts by appellate judges.[2]

Candour requires me to acknowledge that a busy day of criminal appeals, involving sometimes three, four, or more appeals against convictions, puts great pressure on the appeal bench. It virtually forces the sharing of responsibilities so that the three judges are dependent on the industry, perceptions, knowledge, and sensitivity of one of their colleagues, at least to some extent.

A particular problem for appellate review in Australia, described in these pages, is that the High Court of Australia has held that an intermediate court that has reached final, "perfected" orders cannot reopen them without express statutory authority. This is so no matter how plain and egregious are the mis-

2 *Weiss v. The Queen* (2005), 224 C.L.R. 300; *Nudd v. The Queen* (2006), 80 A.L.J.R. 614.

takes called to notice.[3] Moreover, the High Court cannot receive fresh evidence in an appeal, no matter how compelling that evidence may be. This is so because of the character of the strict "appeal" envisaged by the Constitution.[4] There are other problems with the appellate process. But enough is shown in this book to indicate why, in particular cases like Mr. Mallard's, there is a need for something more. That need has appeared most startlingly in recent times as a result of compelling forensic (usually DNA) evidence which tends to show that a wrongful conviction of an innocent person has occurred.[5] There are new and special problems in scientific forensic evidence.[6] There are potential benefits to safeguard the accused against unjust convictions. But there are also dangers that need to be allowed for.

The centrepiece of this book is the examination of the non-curial solutions that have been devised to address the nightmare of wrongful convictions, especially those resulting in prolonged imprisonment of an arguably innocent person. The dangers of petitions to the Executive and *ad hoc* enquiries are well explained, although sometimes these can vindicate the assertion of innocence. Experienced observers will quickly realize that assertions of innocence cannot always be accepted at face value. In any hotly contested criminal trial, resulting in a verdict of guilty and a conviction, the accused will normally continue to protest his or her innocence. Something more is needed to give rise to a well-founded concern that the protest may be justified and warrants redress.

In Australia, the Australian Law Reform Commission was charged to consider possible alternatives to royal commissions and *ad hoc* commissions of enquiry. Naturally, this directed attention to the models adopted in the United Kingdom following community concern about the outcome of the appellate process in a number of Irish cases. As the authors point out, the Royal Commission into the New South Wales Police Services, conducted by Justice James Wood, reported in 1997 that the current system provided a "substantial opportunity for any applicant armed with fresh evidence" to have his or her conviction reviewed on the merits.[7] A report of the Australian Law Reform Commission (ALRC) in 2003 recommended in favour of the establishment of

---

3 *Burrell v. The Queen* (2008), 238 C.L.R. 218, applying *Grierson v. The King* (1938), 60 C.L.R. 431.

4 *Eastman v. The Queen* (2000), 203 C.L.R. 1, applying *Mickelberg v. The Queen* (1989), 167 C.L.R. 259. *Cf. Eastman v. The Queen* (2009), 184 A. Crim. R. 1.

5 See, for example, *R. v. Button*, [2001] QCA 133 at para. 20, Williams J.A.

6 M.D. Kirby, "The Urgent Need for Forensic Excellence" (2008) 32 Criminal Law Journal 205 at 210.

7 *Royal Commission into the New South Wales Police Service: Final Report* (Sydney: Royal Commission into the New South Wales Police Force, 1997) at 447–50.

a national process to review post-conviction applications based on DNA evidence.[8] The limitation to DNA exculpation was understandable, given the context of a report dealing with genetic data. However, it raises difficulties given that sometimes non-genetic evidence can convincingly establish a likelihood of innocence, as it did in Mallard's case. Presumably, this is why the ALRC has now been asked to consider the problem in a wider context.

This book, and the opinions of the authors, will be of great value to the ALRC in developing its proposals. A particular problem exists in Australia, namely, that administration of the criminal law is still substantially the responsibility of states and territories. Creation of a national statutory agency that would have authority to act in each sub-national jurisdiction would present well-known jurisdictional difficulties.

In the United Kingdom, the permanent commissions have received an average of a thousand applications each year. Since their creation in 1997, they have completed a review of more than 12,000 cases. Of these, to 2010, they have referred no fewer than 420 cases for re-determination by the courts. In the result, the courts have quashed nearly 70 percent of the convictions so referred. It is not a high number, but it is high enough, especially for those involved, their families, and friends.

In olden times, judges and lawyers would acknowledge the risk that cases like that of Mallard would arise but shrug their shoulders. They would declare that we must accept a small number of wrongful convictions because of the inherent fallibility of any human institution.

In the current age, we are less inclined to adopt this attitude of resignation. In part, this change may be because judges and lawyers are less formalistic than they were in the past. In part, it is probably because of shocking and repeated reports demonstrating the wrongful conviction and punishment of innocent people. In part, it may have come about because media and academic scrutiny are less deferential today to institutions than once they were. And, in part, the changing view may have arisen because of the pervasive notion of fundamental human rights that instills and reinforces in the legal system a scrupulous attempt to repair arguable injustice wherever it can be demonstrated.

This book collects hundreds of cases across a number of jurisdictions where innocence has been protested and where "the system" has grappled with the challenge, sometimes convincingly and on other occasions, less so. Having

---

8 Australia, Law Reform Commission, *Essentially Yours, The Protection of Human Genetic Information in Australia* (ALRC Report 96) (Sydney: ALRC, 2003) at 19 (Recommendation 42-2).

viewed the scrutiny of challenged criminal convictions, as it is conducted behind the purple curtain, I acknowledge the earnest attempts on the part of many players to correct miscarriages of justice. At the same time, I must also accept the imperfections of the courts and of the present *ad hoc* arrangements to redress arguable injustice where it can be demonstrated.

In the end, the choice before society may be as brutal as this: do we care about the cases like Andrew Mallard's enough to draw the inference that there may be other such cases that never had a chance to secure similar repeated scrutiny? Where the prisoner was odd and could not convince anyone to support a protest? Where funds could not be procured to attract sufficient legal interest? Where the overworked *pro bono* schemes of the legal profession could not be engaged? Where the talent or commitment of the prisoner's supporters waned with the passing of time and a realization of the difficulty of storming this particular citadel? Where the overworked appeal judges missed factual inconsistencies or mistook the governing law? Where the High Court, emphasizing once again that it is not a general court of criminal appeal, declined special leave? Where the Executive could not be persuaded to institute a post-conviction enquiry? Where the government, in the midst of another law and order electoral campaign, declined to create an *ad hoc* enquiry or royal commission?

Do we care enough to create a permanent, expert agency with the patience, determination and skill to review contested convictions? In the United Kingdom, the answer to that question was in the affirmative. The result has not been an intolerable flood, exhausting the resources of the new commissions—it has been the correction of a number of wrongs. The authors make a compelling case for the establishment of such a body in Australia. It would re-affirm the commitment of our society to the highest standards of justice and law in all serious criminal proceedings. If, from the study of individual cases requiring action, systemic improvements of the criminal justice system can be identified and achieved, the result, in the end, may be an enhancement of justice beyond the sum of the cases like Mr. Mallard's which our institutions can correct. Affording real protections from serious miscarriages of criminal justice is a true test for the civilization of a society, such as ours. But will we face and meet that test?

*The Hon. Michael Kirby*
Justice of the High Court of Australia (1996–2009)
Sydney
July 2010

# Acknowledgements

The collaboration behind this book started when Kent Roach contacted Bibi Sangha and Bob Moles to see if they could write a paper on the Australian experience with forensic pediatric pathology and the courts as part of the research program of the Inquiry into Pediatric Forensic Pathology in Ontario, chaired by the Hon. Justice Stephen Goudge. Three years and several trips to Adelaide and Toronto later, the book has arrived. The authors thank Justice Goudge and all those associated with his inquiry for believing in the importance of comparative research and facilitating this collaboration. The views expressed here, like those expressed in the research studies conducted for the Goudge Inquiry, are of course only those of the researchers.

Dr. Harry Harding is a talented forensic scientist who believes that precision in writing will aid clarity in understanding. His critical comments on earlier drafts of the book have helped us to improve its content and the form in which it is expressed, and we are most grateful to him for that.

Julie Goulding is a Commissioner with the Criminal Cases Review Commission and she has added significantly to our understanding of the role and function of the Commission. John Wagstaff is a legal adviser to the Commission and he has generously assisted by responding to our queries and helping us track down elusive case reports. We are most grateful to Julie and John for their willingness to help us when there are no doubt many other pressures upon their valuable time.

Kent Roach would like to thank three excellent research assistants at the University of Toronto's Faculty of Law who assisted with this project over the last three years. They are Andrew Martin, Tom McConnell, and Owen

Goddard. He also acknowledges the generous financial assistance of Canada's Social Sciences and Humanities Research Council for funding this and other work on the comparative study of miscarriages of justice. He also thanks the staff of the Bora Laskin Library for their cheerful and diligent assistance. Finally, he is very grateful to his co-authors for taking him into their home as they worked on the book, as well as for a visit to the excellent vineyards surrounding the beautiful town of Adelaide.

We are all very grateful to Jeffrey Miller, Alisa Posesorski, and all the staff at Irwin Law for their excellent work on this publication. Irwin Law is to be congratulated for producing high quality books at prices that are extremely reasonable in the field of law. Alisa Posesorski and Kate Revington deserve special thanks for the excellent work they did in editing the work of three authors, all with different writing styles.

We hope that this book is of some use to all those that work to prevent and remedy miscarriages of justice. Such people include lay persons and prisoners who may not have ready access to a full law library. In an effort to assist in such efforts, Bob Moles has compiled many of the online sources cited in this book and they are available at his Networked Knowledge website, online: http://netk.net.au and http://netk.net.au/ForensicInvestigationsHome.asp.

Finally, we thank former Australian High Court Justice, Michael Kirby, for his willingness to consider our work worthy of a foreword by him. He is, without doubt, one of the most well known judges of the modern era, and this book is testimony to many of his judgments in which he has expressed views about the adequacy of the legal system in protecting the rights of the vulnerable. He too has many demands upon his time and we are grateful to him for including this work in his busy schedule.

Bibi Sangha<br>
Kent Roach<br>
Robert Moles<br>
Adelaide and Toronto<br>
July, 2010

CHAPTER I

# Overview of the Book

This book discusses miscarriages of justice in three of the major common law jurisdictions—Britain, Canada, and Australia. The objective is to make clear that despite the rules laid down by statutes and decided cases to ensure that criminal trials are properly conducted (the rhetoric), there are many instances where those rules have not been properly applied (the reality).

There is now sufficient experience in all three jurisdictions to show that people have been wrongly convicted of crimes and for us to critically explore pertinent issues. In all three jurisdictions, there have been cases where investigations have fundamentally miscarried and where expert witnesses have given evidence that has been either fraudulent or wrong. Our objective is to bring some clarity to where we are in recognizing and dealing with these problem cases. There are marked differences between the jurisdictions in the procedures available to identify possible errors. We think that the jurisdictions can learn from one another in determining how best to move forward.

We have selected cases as illustrative of the issues and problems that arise. In many respects, the lessons to be learned and the guidance to be gained are not jurisdictionally specific—after all, the laws of physics and of human nature are indifferent to many of the features of those jurisdictions which make them most distinctive.

Each of the three nations is a major common law jurisdiction with a sufficient degree of similarity in its processes to be recognizable, one to the other. The standards that govern police and forensic investigations and prosecutions in each of them have common features. Expert witnesses often give evidence in more than one of them and feel confident about what is required of them.

There are differences in nomenclature between the jurisdictions. The "Crowns" referred to in Canada are often called "prosecutors" elsewhere. The state or territory Supreme Court in Australia is the equivalent of the Crown court in Britain and the provincial courts in Canada. The final appellate court in Australia is the High Court. The final appellate court in Britain and in Canada is called the "Supreme Court."[1]

A word of caution is also in order: by studying "miscarriages of justice," we are looking across a broad range of cases and considering those particular cases where criminal trials and appeals have gone wrong—as identified by the systems' own rules.[2] We are aware of broader debates about the precise meaning of miscarriage of justice. Some argue that miscarriage of justice should be defined broadly to include convictions under unjust laws or through discriminatory systems[3] while others, often influenced by American innocence projects and DNA exonerations, argue that there should be a narrower focus on cases where the accused has been established to be "factually innocent."[4] This book does not attempt to resolve this debate.[5] Nevertheless, it accepts that a

> "miscarriage of justice" is an expression which, although very familiar, is not a legal term of art and has no settled meaning. Like "wrongful conviction" it can be used to describe the conviction of the demonstrably innocent . . . . But, again like "wrongful conviction," it can be and has been used to describe cases in which defendants, guilty or not, certainly should not have been convicted.[6]

---

1 In October 2009, the House of Lords became known as the Supreme Court; see *Constitutional Reform Act 2005* (U.K.), 2005, c. 4.

2 A good theoretical discussion of the conceptual issues involved in "miscarriages of justice" can be found in Charles J. Ogletree Jr. & Austin Sarat, eds., *When Law Fails: Making Sense of Miscarriages of Justice* (New York: New York University Press, 2009).

3 Clive Walker, "Miscarriages of Justice in Principle and Practice" in Clive Walker & Kier Starmer, eds., *Justice in Error* (London: Blackstone, 1993) at 37. See also Michael Naughton, *Rethinking Miscarriages of Justice beyond the Tip of the Iceberg* (New York: Palgrave Macmillan, 2007) at 41*ff.*, proposing an examination of "routine" and "mundane" miscarriages of justice that would involve all successful appeals.

4 Barry Scheck, Peter Neufeld, & Jim Dwyer, *Actual Innocence* (New York: Doubleday, 2000); Daniel Medwed, "Innocentrism" 2008 U. Ill. L. Rev. 1549; Michael Naughton, ed., *The Criminal Cases Review Commission: Hope for the Innocent?* (Houndsmill: Palgrave Macmillan, 2009) [Naughton, *Hope*].

5 But for a discussion of the definition of miscarriages of justice, see Kent Roach & Gary Trotter, "Miscarriages of Justice in the War against Terror" (2005) 109 Penn. St. L. Rev. 967. On the dilemmas of either ignoring or declaring innocence, see Kent Roach, "Exonerating the Wrongfully Convicted: Do We Need Innocence Hearings?" in Margaret Beare, ed., *Honouring Social Justice* (Toronto: University of Toronto Press, 2008) [Roach, "Exonerating"].

6 *R. v. Secretary of State for the Home Department, Ex parte Mullen*, [2004] UKHL 18 at para. 9; Lord Bingham [*Mullen*].

The judge went on to explain that in speaking of those who ought not to have been convicted, he included those cases where the evidence against them may have been fabricated or perjured; their convictions may have been based upon flawed expert evidence; evidence helpful to them may have been concealed or withheld; the jury may have been the subject of malicious interference, or there may have been some judicial unfairness or misdirection. He said that in such cases something has seriously gone wrong in either the investigation of the offence or the conduct of the trial resulting in the conviction of someone who should not have been convicted, although as he made clear, "it may, or more often may not, be possible to say that a defendant is innocent, but it is possible to say that he has been wrongly convicted."[7] No doubt, the advent of DNA technology has improved the chances of proving innocence in some cases. However DNA will not be available in many cases and even in cases where it was available, it may not have been retained.

In this book we restrict our focus to those cases which the respective systems have already identified as being miscarriages of justice. A miscarriage of justice, in our view, includes both the conviction of the innocent and other serious justice errors, such as those arising from lack of full disclosure and the giving of unreliable testimony. In accordance with the standard view of such things, a case cannot be identified as a miscarriage of justice until after normal appeal procedures have been exhausted and the errors have still remained unidentified or uncorrected. Until then, we merely have "alleged" miscarriage of justice cases. A case becomes a miscarriage of justice when subsequently error is recognized and the conviction is overturned. It follows that a jurisdiction such as Australia where it is more difficult to have such cases returned to the courts because the decision is reserved to the Executive, will have fewer miscarriage of justice cases for us to consider than those such as Britain where, since 1997, an independent commission, the Criminal Cases Review Commission, has a mandate to return cases to the appellate courts in cases where there is a real possibility that the conviction would not be upheld if reconsidered by the courts.[8] Canada lies somewhere in between Australia and Britain under a procedure that allows the federal Minister of Justice to conduct or delegate an investigation into a case where appeals have been exhausted and to order a new trial or a new appeal "if the Minister is satisfied that there is a reasonable basis to conclude that a miscarriage of justice likely occurred."[9]

---

7 *Ibid.* at para. 4.

8 *Criminal Appeal Act 1995* (U.K.), 1995, c. 35, s. 13.

9 Canada, *Criminal Code*, R.S.C. 1985, c. C-34, s. 696.3(3)(a).

Lest it be suggested that our approach is defence oriented, we would argue that everyone in the community should have an interest in proper outcomes from the criminal legal process. Wrongful convictions, and their re-investigation and correction, take up considerable resources apart from issues of compensation and the social cost involved. Retrospective reviews take up scarce resources (investigatory and forensic) that otherwise might be directed to dealing with new cases. As Cory J. of Canada said:

> It cannot be forgotten that a wrongful conviction is as much a wrong to the administration of justice and to our society, as it is to the individual prisoner. Wrongful imprisonment is the nightmare of all free people. It cannot be accepted or tolerated.[10]

In Canada especially, prosecutors and the police have to their credit expressed an increased awareness of the reality of wrongful convictions and of means to prevent them in the future.[11]

The book is divided into three broad themes:

- *Part One — The Rhetoric*: This is an account of the principles claimed by the legal system to guide its conduct. We should know how things *ought* to be done before we discuss examples of shortcomings. This part also discusses the legal procedures available in each jurisdiction to identify wrongful convictions.
- *Part Two — The Reality*: Here, we set out the cases on each of our main topics (investigations, forensic science, and forensic pathology) jurisdiction by jurisdiction (Britain, Canada, and Australia) in which the principles set out in Part One have not been properly followed.
- *Part Three — Institutional Responses*: Here, we look at the way in which each system has responded to the growing awareness of miscarriages of justice. The important question, of course, is this: What more needs to be done?

---

10 Justice Peter Cory, "Compensation Recommendation," *The Inquiry Regarding Thomas Sophonow: The Investigation, Prosecution, and Consideration of Entitlement to Compensation* (Winnipeg: Manitoba Justice, 2001).

11 Federal Provincial and Territorial Heads of Prosecutions, *Report on the Prevention of Miscarriages of Justice* (Ottawa: Department of Justice, 2004), online: www.justice.gc.ca/eng/dept-min/pub/pmj-pej/pmj-pej.pdf. For some criticisms of the report, see also Christopher Sherrin, "Comment on the *Report on the Prevention of Miscarriages of Justice*" (2007) 52 Crim. L.Q. 140.

## A. PART ONE — THE RHETORIC: GUIDING PRINCIPLES

### 1) Chapter 2: Prosecutors and Expert Witnesses

We discuss the leading case on the role of the prosecutor in criminal cases: *Boucher v. The Queen*,[12] a Canadian case which has been accepted in each of the other jurisdictions. It said that it could not be overemphasized that the purpose of a criminal prosecution is not to obtain a conviction, but to lay before a jury what the Crown considers to be credible evidence relevant to what is alleged to be a crime. There is no doubt that this sentiment has been repeated in the words of legal judgments,[13] as well as in ethical standards and codes of conduct in Britain and Australia.

There is no difficulty in identifying the appropriate standards in each of these areas. Indeed, it seems to be a right of passage for any prosecutor or forensic expert to state the standards in a clear, forthright, and non-controversial manner. Police forces and prosecutors state frequently that they are objective, fair, unbiased, and open in their dealings with the public and potential suspects. Many senior prosecutors have written papers on the prosecution's duty of disclosure. The laws relating to the admissibility of evidence and the ethical duties proclaimed by bar associations and law societies for the conduct of advocates, solicitors, and barristers aim to ensure fairness in the conduct of criminal cases and the right of people appearing before the courts to be fairly and competently represented. Forensic services are awash with mission statements and ethical codes that are intended to ensure that expert evidence is objectively arrived at, properly substantiated, balanced, and complete in all aspects.

We discuss the fact that in dealing with serious crimes, all those involved should have a good knowledge of the basic principles used by the specialists they call upon to advise them. We discuss the role of expert witnesses and the tests that the courts have laid down to try to ensure that any expert evidence given to the court is relevant and reliable. It is fair to say that, in light of recent experiences of miscarriages of justice, each of the three jurisdictions is carefully examining the issues under discussion here to see how things can be improved.

The law says that experts who assist the court must be objective and impartial as between the defence and prosecution. They are there to inform the court of their findings and observations, and to assist the jury to understand

---

12 *Boucher v. The Queen*, [1955] S.C.R. 16.

13 For example, in Britain, *Randall v. The Queen*, [2002] 2 Cr. App. R. 17; in Australia, *Libke v. The Queen*, [2007] HCA 30.

what their observations mean. Although called by the prosecution or defence, they are the property of neither. They have a duty to ensure that their evidence is not used in a misleading manner.

It was the British Attorney General who said:

> One particular issue was whether we should accord to experts the deference that in the past we had. There is nothing new in this. Some will remember, at least by account, Sir Bernard Spilsbury, who acted in the case of Dr Crippen, the Brides in the Bath murders and the Brighton Trunk murders, amongst many very famous cases. Juries were in awe of him and he was considered invincible in court. Yet, even in the later years of his life (he died in 1947) judges began to express concern about this. His dogmatic manner and unbending belief in his own infallibility gave rise to criticism and some research has indicated that his inflexibility led to miscarriages of justice.[14]

We suggest that the problem of the egotistical or incompetent expert is sometimes compounded by those who lack the confidence to challenge the expert:

> The court does not rise in indignation, the lawyers shaking their fists at the misleading expert. Opposing counsel does not retaliate with the obvious retort, nor ask the revealing, searching question. More often than not, the misleading testimony becomes accepted fact in the eyes of the court. Given the motivation to mislead, the expert witness learns, through ordinary experience in the courts, how to do so effectively.[15]

In the Canadian case of Dr. Charles Smith, who was found to have made many errors in his autopsies in pediatric cases, Goudge J., who had conducted an inquiry into his work, said, "he achieved the status of a leading expert in the field in large part because there was no one who had the training, experience,

---

14 The Rt. Hon. Lord Goldsmith, "Expert Evidence—The Problem or the Solution?" in "The Role of Expert Evidence and Its Regulation" (The John Bolton Memorial Lecture, Academy of Expert Witnesses, 25 January 2007). In Canada, Goudge J. frequently referred to Dr. Smith as "arrogant," "dogmatic," "disorganized," and given to making "false" and "misleading" statements: see, for example, *Report of the Inquiry into Pediatric Forensic Pathology in Ontario: Executive Summary*, vol. 1 (Toronto: Ontario Ministry of the Attorney General, 2008) at 16–19 [Goudge Inquiry].

On Spilsbury, see Colin Evans, *The Father of Forensics: How Sir Bernard Spilsbury Invented Modern CSI* (Thriplow, UK: Icon Books, 2006). For a more critical evaluation, see Andrew Rose, *Lethal Witness—Sir Bernard Spilsbury, Honorary Pathologist* (Stroud, UK: Sutton, 2007).

15 David S. Bell, "The Expert Misleads. The Court Follows" (1995) The Australian Journal of Forensic Sciences 59 at 60.

and expertise to take him on." While the comments of Goudge J. are directed to Dr. Smith's colleagues in the medical community, we think they are equally applicable to the lawyers who failed to properly research and challenge his evidence at the time.

### 2) Chapters 3 to 5: The Law Relating to Miscarriages of Justice

Here, we set out the principles laid down in the legislation and cases, from each of the jurisdictions, concerning what is involved in an appeal and what amounts to a miscarriage of justice. It is interesting to consider that the very idea of appeals in criminal cases is of relatively recent origin. It was previously thought that to overturn a jury verdict on appeal was an unwarranted intrusion into the independence of the jury.

The principles laid down by the highest courts make it clear that fabricating evidence, withholding evidence that might assist someone who has been accused of serious crimes, or providing false or misleading scientific evidence, is not acceptable. The presumption of innocence and the onus of proof (the prosecution must prove its case beyond reasonable doubt) means that an accused person should be given the benefit of any reasonable doubt. An exception in all jurisdictions is made for any error at trial perceived by the appeal courts to be harmless because it does not cause any miscarriage of justice. So, unless one can be confident that a conviction is soundly based, it is liable to be set aside. The legal principles concerning a fair trial have a certain resonance across each of the three jurisdictions.

Of the three jurisdictions, Britain has developed the most substantial experience in dealing with miscarriage of justice cases. The United Kingdom set up the Criminal Cases Review Commission (CCRC) in 1997 following the overturning of the convictions in a number of IRA bombing cases.[16] The number of post-appeal applications and referrals increased dramatically since the CCRC took over the process previously reserved for the Home Secretary.[17] CCRC referrals resulted in some 250 convictions being overturned in the first ten years of the commission's operation. The CCRC has given the appellate courts much work to do and this is why, in each of our chapters, we look to the British experience before looking to that of Canada and Australia.

In Canada, there have been a number of public inquiries into wrongful convictions in recent years. They have each taken place *after* the convictions

---

16 The Scottish Criminal Cases Review Commission (SCCRC) was established in 1999.

17 Laurie Elks, *Righting Miscarriages of Justice?* (London: Justice, 2008) at 334 [Elks].

were overturned by the courts. The inquiries, sometimes taking years to reach their findings, have been major undertakings. They have ensured that the issue of wrongful convictions has been very much in the public mind. There is also a voluntary organization, AIDWYC, which has campaigned on these issues and been responsible for bringing many cases back before the courts.[18] As a result, a significant number of high-profile cases have been overturned and substantial compensation payments made.

In Australia, there is no publicly funded body (such as the CCRC) and no pre-eminent voluntary body such as AIDWYC to bring suspect cases back before the courts.[19] In addition, Australian legal procedures make it much more difficult to obtain reviews of questionable cases.

In each of the three jurisdictions, the contributions from each of the final courts of appeal tend to be more strategic and symbolic as they each deal with relatively small numbers of cases. The bulk of the work in each of the jurisdictions has to be done by the intermediate appellate courts. Britain has a unified, full-time Court of Appeal. Canada is a federal system with full-time appellate judges to hear criminal appeals. In Australia, also a federal jurisdiction, there are some states and territories where the appeal court is comprised of trial judges who on occasion sit together to hear an appeal.[20] This means that upon their appointment as a judge of the Supreme Court (to conduct trials), they can immediately sit to hear appeals. Such an appellate structure can affect the quality of the jurisprudence produced which is why we discuss relatively few intermediate appellate cases in the chapter on Australian law. By comparison, most of the cases discussed in the British chapter are those from the Court of Appeal.[21] Cases in Canada are also heard by separate courts of appeal with considerable experience in criminal appeals.

From our analysis we will see that one outstanding issue is the way in which prosecutors in Britain and to a lesser extent Canada have been prepared

18 AIDWYC—Association In Defence of the Wrongly Convicted.

19 On the emerging role of innocence projects in Australia, see Lynne Weathered, "The Emerging Role of Innocence Projects in the Correction of Wrongful Conviction in Australia" (2003) 12 Griffith L.R. 64. See also Lynne Weathered, "Does Australia Need a Specific Institute to Correct Wrongful Convictions?" (2007) 40 Aust'l. & N.Z. J. Crim. 179.

20 For example, South Australia, Tasmania, and the Northern Territory. See also Stephen Charles, "The First Decade of the Victorian Court of Appeal" in Chris Corns & Gregor Urbas, eds., *Criminal Appeals 1907–2007: Issues and Perspectives* (2008) 26 Law in Context 21.

21 The Hon. Michael Kirby, "Permanent Appellate Courts—The NSW Court of Appeal 20 Years On" (1987) 61 Austl. L. J. 391.

to make concessions in the light of challenges to convictions. Prosecutors have been less prepared to do so in Australia.

Process is important. In all jurisdictions, it is made clear that the task for the appellate courts is not to determine guilt or innocence, but whether or not the person convicted has had a fair trial. The reluctance of the courts to concern themselves explicitly with innocence can be frustrating for the wrongly convicted who often want to clear their name. In addition, findings of innocence are generally required for a person to receive compensation.[22] The British CCRC has been criticized in some quarters for not being concerned enough about the innocence of applicants.[23] At the same time, the conviction of an innocent person is included in any definition of a miscarriage of justice.[24] Moreover, there may be many cases where innocence or guilt is impossible to establish in a definite sense and there is an inherent value in fair process regardless of innocence.

The cases make it clear that we must ensure that the process of investigation accords with basic tenets of scientific and legal knowledge. British law states most clearly that it is contemporary scientific knowledge which must be applied in an appeal and not that which might have been acceptable at the time of the trial.

### 3) Chapter 6: Fraud in Criminal Proceedings

Here we raise a fundamental but not well-recognized issue. Suppose that there has been fraud committed in the presentation of a case at trial, but in circumstances where there is no right of appeal. In a British case it was in relation to charges of driving while over the limit. Blood tests had returned positive results. The accused pleaded guilty. After conviction it was found that the swabs used in taking the blood had contained alcohol, so the results were worthless. Yet there was no provision in the law for an appeal against a guilty plea. Faced with the dilemma the British judges virtually had to invent a procedure so that they could do justice in the case. In Australia there are other real difficulties in getting miscarriage of justice cases back to court.

In this section, we raise the question whether there is a fundamental right to be heard where a person alleges that his or her conviction has been obtained by fraud. We emphasize that this is *not* an appeal, for appeal rights exist where a conviction has been more regularly obtained. We suggest that where a pur-

22 Roach, "Exonerating," above note 5.
23 Naughton, *Hope*, above note 4.
24 *Mullen*, above note 6 at para. 4.

ported conviction has been obtained by fraud, the proceedings were in effect a nullity, and may be set aside even in the absence of any further right of appeal. As is said in a number of cases, the job of the judges is to do justice, and they should not allow procedural rules to prevent them from achieving that goal.

Although there can be many robust discussions about applicable standards, or what *ought* to be done, the main focus of Part One is to explain what the standards are. The next step, which we take in Part Two, is to explain the circumstances in which educated and responsible people have sometimes failed to act in accordance with those standards.

## B. PART TWO — THE REALITY

Here, we look at the cases that have been identified as being miscarriages of justice. It is important to make it clear that some of the cases referred to in Part One have arisen in the normal course of appeals where convictions have been set aside. Others came about because after the first appeal it became apparent that all was not well with the conviction and through various processes, the matter was returned to the courts for further consideration.

However, in all of the cases referred to in Part Two, convictions were upheld on the first appeal. Our particular focus here is on that class of cases where there was some error at trial not detected in the first appeal.

We set out our analysis in relation to three significant areas where errors can occur:

- Chapter 7 deals with investigations and prosecutions;
- Chapter 8 deals with forensic science cases;
- Chapter 9 deals with forensic pathology cases.

In each chapter, we look at the relevant category of cases jurisdiction by jurisdiction.

We begin each chapter by first looking to the British cases because that is where problems have generally been exposed in the most comprehensive manner. We then look in each chapter to Canada, which has made significant progress in recognizing miscarriages of justice and which has been amplified through the work of its public inquiries. Finally, in each chapter we look to the Australian experience where the ability to deal effectively with miscarriages of justice is more difficult and where there have been fewer examples of the recognition of error.

In each jurisdiction, there have been headline cases where errors at many levels have appeared in the one case; where errors of investigation have either led to or been compounded by errors of science. It is for this reason that some cases will be referred to in more than one chapter. Some of the common themes running through the cases are loss of objectivity, lack of disclosure, lack of fidelity to a scientific approach, overconfident scientists, and difficulties in challenging seemingly accomplished forensic witnesses presented by the prosecution.

### 1) Chapter 7: Investigations and Prosecutions

A common theme to have emerged in all jurisdictions in this area is tunnel vision and a lack of objectivity. This is where prosecutors and investigators become too attached to a particular resolution of an issue before the evidence really warrants it and are then drawn to tailor the evidence to attain their desired outcome. There have also been many cases where the loss of objectivity has led to a failure to disclose information that might have been of assistance to an accused person. Sometimes witnesses, wittingly or otherwise, have given unreliable evidence because they have had something to gain and where their interest in the matter has been hidden from the jury.

#### a) The British Experience

A major turning point came with the overturning in the late 1980s and early 1990s of the convictions in the IRA cases from the 1970s: the Guildford Four, the Birmingham Six, the Maguire Seven, and the M62 (Judith Ward) bombings. As it turned out the cases had involved fraudulent scientific evidence and undue pressure to extract confessions or admissions. After the exposure of the errors in those cases, the British government took steps that eventually led to the establishment of the Criminal Cases Review Commission (CCRC).[25] The

25 The Guildford Four: Convicted in 1975 of the bombing of two Guildford pubs; in 1989 their convictions were quashed. The Birmingham Six: Convicted in 1975 of causing explosions and killing people in pub explosions in 1974, they had their convictions quashed in 1991. The Maguire Seven: Convicted in 1976 of possession of the nitroglycerine used in the bombings of the two Guildford pubs, their convictions were quashed in 1991. Judith Ward: Convicted of the M62 and other bombings in 1973–74, her convictions were overturned in 1993 in part because of her psychological vulnerabilities. The CCRC was set up as a result of *The Report of the Royal Commission on Criminal Justice*, Cm 2263 (London: H.M.S.O., 1993) [Runciman Report]. It is interesting to note that Lord Runciman was formerly chairman of the Securities and Investment Board, and as he put it, "I knew next to nothing about the criminal justice system." W.G. Runciman, "An Outsider's View of the Criminal Justice System" (1994) 57 Mod. L. Rev. at 1.

CCRC investigations and reports in its first ten years have given insights into investigations and prosecutions that had occurred in Britain over the previous fifty years.[26]

We set the scene with one of the early cases where public revulsion at what occurred almost certainly skewed the whole of the subsequent process, including a trial which was unbalanced and unfair. In 1998 it was revealed that in the early 1950s, the judge in the trial of Derek Bentley (who had been hanged for the murder of PC Miles) had failed to explain to the jury what the words "beyond reasonable doubt" meant. As the Court of Appeal said in overturning Bentley's conviction:

> . . . it is with genuine diffidence that the members of this court direct criticism towards a trial judge widely recognized as one of the outstanding criminal judges of this century. But we cannot escape the duty of decision. In our judgment the summing up in this case was such as to deny the appellant that fair trial which is the birthright of every citizen.[27]

It took the best part of fifty years to acknowledge the evident deficiencies in the trial judge's handling of the case and his unbalanced summing up in favour of the police and prosecutors. In 1998 the court overturned the conviction of Mahmoud Mattan (a Somali man), who had been convicted and hanged in 1962 for the murder of a female shopkeeper by cutting her throat.[28] Subsequently, it was revealed that the chief Crown witness had most probably committed the crime.

In recent years it was revealed that the West Midlands Major Crime Squad in the 1970s and 1980s had engaged in practices that involved the *torture* of suspects.[29]

There have been a number of cases where investigators and prosecutors withheld evidence that would have assisted the defence. Sometimes, prison informants were found to have been promised undisclosed benefits in return for their evidence incriminating various people accused of serious crimes.

---

26 Elks, above note 17. The CCRC is not, however, without its critics who point out that it does not refer 96 percent of the applications it receives or concern itself with factual innocence. See Naughton, *Hope*, above note 4.

27 *R. v. Bentley (Deceased)*, [1998] EWCA Crim 2516.

28 *R. v. Mattan (Deceased)*, [1998] EWCA Crim 676.

29 *R. v. Keith Twitchell*, Court of Appeal (Criminal Division) 26 October 1999; David Kyle, "Correcting Miscarriages of Justice: The Role of the Criminal Cases Review Commission" (2004) 52 Drake L. Rev. at 657–76.

### b) The Canadian Experience

We see here examples of the tenacity with which investigators and prosecutors have continued to maintain their confidence in the original verdicts, despite sometimes compelling evidence to the contrary.

The Marshall Inquiry found that investigating officers had acted unprofessionally and that their investigation merely sought evidence to support their theory about the killing and failed to consider the evidence that did not support it. The investigators failed to disclose evidence that could have revealed the late Donald Marshall's innocence before he spent ten years in prison for a crime he did not commit. The Sophonow Inquiry found that the causes of the wrongful conviction included unreliable jailhouse informants; inadequate disclosure by the prosecution, and tunnel vision on the part of the police and the prosecution.

In the Morin Inquiry, Commissioner Fred Kaufman stated that the fact that one of the investigators still believed that the informants were telling the truth, in the face of DNA evidence establishing Morin's innocence, amounted to tunnel vision of "the most staggering proportions."[30] This case also involved the presentation of unreliable hair and fibre evidence that was misunderstood by all participants in the trial that convicted Morin. Former Chief Justice Lamer, in his inquiry into a number of wrongful convictions, referred to public pressure to find and convict a perpetrator, investigative theories which he thought were "far-fetched," and the demonizing of a suspect which might lead to corrupt practices. He warned of a "vicious circle" of "tunnel vision" that "is generated by a police and prosecutorial culture that allows the subconscious mind to rationalize a biased approach to the evidence. Moreover, it is mutually re-enforcing among police officers, among prosecutors and in the interaction between these two groups of professionals. It may even affect judges."[31]

### c) The Australian Experience

The investigations into the cases of Lindy Chamberlain and Edward Splatt were examined in considerable detail in royal commissions in the 1980s. Chamberlain was said to have murdered her young baby by cutting her throat at a camp in the Australian outback. Splatt was said to have raped and murdered an elderly woman who lived close to where he lived and worked. In both cases, there were found to be extensive errors by the investigators as well as by

---

30 *Report of the Kaufman Commission on Proceedings Involving Guy Paul Morin* (Toronto: Ministry of the Attorney General, 1998), Executive Summary at 11 [Morin Inquiry].

31 *The Lamer Commission of Inquiry Pertaining to Ronald Dalton, Gregory Parsons and Randy Druken* (St. John's, NL: Department of Justice, 2006) at 71.

the scientists involved. The royal commissions found that in each case, much of the evidence that led to the convictions was fundamentally flawed.

In Western Australia, Andrew Mallard, who was suffering from a psychiatric condition at the time of his arrest, was convicted of a savage murder of a woman in her jeweller's shop. The High Court of Australia set aside his conviction many years later, largely on the basis of failures of disclosure by the Crown. Yet, subsequent to that the chief prosecutor secured Mallard's continued detention in prison for several months on the basis that he was still the main suspect—and would be retried. When Mallard was eventually released from prison, some months later, the same prosecutor said that Mallard was still the main suspect.[32] Several months after that, during a cold case review, it appeared that all along the prosecution had further evidence on file (a palm print) which incriminated another person in the murder, and who had been subsequently convicted of another similar offence.[33] Mallard sued for substantial compensation.[34] A subsequent report found misconduct by both police officers and prosecutors in the case.[35]

### 2) Chapter 8: Forensic Science

It is often said that scientists are the epitome of neutrality and objectivity—working in the laboratories in their white coats:

> For lawyers, jurors and judges a forensic scientist conjures up the image of a [person] in a white coat working in a laboratory, approaching [their] task with cold neutrality, and dedicated only to the pursuit of scientific truth. It is a sombre thought that the reality is sometimes different.[36]

It is disturbing to find the extent to which the scientists have not only been mistaken, but have sometimes gone beyond that to ensure the conviction of

32 Amanda Banks, "Released Man Vows to Solve Murder Case" *The Australian* (22 February 2006).

33 Tony Barrass, "Case Review Clears Mentally Ill Man of Killing" *The Australian* (11 October 2006); Colleen Egan, "No Apologies for Mallard" *The Sunday Times* (22 October 2006).

34 "Mallard Set for Record Compensation Payment" *The West Australian* (22 December 2008).

35 Corruption and Crime Commission, *Report on the Inquiry into Alleged Misconduct by Public Officers in Connection with the Investigation of the Murder of Mrs Pamela Lawrence, the Prosecution and Appeals of Mr Andrew Mallard* (Perth, WA: Corruption and Crime Commission, 2008).

36 *R. v. Ward* (1993) 96 Cr. App. R. 1 at 51.

the innocent. Arrogance, overconfidence, or downright misinterpretation of the evidence to secure a conviction is not as rare as one might expect.

**a) The British Experience**

In the IRA bombing cases the court was told that the evidence showed that the accused had been handling explosives and that the scientific results were clear evidence of that when that was not true. In these cases it was found that scientific witnesses had, either through negligence or wilful misconduct, informed the court that tests confirmed that people had been in contact with explosive substances, when, as it later turned out, the test results might well have been the same if they had been in contact with soap, boot polish, or the plastic backing on playing cards.[37] The scientists were at a loss to explain why they told the jury that the results of the tests for the presence of nitroglycerine were specific and clear when in fact they were neither.

In the British pediatric cases, Professor Sir Roy Meadow told the jury in the Sally Clark case the statistical improbability of multiple child deaths occurring innocently within one family—when he had neither training nor expertise in the field of statistics. In the case of Angela Cannings, Meadow said that in a family one sudden infant death is a tragedy, two is suspicious, and three is murder, until proved otherwise. It was not, of course, the job of the expert inquiring into such matters to reverse the burden or the onus of proof in a criminal trial.

**b) The Canadian Experience**

In the Guy Paul Morin case, there appeared to be fairly conclusive evidence from hairs and fibres that the young girl (who lived nearby and had gone missing) had been in Morin's car shortly before she disappeared. At the subsequent inquiry, long after Morin's conviction for her murder, expert witnesses disclaimed responsibility for such implications. The Canadian scientists said that when they had said that the hairs or fibres in the car were "consistent with" having come from the young girl, they didn't mean to assert any positive or incriminatory connection between the two—and seemed surprised to be told that the jury may not have understood their evidence in that way.

---

37 *R. v. Richardson, Conlon, Armstrong, & Hill*, Court of Appeal (Criminal Division), 20 October 1989 [The Guildford Four]; *R. v. McIlkenny & Ors*, Court of Appeal (Criminal Division), 27 March 1991 [The Birmingham Six]; *R. v. Maguire & Ors*, Court of Appeal (Criminal Division), 26 June 1991 [the Guildford Four follow-on case]; *R. v. Ward, ibid.* [The M62 Bombings].

The James Driskell case also involved hair evidence. In the David Milgaard case, it was DNA testing which caused a re-examination of the previously used scientific evidence. In the Thomas Sophonow case, it was said that all items should be properly tested and that the results of the tests should not be ovestated. It recognized that items such as hairs and fibres cannot usually show any exclusive connection between a crime and a perpetrator.

The various Canadian public inquires have emphasized what should have been obvious: that it was the duty of scientists to be working to challenge or *disprove* a hypothesis rather than to prove one.[38] In addition, sometimes the close working relationships between scientists and the state that employs them or that provides them with much work (and income) contributes to the presentation of unreliable forensic evidence.

### c) The Australian Experience

The prosecution of Edward Splatt seemed to point conclusively to his involvement in the very brutal rape and murder of Mrs. Simper. The case covered different types of forensic evidence involving a good many areas of scientific expertise: fibre evidence, wood particles, paint spicules, bird seeds—and how distinctive or valuable such evidence can be. In the royal commission that followed his conviction, not one of those items of forensic evidence was found to be without error.[39] It is worth noting that the trial which secured the conviction of Splatt took eleven days; the commission that exonerated him took 194 hearing days.

The prosecution of Lindy Chamberlain provided compelling evidence relating to the presence of fetal blood in the car consistent with arterial spurts or sprays and handprints in blood found on the baby's clothes. The royal commission concluded that each and every piece of scientific evidence produced at the trial was fundamentally flawed. The "fetal blood" turned out to be bitumized material used for sound deadening on the underside of the wheel arches of the car. "Arterial spray" turned out to be the distribution of water containing traces of the deadening material as it was blown through a hole in the metal separating the passenger area from the engine compartment. The "handprint" said to have been seen by an eminent British professor brought to Australia for

38 Morin Inquiry, above note 30; *Report of the Commission of Inquiry into Certain Aspects of the Trial and Conviction of James Driskell* (Winnipeg: The Commission, 2007), online: www.driskellinquiry.ca/pdf/final_report_jan2007.pdf; Goudge Inquiry, above note 14 at 538–42, online: www.goudgeinquiry.ca/.

39 *Royal Commission Report concerning the Conviction of Edward Charles Splatt* (Adelaide, AU: Government Printer, 1984).

the case could not now be seen by anyone at the commission. The "blood" of which it was comprised turned out to be sand. The commissioner later stated that if Professor Cameron's evidence had been challenged as inadmissible at trial because it was not within his area of expertise, the challenge no doubt would have been successful.[40] The commissioner said that none of the scientists were willing to take responsibility for the way in which the scientific evidence was put to the jury.[41]

### 3) Chapter 9: Forensic Pathology

Most frequently, forensic pathology involves the evidence of medical practitioners who have conducted autopsies on deceased persons. The involvement of the medical practitioner distinguishes forensic pathology from forensic science. In forensic science, the evidence is given by scientists who are not medical practitioners. However, doctors as well as scientists are required to operate in accordance with established scientific principles. Here again, there is a rich history of medical practitioners who have failed to act in accordance with their scientific and legal duties.

#### a) The British Experience

Forensic pediatric pathology has been at the forefront of concerns in Britain. Prof. Sir Roy Meadow was involved in the series of cases involving child deaths where it was thought that the mothers of the babies had been complicit in their deaths. He had been influential in developing the theory of Munchausen Syndrome by Proxy (MsBP) which claimed that mothers had deliberately harmed their children in order to bring attention to themselves. Sally Clark had been a solicitor and she was convicted of the murder of her two children, in part, based upon the evidence of Meadow. John Batt, a solicitor who acted for Clark in her appeal, said that her imprisonment for life for the murder of her two babies, which existed only in the fevered imaginations of incompetent medical experts, was described in the British Parliament as one of the worst miscarriages of justice in their history. Batt said he had known Sally for thirty years:

---

40 *Royal Commission of Inquiry into Chamberlain Convictions* (Canberra, AU: Government Printer, 1987) c. 10: "Prof Cameron said that what he saw on the clothing indicated that the baby's throat had been cut by an instrument used by human hand . . . . It is doubtful if Prof Cameron would have been permitted to give his evidence at trial if objection had been taken."

41 *Ibid.*, particularly c. 16, "Scientific Evidence Standards."

> I sat beside her at her trial with a watching brief for her family. The worst moment of her life, and probably mine, was when the foreman of the jury said 'guilty' twice. As every lawyer knows, if you are careless enough to step into the path of a miscarriage of justice it consumes you to the exclusion of everything else until it is put right. As a solicitor, I joined Sally's defence team and worked full time on her case for the next three and a half years, when she was freed. As a writer, I felt compelled to tell her story, not only for its own sake which I was able to do from the inside, but because it was symptomatic of what I came to believe were a huge number of miscarriages of justice in the Family and Criminal Courts throughout the English speaking world. These have been brought about largely by experts giving evidence based on *hunches* and not science.[42]

In the same case, a forensic pathologist, Dr. Alan Williams, was found guilty of serious professional misconduct for failing to disclose the results of one of the scientific tests that suggested one of the children might have died from an infection rather than from abuse by their mother.[43] Professor Meadow was ultimately cleared of unprofessional conduct by the Court of Appeal.[44] Clark's conviction was overturned.[45] The damage done to her, though, was too great to be reversed. On 7 November 2007 it was announced that an inquest had ruled she had died accidentally as a result of acute alcohol intoxication.[46]

In the Angela Cannings case, the Court of Appeal said that where a full investigation into two or more sudden unexplained infant deaths in the same family is followed by a serious disagreement between experts about whether natural causes can be excluded, then the parent or caregiver should not be prosecuted, unless there is some additional evidence to show that the infant was deliberately harmed.[47] The court said that it must be mindful that the

---

42 John Batt, *Stolen Innocence—The Story of Sally Clark, A Mother's Fight for Justice* (London, UK: Ebury, 2004).

43 Policy Advisory Board for Forensic Pathology, Dr. A.R. Williams, 28 March 2006, upheld in *Dr. Alan Williams v. General Medical Council*, [2007] EWHC 2603 (Admin).

44 *General Medical Council v. Meadow*, [2006] EWCA Civ 1390.

45 *R. v. Sally Clark*, [2003] EWCA Crim 1020.

46 *BBC News*, "Freed lawyer's accidental death" (7 November 2007).

47 *R. v. Cannings*, [2004] EWCA Crim 1 at paras. 178–79; however, there was a retreat from this position in *R. v. Kai-Whitewind*, [2005] EWCA Crim 1092. For further discussion, see Kathryn Campbell & Clive Walker, "Medical Mistakes and Miscarriages of Justice: Perspectives on the Experience in England and Wales" in Kent Roach, ed., *Independent Research Papers: Pediatric Forensic Pathology and the Justice System*, vol. 2 (Toronto: Ontario Ministry of the Attorney General, 2008) [Goudge Inquiry Research Papers].

dreadful possibility always remains that a mother, brutally scarred by the unexplained death or deaths of a baby, may find herself in prison for life for killing them when she should not be there at all. As the court said, in any civilized community that is abhorrent.

### b) The Canadian Experience

At the age of fourteen, Stephen Truscott was sentenced to death by hanging for the murder of his young school friend, Lynne Harper. Fortunately the sentence was commuted to one of imprisonment. It took over forty years for the system to recognize that a main ingredient of the case upon which the prosecution was based had no scientific validity. The time of death had been based upon an examination of the girl's stomach contents. This was the same method that had been used in the Australian case of Frits Van Beelen (1972)—a case in which the conviction still stands.[48] The Supreme Court affirmed Truscott's conviction in 1966 over a dissent by one judge.[49] When the case was referred by the Minister of Justice back to the courts for a second time, the Ontario Court of Appeal accepted new evidence that it was not scientifically possible to estimate the time of death with the required precision on the basis of the stomach contents.[50]

More recently, the Goudge Inquiry investigated the work of Dr. Charles Smith, a leading pediatric pathologist. He had completed more than 1,000 autopsies. It was found that he had made serious errors in a significant number of his cases. The Gagnon family had to fight for years and spend their life savings to establish that there was no evidence to support a diagnosis of cerebral oedema consistent with blunt force injury as had been found by Dr. Smith. In another case, William Mullins-Johnson had spent twelve years in prison after he was convicted of the rape and murder of his four-year-old niece. It eventually transpired that the murder he was charged with never took place, but was a fiction created by "shoddy" pathological work. Louise Reynolds spent two years in jail for the death of her seven-year-old daughter after Dr. Smith had concluded the child had been stabbed eighty times; however, after an independent review by other pathologists, it was determined that the child had been attacked by a dog.[51]

---

48 *R. v. Truscott*, 2007 ONCA 575; on Van Beelen, see Robert N. Moles, *A State of Injustice* (South Melbourne: Lothian, 2004) c. 5.

49 *Truscott (Re)*, [1967] S.C.R. 309.

50 *Truscott (Re)*, above note 48.

51 Goudge Inquiry, above note 14, vol. 1 and vol. 4, App. 28; the various cases are discussed there.

As Goudge J. stated, the Crown, the defence, and the court (meaning the judges) were responsible for the terrible outcomes involving Dr. Smith.[52] In each of these cases, what appeared to be conclusive and incriminatory evidence at trial later appeared to be unclear and far from incriminating. Dr. Smith agreed in his evidence to the Goudge Inquiry that he may sometimes have overstated the case for the prosecution; and quite remarkably, he told the inquiry that he thought it was his job to help the prosecution gain a conviction. How could he have been so eminent and yet so misguided in understanding his proper role as an expert witness allowed by the court to give opinion evidence?

#### c) The Australian Experience

The case of Frits Van Beelen is very similar to that of the Truscott case in Canada.[53] In both cases, the time of death was said to have been based upon an analysis of stomach contents. In Canada it has been recognized that this was unscientific and unreliable. Van Beelen's case has not yet been accepted for review.

In three baby death cases in South Australia, it was determined that the babies had died from bronchopneumonia. A subsequent coronial inquiry determined that the deaths were almost certainly the result of serious criminal assaults and that there was no proper evidence of bronchopneumonia. These cases reveal how faulty forensic pathology can result in the guilty going free as well as the conviction of the innocent.

## C. PART THREE — RESPONSES TO MISCARRIAGES OF JUSTICE

### 1) Chapter 10: Error Correction and System Reforms

In this chapter we review in some detail the role and function of the CCRC. We look at the procedures it follows in examining the applications it receives. It is interesting to note that although it refers only something like 4 percent of applications to the courts, it is obliged to examine all of them, often in some

52 *Ibid.*, vol. 1 at 19. See also the discussion by Sir Thomas Thorp, *Miscarriages of Justice* (Auckland, NZ: Legal Research Foundation, 2006) at 7, where he surveys the discussions on miscarriages of justice from 1912 to 1960 and points out that Borchard in the United States identified "incompetence of counsel" as a significant factor in the cases he had researched.

53 The Van Beelen case has not yet been recognized as a miscarriage of justice, and as such it represents an exception to our general policy of dealing only with cases that have been officially recognized as miscarriages of justice.

detail, before determining how to respond to them. It gives detailed reasons for decisions and responds to objections to those reasons. Its referral of cases to the Court of Appeal can give rise to tensions between the commission and the court. Some 70 percent of cases referred to the court are successful.

We then look to innocence projects and commissions which amount to the informal and often unfunded inquiries into alleged miscarriages of justice. They frequently involve student review teams. In the United States, they have grown considerably in strength and authority over the years, but they are also found in the Britain, Canada, and Australia. A major focus of such groups has been upon the use of DNA in exonerating the innocent. The innocence projects have influenced the setting up of similar groups in many other jurisdictions.

We then discuss the issue of error correction on the one hand (the CCRC and innocence projects) and the issue of systemic reform (the Canadian inquiries) on the other. We ask whether it is possible to develop a single model to combine both aspects of such inquiries or whether the strategic objects are so distinct as to require separate institutions to deal with them.

### 2) Chapter 11 — Scientific Problems

Here we take a look at broader issues in relation to the science which is used in court proceedings. A report by the National Academy of Sciences (NAS) in the United States states that if one looks at any area of forensic science, one can see that it does not come up to the standard for *reliable* science. Fingerprint evidence, which is often thought to be most reliable, depends in the final analysis on the judgment of a person who is to compare the print from a scene with that taken from a person. The subjectivity of this judgment introduces variability and this is contrary to the requirement of scientific experiments, that they be capable of replication without variation. The *NAS Report* recommends the establishment of a national institute of forensic science. There is a multiplicity of organizations involved in establishing and maintaining standards in forensic laboratories. Some deal with standards of management practices; others deal with reliability of equipment and results. Other organizations have attempted to register or validate practitioners. It has to be said that the current achievements are not encouraging.

In Australia, the Splatt Royal Commission recommended the establishment of a national institute of forensic science. Although a body with this name has been established in Australia, it is established and managed by the police, so does not provide the independence and authority envisaged in the commission's report.

However, nothing can be more important than improving the underlying science. The *NAS Report* and the Goudge Inquiry both recommend improved relationships between forensic science centres, the universities, and the courts. A perennial problem in this area is the combination of misunderstanding and miscommunication between scientists and lawyers. Another is the fact that the various reports in each of our jurisdictions have recommended strategies for implementation, but little or nothing has been done to further that end. Indeed, the Canadian inquiries in later reports have bemoaned the fact that the recommendations of the earlier reports have not been implemented. If we are to close the gap between the rhetoric and the reality, then we need to educate, communicate, and implement the recommendations seriously and vigorously.

### 3) Chapter 12—Recommendations

The final chapter contains our major recommendations for narrowing the gap between the rhetoric of impartial forensic science and prosecutions and the reality of a growing number of recognized miscarriages of justice. We emphasize that both forensic science and the legal system must change and seek to better understand each other.

With respect to forensic science, there needs to be proactive research that identifies areas of controversy and evolving science that are particularly important to the criminal justice system. Adversarial criminal trials are not the best forum for understanding or advancing science. Such reviews can also identify areas where the science may be so suspect that proactive audits of criminal cases that rely on such evidence should be conducted. Some examples where such audits have been conducted in some jurisdictions include cases that rely on evidence about shaken baby syndrome or microscopical hair analysis. Audits can also play an important role in cases where concerns have been raised about the work of a particular expert witness. Audits do not rely on individuals to seek remedies for miscarriages of justice, and they can help restore public confidence in both the forensic science and criminal justice systems.

The major recommendation that we make with respect to the criminal justice system is that all jurisdictions should establish a state-based CCRC-type body with the necessary resources and powers to investigate claims of miscarriages of justice, including those involving forensic science. Volunteer bodies such as innocence projects can play an important role, but they are no substitute for a state-funded, but independent body concerned with miscarriages of justice. Building on the experience of the CCRC, thought should also be given to how a CCRC-type body can participate in proactive audits of cases that rely on suspect forms of evidence; how to best use legal representation for applicants; and how best to make systemic recommendations to prevent miscarriages of justice in the future. The creation of a CCRC-type body in Australia and Canada and elsewhere would be an important reform, but the CCRC should not be seen in isolation from other parts of the forensic science and criminal justice systems that contribute to miscarriages of justice.

We also survey other improvements that the legal system can make when it engages with forensic science. Publication of expert reports before trial may increase the likelihood that scientific error or controversy will be discovered and presented to the court. Judges should also play a more active role both in vetting expert evidence and when necessary supplementing expert evidence with their own experts. The imposition of the standard that forensic evidence offered by the state be demonstrably reliable before it is admitted in court could help prevent miscarriages of justice and also encourage the state to invest in improving the forensic sciences.

PART ONE

# The Rhetoric: Guiding Principles

CHAPTER 2

# Prosecutors and Expert Witnesses

This chapter sets out some of the important elements about how things *ought* to be done — the rhetoric — in the conduct of legal proceedings. The focus is on the role of prosecutors and expert witnesses, both of which play a critical role in presenting forensic evidence to the courts. As will be seen, both prosecutors and expert witnesses are supposed to present evidence in a fair and impartial manner in order to assist the court in making reliable and careful decisions about guilt and innocence.

In this chapter we explain that the duty of a prosecutor is not just to obtain a conviction but to act fairly in presenting relevant evidence to a court. The basic principles that govern the conduct of prosecutors are common to each of our three main jurisdictions. However, the way in which they are applied in practice can be quite different, as we see in Part Two of this book.

We also explain two important aspects relating to the conduct of expert witnesses. The first is what the law requires of them in order to be regarded as an expert and to grant them special privileges in terms of what they can say to the court in the conduct of legal proceedings. The second is to set out some of the ethical principles that are laid down in codes of conduct and meant to guide their conduct before, during, and after they give evidence in court.

Expert witnesses are an exception to the general rule that witnesses are not allowed to express their *opinions* about what the evidence in legal proceedings means. Experts, the law tells us, are people who are appropriately qualified and with proper experience. In certain circumstances, they are allowed to assist the jury by advising what inferences might be drawn from the available evidence. However, it is always up to the jury to determine if they accept the advice.

The UK Law Commission summed up the position in its 2009 Discussion Paper setting out the law relating to the role of expert witness. It referred to the 1984 South Australian case of *R. v. Bonython*[1] as correctly expressing the applicable principles. We explain in this chapter that the more recent Australian case of *Makita v. Sprowles*[2] endorses key aspects of the *Bonython* position, and does so by linking the discussion to important British cases. The net effect, it may be said, is that the Australian and British positions are closely aligned on these issues as is the Canadian position.

In substance, the cases say that an expert opinion must be based upon clearly stated facts that have been (or will be) established by properly admissible evidence in the case (the relevance issue). Scientific principles and the reasoning that relates them to the facts of the case must also be correct and clearly articulated by the expert (the reliability issue). It is clear that an expert witness must not engage in speculation or testify in areas that lie outside of his or her expertise.

There are many codes of conduct to assist experts in properly understanding their role in legal proceedings, and we give details of some of these. The codes are, in effect, simplified expressions of the underlying legal principles. They are usually propounded by the relevant associations as an educational tool to reinforce and remind their members of key aspects of their professional duties. The codes say that expert witnesses are expected to act in a fair and balanced manner; they are not supposed to act in the interests of either the prosecution or the defence. They are there to assist the court to understand the evidence and the issues involved.

Important problems are associated with the introduction of experts into any legal proceedings. Jurors (and judges) may be tempted to accord undue deference to them. The defence may be unable to afford or to find others of similar standing to challenge those put forward by the prosecution.

It will be clear from the cases we look at in Part Two that there have been many cases where inappropriate expert evidence has been admitted. That will give rise to some consideration as to how such evidence was admitted. Was it because the judges were not sufficiently skilled in evaluating the scientific issues involved or had not sufficiently appreciated what the rules set out in this chapter required of them? Had the judges perhaps been too indecisive in keeping questionable evidence from the jury?

---

1 *R. v. Bonython* (1984), 38 S.A.S.R. 45 at paras. 46–47; UK Law Commission, *The Admissibility of Expert Evidence in Criminal Proceedings in England and Wales*, Consultation Paper 190 (Norwich: The Stationery Office, 2009) [Law Commission, "Admissibility"].

2 *Makita (Australia) Pty. Ltd. v. Sprowles*, [2001] NSWCA 305 [*Makita*].

One discussion that we can anticipate in Part Three, which is advanced by the UK Law Commission, will relate to what needs to be done to ensure that the rules set out here become part of the reality and do not simply remain as part of the rhetoric.

## A. PROSECUTIONS

### 1) General Principles

The common law system of criminal trials is essentially adversarial. Some people think this means that each side is focused on winning and may pursue their cause as vigorously as possible before the independent umpire (the judge and jury).

There are, however, significant limitations on this especially with regard to the role of prosecutor and the expert witness. We discuss these two important participants in the criminal process together because of this. Formally, the expert witness is a neutral participant in the trial process and should be indifferent to the outcome. The prosecutor, obviously, is an advocate for a guilty verdict, but even here, we find that the prosecutorial advocacy is muted to some degree.

*Boucher v. The Queen*, an important Canadian case, sets out the principles applying to the duty of the prosecutor in a criminal case, and those criteria have also informed the discussions on this topic in Britain and Australia.[3] It said the duty of the prosecutor is to bring before the court all the relevant evidence and to ask the jury to come to the conclusion that the accused is guilty. The overriding duty is to assist the jury. The prosecutor must not express by inflammatory or vindictive language, his or her personal opinion that the accused is guilty.[4] That is because, as *Boucher* explained, the character or eminence of a barrister is to be wholly disregarded in determining the justice or otherwise of the client's cause, it being an inflexible rule of forensic pleading

---

3 *Boucher v. The Queen*, [1955] S.C.R. 16 [*Boucher*]. See also *Berger v. United States*, 295 U.S. 78 at 88 (1935) and the discussion in Susan Rutberg, "Anatomy of a Miscarriage of Justice: The Wrongful Conviction of Peter J. Rose" (2006) 37 Golden Gate U.L. Rev. 7 at 22*ff.* [Rutberg].

4 The same principle is included within the various bar rules in Australia. For example, *South Australian Barristers' Rules* (Adelaide: South Australian Bar Association, 2005) cl. 9.4, states, "a prosecutor must not (a) by language or other conduct seek to inflame or bias the court against the accused (b) press the prosecution's case for a conviction beyond a full and firm presentation of that case."

that an advocate shall not, as such, express a personal opinion of—or his or her belief in—the client's case.

The purpose of a criminal prosecution, says *Boucher*, is not to obtain a conviction, but to lay before the jury credible evidence relevant to what is alleged to be a crime. While the prosecutor has a duty to see that all available legal proof of the facts is presented, it should be done firmly and pressed to its legitimate strength—it must be done fairly. The role of a prosecutor excludes any notion of winning or losing. The function is

> . . . a matter of public duty than which in civil life there can be none charged with greater personal responsibility. It is to be efficiently performed with an ingrained sense of the dignity, the seriousness and the justness of judicial proceedings.[5]

Prosecuting counsel should regard themselves as being "ministers of justice" and assisting in its administration rather than being seen as strident advocates for a particular outcome.

### 2) Guidelines

The British,[6] Canadian,[7] and Australian[8] prosecution guidelines state that prosecutors must be fair, independent, and objective. Prosecutors must act

---

5 Above note 3 at 24, Rand J. This was endorsed in the United Kingdom by the Privy Council in *Randall v. The Queen*, [2002] 2 Cr. App. R. 17, Bingham L.J., and by the High Court of Australia in *Libke v. The Queen*, [2007] HCA 30 at para. 71, Hayne J. See also *R. v. Stafford*, [2009] QCA 407 at para. 138: "The prosecutor's obligation is to put the case against the accused fairly"; Keane J.A. citing *Richardson v. The Queen* (1974), 131 C.L.R. 116; *R. v. Apostilides* (1984), 154 C.L.R. 563 at 575; and *R. v. Soma* (2003), 212 C.L.R. 299 at para. 31.

6 See, for example, *The Farquharson Guidelines on the Role and Responsibilities of the Prosecuting Advocate* (London: Crown Prosecution Service, 2002); *The Code of Conduct of the Bar of England and Wales*, 8th ed. (London: General Council of the Bar of England and Wales, 2004); and David Corker & Steven Parkinson, *Disclosure in Criminal Proceedings* (Oxford: Oxford University Press, 2009).

7 In Canada at the federal level, the policies and guidelines are set out in the *Federal Prosecution Service Deskbook* (Ottawa: Department of Justice, 2005) and at provincial levels see, for example in Ontario, *Crown Policy Manual* (Toronto: Ministry of the Attorney General, 2005).

8 At the federal level, the policies and guidelines are set out in *Prosecution Policy of the Commonwealth*, 2d ed. (Canberra: Australian Government Publishing Service, 1998). All state and territory Directors of Public Prosecutions have prosecution policies and guidelines: see, for example, South Australian Office of the Director of Public Prosecutions, *Prosecution Policy and Guidelines*, and the New South Wales Office of the Director of

in the interests of justice in assisting the court to arrive at the truth and not solely to obtain a conviction. They should provide guidance and advice to investigators. They are to ensure that the law is properly applied and that all relevant evidence is put before the court. There must be a realistic prospect of a conviction, which is said to be an objective test. They must determine if the evidence in prospect is reliable and in particular if there are any circumstances that might make the evidence of a witness appear unreliable. Obviously, this is particularly important in the context of an expert witness.

Prosecutors must also determine if it is in the public interest for a prosecution to proceed.[9] Their assessment includes the seriousness of the offence and the manner in which it occurred. They might consider, for example, the use of weapons, violence, and whether it was an abuse of trust or an act against a public official. If there was some element of misunderstanding or confusion, or where there has been long delay or the person is elderly or frail, or the matter can be dealt with in some other way, then such issues may be taken into consideration.

Charges must be appropriate to the circumstances, and there must not be any element of elevating the charges so as to encourage a guilty plea to a lesser offence. Prosecutors should always consider alternatives to prosecution. The prosecutor must consider the interests of the victim and of the wider community in deciding whether to accept a guilty plea.

There is also a duty upon prosecutors, as there is for defence lawyers, not to mislead the court. If any evidence might cast doubt upon the accuracy of the evidence of one of its expert witnesses, they must disclose that evidence.[10] Likewise, there is a duty to disclose prior inconsistent statements of one of their witnesses, as that might go to credibility or reliability. They must disclose if there has been any agreement or arrangement with a witness for any offences or circumstances in which they may have been involved.

---

Public Prosecutions, *Prosecution Guidelines* (Sydney: Director of Public Prosecutions, 2007). See also the *South Australian Barristers' Rules*, above note 4.

9 As Sir Hartley Shawcross, British attorney general and former Nuremberg trial prosecutor, speaking in the House of Commons on 29 January 1951, said:

> [i]t has never been the rule in this country . . . that suspected criminal offences must automatically be the subject of prosecution. Indeed the very first Regulations under which the Director of Public Prosecutions worked provided that he should . . . prosecute "wherever it appears that the offence or the circumstances of its commission is or are of such a nature that a prosecution in respect thereof is required in the public interest."

That is still the dominant consideration.

10 Rutberg, above note 3 at 25.

In Britain, the *Attorney General's Guidelines* make it clear that any material in the possession of the prosecutor that comes to light after the conclusion of a case and that casts doubt upon the safety of a conviction must be immediately disclosed.[11] Drawing in part on the experience of the wrongful conviction of the late Donald Marshall, the Supreme Court of Canada has also indicated that the prosecutor has a continuing duty of disclosure.[12]

## B. EXPERT WITNESSES

### 1) General Principles

In considering the role of the expert witness we must first explain that any such people may well have two distinct functions.

The first may be to give evidence in respect of their *observations*—what they have seen or heard. Document examiners may give evidence about documents that came into their possession and what they saw on those documents. Pathologists may give evidence about their observations of tissues or dead bodies. Prof. William Tilstone has said that the basic obligation of the forensic scientist is to "gather evidence" of what has been observed.[13] Having done that, it can be used as the basis for any inferences to be made.

It is important to bear in mind that in this respect, the expert is no different from any other witness. As with any witness, the court or tribunal will need to make an assessment of the reliability of the observations, the circumstances in which they took place, the time of recording of any notes in relation to them, and whether there is any possibility for confusion or error.[14]

Of course, knowing that a certain witness is bringing some degree of expertise to the court or tribunal, there is a greater tendency to assume that the observations of *that* witness are more reliable than those of other witnesses. As we will see in the following chapters, though, such confidence could well be misplaced.

The second and distinctive role of the expert witness in legal proceedings is with regard to their ability to express an *opinion*. Ordinary witnesses will normally be allowed to give evidence of what they saw or heard directly, but

---

11 *Attorney General's Guidelines on Disclosure* (London: Attorney General's Office, 2005) at para. 59.

12 *R. v. Stinchcombe*, [1991] 3 S.C.R. 326.

13 William Tilstone, "Where Now for Forensic Science?" in (1986) 4 Proceedings of the Australian Forensic Science Society 12.

14 The distinction here referred to is discussed in greater detail by Alan D. Gold in *Expert Evidence in Criminal Law: The Scientific Approach*, 2d ed. (Toronto: Irwin Law, 2009) c. 1.

they will not be allowed to express an opinion as to the meaning or interpretation of those observations. This practice is predicated on the notion that in most instances, the fact finders (judge or jury) are just as capable as the witnesses are in drawing inferences or forming opinions from the facts reported by witnesses.[15] In normal circumstances, it would be allowable for a witness to say that he heard "a loud bang," but it may not be acceptable for that witness to say that he heard "a gunshot," for that brings with it a greater element of interpretation. In keeping with this, police custody officers will record an item as being "yellow metal" rather than as "gold." An expert can be invited to assist the jury, however, where it is thought that the jury will not be able to understand what proper inferences can be drawn from the evidence.

### 2) Australia and Britain

In its 2009 discussion paper, the UK Law Commission set out its understanding of the current rules on the admissibility of expert evidence, by reference to the South Australian case of *R. v. Bonython*[16] which said that the trial judge must determine the following:

> (a) whether the subject matter of the opinion is such that a person without instruction or experience in the area of knowledge or human experience would be able to form a sound judgment on the matter without the assistance of witnesses possessing special knowledge or experience in the area [the evidence is necessary to assist jury];
>
> (b) whether the subject matter of the opinion forms part of a body of knowledge or experience which is sufficiently organised or recognized to be accepted as a reliable body of knowledge or experience, as special acquaintance with which by the witness would render his opinion of assistance to the court [the evidence is reliable];
>
> (c) whether the witness has acquired by study or experience sufficient knowledge of the subject to render the opinion of value in resolving the issues before the court [the witness is reliable].[17]

The discussion paper pointed out that there had been a view (established in 1923) that to be admissible, an expert opinion had to be deduced from well-

15 While the jury is frequently the trier of fact in a criminal trial, there are circumstances where a person may opt to be tried before a judge without a jury. See comments on this in Chapter 4.

16 *Bonython*, above note 1 at paras. 46–47.

17 Law Commission, "Admissibility," above note 1 at para. 1.2.

recognized principles that were generally accepted within the relevant scientific specialty (the *Frye* test).[18] That view was subsequently refined to allow for legitimate differences of opinion that had emerged within certain fields of knowledge. In the leading American case of *Daubert v. Merrell Dow*,[19] the US Supreme Court took the view that where opinions are held, but which have not yet had the chance to gain general acceptance, then the knowledge must have been arrived at by an appropriate and accepted scientific *method*. Therefore, where the *knowledge* is not generally accepted, then it must be arrived at by a generally accepted *method*.

*Daubert* said the factors that one must consider in identifying such expertise were as follows:

> The principles used in the derivation of the knowledge must be *testable*. This means that if the knowledge is not capable of being tested (and therefore capable of being falsified, or proved wrong if it is wrong), then whatever it is—it is not science.
>
> The principles used must also have been *tested*.
>
> The knowledge must have been subjected to *peer review* and publication.
>
> It is important to identify the standards for using the method in question, and in particular, for identifying any known *error rate*.[20]

As we will explain in Part Two, the British discussion paper recognized that the cases show that sometimes expert evidence of doubtful reliability was not properly challenged by opposing counsel or was admitted too freely by the court. When that happened, it was not surprising that it was accepted by the jury.

As the discussion paper said, jury deference to the opinions of experts gives rise to serious concerns about the admissibility of such unreliable evidence.

In the Canadian Goudge Inquiry, Goudge J. referred to the comment by former Justice Lesage:

> Did I . . . question the expertise sufficiently? Did defence counsel, or Crown counsel as the case might be, question the expertise, the basis and the underpinnings of it as much as we ought to have? In many cases, no, we didn't.[21]

---

18 *Frye v. United States*, 293 F. 1013 (D.C. Cir. 1923) [*Frye*].

19 *Daubert v. Merrell Dow Pharmaceuticals Inc.* 509 U.S. 579 (1993) [*Daubert*].

20 Robert N. Moles, "The Role and Function of the Expert Witness" (October 2007), online: http://netk.net.au/Reports/ExpertWitness.asp.

21 *Report of the Inquiry into Pediatric Forensic Pathology in Ontario*, vol. 3 (Toronto: Queen's Printer, 2008) at 486 [Goudge Inquiry].

Justice Goudge pointed out that Lesage J., during his long career on the bench, said he had rejected perhaps only half a dozen proffered experts on the grounds they had no basis on which to come to their conclusion. There is a danger of trial judges simply admitting the expert evidence, then leaving any misgivings about reliability to counsel for cross-examination or to the jury in assigning the appropriate weight to give to it.[22]

### 3) Experts to Assist the Jury

It is important to distinguish between those circumstances where jurors can work things out for themselves, and where they really need some expert assistance to properly understand the issues involved. Ordinary members of a jury might be expected to appreciate that when people get drunk, their judgment is impaired and they might drive badly and crash a car. However, they might need some expert assistance to understand how ingested poisons can affect the nervous system and cause death. As was pointed out in *R. v. Turner*,[23] jurors do not need psychiatrists to tell them how ordinary people (not suffering from any mental illness) are likely to react to the stresses and strains of life. So, psychiatric evidence to show that an accused was likely to have been provoked or is likely telling the truth will not usually be admitted.

### 4) Assessment of Reliability: Facts plus Reasoning Essential

The Australian and British positions on the use of expert testimony and its limitations were explained in the Australian case of *Makita*.[24] This decision made it clear that the court must be provided with criteria to enable the expert's

---

22 *Ibid.* at 487. For an interesting recent Australian case on the topic, see *The Queen v. Robert Farquarson*, [2009] VSCA 307 [*Farquarson*], where the appeal court held that it was not essential for an expert medical witness to have specialized in the study of a condition in order to express an opinion concerning its occurrence and ætiology; such factors would go to the *weight* of the evidence, not the *admissibility* of it.

23 *R. v. Turner*, [1975] Q.B. 834 at 841 (C.A.) [*Turner*]. See also the discussion of the work of Gisli Gudjonsson in Chapter 8.

24 Above note 2. The following discussion is based upon the judgment of Heydon J.A. (now a judge of the High Court of Australia). Although dealing with a civil case, the judge made it clear that the same principles apply to criminal cases. He is also the editor of *Cross on Evidence*, a leading practitioners' book. *Makita* was discussed in some detail in *Farquarson*, above note 22. The Canadian position is explained in Gary Edmond, "Pathological Science? Demonstrable reliability and Expert Forensic Pathological Evidence" in Kent Roach, ed., *Independent Research Papers: Pediatric Forensic Pathology and the Justice System*, vol. 2 (Toronto: Ontario Ministry of the Attorney General, 2008) at 105–17.

conclusions to be properly evaluated. In indicating the common approach to these issues across different jurisdictions, the court looked in detail at the way in which these issues had been dealt with in the Scottish case of *Davie v. The Lord Provost*[25] which had involved scientific evidence concerning explosives used in blasting. The court in *Davie* pointed out that the real value of expert evidence depends upon the authority, experience, and qualifications of the expert and above all upon the extent to which the evidence carries conviction, "and not upon the possibility of producing a second person to echo the sentiments of the first."[26]

It was said by the plaintiff in that case that because the defence did not lead counter evidence, then the court was bound to accept the conclusions of the expert. The court said that this must be "firmly rejected" as contrary to the principles in accordance with which expert opinion evidence is admitted. As the court pointed out, expert witnesses, however skilled or eminent, can give no more than evidence. They cannot usurp the functions of the jury or the judge sitting as a jury. The duty of the expert is to furnish the judge or jury "with the necessary scientific criteria for testing the accuracy of their conclusions, so as to enable the judge or jury to form their own independent judgment by the application of these criteria to the facts proved in evidence."[27]

As we will see in Part Two, if this important principle had been complied with, then many of the serious miscarriages of justice that have occurred over the years, in all jurisdictions, might have been avoided. This is particularly so in those cases where the only expert witness is offered by the prosecutor. The court in *Davie* went on to say:

> The scientific opinion evidence, if intelligible, convincing and tested, becomes a factor (and often an important factor) for consideration along with the whole other evidence in the case, but the decision is for the Judge or jury. In particular the bare ipse dixit of a scientist, however eminent, upon the issue in controversy, will normally carry little weight, for it cannot be tested by cross-examination nor independently appraised, and the parties have invoked the decision of a judicial tribunal and not an oracular pronouncement by an expert.[28]

---

25 *Davie v. The Lord Provost, Magistrates and Councillors of the City of Edinburgh*, [1953] S.C. 34 [*Davie*].

26 *Ibid.* at paras. 39–40, cited in *Makita*, above note 2 at para. 59.

27 *Makita, ibid.*

28 *Ibid.*

It was explained in *Makita* that *Davie* was not to be read as reflecting only a principle peculiar to Scottish law. The court in *Davie* referred to the earlier Australian case of *Jenkins*[29] where it was made clear that an expert witness must "explain the basis of theory or experience" upon which the conclusions stated are supposed to rest: "Courts cannot be expected to act upon opinions the basis of which is unexplained."[30] The court in *Makita* pointed to an extensive range of recent writing and authority on the topic.[31]

In the British case of *Gilfoyle*, in approving *Davie*, the Court of Appeal said that the evidence of a psychologist "was not expert evidence of a kind properly to be placed before the court for a number of reasons." One of those reasons was that "his reports identify no criteria by reference to which the court could test the quality of his opinions."[32]

In *Makita* it was said that according to *Phipson on Evidence*, experts may give evidence in chief as to the grounds on which they have reached their opinions, and it goes on to say that, "without the grounds, the opinion is valueless."[33] Justice Heydon said that while it was an accepted practice for experts to refer only to their conclusions in their evidence in chief, doing so is clearly a mistake. Such a practice, he thought, was opposed to a line of authority which said as much.[34] This can be seen as a judicial acceptance of the limits of experience-based forensic evidence in which the expert relies on his or her opinion and experience without explaining the underlying grounds, theories, and evidence that supports the opinion.

The basic principle is that an expert gives an opinion based on facts. Because of that, the expert must either prove by admissible evidence those facts on which the opinion is based or state explicitly the assumptions as to fact on which the opinion is based. One reason why the facts proved must correlate to some degree with those assumed is that the expert's conclusion must have

---

29 *R. v. Jenkins; ex parte Morrison*, [1949] V.L.R. 277 at 303, Fullagar J.

30 *Makita*, above note 2 at para. 60. See also *H.G. v. The Queen* (1999), 197 C.L.R. 414.

31 *Makita, ibid.* at para. 61; Gordon J. Samuels, "Problems Relating to the Expert Witness in Personal Injury Cases" in Harold H. Glass, ed., *Seminars on Evidence* (Sydney: Law Book Co. for New South Wales Bar Association, 1970) 141; *Phipson on Evidence*, 15th ed. (London: Sweet & Maxwell, 2000) at paras. 37-01 and 37-50; *Lysaght v. Police*, [1965] N.Z.L.R. 405 at 409; *Re B. (A Minor) (Care: Expert Witnesses)*, [1996] 1 F.L.R. 667 at 670; *O'Kelly Holdings Pty Ltd v. Dalrymple Holdings Pty Ltd* (1993), 45 F.C.R. 145 at 155, Spender J., quoted by Sweeney and O'Connor JJ.; *Idoport Pty Ltd v. National Australia Bank Ltd*, [2001] NSWSC 123 at para. 13 [*Idoport*]; *R. v. Gilfoyle (No. 2)*, [2001] 2 Cr. App. R. 57 at para. 25 [*Gilfoyle*].

32 *Gilfoyle, ibid.* at para. 25.

33 *Phipson on Evidence*, above note 31 at paras. 37-09 and 37-48.

34 *Makita*, above note 2 at para. 63.

some rational relationship with the facts proved. In *Bugg v. Day*, one reason for criticizing the reception of a motor repairer's evidence of the speed of a taxicab when it hit a motorcycle inspected by him was that it "plainly involved assumptions of fact that were not adverted to by the witness."[35] As Latham C.J. pointed out, he had not been provided with the data that would have been necessary to enable a person to form an estimate of the speed of either vehicle at the moment of the collision. He was not informed as to the weight of the taxicab or as to the distances, after the accident, of the two vehicles from the point of collision.[36]

*Ramsay v. Watson*[37] concerned a patient's medical history. The court said that if the history is not supported by admissible evidence, then the opinion may have little or no value, for part of its basis is gone. The evidence in *Ramsay* was not merely of little or no value—it was inadmissible. The court there took the view that the total failure to seek to prove the factual basis on which the opinion was formed justified total rejection of the evidence.

The court pointed out:

> That some medical witness should go into the box and say only that in his opinion something is more probable than not does not conclude the case. A qualified medical practitioner may, as an expert, express his opinion as to the nature and cause, or probable cause, of a condition, but it is for the jury to weigh and determine the probabilities. In doing so they may be assisted by the medical evidence. But they are not simply to transfer their task to the witnesses. They must ask themselves "Are we on the whole of the evidence satisfied on a balance of probabilities [or beyond reasonable doubt] of the fact?"[38]

The jury cannot weigh and determine the probabilities for themselves if the expert does not fully expose the reasoning relied on.

Underlying these observations is an assumption that the trier of fact (judge or jury) must arrive at an independent assessment of the opinions and their value, and that this cannot be done unless their basis is explained:

> Before a court can assess the value of an opinion it must know the facts upon which it is based. If the expert has been misinformed about the facts or has taken irrelevant facts into consideration or has omitted to consider relevant

---

35 *Bugg v. Day*, [1949] HCA 59, Dixon J., cited in *ibid.* at para. 65.

36 *Ibid.*

37 *Ramsay v. Watson* (1961), 108 C.L.R. 642, cited in *Makita*, *ibid.* at para. 66.

38 *Ibid.* at 645, cited in *Makita*, *ibid.* at para. 67.

> ones, the opinion is likely to be valueless. In our judgment, counsel calling an expert should in examination in chief ask his witness to state the facts upon which his opinion is based. It is wrong to leave the other side to elicit the facts by cross-examination.[39]

A further illustration of the importance that the law attaches to the identification, whether formally or informally, of the assumed facts is *R. v. Fowler*:

> It must be kept steadily in mind that the court (the jury in a jury trial) is the tribunal of fact and that it is no part of the function of a witness to decide what version or interpretation of the facts is to be accepted or rejected. The witness who expresses an opinion . . . must give his opinion upon an assumed state of facts postulated to him or by him for that purpose. Strictly speaking *it is not permissible for him to recount what he has been told*, as distinct from what he assumes as the basis of his opinion, as that would result in hearsay material coming to the notice of the Court.[40]

The court in *Fowler* went on to say that "adherence to the rule is of the utmost importance when the evidence is given before a jury."[41] As the court in *Makita* pointed out, "Examining the substance of an opinion cannot be carried out without knowing the essential integers underlying it."[42] The importance of proving the facts underlying an opinion is that the absence of such evidence deprives the court of an important opportunity of testing the validity of the process by which the opinion was formed, and substantially reduces the value and cogency of the opinion evidence.[43] The court in *Lewis* pointed out:

> Forensic evidence, especially if it goes to a vital issue implicating an accused person in the commission of an offence, may often have a prejudicial effect on the minds of a jury which far outweighs its probative value. The jury, being people without scientific training, may often be impressed by an expert's qualifications, appointments and experience and the confident manner in which he expresses his opinions. And yet it ought not be left to such matters alone to provide a foundation for the jury making an assessment of the

39 *Turner*, above note 23 at 840, Lawton L.J., as cited in *Makita, ibid.* at para. 69.

40 (1985), 39 S.A.S.R. 440 at 442, King C.J., as cited in *Makita, ibid.* at para. 70 [emphasis added].

41 *Ibid.*at 442.

42 *Holtman v. Sampson*, [1985] 2 Qd. R. 472 at 474, as cited in *Makita*, above note 2 at para. 71.

43 *Bell v. F.S. & U. Industrial Benefit Society Ltd.* (9 September 1987) (Supreme Court of New South Wales), McLelland J., as cited in *Makita, ibid.* at para. 72.

> probative value of forensic evidence, particularly where there are conflicts in expert testimony, or where it is acknowledged that other experts of more or less equal distinction are unlikely to agree.[44]

The judge in *Lewis* went on to say:

> For my part I think that whenever the Crown wishes to rely upon forensic evidence the prosecutor has a clear duty, not just to his client, the Crown, but to the trial judge and the jury to acquaint them, in ordinary language, through the evidence he leads, with those aspects of the expert's discipline and methods necessary to put them in a position to make some sort of evaluation of the opinions he expresses. Where the evidence is of a comparatively novel kind, the duty resting on the Crown is even higher: *it should demonstrate its scientific reliability.* It is not an answer to considerations that dictate these things to be done to say the defence may draw it out in cross-examination; that is an abdication of the Crown's primary function in a criminal prosecution. There is a tendency amongst academics, professionals and others who develop skills in a particular area to mystify their field, often by the use of what seems to the outside to be arcane language. It is the role of a prosecutor to strip forensic evidence of its mystery so far as is possible; trial by expert must never be allowed to take the place of trial by jury. The inability to articulate the principal tenets that need to be understood, to describe in ordinary language the methods used and the reasons that point to a particular conclusion, these are the hallmarks of unreliable science and the not-so-qualified expert.[45]

This case recognizes the special obligations of both prosecutors and their expert witnesses to explain the basis for the forensic opinion and "to strip forensic evidence of its mystery so far as it is possible" so that the tier of fact can critically assess all the components of the opinion.

In *National Justice Compania Naviera S.A. (UK)*,[46] Cresswell J. set out a list of duties and responsibilities of expert witnesses as follows:

> 1. Expert evidence presented to the Court should be, and should be seen to be, the independent product of the expert uninfluenced as to form or content by the exigencies of litigation.

44 *Lewis v. R.* (1987), 88 F.L.R. 104 at 123–24; Maurice J., as cited in *Makita, ibid.* at para. 73 [emphasis added].

45 *Ibid.* [emphasis added].

46 *National Justice Compania Naviera S.A. v. Prudential Assurance Co. Ltd. ("The Ikarian Reefer")*, [1993] 2 Lloyd's Rep. 68.

2. An expert witness should provide independent assistance to the court by way of objective unbiased opinion in relation to matters within his expertise. An expert witness in court should never assume the role of an advocate.
3. An expert witness should state the facts or assumptions upon which his opinion is based. He should not omit to consider material facts which could detract from his concluded opinion.
4. An expert witness should make it clear when a particular question or issue falls outside his expertise.
5. If an expert's opinion is not properly researched because he considers that insufficient data is available, then this must be stated with an indication that the opinion is no more than a provisional one. In cases where an expert witness who has prepared a report could not assert that the report contained the truth, the whole truth and nothing but the truth without some qualification, that qualification should be stated in the report.
6. If, after exchange of reports, an expert witness changes his view on a material matter having read the other side's expert's report or for any other reason, such change of view should be communicated (through legal representatives) to the other side without delay and when appropriate to the Court.
7. Where expert evidence refers to photographs, plans, calculations, analyses, measurements, survey reports or other similar documents, these must be provided to the opposite party at the same time as the exchange of reports.[47]

As the judge said in *Makita*, while some of these matters have an ethical dimension, taken together, they point to the need for the trier of fact to be fully informed of the reasoning process deployed in arriving at the expert's opinions. He said that the list just referred to has influenced a number of jurisdictions to devise rules of court to control expert evidence and has also influenced later judicial pronouncements.

The law regulating the admissibility of expert evidence was well summed up in *Makita*:

> If evidence tendered as expert opinion evidence is to be admissible, it must be agreed or demonstrated that there is a field of "specialized knowledge"; there must be an identified aspect of that field in which the witness demon-

47 *Ibid.* at 81–82, Cresswell J., as cited in *Makita*, above note 2 at para. 79.

> strates that by reason of specified training, study or experience, the witness has become an expert; the opinion proffered must be "wholly or substantially based on the witness's expert knowledge"; so far as the opinion is based on facts "observed" by the expert, they must be identified and admissibly proved by the expert, and so far as the opinion is based on "assumed" or "accepted" facts, they must be identified and proved in some other way; it must be established that the facts on which the opinion is based form a proper foundation for it; and the opinion of an expert requires demonstration or examination of the scientific or other intellectual basis of the conclusions reached: that is, the expert's evidence must explain how the field of "specialized knowledge" in which the witness is expert by reason of "training, study or experience", and on which the opinion is "wholly or substantially based", applies to the facts assumed or observed so as to produce the opinion propounded. If all these matters are not made explicit, it is not possible to be sure whether the opinion is based wholly or substantially on the expert's specialized knowledge. *If the court cannot be sure of that, the evidence is strictly speaking not admissible*, and, so far as it is admissible, of diminished weight. And an attempt to make the basis of the opinion explicit may reveal that it is not based on specialized expert knowledge, but, to use Gleeson C.J.'s characterisation of the evidence in *H.G. v. R.* (1999) 197 CLR 414, on "a combination of speculation, inference, personal and second-hand views as to the credibility of the complainant, and a process of reasoning which went well beyond the field of expertise."[48]

Thus there must be specific evidence as to the specialized knowledge of the person in relation to that subject and as to the training, study, or experience upon which that specialized knowledge is based. The further requirement that an opinion be *based on* specialized knowledge would normally be satisfied by the person who expresses the opinion demonstrating the reasoning process by which the opinion was reached. That is, a report in which an opinion is recorded should expose the reasoning of its author in a way that would demonstrate that the opinion is based on particular specialized knowledge. As we will see in subsequent chapters, expert opinions on matters of science and pathology are frequently stated in reports without any reference to the reasoning and substantiation just referred to.

48 *Makita*, *ibid.* at para. 85 [emphasis added].

Similarly, opinion evidence given orally should be shown, by exposure of the reasoning process, to be based on relevant specialized knowledge.[49] Evidence not complying with the principles described might be inadmissible as irrelevant.[50]

## 5) Speculation Not Permitted: Probative versus Prejudicial Value

It follows from what has been said that it is inappropriate for expert witnesses to engage in speculation in the sense of conjectures that are not based upon established facts or upon established scientific research. In the Australian case of *R. v. Straker*,[51] William Straker had been convicted of the murder of George Stafford. The pathologist who had conducted the autopsy noticed a tear in the lining of the anus and that, linked with other physical conditions present, led him to suggest that someone might have had anal intercourse with the deceased before or after death. The Australian High Court said that such speculation in the context of expert opinion evidence is inadmissible:

> . . . great care should be exercised in the use made by the prosecution of the doctor's post-mortem examination performed on the deceased's body, particularly as to the extent to which conclusions from it should be pursued in evidence or in argument. In particular, the doctor performing the examination ought not to be allowed to speculate on possible inferences from the state of the deceased's body. *If no inferred fact is probable, the opinion as to what might possibly be inferred is, at least in the circumstances of the case, inadmissible.*[52]

As the court said, "the evidence of Dr James was so highly prejudicial, and of such slight evidential value, that even if it might be thought to be technically relevant it should have been rejected."[53] It added:

> The real complaint of the appellant [Straker] is that Dr James was permitted to speculate on a *possibility* of which there was no evidence of *probability* . . . The question, therefore, is whether Dr James's speculation on possibilities which had no basis of probability was admissible. I can see no basis upon

---

49 *Ocean Marine Mutual Insurance Association (Europe) O.V. v. Jetopay Pty. Ltd.*, [2000] FCA 1463 at paras. 21–23.

50 *Idoport*, above note 31 at para. 19, Einstein J.

51 *Straker v. The Queen* (1977), 15 A.L.R. 103.

52 *Ibid.* at 108, Barwick C.J. [emphasis added].

53 *Ibid.* at 109.

> which it was admissible . . . he is not entitled to speculate on a possibility directly relevant to the issue or to a fact in issue when the speculation is adverse to the accused person and when there is no evidence which would support a conclusion that the fact was established.[54]

The court went on to say that experts may give evidence that a condition found by them is consistent with a certain cause, but if the cause is in issue in the case, then such expert evidence is admissible against an accused only if other evidence supports a finding of that cause. The jury may be invited to draw inferences from the evidence but not to join an expert witness in speculation on possibilities adverse to the accused.[55]

As it was summed up by the court, the medical evidence was that the deceased's condition was consistent with this having occurred either before or after death—or not having occurred at all. The evidence was speculative and did not justify a conclusion that intercourse had occurred. All this evidence was prejudicial to the accused and should have been rejected as inadmissible.[56] Full disclosure of both facts and reasoning will help to avoid impermissible speculation.

### 6) Duty of Disclosure

In Britain, Dr. Alan Williams had been involved in the case of Sally Clark. She was a solicitor, and it had been alleged that she had killed her two babies. It was subsequently revealed that they may well have died from natural causes (an infection). Her conviction was overturned, and Dr. Williams had to answer a complaint before the General Medical Council [GMC]. In handing down the finding, the GMC said that Dr. Williams had failed in his duty to consider all the possible causes of Christopher's death. It said that his post-mortem examination of Christopher was so impaired that it could not be considered reliable. He had "failed to discharge the duties of a competent pathologist in such circumstances."[57]

The tribunal that heard the complaint against Dr. Williams for the Advisory Board for Forensic Pathology pointed out that in the 1998 edition of *Archbold Criminal Pleading, Evidence and Practice* the existing law was summarized as follows:

---

54 *Ibid.* at 114, Jacobs J. [emphasis added].

55 *Ibid.*

56 *Ibid.* at 115, Murphy J.

57 *Times Online* (28 May 2005). The findings in relation to Dr. Williams are considered in more detail later in this chapter.

> Duty of Disclosure. It is the duty of an expert instructed by the prosecution to act in the cause of justice.[58] It follows that if an expert has carried out a test which casts doubt on his opinion, or if such a test has been carried out in his laboratory and *is known to him*, he is under a duty to disclose this to the solicitor instructing him who has a duty to disclose it to the defence. This duty exists irrespective of any request by the defence. It is not confined to documentation on which the opinion or findings of the expert are based. It extends to anything which might arguably assist the defence. Moreover, it is a positive duty which in the context of scientific evidence, obliges the prosecution to make full and proper inquiries from forensic scientists to ascertain whether there is discoverable material.[59]

In the Guildford Four IRA bombing case, it was emphasized that an expert's duty of disclosure is continuing.[60] In the M62 bombing case (Judith Ward), it was said that the fact that information may ultimately be found to be of no real significance should be wholly excluded from the minds of the prosecution when the question of disclosure is being considered.[61] It was also emphasized that

> . . . "all relevant evidence of help to the accused" is not limited to evidence which will obviously advance the accused's case. It is of help to the accused to have the opportunity of considering all the material evidence which the prosecution have gathered . . . .[62]

The judge explained that the duty is continuous. It applies not only in the pretrial period but also throughout the trial. The duty is also to make timely disclosure.[63]

In its judgment, the tribunal in Dr. Williams's case said that doctors who are engaged in professional consultations with other doctors have a professional duty to disclose all matters within their knowledge, whether believed by them to be relevant or not, which the other doctors would wish to take into consideration. This professional duty is based upon the expectation between doctors that

---

58 *R. v. Ward* (1993), 96 Cr. App. R. 1 [*Ward*].

59 Policy Advisory Board for Forensic Pathology, Dr. A.R. Williams MB. ChB. FRC. Path., Judgment of the Tribunal. 28 March 2006 [Policy Advisory Board—Williams] [emphasis added].

60 *Maguire & Others* (1992), 94 Cr. App. Rep. 133 at 146 [Guildford Four bombing case]; Stuart-Smith L.J., cited in Policy Advisory Board—Williams, *ibid.*

61 *Ward*, above note 58, Glidewell L.J. on "non-disclosure of evidence."

62 *Ibid.* "The duty of disclosure."

63 *Ibid.* "Conclusions on ground A: Material non-disclosure."

they will, at all times, be full and frank in their professional dealings with one another. Professor Berry said that doctors trust each other to follow normal practice and to share basic information.[64] In addition, doctors do, of course, have a professional duty to comply with their legal obligations, and to comply with relevant Practice Guidelines, such as those issued by the Home Office Policy Advisory Board for Forensic Pathology. These require, for example, that a post-mortem report should be of a high standard in presentation and appropriate to the purpose for which it is intended. It must include a detailed description of the post-mortem findings and offer conclusions that interpret those findings and any other relevant investigations undertaken. The findings should be laid out in clear, concise language, which will be readily understood by lay individuals.

In its judgment, the tribunal said that one would have expected all the results to have been set out in or attached to the report: "Dr. Williams, of course, decided not to make any reference to the microbiology he had commissioned and it is for this that he is criticized."[65] The tribunal noted that no professional colleague had been called to defend that decision.

Dr. Williams had said, "It is not my practice to refer to additional results in my post mortem [report] unless they are relevant to the cause of death as the specimens were referred to another consultant, I regard them to be his results. In the same way I have not referred to the reports of Professor Green nor Dr. Smith."[66] He commented that he did not think these results were significant or relevant so he did not bring them to the attention of the police.

The tribunal pointed out that those explanations demonstrated that Dr. Williams was applying entirely the wrong test when deciding whether or not to refer to or disclose the microbiological results. The tribunal said that the doctor's subjective opinion as to relevance or significance (whether or not he thought it would be shared by others) could not be a sufficient reason for failing to disclose results that others (including the defence experts) would reasonably wish to consider. If the results are not referred to, then the report will not contain information that others need to evaluate. If a forensic pathologist were to be entitled not to disclose such information just because he or she had concluded that it was not relevant or potentially relevant, then the underlying reasons for requiring disclosure would likely be defeated. This is not just common sense and good medical practice—it is also good law.[67]

---

64 Policy Advisory Board—Williams, above note 59 at 15.

65 *Ibid.* at 27.

66 *Ibid.* at 29.

67 The Tribunal of the Advisory Board here referred to Glidewell L.J.'s judgment in *Ward*, above note 58, and *R. v. Sally Clark*, [2003] EWCA Crim 1020 [*Clark*].

As the tribunal noted, "It is tantamount to saying 'If I can discount it, nobody else need consider it.' As an approach it only has to be voiced for the inherent danger to be obvious."[68] It also added that Dr. Williams's explanation that he did not disclose or refer to the microbiological results because the reports on such results were produced "by other experts"[69] was entirely without merit and not supported by any other expert.

Dr. Williams claimed that he was under the misapprehension that the microbiological results were known to all and sundry, including the defence experts. He told the tribunal that he thought his view that the samples had been contaminated was shared by them, and that this was the reason why the results had not been mentioned by any of the experts in their own reports. The tribunal observed that this belief is not an excuse for failing to refer to them in his report.

## C. UK LAW COMMISSION REFORMS

The UK Law Commission raised the possibility that the test for the admissibility of expert opinion be elevated to that of a statutory test. It questioned whether a statutory test requiring the judge to take on a "gatekeeping" role in assessing the validity of the principles and methodology underpinning the expert testimony was necessary.[70] It also raised the interesting question as to whether the admissibility and reliability of expert evidence should be examined before the jury is sworn in. It asked whether a pretrial preliminary assessment, perhaps with the assistance of an independent assessor, might be more effective in ensuring compliance with the admissibility rules. We will examine this issue more closely in Part Three.

## D. CANADA

The law relating to the admissibility of expert evidence is set out in the Canadian Supreme Court decision of *R. v. Mohan*.[71] It provides four criteria:

1. Relevance — the probative value must be balanced against the prejudicial value. In *R. v. D.D.* the Supreme Court of Canada took the view

---

68 The tribunal quoted Kay L.J. in *Clark*, *ibid.* at para. 167.

69 Above note 59 at 31.

70 Similar concerns were raised by Goudge J.A. in Goudge Inquiry, above note 21 at 487, "Tools for Judges to Use in Determining Threshold Reliability."

71 *R. v. Mohan*, [1994] 2 S.C.R. 9 [*Mohan*].

that "probative value is determined by considering the reliability, materiality and cogency of the expert testimony"[72]

2. Its necessity in assisting the trier of fact;
3. The absence of any exclusionary rule under the law of evidence;
4. Properly qualified experts. Is the witness shown to have acquired specialist knowledge through study or experience in respect of matters on which he or she undertakes to testify?[73]

Reliability is a factor that plays a decisive role in each of the four *Mohan* criteria.[74] In *R. v. J.-L.J.*, the Canadian Supreme Court analysed the admissibility of expert evidence as it applies to what it termed "novel science," or those areas of scientific knowledge that are new and not yet part of the established view of things.[75] Justice Binnie explained how the law had evolved since *Mohan*. He noted that the "dramatic growth in frequency with which they [experts] have been called upon has led to ongoing debate about suitable controls in their participation; precautions to exclude junk science and the need to preserve and protect the role of the trier of fact."[76] He warned about the dangers of the apparent infallibility of expert evidence.[77] He concluded that a trial judge should take the role of gatekeeper seriously, not allowing too easy an entry to expert evidence.[78]

Justice Binnie noted that *Mohan* kept the door open to novel science but rejected the general acceptance theory as stated in the American case of *Frye v. U.S.*[79] He instead adopted the four factors laid down by the US Supreme Court in *Daubert*[80] as ones that can be helpful in evaluating the reliability of novel science. He noted that while *Daubert* must be read in the light of the specific text of the US *Federal Rules of Evidence* "which differs from our own [Canadian] procedures,"[81] it was reasonable to rely on the criteria used in that case.

More recently, the Supreme Court of Canada in *R. v. Trochym*[82] has shown a willingness to embrace the American evidence jurisprudence to assist with determining reliability even where the issue is not thought to relate to novel

72 *R. v. D.D.*, [2000] 2 S.C.R. 275 at para. 36.
73 *Mohan*, above note 71 at 21.
74 Goudge Inquiry, above note 21 at 478, citing *McWilliams' Canadian Criminal Evidence*, looseleaf (Aurora, ON: Canada Law Book, 2003–) at 12–27.
75 [2000] 2 S.C.R. 600 [*J.-L.J.*].
76 *Ibid.* at para. 25.
77 *Ibid.*
78 *Ibid.* at para. 28.
79 *Frye*, above note 18.
80 *Daubert*, above note 19.
81 *Ibid.* at para. 33.
82 [2007] 1 S.C.R. 239.

science. In *Trochym*, the Court, in stressing that reliability was an essential element of admissibility, said a technique that may be acceptable in a clinical setting may not be reliable enough to be accepted in a criminal trial.[83]

In his report Goudge J. stated in relation to the effects of the *Daubert* decision the following:

> No longer is it enough to obtain the approval of a cohort of the expert's cronies willing to vouch for the technique . . . *Daubert* has focused attention of the importance of examining the underlying theory and technique rather than just the proffered conclusions.[84]

Justice Goudge recommended that in applying the *Daubert* criteria, the trial judge had to play a greater gatekeeping role in relation to the admissibility of expert evidence by ensuring that the evidence complies with scientific methodology (evidence based) rather than simply relying upon the experience of the expert (experience based).[85] He took the view that while the evidence-based approach was not infallible, it was nonetheless easier to falsify.[86] The Ontario Court of Appeal has subsequently affirmed the judge's gatekeeping role in ensuring the threshold reliability of expert evidence, but it has also warned that strict *Daubert* criteria cannot be applied to forms of expert evidence not based on the scientific method.[87] This limitation raises concerns that the courts may not force the forensic sciences to invest in more basic research and testing of their work. It is an important issue, one that we focus on in Chapter 12.

It should be noted that the Canadian Morin Inquiry[88] recommended that no police officer or Crown counsel should take action affecting an accused or a potential accused based upon representations made by a forensic scientist which are not recorded in writing. Indeed, the Morin Inquiry took sworn

---

83 *Ibid.* at paras. 27 and 37.

84 Goudge Inquiry, above note 21 at 481, citing Erica Beecher-Monas, *Evaluating Scientific Evidence: An Interdisciplinary Framework for Intellectual Due Process* (Cambridge: Cambridge University Press, 2007) at 11.

85 Goudge Inquiry, *ibid.* at 483–96.

86 Where an expert justifies a conclusion on the basis of "my experience," it invariably means that the basis for the conclusion is not available for examination or testing. It will not have been documented or scientifically tested. If that had occurred, then the proposition would be evidence based, not experience based.

87 *R. v. Abbey*, 2009 ONCA 624, admitting sociological evidence about the possible meanings of a teardrop tattoo on a gang member accused of murder.

88 *Report of the Kaufman Commission on Proceedings Involving Guy Paul Morin* (Toronto: Ministr of the Attorney General, 1998) [Morin Inquiry].

evidence from Professor Tilstone about the policies in place at the Forensic Science Centre in South Australia. He said:

> There was a fairly lengthy policy on reporting, and that policy said that reports had to contain 5 parts.
>
> 1. They had to have a chain of custody which defined the items which were examined, and where they came from.
> 2. They had to define the tests which were conducted.
> 3. They had to specify the results of that testing.
> 4. They had to specify the conclusions which could be drawn from the testing.
> 5. They had to specify the limitations which could be placed on those conclusions.[89]

Tilstone said that the National Association of Testing Authorities (NATA) program in Australia contained provisions that speak to the issue of how reports should be written.

## E. CODES OF CONDUCT

In addition to statutory requirements and those laid down in reported decisions of the courts, there are also guidelines, policies, regulations, codes of conduct, and ethical requirements. They may be found, for example, in police forensic procedures manuals, the bar rules that govern the conduct of barristers, or the guidelines for prosecutors that exist in all jurisdictions.

In Britain, for example, Criminal Procedure Rules on expert evidence first came into effect in November 2006 and appear within *Criminal Procedure Rules 2010*.[90] They deal with the duty of an expert to the court and they state:

> 1. An expert must help the court to achieve the overriding objective by giving objective, unbiased opinion on matters within their expertise.
> 2. This duty overrides any obligation to the person from whom they receive instructions or by whom they are paid.

---

89 *Ibid.*, vol. 1 at 333.

90 UK Ministry of Justice, *Criminal Procedure Rules 2010* (London: Criminal Procedure Rules Committee, 2010) Part 33 "Expert Evidence." See also "Court Rules Concerning Reception of Expert Evidence in Australian Supreme Courts" in Ian Freckelton & Hugh Selby, *Expert Evidence—Law, Practice, Procedure and Advocacy* (Pyrmont, NSW: Law Book Co., 2005) c. 27.

3. This duty includes an obligation to inform all parties and the court if the expert's opinion changes from that contained in a report served as evidence or given in a statement.[91]

In discussing the rules, the UK Attorney General noted that they also require a party to inform the expert when they have served the expert's report on another party, or on the court. They provide explicitly for pretrial discussion between experts, and they allow the court to order that a single, joint defence expert should give expert evidence for the defence.[92] The rules specify that a party may not introduce expert evidence without the court's permission, or the consent of every other party if the expert has not complied with a direction of the court.[93] As the Attorney General put it:

> The key point is that the expert is not a hired gun. His duty is to the court. But it isn't the court that instructs him—it's one side or the other. An expert can only form an opinion on the basis of the information that he is given. Whilst we gave up trial by combat many years ago, trial by ambush was until recently quite acceptable. As Lord Wilberforce said, "Expert evidence presented to the court should be and be seen to be the independent product of the expert, uninfluenced as to form or content by the exigencies of litigation."[94]

This is another reaffirmation of the rhetoric of the impartial expert witness.

### 1) Forensic Scientists and Pathologists

Every jurisdiction has a code of conduct for forensic scientists and forensic pathologists.[95]

These codes have elements similar to the following. An Australian code says that appropriate methods should be used having regard to the standard

91 *Criminal Procedure Rules 2010*, *ibid.*, Rule 33.2.

92 *Ibid.*, Rule 33.7; this is where more than one defendant wants to introduce expert evidence on an issue at the trial; the court may direct that the evidence on that issue be given by one expert only.

93 *Ibid.*, Rule 33.4.

94 The Rt. Hon. Attorney General, Lord Goldsmith, "Expert Evidence—The Problem or the Solution?" in *The Role of Expert Evidence and Its Regulation* (John Bolton Memorial Lecture delivered for the Academy of Expert Witnesses, 2007).

95 This example is derived from the Australian and New Zealand Forensic Science Society *Code of Ethics* (Brisbane, Qld: ANZFSS). The UK equivalent is the Home Office and Royal College of Pathologists *Code of Practice and Performance Standards for Forensic Pathologist* (London: Home Office, 2004). The latter contains much information that in South Australia has been included in the *Police Procedures Manual.*

of proof that is required and can be reasonably achieved. Objectivity should be maintained at all times. Relevant experimental controls should be used and, where appropriate, results verified by re-testing or by applying additional or alternative techniques. The codes emphasize that opinions should not be expressed beyond the limits of an expert's expertise. Where applicable, the physical results of tests, field notes, test notes, reports, and photographs should be retained for as long as possible or at least during the currency of any relevant legal proceedings. Distinctions should be made between the *results* of tests and examinations, and *opinions* based on these. If any limitations apply to the test results and conclusions, then they should be explained. Opinions should be expressed in simple, precise, and unambiguous terms.

Beyond that, an expert should be prepared to concede that other opinions, being contrary to or at variance with one's own, can be honestly held. In a report, the expert should refer to all items examined or tested. The nature and character of all tests and examinations and their results should be available to the court.

On the understanding that there is no property in expert scientific witnesses, the prospective witness should be reasonably available for discussion with professional representatives of all parties involved with the proceedings. Any retainer offered should be refused if it is suspected that a purpose of the offer is to prevent relevant evidence being presented to a court. No services should be rendered where the fee is dependent on the outcome of the examination. Witnesses should appeal to the presiding judicial officer (in the absence of the jury if the trial is by judge and jury) if they believe that the manner in which the evidence is being elicited is such as to prevent the disclosure of a significant relevant matter or circumstance.

It is proper to advise a lawyer concerning the reports and evidence of another expert, and such advice may be used in the cross-examination of that expert. To this end, co-operation in the provision of notes and records should be given with, if desired, the proviso of open consultation and discussion with the reviewing expert.

Professional and personal behaviour consistent with membership of a skilled profession should be observed. Colleagues should be treated with due respect and inappropriate criticism of them avoided. Errors or omissions discovered prior to, during, or *after* any hearing should be disclosed. This last provision is particularly important where errors are detected after a trial's conclusion, and in some of the cases, this has occurred many years later.

## F. INTERNATIONAL COLLABORATION

Nowadays experts are frequently called upon to give evidence in several jurisdictions. Prof. William Tilstone is an exemplar of the modern transnational approach to these issues. He was professor of Forensic Science at Strathclyde University, Scotland, but has been based in the United States for many years and has given evidence to Canadian inquiries on proper methods in forensic science. He was also the director of the Forensic Science Centre in Adelaide, South Australia, for some years.

Similarly, Prof. Stephen Cordner, the head of the Victorian Institute of Forensic Medicine in Melbourne, Australia, has also given evidence in British cases and was also an important witness to the Goudge Inquiry in Canada. Problems in the pathology work of Dr. Charles Smith were first revealed when the files were subject to peer review by five experts, the majority of whom worked outside of Canada.

A few British experts have played key roles. Prof. Jack Crane from Northern Ireland was retained as an expert by authorities in Toronto to look at some of the cases of Dr. Charles Smith. Professor Cameron from Britain gave evidence at the Lindy Chamberlain trial in Australia. In the Splatt Royal Commission in Australia, they also derived great benefit from British scientific experts.

Indeed, the international aspect of many areas of expert evidence, particularly in the areas of forensic science and pathology, is becoming increasingly important. For this reason there must be some degree of coherence and consistency in terms of the standards employed and expected of such experts. International collaboration can also provide a valuable form of peer review to help ensure that the work of scientists in a particular jurisdiction does not fail to meet basic standards.

## G. CONCLUSION

In this chapter we have set out the *rhetoric* in relation to prosecutors and experts. The formal rules that state what should be done and how it should be done appear to be sensible and to have a reasonable degree of similarity across Britain, Canada, and Australia. In matters as serious as criminal trials, one would hardly expect the rules to state anything other than that the prosecutors and experts should be diligent, fair, and properly qualified, and that they should submit to courts only evidence that is accurate and reliable.

The challenge to our sense of well-being will arise in Part Two when we outline the types of cases in which expert evidence has led to serious miscarriages of justice in all jurisdictions. The thoughtful reader might anticipate that such cases involve technical issues where the intricacy of the science or processes involved has led to some unfortunate misunderstandings. Regrettably, the *reality* is not so. The errors have been far more basic, and the gap between the rhetoric and the reality much wider than we might care to admit.

CHAPTER 3

# Law on Miscarriages of Justice: Britain

In this chapter, we look first to the evolution of appeals in criminal cases. The UK system of appeals has had a significant influence upon the development of the appellate system in both Canada and Australia. However, it should be borne in mind that in recent years the appellate system in Britain has gone through a number of changes that have not yet been reflected in those other jurisdictions, such as the simplification of the grounds of appeals which we discuss shortly.

A most significant development — and one that distinguishes UK criminal appeals in recent years from those of Canada and Australia — has been the development of the Criminal Cases Review Commission (CCRC) as an initiator of renewed appeals.[1] After an investigation, the CCRC is empowered to refer appropriate cases to the Court of Appeal for a rehearing. On receipt of the referral, the Court of Appeal is bound to rehear the matter. As a result, in a significant number of cases, the court has overturned convictions — those cases provide much of the basis for the discussion in this chapter. By definition, they are "miscarriage of justice" cases because the CCRC cannot normally commence its review until all of the appellate procedures have been exhausted. So, the discussion in this chapter is almost exclusively on the Court of Appeal cases — *Pendleton*[2] is the obvious exception being a House of Lords (Supreme Court) decision.

By contrast, in Canada and Australia, working without a body such as the CCRC, we have to depend upon our understanding of the principles relevant

1 We discuss the procedures in more detail in Chapter 10.

2 *R. v. Pendleton*, [2001] UKHL 66 [*Pendleton*].

to miscarriage of justice cases from the royal commissions (Australia) or public inquiries (Canada), which are relatively infrequent, and otherwise by extrapolation from the more usual appellate cases. The emphasis in Chapters 3 and 4 is predominantly upon the more regular superior court appellate cases and also in Canada, on the relatively rare cases referred back to the courts by the Minister of Justice. In Chapter 5, on the Australian law, the emphasis is almost exclusively on the High Court cases, with relatively little discussion of the cases in the intermediate appellate courts. The discussion of the Canadian law, which is in Chapter 4, is more balanced between Supreme Court and intermediate appellate court cases, reflecting the more established and full-time nature of their appellate jurisdiction by contrast to the sometimes part-time nature of the intermediate appeals in Australia.[3]

In each of the three chapters, the tone of the discussion will vary, and this to some extent reflects the nature of the sources being used.

As we move into the discussion of the UK cases, we first look at the history of the appellate system and then the current appeal provisions. We then look in general terms at the process of appeals before turning our attention to the types of cases that have arisen as sources of error at trial.

## A. HISTORY OF APPEALS

Some may be surprised to learn that the right of a convicted person to appeal the decision and sentence of a criminal trial court is a relatively modern development. It was introduced in Britain in 1907.[4] It is also a relatively modern development that an accused person has been able to have a lawyer speak in his or her defence, or that the accused be allowed to give evidence.[5] The main process used by the courts in common law countries for criminal trials is adversarial. It has been said that the real effect of that system has been to suppress the truth, rather than to reveal it:

---

3 As mentioned in Chapter 2, in some Australian jurisdictions, the appeal court is made up of trial judges sitting together as the Court of Appeal.

4 *Criminal Appeal Act, 1907* (U.K.), 7 Edw. VII, c. 23. See also Richard Nobles & David Schiff, "The Right to Appeal and Workable Systems of Justice" (2002) 65 Mod. L. Rev. 676; Ken Whiteway, "The Origins of the English Court of Criminal Appeal" (2008) 33 Canadian Law Library Review 309 [Whiteway]; Leon Radzinowicz & Roger Hood, *A History of English Criminal Law* (London: Stevens, 1986) [Radzinowicz & Hood]; Rosemary Pattenden, *English Criminal Appeals 1844–1994* (Oxford: Oxford University Press, 1996) [Pattenden].

5 John H. Langbein, *The Origins of the Adversary Criminal Trial* (Oxford: Oxford University Press, 2003).

> In an Anglo-American trial, the job of each adversary is to win the courtroom struggle. Winning often reveals tactics that distort or suppress the truth, for example, concealing relevant witnesses, withholding information that would help the other side, preparing witnesses to affect their testimony at trial (coaching), and engaging in abusive cross-examination.[6]

Prior to the enactment of the *Criminal Appeal Act, 1907*, the two limited procedures for appeals against conviction on indictment were by way of a "writ of error" or by "case-stated." The ancient writ of error was a process by which the decision of an inferior court could be challenged for "error on the face of the record." The circumstances in which this could occur were limited, and sometimes a decision was set aside for unmeritorious technical error.[7] The case-stated procedure was also used sparingly. It gave the trial judge the sole discretion to refer points of law to the Court of Crown Cases Reserved. The court could either affirm or discharge the verdict of the trial judge but had no power to direct a new trial.

This lack of a proper system of criminal appeals was partly responsible for the perpetuation of several miscarriages of justice. There were widespread concerns about some perceived miscarriage of justice cases, culminating in the two highly publicized cases of Adolph Beck and George Edalji.[8]

In the first, Thomas Smith was convicted and sentenced to five years of imprisonment in 1877 for defrauding a number of women. Shortly after his release, similar offences occurred. Beck, a Norwegian of dubious character, was arrested for the offences. At his trial, eight of the ten women who gave evidence for the prosecution positively identified him as the perpetrator. A retired police officer who had arrested Smith in 1877 gave evidence that Beck was the person convicted back then. A handwriting expert also testified that documents written by Smith in 1877 were in Beck's disguised handwriting. What the court never heard was that in 1877 Beck was in South America and could not have been the author of those documents. Beck was convicted and sentenced to seven years of imprisonment. He submitted many petitions to the Home Secretary for a re-examination of his case, but they were all denied.[9]

---

6 *Ibid.*, Introduction at 1. See also Evan Whitton, *Our Corrupt Legal System* (Coopers Plains, Qld: Book Pal Australia, 2009).

7 Roger J. Traynor, *The Riddle of Harmless Error* (Columbus, OH: Ohio State University Press, 1970).

8 See Pattenden, above note 4 at 28–30; See Whiteway, above note 4.

9 Tim Coates, *The Strange Case of Adolph Beck* (London: H.M.S.O., 2001).

In 1904, three years after Beck was released from prison, he was again arrested and convicted for further similar offences. This time the judge had some doubts and reserved sentence so that more inquiries could be made. During this time Smith was arrested and confessed to committing all of the offences. Beck was eventually pardoned in respect of both convictions and paid compensation.

The second case concerned George Edalji, a solicitor, who in 1903 was wrongly convicted of harming and killing animals near his parents' vicarage. He was convicted despite the fact that he had an alibi and was in custody when some of the offences took place. A petition submitted on his behalf to the Home Secretary was unsuccessful. After three years into his seven-year sentence he was released without explanation. Following much public agitation, including by Sir Arthur Conan Doyle, an inquiry set up by the Home Office found his conviction to be unsatisfactory. Although he was eventually pardoned, no compensation was paid.

The mishandling of the Beck and Edalji cases was largely attributed to the lack of a proper appeal process. The push for reforms by high-profile lawyers, newspaper editors, and some members of Parliament resulted in some twenty-eight bills being introduced into Parliament with a view to setting up a system of appeals in criminal cases. These efforts culminated in the passing of the 1907 Act.[10]

The *Criminal Appeal Act 1907* set up the new Court of Criminal Appeal and abolished the ancient writ of error and the Court of Crown Cases Reserved. The Act gave this new appeal court the power to determine any questions necessary for the purpose of doing justice in the case before the court. The grounds set out for overturning a jury verdict were that the verdict was unreasonable; that it could not be supported having regard to the evidence; or that there had been a wrong decision on any question of law or on any ground signifying a miscarriage of justice.[11]

A failure to establish any of those grounds meant that the court was required to dismiss the appeal. The Act also contained a proviso which said that notwithstanding that the court may have decided a point or points raised in the appellant's favour, it could still dismiss the appeal if it considered that no substantial miscarriage of justice had occurred.[12] Apart from reviewing a conviction, the Court of Criminal Appeal could also entertain an appeal on the

10 Lester B. Orfield, "History of Criminal Appeal in England" (1936) 1 Mod. L. Rev. 326 at 336.

11 *Criminal Appeal Act, 1907*, above note 4, s. 2. The issues here are set out and explained in *Pendleton*, above note 2 at para. 8*ff.*

12 *Criminal Appeal Act, 1907*, *ibid.*, s. 3.

sentence. The 1907 Act had no restriction on the admission of fresh evidence as long as it was thought to be necessary or expedient in the interest of justice.

The passing of this legislation received mixed responses.[13] Many senior judges expressed deep concern that a convicted person would be able to abuse the system. In their view, owing to the high standard of proof required, the possibility of an innocent person being convicted was too remote. Furthermore, they thought, an appeal against conviction would have the effect of undermining the role of the jury in a criminal trial. They also saw the need for finality in criminal proceedings as another overriding consideration. These judicial attitudes had an effect on the way the Court of Appeal, despite its rather broad statutory grounding, exercised its role. Indeed, historically judges in England resisted the introduction of appeals, maintaining that the rate of error was low and could be dealt with by pardons from the executive.[14]

The 1907 Act did not give the Court of Appeal the power to order a retrial upon a successful appeal—it could only confirm, set aside, or modify the conviction.[15] Subsequently, significant reforms were made to the 1907 Act. Only in 1964 was the Court of Appeal given limited power to order a retrial and not until 1988 was it granted unconditional power to order a retrial. In 1968 the Court of Criminal Appeal was renamed the Court of Appeal (Criminal Division). Further significant changes were brought about in 1995 in response to the series of miscarriage of justice cases that we will examine in later chapters (the IRA bombing cases).[16] They included the alteration of the grounds of appeal to a single requirement that the conviction was "unsafe"—and the transfer of responsibility for considering the safety of a conviction, and any subsequent reference to the Court of Appeal, from the Home Secretary to the CCRC.

## B. CONTEMPORARY APPEAL PROVISIONS

The current position is as follows. After a conviction for more serious (indictable) offences, a person has a right of appeal on any issue of law without the need to obtain permission (leave); on issues of fact or mixed issues of law and

---

13 Pattenden, above note 4 at 22–27. See also Radzinowicz & Hood, above note 4, vol. 5 at 765.

14 Benjamin Berger, "Criminal Appeals as Jury Control" (2007) 10 Can. Crim. L. Rev. 1 at 29–31.

15 See *Woolmington v. D.P.P.*, [1935] A.C. 462.

16 See Richard Nobles & David Schiff, "The Criminal Cases Review Commission: Establishing a Workable Relationship with the Court of Appeal" (2005) Crim. L. Rev. 173; Clive Walker & Keir Starmer, eds., *Justice in Error* (London: Blackstone Press, 1993).

fact, the person may appeal only with the leave of either the trial judge or of the Court of Appeal.[17] This distinction has its basis in the traditional deference due to the jury as the trier of facts in a criminal case. It is harder to overturn a verdict by a challenge to the facts upon which the verdict is based.

The principal provision that was contained in the 1907 Act is now expressed succinctly in the *Criminal Appeal Act 1968* (as amended in 1995). It states that the Court of Appeal "shall allow an appeal against conviction if they think that the conviction is unsafe."[18] Otherwise, it is required to dismiss the appeal.[19]

The legislation prior to 1995 used the expression "unsafe or unsatisfactory." There was some debate as to whether the 1995 amendment was designed to narrow the ground of appeal in the shift from "unsafe and unsatisfactory" to "unsafe." It was thought "unsatisfactory" might encompass cases where the court of appeal may have been convinced that the accused was guilty (so in that sense the conviction was "safe") but because of some procedural error (non-disclosure of police misconduct, for example) they felt that the accused had not had a fair trial. However, as we will see shortly, cases decided under the new formula have shown that the Court of Appeal has not adopted such a restrictive interpretation. For example, in *R. v. Smith (Patrick Joseph)* a conviction was quashed as unsafe because of trial irregularities, even though the accused had admitted his responsibility for the crime under cross-examination at his trial.[20]

The specific terms of what we have referred to as "the proviso" were not continued after the 1995 amendments. It is, however, accepted that factors similar to those of the proviso have been incorporated into the general consideration of whether the verdict was safe.

## C. THE PROCESS OF APPEAL

The appeal does not usually take the form of a rehearing of the case although the court does have the power to hear additional or new evidence. The Act allows the Court of Appeal, if it thinks it necessary and expedient in the interests of justice, to order the production of any document, exhibit, or other thing

17 *Criminal Appeal Act 1968* (U.K.), 1968, c. 19, s. 1.

18 *Ibid.*, s. 2(1).

19 The history and legislative background to the provision is set out in *Pendleton*, above note 2.

20 *R. v. Smith & Ors*, [1999] EWCA Crim 1525.

that appears necessary for the determination of the case.[21] It can also order any witness who would have been a compellable witness at the trial to attend and be examined, whether they were or were not called at the trial.

In hearing an appeal the court will usually have a considerable body of material before it (the *Appeal Book*) which might well take up several volumes.[22] These will include the application and the grounds of appeal, transcripts (the judge's summing up to the jury, relevant passages in the evidence, and rulings given before or in the course of the trial), plans, photographs, and expert reports.

Given that a jury does not give reasons for its decision, the court will have to draw any necessary inferences about the facts from the verdict. If, for example, the issue in a rape case was that of consent, then the jury in order to convict must have been sure that the victim did not consent. If the issue was that of identification, then the jury, if it convicted, must have been sure that the evidence identifying the defendant was reliable. If a proper judicial direction has been given, it will ordinarily be safe for the Court of Appeal to infer that the factual ingredients essential to prove guilt were established to the jury's satisfaction.

However, the Court of Appeal cannot know what points the jury may have had difficulty with. The jury's process of reasoning is not available for scrutiny and if a number of witnesses gave evidence bearing on a single question, the Court of Appeal will never know which of those witnesses the jury accepted and which, if any, they doubted or rejected.

The House of Lords in *Pendleton* said it was right to emphasize the central role of the jury in a trial on indictment. They said that this role is an important and greatly prized feature of the common law system. As they pointed out, "trial by jury does not mean trial by jury in the first instance and trial by judges of the Court of Appeal in the second."[23] The Court of Appeal is entrusted with a power of *review* to guard against the possibility of injustice—but this power must be exercised with caution, mindful that the Court of Appeal is not privy to the jury's deliberations and must not intrude into territory that properly belongs to the jury.

In practice, in order to succeed on appeal, the accused will need to identify some procedural error at the trial or show some fresh or new evidence casting doubt on the original conviction. In 2005, the Court of Appeal allowed

---

21 *Criminal Appeal Act 1968*, above note 17, s. 23(1).

22 This part of the discussion has been adapted from the decision in *Pendleton*, above note 2.

23 *Ibid.* at para. 17.

228 conviction appeals and twenty-eight of these were on referral from the Criminal Cases Review Commission.[24] A study of the first 300 appeals heard by the Court of Appeal in 2002 revealed that "lurking doubt" about the conviction was raised in only seven of the appeals, and the appeal was allowed on that basis in only one of the appeals. Fresh evidence was raised as a ground of appeal in thirty-seven of these 300 cases and was successful in nine of them.[25]

## D. APPELLATE DISCRETION TO ENTER ACQUITTAL OR ORDER A NEW TRIAL

Following a successful appeal the Court of Appeal will quash the conviction and either enter a verdict of acquittal or order a retrial.[26] In some cases, it is said that the decision to allow an appeal is closely associated with the decision to order a retrial. As was said in *Pendleton*, this is clearly understandable, but it is wrong.

In *Pendleton* it was said that if the court thinks a conviction is unsafe, then its clear duty is to allow the appeal and quash the conviction. Whether there can be a retrial is a separate issue and must not be allowed to influence the decision about the safety of the verdict. It would be wrong to say that a conviction can be thought to be unsafe—so long as a retrial is available. Otherwise, it will be taken to be safe. Only when an appeal has been allowed can any question of a retrial properly arise.

Before 1988 a retrial could be ordered only if the successful appeal was allowed by reason of fresh evidence and "it appears to the court that the interests of justice so require."[27] The earlier limitation on the requirement of fresh evidence was removed by the *Criminal Justice Act 1988*.[28] The court now has a complete discretion to order a retrial in any successful appeal where the interests of justice so require.

Normally, a person can be retried only for an offence for which he or she was or could have been convicted when first tried. So, if an accused was

24 Michael Naughton, *Rethinking Miscarriages of Justice: Beyond the Tip of the Iceberg* (New York: Palgrave Macmillan, 2008) at 40. In 2004, the respective figures were 240 appeals allowed, twenty-six on referral from the CCRC; in 2003, 178 appeals were allowed, twenty-nine on referral from the CCRC; in 2002, 166 appeals were allowed, twenty-two on referral from the CCRC.

25 Stephanie Roberts, "The Royal Commission of Justice and Factual Innocence: Remedying Wrongful Convictions in the Court of Appeal" (2004) 1 Justice Journal 86.

26 See also the discussion of this topic in Chapter 4, which is on Canadian law.

27 *Criminal Appeal Act 1968*, above note 17, s. 7(1).

28 *Criminal Justice Act 1988* (U.K.), 1988, c. 33, s. 43.

convicted for a non-existent or wrong offence, a retrial is not possible, however strong the evidence. The Court of Appeal has not provided any formal directions as to when it will order a retrial. Factors such as the strength of the evidence for the prosecution and the seriousness of the offence have been mentioned as reasons for a retrial.[29] Factors such as excessive delay and unavailability of witnesses would mitigate against a retrial.[30]

## E. CROWN APPEALS

Following an acquittal, the prosecution originally had no right of appeal, but over the years a series of piecemeal changes have given them limited rights of appeal. For example, following an acquittal, under the *Criminal Justice Act 1972*,[31] section 36(b), the prosecution can refer a point of law to the Court of Appeal which it believes the trial judge applied wrongly. If the Court of Appeal upholds the reference, it can publicly say so for the benefit of the trial judges in future cases. The acquittal, however, stands.

The prosecution can also appeal against an inadequate sentence. The Court of Appeal has the power to overturn the trial judge's decision on the sentence and to increase it.[32]

In limited circumstances the prosecution can apply to the High Court against a "tainted acquittal" procured by intimidation of witnesses or jurors, and if the Court upholds the application, the acquittal is quashed and the accused is liable to be retried.[33]

Since 2003 retrials following acquittals are now allowed if there is "new and compelling" evidence for crimes of murder, manslaughter, kidnapping, rape, armed robbery, and such serious offences, all of which carry sentences of life imprisonment. However, any such retrial must be approved in writing by the director of Public Prosecutions, and the Court of Appeal must agree to quash the original acquittal.[34] The retrial must take place on an indictment preferred by the direction of the Court of Appeal, and the arraignment must take place within two months of the order for retrial unless the court allows a longer period.[35]

---

29 *R. v. Bey*, [1993] 3 All E.R. 253 re strength of evidence; *R. v. Theodosi*, [1993] R.T.R. 179 re seriousness of offence.

30 *Reid v. R.*, [1980] A.C. 343 (P.C.).

31 (U.K.), 1972, c. 71.

32 *Criminal Justice Act 1988*, above note 28, ss. 35–36.

33 *Criminal Procedure and Investigations Act 1996* (U.K.), 1996, c. 25, s. 54.

34 *Criminal Justice Act 2003* (U.K.), 2003, c. 44, ss. 75–76.

35 *Ibid.*, s. 84.

## F. WHERE APPEALS HAVE BEEN EXHAUSTED

Prior to 1995 the only option to secure a further review of a case was by lodging a petition with the Home Office through the C3 department.[36] Under this process the initial hurdle of preparing and presenting a petition was considerable. The first evaluation of the petition would be made by public servants operating within strict, self-imposed guidelines and if further investigations were required, they would usually be carried out by individuals, for example, police officers, who may be reluctant to unearth their own or their colleagues' potential misconduct or shortcomings. Even if the petition was passed to the Home Secretary, who had the sole discretion to refer the case back to the Court of Appeal, the overriding principle governing the use of this power was to avoid giving the appearance of executive interference with the role of the judiciary.[37]

From 1981 to 1988, the Home Secretary referred only thirty-six convictions involving forty-eight appellants back to the Court of Appeal under the petition procedure.[38] From 1989 to 1992, however, twenty-eight cases involving forty-nine appellants were referred by the Home Secretary, including cases involving terrorism and the West Midlands Serious Crime Squad.[39] This dramatic increase in referrals as well as the high profile of many of these miscarriages of justice contributed to the creation of the CCRC in 1995.

In 1994, C3 had twelve caseworkers and two-and-half senior staff working full time on miscarriages of justice.[40] C3 was widely criticized for its failure to investigate cases independently. A 1989 report by the rights group JUSTICE, for example, stated:

---

36 *Criminal Appeal Act 1968*, above note 17, s. 17. This issue is discussed in more detail in Chapter 10.

37 Home Office Memoranda (1991) 4.5:

> Successive governments have taken the view that it is fundamental to our system of justice that questions of guilt or innocence are matters for the court to decide, free from interference from ministers. Juries are arbiters of fact and it is not for the Home Secretary to seek to set aside a verdict simply because he or others who have interest themselves in a case have drawn different conclusion about the convicted persons' guilt based on their own assessment of the evidence which was before the court. Similarly, questions of law are matters for the judge, not the Secretary of State; it is not for him to substitute his view on such question.

38 *Report of the The Royal Commission on Criminal Justice* Cm 2263 (London: H.M.S.O., 1993) at 181.

39 *Ibid.*

40 Michael Naughton, "Introduction" in Michael Naughton, ed., *The Criminal Cases Review Commission: Hope for the Innocent?* (Basingstoke, UK: Palgrave Macmillan, 2009) at 14, n 9 [Naughton].

> The officials employed to investigate cases do not have any legal expertise. This may not be important when the matter is one of factual analysis, but it can be disadvantageous when regard must be had to the quality of trial or the appeal or the competence or conduct of trial counsel. Moreover, the officials do not themselves investigate, but usually ask the same police force which investigated the offence to carry out the further investigation. This, in our view, is inherently unsatisfactory . . . In JUSTICE's experience, the nature of the re-investigation seems more often an attempt to shore up the case against the defendant than a disinterested examination of the complaints.[41]

JUSTICE proposed the creation of an independent body that could investigate and hold hearings and make recommendations to the Home Secretary that cases be referred back to the Court of Appeal.[42]

Since 1995 the Criminal Cases Review Commission has had the power to refer a case back to the Court of Appeal. It can make such a reference after assessing the merits of the case upon an application by the accused or another interested party. The CCRC also has the power to consider a case for reference without any application having been made to it. It may exercise this power when the application by one party throws doubt on the conviction of a co-accused or where evidence unearthed in one case renders a series of convictions open to doubt.[43] The CCRC does still, on occasion, appoint police officers to conduct outside investigations,[44] but as will be discussed in Chapter 10, it receives many more applications and refers many more convictions to the Court of Appeal than did the Home Secretary.

## G. PROCEDURAL ERROR: THE RIGHT TO A FAIR TRIAL

The objective of the appellate process is to conduct reviews of trial procedures to ensure that every person who has been convicted has had a fair trial.

- *R. v. Bentley*: In November 1952 Police Constable Sidney Miles was shot dead in the execution of his duty on the roof of a warehouse in Croy-

---

41 Sir George Stanley Waller, *Miscarriages of Justice* (London: Justice, 1989) at 5.15.

42 *Ibid.* at 5.2.5.

43 For example, cases involving the now disbanded West Midlands Serious Crimes Squad are discussed in detail in Chapter 7.

44 Laurie Elks, *Righting Miscarriages of Justice* (London: Justice, 2008) at 22 [Elks] (investigating officers appointed in thirty-three cases in the first ten years of the CCRC, with eighteen cases going to officers from an outside force and referrals being made to the Court of Appeal in sixteen of the cases).

don. Two males were convicted of the murder: Christopher Craig (aged sixteen) and Derek Bentley (aged nineteen). Bentley's case contained a recommendation to mercy. The trial judge passed on each the only sentence permitted by law: Craig, because of his age, was to be detained during Her Majesty's Pleasure. Bentley was sentenced to death and executed on 28 January 1953. In 1993, forty years later, Bentley was granted a posthumous royal pardon in respect of the death sentence. In 1998 following a reference by the CCRC, his conviction was overturned by the Court of Appeal. The court was critical of the role of the judge at the trial who had unfairly emphasized the strength of the prosecution case. In its judgment the Court of Appeal said a fair trial is the birthright of every citizen.[45]

- *R. v. Mattan*: In July 1952 Mahmoud Mattan, a Somali man, was convicted of the murder of a shop assistant and sentenced to death. He was hanged on 8 September. The deceased (Mrs. Volpert) kept a shop near Cardiff docks. About £100 was stolen and she was found with her throat cut from side to side from behind. The key witness for the prosecution was a man named Harold Cover. He said he saw Mattan coming from the doorway of the shop at 8:15 p.m., the time when the murder must have been committed. It subsequently transpired that Cover had later attacked someone else in circumstances similar to that of Mrs. Volpert. In allowing Mattan's posthumous appeal against his conviction, the Court of Appeal in 1998 said that the duty to ensure a fair trial is not just the duty of the judge, but the duty of everyone associated with the criminal justice system, be they prosecutors, defence counsel, or judges. Injustices can be avoided only if all concerned in the investigation and prosecution of crime observe the highest standards of integrity, conscientiousness, and professional skill.[46]

Indeed, as we will see from some of the UK cases, those people who have been accused of crimes have often had an extensive criminal history.[47] Yet, the Court of Appeal has made it clear that both the innocent and the guilty are entitled to fair trials. If the trial process is not fair, if it is distorted by deceit or

---

45 *R. v. Bentley (Deceased)*, [1998] EWCA Crim 2516 [*Bentley*].

46 *R. v. Mattan (Deceased)*, [1998] EWCA Crim 676 [*Mattan*].

47 In *R. v. Maynard & Ors*, [2002] EWCA Crim 1942 at para. 11 [*Maynard*]: Mantell L.J. observed, "It would not be unfair to observe that most of the principal personalities . . . concerned in the events which gave rise to the charges were either convicted criminals, or members of the families or friends of convicted criminals."

by material breaches of the rules of evidence or procedure, then the liberties of all are threatened.[48]

In some of the cases we examine, both in this and the following chapters, it is clear that the investigatory and trial procedure was less than rigorous. In some cases, the appalling nature of the crimes and the desire to hold *someone* accountable — as perhaps in the cases of Bentley and Mattan — may have affected the procedure. Yet, as the courts have said, both judge and counsel must ensure that the trial process is not compromised by the desire to apportion blame.

The objective of an appeal is not to allow people to have their matter retried before appeal court judges, but to test out the reliability of the trial that was conducted before the jury. The goal, therefore, is not so much for the court of appeal to *do justice* — in the sense of determining the appropriate outcome (guilty or not guilty) — but to *prevent injustice* being done at trials. As the appeal court has said repeatedly throughout these decisions, it is not for appeal court judges to determine if the accused was guilty or innocent, but to ensure that even if guilty, they have been subjected to an open and fair trial process.

While there have been many changes of detail over the years, the fundamental principles have not changed. No doubt, the abolition of capital punishment in 1969 and the ability from 1964 to order a retrial meant that the choices available to the appeal court have become less stark.[49] After all, it might be easier for the judges to recognize a possible miscarriage of justice if they feel that a jury will have another chance to ensure that justice is done. Nevertheless, the appeal courts must remain committed to preventing injustices regardless of whether a new trial is possible.

Some of the most difficult cases to deal with are those where there has been a serious irregularity in the trial, and yet there seems to be sufficient evidence of guilt. This situation raises the broader issue of more general concern with miscarriages of justice, defined to include unfair trials and not just wrongful convictions of the innocent. This emphasis points to an important difference between the approach of various innocence projects which emphasize "factual

---

48 *R. v. Davis & Ors*, [2000] EWCA Crim 109 [*Davis*].

49 *Pendleton*, above note 2 at para. 8:

> Although the 1907 Act has been repeatedly amended, the scheme of the Act has not been fundamentally altered. The most notable change has been the granting by the *Criminal Appeal Act 1964* and the extension by the *Criminal Justice Act 1988* of a power, on the allowing of an appeal against conviction, to order a retrial.

The last hanging in the United Kingdom was in 1964; capital punishment was abolished there in 1969.

innocence" and that of the CCRC which does not limit its concerns to factual innocence.[50]

Here again, the approach of the UK courts has been principled. Unless the requirements of a fair trial have been complied with, the conviction cannot remain undisturbed, and a material irregularity can result in the quashing of a conviction when evidence as to guilt is nevertheless overwhelming.[51] The view taken is that it is a fundamental constitutional requirement that even a guilty defendant is entitled, before being found guilty, to have a trial which conforms with the minimum standards of what is regarded as an acceptable trial. Such standards include a safeguard against serious procedural (but not technical) unfairness.[52] As such, they should not be disparaged as "technicalities."[53]

The distinction was referred to in the Privy Council decision in *Randall v. R.*:

> . . . it is not every departure from good practice which renders a trial unfair . . . . It would emasculate the trial process, and undermine public confidence in the administration of criminal justice, if a standard of perfection were imposed that was incapable of attainment in practice. But the right of a criminal defendant to a fair trial is absolute. There will come a point when the departure from good practice is so gross, or so persistent, or so prejudicial, or so irremediable that an appellate court will have no choice but to condemn a trial as unfair and quash a conviction as unsafe, however strong the grounds for believing the defendant to be guilty. The right to a fair trial is one to be enjoyed by the guilty as well as the innocent, for a defendant is presumed to be innocent until proved to be otherwise in a fairly conducted trial.[54]

---

50 Graham Zellick, "Facing Up to Miscarriages of Justice" (2005–2006) 31 Man. L.J. 555. Zellick was formerly the chair of the CCRC. See also the development of this point in Chapter 10.

51 *Davis*, above note 48, Mantell L.J. in reference to *R. v. Weir*, *The Times* (16 June 2000).

52 *R. v. Hanratty*, [2002] EWCA Crim 1141 at para. 95 [*Hanratty*].

53 For example, Michael Naughton warns that the cases referred by the CCRC "includes cases that the CCRC refers back to the [Court of Appeal] on technicalities that are not deemed eligible 'claims of innocence' by Innocence Network UK (INUK) to be referred to one of its member innocence projects for further investigation." Michael Naughton, "Introduction" in Naughton, above note 40. Laurie Elks, a former CCRC commissioner, concedes that some of the referrals by the CCRC are based on "technical-legal" grounds often related to changes in the law or errors in the judge's instructions to the jury and that some "lack any intrinsic appeal to one's sense of justice." He warns, however, that the CCRC would be subject to judicial review if it had not referred these cases and that some of the cases "do raise genuine concerns as to possible injustice." Elks, above note 44 at 344.

54 *Randall v. R.*, [2002] UKPC 19 at para. 28. See also the "sleeping judge" case in Australia—*Cesan v. The Queen; Mas Rivadavia v. The Queen*, [2008] HCA 52.

It should be noted that Britain has the added protection of a system of external review to ensure the maintenance of proper standards: Article 6 of the *European Convention for the Protection of Human Rights and Fundamental Freedoms*[55] confers on everyone the right to a fair trial. This is now enacted in Article 6 of Schedule 1 of the *Human Rights Act 1998*.[56] However, in *Davis*, the Court of Appeal made it clear that a breach of some procedure that forms part of the right to a fair trial does not automatically make the conviction unfair or unsafe. That would depend on the nature and degree of the breach.[57]

## H. FRESH EVIDENCE ON APPEAL

One reason for a conviction being unsafe is that new evidence that casts doubt on the safety of the conviction has come to light. The *Criminal Appeal Act 1968*, section 23(1)(c), allows the Court of Appeal to receive evidence that was not adduced at the trial. However, in deciding whether to receive such evidence the court will have regard to these four criteria set out in section 23(2):[58]

- Is it capable of belief?
- Does it provide any ground for allowing the appeal?
- Would it have been admissible in the trial?
- Is there a reasonable explanation for failing to produce the evidence at trial?

When considering such an application, the court will have before it a written statement of the evidence that the witness proposes to give. If on reading it, the court does not view the statement as even capable of belief, then it will proceed no further. Likewise, if having read the statement the court takes the view that it will not afford any ground for allowing the appeal (that is, that the conviction is unsafe), then it will proceed no further.

On the other hand, the appeal court will sometimes admit additional evidence even if all the section 23(2) requirements are not complied with.[59] Such a flexible approach may be consistent with the Court of Appeal's role in preventing injustice.

---

55 *European Convention for the Protection of Human Rights and Fundamental Freedoms* (1950), E.T.S. No. 005.

56 *Human Rights Act 1998* (U.K.), 1998, c. 42.

57 Above note 48.

58 This issue is discussed in detail in *Pendleton*, above note 2 at para. 11, citing *R. v. D. and J.*, [1996] 1 Cr. App. R. 455.

59 *R. v. Pinfold & Anor*, [2003] EWCA Crim 3643 at para. 10 [*Pinfold*].

In *R. v. Gilfillan*,[60] the accused had been playing loud music in his apartment and had become involved in a fight with his neighbour Purbrick about it. It appears Purbrick had been subjected to severe kicks and punches from which he died. Gilfillan was convicted of murder and sentenced to life imprisonment. In his appeal, Gilfillan wanted to argue that he was suffering from such an abnormality of mind as substantially impaired his mental responsibility for his acts in relation to the killing. If successful this argument would have meant that he should have been convicted only for manslaughter, not murder. The issue had not been raised at the trial because Gilfillan did not make any disclosure in support of such a plea to those who examined him medically. However, the Court of Appeal said that even where there was no reasonable explanation for the failure to adduce the evidence at the trial, the duty of the court was to have regard to what it considered necessary or expedient in the interests of justice.

As the House of Lords said in *Pendleton*, in practice, and often with the consent of the Crown, the court will hear *de bene esse* the evidence of a witness, without preliminary argument about whether the requirements set out above have been met.[61] The court in *Pendleton* said it had no objection to this practice; however, if it receives the evidence, or hears it *de bene esse*, it must then undertake its second task: that of deciding whether or not to allow the appeal.

The court's approach to such fresh evidence issues is not necessarily passive. The court is empowered to appoint someone to interview witnesses on its behalf.[62] Or it can appoint a special commissioner to investigate any scientific or other issues that could not be examined in court and to report back (section 23A). It can also appoint people with special expert knowledge as assessors to assist the court. In *Nicholls*, the court considered taking evidence "on Commission" because a witness was suffering from terminal illness and might not be available for the later hearing of the court.[63] Although the Court of Appeal operates in an adversarial system, sometimes a more proactive approach may be helpful in preventing injustices.

One way of assessing the safety of a conviction is to consider the views being expressed by the relevant experts. An important area where new insights

---

60 *R. v. Gilfillan*, [1998] EWCA Crim 3466, Lord Bingham L.C.J. [*Gilfillan*].

61 *Pendleton*, above note 2 at para. 11, citing *R. v. Parks*, [1961] 1 W.L.R. 1484. *De bene esse*, a Latin expression meaning of well-being; usually understood in legal proceedings to mean provisionally, or conditionally or in anticipation of future need, *Blacks Law Dictionary*, 5th ed.

62 *The Criminal Appeal Act 1968*, above note 17, s. 23(4).

63 *R. v. Nicholls*, [1998] EWCA Crim 727 (bail application).

have been gained in this respect is that of psychiatry and psychology. The cases show that one of the most common problems has been a deficient understanding of the extent to which people might go to mislead others.[64] Sometimes it has been by way of false confessions, to gain favour with the investigators;[65] other times it has been to assert knowledge of things that could not have been known (the notorious "jailhouse" confessions).[66] The words "suggestibility," "compliance," and "vulnerability" have been often used in these judgments to refer to things said and done by the accused and by witnesses.[67] In a number of cases the Crown did not oppose the putting forward by the defence of fresh evidence about the mental state of the accused.[68]

It is obviously relevant to consider whether the fresh evidence would have been admissible at the trial. If the evidence could have been put to the court at the trial, and the accused or the accused's lawyers made the tactical decision not to do so, then they cannot expect to come back later and have a second go. However, as we shall see later, if the failure results from a failure of counsel to provide proper advice, then such evidence can be admitted.

---

64 In *R. v. Ward*, [1993] 2 All E.R. 577, it was said that the courts must be vigilant to ensure that they can identify confessions that may be untrue.

65 In *R. v. Kelly & Anor*, [2003] EWCA Crim 2957 [*Kelly*], it was said that if it wasn't for Graham's [untrue] evidence, Kelly would not have been convicted [and hanged]. The Under Secretary had confirmed the Secretary of State's decision to recommend the remission of the remainder of Graham's sentence and his immediate release from custody following upon his "assistance" in this matter.

66 In *Kelly*, *ibid.*, Graham had said that he had also heard a confession from Johnson to having committed the crime.

67 G.H. Gudjonsson, *The Psychology of Interrogations, Confessions, and Testimony* (New York: Wiley, 1992); G.H. Gudjonsson, *The Psychology of Interrogations and Confessions: A Handbook* (Hoboken, NJ: Wiley, 2003) [Gudjonsson]; Saul M. Kassin & Gisli H. Gudjonsson, "The Psychology of Confessions, A Review of the Literature & Issues" (2004) 5 Psychological Science in the Public Interest 33. Professor Gudjonsson has been responsible for the overturning several convictions in the United Kingdom and Scotland; see, for example, *Raymond McKenzie Gilmour v. Her Majesty's Advocate*, [2007] HC HCJAC 48 (Scot.); *Robert Adams v. The Queen*, [2006] NICA 6; *R. v. Friend*, [2004] EWCA Crim 2661; *R. v. Fell*, [2001] EWCA Crim 696; *Pendleton*, above note 2; *R. v. O'Brien & Ors*, [2000] EWCA Crim 3 [*O'Brien*]. It should be noted that Gudjonsson's work and evidence was used in the Canadian case of *R. v. Phillion*, 2009 ONCA 202, where the prosecutor referred to it as not being proper "science." The court held that it failed the cogency test and therefore would not be admitted as fresh evidence. The appeal was allowed on other grounds.

68 *Gilfillan*, above note 60, Bingham L.C.J; *R. v. Haddon*, [2003] EWCA Crim 284 at para. 9, Rose L.J.; *R. v. Samra*, [2004] EWCA Crim 1797 at para. 18, Kennedy L.J. [*Samra*]; *R. v. Steel*, [2003] EWCA Crim 1640 at para. 5, Rix L.J.; *R. v. Green*, [2002] NICA 14; Carswell L.C.J.; *R. v. James*, [1998] EWCA Crim 2521 [*James*]; *R. v. M.F.*, [2003] EWCA Crim 1173 at paras. 24–26; *R. v. Smith*, [2002] EWCA Crim 840 at para. 29 [*Smith*].

When the Court of Appeal receives fresh evidence it must assess its quality. If it takes the view that it might have caused a properly directed jury to acquit, then the appeal will be allowed. As we have noted, an appeal is not to be seen as an opportunity for the appeal court judges to substitute their own opinions for that of members of the jury. On the other hand, it would not be possible to separate entirely their judgment from the judgment of the jury. It would be anomalous for the court to say that the evidence raised no doubt in their minds—but might have raised a reasonable doubt in the minds of the jury. *Pendleton* stands for the principle that the Court of Appeal must consider whether the conviction is safe and not whether the accused is guilty. Two important points should then be kept in mind:

- First: The Court of Appeal is not and should never become the *primary* decision-maker.
- Second: The Court of Appeal has an imperfect and incomplete understanding of the processes that led the jury to convict.

Therefore, *Pendleton* concludes that the Court of Appeal can make its own assessment of the reliability and significance of the fresh evidence *it* has heard; what it cannot do is to then relate that evidence to the rest of the evidence that *the jury* had heard. In any case of difficulty, the proper test is to ask whether the new or additional evidence, if given at the trial, might reasonably have affected the decision of the trial jury to convict. If it *might* have done, then the conviction *must* be thought to be unsafe.

Having said that, however, we must bear in mind the views expressed in the following case which, to some extent, sit uneasily with the foregoing and represent a continued deference by the Court of Appeal to the jury.

## I. DEFERENCE OF APPEAL COURT TO THE JURY

In *R. v. Hanratty*,[69] the accused had been convicted of the murder of Michael Gregsten. In August 1961, Gregsten and his girlfriend Valerie Storie were together in a car in Buckinghamshire. It was getting dark, when they were approached by a man who threatened them with a gun. On his instruction, the car was driven onto the A6 motorway. In the early hours of the following morning, at a lay-by south of Bedford, Gregsten was shot twice at close range; he died almost instantly. Storie was raped and also shot, but survived. Hanratty was convicted and executed on 4 April 1962.

69 *Hanratty*, above note 52.

In 2002, following a reference by the CCRC, the Court of Appeal accepted that certain material had been withheld during the trial. It was said the prosecution had failed to disclose material to the defence in relation to identification and interview issues; however, there was also new DNA evidence which the prosecution introduced and which, they said, supported Hanratty's guilt. In light of this DNA evidence, the Court of Appeal said that the effect of the new evidence produced by the defence had not undermined confidence in the jury's verdict. In evaluating the significance of the evidence, the court said it acknowledged that in carrying out such an exercise, it was trespassing upon what at trial would be the function of the jury, but it took the view that "that is the inevitable consequence in any case involving fresh evidence."[70]

The appeal court's justification for not interfering with the jury's findings on factual matters may be justified on both constitutional and rational grounds. Constitutionally, an accused person should be convicted by the judgment of their peers and not by what appeal judges believed or reasoned. Rationally, it is said, the jury can see and hear the witnesses giving evidence (unlike the appellate court) and can draw upon a wider range of experiences.[71]

In *R. v. Trevor Campbell*,[72] a widow eighty-four years old was brutally murdered in her home in June 1984. On the following day an unsuccessful attempt was made to set fire to her house where her body was. Two people were tried for her murder. Trevor Campbell, then aged nineteen, and his fifteen-year-old girlfriend Christine were both convicted, and leave to appeal was denied. Following a reference by the CCRC, the Court of Appeal ruled the convictions to be unsafe. In quashing the convictions they observed that the police officers in the case had been the subject of adverse findings in previous cases which concerned their improper treatment of suspects and the fabrication of witness statements. As the Court of Appeal said, if those factors about the officers' background had been known at the time, then they could have been more effectively cross-examined by counsel for the accused. The court said the police would have been driven to make admissions that would and should have caused the jury to entertain doubts about their evidence. As the court said, even if the jury were still inclined to believe the officers, it is hard to see how rationally and conscientiously they could have been *sure* of what they had to say.[73]

---

70 *Ibid.* at para. 103.

71 Richard Nobles & David Schiff, *Understanding Miscarriages of Justice* (Oxford: Oxford University Press, 2000) at 89.

72 *R. v. Campbell*, [1999] EWCA Crim 2264 [*Campbell*].

73 *Ibid.*, Lord Bingham L.C.J.

It was therefore important that all the information should have been before the jury, to enable it to make that important choice. As it turned out, in making their choice on credibility, the jury did not know of matters that threw severe doubt on the honesty and professional integrity of those officers.[74]

In *Campbell*, the court made it clear that it was in no position to make findings of fact about what happened:

> It is not for us to hold as a fact-finding tribunal that the appellant was or was not involved in the murder . . . Nor are we a fact-finding tribunal who can determine whether the . . . officers misconducted themselves in the manner which the appellant has claimed. *That is simply not our function.*[75]

The court said its sole function was to form a judgment whether, in the light of the material now known (but not known to the judge, the jury, or counsel at the time of the trial) the verdict was unsafe. An important issue in that case was to determine the conflict in the evidence between the police on the one hand and Campbell on the other. The jury had to be sure that Campbell's account was false in material respects to be sure of his guilt.[76]

It is important to appreciate that the Court disavowed any ability to be determinative as to what the outcome would have been if all of the relevant information had been available.

> . . . what would have been the effect if the new material had been considered, the court feels bound to observe that it would be speculating. *It would have been a different case* and not the case which the jury were in fact sent out to resolve . . . . There are many questions that could be raised [about a witness], *but this is to conduct a post mortem on a body which the jury were never asked to dissect.*[77]

Speculating about the detailed thought processes of the jury is something the court has consistently steered away from. The closest they allow themselves to come to this is to ask if the factor might reasonably have affected the decision of the jury. If it *might* have done, then the court *must* set aside the conviction.

In *Maynard, Dudley, Bailey and Clarke*,[78] the accused were variously convicted in 1977 of murder and conspiring to cause grievous bodily harm to Mi-

---

74 *Ibid.*
75 *Ibid.* [emphasis added].
76 *Ibid.*
77 *Ibid.* [emphasis added].
78 *Maynard*, above note 47.

chael Cornwall. His body and various body parts were washed up at separate locations on the Thames foreshore in Essex.

In their appeal in 2002, there was new evidence to the effect that a statement said to have been taken by the police could not have been written within the times stated. The court was invited to accept that either the commencement time of the interview or the finishing time must have been noted incorrectly. While the court accepted that could well have been a possibility, they also accepted that there could have been other less innocent explanations. It was not for them to determine which one of them was correct. Once they had determined that there had been a defect in the evidence—not disclosed at trial—and that defect *might* have affected the jury's decision, then they were obliged to overturn the verdict. Indeed, the court determined that the defect in one statement could have led the jury to look at other pieces of evidence (against the other co-accused) differently. As a result, they overturned all four convictions, even though the statements that the others had given appeared to be without such defects. The court said the suggestion that the jury concluded that the police made a mistake would require the appeal court to look into the minds of the jury and to speculate as to their reasoning in a way that is clearly forbidden by *Pendleton*.[79] Instead, the court asks whether the evidence, if given at trial, might reasonably have affected the decision of the trial jury to convict.[80]

In assessing the criticisms of the trial, the court does not have to evaluate each of the criticisms in isolation. The evidence has to be looked at as a whole[81] and the cumulative effect of the criticisms has to be evaluated.[82] As the court said, it is unnecessary to say that one of those matters, or any combination of them, is decisive. It is sufficient to say that *in their totality* they must be able to persuade the court that the convictions are no longer safe.[83] The court has also made it clear that once it has formed the view that it has identified a sufficient basis upon which to allow the appeal, it does not necessarily have to consider all of the other issues or arguments that have or could be raised.[84]

---

79 *Pendleton*, above note 2.

80 *Maynard*, above note 47 at para. 50.

81 *R. v. Murphy & Anor*, [2002] EWCA Crim 120 at para. 93 [*Murphy*].

82 *R. v. Cooper & Anor*, [2003] EWCA Crim 2257 at para. 2 [*Cooper*].

83 *Ibid.* at para. 46 [emphasis added].

84 *R. v. Wickens*, [2003] EWCA Crim 2196 at para. 15 [*Wickens*].

## J. CONTEMPORARY STANDARDS

In recent years, largely as a result of the activities of the CCRC, the Court of Appeal has been required to re-examine the conduct of trials that took place many years previously. When looking back at a case after many years, there may well have been many alterations and developments in applicable standards for the conduct of such trials. The court has taken the view that where there has been some development in scientific or investigatory standards, then that may well be taken into account in considering the safety of the verdict. However, where the change is merely a development of the applicable *legal* standards, then it may or may not have that effect.[85]

In *Bentley*,[86] the Court of Appeal held that the statutory law of homicide had to be taken as it was at the time of the trial, but that the common law was that current at the time of review. Likewise, the conduct of the trial, including the judge's direction to the jury, had to be judged by contemporary standards. The court said that where, between conviction and appeal, standards of fairness have changed significantly, the court might well apply legal rules and procedural criteria that were not and could not reasonably have been applied at the time.

In *R. v. O'Brien and Ors*,[87] the accused had been convicted of the murder of a Cardiff newsagent, who was attacked and robbed as he returned to his home in October 1987. An important aspect of the prosecution case was based on an alleged confession by one of the co-accused (Hall). The first appeal was dismissed. In 1999, following a reference by the CCRC, the Court of Appeal quashed the convictions after hearing expert psychiatric evidence suggesting that Hall suffered from a mental abnormality which predisposed him to fabricate and fantasize, and to improperly implicate himself and others in the crime. It was also said that there had been other irregularities in the police investigation with Hall being denied access to legal representation during his interrogation when he made the alleged confession. Running the legal and investigatory issues together, the appeal court said that it would judge the conduct of the investigation of the case, the conduct of the trial, the directions to the jury, and the reliability of the evidence on which the jury acted in accordance with "the standards that this court now applies"; the practices followed and the reliability of evidence thus obtained are to be judged by "present" standards.[88]

---

85 *Hanratty*, above note 52 at para. 98.

86 *Bentley*, above note 45.

87 *R. v. O'Brien & Ors*, [2000] EWCA Crim 3.

88 *Ibid.* [emphasis added].

That view, however, should be seen in the context of the later decision in *Hanratty*, where the Court of Appeal said that because contemporary rules have not been complied with does not mean that a trial which took place many years ago must be judged on the false assumption it was tried yesterday. Such an approach, it said, could achieve injustice because the non-compliance with certain rules does not necessarily mean that a defendant has been treated unfairly.[89] As the court said in *Hanratty*, non-compliance with rules that were not current at the time of the trial may have to be treated differently from rules that were in force at the time of the trial. If certain of the current requirements of, for example, a summing up are not complied with at a trial that takes place today, this almost automatically results in a conviction being set aside but, the court said, this approach should not be adopted in relation to trials that took place before the rule was established.[90]

The judicial approach to the application of contemporary standards seems somewhat inconsistent, and there is some reluctance to apply all contemporary standards to past events. As Laurie Elks has pointed out, the court noted that, despite the warnings following the decision in *Bentley*, there has been no flood of "modern standards of fairness" appeals.[91]

## K. MEANING OF "BEYOND REASONABLE DOUBT"

One point emphasized by the Court of Appeal in its decisions is the fact that in criminal trials the *burden* of proof is on the prosecution, and the *onus* of proof is "beyond reasonable doubt."[92] However, there are some cases where the public demand for someone to be held accountable, especially when facing an outraged media, can often appear to constrain choices which otherwise might be available.

In *Bentley*, the public were outraged at the shooting of Police Constable Miles when trying to apprehend the youths who had broken into a warehouse. As the court pointed out in the more recent appeal, the killing of the police officer had, very understandably, aroused widespread public sympathy for the victim and his family, and a strong sense of public outrage at the circumstances of his death. The court said this background made it more important that the jury should approach the issues in a dispassionate manner if the accused were to receive a fair trial. However, far from encouraging the jury to

89 *Hanratty*, above note 52 at para. 98.

90 *Ibid.*

91 Elks, above note 44 at 142.

92 But on appeal, the burden is, initially at least, on the appellant.

approach the case in a calm frame of mind, the trial judge's summing up had the opposite effect.[93]

It seems strange in hindsight that it took the British judicial system more than forty years to recognize that basic errors were made in the conduct of the Bentley trial by a senior and experienced judge.[94]

The issue of ambiguity frequently arises in this context. There arises a possible explanation of a circumstance which does not quite fit with the rest of the explanations available and which might well be incriminatory. In such a case, it is often tempting to overlook the one piece of inconsistent evidence. But again, it takes only a moment's reflection to realize that just one piece of exculpatory evidence might well be sufficient to determine the case. As Professor Pounder has stated, "you only need one item of evidence which says it *couldn't* have happened — to prove it *didn't* happen."[95]

In *R. v. James*,[96] the accused was a veterinarian whose wife had died by ingesting a toxic substance used in the treatment of animals. The question was whether she had taken it (suicide) or whether he had given it to her (murder). He had been convicted of her murder. Some time after, when clearing out a cupboard at his home, a note was found in a magazine. It was in his wife's handwriting and consisted of just two sentences. It could not be determined when it was written, or indeed, if the thoughts were suicidal. As the Court of Appeal said, more than one interpretation is capable of being placed upon the note in the circumstances, but none is conclusive and one is undoubtedly consistent with an intention to commit suicide. It held that the jury's verdict given in ignorance of the note must be regarded as unsafe. It therefore quashed the conviction on that single ground.

So, the court was faced with a single piece of evidence, not by any means unambiguous, yet one interpretation of which was possibly inconsistent with the guilt of the accused. It didn't prove by any means that James didn't commit the murder. But as we have just seen, that is not the system of justice that the British cases subscribe to. "Beyond a reasonable doubt" means that if there is a doubt — which is reasonable — then it is unreasonable to convict in those circumstances. Or, put the other way around, the *possibility* that the accused is guilty has to be more than just a hypothesis: ". . . the Crown's case has to be that this 'possibility' [of guilt] is by no means a mere possibility, but a fact

93 *Bentley*, above note 45, Bingham L.C.J.

94 *Ibid.*

95 Television interview on *Today Tonight* (9 June 2003), Channel 7, Adelaide.

96 Above note 68.

established to the criminal standard to the satisfaction of this court."[97] In other words, it must be sufficient to be able to exclude *all* reasonable doubts.

Without witnesses to what had happened, we have what is called a "circumstantial" case. With such cases, it is often said that the circumstances must be such as to be inconsistent with *any* rational hypothesis in support of the innocence of the accused. The reason for this is clear. Once we have such a rational hypothesis, then we have an explanation of the known facts consistent with the innocence of the accused and no rational way of choosing between the hypotheses that support the innocence or guilt of the accused. Of course, in wrongful death cases, a circumstantial case can be no stronger than the circumstance determinative of the cause of death. Unless the cause of death can be determined beyond reasonable doubt as being homicidal, then no combination of surrounding circumstances can overcome that weakness. A suspicious death clearly has to be determined to be an *unlawful* death before anyone can be held to account for it in a criminal sense.

One way to describe the issue under discussion is to say that we are seeking a form of "narrative coherence"—the way in which statements hold together as part of some intelligible account of what has occurred. In some respects, the use of fresh evidence often creates an inconsistency between the previously settled view of things and that which is now being proposed. This situation does not mean that opinions cannot change or that statements cannot be inconsistent with each other; it means that there must be some satisfactory explanation for any inconsistencies, if the evidence is to be believed. Clearly, such an explanation cannot be forthcoming if statements inconsistent with the primary statement have been concealed.

In *Kelly*, before pointing the finger at those accused, the witness had laid the blame at someone else's door. When it came to trial, the prior inconsistent statement was not disclosed. As the Court of Appeal pointed out, the non-disclosure of the inconsistency led to the conclusion that all the evidence was false and probably deliberately so.[98] The court decided—and this is important—that statements given in relation to the same matter, but at different times, require careful analysis. An inability to explain differences can, of course, result in challenges to credibility. As the court observed, a comparison of earlier statements with later statements, with evidence given at committal and at trial, may have affected those witnesses' credibility. If such factors had been disclosed, the defence would have been able still further to undermine the

---

97 *R. v. Shirley*, [2003] EWCA Crim 1976 at para. 12, Laws L.J.
98 *Kelly*, above note 65 at para. 4, Rix L.J.

prosecution case.[99] The court was particularly critical where the non-disclosure of highly relevant material was due to deliberate concealment.[100]

In *R. v. Downing*, the CCRC obtained further independent forensic reports relating to the pattern of bloodstaining found on the clothing of the assailant. The Court of Appeal, upon referral by the CCRC, decided that because the scientific evidence is as consistent with innocence as with guilt the conviction had to be overturned.[101]

When detailed reports have been prepared by eminent experts, the UK court has not infrequently taken the view that there is little need to cross-examine those who have prepared them. In *Samra* the judges said (in relation to psychiatric evidence) that they did not need to hear the evidence orally from those who wrote the reports in order to conclude that the conviction for murder could no longer be regarded as safe.[102]

In *R. v. Josephine Smith*, the Court of Appeal determined that a new view put by a psychiatrist—who had given evidence at trial—amounted to fresh evidence.[103] This determination was made without there being any suggestion that the expert had not done his job properly at trial. It was simply that experts can work only with the information available. If given new evidence, then the opinion that an expert expresses will most likely change. As the court said:

> Professor Eastman's evidence proffered to this Court, notwithstanding that he gave evidence at trial, is fresh evidence. It was truly fresh evidence rather than an expression of view based upon material available at trial about which he could have been asked then.
>
> In these circumstances, we think it expedient, in the interests of justice, to admit Professor Eastman's evidence, without embarking on any further, more precise, analysis as to whether it can properly be characterised as fresh evidence or not.[104]

Again, this related to information about the state of mind of the accused. However, there can be no difference in principle between the interpretation of that type of evidence and the interpretation of physical evidence.

As we have seen, in *Mattan*, the Court of Appeal recognized that because the evidence of the key witness at the trial was inconsistent with prior state-

99 *Ibid.* at para. 11.
100 *Ibid.*
101 *R. v. Downing*, [2002] EWCA Crim. 263 at para. 13.
102 *Samra*, above note 68 at para. 21, Kennedy L.J.
103 *R. v. Smith*, [2002] EWCA Crim 2671, Rose L.J.
104 *Ibid.* at para. 28.

ments that, at least, rendered the evidence unreliable. It was then recognized that because this evidence was a key element of the case, the whole case collapsed.[105] A not dissimilar situation arose in *Maynard*, where the non-disclosure related to the unreliability of the evidence relating to a statement which was said to have been made. After the trial it was said that the statement could not have been made within the time alleged; therefore, the time of 4:28 had been written down in error for the time of 4:08. While this was one way to adjust the facts consistently with the finding of guilt, the appeal court thought it to be inappropriate:

> If it is possible, . . . that the evidence . . . demonstrates that some police officers must have lied on the issue of contemporaneous recording, it is no less possible, as the Crown suggest, that the evidence demonstrates that the police made a simple error in recording the time, and mistakenly but honestly repeated that error in their evidence. Deciding between those alternatives would require hearing all the relevant witnesses and is the exclusive territory of the jury into which we must not and do not enter.[106]

In evaluating the significance of the evidence of the handwriting expert in *Maynard* the court said it was a piece of independent, expert evidence of unquestioned integrity. It demonstrated that the police account as to some aspects of a crucial interview was necessarily wrong and unreliable; either the times were incorrectly recorded or the notes were not contemporaneous. Arguably, the court said, the issue went to the core of the single most damaging and cogent evidence against one of the accused. It said it was in no doubt that the evidence might reasonably have affected the decision of the jury to convict him of either or both murders. As a result, the court took the view that his convictions were unsafe.[107]

The court went on to say that because the evidence of the handwriting expert demonstrated a basic flaw in *the system*, then all other evidence generated by that same system must be taken to be defective. As the the court said:

> . . . the . . . *system* was central to the case against every appellant. If the jury might have been affected by the evidence of [the handwriting expert] in relation to any one interview, then that reasonably might have — and indeed

105 *Mattan*, above note 46, Rose L.J.
106 *Maynard*, above note 47 at para. 47, Mantell L.J.
107 *Ibid.* at para. 54.

> probably would have—caused them to look more cautiously at the integrity of every other interview.[108]

The above cases demonstrate two things: First, there is often no clear evidence of innocence in miscarriage of justice cases; second, the constitutional requirement that guilt be proven beyond a reasonable doubt means that convictions should be overturned on the basis of single items of evidence that might rationally be inconsistent with guilt as well as by reasonable concerns about the reliability of the prosecution's evidence.

## L. THE ROLE OF DEFENCE LAWYERS AND INEFFECTIVE ASSISTANCE OF COUNSEL

Incompetent representation at trial is not in itself a basis for appeal.[109] There are, however, cases where the court has taken the view that the failure of counsel was such as to result in an unfair trial, thereby making the verdict unsafe.

As mentioned earlier, where the accused has made a clear strategic decision at trial not to pursue a line of defence, the Court of Appeal is unwilling to allow that defence to be pursued after a finding of guilty. However, different considerations might well apply when the failure to explore a defence or to expose a weakness in the prosecution case results from the failure of trial counsel. In *Murphy*[110] it was argued that the accused Brannan and Murphy acted in self-defence when Pollitt (the deceased) was going to shoot them. Therefore, they had an answer to the charges. As the Court of Appeal recognized, the legal advisers had been told about Pollitt having a gun, but they had told the accused that it was irrelevant to the defence.[111]

The report of the appeal case makes it clear that Brannan was not the easiest of people to deal with. At trial he did not give evidence and did not call witnesses. When interviewed by the police he had exercised his right of silence and refused to answer any questions. Even in his previous appeal he had "stuck to his rights." During the earlier appeal proceedings, Brannan had not waived the legal privilege that bound his legal advisers, with the result that the appeal court had not seen the proofs or instructions given by Brannan to his solicitors before trial. The court said that it was entitled to draw an inference from this.[112]

---

108 *Ibid.* at para. 57 [emphasis added].

109 *R. v. Day*, [2003] EWCA Crim 1060.

110 Above note 81.

111 *Ibid.* at para. 38, Keene L.J.

112 *Ibid.* at para. 28.

In the later appeal, the Court of Appeal said that it was clear from the judgment of the earlier appeal that the "late invention" of Pollitt having a gun was thought to be just a ruse. In the more recent appeal, legal privilege was waived and it was clearly seen that the existence of the gun was mentioned to the legal advisers from the outset. Also, the police had been informed by a number of other people that they saw Pollitt with a gun, but they had not disclosed this to the defence.

The court could have taken the view that Brannan and Murphy had in some way been responsible for the outcome. However, if we bear in mind the earlier observation—that it is not for the accused to prove their innocence, but for the prosecution to prove their guilt—then clearly they could not have discharged that burden if the prosecution (which includes the police) was withholding relevant information. As we have noted, the duty of the prosecution goes beyond gaining convictions; it is to ensure that all relevant evidence is before the court, and the court cannot discharge its duty unless sure that both sides of the issue have been fully and fairly presented to it.[113]

Sometimes the failure of counsel can arise from either inadvertence or perhaps a form of misplaced paternalism. This problem is more likely in those cases where the accused is intellectually or mentally challenged.[114] The key point, however, is that so long as the failure to challenge did not arise from a specific decision of the accused, then that failure cannot be fatal to the success of the appeal.

In *Smith*,[115] the accused was convicted of murder in 1977 when he was eighteen years of age. In his appeal in 2002, the issue was raised whether he should have been found guilty of manslaughter by reason of diminished responsibility. Much medical evidence before the Court of Appeal had not been before the trial court and that evidence suggested that the accused may have been suffering from diminished responsibility. He had savagely beaten a man who had made homosexual advances to him. After Smith had started to serve his sentence, some two years or so later, in July 1979, he killed his cell mate. It was then found that he suffered from a serious psychopathic disorder such as to substantially impair his mental responsibility for his actions at the time of the killing.

It is apparent that the question of diminished responsibility was not raised or discussed with the appellant at the time of his first trial. The Court of Ap-

113 *James*, above note 68.

114 See also the references to Gudjonnson, above note 67, and the cases referred to earlier.

115 *Smith*, above note 68.

peal held that it was not a case in which any tactical decision was made at first trial not to run diminished responsibility and therefore the matter should be taken into consideration in the appeal.

In *R. v. Kamara*,[116] the manager of a betting shop in Liverpool was robbed and stabbed to death at his shop in March 1981. The deceased had been tied up, and after failing to give the safe combination quickly enough because of a speech impediment, he was stabbed nineteen times. The prosecution case was that Gilbert did the stabbing, while Kamara was present and assisting. The trial commenced initially with Gilbert and Kamara as co-accused. Shortly after it began, Gilbert changed his plea to guilty. The question then arose as to whether the trial could continue in respect of Kamara who maintained his plea of not guilty or start again with a fresh jury. It was clear from the evidence given on the appeal that the legal advisers had discussed the issue in the absence of their client and determined to press ahead with the trial.[117] As it turned out, some of the evidence already admitted in relation to the co-accused was thought to be prejudicial to Kamara and sufficient to overturn his conviction.

In *R. v. Poole & Anor*, a police officer's statement contained a comment from a witness in which it was suggested that the accused had intended to "beat up" the deceased.[118] That witness was not produced before the court. The comment was clearly hearsay and not capable of being dealt with in cross-examination. The court did not know how much weight, if any, the jury would have given to it. The Court of Appeal said that it was surprising that defence counsel did not seek the exclusion of those comments.[119] This observation clearly suggested some shortcoming with defence counsel. However, the appeal court pointed out that its function was not to act as some sort of professional conduct tribunal. Its primary concern was to consider the effect that the critical hearsay material would have had upon the jury and upon the safety of their verdict. It took the view that the hearsay was capable of having had a seriously and unfairly prejudicial effect on the jury's deliberations.[120]

Of course, there may well have been a quite proper basis for the way in which defence counsel acted and which was not known to the Court of Appeal. Without intimate knowledge of the instructions from the client, it is often difficult to be determinative of such things. But clearly, that is not the focus of the court on the appeal.

---

116 [2000] EWCA Crim 37.
117 *Ibid.*, Otton L.J.
118 [2003] EWCA Crim 1753.
119 *Ibid.* at para. 81, Auld L.J.
120 *Ibid.* at paras. 81–82.

## M. PROPER INVESTIGATIONS AND THE NEED FOR DISCLOSURE

In Britain, proper investigations have been regarded as an essential part of the road to justice:

> The code of practice pursuant to the *Criminal Procedure and Investigations Act 1996* requires: In conducting an investigation the investigator should pursue all reasonable lines of inquiry, whether these point towards or away from the suspect. What is reasonable in each case will depend upon the particular circumstances.[121]

In *Cooper*,[122] the court said that it had become increasingly apparent that there were serious grounds for concern about the way in which the police investigated the matter and put the prosecution case together.[123] Judicial review of investigative techniques must clearly be the basis upon which a judgment can be made about whether there exist any reasonable doubts as to the guilt of an accused. Clearly, it would be inappropriate for police or prosecutors to try to shore up a weak case by failing to investigate matters that might be exculpatory.

It is also worth bearing in mind that the status of those involved in the investigation can lead to an element of prejudice. As the Court of Appeal said in *Bentley*, there is an obvious risk of injustice if a jury is invited to approach the evidence on the assumption that police officers because they are police officers are likely to be accurate and reliable witnesses, and defendants, because they are defendants, likely to be inaccurate and unreliable.[124]

As we have seen, a frequent concern expressed throughout these cases has been with the issue of non-disclosure of relevant material. As the court said in *Murphy*, evidence which has "some bearing" on the offence charged and the surrounding circumstances of the case should be disclosed.[125] It said the reason for disclosure is to enable the defence to utilize such material as part of their cross-examination of the witness and that non-disclosure may prevent the defence from putting such references in cross-examination of prosecution witnesses.[126]

---

121 *R. v. Causley*, [2003] EWCA Crim 1840 at para. 92 [*Causley*] [emphasis added], citing para. 3.4 of Prosecution Code and Practice introduced pursuant to the *Criminal Procedure and Investigations Act 1996* (U.K.) 1996, c. 25.

122 Above note 82.

123 *Ibid.* at para. 2, Kennedy L.J.

124 *Bentley*, above note 45, Bingham L.C.J.

125 *Murphy*, above note 81 at para. 83, Keene L.J.

126 *Ibid.* at para. 84.

In *Cooper*, the appeal court said it would have been important to know the status of the witness. As it pointed out, what those acting for the accused at the trial did not know, and what is now agreed, is that an important witness was a police informant. On the recommendation of a senior police officer, the informant had received a financial reward from the Post Office following the robbery. The court said the information which was not disclosed, but at the time of the appeal would be regarded as disclosable, would have helped the defence greatly. It added that the inescapable conclusion was that at the trial, without judicial approval, the evidence of the witness was presented by the prosecution in a way that was deliberately misleading.[127] Also, the non-disclosure of a large number of witness statements was seen to be a serious shortcoming in that case.[128] Part of the reason, as we have seen, is that non-disclosure of a witness's prior inconsistent statement—a statement which seriously contradicts the evidence being given in court—prevents the defence from being able to cross-examine the witness in relation to it.[129]

In *Nicholls*, the accused used to go to a pub in 1975 where he would sometimes have a drink with a woman of seventy-four years who also went there. One day the woman's housemates returned home to find her lying at the foot of the stairs dead. The prosecution said that Nicholls had gone to her home to rob her, that he had assaulted her and brought about her death from heart failure. The forensic evidence was that her body had been dumped at the foot of the stairs and that she could not have been in that position if she had fallen or collapsed from natural causes. A subsequent review of the forensic evidence said that the conclusions were inadequate, inappropriate, and misleading and that the cause of death was incorrectly stated.

The appeal court in *Nicholls* said, "there was still a very strong circumstantial case against the appellant which was true once it was accepted that this was an unlawful killing."[130] Once it has been determined that there is an unlawful killing, then it has to be explained and the evidence will be construed within that context. However, if the unlawful killing is in doubt, or it is established that it did not occur, then the evidence will have be viewed differently.[131]

Interestingly, in *R. v. Wickens* the court pointed out that if anyone had been suspected or charged with murder at an early stage of an investigation,

---

127 *Cooper*, above note 82 at paras. 18–21.
128 *Ibid.* at para. 36, Kennedy L.J.
129 *Ibid.* at para. 38.
130 *R. v. Nicholls*, [1998] EWCA Crim 1918, Roch L.J. [*Nicholls*]. This case is discussed further in Chapter 9.
131 *Pinfold*, above note 59 at para. 64.

an autopsy could have been called.[132] The court went on to express surprise in *Wickens* that independent pathological evidence was not obtained, particularly as there was a dispute about time of death.[133] When a further report from the Crown pathologist (who had given evidence at the trial) was provided, it was sufficient for the court to overturn the conviction as unsafe: the important professional judgment of the Crown's pathologist about the time of death was never available to the jury.[134]

As we have already seen, in several cases there was subsequent disclosure of material related to the unreliability of witnesses (sometimes police witnesses) and occurring prior to trial. The important issue is that if such information had been available to defence counsel at the time of the trial, then it could have been used to undermine the credibility of the witness.

In *Campbell*,[135] the accused, at his trial had made allegations of improper conduct on the part of some of the police officers who had interviewed him. He was unaware that those officers had been the subject of prior disciplinary proceedings. When he found out about it, he thought that the reliability of the two officers who had worked together had been seriously undermined.[136] The Court of Appeal said that the method used by the police to obtain evidence could only be described as "unorthodox," which amounted to the officers concerned having "engaged in fabricating evidence." The court observed that it would have directed that the papers be sent to the Director of Public Prosecutions had this not already been done.[137]

In *Maynard*, the court said, "if chicanery of that kind had taken place who is to say that other members of the team . . . had not resorted to the same dishonest technique?"[138] The point being, that if the system of due process fails to expose those who have compromised that process, then there is more to be concerned about than just the conduct of the individual.

The failure to be able to explain prior shortcomings in the conduct of a trial should not be seen as a reason for not examining them. Certain types of failures cannot be explained away as the result of some tactical decision, unless it can be seen to make tactical sense. In *Bentley*, the appeal court said that it was unable to discover any reasonable explanation for the failure to adduce in

---

132 *Wickens*, above note 84 at para. 20, Kay L.J. This case is discussed further in Chapter 9.
133 *Ibid.* at para. 21.
134 *Ibid.* at paras. 54–55.
135 Above note 72.
136 *Ibid.*, Bingham L.C.J.
137 *Ibid.*
138 *Maynard*, above note 47 at para. 43, Mantell L.J.

the trial in 1952 the evidence now reflected in the psychiatric and psychological reports. In that context, it thought, tactical considerations could not normally be regarded as a reasonable explanation.[139]

In *Mattan*,[140] the court made a list of the extensive range of matters which were not before the jury and of which they should have been informed. A deficiency in the information concerning the antecedents of police and other prosecution witnesses can arise without there being any conscious awareness of that by the prosecution. In *Causley*, the prosecution said that if the material facts that undermined the integrity of the witness had been known at the time of the trial, they would have been obliged not only to disclose it but also to consider whether in the light of that evidence, they ought to rely upon the witness. Because they knew nothing of that background, that process never took place.[141]

## N. PROSECUTORIAL CONCESSIONS

An important element in the recent British cases is the number of occasions where the Crown, at the appeal, has accepted the evidence or the arguments put forward by the defence without objection. As we have seen from Chapter 2, the duty of the Crown is to ensure a fair trial. Once in possession of compelling evidence that the trial process was inappropriately compromised, they have the duty to ensure that remedial steps are taken. Of course, it is not for the Crown to tell the Court of Appeal that they think that the appeal should be allowed, but they can tell the court they don't object to such a course of action.

In *Bentley*, some fifty years after Bentley had been hanged, the Crown decided to make no objection to the reception of the fresh evidence on the appeal.

In *Kelly*, the manager and assistant manager of the Cameo Cinema in Liverpool were shot dead in the course of a robbery. It was alleged that Kelly was the gunman and Connolly the lookout. Kelly was convicted and hanged in 1949. Part of the evidence against Kelly was from a prison informant who said that Kelly had confessed to him his involvement in the murders. However, what was not known was that the informant had previously provided a statement to say that another person had also confessed to his role in the murder. On the appeal, the Crown accepted that even under the duties of disclosure that applied

139 *Bentley*, above note 45, Bingham L.C.J.

140 *Mattan*, above note 46.

141 See *Causley*, above note 121 at para. 83.

in 1949, the previous statement should have been disclosed but was not. The implication of this was of fundamental importance to the case: "The Crown therefore did not seek to uphold the conviction of Kelly for murder."[142]

In *Mattan* the prosecution made it clear that they no longer relied on the evidence of one of the key witnesses (Mrs. Gray) as being credible.[143] They also accepted that the evidence of the chief prosecution witness at the trial was no longer reliable since that witness might well have been the perpetrator.

In *R. v. Causley*, there was much to be said against the accused. He had told lies over a long time about the whereabouts of his wife. He had forged insurances on her life to take advantage of her disappearance and had fraudulently transferred title on their home. He had also established a relationship with another woman.[144] Nevertheless, he was convicted in part on the evidence of a jailhouse informant, and the jury did not know that the same witness had earlier been involved in another case where he had also claimed to have heard a jailhouse confession.

In both the previous and the current case, the jailhouse informant said that the information was received in walks around the prison, notes were made on the back of an envelope, and the confessor had derived inspiration for his deeds by picking up details from detective books. The jury in *Causley* did not know that the witness had appeared in a previous case in remarkably similar circumstances. The court said that if material that ought to have been available to the defence might have caused doubt to be cast about the witness's evidence, then the fact that that evidence was not available at the trial must lead to the conclusion that the resulting conviction was unsafe. What is most noteworthy is the Crown's concession that the conviction should be overturned:

> Recognising that the ultimate responsibility lies with the court, the view taken on behalf of the prosecution is that the court should conclude that the conviction is unsafe and therefore needs to be set aside.
>
> If there is material that ought to have been available to the defence which might have caused doubt to be cast about [the witness's] evidence, then the fact that that evidence was not available at the trial must lead to the conclusion that the resulting conviction was unsafe. That is the proposition that the Crown have accepted in relation to the matter.[145]

---

142 *Kelly*, above note 65 at para. 16, Rix L.J.
143 *Mattan*, above note 46, Rose L.J.
144 *Causley*, above note 121 at para. 30.
145 *Ibid.* at paras. 2 and 86.

Despite the admitted and extensive wrongdoing of Causley and the possibly benign nature of the non-disclosure, the Crown nevertheless accepted that that breach was such that these interviews should have been excluded. As it said, if that had happened, the case would have been stopped at the conclusion of the evidence for the prosecution, and there would have been effectively no evidence on which a jury could safely convict.[146]

Clearly, the Crown in Britain has acted with responsibility and fairness in not putting appellants to further and unnecessary stresses and strains, when in their judgment, recognizable and reviewable error had been detected. The recent appeals also give us a much better insight into the perhaps related issues of false confessions which the Court of Appeal has acknowledged is now much better than it was twenty years ago.[147]

## O. CONCLUSION

The analysis of the development of a right of appeal in Britain has given us a basis from which to compare similar developments, which have been based upon the British legislation, in Canada and Australia. It is noticeable that only one decision discussed in this chapter has been from the House of Lords (now the Supreme Court).[148] All of the others are from the Court of Appeal. This contrasts markedly with the Australian position, where most of the cases we will discuss are from the Australian High Court. Clearly, the UK Court of Appeal has had a good deal of work to do in recent years because of the advent of the CCRC and its ability and willingness to refer cases to the court for reconsideration. The lack of a similar development in Canada and Australia perhaps accounts to some extent for the more limited numbers of cases we have to work with specifically on miscarriage of justice appeals. However, the courts in both of those jurisdictions have provided guidance on what constitutes a miscarriage of justice.

In many respects, as we will see, the principles are often comparable with those of the British courts. The real difference is perhaps in the increased difficulty in Australia and Canada to get the cases into the appellate courts for review.

146 *Ibid.* at para. 4.

147 *O'Brien*, above note 67; and the previous reference to Gudjonsson, above note 67; and the related cases referred to earlier.

148 *Pendleton*, above note 2.

CHAPTER 4

# Law on Miscarriages of Justice: Canada

Canada has had a number of high-profile wrongful convictions revealed in recent years. Governments have been forced by these circumstances to appoint seven public inquiries that have examined the causes of these wrongful convictions and have made recommendations to lessen the risk of convicting the innocent in the future.[1] Public inquiries are appointed at the discretion of the provincial governments and have been appointed in only a minority of all cases in which wrongful convictions have been recognized. The public inquiries generally make factual findings about the causes of the wrongful convictions being examined and recommendations about ways to prevent wrongful convictions in the future. They are precluded from making determinations of criminal or civil liability. Once an inquiry has been appointed, it performs its work independently of government, a point underlined by the fact that all of

1 *The Royal Commission on the Donald Marshall Jr. Prosecution* (Halifax: The Commission, 1989) [Marshall Inquiry]; *Report of the Kaufman Commission on Proceedings Involving Guy Paul Morin* (Toronto: Ministry of the Attorney General, 1998) [Morin Inquiry]; The *Inquiry Regarding Thomas Sophonow* (Winnipeg, MB: Manitoba Justice, 2001) [Sophonow Inquiry]; *The Lamer Commission of Inquiry Pertaining to the Cases of Ronald Dalton, Gregory Parsons and Randy Druken* (St. John's, NL: Department of Justice, 2006) [Lamer Inquiry]; *Report of the Commission of Inquiry into Certain Aspects of the Trial and Conviction of James Driskell* (Winnipeg: The Commission, 2007) [Driskell Inquiry]; *Report of the Commission of Inquiry into the Wrongful Conviction of David Milgaard* (Saskatoon, SK: The Commission, 2008) [Milgaard Inquiry]; *Report of the Inquiry into Pediatric Forensic Pathology in Ontario* (Toronto: Ministry of the Attorney General, 2008) [Goudge Inquiry].

the inquiries have been headed by either sitting or retired judges.[2] The work of the inquiry often spans several years. Inquiries have had multi-million dollar budgets to conduct hearings and research, and they have produced recommendations that have attracted the attention of policy makers and courts in Canada and abroad.[3] There is, however, no requirement that their recommendations be implemented, and the federal government has generally been resistant to implementing the recommendations of the provincial inquiries into wrongful convictions.

Recommendations of the inquiries will be discussed at various junctures in this chapter which will examine aspects of procedural and evidential law as they affect miscarriages of justice in Canada. A common recommendation of all but one of the seven inquiries is that the government should create a permanent independent commission like the UK Criminal Cases Review Commission (CCRC) to investigate claims of wrongful convictions. The government has refused to implement these recommendations. Some minor changes were made in 2002 to the procedure by which the federal Minister of Justice considers petitions to reopen cases by ordering new trials or appeals, where there is a reasonable basis for concluding that a miscarriage of justice likely occurred.[4] In addition, this chapter will examine appeal rights and procedures in Canada, including the ability of appeal courts to consider fresh evidence, appellate discretion to order a new trial or enter an acquittal, the role of pardons, the application of contemporary standards on appeals, and the meaning of proof of guilt beyond a reasonable doubt. It will also examine how a broad constitutional right to disclosure of all relevant evidence has been fashioned in Canada with special attention to the danger of wrongful convictions. Finally, the chapter examines how the test for the admissibility of expert evidence, including evidence from forensic scientists, affects the risk of wrongful convictions based on faulty forensic science.

Despite Canada's failure to create a permanent commission of inquiry to investigate claims of wrongful convictions, increased recognition of the reality of wrongful convictions has undeniably affected Canadian law. The most

2 On the Canadian inquiries, see Kathryn Campbell, "Policy Responses to Wrongful Conviction in Canada: The Role of Conviction Review, Public Inquiries and Compensation" (2005) 41 Criminal Law Bulletin 145; Kent Roach, "Inquiries and the Processes of Accountability" in Philip Stenning, ed., *Accountability for Criminal Justice* (Toronto: University of Toronto Press, 1995).

3 See, for example, *Report of the Commission on Capital Punishment* (Springfield, IL: Governor's Commission on Capital Punishment, 2002) which relied heavily on the Canadian inquiries which had reported up to that time.

4 *Criminal Code*, R.S.C. 1985, c. C-46, s. 696.3.

dramatic change is probably the Supreme Court of Canada's 2001 decision in the *United States of America v. Burns and Rafay*.[5] Here, the Supreme Court held that it would violate the principles of fundamental justice protected under the *Canadian Charter of Rights and Freedoms*,[6] to extradite a fugitive to any foreign country without assurances that the death penalty would not be applied. In making this decision, the Supreme Court reversed decisions made a decade earlier that allowed fugitives to be extradited to face the death penalty in the United States.[7] It did so mainly on the basis that the 1990s had revealed an increased risk of error in criminal justice systems throughout the world, including in Canada, the United Kingdom, and the United States. The *Burns and Rafay* decision recognizes that while DNA has helped reveal wrongful convictions, such evidence will not be available in most cases.[8] The case is also noteworthy in its recognition that "a fair trial does not always guarantee a safe verdict."[9] *Burns and Rafay* presents a challenge to all courts and policy makers to do better in responding to the risk of wrongful convictions.[10]

The Supreme Court has recognized the risk of wrongful convictions in other cases. The Court's most important decision in this respect is probably *R. v. Stinchcombe* in which it recognized that the accused had a broad constitutional right to the disclosure of all relevant non-privileged information held by the Crown prosecutor, including a right to continuing disclosure.[11] This decision was in large part based on the commission of inquiry that recognized that lack of disclosure was a significant factor in Donald Marshall's wrongful conviction and recommended that Parliament enact legislation requiring full disclosure. This decision will be examined in greater depth in later parts of this chapter.

---

5 [2001] 1 S.C.R. 283 [*Burns and Rafay*].

6 *Canadian Charter of Rights and Freedoms*, Part I of the *Constitution Act, 1982*, being Schedule B to the *Canada Act 1982* (U.K.), 1982, c. 11.

7 *Re Ng Extradition (Canada)*, [1991] 2 S.C.R. 858; *Kindler v. Canada (Minister of Justice)*, [1991] 2 S.C.R. 779.

8 The Court noted that many British miscarriages of justice revealed by the CCRC did not depend on DNA testing and concluded that "these cases demonstrate that the concern about wrongful convictions is unlikely to be resolved by advances in forensic sciences, welcome as these advances are from the perspective of protecting the innocent and punishing the guilty." *Burns and Rafay*, above note 5 at para. 116.

9 *Ibid.* at para. 98. In reference to the David Milgaard case, the Supreme Court stated: "Milgaard was represented by able and experienced counsel. No serious error in law or procedure occurred at the trial. Notwithstanding the fact that the conviction for murder followed a fair trial, new evidence surfaced years later."

10 For an assessment of how Canadian courts have responded to this challenge, see Kent Roach, "The Protection of Innocence under Section 7 of the *Charter*" (2006) 34 Sup. Ct. L. Rev. (2d) 249.

11 [1991] 3 S.C.R. 326 [*Stinchcombe*].

In a 2000 decision in *R. v. Oickle*, the Court recognized false confessions as a cause of wrongful convictions and held that one of the purposes of the voluntariness rule is to prevent false confessions.[12] That said, concerns have been voiced that the test for determining whether a confession is voluntary is not sensitive enough to characteristics of the accused, such as mental disabilities or instabilities and drug withdrawal, which could help produce false confessions.[13] In tightening the rules for the admissibility of expert evidence and excluding post-hypnosis evidence as unreliable, the Court has recently recognized the contribution that unreliable evidence has made to many wrongful convictions.[14] The Court has also recognized the ability of people to bring civil suits with respect to malicious prosecution[15] and with respect to negligent forms of investigation.[16]

The Court's performance on issues relating to wrongful convictions has not been uniformly positive. Despite the recognition by a number of inquiries of the role that jailhouse informants have played in a number of wrongful convictions, the Court has not prevented jailhouse informants from testifying or even required that warnings be given about their unreliability in all cases.[17] Despite the widespread recognition that faulty eyewitness identification is a leading cause of wrongful convictions, the Supreme Court has allowed witnesses to make in-dock identifications of the accused despite their limited probative value.[18] It has also held that improprieties in obtaining identifications do not affect their admissibility.[19] Parliament has also fallen down with respect to the prevention of wrongful convictions. It has not enacted legislation to ensure that best practices are followed in identification or interrogation procedures. Moreover, it has not created a permanent independent commission to investigate allegations of wrongful convictions.

## A. HISTORY OF APPEALS

Before the enactment of the *Criminal Code* of Canada in 1892, appeals from convictions were limited to those recognized by common law writs, such as

12 [2000] 2 S.C.R. 3 [*Oickle*].

13 Christopher Sherrin, "False Confessions and Admissions in Canadian Law" (2005) 30 Queen's L.J. 601.

14 *R. v. Trochym*, [2007] 1 S.C.R. 239.

15 *Nelles v. Ontario*, [1989] 2 S.C.R. 170; *Proulx v. Quebec (Attorney General)*, [2001] 3 S.C.R. 9; *Miazga v. Kvello Estate*, [2009] SCC 51.

16 *Hill v. Hamilton-Wentworth Regional Police Services Board*, [2007] 3 S.C.R. 129.

17 *R. v. Brooks*, [2000] 1 S.C.R. 237.

18 *R. v. Hibbert*, [2002] 2 S.C.R. 445.

19 *R. v. Mezzo*, [1986] 1 S.C.R. 802.

*habeas corpus*. The writs tended to focus on matters of procedure rather than substantive error.[20] Writs of appeals and writs of error were used, but often in cases where the accused was believed to have been wrongfully acquitted. The royal pardon remained the most viable means of redress on the merits. In the *Murder Act, 1752*,[21] the time between conviction and execution was fixed at three days in order to forestall campaigning for a pardon.[22] Historically

> . . . verdicts that were unsupported by the evidence, or even perverse ones, could not be set aside or even challenged. There was no jurisdiction in the Court for Crown Cases Reserved to direct a new trial. It affirmed or it discharged. So the Royal Prerogative of pardon, inherited in 1837 by the Home Secretary, was the only real relief that could be claimed following a bad conviction. Stephen was appalled by the necessity of having to pardon a man for his own innocence.[23]

Although most Canadian provinces had appellate courts mirrored after the Court for Crown Cases Reserved in England, these courts, as well as the Supreme Court of Canada (created in 1875), were mainly concerned with legal issues certified for review by trial judges. Canada did not follow England when it adopted its *Criminal Appeal Act, 1907* in response to concerns about miscarriages of justice.[24]

The appeal rights originally recognized in the 1892 Canadian *Criminal Code* were quite limited, but they did not encounter the same resistance from judges as the creation of the Court of Appeal in 1907.[25] For the accused, the leave of the trial judge was required and if this was refused, the leave of the Attorney General was required. In the course of dismissing the idea that the *Canadian Charter of Rights and Freedoms*, enacted as a constitutional bill of rights in 1982, provided for a constitutional right to appeal or a constitutional right to publicly provided lawyers or transcripts for appeals, the Alberta Court of Appeal has stated:

> . . . despite the 1892 adoption of a comprehensive Canadian *Criminal Code* which catalogued crimes and review procedures, no comprehensive right of

20 S. Casey Hill & Peter K. McWilliams, *McWilliams' Canadian Criminal Evidence*, 4th ed. (Aurora, ON: Canada Law Book, 2003) as updated at 35.10.

21 25 Geo. 2, c. 37.

22 This history is recounted in *R. v. Robinson*, [1989] A.J. No. 950 (C.A.) [*Robinson*].

23 *Ibid.* at para. 35.

24 (U.K.), 7 Edw. VII, c. 23. See Ken Whiteway, "The Origins of the English Court of Criminal Appeal" (2008) 33 Canadian Law Library Review 309.

25 Benjamin Berger, "Criminal Appeals as Jury Control" (2007) 10 Can. Crim. L. Rev. 1 at 34.

review was conferred upon the Canadian prisoner who considered himself aggrieved by his conviction.[26]

In 1923, however, the *Criminal Code* was amended to embrace wider appeal rights. The accused was given a right to appeal on questions of law and with leave of the trial judge or with leave from the Court of Appeal on questions of fact or mixed law and fact. The Attorney General also had a right of appeal alleging errors of law. Unlike in England at the time, new trials could be ordered so that in a case of a successful appeal by the accused, the provincial Court of Appeal had the option of a entering an acquittal or ordering a new trial.

## B. CONTEMPORARY APPEAL PROVISIONS

At present, the accused has a right to appeal convictions to the Court of Appeal with respect to indictable offences. The accused can appeal as of right on any matter that involves a question of law alone and with leave of the Court of Appeal or certification by the trial judge can appeal questions of fact, questions of mixed fact and law, and any other matter.[27] The *Criminal Code* provides that on an appeal from conviction, the Court of Appeal may allow the appeal where it is of the opinion that

(i) the verdict should be set aside on the ground that it is unreasonable or cannot be supported by the evidence,
(ii) the judgment of the trial court should be set aside on the ground of a wrong decisions on a question of law, or
(iii) on any ground there was a miscarriage of justice.[28]

In what is commonly called "the proviso," the Court of Appeal can dismiss an appeal in cases where even though the trial judge made an error of law, the Court of Appeal "is of the opinion that no substantial wrong or miscarriage of justice has occurred."[29]

The Ontario Court of Appeal has characterized the accused's appeal rights, combined with the power to admit fresh evidence and hear evidence from witnesses under section 683 of the *Criminal Code* "in the interests of justice" as "broad rights of appeal." It has stated that "the broad rights of appeal, the power to receive fresh evidence, and the court's wide remedial powers are all

---

26 *Robinson*, above note 22 at para. 50.
27 *Criminal Code*, above note 4, s. 675.
28 *Ibid.*, s. 686(1)(a).
29 *Ibid.*, s. 686(1)(b)(iii).

designed to maximize protection against wrongful convictions."[30] This statement was made in the course of a ruling in which the accused sought disclosure of material related to Dr. Charles Smith, a pathologist whose faulty work led to the appointment of the Goudge Inquiry into Pediatric Forensic Pathology in Ontario and the recognition of a number of wrongful convictions. The Supreme Court eventually ordered a new trial in the case despite the Crown's argument that a conviction could be sustained without Dr. Smith's testimony given the pattern of child abuse. The Supreme Court held that it was

> . . . neither safe nor sound to conclude that the verdicts on any of the charges would necessarily have been the same but for Dr. Smith's successfully impugned evidence. To attempt at this stage to insulate the effect of Dr. Smith's evidence on one count from its possible effect on the others would amount to an unwarranted exercise in appellate speculation.[31]

The reference in the Supreme Court's decision in *R. v. Trotta* to a concern about the safety of the guilty verdict may respond to criticisms that, unlike in Britain or Australia, the Canadian *Criminal Code* does not specifically authorize appeals to be allowed because of concerns about the safety of verdicts. Justice Kaufman, in his commission of inquiry report on the Guy Paul Morin case, recommended that consideration should be given to changing the powers of the Court of Appeal so that they could "set aside a conviction where there exists a lurking doubt as to guilt."[32] Justice Kaufman reviewed appellate court authority as of his 1998 report and found that appellate courts implicitly and in a few cases explicitly considered the safety of verdicts when determining whether a conviction was reasonable or cannot be supported by the evidence under *Criminal Code*, section 686(1)(a)(i). He stressed:

> . . . an appellate court can overestimate the importance of seeing or hearing the witnesses. A substantial part of credibility is the internal consistency of a witnesses' testimony (however well or badly that witness presents) and its consistency with other known facts. If the record produces a lurking doubt or a sense of disquiet about the verdict of guilt, should an appellate court not

30 *R. v. Trotta* (2004), 23 C.R. (6th) 261 at para. 24 (Ont. C.A.).

31 *R. v. Trotta*, [2007] 3 S.C.R. 453 at para. 14. This decision reversed an earlier one of the Ontario Court of Appeal that had upheld the conviction on the basis that "there was cogent, if not overwhelming, evidence that Paolo was a battered child and that Marco was his abuser." *R. v. Trotta* (2004), 190 C.C.C. (3d) 199 at para. 31 and on the basis that the Crown had provided overwhelming evidence that the child was abused during his eight-month life and that "there will never be a perfect trial." *Ibid.* at para. 98 (C.A.).

32 Morin Inquiry, above note 1, vol. 2 at 1176.

> be empowered to act upon that sense after fully articulating those aspects of the record that have produced that doubt? No doubt, many appellate judges who sense a potential injustice do this—sometimes indirectly—through their determination of whether there was a legal error at trial. With respect, a disquieting conviction may compel an appeal to be allowed on the most esoteric misdirection relating to a point of law that only legal scholars might appreciate. It is well arguable that a slightly broadened scope for appellate intervention permits the Court to do directly what some judges now do indirectly. It recognizes the most important, though not exclusive, function of a criminal appellate court: to ensure that no person is convicted of a crime that he or she did not commit.[33]

Despite this recommendation, section 686 has not been amended to mirror English law that since 1968, has authorized appellate courts to overturn convictions when they are found to be unsafe or unsatisfactory.[34] With the 1995 British reforms, discussed in Chapter 3, appellate courts can also allow convictions to be overturned if they are unsafe.

Before the various grounds of appeal that are available in Canada are discussed in greater depth, a word about Canadian criminal procedure and mode of trials is necessary. The accused has a right under section 11(f) of the *Canadian Charter of Rights and Freedoms* to trial by jury if he or she faces five years of imprisonment or more. Nevertheless, for all commonly charged crimes except murder, the accused can elect to have a trial by judge and jury or trial by judge alone. In most of these cases, the accused elects to be tried by the judge without the jury. Even with respect to murder, the accused can be tried by judge alone if both the accused and the Attorney General elect for a bench trial. As will be seen, the distinction between judge alone and jury trials has a practical influence on appeal remedies in large part because trial judges in Canada are obliged to give reasons for their verdicts.[35] These reasons, including judgments about credibility and other factual matters, are exposed to appellate scrutiny. A jury does not provide reasons for its verdicts. Indeed, the Supreme Court of Canada has affirmed broad common law privileges which prevent the introduction of evidence about the jury's deliberation in order to challenge the jury's verdict.[36]

---

33 *Ibid.* at 1187–88.
34 *Criminal Appeal Act 1969* (U.K.), 1969, c. 35, s. 2.
35 *R. v. Sheppard*, [2002] 1 S.C.R. 869.
36 *R. v. Pan*, [2001] 2 S.C.R. 344.

## C. APPEALS BY THE DEAD

The Supreme Court has rejected arguments that the courts do not have jurisdiction to hear appeals from persons who have died. The Court has, however, warned that the discretion to hear moot appeals in criminal cases should be used sparingly and reserved for cases with special circumstances. The Court refused to exercise this discretion in a case where those acting on behalf of the accused wanted to argue that statements the accused had made to the police were inadmissible.[37] It distinguished the case from another case in which an appeal from a dead person was heard when the appellate court was

> . . . confronted with fresh evidence that suggested the factual innocence of the convicted offender. The opportunity to clear the name of the deceased appellant was of major significance to his family, and their determination to establish his factual innocence supplied the adversarial context. In the presence of such an apparent miscarriage of justice, "scarce judicial resources" could seldom be a disqualifying consideration. The issues surrounding the perjured testimony were quintessentially for the courts, not the legislature, to resolve. For the court to have declined to look into a serious abuse of its own process would clearly not have been "in the interests of justice".[38]

The distinguished case in which a moot appeal from a dead person was heard also "raised issues of broad public importance concerning police conduct and a potential systemic failure in the justice system, as well as the spectre of a serious injustice to the deceased and his family."[39] This case is also significant because of the weight the Court places on "factual innocence," something not officially recognized in the grounds of appeal available to the accused.

## D. THE GROUNDS FOR APPEAL

The ground of appeal that is, in some respects, most relevant to wrongful convictions and that has been the most controversial is *Criminal Code*, section 686(1)(a)(i), which authorizes an appeal court to overturn a conviction "on the ground that it is unreasonable or cannot be supported by the evidence." In the

---

37 *R. v. Smith*, [2004] 1 S.C.R. 385 [*Smith*].

38 *Ibid.* at para. 47, discussing *R. v. Jetté* (1999), 141 C.C.C. (3d) 52 (Que. C.A.) in which an appeal was allowed and a stay of proceedings entered in a case where fresh evidence was admitted suggesting that the accused's statements had been extracted involuntarily and that perjured testimony about the accused making an incriminating statement to an informant had been introduced at trial.

39 *Smith*, *ibid.* at para. 48.

absence of statutory change, this ground has been the site of a judicial struggle over whether convictions should be overturned because of concerns about their safety or because of a lurking doubt about guilt.

In 1975, a majority of the Supreme Court in *R. v. Corbett* stated that under section 686(1)(a)(i)

> . . . the Court of Appeal must satisfy itself not only that there was evidence requiring the case to be submitted to the jury, but also that the weight of such evidence is not so weak that a verdict of guilty is unreasonable. This cannot be taken to mean that the Court of Appeal is to substitute its opinion for that of the jury. The word of the enactment is "unreasonable", not "unjustified". The jurors are the triers of the facts and their finding is not to be set aside because the judges in appeal do not think they would have made the same finding if sitting as jurors. This is only to be done if they come to the conclusion that the verdict is such that no twelve reasonable men could possibly have reached it acting judicially.[40]

Justice Laskin dissented and stressed that the Court of Appeal's jurisdiction under the section must go beyond finding errors of law and suggested that an unsafe or unsatisfactory verdict as defined under British legislation would also be an unreasonable verdict under the Canadian provision. He added:

> The members of that Court must surely weigh the evidence in bringing their own judgment to bear on the issue whether the jury's verdict is unreasonable or cannot be supported by the evidence. They are quite entitled to substitute their opinion for that of the jury on that issue. I have already adverted to the fact that an appellate Court may be reluctant to upset a jury verdict on simply a scrutiny of a lifeless record. Such reluctance must not, however, be translated into a principle of non-reviewability, and this, in my opinion, is what has happened in the present case.[41]

Even though the Laskin position is supported by Canada's subsequent experience with wrongful convictions, it has not yet become the law in Canada.[42]

In *R. v. Yebes*, the Supreme Court of Canada considered whether a murder conviction was unreasonable in a case where a pathologist determined that two boys died before a fire was deliberately set in their home, but the cause of death

---

40 [1975] 2 S.C.R. 275 at 278–79 [*Corbett*].

41 *Ibid.* at 289.

42 Andrew Furgiuele, "The Self-Limiting Appellate Courts and Section 686" (2007) 52 Crim. L.Q. 237.

was unascertained.[43] The Supreme Court held that appellate courts must go beyond finding whether there is some evidence that if believed by the jury would support the conviction and ask themselves whether the verdict was one that a properly instructed jury acting judicially could render. The Court added that the test of whether the impugned verdict could *possibly* have been reached would render review on appeal under the subsection almost impossible. The concept of reasonableness is clearly expressed in the section that speaks of an unreasonable verdict. Therefore, curial review is invited whenever a jury goes beyond a reasonable standard. It seems, then, *Corbett* is the governing case and the test is "whether the verdict is one that a properly instructed jury acting judicially, could reasonably have rendered."[44]

Although this process does not call for the appellate court to substitute its opinion for that of the trier of fact, it requires the court to some extent to reconsider and reweigh the evidence before the court. The murder conviction was upheld on the basis that the accused had a motive to kill the boys because of splits in the family as well as the exclusive opportunity, there being no evidence of the presence of another person in the house that night. It was upheld even though the door was unlocked and the appellant's estranged wife had been in the house earlier that night, and she also had a motive to kill the boys.

The above decision was rendered in 1987 before the experience with wrongful convictions was widely revealed—that happened throughout the 1990s. This revelation led to the Supreme Court changing its approach to extradition to face the death penalty because of a recognition of the risk of a wrongful conviction. In 1996, the Supreme Court held that historical indecent assault convictions against a priest were unreasonable in large part because of inconsistencies in the complainant's stories. Although deference should be paid to findings of credibility made by the trial judge, "the court of appeal retains the power, pursuant to s. 686(1)(*a*)(i), to reverse the trial court's verdict where the assessment of credibility made at trial is not supported by the evidence."[45] It is a power which would be used sparingly by the appellate court:

> This is not to say that an appellate court should shrink from exercising the power when, after carrying out its statutory duty, it concludes that the conviction rests on shaky ground and that it would be unsafe to maintain it. In conferring this power on appellate courts to be applied only in appeals by the

---

43 [1987] 2 S.C.R. 168 [*Yebes*].

44 *Ibid.* at para. 23.

45 *R. v. Burke*, [1996] 1 S.C.R. 474 at para. 5.

> accused, it was intended as an additional and salutary safeguard against the conviction of the innocent.[46]

In the end, the conviction was overturned on the basis that "no properly instructed jury acting in a judicial manner could reasonably have accepted the claims of these complainants."[47]

The above case was decided by a trial judge alone and can be contrasted with the Supreme Court's 4:3 decision to uphold a historical rape conviction in another case that was tried before a jury. In that case, the majority stressed that the inferences drawn by the jury could not be known and that a jury's verdict was not unreasonable simply because there were inconsistencies in the complainant's testimony. The majority of the Court stressed the jury's advantage in assessing the witness's demeanour and applying its own common sense. It concluded that the jury could have resolved these inconsistencies by accepting the complainant's explanations for them, including that the complainant had a repressed memory of the events. Three judges in dissent stressed that juries are not infallible and that the inconsistencies in the complainant's testimony meant that it was unreasonable for the jury not to have a reasonable doubt about the accused's guilt.[48] As Kaufman J. suggested in the Morin Inquiry, appellate courts can overestimate the importance of seeing and hearing the witnesses, and they have the ability to detect flaws at trial that may reveal doubts about guilt.

The differences between the degree of review of judge alone and jury verdicts in the two cases discussed above may have been somewhat narrowed by a more recent decision, where a narrow majority of the Supreme Court stressed that appellate courts should focus on whether the verdict as opposed to the trial judge's reasons for the verdict are unreasonable.[49] A minority in that case stressed that no one should be convicted on the basis of bad or illogical rea-

---

46 *Ibid.* at para. 6.

47 *Ibid.* at para. 7.

48 *R. v. François*, [1994] 2 S.C.R. 827.

49 *R. v. Beaudry*, [2007] 1 S.C.R. 190 at para. 62 [*Beaudry*]:

> I readily appreciate that the deference owed to a trial court's findings of fact must not become a pretext for an appellate court to evade its responsibility to set aside an unreasonable verdict. This is why no finding of fact is entirely exempt from appellate court scrutiny. Nonetheless, as this Court has consistently said, the integrity of our judicial system requires that the trial judge's privileged position in assessing the facts be respected. It should also be borne in mind that the question whether a verdict is unreasonable is not the same as the question whether a different verdict would have been reasonable had the evidence presented at trial been interpreted differently.

sons.[50] In respect to overturning unsafe convictions, this more recent case is a step backward because it could allow a conviction to be upheld despite inconsistencies in the trial judge's reasons for the verdict.

The leading case interpreting the provision that allows verdicts to be overturned on grounds that they are unreasonable or not supported by the evidence is *R. v. Biniaris*.[51] In that case, the Court upheld a murder conviction even though the Crown pathologist changed her testimony after having consulted with the defence pathologists: she then said that the accused's actions in stomping on the deceased did not cause death, it having been caused by a fall that occurred after the deceased was assaulted by another person. Following Kaufman J.'s recommendations in the report of the commission of inquiry into the Guy Paul Morin case, the Court was urged to adopt the "lurking doubt" standard for reversal of a conviction but refused to do so. Justice Arbour stated for the Court:

> It is insufficient for the court of appeal to refer to a vague unease, or a lingering or lurking doubt based on its own review of the evidence. This "lurking doubt" may be a powerful trigger for thorough appellate scrutiny of the evidence, but it is not, without further articulation of the basis for such doubt, a proper basis upon which to interfere with the findings of a jury. In other words, if, after reviewing the evidence at the end of an error-free trial which led to a conviction, the appeal court judge is left with a lurking doubt or feeling of unease, that doubt, which is not in itself sufficient to justify interfering with the conviction, may be a useful signal that the verdict was indeed reached in a non-judicial manner. In that case, the court of appeal must proceed further with its analysis.[52]

The lurking doubt standard was thus rejected by the Supreme Court even though the Ontario Court of Appeal had previously indicated it was prepared to adopt this and the related standard of a safe verdict under the notion in section 686(1)(a)(i) of verdicts being reasonable and supported by the evidence.[53]

Although the Supreme Court of Canada rejected the lurking doubt standard and recognized that it was more difficult to find that verdicts rendered by a jury as opposed to those explained by a trial judge were unreasonable, the Court did not insulate jury verdicts from review. Justice Arbour stated:

---

50 *Ibid.*

51 [2000] 1 S.C.R. 381 [*Biniaris*].

52 *Ibid.* at para. 38.

53 *R. v. Malcolm* (1993), 81 C.C.C. (3d) 196 (Ont. C.A.). Note that this decision was not followed by other courts of appeal. See *R. v. Guyatt* (1997), 119 C.C.C. (3d) 304 (B.C.C.A.).

> When a jury which was admittedly properly instructed returns what the appeal court perceives to be an unreasonable conviction, the only rational inference, if the test in *Yebes* is followed, is that the jury, in arriving at that guilty verdict, was not acting judicially. This conclusion does not imply an impeachment of the integrity of the jury. It may be that the jury reached its verdict pursuant to an analytical flaw similar to the errors occasionally incurred in the analysis of trial judges and revealed in their reasons for judgment. Such error would of course not be apparent on the face of the verdict by a jury. But the unreasonableness itself of the verdict would be apparent to the legally trained reviewer when, in all the circumstances of a given case, judicial fact-finding precludes the conclusion reached by the jury.[54]

The Court defended the role of "judicial experience" in evaluating the reasonableness of the verdict when it stated that if an appellate court concludes on a mix of objective and subjective factors that a jury's verdict is unreasonable, it is not acting illegitimately as a thirteenth juror or claiming that the jury had wrongfully acted partially or went beyond the evidence. Rather, the appellate court was examining the verdict "through the lens of judicial experience which serves as an additional protection against an unwarranted conviction."[55]

The most common ground of appeal from convictions is the reference in section 686(1)(a)(ii) to the verdict being based on an error of law. As discussed above, the accused has a right to appeal only on questions that involve an error of law. Some recent studies have suggested that appeals of legal errors have not been an effective means to prevent wrongful convictions, at least in American cases of proven DNA exonerations.[56] Although it would be an error of law to convict a person in the absence of evidence relating to all the elements of an offence, it would not likely be an error of law if a trial judge or a jury reached an erroneous conclusion when assessing the credibility of a witness.

Unlike the other grounds of appeal based on unreasonable verdicts or miscarriages of justice, however, this ground is qualified by a proviso under section 686(1)(b)(ii) which allows the appellate court to dismiss the accused's appeal on the basis that "no substantial wrong or miscarriage of justice has occurred." In other words, appeals on grounds of errors of law made by the trial judge or in the trial judge's charge to the jury can be held as harmless to the verdict. The

---

54 *Biniaris*, above note 51 at para. 39.

55 *Ibid.* at para. 40.

56 Brandon Garrett, "Judging Innocence" (2008) 108 Colum. L. Rev. 55; finding appeal success rates in cases of DNA exonerees is not different from appeal success rates in comparable cases where there is no reason to question the guilt of the accused.

proviso at least requires the appellate court to address its mind to the question of whether there has been a miscarriage of justice. Nevertheless, a recent American study has shown that appellate courts have applied a similar harmless error rule in cases where DNA exonerations were subsequently obtained.[57]

The Supreme Court of Canada has recognized that some errors of law will be so minor that they will not affect the verdict. Even if the error is not characterized as minor, the proviso can be applied to even a major error of law but "only if it is clear that the evidence pointing to the guilt of the accused is so overwhelming that any other verdict but a conviction would be impossible."[58] A new trial should be ordered after a finding of an error of law unless there is no reasonable possibility that the verdict would have been different if the error had not been made.[59] In cases where the error of law was the exclusion of exculpatory evidence, any reasonable effect that the evidence could have had on the jury should be considered.[60] In cases where the error of law was the inclusion of inadmissible evidence, the appeal should be allowed and a new trial ordered if there is any possibility that a trial judge would have had a reasonable doubt about the accused's guilt on the basis of the admissible evidence.[61]

The final ground for allowing appeals is found under the *Criminal Code*, section 686(1)(a)(iii), which refers to allowing an appeal "on any ground that there was a miscarriage of justice." The Supreme Court has stated, "In every case, if the reviewing court concludes that the error, whether procedural or substantive, led to a denial of a fair trial, the court may properly characterize the matter as one where there was a miscarriage of justice."[62] In such cases a new trial is the minimal remedy that the appellate court must order. In early cases, the Supreme Court has stressed, "A person charged with the commission of a crime is entitled to a fair trial according to law. Any error which occurs at trial that deprives the accused of that entitlement is a miscarriage of justice."[63] There may also be a miscarriage of justice where the trial judge misapprehended evidence on matters of substance rather than detail, but only if such matters are material to the verdicts and the error plays "an essential part not just in the narrative of the judgment but 'in the reasoning process resulting in a conviction.'"[64]

---

57 *Ibid.* at 108; 32 percent of exonerees had error made at trial judged to be harmless.
58 *R. v. Khan*, [2001] 3 S.C.R. 823 at para. 31 [*Khan*].
59 *R. v. Bevan*, [1993] 2 S.C.R. 599.
60 *R. v. Wildman*, [1984] 2 S.C.R. 311.
61 *R. v. S.(P.L.)*, [1991] 1 S.C.R. 909.
62 *Khan*, above note 58 at para. 27.
63 *R. v. Fanjoy*, [1985] 2 S.C.R. 233 at 240.
64 *R. v. Lohrer*, [2004] 3 S.C.R. 732 at para. 2.

The miscarriage of justice ground for allowing an appeal is of particular relevance in cases where new evidence is admitted on appeal. In its *Truscott Reference*,[65] the Ontario Court of Appeal commented that on appeals that consider fresh evidence

> . . . section 686(1)(a)(iii) is the only provision that is potentially relevant. It allows an appellate court to grant an appeal 'on any ground there was a miscarriage of justice'. This power can reach virtually any kind of error that renders the trial unfair in a procedural or substantive way. The section has been applied on appeals where there was no unfairness at trial, but evidence was admitted on appeal that placed the reliability of the conviction in serious doubt. In these cases, the miscarriage of justice lies not in the conduct of the trial or even the conviction as entered at trial, but rather in maintaining the conviction in the face of new evidence that renders the conviction factually unreliable.[66]

Appeals on grounds of miscarriages of justice in Canada thus allow convictions to be quashed both on the basis that the trial was not fair and on the basis that new evidence places the reliability of the conviction in serious doubt. This decision demonstrates the flexibility of the legal term "miscarriage of justice" and its ability to include but not be limited to cases of factual innocence.

## E. APPELLATE DISCRETION TO ENTER AN ACQUITTAL OR ORDER A NEW TRIAL

If the accused is successful on the appeal, the appellate court has, under section 686(2) of the *Criminal Code*, a discretion to enter an acquittal or to order a new trial. Even if a new trial is not held because the prosecutor declines to proceed due to no reasonable prospect of conviction, the choice between these two remedies can have a profound effect on those who may have been wrongfully convicted. An acquittal means that the accused has been found not guilty and the presumption of innocence has been restored whereas a new trial order may either place the accused in continued jeopardy or result in a prosecutorial stay of proceedings which, as will be discussed below, may produce residual stigma in the case of an accused who has previously been convicted.

There is a long but not invariable practice of entering acquittals in cases where the accused likely suffered a miscarriage of justice. The Manitoba Court of Appeal entered an acquittal after Thomas Sophonow's third trial in part be-

65 2007 ONCA 575.

66 *Ibid.* at para. 110.

cause he had already faced three trials and served close to four years in jail and because the identification evidence in the case was not reliable.[67]

In *R. v. Hinse*,[68] the Supreme Court of Canada set aside a stay of proceedings entered by the Quebec Court of Appeal in a case of a thirty-year-old robbery conviction that was a suspected miscarriage of judgment and entered an acquittal on the basis that the "evidence could not allow a reasonable jury properly instructed to find the appellant guilty beyond a reasonable doubt."[69]

In the *Truscott Reference*, a five-judge panel of the Ontario Court of Appeal addressed how appellate discretion to order a new trial or enter an acquittal should be exercised. It stated:

> Relatively little has been written about the principles guiding the exercise of the remedial discretion in s. 686(2). It is clear that if the appeal court is satisfied based on the trial record as augmented by the fresh evidence, that no reasonable jury could convict, the appeal court's discretion must be exercised in favour of ordering an acquittal. An acquittal is the only appropriate order in this circumstance since a conviction following a retrial would presumably be quashed as an unreasonable verdict. An appeal court will not order a new trial to give the Crown an opportunity to make a case against an appellant when, as matters stood at the end of the proceedings in the court of appeal, no reasonable jury could convict.
>
> Apart from those cases where an acquittal is mandatory, the manner in which an appeal court should exercise its remedial discretion is more uncertain. As a general rule, if the appeal court is satisfied that the entirety of the record at the end of the appeal admits of a reasonable possibility of a conviction on a retrial, the appeal court will order a new trial.
>
> There are, however, cases where an appeal court has entered an acquittal even in the face of evidence that could reasonably support a conviction on a retrial. For example, acquittals have been entered where an appellant has fully served his or her sentence, or has already been subjected to several trials. These authorities offer little guidance as to when an acquittal should be entered as opposed to ordering a new trial with a direction that the trial be stayed.[70]

After an exhaustive review of new evidence, including new forensic evidence and material not disclosed to the accused at the time of his original 1959

---

67 *R. v. Sophonow* (1985), 38 Man. R. (2d) 198 at 202 (C.A.).

68 [1997] 1 S.C.R. 3 [*Hinse*].

69 *Ibid.* at para. 2.

70 *Truscott Reference*, above note 65 at paras. 247–49.

murder trial or on the 1967 reference, the Court of Appeal concluded that an acquittal should be entered. It explained:

> This is one of those cases where a new trial could result in an acquittal or a conviction. In most cases, that conclusion would lead to an order for a new trial. However, to order a new trial in these circumstances merely because the remaining evidence clears a relatively low evidentiary threshold, knowing full well that a new trial will never be held, would be unfair to the appellant and does a disservice to the public. Nor would an order for a new trial accompanied by a further order staying the new trial be an adequate remedy. It would remove the stigma of the appellant's conviction, but leave in place the stigma that would accompany being the subject of an unresolved allegation of a crime as serious as this one.[71]

Although the Court of Appeal was not prepared to conclude that no properly instructed jury could convict the accused, it went on to find that it was clearly more probable than not that the accused would be acquitted at a hypothetical new trial. On this latter basis, and given the age and history of the case, the Court of Appeal entered an acquittal.

In other miscarriage of justice cases, courts of appeal have concluded that an acquittal should be entered because no reasonable jury would convict the accused. In *R. v. Walsh*, the New Brunswick Court of Appeal entered an acquittal after hearing new evidence from a variety of witnesses, as well as examining archival material that should have been disclosed to an accused who had served twenty-seven years' imprisonment on a murder charge. It stressed that the Crown had agreed that the fresh evidence should be admitted, that there was a miscarriage of justice, and that a new trial was not feasible.[72] It concluded:

> In view of the fact we have a complete record, we have considered the entire case as it was presented to the judge and jury. We have also considered the fresh evidence. On the evidence as it now stands, the trial record as augmented by the fresh evidence, we are of the opinion that no reasonable jury could convict Walsh of murder.[73]

In the William Mullins-Johnson case, an acquittal was also entered, with the agreement of the Crown, after the Ontario Court of Appeal had considered fresh pathological evidence indicating that the cause of death of Mullins-John-

71 *Ibid.* at para. 265.

72 *Re Walsh*, 2008 NBCA 33 at para. 96.

73 *Ibid.* at para. 91.

son's niece was undetermined and that the medical evidence did not support the original conviction of murder and sexual assault.[74]

The practice of entering acquittals is not invariable. The Ontario Court of Appeal refused to enter an acquittal when overturning a 1972 murder conviction in Romeo Phillion's case. The Court of Appeal stated that a new trial was necessary because "depending on how the fresh evidence were to unfold at a new trial, it would be open to a jury to reject the defence of alibi and conclude, essentially on the basis of the appellant's confessions" that the accused was guilty. It concluded both that "substituting a verdict of acquittal on the basis that the fresh evidence is 'clearly decisive' of innocence is not a tenable position."[75] Phillion had not established under the *Truscott* test that it was more probable than not that he would be acquitted at a hypothetical new trial even though there was new alibi evidence that "may well have left the jury in a state of reasonable doubt."[76] One judge dissented in this appeal and would have upheld the conviction. As in *Truscott*, a new trial was impossible given the age of the events and the prosecutor subsequently decided to withdraw the charge. This act was challenged on the basis that it deprived Phillion of the right to receive a not guilty verdict, but was upheld.

## F. PROSECUTORIAL USES OF STAYS OF PROCEEDINGS

If a new trial as opposed to an acquittal is ordered in a case of a suspected miscarriage of justice, the prosecutor must decide whether to proceed with the new trial or enter a prosecutorial stay. This issue has arisen in a number of wrongful conviction cases, including the David Milgaard case where the prosecutor had issued a prosecutorial stay under section 579 of the *Criminal Code*. In such cases, the protections of *res judicata* and double jeopardy do not apply and the prosecution could in theory be revived.

Two public inquiries have expressed strong criticism of the use of prosecutorial stays in cases involving suspected miscarriages of justice. Antonio Lamer, the late former chief justice of Canada, expressed these concerns:

> A stay of proceedings may leave an impression with the public that the charge is merely being "postponed" or "the authorities", in a broad sense, still believe in the validity of the charge. That impression is likely to be magnified where,

---

74 *Re Mullins-Johnson*, 2007 ONCA 720 [*Mullins-Johnson*].

75 *Re Phillion*, 2009 ONCA 202 at para. 244. See also *R v. Phillion*, 2010 ONSC 1604, upholding the subsequent decision to withdraw charges from *Charter* challenge.

76 *Ibid.* at para. 246.

> as in this case, the accused had already been convicted and spent years in prison prior to his successful appeal.[77]

Similarly, Patrick Lesage, the former chief justice of the Ontario Superior Court, expressed concerns that a prosecutorial stay leaves "a residual stigma"[78] and is not an appropriate remedy when the Minister of Justice has ordered a new trial under the petition procedure of section 696.1.[79] He recommended that a stay should be entered only by the Attorney General when there is an active investigation of the accused and that the preferable course in most cases of a suspected miscarriage of justice is for the Crown to call no evidence: the accused then receives an acquittal and is protected by double jeopardy provisions from further prosecutions for the alleged offence.[80]

A third commission of inquiry recognized that a prosecutorial stay in 1992 in David Milgaard's case "left him with significant stigma" that was not dispelled until DNA exonerated him in 1997, but that it was nevertheless a reasonable decision.[81] That said, the Milgaard Inquiry also endorsed the recommendations of Lesage J. about the limited use of prosecutorial stays in cases of suspected miscarriages of justice.

In the Romeo Phillion case discussed above, the prosecutor withdrew charges rather than stay proceedings when a new trial was ordered but was not possible in a historical murder case. Phillion challenged this decision under the *Charter* and argued that he is entitled to a not guilty verdict. The Crown's decision to withdraw charges was upheld, but it is fair to say that either way the Canadian inquiries and now the courts have given much attention to the proper disposition in cases involving miscarriages of justice.

## G. PARDONS

The *Criminal Code* provides that when the Governor in Council grants a free pardon "that person shall be deemed thereafter never to have committed the offence in respect of which the pardon is granted."[82] Despite the association of the word "pardon" with mercy as opposed to innocence, this provision suggests that a free pardon may be a means to recognize innocence in Canada. This approach is also supported by the fact that, in its 1992 decision in the David Mil-

77 Lamer Inquiry, above note 1 at 317–18.
78 Driskell Inquiry,above note 1 at 139.
79 *Criminal Code*, above note 4.
80 Driskell Inquiry, above note 1 at 129–39.
81 Milgaard Inquiry, above note 1 at 336.
82 *Criminal Code*, above note 4, s. 748(3).

gaard reference, the Supreme Court indicated that a free pardon would be the appropriate remedy if Milgaard satisfied the very high standard of establishing his innocence beyond a reasonable doubt.[83] Milgaard was unable to satisfy that standard in large part because DNA testing was not done until 1997.

Despite the above pronouncements, pardons are problematic as a means to recognize an accused's innocence. One problem is the connotation of pardons with mercy. Another problem is that pardons are granted by the federal Cabinet and not by the courts. A public inquiry in Canada recommended that three women be given free pardons because either they killed in legitimate self-defence or there was a reasonable doubt about whether they were guilty. The Cabinet, however, refused to grant the free pardons because of concerns about public safety and the lack of compassionate grounds not related to the question of guilt or innocence.[84]

## H. CROWN APPEALS

The prosecutor in Canada can appeal acquittals, but only with respect to questions of law.[85] Unlike the accused, the prosecutor cannot appeal on the basis that the acquittal is unreasonable or not supported by the evidence.[86] The trial judge can err in law, however, if he or she finds all the facts necessary for a legal conclusion but does not draw the necessary legal conclusion, fails to appreciate evidence because of a misapprehension of a legal principle, or fails to consider all the relevant evidence in relation to a legal issue.[87]

The Crown successfully appealed Guy Paul Morin's original acquittal, and he was wrongfully convicted at his second trial. The Supreme Court held that the trial judge had erred in law by inviting the jury to apply the "reasonable doubt" standard to each piece of evidence.[88] The Morin Inquiry into Morin's wrongful conviction recommended that the *Criminal Code* be amended to require the Crown to demonstrate that the verdict likely would have been different had the trial judge not made the error of law.[89] The Supreme Court has subsequently held that an error of law proven by the prosecutor when appeal-

---

83 *Reference re Milgaard*, [1992] 1 S.C.R. 866. See also *Re Therrien*, [2001] 2 S.C.R. 3 at para. 121, recognizing the distinct nature of the free pardon.

84 Gary Trotter, "Justice, Politics, and the Royal Prerogative of Mercy: Examining the Self-Defence Review" (2001) 26 Queen's L.J. 353 at 392.

85 *Criminal Code*, above note 4, s. 676.

86 *R. v. Sunbeam Corp.*, [1969] S.C.R. 221.

87 *R. v. Morin*, [1992] 3 S.C.R. 286.

88 *R. v. Morin*, [1988] 2 S.C.R. 345.

89 Morin Inquiry, above note 1 at 1190.

ing an acquittal must be reasonably thought to have a material bearing on the acquittal. That said, the prosecutor does not have to establish that the verdict would have been different in order to receive an order for a new trial after a successful prosecutorial appeal from an acquittal.[90]

## I. FRESH EVIDENCE ON APPEAL

The ability of appellate courts in Canada to consider fresh evidence on appeal is of particular importance in the wrongful conviction context. Section 683 of the *Criminal Code* provides courts of appeal with broad powers to consider fresh evidence, including powers to order production of things and to provide for the examination and cross-examination of witnesses before the Court of Appeal or other body. The Court of Appeal can appoint a special commissioner to inquire and report back on matters, including scientific matters that cannot "conveniently be inquired into before the court of appeal."[91] This provision is an interesting inquisitorial aspect of the appellate process in Canada. The addition of inquisitorial aspects to the adversary system could, in some cases, help prevent or remedy wrongful convictions by demonstrating an official commitment that the state should take efforts to discover the truth.

Under *R. v. Palmer* the basic test for the admission of fresh evidence is that

(1) the evidence must bear on a decisive or potentially decisive issue;
(2) the evidence must be credible;
(3) the evidence, if believed, could affect the result; and
(4) the evidence should generally not have been obtainable at trial by due diligence.[92]

From the start, courts have held that the due diligence requirement should not be applied as strictly in criminal as in civil cases. In a case decided in 2000, the Supreme Court made clear that the due diligence requirement was not essential and must yield where a miscarriage of justice would otherwise result.[93] In that case, however, the Court held that a miscarriage of justice had not occurred when the fresh evidence consisted of a secretly recorded conversation of a complainant in a sexual assault case where she denied that the accused had sexually assaulted her. The Court determined that defence counsel was aware of the tape

90 *R. v. Graveline*, [2006] 1 S.C.R. 609.
91 *Criminal Code*, above note 4, s. 683(1)(e).
92 [1980] 1 S.C.R. 259 [*Palmer*].
93 *R. v. G.D.B.*, [2000] 1 S.C.R. 520 at para. 37 [*G.D.B.*].

but decided not to use it as exculpatory evidence given that the complainant's statements were not convincing and were made in response to leading questions from her mother. The Court also held that the defence counsel's decision did not result in ineffective assistance. The due diligence standard can also be satisfied in cases where the lack of due diligence can be explained by ineffective assistance of counsel in the form of unreasonable conduct by defence counsel that may have contributed to a miscarriage of justice.[94]

## J. CONTEMPORARY STANDARDS

Canadian courts have not given as much thought to the problem of applying contemporary standards in historical cases as the British courts have. In the 2007 *Truscott Reference*, the Ontario Court of Appeal ruled that it was unnecessary to decide whether Truscott had been treated unfairly at his 1959 trial or his subsequent reference to the Supreme Court in 1966. The Court noted that disclosure requirements and trial practices were very different at that time and that there was potential unfairness both in attempting to determine what happened and applying contemporary standards to past cases.[95] The Canadian courts have also taken a strict view of *res judicata* so that an accused cannot benefit in changes of laws if his or her appeals have been exhausted.[96] In such cases, it would be necessary to successfully petition the federal Minister of Justice to reopen the case.[97] In his report on the matter, Kaufman J. took the position that the fact that a trial was fair under the standards existing at the time should not immunize the conviction from ministerial review.[98]

## K. MEANING OF GUILT BEYOND A REASONABLE DOUBT

The Canadian courts have taken some recent steps to define the meaning of proof of guilt beyond a reasonable doubt at trial. The Supreme Court of Canada has indicated that juries should be instructed that the reasonable doubt standard is related to the presumption of innocence and requires the Crown to establish

94 *Ibid.*; *R. v. Appleton* (2001), 55 O.R. (3d) 321 (C.A.).

95 *Truscott Reference*, above note 65 at paras. 122–23.

96 *R. v. Sarson*, [1996] 2 S.C.R. 223.

97 Gary Trotter, "Justice, Politics and the Royal Prerogative of Mercy: Examining the Self-Defence Review" (2001) 26 Queen's L.J. 339.

98 Hon. Fred Kaufman, *In the Matter of an Application by Steven Murray Truscott pursuant to Section 690 (Now 696.1) of the Criminal Code: Report to Minister of Justice* (Ottawa: Department of Justice, 2004) at para. 177 [Kaufman].

guilt. A reasonable doubt is based on reason and common sense and not on sympathy or prejudice, and it cannot be an imaginary or frivolous doubt. Although the Crown does not have to establish guilt to an absolute certainty, it is not enough for the Crown to establish that the accused is probably guilt.[99] Thus the reasonable doubt standard is closer to certainty than probability.[100]

Once the accused has been convicted, the reasonable doubt standard does not operate in the same way. The accused has to establish grounds of appeal, even on an appeal that has been ordered by the Minister of Justice, because there is a reasonable basis to believe that a miscarriage has likely occurred. Nevertheless, appellate standards relating to the reasonableness of the verdict, the existence of a miscarriage of justice, and the effect of the introduction of new evidence appropriately take into the account the reasonable doubt standard when deciding whether a conviction should be overturned.

## L. CROWN CONCESSIONS

In recent years, prosecutors have become more aware of the possibilities of wrongful convictions. The idea that the Crown is concerned with justice as opposed to winning is consistent with *Boucher*.[101] Prosecutors have made some important concessions in wrongful conviction cases. In the 1983 Marshall reference, the Crown conceded that the late Donald Marshall's appeal should be allowed.[102] In the Erin Walsh case,[103] the Crown also conceded that the appeal should be allowed but took issue with the Court's decision to enter an acquittal. In at least two cases arising from the testimony of discredited pathologist Dr. Charles Smith, the Crown has conceded that convictions should be overturned.[104] In other cases, such as the Stephen Truscott and Romeo Phillion cases, the Crown has taken an adversarial position.

## M. WHEN APPEALS HAVE BEEN EXHAUSTED: THE PETITION PROCEDURE

Once a person's appeals have been exhausted, the only means to reopen a case is to petition the federal Minister of Justice, an elected official who also serves as

99 *R. v. Lifchus*, [1997] 3 S.C.R. 320.
100 *R. v. Starr*, [2000] 2 S.C.R. 144.
101 *Boucher v. The Queen*, [1955] S.C.R. 16 [*Boucher*].
102 *R. v. Marshall* (1983), 57 N.S.R. (2d) 286 (S.C.A.D.).
103 *Re Walsh*, above note 72.
104 *Mullins-Johnson*, above note 74; *R. v. Sherret-Robinson*, 2009 ONCA 886 [*Sherret-Robinson*].

the Attorney General of Canada.[105] This power is related to the royal prerogative of mercy and was recognized in Canada's first *Criminal Code* enacted in 1892. It provided:

> 748. If upon any application for the mercy of the Crown on behalf of any person convicted of an indictable offence, the Minister of Justice entertains a doubt whether such person ought to have been convicted, he may, instead of advising Her Majesty to remit or commute the sentence, after such inquiry as he thinks proper, by an order in writing direct a new trial at such time and before such court as he may think proper.[106]

In 1927, the *Criminal Code* was amended to give the Minister of Justice the option of referring the case to a Court of Appeal pursuant to the wider appeal powers enacted a few years earlier (and discussed above). In 1955, the provision was reworded to provide that the minister could direct a new trial or a new appeal at his discretion as opposed to cases where the minister "entertains a doubt." The former "doubt" standard both provided more statutory guidance to the minister and accorded with basic principles of criminal justice—these require guilt to be proven beyond a reasonable doubt.

In Canada, most criminal prosecutions are conducted by the provincial Attorneys General, but the Attorney General of Canada has some concurrent prosecutorial responsibilities, for example, with respect to terrorism prosecutions. The Attorney General of Canada also prosecutes drug offences and criminal offences in Canada's three northern territories. In recommending that the petition process be replaced by an independent and permanent commission, such as the English CCRC, a number of public inquiries have noted that the federal Minister of Justice is in a perceived and sometimes real conflict of interest in deciding whether to reopen a criminal conviction.[107] The Milgaard Inquiry has documented a lack of transparency in the petition process which saw Milgaard's petitions originally denied but then granted after the prime minister intervened in the matter.[108]

---

105 Kerry Scullion, "Wrongful Convictions and the Criminal Conviction Review Process pursuant to Section 696.1 of the *Criminal Code* of Canada" (2004) 46 Canadian Journal of Criminology and Criminal Justice 189. See also Hon. Justice Peter H. Howden, "Judging Errors of Judgment: Accountability, Independence and Vulnerability in a Post-Appellate Conviction Review Process" (2002) 21 Windsor Y.B. Access Just. 569.

106 *Criminal Code, 1892*, S.C. 1892, c. 29.

107 See, for example, the Milgaard Inquiry, above note 1, c. 6.

108 *Ibid.* at 376–77.

Until amendments in 2002, the petition procedure was explicitly tied to applications for the mercy of the Crown. Under what until 2002 was known as section 690 of the *Criminal Code*, the Minister of Justice had discretion to

> (a) direct, by order in writing, a new trial or, in the case of a person under sentence of preventive detention, a new hearing, before any court that he thinks proper, if after inquiry he is satisfied that in the circumstances a new trial or hearing, as the case may be, should be directed;
> (b) refer the matter at any time to the court of appeal for hearing and determination by that court as if it were an appeal by the convicted person or the person under sentence of preventive detention, as the case may be; or
> (c) refer to the court of appeal at any time, for its opinion, any question on which he desires the assistance of that court, and the court shall furnish its opinion accordingly.[109]

This provision provided no rules to govern the Minister of Justice's exercise of discretion. Judges in Canada have quoted in relation to section 690 with approval a 1976 statement by Lord Diplock in *Freitas v. Benny*:

> Mercy is not the subject of legal rights. It begins where legal rights end. A convicted person has no legal right even to have his case considered by the Home Secretary in connection with the exercise of the prerogative of mercy. In tendering his advice to the sovereign the Home Secretary is doing something that is often cited as the exemplar of a purely discretionary act as contrasted with the exercise of a quasi-judicial function. [110]

These statements taken on their own would suggest that a person who seeks to reopen a case after conviction has no rights.[111]

In Canada, however, these statements have been qualified somewhat by a recognition that basic principles of procedural fairness and the *Charter* would apply to the exercise of ministerial powers under the petition procedure. Justice Rothstein has stated in the course of a judicial review of Colin Thatcher's application:

> An adverse decision by the Minister in exercising his discretion under section 690 can result in the continuation of a lengthy, if not lifetime, incarceration of a convicted person. This deprivation of liberty is what engages the appli-

109 Repealed S.C. 2002, c. 13, s. 70.
110 [1976] A.C. 239 at 247 (J.C.P.C.).
111 See also the discussion of this issue in Chapter 5, on Australian law.

> cant's rights under section 7 of the *Charter*, and requires that the Minister act fairly in exercising his discretion. However, it is important to remember, even in the context of the *Charter*, that the applicant is asking for mercy. In this respect, there is no *lis* between the applicant and the Minister, and the applicant has already had the full benefit of the *Charter* in the antecedent judicial proceedings leading to the conviction.
>
> Having regard to the nature of proceedings under section 690 and the consequences to the individual, I am of the view that the content of the Minister's duty of fairness under section 690 is less than that applicable to judicial proceedings. In exercising his discretion under section 690, the Minister must act in good faith and conduct a meaningful review, provided that the application is not frivolous or vexatious. The convicted person should have a reasonable opportunity to state his case. However, proceedings under section 690 do not constitute an appeal on the merits. There is no general right of disclosure to everything considered by the Minister or his officials.[112]

Several judicial reviews of negative decisions by the Minister of Justice to refer cases to the courts have been made but all without success.[113]

In 1994, Minister of Justice Allan Rock announced a number of principles that guided his decision making under the petition procedure. They included the idea that the petition remedy was extraordinary and not intended to allow the minister to substitute his opinion for that of the court or jury or to create a fourth level of appeal. Moreover, applications should ordinarily be based on new matters that had not been considered by the courts. The minister will investigate new evidence that is presented to determine its reliability and significance. Although an applicant does not have to establish innocence to be successful, the applicant would have to establish a basis that a miscarriage of justice likely occurred.[114] The reactive nature of this enterprise was outlined in the Milgaard Inquiry when it heard the following from a former federal official:

> Q . . . A convicted person can't come to you and say "look, I'd like you to investigate, I'm innocent, I don't know what went wrong but would you

---

112 *Thatcher v. Canada*, [1997] 1 F.C. 289 at paras. 12–13.

113 *Ibid.*; *W.R. v. Canada (Minister of Justice)*, [1999] F.C.J. No. 1059 (T.D.); *Bonamy v. Canada (Minister of Justice)* (2001), 156 C.C.C. (3d) 110 (F.C.T.D.); *Daoulov v. Attorney General (Canada)*, 2008 FC 544; *Bilodeau v. Canada (Minister of Justice)*, 2008 QCCS 1036, aff'd (*sub nom Bilodeau v. Canada (Ministre de la Justice)*) 2009 QCCA 746.

114 Patricia Braiden & Joan Brockman, "Remedying Wrongful Convictions through Applications to the Minister of Justice under Section 690 of the *Criminal Code*" (1999) 17 Windsor Y.B. Access Just. 3 at 9–10.

people please go and investigate this and find out why I was wrongfully convicted"?

A We would say to that person "that is not the role of the department or of the Minister". Certainly, if you've been through the process, sat in on your trial, heard the evidence, you're in the best position to identify to us what it is you say constitutes wrongful—or what the errors were and why they constitute a miscarriage of justice.

Q And what you are telling us, then, it would be incumbent upon Mr. Milgaard and/or his counsel to identify significant grounds that might provide a basis for a remedy under Section 690?

A Yes.[115]

These principles establish a number of significant hurdles for an applicant to pass before the Minister of Justice orders that the courts reconsider a conviction. As will be seen, these principles have now largely been codified in the 2002 reforms.

A new trial or a new appeal would be subject to the normal appeal procedures, but there was no appeal from an advisory opinion under section 690(c) of the *Criminal Code*.[116] The ability of the Minister of Justice to refer matters to courts of appeals for advisory opinions is now retained under section 696.3(2). In addition, the Minister of Justice has a power to refer cases directly to the Supreme Court, something that has been done in at least three cases of suspected miscarriages of justice.[117]

In 2002, the section 690 prerogative of mercy provisions were replaced with new procedures under section 696.1–6. The new procedures were designed to make the petition process more transparent by providing the Minister of Justice with legal standards for making decisions. The most important provision is section 696.3(3) and (4):

> (3) On an application under this Part, the Minister of Justice may
> (a) if the Minister is satisfied that there is a reasonable basis to conclude that a miscarriage of justice likely occurred, direct, by order in writing, a new trial before any court that the Minister thinks proper or, in the case of a person found to be a dangerous offender or a long-term offender under Part XXIV, a new hearing under that Part, or refer the matter at any time to the court of appeal for hearing and determination by that court as if

115 Milgaard Inquiry, above note 1 at 358.

116 *R. v. Kelly*, [2001] 1 S.C.R. 741.

117 *Re Coffin* (1955), 116 C.C.C. 215; *Re Truscott*, [1967] S.C.R. 309; *Reference re Milgaard*, above note 83.

it were an appeal by the convicted person or the person found to be a dangerous offender or a long-term offender under Part XXIV, as the case may be; or

(b) dismiss the application.

(4) A decision of the Minister of Justice made under subsection (3) is final and is not subject to appeal.

The statutory criterion that the Minister of Justice must conclude that a miscarriage of justice likely occurred seems higher than the CCRC's standard of there being "a real possibility" that the conviction would not be upheld if referred to the Court of Appeal. A reasonable likelihood is a higher standard than a real possibility.

The term "miscarriage of justice" is not defined in the Canadian legislation. In the appeal context, a miscarriage of justice is a separate ground of appeal from those based on unreasonable verdicts and errors of laws. A miscarriage of justice would include both trials that have been unfair and trials

> . . . where there was no unfairness at trial, but evidence was admitted on appeal that placed the reliability of the conviction in serious doubt. In these cases, the miscarriage of justice lies not in the conduct of the trial or even the conviction as entered at trial, but rather in maintaining the conviction in the face of new evidence that renders the conviction factually unreliable.[118]

Justice Kaufman, in his exhaustive report for the Minister of Justice in connection with Stephen Truscott's application for ministerial review, stressed that consistent with the appellate jurisprudence, a miscarriage of justice would occur both if the conviction of a factually innocent person was established but also if new evidence could reasonably have affected the verdict. He stressed that in the latter circumstances "it would be unfair to maintain the accused's conviction without an opportunity for the trier of fact to consider new evidence."[119]

In deciding whether to reopen a conviction by ordering a new trial or a new appeal, section 696.4 instructs that the Minister of Justice shall take into account all matters that the minister considers relevant, including

(a) whether the application is supported by new matters of significance that were not considered by the courts or previously considered by the Minister in an application in relation to the same conviction or finding under Part XXIV;

---

118 *Truscott Reference*, above note 65 at para. 110.

119 Kaufman, above note 98 at para. 164.

(b) the relevance and reliability of information that is presented in connection with the application; and

(c) the fact that an application under this Part is not intended to serve as a further appeal and any remedy available on such an application is an extraordinary remedy.[120]

This section codifies many of the principles contained in Minister of Justice Rock's 1994 statement. It does not insist that new evidence or new matters be presented, but as a practical matter, doing this is almost required given that the petition procedure is not intended to be a further level of appeal. Indeed, the Department of Justice's website presents the need for new matters to be presented as a requirement.[121]

These internal procedures are used: (1) a preliminary assessment to determine whether there are new matters that provide an air of reality to the claim of a miscarriage of justice; (2) an investigation in which counsel within the department verifies the information, collects new information, and makes a recommendation to the minister; (3) preparation of an investigative summary that is prepared by counsel and disclosed to the applicant for comments; and (4) the preparation of final legal advice for the Minister of Justice's decision. A special adviser within the department can offer advice at various stages of the investigation. The Milgaard Inquiry, however, concluded that the post-2002 changes have not changed the fundamental nature of the process:

> While the changes have improved the conviction review process since *Milgaard*, the fundamental aspects have not changed. The process remains re-active. The federal Minister does not conduct a proactive investigation on receipt of an application, but rather relies on the applicant, lacking in investigative expertise, to identify the grounds for an alleged miscarriage of justice. The test for the exercise by the Minister of his or her discretion to refer a matter to the Court system has not changed. Finally, the decision as to whether a

---

120 *Criminal Code*, above note 4.

121 Department of Justice Canada, "Addressing Possible Miscarriages of Justice" in *Annual Report 2008* (Ottawa: Department of Justice, 2008), online: www.justice.gc.ca/eng/pi/ccr-rc/rep08-rap08/02.html:

> An application for ministerial review must be supported by "new matters of significance" — generally new information that has surfaced since the trial and appeal and therefore has not been presented to the courts, and has not been considered by the Minister on a prior application. Only after a thorough review of the new matters of significance will the Minister be in a position to determine whether there is a reasonable basis to conclude that a miscarriage of justice likely occurred.

convicted person can have access to the Court to challenge a conviction still lies with the federal Minister, an elected politician.[122]

The new procedure, codified in 2002, allows the Minister of Justice to appoint individuals to investigate claims of wrongful conviction. Those individuals must be retired judges, members of the bar, or those with similar qualifications. They have powers to take evidence, issue subpoenas, and compel people to give evidence.[123] These powers are broad and unlike the CCRC include a power to obtain documents from private persons.

The initial application must include material such as true copies of trial transcripts and material filed on appeal. If an investigation is conducted, it will be disclosed to the applicant who has an opportunity to respond to the investigation.

From November 2002 when the new provisions came into force to 31 March 2009, the Minister of Justice has made decisions on eighty-three applications. Sixty-one, or 73 percent, of the applications were closed after a preliminary assessment on the basis that there were no grounds for further investigation. The remaining applications went to investigation with twelve of those cases (14 percent of total applications) being referred back to the courts and ten (12 percent of total applications) being dismissed by the Minister of Justice. These statistics suggest that the Minister of Justice refers a greater percentage of applications (12 percent compared to 4 percent) to the courts than the British CCRC, but that the CCRC receives many more applications each year than the Minister of Justice and conducts more preliminary investigations.[124] Although the Canadian system does allow the minister or a delegate to conduct an investigation, there is an expectation that the application be complete and generally present new evidence to the minister.

There have been many criticisms of the delay in processing petition applications which, in some cases, can take years. One response to this delay is that in a number of cases, the courts have fashioned a remedy that allows an applicant to obtain bail pending consideration by the Minister of Justice.[125]

---

122 Milgaard Inquiry, above note 1 at 364.

123 *Criminal Code*, above note 4, s. 696.2.

124 Department of Justice Canada, "Applications for Ministerial Review" in *Annual Report 2009* (Ottawa: Department of Justice, 2009), online: www.justice.gc.ca/eng/pi/ccr-rc/rep09-rap09/p5.html. See Chapter 10, below, for more discussion of the operation of the CCRC.

125 *R. v. Phillion*, [2003] O.J. No. 3422 (S.C.J.); *R. v. Driskell*, 2004 MBQB 3; *R v. Unger*, 2005 MBQB 238.

There are also statutory provisions that allow a person to obtain bail pending appeal.[126]

## N. THE HEARING OF APPEALS AS A RESULT OF THE PETITION PROCEDURE

In recent years when the petition procedure has been used, the preferred remedy by the Minister of Justice has been to refer a case for an appeal as opposed to a new trial. A new appeal is especially useful in historical cases where a new trial is not possible. As discussed above, appeal courts can consider new evidence on appeals and even hear testimony or appoint special commissioners to inquire into defined matters. Starting with the 2007 *Truscott Reference*, the courts of appeal have also been willing to decide whether an acquittal is more probable than not at a hypothetical new trial and if so enter an acquittal. The trend towards relying on new appeals as opposed to new trials also mirrors the practice in Britain, where the CCRC must refer a case to the Court of Appeal and is not able to direct a new trial.

The Royal Commission on the Donald Marshall Jr. Prosecution criticized the use of an appeal remedy because it places the onus on the accused and could result in a new trial. At the same time, however, there has been a danger that an order of a new trial could, as discussed above, result in a prosecutorial stay that would deprive the accused of any verdict and result in a residual stigma.

The Minister of Justice ordered a new appeal in the Stephen Truscott case, though one limited to matters of new evidence. A special five-judge panel of the Ontario Court of Appeal heard extensive new evidence from forensic pathologists and entomologists relating to the victim's time of death as well as archival material relating to matters that were not disclosed to Truscott at his 1959 trial or during the 1966 reference to the Supreme Court. The Ontario Court of Appeal concluded that the new evidence was admissible under the tests described earlier. The new evidence was such that Truscott's murder conviction was no longer reliable and should be quashed. The Court of Appeal then decided that the appropriate remedy would be to enter an acquittal rather than to order a new trial. In reaching this conclusion, the Court of Appeal decided that it was more probable than not that a hypothetical new trial would end in acquittal. It also took note of the reality that a new trial was impossible given that the last trial took place almost fifty years earlier.

---

126 *Criminal Code*, above note 4, s. 679.

In the *Mullins-Johnson* case, the Court of Appeal heard evidence from Ontario's chief forensic pathologist that a crime did not occur despite Mullins-Johnson's conviction of murdering his niece and his eleven years' imprisonment. This decision is also noteworthy because both the Crown and the Court of Appeal offered an apology to Mullins-Johnson for his wrongful conviction.[127] At the same time, the Court of Appeal held that because it was hearing an appeal, it did not have jurisdiction to determine or make a declaration of factual innocence.[128] Rather, the only remedies available to it when deciding an appeal were to order a new trial or enter an acquittal. Given the new pathology evidence that there was no evidence of a crime, the Court of Appeal entered an acquittal.

The year before, the Driskell Inquiry examined the question of whether some procedure should be available in Canadian law to allow those who have been wrongfully convicted to seek a declaration of innocence. Both the inquiry and the Ontario Court of Appeal in *Mullins-Johnson* expressed concern that such a new procedure could undermine the meaning of the not guilty verdict, creating two classes of people found not guilty, namely, those who are declared innocent and those who are not. That said, the Driskell Inquiry recognized that Canadian governments generally require evidence of innocence for purposes of compensating the wrongfully convicted and recommended that the issue of innocence determinations be subject to further study along with the issue of compensation.[129]

## O. THE ROLE OF THE PROSECUTOR AND DISCLOSURE

Lack of full disclosure of relevant material in the prosecutor's possession has been an important factor in many wrongful convictions. Indeed, some wrongful conviction cases, such as those of Stephen Truscott and Erin Walsh, have

---

127 Similarly, in *Re Walsh*, above note 72 at para. 45, the New Brunswick Court of Appeal stated:

> The present case became atypical when, upon the s. 696.1 reference to this Court, the Crown joined in the motion for the admission of fresh evidence and conceded that: (1) Mr. Walsh suffered a miscarriage of justice; (2) he was wrongfully convicted; and (3) the conviction ought to be quashed. Thus, it is not necessary for the Court to subject the proffered fresh evidence to the *Palmer* criteria. We are entitled "in the interest of justice", therefore, to receive the proffered evidence as admissible fresh evidence and conclude that it would, taken together with the other evidence adduced at trial, disclose that Mr. Walsh has been the victim of a miscarriage of justice.

128 *Mullins-Johnson*, above note 74.

129 Driskell Inquiry, above note 1 at 123–43.

featured the introduction of material taken from the archives that would have helped the defence had it been disclosed at the original trial.

As discussed earlier, the wrongful conviction of Donald Marshall Jr. led to the appointment of the first commission of inquiry into a wrongful conviction in Canada. The Marshall Inquiry found that a failure of the Crown to disclose inconsistent statements made by witnesses who lied that they had seen Marshall stab the victim after having been subjected to suggestive interviews by the police was an important factor in Marshall's wrongful conviction. In addition, a companion of the real killer told the police that Marshall was not the killer shortly after Marshall's conviction — but this critical information was not disclosed to Marshall or his lawyer. In response to these findings, the Marshall Inquiry recommended that Parliament amend the *Criminal Code* to place on the prosecution a continuing statutory duty of disclosure. As is unfortunately often the case, legislative reform to minimize the risk of wrongful convictions was not a priority and Parliament has yet to enact a statutory code of disclosure. In this area Parliament has sought only to place limits on the disclosure of therapeutic records of complainants in sexual assault cases.

In 1991, the Supreme Court of Canada decided the landmark case of *Stinchcombe*.[130] Justice Sopinka for a unanimous Court stated:

> The right to make full answer and defence is one of the pillars of criminal justice on which we heavily depend to ensure that the innocent are not convicted. Recent events have demonstrated that the erosion of this right due to non-disclosure was an important factor in the conviction and incarceration of an innocent person. In the *Royal Commission on the Donald Marshall, Jr., Prosecution*, Vol. 1: *Findings and Recommendations* (1989) (the "Marshall Commission Report"), the Commissioners found that prior inconsistent statements were not disclosed to the defence. This was an important contributing factor in the miscarriage of justice which occurred and led the Commission to state that "anything less than complete disclosure by the Crown falls short of decency and fair play" (Vol. 1 at p. 238). The Commission recommended an extensive regime of disclosure of which the key provisions are as follows (Vol. 1 at p. 243):
>
> 2 (1) Without request, the accused is entitled, before being called upon to elect the mode of trial or to plead to the charge of an indictable offence, whichever comes first, and thereafter:
>
> (a) to receive a copy of his criminal record;

130 Above note 11.

(b) to receive a copy of any statement made by him to a person in authority and recorded in writing or to inspect such a statement if it has been recorded by electronic means; and to be informed of the nature and content of any verbal statement alleged to have been made by the accused to a person in authority and to be supplied with any memoranda in existence pertaining thereto;
(c) to inspect anything that the prosecutor proposes to introduce as an exhibit and, where practicable, receive copies thereof;
(d) to receive a copy of any statement made by a person whom the prosecutor proposes to call as a witness or anyone who may be called as a witness, and recorded in writing or, in the absence of a statement, a written summary of the anticipated testimony of the proposed witness, or anyone who may be called as a witness;
(e) to receive any other material or information known to the Crown and which tends to mitigate or negate the defendant's guilt as to the offence charged, or which would tend to reduce his punishment therefore, notwithstanding that the Crown does not intend to introduce such material or information as evidence;
(f) to inspect the electronic recording of any statement made by a person whom the prosecutor proposes to call as a witness;
(g) to receive a copy of the criminal record of any proposed witness; and
(h) to receive, where not protected from disclosure by the law, the name and address of any other person who may have information useful to the accused, or other details enabling that person to be identified.

2 (2) The disclosure contemplated in subsection (1), paragraphs (d), (e) and (h) shall be provided by the Crown and may be limited only where, upon an *inter partes* application by the prosecutor, supported by evidence showing a likelihood that such disclosure will endanger the life or safety of such person or interfere with the administration of justice, a justice having jurisdiction in the matter deems it just and proper.[131]

In some respects, the new constitutional rule of disclosure created in *Stinchcombe* was broader than the statutory rule proposed by the Marshall Inquiry because it applied to all relevant information regardless of whether the evidence was classified as exculpatory and regardless of whether it related to a person that the prosecutor proposed to call as a witness. The only exceptions recognized by the Court related to evidentiary privileges, such as the informer

131 *Ibid.* at 336.

privilege and the timing of the disclosure. The Crown also based the broad disclosure duty of the prosecutor on the idea that the prosecutor was not a pure adversary, but had special duties to see that justice be done.[132] Finally, the Court made clear that the duty of disclosure was a continuing one.

Subsequent decisions of the Supreme Court of Canada have continued to define disclosure rights broadly to include relevant material that might open up lines of inquiry for the accused.[133] The obligation to disclose relevant information also entails a duty to preserve such information.[134] In 2003, the Supreme Court observed:

> . . . the way in which the disclosure of evidence was viewed in the past—as an act of goodwill and cooperation on the part of the Crown—played a significant part in catastrophic judicial errors. On this point, we need only recall that the Royal Commission on the Donald Marshall, Jr., Prosecution identified the failure to disclose all the relevant evidence as one of the causes of the judicial error that deprived Donald Marshall of his liberty for 11 years, for a crime he had not committed.[135]

Indeed, a recent decision has affirmed that the police have a duty under *Stinchcombe* to disclose relevant material to the Crown prosecutor and that, in some cases, the duty may extend to disciplinary records of a police officer.[136] In that case, Charron J. defined the right to disclosure in the following broad terms:

> The Crown's obligation to disclose all relevant information in its possession relating to the investigation against an accused is well established. The duty is triggered upon request and does not require an application to the court. *Stinchcombe* made clear that relevant information in the first party production context includes not only information related to those matters the Crown intends to adduce in evidence against the accused, but also any information in respect of which there is a reasonable possibility that it may assist the accused in the exercise of the right to make full answer and defence (pp. 343–44). The Crown's obligation survives the trial and, in the appellate context, the scope of relevant information therefore includes any information in respect of which there is a reasonable possibility that it may assist the appellant in prosecuting an appeal.

---

132 *Ibid.*, quoting *Boucher*, above note 101.
133 *R. v. Dixon*, [1998] 1 S.C.R. 244; *R. v. Tallifer and Duguay*, [2003] 3 S.C.R. 307.
134 *R. v. La*, [1997] 2 S.C.R. 680.
135 *R. v. Tallifer and Duguay*, above note 133 at para. 1.
136 *R. v. McNeil*, 2009 SCC 3.

> While the *Stinchcombe* automatic disclosure obligation is not absolute, it admits of few exceptions. Unless the information is clearly irrelevant, privileged, or its disclosure is otherwise governed by law, the Crown must disclose to the accused all material in its possession. The Crown retains discretion as to the manner and timing of disclosure where the circumstances are such that disclosure in the usual course may result in harm to anyone or prejudice to the public interest. The Crown's exercise of discretion in fulfilling its obligation to disclose is reviewable by a court.[137]

This passage recognized that the duty to disclose is continuing and includes material that may assist the accused on appeal. The importance of the Court's broad approach to disclosure is confirmed in two recent references from the Minister of Justice involving Stephen Truscott and Erin Walsh.[138] In both cases extensive evidence culled from the archives was admitted as fresh evidence and played a role in decisions by the Court of Appeal to quash convictions that were originally entered in 1959 and 1975 respectively.

## P. THE ROLE OF DEFENCE LAWYERS AND INEFFECTIVE ASSISTANCE OF COUNSEL

Although the Crown prosecutor has special obligations to make full disclosure, ineffective assistance of counsel can also play a role in wrongful convictions. The Marshall Inquiry, for example, criticized Marshall's lawyers for not requesting disclosure or conducting their own investigations. The Goudge Inquiry into pediatric forensic pathology stressed the need for lawyers to be adequately trained and funded to deal with complex issues of pediatric forensic pathology. Guilty pleas were entered in some of the cases involving Dr. Smith and in some cases,[139] no competing forensic pathology evidence was called by the defence. In a recent case, the Ontario Court of Appeal reversed a conviction in a case where an accused accepted a plea bargain after mistakenly being identified as the perpetrator of a break-in and sexual assault.[140] The case raises issues of whether it is competent and ethical for a defence lawyer to enter a guilty plea on behalf of a client who maintains his or her innocence so as to

---

137 *Ibid.* at paras. 17–18.

138 *Re Walsh*, above note 72.

139 *Sherret-Robinson*, above note 104, reversing conviction in child death case entered on the basis of a guilty plea.

140 *R. v. Hanemaayer*, [2008] ONCA 580.

receive a lighter sentence than will be imposed should the client be convicted after the completion of a trial.

In *R. v. G.D.B.*,[141] the Supreme Court recognized that the right to effective assistance of counsel was a fundamental principle of justice protected under section 7 of the *Charter*. The Court held that this right would be violated only if counsel's conduct was unreasonable and incompetent and if the conduct resulted in a miscarriage of justice. There is a strong presumption that counsel's conduct is reasonable and generally this issue will not be determined unless the accused can demonstrate that the alleged incompetence resulted in a miscarriage of justice. The Court added, "miscarriages of justice may take many forms in this context. In some instances, counsel's performance may have resulted in procedural unfairness. In others, the reliability of the trial's result may have been compromised."[142] In the result, the Court found that counsel had made a tactical decision not to use a tape where the complainant was being sexually abused by the accused. The Court held that the lack of use of the tape did not affect the reliability of the conviction.

## Q. EXPERT EVIDENCE

A number of wrongful convictions in Canada have been caused by faulty forensic evidence. The Morin Inquiry recommended in 1998 that trial judges should

> undertake a more critical analysis of the admissibility of hair comparison evidence . . . . evidence that shows only that an accused cannot be excluded as the donor of an unknown hair . . . is unlikely to have sufficient probative value to justify its admission as circumstantial evidence of guilt.[143]

The inquiry raised similar concerns about fibre analysis and called for greater quality assurance and more careful use of language by the Ontario Centre of Forensic Sciences: it recommended better training and monitoring of courtroom testimony. Many of these same themes re-emerged a decade later when the Commission of Inquiry into Pediatric Forensic Pathology in Ontario recommended similar reforms to the practice of forensic pathology.

That commission, known as the Goudge Inquiry, recommended that "trial judges should be vigilant in exercising their gatekeeping role" with respect to the admissibility of scientific evidence and exclude such evidence if it "does not

141 Above note 93.

142 *Ibid.* at para. 28.

143 Morin Inquiry, above note 1, Report Recommendation 1.

satisfy standards of threshold reliability . . . whether or not the science is classified as novel or not."[144] Threshold reliability requires an assessment of the reliability of the proposed witness, the field of science, and the opinion offered in the particular case,[145] with attention paid to the limits of the proposed witness's expertise and the language used to express the opinion. The Goudge Inquiry stressed that judges needed to examine the details of the proposed expert evidence and had the ability to allow some parts of the expert's proposed opinion but not other parts.[146]

The increased scrutiny of expert scientific opinion is supported by the evolution of Canadian law on the subject of expert evidence. The courts have moved away from tests that focused on whether there was general acceptance of the proposed testimony and whether the expert had special knowledge through education or experience to more rigorous tests that require that the expert opinion evidence be necessary in assisting the trier of fact; that it be given by a properly qualified expert; and that it not be excluded by an exclusionary rule, such as the general rule that the prejudicial effect of the evidence should not outweigh its probative value.

In 1994, the Supreme Court of Canada warned about

> . . . a danger that expert evidence will be misused and will distort the fact-finding process. Dressed up in scientific evidence which the jury does not easily understand and submitted through a witness of impressive antecedents, this evidence is apt to be accepted by the jury as being virtually infallible and as having more weight than it deserves.[147]

The Court subsequently recognized the relevance of the approach in American jurisprudence which examines whether the theory behind the testimony has been tested, subject to peer review and inquiry into its known or potential error rate as well as its general acceptance.[148] The Supreme Court has repeatedly stressed that science that might be accepted in a clinical setting to treat a patient may have too high an error rate to justify its use as forensic evidence in criminal proceedings.[149]

There is a new emphasis in Canada on evidence-based as opposed to experience-based expert scientific opinion. In the 2007 Stephen Truscott appeal,

---

144 Goudge Inquiry, above note 1, Report Recommendation 130.
145 *Ibid.*, Report Recommendation 131.
146 *Ibid.*, Report Recommendation 133.
147 *R. v. Mohan*, [1994] 2 S.C.R. 9 at para. 19.
148 *Daubert v. Merrell Dow Pharmaceuticals*, 509 U.S. 579 (1993).
149 *R. v. J.-L.J.*, [2000] 2 S.C.R. 600.

for example, the Ontario Court of Appeal disregarded two opinions offered by an expert forensic pathologist and an entomology expert respectively about the time of death because they were simply based on the admittedly considerable experience of the Crown's experts and did not engage with the scientific literature or other attempts to test the experience of the expert witnesses.[150]

In a more recent case, the Ontario Court of Appeal has affirmed that trial judges have a discretion to exclude expert evidence that otherwise satisfies the criteria for admissibility because of concerns about its threshold reliability and possible prejudicial effect. Nevertheless, the Court of Appeal found that the trial judge had erred by excluding evidence from a sociologist about the possible meaning of a teardrop tattoo on an accused charged with a gang-related murder. The Court of Appeal stressed that the trial judge's concerns about the unknown error rate and lack of a random sample for the sociologist's research were inappropriate given the nature of sociology and that the sociologist would testify only about a range of possible meanings of the tattoo and not to the effect that the tattoo meant that the accused was guilty.[151] A critical question is whether similar concerns will allow various kinds of evidence from forensic sciences to continue to be used in the absence of basic research on the validity of the experience-based opinion drawn by fingerprint and handwriting analysts, and forensic pathologists.

In 2007, the Supreme Court in a 4:3 decision in *R. v. Trochym* excluded the post-hypnosis testimony of a witness who purported to provide eyewitness identification.[152] The majority stressed the importance of determining the threshold reliability of the evidence and started its judgment by noting the following:

> In recent years, a number of public inquiries have highlighted the importance of safeguarding the criminal justice system — and protecting the accused who are tried under it — from the possibility of wrongful conviction. As this Court has previously noted, "[t]he names of Marshall, Milgaard, Morin, Sophonow and Parsons signal prudence and caution in a murder case": *United States v. Burns*, [2001] 1 S.C.R. 283, 2001 SCC 7, at para. 1. In the case at bar, we consider once again the need to carefully scrutinize evidence presented against an accused for reliability and prejudicial effect, and to ensure the basic fairness of the criminal process. More specifically, the decisions at trial to admit post-

---

150 *Truscott Reference*, above note 65 at paras. 165–69, 313–14.

151 *R. v. Abbey*, 2009 ONCA 624.

152 Above note 14.

> hypnosis evidence and similar fact evidence in this case constitute errors of law that are neither harmless nor negligible.[153]

In deciding that post-hypnosis testimony should be excluded, the Court was not deterred by the fact that it had been accepted in previous cases and might not be characterized as novel science, noting that "the admissibility of scientific evidence is not frozen in time."[154] The Court stressed that what was "most troubling" about post-hypnosis evidence was

> . . . the potential rate of error in the additional information obtained through hypnosis when it is used for forensic purposes. At the present time, there is no way of knowing whether such information will be accurate or inaccurate. Such uncertainty is unacceptable in a court of law.[155]

In this case the majority of the Supreme Court demonstrated an appropriate concern about the risk of wrongful convictions and the risk of relying on evidence of unknown reliability.

## R. CONCLUSION

This chapter has provided an overview of Canadian law as it relates to wrongful convictions. Although convictions can be overturned by appellate courts on the basis that they are unreasonable, not supported by the evidence, or involve a miscarriage of justice, Canadian law has not adopted the concerns about the safety of verdicts, including lurking doubts about guilt, that are found in English law. The Canadian approach is somewhat balanced out, however, by a generous approach to the admissibility of fresh evidence on appeals in the interests of justice. Canadian courts have also become more aware of the reality and risk of wrongful convictions, and this has resulted in the recognition of broad rights of disclosure and stricter scrutiny of the threshold reliability of scientific evidence.

Despite recommendations from six public inquiries, Canada has not yet created an independent agency such as the CCRC to investigate claims of wrongful convictions. A person who has exhausted his or her appeal rights must still apply to the federal Minister of Justice who has the power to order a new trial or a new appeal if there is a reasonable basis to conclude that a miscarriage of justice has likely occurred. Although the Minister of Justice or dele-

---

153 *Ibid.* at para. 1.
154 *Ibid.* at para. 31.
155 *Ibid.* at para. 55.

gates have wide investigative powers, it is generally expected that the applicant will produce new evidence when applying to reopen the case. This expectation places a great burden on the applicants and leads to considerably fewer applications to the Minister of Justice and fewer referrals back to the courts than in the United Kingdom on a per capita basis.

CHAPTER 5

# Law on Miscarriages of Justice: Australia

The current appeal provisions in Australia are similar to those that prevailed in Britain before the more recent amendments simplifying the grounds of appeal. Before we discuss them and their specific implications, however, a broader structural issue to the Australian appellate system needs to be canvassed.

Once a person has been convicted at trial and then has had an unsuccessful appeal, that person has no legal right to a further appeal based upon the discovery of fresh evidence. Even where an important prosecution witness subsequently gives sworn evidence in other proceedings that the evidence given at a criminal trial was wrong, the person convicted will still have no *legal* right to a rehearing. This is because the Australian appeal courts have determined that following an unsuccessful appeal, they cannot reopen an appeal. That view has been endorsed by the High Court of Australia.[1]

The High Court in Australia, unlike its counterparts in Britain or Canada, has taken the view that it cannot hear fresh evidence. The only remaining procedure in such a case is to petition the Attorney General of the relevant state or territory to refer the matter back to the appeal court for a rehearing. There is, however, legal authority to suggest that the petition procedure is a matter of discretion and does not give rise to legally enforceable rights: that means that petition cases can be ignored or delayed for years without redress.

As we have seen, in Britain in recent years, there have been a significant number of cases where appeals have been allowed following the discovery of fresh evidence and the subsequent referral of the case to the appeal court by

1 The cases in support of these propositions are set out in the sections following the discussion in Section A, below in this chapter.

the Criminal Cases Review Commission (CCRC). Much of our discussion in Chapter 3 was based upon those cases. In Australia, however, although there have clearly been defective trials—and many of them based upon defective evidence—those convicted have been unable to obtain the necessary "permission" to enable them to be referred back to the courts.[2] It follows therefore that the discussion of appeals and fresh evidence issues in this chapter has to be based upon those cases where the fresh evidence has come to light before the normal appellate process has been exhausted. From the British experience, it is clear that this would occur only rarely. The more usual situation is where the fresh evidence comes to light many years after the original trial.

The discussion of the relevant legal principles in this chapter can be contrasted with the very different tone of the discussion in relation to the British law in Chapter 3. There, we were able to refer to the interesting circumstances, subsequently revealed, which led to the appeal court being critical of the conduct of trials that took place many years previously. In this chapter, we refer to few decisions of the intermediate appeal courts. Instead, we rely upon declarations of principles by the ultimate appellate court in Australia: the High Court. Because of its inability to hear fresh evidence, however, its judgments are limited to explaining and clarifying the relevant legal principles.

In this chapter, we will discuss the current appeal provisions before returning to a more detailed discussion of the difficulties in reopening appeals in Australia.

## A. CONTEMPORARY APPEAL PROVISIONS

Under the Australian Constitution, each state and territory has jurisdiction over the enactment and enforcement of its own criminal law.[3] In most instances, a trial in serious criminal cases may be heard in the state supreme court. Although an accused person can elect to be tried by a judge alone, this is an exception to the more usual trial by jury.[4] Upon conviction, an appeal may lie to the state court of appeal constituted within the supreme courts on an issue of law (without leave) or on an issue of law and fact (with leave of the trial judge

2 See, for example, the cases discussed in Robert N. Moles, *A State of Injustice* (South Melbourne: Lothian Books, 2004); *Losing Their Grip—The Case of Henry Keogh* (Adelaide: Elvis Press, 2006).

3 *Commonwealth of Australia Constitution Act, 1900* (U.K.), 1900, 63 & 64 Victoria, c. 12, s. 51 [Constitution].

4 See Vicki C. Waye, "Judicial Fact-Finding: Trial by Judge Alone in Serious Criminal Cases" (2003) 27 Melbourne U.L. Rev. 423. It is also different from the Canadian practice as we have seen above in Chapter 4.

or of the appeal court).[5] Any further appeal to the High Court of Australia can take place only with the leave of that court.[6]

While a number of the states have permanent courts of appeal, with full-time appellate judges, some states such as South Australia use the "Full Court" whereby three or more supreme court trial judges sit on a rotating basis as the court of appeal. This means that upon appointment as a judge of the supreme court, to conduct trials, such a judge can immediately sit to hear appeals.[7]

As with Britain and Canada, the appellate jurisdiction in criminal cases in Australia is statute based. Appeals are modelled on the British *Criminal Appeal Act, 1907*.[8] The power to overturn convictions on the grounds specified in the 1907 Act have been replicated in what are known as the "common form" provisions of each of the Australian states and territories.

The standard legislative provisions that apply in all jurisdictions in Australia (apart from the Australian Capital Territory (ACT)[9]) state that the court shall allow an appeal under these conditions:

> It is of opinion that the verdict of the jury should be set aside on the ground that it is unreasonable, or cannot be supported, having regard to the evidence; or the judgment of the court of trial should be set aside on the ground of the wrong decision of any question of law; or on any other ground whatsoever there was a miscarriage of justice.[10]

---

5 See, for example, the *Criminal Law Consolidation Act 1935* (S.A.), s. 352:

> Right of appeal in criminal cases
>
> (1) Appeals lie to the Full Court as follows:
>
> (a) if a person is convicted on information
>
> (i) the convicted person may appeal against the conviction as of right on any ground that involves a question of law alone; (ii) the convicted person may appeal against the conviction on any other ground with the permission of the Full Court or on the certificate of the court of trial that it is a fit case for appeal.

The "Full Court" is the appeal court sitting with three judges. See also the discussion of this issue above in Chapter 3.

6 *Judiciary Act 1903* (Cth.), s. 35A.

7 See Stephen Charles, "The First Decade of the Victorian Court of Appeal" in Chris Corns & Gregor Urbas, eds., *Criminal Appeals 1907–2007 Issues and Perspectives* (2008) Law in Context 21 [Corns & Urbas].

8 *Criminal Appeal Act, 1907* (U.K.) 7 Edw. VII, c. 23.

9 In the ACT, the *Supreme Court Act 1933* does not specify specific grounds for allowing an appeal. See Chris Corns, "The Discretion of a Court of Appeal to Order a New Trial or a Verdict of Acquittal" (2006) 30 Crim. L.J. 343.

10 *Criminal Law Consolidation Act 1935* (S.A.), s. 353; *Criminal Appeal Act 1912* (N.S.W.), s. 6; *Crimes Act 1958* (Vic.), s. 568; *Criminal Code Act 1899* (Qld.), s. 668E; *Criminal Code*

This is subject to the usual proviso derived from the 1907 Act that the court may dismiss the appeal, notwithstanding it is of the opinion that the point or points raised by the appeal may be decided in the appellant's favour, if it considers that no substantial miscarriage of justice has occurred.[11] In Chapter 3 we explained that the British provision is now contained in the *Criminal Appeal Act 1968* (as amended in 1995)[12] which says the court will allow an appeal where it thinks that the conviction is "unsafe" and is without a separate proviso. The Canadian position is similar to that of Australia. It allows convictions to be quashed on the grounds that the verdict is unreasonable or cannot be supported by the evidence, that there has been an error of law, or on any ground that there was a miscarriage of justice.[13] It also has a proviso.[14]

Unlike Britain where significant reforms have been made, the Australian statutory powers have remained virtually unchanged since their incorporation into Australian criminal legislation. It has been determined that whether there is evidence to support the verdict is not a question of law but of "*fact* which the court must decide by making its own independent assessment of the evidence."[15] The significance of this distinction is important where a notice of appeal claims that the verdict is unsound because it is unsupported by the weight of the evidence. If the claim is regarded as involving a question of law, it would give rise to an automatic right of appeal. Being a question of fact, leave is required to proceed with an appeal.

The third ground of appeal is stated in the broadest terms: "on any other ground whatsoever there was a miscarriage of justice."[16] In *Chamberlain v. The Queen (No. 2)* Brennan J. explained that it "confers on the court a power, to be

---

(N.T.), s. 411; *Criminal Code Act Compilation Act 1913* (W.A.), s. 689; *Criminal Code Act 1924* (Tas.), s. 404(1).

11 It is also interesting to note that while the New Zealand provision is similar, it has the additional component that the court must allow the appeal if it is of the opinion that "the trial was a nullity." *Crimes Act 1961* (N.Z.), 1961/43, s. 385(d). See the discussion of these provisions and the British context in which they arose in Hon. Justice Grant Hammond, "The New Miscarriages of Justice" (The Harkness Henry Lecture delivered at the University of Waikato, 2006). The nullity issue relates to our discussion of fraud in criminal proceedings in Chapter 6.

12 *Criminal Appeal Act 1968* (U.K.), 1968, c. 19, as amended by *Criminal Appeal Act 1995* (U.K.), 1995, c. 35, s. 2(1).

13 *Criminal Code* of Canada, R.S.C. 1985, c. C-46, s. 686(1).

14 *Ibid.*, s. 686(b)(iii): Courts of appeal in Canada can dismiss appeals under this section if, despite finding that the trial judge made an error of law, they conclude "no substantial wrong or miscarriage of justice occurred."

15 *Gipp v. The Queen*, [1998] HCA 21 at para. 169 [*Gipp*], Kirby J. referring to *M. v. The Queen* (1994), 181 C.L.R. 487 at 492–93 (H.C.A.) [emphasis added].

16 *Criminal Appeal Act 1912* (N.S.W.), s. 6.

exercised with discrimination and caution, to set aside some verdicts which the court could not otherwise set aside as unreasonable or not supportable having regard to the evidence."[17] In *Gipp* Callinan J. pointed out that the issues can be simplified by going back to the earlier stage of the legislative provision.[18] He noted that in speaking of the *Criminal Appeal Act 1912* (NSW) Isaacs J. in *Hargan v. The King* had said:

> If [the appellant] can show a miscarriage of justice, that is sufficient. That is the greatest innovation made by the Act, and to lose sight of that is to miss the point of the legislative advance.[19]

In this context, the concepts of justice and miscarriage of justice bear two aspects: *outcome* and *process*. They are different, but related. In *Davies and Cody v. The King*,[20] the High Court said:

> From the beginning, [the English Court of Criminal Appeal] has acted upon no narrow view of the cases covered by its duty to quash a conviction when it thinks that *on any ground* there was a miscarriage of justice, . . . It has consistently regarded that duty as covering not only cases where there is affirmative reason to suppose that the appellant is innocent, but also cases of quite another description. For it will set aside a conviction whenever it appears unjust or unsafe to allow the verdict to stand because some failure has occurred *in observing the conditions* which, in the court's view, *are essential to a satisfactory trial*, or because there is some feature of the case raising a substantial possibility that, either in the conclusion itself, or in the manner in which it has been reached, *the jury may have been mistaken or misled*.[21]

In *Gallagher v. The Queen* it was said that the issue as to whether the jury was mistaken or misled really "subsumes the issue of credibility."[22] Justice Kirby, in his dissenting judgment in *Bounds v. The Queen*, said the accused was entitled to a trial before a jury uncomplicated by extraneous and legally impermissible considerations.[23]

---

17 (1984), 153 C.L.R. 521 at para. 604 [*Chamberlain*].

18 Above note 15 at para. 121.

19 (1919), 27 C.L.R. 13 at 23.

20 (1937), 57 C.L.R. 170 [*Davies*].

21 This citation from *Davies*, *ibid.* at 180 [emphasis added] was referred to by Gleeson C.J. in *Nudd v. The Queen*, [2006] HCA 9 at para. 4 [*Nudd*]. See also the discussion of this issue in *R. v. Stafford*, [2009] QCA 407 at para. 149 [*Stafford*].

22 [1986] HCA 26 at para. 7, Gibbs C.J. [*Gallagher*].

23 [2006] HCA 39 at para. 42.

It is worth noting Kirby J.'s view that although the form in which such principles are expressed in the various common law jurisdictions may differ, their underlying effect is substantially similar.[24]

Australia's appeal provisions (in this respect, similar to those of Britain and Canada) also provide appellate courts with supplemental powers to conduct investigations or to commission reports into aspects of the evidence that might be of concern or interest in the appeal. However, it appears to be a power not often used.[25] It is interesting to note that this would allow any "scientific" investigation to be conducted in this way. (This matter will be taken up again in Chapter 12.)

## B. REOPENING AN APPEAL

The legislative appeal provisions in Australia are interpreted as allowing the intermediate appellate courts the jurisdiction to hear one appeal only, thereby providing no right to reopen an appeal.[26] However, the foundation for that view is based upon flimsy ground. It goes back to the 1938 decision of *Grierson v. The King* in which an application for special leave to appeal to the High Court was dismissed.[27] However, more recent decisions of the High Court make it clear that a refusal of an application for leave to appeal has not engaged the jurisdiction of the court, and therefore, one would think that the reasoning in support of such a refusal could hardly count as a binding decision of the High Court:

> Until the grant of leave or special leave, there are no proceedings *inter partes* before the Court. This is so even in a case in which the application for leave or

---

24 *Mallard v. The Queen*, [2005] HCA 68 at para. 67, Kirby J. [*Mallard*].

25 *Criminal Law Consolidation Act 1935* (S.A.), s. 359:

> (d) where any question arising on the appeal involves prolonged examination of documents or accounts or any scientific or local investigation which cannot, in the opinion of the Full Court, conveniently be conducted before the Court, order the reference of the question in the manner provided by rules of court for inquiry and report to a special commissioner appointed by the Court and act on the report of any such commissioner so far as it thinks fit to adopt it; and (e) appoint any person with special expert knowledge to act as assessor to the Full Court in any case where it appears to the Court that such special knowledge is required for the proper determination of the case.

26 *Commonwealth of Australia Constitution Act 1900*, above note 3, ss. 73–76; *Mickelberg v. The Queen*, [1989] HCA 35; *Eastman v. The Queen* (2000), 203 C.L.R. 1 [*Eastman*] *R. v. Keogh*, [2007] SASC 226, citing *Grierson v. The King*, [1938] HCA 45 [*Grierson*], based upon *R. v. Edwards (No. 2)*, [1931] SASR 376; *Grierson v. The King* (1938) NSW CCA.

27 *Grierson*, *ibid.*

> special leave is opposed . . . ; In *Eastman v. Director of Public Prosecutions (ACT)* (2002), I pointed out, consistently with this passage in *Collins*, that before the grant of leave there is no matter engaging the Court's jurisdiction.[28]

In *Burrell v. The Queen*, the NSW Court of Appeal had issued its decision rejecting an appeal. Within a day or two, it realized that it had (in part) made its decision upon an incorrect factual basis. It had assumed that a document on the prosecution file represented facts accepted by the prosecution, when it was merely a submission from the defendant. The court immediately recalled its decision and reissued its judgment. In the subsequent appeal, the High Court said that it ought not to have done so. It said that once the decision of the Court of Appeal has been "perfected," it thereafter has no jurisdiction to reconsider the matter.[29] In *Burrell*, Kirby J. stated, "I regard it as unfortunate that the inherent power of an appellate court does not extend to varying its own orders when the interests of justice require it."[30]

The High Court accepts few applications for leave to appeal in criminal cases. A case cannot be heard before the High Court unless the court itself gives leave. The High Court will hear cases only where it feels that broad principles of public importance are involved.

A further limitation is that, unlike the intermediate appellate courts, the High Court has no power to receive fresh evidence in a criminal appeal. In opening his judgment in *Mickelberg v. The Queen*, Mason C.J. stated:

> The applicants sought to place before this Court additional evidence which was not before the Court of Criminal Appeal. Over the years this Court has consistently maintained that it has no power to receive fresh evidence in the exercise of its appellate jurisdiction. The applicants argued that the relevant decisions are wrong and should not be followed.[31]

The appellate jurisdiction of the High Court is conferred by section 73 of the Constitution.[32] Under the "common form" statutes establishing the state

---

28 *Milat v. The Queen*, [2004] HCA 17 at para. 26, McHugh J., citing Barwick C.J., Stephen, Mason, and Jacobs JJ. in *Collins v. The Queen*, [1975] HCA 60. See also *Burrell v. The Queen*, [2008] HCA 34 [*Burrell*].

29 *Burrell*, *ibid*. The "perfecting" of the record means the formal entering of the judgment on the court files.

30 *Ibid*. at para. 37. Justice Kirby referred to his previous judgments in *DJL v. Central Authority*, [2000] HCA 17 at paras. 98–99; and *Postiglione v. The Queen*, [1997] HCA 26. See also Bibi Sangha, "Extending the Scope of Post-conviction Reviews" (2007) 30 Austl. Bar Rev. 90 [Sangha], as discussed in Chapter 6.

31 [1989] HCA 35 at para. 2 [*Mickelberg*].

32 Above note 3.

courts of appeal, if the High Court was to admit fresh evidence that would require it to make "an independent and original decision" based on its assessment of the evidence resulting in its exercising an *original* rather than truly *appellate* jurisdiction. The suggestion is that because the conferral of original jurisdiction under section 75 of the Constitution is limited to certain federal matters, any exercise of original jurisdiction by the High Court would be unconstitutional and equivalent to investing the High Court with original jurisdiction over matters falling within state judicial power.[33]

Chief Justice Mason in *Mickelberg* went on to point out that the powers of the Court "are of the widest character which true appellate jurisdiction may possess." He added, interestingly, that section 73 of the Constitution "contains no express fetter preventing the Court from considering fresh evidence." [34] The following has been pointed out elsewhere:

> In regard to the interpretation of the legislation, the High Court has stated: It is quite inappropriate to read provisions conferring jurisdiction or granting powers to a court by making implications or imposing limitations which are not found in the express words.[35]

If there are no express words inhibiting the reception of fresh evidence, then it might be only a matter of custom and convention that has inhibited the High Court from exercising this power. After all, it was only a Practice Statement that transformed the practice of the House of Lords in Britain in regard to its adherence to its own previous decisions.[36] As the Chief Justice summarized the position in *Mickelberg*:

> The authorities in this Court stand clearly for the proposition that the reception of fresh evidence is not a part of the appellate jurisdiction of the Court. The applicants challenged the reasoning on which these authorities are based on the ground that the reasoning depended on old English authorities which have been overtaken by more recent decisions. The applicants made the point that, at a time when an appeal lay from this Court to the Privy Council, the Court was influenced by the circumstance that the Court of Appeal and the House of Lords did not receive fresh evidence. As it is now clearly established

33 *Mickelberg*, above note 31 at para. 16; Toohey and Gaudron JJ., citing Isaacs J. in *Werribee v. The Queen* (1928), 42 C.L.R. 1 at para. 20. See also the text accompanying note 38.

34 *Mickelberg*, *ibid.* at para. 6, citing *Victorian Stevedoring and General Contracting Co. Pty. Ltd. and Meakes v. Dignan* (1931), 46 C.L.R. 73 at 87.

35 *Shin Kobe Maru v. Empire Shipping Co. Inc.*, [1994] HCA 5; discussed in Sangha, above note 30.

36 See *Practice Statement (Judicial Precedent)*, [1966] 1 W.L.R. 1234.

> that both the Court of Appeal and the House of Lords receive fresh evidence, there has been a material development which justifies reconsideration of the existing authorities.[37]

While the invitation to extend the powers of the High Court to receive fresh evidence was not taken up in *Mickelberg*, the broader evolution of the principles relating to miscarriages of justice, and the evident harmony of those principles between each of the major common law jurisdictions which we have referred to, makes it a promising prospect for reconsideration.

Indeed, Kirby J. urged a more liberal interpretation of the term "appeal" in his strong dissenting judgment in *Eastman v. The Queen* where he said that there were many instances where the Constitution had been approached in the way he favoured. So, he thought that a jury trial to which section 80 of the Constitution referred would, in 1900, undoubtedly have meant a jury comprising men only, and then, chosen by reference to their property qualifications. Yet, he pointed out, the High Court rejected those requirements as inherent in that feature of legal procedure inherited from England. Why, he asked, is the notion of appeal stamped indelibly with certain limitations yet the notion of a jury is not?[38]

### 1) The Petition Procedure

The inability to reopen an appeal in combination with the principle that the High Court considers that it is unable to hear fresh evidence means that significant obstacles are in the way of achieving justice. As Kirby J. has pointed out:

> The rule [prohibiting the High Court from receiving fresh evidence] means that where new evidence turns up after a trial and hearing before the Court of Criminal Appeal are concluded, whatever the reason and however justifiable the delay, the High Court, even in a regular appeal to it still underway, can do nothing. Justice, in such cases, is truly blind. The only relief available is from the Executive Government or the media—not from the Australian judiciary.[39]

---

37 *Mickelberg*, above note 31 at para. 7.

38 *Eastman*, above note 26 at paras. 240–43.

39 Justice Michael Kirby, "Black and White Lessons for the Australian Judiciary" (2002) 23 Adel. L.R. 195 at 206. See also *Sinanovic's Application* (2001) 180 A.L.R. 448 at 451, Kirby J.

> By authority of this court [High Court of Australia] such fresh evidence, even if it were to show a grave factual error, indeed, even punishment of an innocent person,

In Australia, claims for the exercise of statutory power to refer convictions back to the court of appeal are handled by the respective states. The Australian petition procedure is similar to that which existed in Britain as the major vehicle for review prior to the advent of the CCRC.[40] It involves an application to the state governor for the exercise of "Her Majesty's mercy"; there is then a statutory power which states that on such an application, the Attorney General

> may, if he thinks fit, at any time, either—(a) refer the whole case to the Full Court, and the case shall then be heard and determined by that Court as in the case of an appeal by a person convicted; or
>
> (b) if he desires the assistance of the judges of the Supreme Court on any point arising in the case with a view to the determination of the petition, refer that point to those judges for their opinion and those judges, or any three of them, shall consider the point so referred and furnish the Attorney-General with their opinion accordingly.[41]

What appears initially as an application for mercy, the exercise of a prerogative power, is, in effect, a statutory power to be exercised by the Attorney General. There is some authority for the view that the exercise of that power is entirely a matter of discretion—the exercise of which (or the non-exercise of which) is not subject to review by the courts.[42] However, the exercise of a statutory power may well be subject to judicial review for "unreasonableness."[43]

In a number of respects the Australian petition process differs from the Canadian procedure. In Canada, a petition is addressed to the federal Attorney General. In Australia, the application is to the state Attorney General who may well be more influenced by local issues and the politics of the case. In

---

> cannot be received by this court exercising its appellate jurisdiction . . . [the prisoner] would be compelled to seek relief from the Executive.

40 Lynne Weathered, "Does Australia Need a Specific Institution to Correct Wrongful Convictions?" (2007) 40 Austl. & N.Z. Crim. J. 179.

41 *Criminal Law Consolidation Act 1935* (S.A.), s. 369.

42 *Von Einem v. Griffin and Anor* (1998), 72 S.A.S.R. 110 at 115, Prior J.:

> There is still no clear decision in this country for the issue of an order in the nature of *mandamus* against the Crown with respect to the prerogative of mercy nor with respect to a statutory power as opposed to a statutory duty. The approach in *Horowitz* and *Burt* is against the power to compel the reference.

References are to *Horowitz v. Connor* (1908), 6 C.L.R. 38; and *Burt v. Governor General*, [1992] 3 N.Z.L.R. 672 (C.A.). In New South Wales an application can be made directly to the Chief Justice for judicial reference under the NSW *Crimes Act 2001*.

43 *Keogh v. The Queen*, [2007] HCA Trans 693 (16 November 2007).

Australia, the state Attorney General has no power to order a retrial as does the federal Minister of Justice.[44] In Australia, the petitioner does not get to see or comment upon the investigative brief before the advice is provided to the Minister of Justice, as happens in Canada.[45] In Australia, there are no guidelines on the decision-making process as there are in Canada.[46] In Canada, the federal Minister of Justice will review prosecutions undertaken by provincial Attorneys General and prosecutors whereas in Australia, the petitioner will ask the state government to review prosecutions undertaken by state officials and prosecutors.

If, however, we can accept that there are substantial impediments to bringing such cases before the courts, there are also specific considerations that apply to the hearing of such cases.

If the Attorney General were to refer the whole case to the appeal court (as an appeal), it is then important to bear in mind that

> . . . when an appeal is lodged, the entire matter is before the court to which the appeal is brought and, unless there is some statutory provision to the contrary, that court "can entertain any matter, however arising, which shows that the decision of the Court appealed from is erroneous."[47]

It therefore follows that in any subsequent appeal to the High Court

> . . . because a court of criminal appeal must decide whether there has been an error occasioning a miscarriage of justice and, on appeal, this Court [the High Court] must decide whether that decision was right or wrong, that an appeal may succeed in this Court on a point neither taken at trial nor in the subsequent appeal to a court of criminal appeal.[48]

---

44 "Manitoba Murder: Retrial Ordered in Brutal 1990 Sex Slaying" *Globe and Mail* (12 March 2009): "It was only the fourth time that a justice minister has sent a case straight to a retrial, skipping the time-consuming and arduous step of having a provincial appellate court conduct a full review."

45 Kerry Scullion, "Wrongful Convictions and the Criminal Conviction Review Process pursuant to Section 696.1 of the *Criminal Code* of Canada" (2004) 46 Canadian Journal of Criminology and Criminal Justice 189.

46 See Chapter 3 discussion of the Canadian *Criminal Code*, above note 13, s. 696.4.

47 *Gipp*, above note 15 at para. 23, Gaudron J., citing Griffith C.J. in *Ah Yick v. Lehmert* (1905), 2 C.L.R. 593 at 601.

48 *Gipp*, *ibid.* at para. 24. Justice Gaudron cited the following cases in support of the proposition: *De Jesus v. The Queen* (1986), 61 A.L.J.R. 1; *Bahri Kural v. The Queen* (1987), 162 C.L.R. 502 at 512; *Robinson v. The Queen* (1991), 180 C.L.R. 531 at 536; *KBT v. The Queen* (1997), 72 A.L.J.R. 116 at 119; *Stirland v. Director of Public Prosecutions*, [1944] A.C. 315 at 327–28.

The reason why that issue was not raised earlier is not so important. The failure might have arisen from some degree of incompetence in the representation of the accused at the earlier hearing. As long as the appellant was not personally responsible for the failure to raise the objections to the trial which have now been expressed, then, the court says, it would be wrong not to attend to those issues on the appeal. As Kirby J. said: "Any other rule would give priority to *form* over *substance*. It would permit procedural rules to defeat the correction of a serious miscarriage of justice that has come to the notice of a court of justice."[49] It was said that even though there may well be evidence upon which a jury might convict, it may be dangerous in all the circumstances to allow the verdict of guilty to stand.[50] A verdict may be unsafe or unsatisfactory for reasons that lie outside the formula requiring that it not be "unreasonable" or incapable of being "supported having regard to the evidence." As Callinan J. pointed out in *Gipp*, the wording states that a verdict which is unsafe or unsatisfactory *for any other reason* may also constitute a miscarriage of justice requiring the verdict to be set aside. In this one respect, the Australian practice compares favourably to the British where, since 2003, appeals on referral by the Criminal Cases Review Commission are limited to the grounds of appeals identified by the CCRC.[51]

In the Andrew Mallard case, following a reference by an Attorney General the intermediate appeal judges thought that they were not to reconsider evidence which had been dealt with at trial.[52] As the High Court said, in that appeal much was made of the difference between "new evidence"—that is, evidence available but not adduced at trial—and "fresh evidence," which appellate courts ordinarily will receive, on the basis that it did not then exist, or, if it did, could not then have been discovered with reasonable diligence. The Court of Appeal then proceeded as if there were serious inhibitions upon that court's jurisdiction to consider, not just the evidence that was adduced at the trial, but also its relevance to the further evidence that the appellant sought to introduce and rely upon in the reference. The High Court said that this approach was erroneous.[53]

In a reference to the court under the petition procedure, the legislation states that the Attorney General "may refer the whole case" to the Court of

49 *Gipp, ibid.* at para. 136, Kirby J. [emphasis added].
50 *Ibid.* at para. 169, Callinan J., citing *Hayes v. The Queen* (1973), 47 A.L.J.R. 603 at 604.
51 *Criminal Justice Act 2003*, (U.K.) 2003, c. 44, s. 315.
52 *Mallard*, above note 24.
53 *Ibid.* at 131.

Criminal Appeal, to be dealt with as an appeal under the relevant statute.[54] The High Court said the reference to "the whole case" conveys no hint of any inhibition upon the jurisdiction of the Court of Criminal Appeal on a reference. The words embrace the whole of the evidence properly admissible, whether "new, fresh or already considered in earlier proceedings, however described."[55] The Court said that it was "*elementary* that some matters may assume an entirely different complexion in the light of other matters and facts either ignored or previously unknown."[56] In considering the additional material, the Court said that it was irrelevant (except in consideration of the proviso) that the whole of the other evidence at trial may have been thought to be sufficient to sustain a verdict of guilty.

### 2) A Pardon Not Sufficient

In this context, it is often suggested that any application for the exercise of mercy can be seen as an application to pardon a convicted person. The words of the pardon state:

> Now know ye that We in consideration of some circumstances humbly represented unto Us, are Graciously pleased to extend our Grace and Mercy unto the said [Petitioner] and to grant him Our Free Pardon in respect of the said conviction, thereby pardoning, remitting and releasing unto him all pains penalties and punishments whatsoever that from the said conviction may ensue.[57]

In the Australian case of *R. v. Cosgrove*, it was held that a pardon when granted is not the equivalent of an acquittal and does not wipe out the crime *ab initio*.[58] In *R. v. Foster* it was noted that the *Shorter Oxford English Dictionary* defines a pardon as a "remission, either free or conditional of the legal consequences of crime."[59] Likewise, in *Re Royal Commission on Thomas Case*, Thomas was granted a pardon in respect of the murders of David and Jeanette Crewe. It held that a pardon clears the person from all *consequences* of the offence, but does not eliminate the conviction itself. That is, the prerogative of mercy cannot remove a conviction, but only pardon its effects.[60] In *R. v. Foster*, the court

---

54 See, for example, *Criminal Law Consolidation Act 1935* (S.A.), s. 369.
55 *Mallard*, above note 24 at para. 6, Gummow, Hayne, Callinan, and Heydon JJ.
56 *Ibid.*, at para. 13 [emphasis added].
57 As cited in *R. v. Foster*, [1985] Q.B. 115 [*Foster*].
58 *R. v. Cosgrove*, [1948] Tas. S.R. 99 at 105–6, Morris C.J. [*Cosgrove*].
59 *Foster*, above note 57 at 127.
60 *Re Royal Commission on Thomas Case*, [1980] 1 N.Z.L.R. 602 at 620.

said that the only body with the statutory power to remove a conviction is the Court of Appeal.[61] As Kirby J. explained in *Eastman v. DPP*:

> At common law the pardon "is in no sense equivalent to an acquittal. It contains no notion that the man to whom the pardon is extended never did in fact commit the crime, but merely from the date of the pardon gives him a new credit and capacity." In England it has been held that at common law, "the effect of a free pardon is such as, in the words of the pardon itself, to remove from the subject of the pardon, 'all pains penalties and punishments whatsoever that from the said conviction may ensue,' but not to eliminate the conviction itself". This type of outcome is not the outcome which a person convicted of a crime and claiming to be innocent of it would desire.[62]

He went on to say that the common law conception of a conviction is that, by it, the convicted person receives justice; the common law conception of a pardon is that, by it, the convicted person receives mercy, notwithstanding the demands of justice. It therefore follows that once it is apparent that the conviction is unjust, the convicted person should receive something different from a pardon, which grants mercy but assumes the validity of the conviction. As he pointed out, "At the heart of the pardoning power there is a paradox. To pardon implies to forgive: if the convicted person is innocent there is nothing to forgive."[63]

### 3) Royal Commissions

Royal commissions have played an important but limited role in correcting miscarriage of justice cases in Australia. In both the Chamberlain and Splatt Royal Commissions, the convictions were overturned by the appellate courts following the recommendations from the commissions. Unlike in Canada, these commissions were appointed before the conviction was overturned. In this way, the Australian commissions contributed directly to the correction of errors in addition to making recommendations about systemic reform to lower the risk of miscarriages of justice in future cases. From reading their reports,

---

61 *Foster*, above note 57.

62 *Eastman v. Director of Public Prosecutions (ACT)*, [2003] HCA 28 at para. 98, Kirby J. [*Eastman v. DPP*] citing (in part) *Cosgrove*, above note 58 at 106, approved by the English Court of Appeal in *Foster*, above note 57, which was referred to without disapproval by Wilson J. in *Kelleher v. Parole Board (NSW)*, [1984] HCA 77; and Rosemary Pattenden, *English Criminal Appeals 1844–1994* (Oxford: Clarendon Press, 1996) at 383.

63 *Eastman v. DPP*, *ibid.*

however, it is clear they were essentially reconsiderations of the factual bases upon which the convictions were obtained, specifically including the scientific reports and reasoning involved and which led to the convictions. Unlike their Canadian counterparts, the Australian royal commissions did not conduct comparative analyses with other jurisdictions or with other similar cases. No doubt, they were subject to the restrictive terms of reference that usually accompany such commissions.

## C. THE PROVISO

As mentioned, the statutory appeal provisions in Australia provide an exception to the grounds of appeal:

> Provided that the Court of Appeal may, notwithstanding that it is of opinion that the point raised in the appeal might be decided in favour of the appellant, dismiss the appeal if it considers that no substantial miscarriage of justice has actually occurred.[64]

The proviso has the strongest application to the second and third grounds of appeal. As Stephen Odgers put it:

> It is fairly apparent that the proviso only has practical application to the second and third grounds for success in an appeal. Substantively, the first ground is concerned with cases where there is insufficient evidence to support the verdict and the conviction must be quashed and a verdict of acquittal entered.[65]

The proviso does not authorize the Australian courts to allow an appeal on an intuitive or speculative basis, or the "lurking doubt" referred to by Lord Widgery in the UK cases.[66] This limitation was explained in *M. v. The Queen*, where the High Court said that the approach in Britain allowed the Court of Appeal to set aside a conviction because it was unsafe or unsatisfactory.[67] It also pointed out that in *R. v. Cooper* Widgery L.J. had said:

> That means that in cases of this kind the court must in the end ask itself a subjective question, whether we are content to let the matter stand as it is, or

---

64 *Criminal Law Consolidation Act 1935* (S.A.), 353(1).

65 "The Criminal Proviso: A Case for Reform?" in Corns & Urbas, above note 7 at 105.

66 See also the discussion of this point in Chapter 4 in the context of Canadian law.

67 This part of the discussion is taken from *M. v. The Queen*, [1994] HCA 63, 181 C.L.R. 487 at para. 4 [*M.*].

> whether there is not some lurking doubt in our minds which makes us wonder whether an injustice has been done. This is a reaction which may not be based strictly on the evidence as such; it is a reaction which can be produced by the general feel of the case as the court experiences it. [68]

The court in *M.* pointed out that this passage was cited with approval in *Stafford v. DPP* where Viscount Dilhorne had said it "is not to be doubted" that this is the effect of the legislation.[69] The Australian view, however, was expressed as follows:

> In *Whitehorn v. The Queen* (1983) [152 C.L.R. 657 at 688–89] the view was expressed in this Court that this interpretation extends the power of the Court of Appeal in England beyond that of courts of criminal appeal in Australia. [See also *Ratten v. The Queen* (1974), 131 C.L.R. 510 at 515–16; *Chamberlain v. The Queen (No 2)* (1984), 153 C.L.R. 521 at 533.] It was said that: "Wide as the powers of an Australian court of criminal appeal are, they do not, under the legislation which prevails in this country, empower a court to set aside a verdict upon any speculative or intuitive basis." Nevertheless, the criminal appeal provisions which are in common form in this country allow a verdict that is unsafe or unsatisfactory to be set aside, notwithstanding that those words do not appear in the legislation.[70]

As the courts have pointed out, however, the task of construing this section is not accomplished by simply taking the text of the statute in one hand and a dictionary in the other.[71]

The fundamental task committed to the appellate court by the common form of criminal appeal statute is to decide the appeal. Insofar as that task requires considering the proviso, it is not to be undertaken by attempting to predict what a jury (whether the jury at trial or some hypothetical future jury) would or might do.[72] Rather, in applying the proviso, the task is to decide

---

68 [1969] 1 Q.B. 267 at 271.

69 [1974] A.C. 878 at 892.

70 *M.*, above note 67 at paras. 4–5.

71 *Weiss v. The Queen*, [2005] HCA 81 at para. 10 [*Weiss*], Gleeson C.J., Gummow, Kirby, Hayne, Callinan, and Heydon JJ. In this judgment the court undertakes an historical analysis of the proviso, noting its origins in the UK Act of 1907 and the strict rule which prevailed prior to that: In *R. v. Gibson*, Lord Coleridge C.J., speaking in 1887, stated the rule as being that "if any bit of evidence not legally admissible, which might have affected the verdict, had gone to the jury, the party against whom it was given was entitled to a new trial."

72 For a contrasting approach, see the Canadian case *R. v. Truscott*, 2007 ONCA 575 at para. 277*ff.* (Part V—A Hypothetical New Trial).

whether a "substantial miscarriage of justice has actually occurred . . . when the proviso falls for consideration, the appellate court has decided that there was some irregularity at trial. If there was not, there is no occasion to consider the proviso."[73]

Thus, the appellate court first must decide whether a substantial miscarriage of justice has occurred. Its second task is then an objective task not materially different from other appellate tasks: it is to be performed with whatever are the advantages and disadvantages of deciding an appeal on the record of the trial—it is not an exercise in speculation or prediction. Third, the standard of proof of criminal guilt is beyond reasonable doubt. The court is not "to speculate upon probable reconviction and decide according to how the speculation comes out." It may readily be accepted that the trial jury did accept the evidence given against the accused and rejected the contrary evidence; however, the possibility that the jury took account of wrongly admitted evidence in deciding what evidence to accept or reject cannot be excluded.[74]

The appellate court must make an independent assessment of the evidence. Making due allowance for the natural limitations in the case of an appellate court proceeding wholly or substantially on the record, it must determine whether the accused was proved beyond reasonable doubt to be guilty of the offence on which the jury returned its verdict of guilty.[75] So, in any of the cases, a question is bound to arise whether, despite any apparent miscarriage of justice, the proviso should be applied.

In *Grey*[76] Kirby J. pointed out that the proviso appears in a section that does not negate the fundamental principle of the administration of criminal justice in Australia, namely, that no person should be convicted of a serious crime except by the verdict of a jury after a fair trial held according to law. If the trial ceases to be a fair trial according to law, the verdict of guilty, as well as the criminal conviction that follows it, is intrinsically flawed.[77]

*Grey* referred to two types of defect in a trial. One was where there had been a significant denial of procedural fairness. The other was where there had been a sufficiently serious breach of the presuppositions of the trial. This latter defect refers to a trial that has miscarried to such an extent as hardly to

73 *Weiss*, above note 71 at paras. 35–36.

74 The points referred to in this paragraph are from *ibid.* at para. 50, Gleeson C.J., Gummow, Kirby, Hayne, Callinan, and Heydon JJ.

75 *Darkan, Deemal-Hall and McIvor v. The Queen*, [2006] HCA 34 at para. 4, Gleeson C.J., Gummow, Heydon, and Crennan JJ.

76 *Grey v. The Queen*, [2001] HCA 65 [*Grey*].

77 *Ibid.* at para. 53, Kirby J.

be a trial at all, or to an irregularity that is such a departure from the law's essential requirements that it goes to the root of the proceedings. It is then no part of the function of a court of criminal appeal to hold that the accused is "so obviously guilty that the requirement of a fair trial according to law can be dispensed with."[78] As Kirby J. pointed out, "the proviso has no application to such a case":

> It is not the purpose of the proviso to substitute for trial by jury, in effect, trial "with the Court of Criminal Appeal as the tribunal of fact."[79]

He went on in *Grey* to say that a conclusion of "not guilty" does not have to be a conclusion that a jury would necessarily have reached; perhaps, it does not represent the most probable verdict of a reasonable jury—it just needs to be a definite possibility. He said that Grey was deprived of such a conclusion because he did not have access to information that, forensically, would have strengthened his attack on the credit of the prosecution witnesses:

> The prosecution should gain no such advantage from its conceded default in [failing to disclose] this important information to the defence.[80]

The non-presentation of evidence that has significant forensic value is sufficient to *exclude* the application of the proviso. The Court of Criminal Appeal is *obliged* to consider the cumulative effect of non-disclosed relevant evidence that was in the hands of the police (or forensic experts) and thus available to the prosecution.

However, the proviso, where it applies, does bring with it a shift in the onus of proof. Once a miscarriage of justice is demonstrated, *the prosecution* bears the burden of persuasion that the accused had not lost "a chance which was fairly open to him of being acquitted" or "a real chance of acquittal."[81]

---

78 *Ibid.* However, in *Nudd*, above note 21, Gleeson C.J. said that the proviso was considered recently by the High Court in *Weiss*, above note 71. He cited Barwick C.J. in *Ratten*, below note 98, where he indicated that some irregularities "may" involve no miscarriage of justice if the appellate court forms a certain opinion about the strength of the case against the appellant. In *Nudd*, the court said that trial counsel put some hopeless arguments. He had an erroneous view of the law on one point, and the court took the view that nothing in the material before the Court of Appeal suggested there was any real doubt about Nudd's guilt.

79 *Grey, ibid.* at para. 56, Kirby J. A similar point was made in *Cesan v. The Queen; Mas Rivadavia v. The Queen*, [2008] HCA 52 [*Cesan*], French C.J.

80 *Grey, ibid.*at para. 72.

81 *Ibid.*, at para. 25, Gleeson C.J., Gummow and Callinan JJ., citing *R. v. Storey* (1978), 140 C.L.R. 364 at 376.

## D. APPELLATE DISCRETION TO ENTER AN ACQUITTAL OR ORDER A NEW TRIAL

Upon quashing a conviction, the Court of Appeal has statutory power to either enter a verdict of acquittal or order a new trial.[82] Although the exercise of this power involves significant considerations of public policy, there is no legislative guidance on its exercise. In *DPP (Nauru) v. Fowler*, the High Court said that the overall consideration was what the interests of justice required in the circumstances of the case.[83] This is set out in a two-stage test. The first is "whether the admissible evidence given at the original trial was sufficiently cogent to justify a conviction." If it was not, then an acquittal would be the appropriate order as "it would be wrong by making an order for a new trial to give the prosecution an opportunity to supplement a defective case." If, on the other hand, the evidence was sufficiently cogent to justify a conviction, then the second test applies, which is as follows:

> . . . the court must take into account any circumstances that might render it unjust to the accused to make him stand trial again, remembering however that the public interest in the administration of justice must be considered as well as the interests of the individual accused.[84]

In deciding whether to order a retrial, the court will take into account the nature of the miscarriage of justice, the strength of the prosecution case, the balance between public interest and the personal interest of the appellant.[85] This may be case where the appellant has served a significant part of the custodial sentence or there is an extensive delay between the date of the alleged offence and date of any retrial.[86] An order of acquittal was entered where the prosecution case was so fundamentally flawed that the accused should never have been charged in the first place[87] or no jury could have convicted on the available evidence.[88]

The courts have generally been reluctant to enter an acquittal following a successful appeal for fear of appearing to usurp the prosecutorial function. In

---

82 *Criminal Law Consolidation Act 1935* (S.A.), s. 353(1); *Criminal Appeal Act 1912* (N.S.W.), ss. 6 and 8; *Crimes Act 1958* (Vic.), s. 568(2); *Criminal Code Act 1899* (Qld.), s. 669(1); *Criminal Code 1913* (W.A.), s. 690(3); *Criminal Code Act 1924* (Tas.), above note 10, s. 402(3).

83 *DPP (Nauru) v. Fowler* (1984), 154 C.L.R. 627 at 630.

84 *Ibid.*

85 *Edwards v. R.* (1993), 178 C.L.R. 193; *R. v. Thomas (No. 4)*, [2008] VSCA 107.

86 *R. v. Patton* (1995), 80 A. Crim. R. 595.

87 *Fingleton v. The Queen* (2005), 216 A.L.R. 474, [2005] HCA 34.

88 *DPP v. Ryan*, [2002] VSCA 176; *R. v. Hanson and Ettridge*, [2003] QCA 488.

*Mallard v. the Queen*, the High Court while not entering a verdict of acquittal nonetheless hinted that a retrial could be avoided.[89] The power to order a new trial extends to a new offence for which the appellant could have been convicted at the time of the trial (a lesser alternative offence under the statute). As discussed above in Chapter 4, the Canadian inquiries have recognized that an order of a new trial followed by a refusal of the prosecutor to proceed may leave the person in limbo and without an acquittal.

## E. CROWN APPEALS

There is no general right of an appeal by the prosecution against an acquittal.[90] However, there are a number of limited avenues of appeals by the Crown. For example, the Attorney General or the DPP (Director of Public Prosecutions) may, after the conclusion of the trial, submit any question of law of general importance to the Court of Appeal. The decision of the Court of Appeal will not affect the verdict of the trial court, although it will provide guidance to future trial judges.[91]

## F. IMPORTANCE OF THE JURY

Like Britain, the Australian appeal courts have generally been reluctant to interfere with jury verdicts for fear of upsetting the jury's constitutional role as fact finders. However, where the accused can cast doubt upon the safety of a conviction, then the Court of Appeal will quash the conviction and either enter a verdict of acquittal or order a new trial.[92]

---

89 *Mallard*, above note 24 at paras. 91–93; Kirby J. said:

> . . . retrial is the normal order in such circumstances. This leaves it to the prosecution, within the Executive Government, to take into account all relevant considerations and to ensure consistency in the treatment of like cases in ordering a retrial . . . Whether in all the circumstances, a retrial should be had, is a question properly left to the Director of Public Prosecutions. The matters disclosed in this appeal will doubtless be of assistance to him in making his decision.

See also the discussion of this topic in *Stafford*, above note 21 at paras. 166–68, Keane J.A., citing *Dyers v. The Queen* (2002), 210 C.L.R. 285 at paras. 88–90, where Kirby J., in a dissenting judgment, sets out various circumstances in which a retrial should *not* be ordered.

90 In Western Australia and Tasmania, the prosecution can appeal against an acquittal on the basis of an error of law at trial.

91 Nicholas Cowdery, "Prosecution Appeals in New South Wales: New Rights, Roles and Challenges for the Court of Criminal Appeal and the DPP" in Corns & Urbas, above note 7.

92 *Chamberlain*, above note 17 at 534.

The criteria to be applied were explained by the High Court in *M. v. The Queen*:

> In most cases a doubt experienced by an appellate court will be a doubt which a jury ought also to have experienced. It is only where a jury's advantage of seeing and hearing the evidence is capable of resolving a doubt experienced by a court of criminal appeal that the court may conclude that no miscarriage of justice occurred. That is to say, where the evidence lacks credibility for reasons which are not explained by the manner in which it was given, a reasonable doubt experienced by the court is a doubt which a reasonable jury ought to have experienced. If the evidence, upon the record itself, contains *discrepancies*, displays *inadequacies*, is *tainted* or otherwise *lacks probative force* in such a way as to lead the Court of Criminal Appeal to conclude that, even making full allowance for the advantages enjoyed by the jury, there is a significant possibility that an innocent person has been convicted, then the court is *bound* to act and to set aside a verdict based upon that evidence.[93]

In a trial before judge and jury, it is important to appreciate that it is the jury which determines what the facts are, and based upon those facts, it then has the responsibility to determine guilt or innocence.[94] In doing this, the jury has had the benefit of having seen and heard the witnesses. If a trial has miscarried, a guilty verdict cannot be upheld on a basis not left to the jury because that would be to trespass on the constitutional function of the jury.[95] If the conviction is to be upheld, it can be upheld only on the basis that was left to the jury.[96]

It follows then that it is not correct to speculate on what might have happened if the prosecution had presented the case on some other basis. It is not for the appellate courts to speculate about the impact of potentially exculpatory evidence which had not been disclosed. Equally, it is not for a "Court of Criminal Appeal to seek out possibilities, obvious or otherwise, to explain away troublesome inconsistencies which an accused had been denied an opportunity to explain and exploit forensically."[97]

---

93 Above note 67 at para. 9 [emphasis added]. The High Court referred to *Chamberlain, ibid.* at 618–19; and *Chidiac v. The Queen* (1991), 171 C.L.R. 432 at 443–44 [*Chidiac*]. See also Gaudron J. in *Gipp*, above note 15 at para. 49, citing *Jones v. The Queen* (1997), 72 A.L.J.R. 78 [*Jones*].

94 Clearly these considerations do not apply where the accused elects to be tried by a judge alone. In Canada, the vast majority of trials are judge-alone trials; this would not reflect the Australian experience.

95 *Osland v. The Queen*, [1998] HCA 75 at para. 20, Gaudron and Gummow JJ.

96 *Ibid.* at para. 21.

97 *Mallard*, above note 24 at para. 23, Gummow, Hayne, Callinan, and Heydon JJ.

In *Gipp v. The Queen* it was pointed out that the ultimate interest of the courts in the administration of justice must be to ensure that people are not victims of the system. As was said in that case, the language used in the judgments is that the decision was "unreasonable" or that it was "unsafe or unsatisfactory," "unjust or unsafe," or "dangerous or unsafe."[98] This, said the judge, was a reflection of the "unsafe or unsatisfactory" criterion that had been included in the *Criminal Appeal Act 1968* (UK).[99] However, "in Australia, the statutory provisions are differently expressed and it is those provisions which must be applied."[100]

## G. ERROR OF LAW AND PROCEDURAL ERROR

Australian courts have tended to overturn a conviction where there has been some misdirection by the judge or some other error of law, such as where the trial judge has wrongly admitted or excluded evidence.[101] These are cases where the appellant has been denied procedural fairness. In *Evans v. The Queen* the High Court said that "the graver the departure from the requirements of a fair trial, the harder it is for an appellate court to conclude the guilt is established beyond reasonable doubt."[102]

The cases make clear that where there has been a departure from the requirements of a properly conducted trial, it cannot be said that there has been no substantial miscarriage of justice. In *Nudd* Gleeson C.J. said the process itself is judged:

> . . . every accused person is entitled to a trial in which the relevant law is correctly explained to the jury and the rules of procedure and evidence are strictly followed. If there is a failure in any of those respects and the appellant may thereby have lost a chance which was fairly open to him of being acquitted, there is, in the eyes of the law, a miscarriage of justice. [103]

That well-known passage relates the failure of process to the loss of a chance of acquittal.

---

98 *Gipp*, above note 15 at para. 169, Kirby J. referring to *Davies*, above note 20 at 180, and *Ratten v. R.* (1974), 131 C.L.R. 510 at 515 [*Ratten*].

99 Above note 12.

100 *Gipp*, above note 15 at para. 126, Kirby J.

101 *R. v. Pantoja*, [1998] NSWCA 565.

102 [2007] HCA 59 at para. 42, Gummow and Hayne JJ.

103 *Nudd*, above note 21 at para. 6, Gleeson C.J., citing Fullagar J. in *Mraz v. The Queen* (1955), 93 C.L.R. 493 at 514 [*Mraz*].

In *Cesan*, it was said that the judge had been sleeping at various stages during the conduct of the trial.[104] In the High Court, the Chief Justice said that there may be cases in which there is a process failure of such significance that, whatever the apparent weight of the evidence against the accused person, it cannot be said that there has not been a substantial miscarriage of justice. That may be because the process failure has deprived the appeal court of the capacity to assess whether the appellant may have lost a fair chance of an acquittal.[105] He pointed out that "the irregularity may be so material that of itself it constitutes a miscarriage of justice without the need to consider its effect on the verdict."[106] He added, "The corollary of that proposition is that a defect in process may be of such a nature that its effect cannot be overcome by pointing to the strength of the prosecution case."[107] In such a case the proviso cannot apply.[108]

The cases refer to the applicant who may have lost *a chance* which was fairly open of being acquitted or "a real chance of acquittal."[109] Where an accused person has lost such a chance, then that is a miscarriage of justice.[110] It is said that the loss of such a chance of acquittal cannot be anything but a substantial miscarriage of justice. Otherwise, there would be the equivalent of a trial by appellate judges who had seen no witnesses, heard no evidence, and had no direct contact with the nuances of the trial.[111]

In *R. v. Stafford*,[112] the appeal court accepted that it was a procedural error for the prosecution to have put a scenario to the jury which was not fairly open on the evidence, as that evidence was subsequently accepted by the Court of Appeal. At trial, the prosecution claimed that the accused had beaten the deceased with a hammer in the bathroom at their home and hidden the body in the trunk of the car for some time before disposing of the body in the bush some distance from the house. On the appeal, the court accepted what it referred to as "new" evidence, which really amounted to new opinions based upon the evidence that had been given at the trial; that was to the effect that

---

104 *Cesan*, above note 79.

105 *Ibid.* at para. 81.

106 *Ibid.* at para. 82 in reference to *TKWJ v. The Queen*, [2002] HCA 46 [*TKWJ*], McHugh J.

107 *Ibid.* at para. 83 in reference to *Nudd*, above note 21, Gleeson C.J.

108 *Ibid.* at para. 82 in reference to *TKWJ*, above note 106, McHugh J.

109 For example, *Wilde v. The Queen*, [1988] HCA 6 at para. 9 [*Wilde*].

110 *Mraz*, above note 103; *Wilde, ibid.*; *Grey*, above note 76; *Beamish v. The Queen*, [2005] WASCA 62 [*Beamish*].

111 *Beamish, ibid.* at para. 319, Steytler, Wheeler, and McLure JJ. citing *Wilde* and *Grey*, *ibid.*

112 Above note 21. This Australian case was one of the few to have resulted from a second reference under the petition procedure. See also above note 21.

the quantity of blood traces in the bathroom and in the car trunk were not really consistent with the death having occurred in the circumstances put forward by the prosecution. If the deceased had been beaten to death in the bathroom or if her body had been kept in the trunk of the car for some time, the blood (and other) traces found would have been greater.

## H. FRESH EVIDENCE ON APPEAL

Subject to what we said earlier about the difficulties in reopening appeals in Australia, like Britain and Canada, the intermediate appeal courts in Australia are explicitly granted powers to receive more evidence if it is deemed necessary and expedient in the interests of justice.[113] As mentioned, the appeal courts have rarely used the broad statutory powers to order production of things, allow for the examination and cross-examination of witnesses, and appoint a special commissioner to inquire and report back on matters (including scientific issues) that cannot conveniently be conducted before the court.[114]

In *Chamberlain v. The Queen* it was said that additional evidence had to be "fresh" and "cogent."[115] "Fresh" refers to evidence that could not "with reasonable diligence" have been discoverable before or at the time of trial.[116] "New" evidence is evidence that was available or could with due diligence have been discoverable at the time of the trial. "Cogent" means that the evidence must be capable of belief.[117]

In certain cases, the presence of new evidnece will be more obvious than others. For example, in *Mallard v. The Queen* the High Court said that it was self-evident that the evidence relied upon could not, with reasonable diligence, have been produced by the accused at the trial because it had been in the possession of the prosecution and not disclosed to the defence. In *Christie v. The Queen* the Western Australian Court of Appeal stated:

---

113 As we have seen, the High Court cannot receive fresh evidence. *Criminal Appeal Act 1912* (N.S.W.), s. 12; *Crimes Act 1958* (Vic.), s. 574; *Criminal Code Act 1899* (Qld.), s. 671B; *Criminal Code* (N.T.), s. 419; *Criminal Code Act Compilation Act 1913* (W.A.), s. 697; *Criminal Code Act 1924* (Tas.), s. 409(1); *Criminal Law Consolidation Act 1935* (S.A.), s. 359.

114 *Criminal Law Consolidation Act 1935* (S.A.), *ibid.*

115 (1983), 46 A.L.R. 493 at para. 499. In *Ratten*, above note 98 at para. 516, Barwick C.J. said that cogency means that the evidence must be such as to convince the appellate court that if it had been placed before the jury together with the other evidence, a different verdict might reasonably have resulted.

116 *Ratten*, *ibid.* at para. 21, Barwick C.J.; and *Gallagher*, above note 22 at para. 4, Gibbs C.J.

117 *Ibid.*

> Great latitude must of course be extended to an accused in determining what evidence by reasonable diligence in his own interests he could have had available at his trial, and it will probably be only in an exceptional case that evidence which was not actually available to him will be denied the quality of fresh evidence.[118]

Where the evidence is clearly of importance, the appellate courts will always receive fresh evidence if it can be clearly shown that a "failure to receive such evidence might have the result that an unjust conviction or an unjust sentence is permitted to stand."[119]

In *Cooley v. The Queen* a doctor had been called by the prosecution to give evidence at a criminal trial.[120] The Medical Board had made adverse findings on his credit some five months before the trial, but five months after the trial his credit was restored. On Cooley's appeal, which took place after the restoration of the doctor's credit, it was argued that at his trial Cooley was denied the opportunity of challenging the doctor's credibility in his cross-examination, based upon the then existent adverse findings of the Medical Board. The Medical Board had found that the witness deliberately attempted to mislead the tribunal. The appeal held that this was significant material which may have affected the jury's assessment of the doctor's credibility at trial:

> In this context, it is not enough for the prosecution to say simply that the information was in the public domain, or that the applicant should have made inquires which would have revealed it. The defence was entitled to assume that a professional expert witness called by the State was a witness of integrity and credibility and that if there was *any material* showing otherwise, the State would disclose it. The failure of the State to do so deprived the applicant of the opportunity to cross-examine Dr Srna on an issue which bore directly on his credibility, in circumstances in which the jury's assessment of that may have led to a different verdict. There was accordingly a miscarriage of justice.[121]

In fresh evidence cases, the court is required to consider if there is a "significant possibility" of a wrongful conviction; or that the jury, acting reasonably, would have acquitted had the fresh evidence been before it at the trial. If such

118 *Christie v. The Queen*, [2005] WASCA 55 at para. 237 [*Christie*], Le Miere and Jenkins JJ.
119 *Gallagher*, above note 22, Gibbs C.J., referring to King C.J. in *R. v. McIntee* (1985), 38 S.A.S.R. 432 at 435.
120 *Cooley v. The State of Western Australia*, [2005] WASCA 160 at para. 67 [*Cooley*].
121 *Ibid.* at para. 67, Roberts-Smith J.A. [emphasis added].

a possibility exists, then the court is *bound* to set aside the verdict.[122] "Once the appellate court comes to the conclusion that any of the pre-conditions to the exercise of its statutory jurisdiction is made out . . . , it is *obliged* to ("shall") allow the appeal."[123] As can be seen, the court in both *Christie* and *Cooley* took the view that the categorization of evidence as either "fresh" or "new" was not as important as determining if there had been a miscarriage of justice.

## I. THE ROLE OF THE PROSECUTOR AND DISCLOSURE

The miscarriage of justice ground may be used where the prosecution fails to disclose all the relevant evidence to the defence. In order for there to be a fair trial, the prosecution is obliged to disclose to the defence *all material* available to it which is relevant or possibly relevant to any issue in the case.[124] This point was reinforced by the High Court in *Mallard v. The Queen*.[125] The duty of disclosure includes the obligation to make inquiry to ascertain whether discoverable matter exists and to ensure its preservation.[126] Discoverable matter includes material that goes to the credit of prosecution witnesses. It may include,

---

122 *Gipp*, above note 15 at para. 18, Gaudron J., citing *M.*, above note 67 at 494 (C.L.R.), Mason C.J., Deane, Dawson, and Toohey JJ., referring to *Chamberlain*, above note 17 at 618–19; *Chidiac*, above note 93 at 443–44; *Jones*, above note 93.

123 *Gipp*, *ibid.* at para. 119, Kirby J. [emphasis added].

124 *Grey*, above note 76 at para. 46, Gleeson C.J., Gummow, and Callinan JJ., referring to the consideration of this matter by the Court of Criminal Appeal of New South Wales in *R. v. Grey* (2000), 111 A. Crim. R. 314 at 322 noted that there it was observed that Rule 66 of the New South Wales Bar Association provided:

> A prosecutor must disclose to the opponent as soon as practicable all material available to the prosecutor or of which the prosecutor becomes aware which constitutes evidence relevant to the guilt or innocence of the accused, unless such disclosure, or full disclosure, would seriously threaten the integrity of the administration of justice in those proceedings or the safety of any person.

125 *Mallard*, above note 24 at para. 17, Gummow, Hayne, Callinan, and Heydon JJ:

> At this point it is relevant to note that the recent case of *Grey v. The Queen* in this Court stands as authority for the proposition that the prosecution must at common law also disclose all relevant evidence to an accused, and that a failure to do so may, in some circumstances, require the quashing of a verdict of guilty. As will appear, the evidence which was not produced before or at this trial, was certainly no less cogent than the evidence which was not disclosed in *Grey*.

126 In *Cooley*, above note 120 at para. 57, Roberts-Smith J.A. said [in reference to the earlier case of *Bradshaw v. The Queen* (13 May 1997), Library No 970228 (WASC CCA), Malcolm C.J. [*Bradshaw*] with whom Pidgeon and Owen JJ. agreed]:

> The Chief Justice observed that it was noted in par. 4.273 of *Archbold* that the above was by no means an exhaustive list and went on to say (at 11):

for example, a previous inconsistent statement or *any other matter* adverse to the character of a prosecution witness.[127]

In *Cooley*, the relevant evidence that went to the credit of the expert witness was on the public record:

> At the date of trial, the material upon which Cooley seeks to rely, namely the findings of the Board given in September 2003, are neither "new", nor "fresh" evidence . . . That material was in existence and available to Cooley by reasonable diligence; indeed the proposition that it was in the public domain is not challenged *the question is always whether or not what occurred has resulted in a miscarriage of justice . . . .* [128]

The court held that on the basis of other Australian authorities, the principles in the British cases of *R. v. Keane*[129] and *R. v. Brown (Winston)*[130] should be taken as applying in New South Wales and Western Australia. There, the duty of a prosecutor to disclose information was defined in the following way:

> . . . the prosecution must disclose documents which are material . . . documents are material if they can be seen on a sensible appraisal by the prosecution, (a) to be relevant or possibly relevant to an issue in the case, (b) to raise or possibly raise a new issue the existence of which is not apparent from the prosecution case, or (c) to hold out a real (as opposed to a fanciful) prospect of providing a lead on evidence going to either (a) or (b).[131]

As the court said, even an innocent failure to disclose relevant material may nonetheless constitute a miscarriage of justice.[132]

If, after conviction, the Crown discloses that it had in its possession or available to it documentary material that had been requested, but innocently

---

> it was submitted that the duty of disclosure included the obligation to make enquiry to ascertain whether discoverable matter existed and to ensure its preservation: *Archbold* [4.268]. Further, if material was available to the Crown, on the basis that it was known to the police, for example, the accused was entitled to it, whether or not its existence was known to prosecuting counsel: *R. v. Ward* (1993) 93 Cr. App. R. 1. I accept these submissions.

127 *Cooley, ibid.* at para. 65, Roberts-Smith J.A.

128 *Ibid.* at para. 53, Roberts-Smith J.A. [emphasis added]

129 [1994] 2 All E.R. 478.

130 [1998] A.C. 367.

131 *Cooley*, above note 120 at para. 58; Robert-Smith J.A. observed that the relevant law was discussed by Hodgson J.A. in *R. v. Reardon (No. 2)* (2004), 60 N.S.W.L.R. 454 at para. 54.

132 *Button v. The Queen*, [2002] WASCA 35 at para. 58 [*Button*], Malcolm C.J. citing *Clarkson v. DPP*, [1990] V.R. 745 at 755; and *R. v. Apostolides* (1984), 154 C.L.R. 563.

denied by the Crown, that is a situation which could lead to a miscarriage of justice.[133]

## J. "THE PROSECUTION" INCLUDES POLICE AND OTHERS

In *Cooley*, as we just noted, it was said:

> . . . if material was available to the Crown, on the basis that it was known to the police, for example, the accused was entitled to it, whether or not its existence was known to prosecuting counsel: *R v Ward* (1993) 93 Cr App R 1. I accept these submissions.[134]

In such a case, it is not necessary for the appellate court to determine whether there was any *fault* on the part of the prosecutor.

In *Mallard v. The Queen*, the court said:

> On the reference however, further evidence was adduced. It also became apparent that a deal of it had been in the possession of investigating police before, and during the trial, and had not then been disclosed to the appellant. (Whether any of it was in the possession of the Director of Public Prosecutions is a question that is unnecessary to investigate.)[135]

Whether or not certain deficiencies in the evidence of a prosecution witness may have led to a miscarriage of justice will depend upon the importance of the witness's evidence and whether there was any issue of witness credibility with respect to it. In *Grey v. The Queen* Kirby J. said:

> In cases where credibility is in issue and where the jury's assessment of the truthfulness of a vital prosecution witness might be important for their verdict, the admission of inadmissible evidence, the rejection of admissible evidence or the unavailability of significant and relevant evidence that later comes to light may, in a particular case, occasion such a miscarriage of justice that a guilty verdict should not stand.[136]

The issue in *Grey* was that a Crown witness had in a previous case been provided by the police with a reference (a "letter of comfort") although they

---

133 *Button, ibid.* at para. 58, Malcolm C.J., citing his judgment in *Bradshaw*, above note 126 at paras. 11–12.

134 *Button, ibid.*, Malcolm C.J., citing his judgment in *Bradshaw, ibid.*

135 *Mallard*, above note 24 at para. 16, Gummow, Hayne, Callinan, and Heydon JJ.

136 *Grey*, above note 76 at para. 55.

knew that he had been engaged in previous questionable activities.[137] The witness was presented by the Crown in that case as a reliable witness. The High Court said that "this was a disingenuous basis upon which to present [the witness]." Because of this conduct, the accused had been prevented from opening up "a fertile ground of cross-examination."[138] As a result, there had been a miscarriage of justice and the conviction was quashed. It was not the sort of miscarriage to which the fresh evidence rule applied. As the court said, it may be "one thing to say that the defence knew or could have found out about various aspects of the unsavoury behaviour on the part of [the witness], but it was an altogether different thing to say that it knew of the special relationship between [that witness] and the police."[139]

## K. PUBLIC CONFIDENCE IN THE TRIAL PROCESS

The central question is whether in the absence of material evidence, the accused received a fair trial—understood as a trial resulting in a verdict "worthy of confidence"; the "fruits of investigation" are the "property of the *public* to be used to ensure that justice is done."[140] The fundamental issue is whether the exculpatory evidence not presented to the jury led to a conclusion that the trial cannot enjoy public confidence.[141] In *Antoun v. The Queen* Kirby J. said:

> I would repeat the words I used in *Goktas v. Government Insurance Office (NSW)*: Our system of justice must do better. This Court must accept its obligation to ensure against wrongs which can be proved and then corrected. At stake is something greater even than the interests of the parties to the case. At stake is the integrity of our system of law and justice.[142]

---

137 *Ibid.*

138 *Ibid.* at para. 18, Gleeson C.J., Gummow and Callinan JJ.

139 *Ibid.* at para. 23.

140 *Mallard*, above note 24, Kirby J. [emphasis added], discussing the provisions of the *Canadian Charter of Rights and Freedoms*, Part 1 of the *Constitution Act, 1982*, being Schedule B to the *Canada Act 1982* (U.K.), 1982, c. 11 [*Charter*].

141 *Mallard*, *ibid.* at para. 98, Kirby J. In *Antoun v. The Queen*, [2006] HCA 2 at para. 28 [*Antoun*], Kirby J. said:

> the manifest observance of fair procedures is necessary to satisfy the requirements not only of fairness to the accused but also of justice before the public so that they may be satisfied, by attendance or from the record, that the process has followed lines observing basic rules of fairness.

142 *Antoun*, *ibid.* at para 47.

He then went on to say that while it might always be possible that a prosecution witness was willing to divulge the information but was not asked, the defence lawyer should not be put in the position of having to find out in front of the jury if such material exists. As Kirby J. said, if the defence is unaware of what evidence is available, a lucky (if extremely risky) question of the witness might have elicited an answer which revealed the existence of the problems relating to the witness's credibility. However, there was no reason why the defence in a criminal trial should be obliged to "fossick for information" of this kind and to which it was entitled.[143] In *Mallard* Kirby J. said, "I would accept this as a statement expressing the common law rule in this country."[144] He pointed out that a similar principle of disclosure is also the rule in Scotland, Ireland, and New Zealand.

In *Grey*, Kirby J. stated that to treat that type of disclosure issue as one amenable to the rules governing fresh or new evidence following a criminal trial is effectively to convert the prosecutor's duty to disclose into an accused's obligation to find out.[145] An essential question is this: if the jury had known about the additional material, would it have cast doubt on the essential features of the prosecution case? Or, to put that another way, was the body of evidence not presented to the jury potentially significant?[146]

The point of appellate review is not to discover whether there was misconduct by the prosecution. Instead, it is to determine whether the non-disclosed material was relevant to the credibility and reliability of the prosecution witnesses or the prosecution case.

In *Mallard*, the specific issue was non-disclosure to the defence. The High Court has made it clear, however, that the fundamental question is whether there has been non-disclosure "to the jury." For example, there may have been evidence or facts that were either ignored or overlooked by the defence. In this respect, it is important to bear in mind that where a miscarriage of justice is said to arise from a failure of process, the *process* is judged, not the performance of the participants in the process. Where the conduct of counsel is said to give rise to a miscarriage of justice, what is significant is what was done or omitted, rather than *why* something occurred.[147]

In *Mallard*, Kirby J. cited *Berger v. United States*[148] in stating that the prosecutor is

143 *Mallard*, above note 24 at para. 66, Kirby J. citing *Grey*, above note 76.

144 *Mallard*, *ibid.* at para. 74.

145 *Grey*, above note 76 at para. 50, Kirby J.

146 *Mallard*, above note 24 at paras. 23–24, Gummow, Hayne, Callinan, and Heydon JJ.

147 *Nudd*, above note 21 at para. 8, Gleeson C.J.

148 295 U.S. 78 at 88 (1935).

> the representative not of an ordinary party to a controversy, but of a sovereignty whose obligation to govern impartially is as compelling as its obligation to govern at all; and whose interest, therefore, in a criminal prosecution is not that it shall win a case, but that justice shall be done.[149]

There was much discussion in *Mallard* of the guidelines for prosecutors as well as the influence of other common law jurisdictions and the effect of international human rights issues.

## L. THE ROLE OF DEFENCE LAWYERS AND INEFFECTIVE ASSISTANCE OF COUNSEL

In some cases, those convicted of crimes might suggest that the fault was not theirs but of the way in which they were defended by their counsel at trial. In such cases, "the defendant must show that there is a reasonable probability that, but for counsel's unprofessional errors, the result of the proceeding would have been different. A reasonable probability is a probability sufficient to undermine confidence in the outcome."[150] The general rule is that a client is bound by counsel's conduct. There is a qualification, however. Where the client might have suffered some injustice as a result of conduct incapable of rational explanation on forensic grounds, the conviction may be quashed.[151] The basic standard for a claim of inadequate counsel is "flagrant incompetence."[152]

It is also possible for a miscarriage of justice to arise from the combined effect of various errors of trial counsel and of the trial judge.

The court pointed out in *Nudd* that in the United States and Canada accused persons have a constitutional or quasi-constitutional right to *effective* assistance from counsel. Yet even in those jurisdictions, the courts have stressed the objective nature of the standard to be applied. In *Strickland v. Washington*, the US Supreme Court held that, when a complaint is made of counsel's ineffectiveness, the appellant must show both that counsel's conduct fell below an objective standard of reasonableness and that prejudice resulted:[153]

---

149 *Mallard*, above note 24 at para. 70. For further discussion on this topic, see also *Benedetto v. R.*, [2003] UKPC 27 (appeal from Eastern Caribbean Court of Appeal); *Randall v. R. (Cayman Islands)*, [2002] UKPC 19; *Boucher v. The Queen*, [1955] S.C.R. 16.

150 *Nudd*, above note 21 at para. 13, Gleeson C.J. citing *Strickland v. Washington*, 466 U.S. 668 at 669 (1984) [*Strickland*].

151 *Nudd*, *ibid.* at para. 16, citing Lord Lane C.J. in *R. v. Ensor*, [1989] 1 W.L.R. 497 at 502.

152 *R. v. Birks* (1990), 19 N.S.W.L.R. 677 at 685 [*Birks*].

153 *Nudd*, above note 21 at para. 13, referring to *Strickland*, above note 150 at 669.

> This requires showing that counsel's errors were so serious as to deprive the defendant of a fair trial, a trial whose result is reliable . . . a breakdown in the adversary process that renders the result unreliable . . . . The defendant must show that there is a reasonable probability that, but for counsel's unprofessional errors, the result of the proceeding would have been different. A reasonable probability is a probability sufficient to undermine confidence in the outcome.[154]

The court in *Nudd* said that in Canada, the right to effective assistance of counsel has been held to be derived from certain provisions of the *Criminal Code* and the *Canadian Charter of Rights and Freedoms*.[155] In *R. v. G.D.B.*, the Supreme Court of Canada followed the approach in *Strickland*.[156] A significant feature of the Canadian cases is that, although they turn upon a legal right to effective assistance from counsel—and complaints are expressed in terms of a denial of the right—the complaints are dealt with by asking a question which, upon analysis, is similar to the question whether there has been a miscarriage of justice.[157]

It is important to note the significance of any combination of the errors involving trial counsel and the judge. This type of cumulative error can provide a good illustration of the way in which the adversary system can lead to a failure of the trial process.[158] In *Nudd*, Gleeson C.J. referred to a number of cases in the Criminal Division of the English Court of Appeal in the late 1980s "where tactical decisions made by counsel without instructions from the client were claimed to have given rise to miscarriages of justice."[159]

However, it must be borne in mind that the adversary system means that criminal trials are conducted as a contest. The High Court made the point in *Nudd* that the system does not require that the adversaries be of equal ability. It said that while opposing counsel may be mismatched, this does not make the process relevantly unfair. "The reluctance of courts of criminal appeal to enter upon an assessment of the performance of trial counsel is well-founded in considerations both of principle and of pragmatism."[160]

It is also interesting to note in passing that, unlike their counterparts in the Britain, Australian prosecutors are not so willing to make concessions.[161] This

154 *Ibid.*
155 *Criminal Code*, above note 13; *Charter*, above note 140.
156 *R. v. G.D.B.*, [2000] 1 S.C.R. 520 [*G.D.B.*].
157 *Nudd*, above note 21 at para. 14, referring to *G.D.B.*, *ibid.*
158 *Nudd*, *ibid.* at para. 18, Gleeson C.J., citing *Birks*, above note 152.
159 *Nudd*, *ibid.* at para. 16.
160 *Ibid.* at para. 12.
161 In *Burrell*, above note 28 at para. 92, Kirby J. stated, "During more than 12 years on this Court I have seen joint support from the prosecution and the prisoner to permit the case of an accepted mistake in the reasoning of the intermediate court but once."

attitude contrasts markedly with the British treatment of what might be called the "knock-on" effect discussed in Chapter 7.[162]

## M. FRAGMENTED APPELLATE STRUCTURE

As with the final courts of appeal in Canada and Britain, the High Court of Australia grants leave to appeal only where matters of particular public importance are involved. In other words, the cases that it hears are selected for their strategic importance in allowing the High Court to implement the principled development of the law. In the early days, the High Court rarely entertained appeals on criminal law, criminal practice, and sentencing, but in recent years the number of such cases has increased.[163] However, it still accepts comparatively few criminal cases for appeal.[164] Having said that, as we have seen, in the last few years a number of significant High Court cases have dealt with criminal appeals where the principles relating to miscarriages of justice have been set out with admirable clarity. These accord with similar principles enunciated by the British appeal courts.

One statutory ground for the grant of special leave to appeal to the High Court is that the interests of the administration of justice require the reconsideration of the case.[165] This ground brings in the special issue of policy which applies with greater emphasis in the High Court of Australia than it does in the lower or intermediate courts.

At the intermediate appellate court level, however, the principles set out in the Australian High Court cases appear not to have been fully implemented.[166] For example, the Western Australia Supreme Court decided unanimously to reject the appeal of Andrew Mallard in *Mallard v. The Queen*.[167] However, the

---

162 See, particularly, *R. v. Maynard & Ors*, [2002] EWCA Crim 1942 at paras. 54–57, as discussed in Chapter 3, Section G.

163 The Hon. Justice Michael Kirby, "Why Has the High Court Become More Involved in Criminal Appeals?" (2002) 23 Austl. Bar Rev. 4. See also *Burrell*, above note 28 at paras. 89–90.

164 In *Burrell*, *ibid.*, Kirby J. pointed out that in the *High Court of Australia Annual Report 2006–07*, there were 106 applications for special leave to appeal in criminal matters filed and twenty-four grants of special leave.

165 *Gipp*, above note 15 at para. 135, Kirby J. *Judiciary Act 1903* (Cth.), s. 35A(b).

166 Susan Rutberg, "Anatomy of a Miscarriage of Justice: The Wrongful Conviction of Peter J. Rose" (2006) 37 Golden Gate U.L. Rev. 7 at 32: "Lofty sentiments about justice and the role of lawyers expressed in appellate opinions are clearly insufficient to protect the innocent."

167 (2003), 28 W.A.R. 1.

High Court then unanimously allowed the appeal.[168] Equally, in the case of *R. v. Cesan*, the Court of Appeal of NSW (by majority) rejected the appeal in the case of a judge who had fallen asleep at significant stages of the trial before a jury; however, the High Court unanimously allowed the appeal without having to reserve their judgment.[169]

Roseanne Catt was convicted on several charges relating to assault, malicious wounding, and an attempt to poison her former husband. Catt said that he was involved in a conspiracy with the investigating police officer (a friend of his) to cause damage to her by having her charged and convicted for these offences. At the trial it was made clear that either she was a malicious person and a liar, or else the investigating officer had engaged in serious misconduct. After Catt had spent more than ten years in prison, her case was referred back to the courts. A judicial inquiry established the following:

> The verdict of guilty on eight of the nine counts meant that the jury essentially accepted the Crown version of events and rejected the defence case of a conspiracy. However, those verdicts now require careful reconsideration having regard to the fact that there is significant fresh evidence available which, if accepted by a jury, would support the conspiracy allegation.[170]

The appeal court judge also said in respect of the investigating officer that he had

> . . . a propensity to improperly use his office to damage Ms Catt irrespective of the risk of gratuitous collateral damage to others . . . it indicates a lack of objectivity having descended into malice and abuse of power.[171]

The appeal court judge went on to say that the officer may well have committed perjury and improperly influenced most of the witnesses in the case. Yet, remarkably, the appeal court overturned only six of the eight convictions on the basis that it was unclear to them how the improper conduct of the officer could have affected the jury's assessment on the remaining two matters.[172] This

---

168 *Mallard*, above note 24.

169 *Cesan and Rivadavia v. DPP (Cth.)*, [2007] NSWCCA 273; *Cesan and Rivadia v. The Queen*, [2008] HCATrans 320 (3 September 2008); *Cesan*, above note 79.

170 *R. v. Catt*, [2005] NSWCCA 279 at para. 61 [*Catt*], McClellan J.A. See also Roseanne Beckett [formerly Catt], Mark Whittaker, & Amy Willesee, *Roseanne Catt—Ten Years* (Sydney: Pan Macmillan, 2005).

171 *Catt, ibid.* at paras. 80–81, McClellan J.A.

172 It also compares most unfavourably with the UK cases, especially that of *R. v. Cooper*, [2003] EWCA Crim 2257.

approach is clearly quite different and far more conservative than what we have seen in the British cases.

Another component of the explanation for the imperfect implementation of the standards set down by the Australian High Court may be that there is no unified appellate court system in Australia. For example, while New South Wales has a permanent appeal court, South Australia does not. In South Australia, an appeal is heard, as we mentioned, by three trial-court judges assigned by the Chief Justice to sit together as the Court of Appeal. Given the fragmented appeal court structure between the various states and territories, the facts that the appeal court cannot reopen a case, the High Court cannot hear fresh evidence, and the clear and unchallengeable reluctance on the part of state Attorneys General to refer cases back to the appeal court, it is clear that the volume of work on these issues in any appeal court in Australia represents only a fraction of that done by their equivalents in Britain.[173]

In addition, the UK Court of Appeal is no doubt appreciative of the fact that deficient decisions might well lead to cases being referred back to them by the CCRC.[174] All of this might well lead to the view that reforms, such as a unified judiciary and the establishment of a body equivalent to that of the CCRC, would be appropriate for Australia.

## N. CONCLUSION

On their face, appeal provisions in Britain, Canada, and Australia give appellate courts a wide mandate to correct miscarriages of justice and to overturn unsafe or unreasonable convictions. That said, appellate courts in all three countries have expressed reluctance to second-guess determinations of fact made at trial and especially by juries. The appellate courts have also tempered their mandate to do justice with concerns about the finality of verdicts that are not explicitly mandated in the statutes authorizing appeals from convictions.

When compared with British cases, the Australian cases involving suspected miscarriages of justice are hampered by the lack of open and transparent referral processes; the inability of the appellate courts to reopen appeals in meritorious cases; and the inability of the High Court to consider fresh evi-

173 It is to be noted that the Victorian Attorney General has called for the establishment of a national judiciary: "Vic A-G Calls for a National Judiciary" *The Australian* (27 June 2008). See also Robert N. Moles, *A State of Injustice* (South Melbourne: Lothian, 2004) c. 16.

174 See Richard Nobles & David Schiff, "The Right to Appeal and Workable Systems of Justice" (2002) 65 Mod. L. Rev. 676.

dence. When these limitations are combined with the lack of a full-time and unified appellate court structure, with clearly deficient decisions being issued at the intermediate level and almost insurmountable hurdles to reach the highest level, there is much that can—and should—be done. In Chapter 6, we consider the issue of a claim of fraud in criminal proceedings as one way of enabling courts in all jurisdictions to reconsider meritorious cases.

CHAPTER 6

# Fraud in Criminal Proceedings

In this chapter we examine a special type of miscarriage of justice. In accordance with our previous discussion, we must be dealing with a situation where there has been a trial, a conviction, and an unsuccessful appeal. Suppose that it was then discovered that the conviction had been obtained by serious misconduct amounting to fraud. In such a situation, we ask if there is a right to be heard by the court system, and if the claim is made out, for the conviction to be set aside.[1]

There may well be many circumstances where resorting to such a right would not be necessary. In the United Kingdom, for example, the Criminal Cases Review Commission (CCRC) would, no doubt, refer the matter to the Court of Appeal. In Canada and Australia, the relevant Attorney General might refer the matter back to the court under the relevant statutory power. However, were those things not to happen, we ask whether there is a residual right for the court to address these issues upon application, without the necessity for a reference upon a petition and in the absence of any right of appeal. This issue raises important constitutional questions about the separation of powers between the judiciary and the executive, and whether the judiciary has an ongoing responsibility to ensure that verdicts rendered by the courts are not the results of frauds that have been perpetrated on them.[2]

1 An earlier version of this discussion was published in Bibi Sangha, "Extending the Scope of Post-conviction Reviews" (2007) 30 Austl. Bar Rev. 90.

2 The courts have recognized a related concern about abuse of process. See, for example, *Connelly v. Director of Public Prosecutions*, [1964] A.C. 1254; *R. v. Jewitt*, [1985] 2 S.C.R. 128. See also Gino Dal Pont, "Judgments Fraudulently Obtained: The Forgotten Equity" (1995) 14 U. Tasm. L. Rev. 129.

Suppose, for example, that a situation such as the IRA bombing cases had occurred in Australia or Canada in recent times. After conviction and appeal, it is then found out that the expert witnesses had given fraudulent evidence to the court in relation to their tests or results. From what we have already explained, we know, for example, that the Australian appeal courts cannot reopen an appeal after its order has been formally recorded (or "perfected") and that the High Court cannot receive fresh evidence. The only avenue left is a reference back to the court by the state Attorney General or in Canada, by the federal Minister of Justice. There could, however, be widespread concern that adverse findings against such expert witnesses might lead to the reopening of many other cases. In such circumstances, an Attorney General might well refuse to refer the matter back to the court. Would that mean that a possibly innocent person would have to serve out the remainder of a sentence—or can something more be done? In this chapter, we explore the possibility that there is a residual right to be heard.

## A. CIVIL AND CRIMINAL CASES

It is worth stating at the outset that some of the cases we refer to in this chapter are civil as opposed to criminal cases. It might well be argued that where certain rights to further consideration are available in civil proceedings, then similar rights ought to be available in criminal cases, given the more serious consequences that follow from such adverse findings. We also find that much cross-referencing takes place between both civil and criminal cases in this area, as one might expect when dealing with the most fundamental issues of court procedure. For example, in *Burrell v. The Queen*,[3] a recent and important Australian criminal case, it was said:

> Secondly, it is important to recognize that underpinning consideration of the issues presented in this matter are fundamental principles about finality of litigation . . . . A central and pervading tenet of the judicial system is that controversies, once resolved, are not to be reopened except in a few, narrowly defined, circumstances. That tenet finds reflection in the restriction upon the reopening of final orders after entry and in the rules concerning the bringing of an action to set aside a final judgment *on the ground that it was procured by fraud*.[4]

---

3 *Burrell v. The Queen*, [2008] HCA 34 [*Burrell*].

4 *Ibid.* at para. 15, Gummow A.C.J., Hayne, Heydon, Crennan, and Kiefel JJ. [emphasis added], referring to *D'Orta-Ekenaike v. Victoria Legal Aid*, [2005] HCA 12, Gleeson C.J.,

The authority cited for that proposition was *D'Orta* which was a civil case. *Burrell* also referred to *DJL v. The Central Authority* (another civil case) where it was said:

> In addition to these methods of overcoming the mistakes and injustices that can sometimes arise in perfected orders, the law has devised means of permitting collateral attack on such orders. This can be mounted in separate proceedings where it is alleged that the judgment was obtained through fraud. But it can also arise where it can be shown that there has been a serious denial of procedural fairness. Such remedies are necessary to maintain the integrity of the court process.[5]

So, *DJL* refers to the need for *separate proceedings*, perhaps emphasizing the fact that we are not dealing with an appeal. It also said that the proceedings are based upon the allegation of fraud, and the purpose is to maintain "the integrity of the court process."[6]

The recent Australian decision of the High Court in *SZFDE v. Minister for Immigration and Citizenship* also accepted that fraud can be such as to vitiate the proceedings.[7] In that case, a family seeking asylum in Australia sought to have their case reconsidered by the Refugee Review Tribunal on the grounds that they had been defrauded by their lawyer into not appearing before the tribunal. The Minister for Immigration argued that any fraud that existed had been upon a party to the tribunal proceedings and not upon the tribunal itself and that such a "third party fraud" was not by or on the decision maker; it therefore did not affect the tribunal's decision. The High Court held that such a fraud was on the tribunal as well as upon the party, and was therefore effective to vitiate the decision.

## B. REOPENING AN APPEAL

It can be seen from what was said in *Burrell* that a reopening of an appeal may always be an alternative to what is being suggested here. We also see that *DJL* refers to the need for *separate proceedings*. Later in this chapter we discuss the

---

Gummow, Hayne, and Heydon JJ. [*D'Orta*]; *Taylor v. Lawrence*, [2002] EWCA Civ 90 also makes it clear that the existence of fraud might allow the reopening of an appeal.

5 *DJL v. The Central Authority*, [2000] HCA 17 at para. 94 [*DJL*] [citations omitted in original].

6 *Ibid.*

7 *SZFDE v. Minister for Immigration and Citizenship*, [2007] HCA 35 [*SZFDE*].

case of *R. v. Bolton Justices; Ex parte Scally*,[8] where those accused of a criminal offence entered a guilty plea and therefore had no right of appeal. There may be other circumstances where those convicted had not appealed and therefore would not have any right to reopen an appeal. In his work, referred to in Chapter 3, Gudjonsson details several cases where people, affected by drink, drugs, or mental incapacity, come to believe that they have committed a crime subsequently proven either not to have taken place or to have been committed by someone else. Baldwin and McConville have also detailed numerous cases where innocent people have plea-bargained and entered a guilty plea to obtain a lesser sentence.[9] In such cases where there has been no appeal or no right of appeal, the reopening of the appeal alternative is clearly not available.

## C. LINKS FROM AUSTRALIAN TO BRITISH CASES

In *SZFDE*, the Australian High Court considered some factors that may be of assistance in further cases. For example, it mentioned that in *Reddaway v. Banham*,[10] Lord MacNaghten spoke of the various guises in which fraud appears in the conduct of human affairs, by saying "fraud is infinite in variety." It also said the following text, expressed by Kerr in *Treatise on the Law of Fraud and Mistake* (1929), served as a corollary: "The fertility of man's invention in devising new schemes of fraud is so great, that the courts have always declined to define it . . . reserving to themselves the liberty to deal with it under whatever form it may present itself." The court discussed notions of fraud, with related notions of bad faith, abuse of power, and "*Wednesbury* unreasonableness."[11] It referred to the following observation in a leading English text as being in point: "These add very little to the true sense, and are hardly ever used to mean more than that some action is found to have a lawful or unlawful purpose."[12] It also contrasted those types of fraud in public law with the "red blooded" species of fraud that engages the common law. It noted that in *Farley (Aust.) Pty. Ltd. v. J.R. Alexander & Sons (Q) Pty. Ltd.*[13] it had said:

---

8 [1991] 1 Q.B. 537 [*Ex parte Scally*].

9 John Baldwin & Michael McConville, *Negotiated Justice: Pressures to Plead Guilty* (London: Martin Robertson, 1977).

10 *Reddaway v. Banham*, [1896] A.C. 199 at 221.

11 "*Wednesbury* unreasonableness" refers to the British case of *Associated Provincial Picture Houses v. Wednesbury Corporation*, [1948] 1 K.B. 223, where it was said that sometimes a decision is so unreasonable that no reasonable decision maker could have come to such a conclusion.

12 The court was referring to William Wade & Christopher Forsyth, *Administrative Law*, 9th ed. (Oxford: Oxford University Press, 2004) at 416.

13 (1946), 75 C.L.R. 487 at 493.

> Fraud is conduct which vitiates every transaction known to the law. It even vitiates a judgment of the court. It is an insidious disease, and if clearly proved spreads to and infects the whole transaction (*Jonesco v. Beard*[14]).

The High Court in *SZFDE* drew attention to the comment by Denning L.J. in *Lazarus Estates Ltd v. Beasley*:

> No court in this land will allow a person to keep an advantage which he has obtained by fraud. *No judgment of a court,* no order of a Minister, can be allowed to stand if it has been obtained by fraud. *Fraud unravels everything.* The court is careful not to find fraud unless it is distinctly pleaded and proved; but once it is proved, it *vitiates judgments,* contracts and all transactions whatsoever.[15]

The Court said that its approach would be as follows:

> Any application of a principle that "fraud unravels everything", requires consideration first of that which is to be "unravelled", and secondly of what amounts to "fraud" in the particular context. It then is necessary to identify the available curial remedy to effect the "unravelling".[16]

The Court also noted:

> It has been said in this Court that, except in very exceptional cases, fraud constituted by perjury by a witness or witnesses acting in concert is not a sufficient ground for setting aside a judgment.[17] The precept engaged here has been identified as that favouring the finality of litigation.[18]

It is clear that this consideration of the "finality principle" was restricted to the context of "civil actions and suits." However, as Graham Zellick has stated, "finality in civil proceedings has everything to commend it: finality in criminal proceedings, where liberty and reputation are at stake, is a singular evil."[19]

As the High Court pointed out, "a rather different trend has appeared in public law, particularly respecting the administration by superior courts of cer-

---

14 [1930] A.C. 298 at 301–2.

15 *Lazarus Estates Ltd. v. Beasley*, [1956] 1 Q.B. 702 at 712-13 [emphasis added], as discussed in *SZFDE*, above note 7 at para. 15.

16 *SZFDE*, *ibid.* at para. 29.

17 See the remarks of Windeyer J. in *McDonald v. McDonald* (1965), 113 C.L.R. 529 at 544, citing those of Williams J. in *Cabassi v. Vila* (1940), 64 C.L.R. 130 at 147-48.

18 *Owens Bank Ltd v. Bracco*, [1992] 2 A.C. 443 at 483. See also *D'Orta*, above note 4 at para. 43.

19 Graham Zellick, "Facing Up to Miscarriages of Justice" (2006) 31 Man. L.J. 555 at 556.

tiorari to supervise the exercise of jurisdiction by inferior courts and tribunals."[20] It went on to say that in *Craig v. South Australia*,[21] Brennan, Deane, Toohey, Gaudron, and McHugh JJ. had said of the scope of certiorari:

> Where available, certiorari is a process by which a superior court, in the exercise of original jurisdiction, supervises the acts of an inferior court or other tribunal. *It is not an appellate procedure* enabling either a general review of the order or decision of the inferior court or tribunal or a substitution of the order or decision which the superior court thinks should have been made. Where the writ runs, it merely enables the quashing of the impugned order or decision upon one or more of a number of distinct established grounds, most importantly, jurisdictional error, failure to observe some applicable requirement of procedural fairness, fraud and "error of law on the face of the record". Where the writ is sought on the ground of jurisdictional error, breach of procedural fairness or fraud, the superior court entertaining an application for certiorari can, subject to applicable procedural and evidentiary rules, take account of any relevant material placed before it.[22]

The Court in *SZFDE* pointed out that their Honours had noted that in this context "fraud" was used in a broad sense which encompasses bad faith.[23] It went on to say that so strong was the policy protecting the due administration of justice that a privative clause by which the legislature sought to exclude or attenuate the jurisdiction of superior courts to issue certiorari was ineffective to exclude the remedy where "manifest fraud" was shown on the part of the party which had obtained the order in the inferior court.[24]

Interestingly, the High Court pointed out that in the English case of *R. v. Wolverhampton Crown Court; Ex parte Crofts*[25] it was held that the double jeopardy rule had no application where the Queen's Bench Division granted certiorari to quash an order of acquittal obtained on the perjured evidence of the appellant to Quarter Sessions against his conviction by justices. The effect of certiorari was to leave standing the regularly obtained conviction. The High

---

20 *SZFDE*, above note 7 at para. 17.

21 (1995), 184 C.L.R. 163 [*Craig*].

22 *Ibid.* at para. 8 [emphasis added; footnotes omitted] as cited in *SZFDE*, above note 7 at para. 17.

23 *Craig, ibid.* at para. 8, n. 11.

24 *The Colonial Bank of Australasia v. Willan* (1874), L.R. 5 P.C. 417 at 442; *Minister for Immigration and Multicultural and Indigenous Affairs v. SGLB* (2004), 78 A.L.J.R. 992 at paras. 55-56 as discussed in *SZFDE*, above note 7 at para. 18.

25 [1983] 1 W.L.R. 204 at 207 [*Crofts*].

Court said that Mason and Brennan JJ. in *Davern v. Messel*[26] saw *Ex parte Crofts* as displaying a proper balance between the protection of the defendant *as the weaker party in a criminal case* and the interests of society in ensuring the due administration of justice.[27]

In *SZFDE* the High Court pointed out that in *Al-Mehdawi v. Secretary of State for the Home Department* Lord Bridge gave as an example of "the principle that fraud unravels everything" a line of authority which he identified as follows:

> In *R. v. Gillyard*[28] the court quashed by certiorari a conviction by justices shown to have been obtained by fraud and collusion. This was followed in *R. v. Recorder of Leicester*[29] and extended in *R. (Burns) v. County Court Judge of Tyrone*[30] to allow the quashing of an affiliation order obtained on the strength of perjured evidence of witnesses called to furnish the required corroboration of the evidence of the complainant, although it was not shown that the complainant herself was party to the perjury.[31]

The High Court in *SZFDE* then added that when extending certiorari to cases of "third party fraud" in *R. (Burns) v. County Court Judge of Tyrone*, Lord MacDermott L.C.J. dealt as follows with the submission that the perjury must be by a party or the party must be privy to it:

> The supervisory jurisdiction of this court is not at large; but the general aim of that jurisdiction is to promote the due administration of justice, and if a distinction is to be drawn between cases where a decision is procured by perjury and cases where a decision is procured by perjury to which one of the parties is privy, it ought to rest on some basis of principle. I am unable to discern any such basis here. Litigation between parties, whether civil or criminal, does not necessarily mean that there are not others anxious or interested to sway the issue one way or the other, and it would, I think, be a grave defect in the procedure of this court if one of these forms of fraud could be noticed but not the other. I can find no rational ground for the sort of discrimination which must prevail if we are to accede to the submission under discussion. If

---

26 (1984), 155 C.L.R. 21 at 58-59.

27 *SZFDE*, above note 7 at para. 18.

28 (1848), 12 Q.B. 527 [*Gillyard*].

29 [1947] K.B. 726 [*Ex parte Wood*].

30 [1961] N.I. 167 [*Burns*].

31 *SZFDE*, above note 7 at para. 19, referring to *R. v. Secretary of State for the Home Department; Ex parte Al-Mehdawi*, [1990] 1 A.C. 876 at 895 [*Ex parte Al-Mehdawi*].

> certiorari does not lie in such circumstances there is no other redress and an order undoubtedly founded on perjury remains effective.[32]

## D. THE DUE ADMINISTRATION OF JUSTICE

The High Court said that the concern with the due administration of justice manifested in these decisions has, in England, been adapted to the position occupied in the legal system by administrative bodies and tribunals. It gave as an example *R. v. Fulham, Hammersmith and Kensington Rent Tribunal; Ex parte Gormly* in which Lord Goddard C.J. said:

> . . . if some collusive proceedings were taken, it would amount to a fraud on the tribunal, and where a fraud was proved I have little doubt that this court could intervene if necessary by an order of certiorari to get rid of a decision which the tribunal had been misled into making.[33]

The High Court in *SZFDE* then pointed out that there is another practical aspect of fraud in public law that may tend in a particular case to set it apart from fraud in relation to civil suits in general. Often, a victim of it will have no useful remedy except to have the fraudulently affected result set aside and a fresh untainted hearing conducted. It noted that *Ainsworth v. Criminal Justice Commission* is an example of the inadequacy of a conventional remedy such as damages.[34] The same may apply to some proceedings before administrative tribunals, for example, an application under the *Freedom of Information Act 1982* (Cth.).

The High Court in *SZFDE* went on to point out that with respect to certiorari to quash summary convictions by reason, for example, of guilty pleas fraudulently induced by the conduct of police officers, the reasoning in the English authorities was applied in Australia in *R. v. The Justices at Biloela, Ex parte Marlow (No. 2)*.[35] It said that in a sense the police officers are "third parties" in this setting, albeit persons in authority or acting under colour of authority.[36]

The High Court in *SZFDE* noted that in a case of alleged fraud the court exercising judicial review may, subject to any applicable procedural and evi-

---

32 *SZFDE*, *ibid.* at para. 20, citing *Burns*, above note 30 at 172 [emphasis added].

33 *SZFDE*, *ibid.* at para. 21, citing *R. v. Fulham, Hammersmith and Kensington Rent Tribunal; Ex parte Gormly*, [1951] 2 All E.R. 1030 at 1034.

34 *SZFDE*, *ibid.* at para. 22, citing *Ainsworth v. Criminal Justice Commission* (1992), 175 C.L.R. 564.

35 [1983] 1 Q.R. 552.

36 *SZFDE*, above note 7 at para. 23.

dentiary rules, take account of any relevant material placed before it.[37] It said that while in *SZFDE* the person perpetrating the fraud was absent from the proceedings and a finding of fraud was a serious matter, the identification of the motives of that person in acting as he did "may be a matter of inference drawn from the available material."[38]

The High Court then concluded that the prevailing circumstances merited the description of the practice of fraud "on" the tribunal. The consequence of that, it said, was that the decision made by the tribunal is properly regarded, in law, *as no decision at all*. In the sense of the authorities, *the jurisdiction remains constructively unexercised*.[39] This understanding raises the interesting point as to whether the court is in effect "quashing" the purported decision or merely declaring that the purported decision is really no decision. As the High Court noted, French J. (in dissenting) in the intermediate appeal had correctly emphasized that there are sound reasons of policy why a person whose conduct before an administrative tribunal has been affected to the detriment of that person by bad or negligent advice or some other mishap should not be heard to complain that the detriment vitiates the decision made.[40] The outcome in the present appeal, it was said, stands *apart from* and *above* such considerations.[41]

## E. PUBLIC LAW—CRIMINAL

The question that now arises is how such principles might translate into the conduct of criminal proceedings that have been vitiated by fraud. A related matter which appears not to have been explored (at least in Australia) concerns the powers to quash a conviction *in the absence of a right of appeal*—a power that has been well used in the United Kingdom in the very group of cases to which the High Court referred in its reasons in *SZFDE*.

The transition from more traditional public law cases to criminal law cases has eventuated in the United Kingdom and, it is suggested, there is no reason in principle why the same extension would not be applicable in Australia and in Canada. In *R. v. West Sussex Quarter Sessions; Ex parte Albert and Maud Johnson Trust Ltd.* it was accepted that in the circumstances of that case, there

---

37 *Ibid.* at para. 38.

38 See the discussion of principle by Lindgren J. in *Wati v. Minister for Immigration and Ethnic Affairs* (1996), 71 F.C.R. 103 at 113–14.

39 *SZFDE*, above note 7 at paras. 51–52.

40 *SZFDE v. Minister for Immigration and Citizenship* (2006), 154 F.C.R. 365 at 399. It should be noted that French J. is now Chief Justice of the High Court of Australia.

41 *Ibid.* at para. 53.

was no right of appeal except on a point of law, which did not apply there.[42] Lord Denning said that if a decision had been arrived at because the court was misled by false evidence or there was fresh evidence that vitiated the decision, then as a matter of *principle* there should be some way of setting the decision aside and ordering a new trial.[43] In these circumstances, he said, the only way to achieve that goal would be by way of certiorari, which would have the effect of setting the decision aside. As he said, "It is not an appeal." He made it clear, however, that despite it not being an appeal the following held true:

> If the inferior court exceeds its jurisdiction, or makes an error of law which appears on the face of the record, or if it is affected by bias, or contravenes the rules of natural justice, certiorari will lie to bring up the record.[44]

Lord Denning said that there is ample authority for holding that, where there is evidence that the decision of the inferior court has been obtained by fraud of a party or by collusion, the court will order it to be brought up and will quash it.[45] The same would apply if a party has been guilty of perjury.[46] It would also apply where one of the *witnesses* had committed perjury.[47] Previous cases had allowed certiorari only for fraud or perjury, but as Lord Denning reasoned, a decision may well be vitiated by mistake as much as by fraud (or perjury). "A witness may say something which is entirely wrong—fraudulently knowing it is false—or incorrectly believing it to be true." If the court believes the witness and bases its decision upon that evidence, then

> . . . on discovering the untruth the decision should be set aside—without embarking on an enquiry whether he was fraudulent or not.[48]

Lord Denning pointed out that where an accused person has been convicted as a result of an error, it matters little to him whether the error was engaged in deliberately or inadvertently by either the police or the prosecutors:

> In such cases the fresh evidence is admitted by affidavit to prove the fraud or mistake. It is proved by something that has happened since the trial. Those

---

42 [1973] 3 All E.R. 289 [*Ex parte Albert and Maud Johnson Trust*].

43 *Ibid.* at 295, Lord Denning, dissenting as to whether fresh evidence discovered after the close of proceedings could be a ground of an order for certiorari; see *Ex parte Scally*, above note 8 at 551, Watkins L.J.

44 *Ex parte Albert and Maud Johnson Trust*, *ibid.* at 296.

45 *Ibid.*, citing *Gillyard*, above note 28.

46 *Ibid.* at 296, citing *Ex parte Wood*, above note 29.

47 *Ibid.*, citing *Burns*, above note 30.

48 *Ibid.* at 296.

> cases are in my opinion only instances of the wide principle upon which fresh evidence is admitted: and that is, when it is necessary to do justice between the parties.[49]

Several examples serve to illustrate the point. *R. v. Leyland Magistrates; Ex parte Hawthorn*[50] referred to *Ex parte Albert and Maud Johnson Trust* to say that one cannot apply for certiorari so that fresh evidence may be called upon a retrial. The claim, it was said, had to involve the denial of the benefit of the rules of natural justice. *Ex parte Hawthorn* involved the conviction of Hawthorn for driving without due care and attention. Afterwards, Hawthorn's insurance company received particulars of two further witnesses whose details had not been provided to him by the time of the trial. He appealed to quash the conviction, claiming that the failure by the police to notify him of the existence of the witnesses amounted to a failure of natural justice. The appeal court (Lord Widgery C.J.) referred to *Halsbury's Laws*, stating that certiorari is the appropriate remedy where a conviction has been obtained by collusion or fraud or where an error appears on the face of the proceedings.[51] The Chief Justice said that there was no doubt that an application could be made by certiorari to set aside an order on the basis that the tribunal failed to observe the rules of natural justice. However, here it was accepted that the police prosecutors, not the tribunal, had made the error. The Chief Justice concluded:

> However, if fraud, collusion, perjury and such like matters not affecting the tribunal themselves justify an application for certiorari to quash the conviction, if all those matters are to have that effect, then we cannot say that the failure of the prosecution which in this case has prevented the tribunal from giving the defendant a fair trial should not rank in the same category .... Fully recognizing the fact that the blame falls on the prosecutor and not on the tribunal, we think that it is a matter which should result in the conviction being quashed.[52]

May and Tudor Evans JJ. agreed.

*R. v. Crown Court at Knightsbridge; Ex parte Goonatilleke*[53] involved a conviction that had been obtained as a result of perjured evidence. It was reheard

---

49 *Ibid.*

50 *R. v. Leyland Justices; Ex parte Hawthorn*, [1979] 1 Q.B. 283 [*Ex parte Hawthorn*].

51 *Ibid.* at 286.

52 *Ibid.*

53 *R. v. Crown Court at Knightsbridge; Ex parte Goonatilleke*, [1985] 2 All E.R. 498 [*Ex parte Goonatilleke*].

by way of judicial review to obtain certiorari to quash the conviction on the basis that it had been obtained by fraud. The court found that a witness had chosen to commit perjury by concealing evidence about his credibility. The concealment amounted to a fraudulent misrepresentation of a material fact (that he was honest and truthful) and its purpose was to deprive the court of the opportunity to make a full and public assessment of the value of his evidence. The court found the applicant had lost a real chance of acquittal because of the witness's perjury. Lord Justice Watkins (who has played an important role in this line of cases) said:

> It is beyond doubt that it is the duty of the prosecution to give that kind of information about a witness to the defence if, of course, they are aware of it. It is simply unbelievable, if the defence here had known about Tanikie in this respect, that they would not have cross-examined him about it, with probably telling effect. Counsel for the applicant submits that a matter going to the credit of a witness in a criminal case cannot be said to be collateral to the vital issue, that is to say guilt or otherwise, especially where, as here, the witness in question provides the only evidence on that issue. In the circumstances of this case I wholly agree with him. Tanikie's evidence was indispensable to the prosecution and his credit, therefore, is of the highest importance.[54]

It was said that the trial had been vitiated by the misconduct of the witness or by his perjury or fraud in suppressing the truth of what had occurred. His character at the time of the trial as well as the use made of it was important. Usefully, Watkins L.J. explained the historical development of the court's right to interfere with a conviction, and he referred to the following cases:

In *Gillyard* (cited with approval in *SZFDE*) Coleridge J. had said that the conviction had been

> . . . a fraud and mockery, the result of conspiracy and subornation of perjury. When the Court observes such dishonest practices, it will interfere, although judgment has been given . . . . I think no honest man ought to think it beneath him, or a hardship upon him, to answer upon affidavit a charge of dishonesty made upon affidavit against him. If a man, when such a serious accusation is preferred against him, will not deny it, he must not complain if the case is taken *pro confesso*.[55]

54 *Ibid.* at 502–3. See also *Cooley v. The State of Western Australia*, [2005] WASCA 160.
55 *Gillyard*, above note 28 at 966.

Lord Justice Watkins then referred to *Ex parte Wood* where Goddard C.J. said he approved of what had been said in *Gillyard*, and he also applied what Lord Coleridge had said in that case.[56]

Lord Justice Watkins cited *R. v. Kent Justices; Ex parte Ashford* where the court said it would quash an order of an inferior court on the basis of fraud where the fraud was clear and manifest.[57] That court said the power to quash an order cannot be used where there is simply a dispute about the facts.

Lord Justice Watkins, then discussing *Ex parte Albert and Maud Johnson Trust*, referred to the majority view that certiorari was limited to cases where it was shown there had been "defects or irregularities" at the trial which vitiated the proceedings.[58]

Lord Justice Watkins rounded off his review with *Burns* (also cited in *SZF-DE*), where Lord MacDermott L.C.J. (Northern Ireland) held that the fraud and perjury alleged did not need to be that of one of the parties to the proceedings. It could be committed by a witness other than the parties themselves.[59]

Having considered these cases in *Ex parte Goonatilleke*, Watkins L.J. went on to say that De Smith in *Judicial Review of Administrative Action* stated that grounds apart from fraud (such as breach of natural justice) may give rise to this type of relief (certiorari) and that breach of the rules of natural justice must be established by affidavit. "The affidavits of the applicant's solicitor will do for that purpose in this case." The witness in question had been a police officer for a short time:

> Albeit his service in the Metropolitan police was comparatively short lived, I do not doubt that it must have made him aware of the importance of evidence of bad character in criminal proceedings. It would have been an elementary part of his early training. The applicant was entitled to know the unsavoury part of the character of his accuser and he, Tanikie, the only person in court to have made that known to him, deliberately contrived to keep him in ignorance . . . I see no essential difference in the unusual circumstances of this case between Tanikie's conduct and the conduct of the prosecution in professional hands knowingly to fail to provide the defence with evidence of a previous conviction of a witness.[60]

---

56 *Ex parte Wood*, above note 29.
57 *R. v. Kent Justices; Ex parte Ashford (No. 2)*, [1956] 1 Q.B. 167.
58 *Ex parte Goonatilleke*, above note 53 at 506.
59 *Burns*, above note 30.
60 *Ex parte Goonatilleke*, above note 53 at 506.

By being denied the ability to cross-examine on such matters, the applicant had been denied the opportunity for a fair trial. Lord Justice Watkins said that natural justice had been denied in this case by the witness's "scandalous and wilful conduct."[61] He said that the applicant was entitled to know and put to use the issues going to the credibility of the witness who was much more than a mere witness; he not only intended that the applicant be prosecuted—but he ensured that he was. His conduct "was conscious and malevolent. He was bent on securing the applicant's conviction and went about it unscrupulously."[62]

In *Ex parte Scally* a number of people had been arrested and charged with driving while having excess alcohol in their systems.[63] Each had given a sample of blood for testing, and the results showed that each was over the prescribed limit. The accused entered guilty pleas. It was later discovered that the swabs that had been used in the taking of blood samples had contained alcohol (ethanol). As no point of law was involved in their convictions, those convicted had no right of appeal. They therefore applied for judicial review of the convictions. The question then arose as to whether the court had jurisdiction to grant an order to quash the convictions on the basis that the trial had been flawed by the use of unreliable evidence or the suppression of reliable evidence. Lord Justice Watkins acknowledged the argument that the circumstances were so unfair as to amount to a breach of natural justice or were "analogous to fraud."[64] He also acknowledged that it had been argued that the court accepted jurisdiction in analogous cases where valuable evidence had not been disclosed without fraud on the part of those concerned.[65]

Lord Justice Watkins recognized that there was no process of appeal available *and that the prerogative of mercy is very difficult in some cases*. He said that the fault in this case was that of the police, and in the court's view, the police are part of the prosecution process. He referred with approval to *R. v. Birmingham Crown Court; Ex parte Ricketts*.[66] There it was said that the prosecution does not refer to any particular body or group but includes all those responsible for the conduct of the prosecution. That can involve the police as well as the

61 *Ibid.* at 505.

62 *Ibid.* at 505.

63 *Ex parte Scally*, above note 8.

64 *Ibid.* at 556.

65 Here, Watkins L.J. referred to *Ex parte Hawthorn*, above note 50; *R. v. Kingston-upon-Thames Justices; Ex parte Khanna*, [1986] R.T.R. 364 [*Ex parte Khanna*]; *Ex parte Goonatilleke*, above note 53; *R. v. Liverpool Crown Court; Ex parte Roberts*, [1986] Crim. L.R. 622.

66 Unreported (8 June 1990), Farquharson J.

prosecution service: "They are collectively, whether one is responsible for the other or not, the prosecution for purposes of this section."[67]

Lord Justice Watkins dealt at some length with *Ex parte Hawthorn* and the comments by Lord Widgery C.J. when he had said that if fraud, collusion, and perjury justify certiorari, then a case where the prosecutor prevented the tribunal from giving the accused a fair trial should rank in the same category.[68] Lord Justice Watkins referred to Lord Bridge's analysis of *Ex parte Hawthorn* in *R. v. Secretary of State for the Home Department; Ex parte Al-Mehdawi* (also cited in *SZFDE*) in suggesting that the suppression of the truth had the same effect as putting forward a falsity and thus distorted the process leading to the conviction.[69] He pointed out that in *Ex parte Albert and Maud Johnson Trust*, all of the judges accepted that fraud or perjury would vitiate the proceedings.[70]

Lord Justice Watkins continued his exposition in *Ex parte Scally* by looking at the judgment in *Ex parte Goonatilleke*. He said, "In my view, *Ex parte Goonatilleke* was clearly a case 'analogous to fraud'." He said that in *Ex parte Khanna* he had already expressed his agreement with Orr L.J. in *Ex parte Albert and Maud Johnson Trust* that the intention was not to limit the grounds to fraud. He said that grounds other than fraud (on the authority of *Ex parte Al-Mehdawi*[71]) can be regarded as "irregularities at the trial" so as to invoke the jurisdiction, "provided that they are analogous to fraud."[72] He repeated his own comments from *Ex parte Khanna* as follows:

> It would be a monstrous injustice if this court was disabled from bringing down a conviction which was obtained in circumstances where it should have been apparent to the prosecutor that there was no case against the applicant . . . .[73]

Lord Justice Watkins pointed out that it had been argued that any tinkering with the boundaries of this important jurisdiction would put in peril the well-established principles of finality and certainty in litigation, outside the boundaries of fault on the part of the tribunal or fraud or collusion on the part of the prosecutor. But he went on to say that *the overriding principle* must be to ensure that "justice be done" and any principle that stands in its way must be

---

67 *Ex parte Scally*, above note 8 at 549.

68 *Ibid.* at 550, citing *Ex parte Albert and Maud Johnson Trust*, above note 42 at 285–86.

69 *Ex parte Al-Mehdawi*, above note 31, cited by Watkins L.J. in *Ex parte Scally*, *ibid.* at 551.

70 *Ex parte Scally*, *ibid.* at 552, citing Orr L.J. in *Ex parte Albert and Maud Johnson Trust*, above note 42 at 298.

71 Above note 31.

72 Lord Justice Watkins in *Ex parte Scally*, above note 8 at 554.

73 Lord Justice Watkins in *ibid.* at 553, citing his judgment in *Ex parte Khanna*, above note 65 at 371.

carefully examined and done so without giving undue weight to the floodgates argument.[74]

As Lord Justice Watkins pointed out, in a case such as this, the accused can have no possible way of knowing that the procedures contained some hidden error. If the analyst's certificate contained some hidden untruth, then its admission into evidence would be akin to perjury, although unwittingly committed. He said that to deprive an accused of an opportunity to establish a complete defence to a charge was conduct analogous to fraud, collusion, or perjury. This was, he thought, a classic case where the supervisory role of the court was required to be exercised.[75]

There has been much discussion of the role of certiorari which applies where a superior court is reviewing a conviction of an inferior court. Obviously, analogous principles must apply where the original conviction was obtained in a superior court. Much in what has been said supports the view that the important matter is to set aside the decision in question. If the appellate court has power to set aside a decision of a magistrate's court on the basis that it was obtained by fraud, in the absence of a right of appeal, then *a fortiori* it must have the authority to set aside a decision of a higher level trial court which has been obtained in similar circumstances. If, in effect, such a decision was "no decision at all," then the greater the authority of the misled court, the greater the evil that has been perpetrated and the necessity to declare it to be so. The principle that form must not be seen to prevail over substance in the presence of a fraud upon the system is obviously of more significance where the fraud has been perpetrated upon a superior court rather than an inferior court.

The question that then arises is whether the application for review of certain issues should be addressed to the trial court or to the intermediate appellate court. In *Heron v. The Queen*[76] in the Australian High Court, Kirby J. spoke of the primacy of the High Court in correcting errors; however, he also spoke of the importance of the trial and of the function of the Court of Criminal Appeal. He remarked on the value of ensuring the availability of the consideration of questions of law and fact by the intermediate court of appeal. He also commented on the respect for the special experience of the intermediate court judges, both at trial and in the appeal.

It is argued here that there is a sensible distinction between the role of the final appellate court in *developing* the policy of the law in relation to errors

74 *Ex parte Scally*, *ibid.* at 555.

75 *Ibid.* at 556.

76 *Heron v. The Queen*, [2003] HCA 17.

and miscarriages of justice, and the *implementation* of those policies by the intermediate appellate courts. In cases where fraud, deceit, or manifest error are being asserted in relation to the conduct of the criminal trial, the court best suited to settling the factual issues and determining whether such vitiating factors have occurred is the intermediate appellate court. It might even be argued that an application in relation to a claim of fraud should be made to the court in which the fraudulent decision was obtained, and preferably to the judge who was the subject of the fraudulent evidence.

## F. INHERENT POWER

The power of the court to set aside a conviction on the basis of fraud and in the absence of a right of appeal is said to arise from the "inherent power" of the court. Lacey has described the nature of this power.[77] She points out that Jacob explained

> . . . the essential character of a superior court of law necessarily involves that it should be invested with a power to maintain its authority and to prevent its process being obstructed and abused. Such a power is intrinsic in a superior court; it is its very life-blood, its very essence, its immanent attribute. Without such a power, the court would have form but would lack substance. The jurisdiction, which is inherent in a superior court of law, is that which enables it to fulfil itself as a court of law. The juridical basis of this jurisdiction is therefore the authority of the judiciary to uphold, to protect and to fulfil the judicial function of administering justice according to law in a regular, orderly and effective manner.[78]

According to Jacob, the inherent jurisdiction may be seen as an independent and separate basis of jurisdiction possessed by superior courts of record. Its essential function is to provide such courts with an array of powers necessary to protect their capacity to administer justice and to retain their very nature as superior courts. It constitutes that residual or reserve source of powers "which the court may draw upon as necessary whenever it is just or equitable to do so, and in particular to ensure the observance of the due process of law, to prevent

---

77 Wendy Lacey, "Inherent Jurisdiction, Judicial Power and Implied Guarantees under Chapter III of the Constitution" (2003) 31 Federal Law Review 2.

78 Isaac H. Jacob, "The Inherent Jurisdiction of the Court" (1970) 23 Curr. Legal Probs. 23 at 27–28 [citations omitted].

improper vexation or oppression, to do justice between the parties and to secure a fair trial between them."[79]

It is clear that a superior court's inherent jurisdiction derives independently of statute or other rule of law and arises from its very nature as a superior court of record. This distinction was discussed by Menzies J. in *R. v. Forbes; Ex parte Bevan* as follows:

> Inherent jurisdiction is not something derived by implication from statutory provisions conferring particular jurisdiction; if such a provision is to be considered as conferring more than is actually expressed that further jurisdiction is conferred by implication according to accepted standards of statutory construction and it would be inaccurate to describe it as "inherent jurisdiction", which as the name indicates, requires no authorizing provision.[80]

As Lacey says, it is difficult to list in a comprehensive manner the array of powers that fall within the ambit of a court's inherent jurisdiction. These powers are many and varied, and are subject to variation in nature and scope, both over time and between different cases. Several commentators, however, have attempted to list some of the powers, and Keith Mason classified each power according to the particular function of inherent jurisdiction to which the power relates.[81] Examples would include the following powers:

- to remedy breaches of the rules of natural justice;
- to correct, vary, or extend an order to prevent injustice;
- to dismiss an action for want of prosecution, including cases where a prolonged or inordinate delay means that the defendant is likely to suffer prejudice;
- to compel observance of the court's process and obedience of and compliance with its orders;
- to punish for contempt of court, including any conduct calculated to interfere with the due administration of justice; and
- to aid superior courts and aid or control inferior courts and tribunals.

## G. CONCLUSION

Nothing in the statutory provisions prevents an appellate court from accepting jurisdiction where a miscarriage of justice is asserted. This miscarriage of justice

79 *Ibid.* at 51.
80 [1972] HCA 34.
81 Keith Mason, "The Inherent Jurisdiction of the Court" (1983) 57 Austl. L. J. 449 at 458.

may have come about because the court at trial was misled by fraud, deceit, or manifest error.

When both the UK and Australian experiences are taken together, the case for a more interventionist role by the criminal appeal courts is compelling. The development of the caselaw in the United Kingdom makes clear that appellate courts have a *duty* to ensure that their processes are not misused. Those cases can then be placed in the context of recent decisions of the High Court of Australia. The Australian decisions state that fundamental conditions must be observed in order for a trial to be considered fair and that the court has the duty to ensure that the public is confident in the judicial process.

It is therefore important to clarify the principles that apply to reconsidering matters by the intermediate appellate courts in accordance with the principles that have been outlined here. Yes, the petition procedure in both Australia and Canada should be improved, and the case for a criminal cases review commission, such as that in the United Kingdom, is compelling; however, there persists a need for *all* courts to be able to correct frauds that may have been perpetrated on them. This need for correction is especially great when the result of fraud is a miscarriage of justice and an unreliable guilty verdict.

PART TWO

# The Reality

CHAPTER 7

# Investigations and Prosecutions

In this and the next two chapters, we will look at some of the major wrongful conviction cases that have occurred in Britain, Canada, and Australia. The important thing to bear in mind is that if the rules (as stated in Part One) had been followed, then we would not have much to report on in this section of the book. Regrettably, the reality is that there have been far too many non-compliant cases—and those included in this section are only a few. It is fair to say, from the cases we discuss here, that some police, lawyers, scientists, and doctors have engaged in conduct that ranges from the scandalous to the seriously deficient. While we accept that this is not a fair description of the majority of such people, the fact that *any* deficiencies of that nature have occurred means that we should be alert to the possibility of them.

In this chapter, we look at the criminal cases from Britain, Canada, and Australia where serious errors have occurred at the investigation and prosecution stages. Some of the conduct we report on, such as that by the West Midlands Serious Crime Squad (involving as it did the torture of suspects) is clearly abhorrent. Other conduct, such as the premature or erroneous targeting of suspects, can be seen as the result of an imperfect understanding of role responsibilities and procedural errors. It is important for us to consider not only how they occurred, but why they were allowed to continue as long as they did.

One important factor to emerge from our study is that individual cases invariably involve errors covering a range of issues and emanating from a number of the specialists involved at different stages of the investigation. This finding suggests that errors which originate with investigators might well influence forensic scientists and the forensic pathologists (and vice versa). Strictly speaking, this relationship ought not to occur. The scientists are supposed to maintain their objectivity. Their role is neither to assist nor hinder the securing of a conviction — but to report accurately what they find.

Bruce MacFarlane, in trying to understand this phenomenon, attributes it to a combination of factors that he describes as "predisposing circumstances." Predisposing circumstances include horrific crimes, public pressures to charge the perpetrator, and accused who are marginalized or unpopular.[1] While objective rules govern investigations, prosecutions, and trials, subjective factors can influence how those rules are understood or applied. The various people involved bring their own perspectives, experiences, aspirations, and fears to the decisions they make. Those perspectives can be influenced by public pressure which inevitably arises in cases seen to be particularly alarming, whether it be the threat to public safety (as in the IRA bombing cases) or the threat to shared values (as in the deaths of babies or young children). The concerns are exacerbated when the person suspected is perceived to be "odd" in some way: Lindy and Michael Chamberlain in Australia were "Seventh Day Adventists"; Donald Marshall in Canada was a young Aboriginal person; and Barry George, who was convicted of shooting Jill Dando in Britain, was a fantasist who stalked and photographed hundreds of women.[2] It is possible in such circumstances for those representing the public interest to perceive that they must succeed even if doing so involves bending the rules. Being a team player can be closely aligned with "noble cause corruption."

So, the scientists and doctors, who should be the first check upon investigatory theories that are going off course, might well be caught up in the aversion to terrible crimes, and their potential to assist in their speedy and effective resolution. Public alarm becomes public pressure to obtain a result. In those circumstances, a *likely* suspect might well be promoted to *the* suspect before the evidence warrants it. Once that happens, an investigation might be difficult to turn around, and as more time and money become invested in pursuing a particular result, tunnel vision or "confirmation bias" can set in. "Confirmation bias" refers to a process where evidence that is inconsistent with the prime suspect's guilt is either not collected or interpreted by the investigators in a manner consistent with the suspect's guilt.

Equally, of course, scientists and doctors can behave badly without there being any encouragement from someone else. In such circumstances, the in-

1 Bruce MacFarlane, "Convicting the Innocent: A Triple Failure of the Justice System" (2006) 31 Man. L.J. 403 at 435.

2 These cases are discussed in some detail in this chapter and in Chapter 8.

vestigators should provide the necessary check in the system for faulty evidence and opinions emanating from those sources. Where that does not occur, one might expect that the prosecutors or the defence lawyers will detect correctable error where it occurs. Eventually, one might look to the judge to be the gatekeeper for what counts as admissible evidence. As we will see throughout these chapters, though, on occasion, manifestly inadequate evidence has surmounted each and every one of these barriers. Miscarriages of justices will often be the product of the failure of multiple systems. They will involve failures of the police, forensic scientists, prosecutors, defence counsel, judges and juries, and appellate courts.

Clearly, consideration will have to be given to systemic improvements to ensure that such occurrences are reduced as much as possible in the future. Before that can be considered, however, we need to develop an appreciation of what we mean by "detectable" or "correctable" error.

## A. THE POLICE

It is common for the police to provide written guidance to officers about how to conduct investigations.[3] The usual police manual provisions are the *minimum* operating standards that crime-scene examiners must follow in their investigations. They spell out the command and responsibility issues, such as who is in charge of each situation and who does what. Manuals cover matters such as the securing of the scene, the role and responsibilities of the crime-scene investigators, preparations and procedures for the examination of crime scenes, and the preservation of evidence, communications (codes and procedures), and case management. They deal with practical topics, such as photography, equipment, and supplies required (such as adhesive tapes, fingerprint powders, plastic bags, gloves, overalls, cameras, and film). They state that the police are trained to treat every unexplained death as suspicious (a homicide) until an explanation either confirms or removes the suspicion. Indeed, the South

---

3 For example, South Australia Police, *Crime Scene and Forensic Procedures Manual* (Adelaide: South Australia Police, 1996); Gerald Uelman, ed., *Final Report, California Commission on the Fair Administration of Justice* (Santa Clara, CA: The Commission, 2008) sets out guidelines for investigators in dealing with eyewitness identifications, false confessions, informant testimony, scientific evidence, and the responsibilities of defence and prosecution lawyers; Robin Napper in Australia refers to the *European Crime Scene Management, Good Practice Manual*, developed in 1997, adopted by all countries in the European Community to identify good practice for the management of crime scenes; see his affidavit referred to in *R. v. Stafford*, [2009] QCA 407. The references in this section are taken from the South Australian manual.

Australia Police *Crime Scene and Forensic Procedures Manual* states specifically: "Initially (regardless of the probable category) crime scene investigators must *treat every death as a homicide* to ensure that no vital evidence is lost."[4] Yet, on a regular basis, events are reported in the media stating that a dead person has been found, that the police are still investigating, and that the police do not regard the death as suspicious.

### 1) Investigations

Police investigations are often found to be at the heart of wrongful convictions. It is clear that any expert (and by this we include police investigators) must have their hunches, instincts, questions, and theories as part of the process of directing them to facts, issues, and people who may be relevant to their inquiries. As Karl Popper put it in the theory of science, a hungry dog will divide the world into things that it can eat and things that it can't; a frightened person sees the world in terms of places of safety and other places.[5] Lord Runciman, in speaking of his work on the Royal Commission on Criminal Justice,[6] said, "I brought with me a bundle of preconceptions derived from my upbringing, or my schoolteachers, or the media."[7] However, the process can become unbalanced when the investigator develops some form of intellectual or emotional attachment to some preferred outcome, irrespective of the available data. Known as "tunnel vision," this has been the cause of significant miscarriages of justice. Sometimes, the impetus to act inappropriately might arise from the sense of moral panic or the hue and cry precipitated by outrages against individuals or groups of people.[8] Offences against children and civilian bombings are the types of situations that have commonly given rise to the greatest pressures upon investigators to identify and apprehend the wrongdoers.[9] Police

---

4 *Crime Scene and Forensic Procedures Manual*, *ibid.* at Part C(5).

5 K.R. Popper, *Conjectures and Refutations*, 4th ed. (London: Routledge and Kegan Paul, 1972). On Popper and related issues of perception, see Robert N. Moles, *Definition and Rule in Legal Theory* (Oxford: Blackwell, 1987) c. 6, "Epistemology—The Common Ground."

6 UK, *The Report of the Royal Commission on Criminal Justice*, Cm 2263 (London: HMSO, 1993) [Runciman Report].

7 W.G. Runciman, "An Outsider's View of the Criminal Justice System" (1994) 57 Mod. L. Rev. at 1. It is interesting to note that this important commission was headed by a person with no previous legal experience.

8 Kathryn Campbell & Myriam Denov, "The Burden of Innocence: Coping with a Wrongful Imprisonment" (2004) 46 Canadian Journal of Criminology and Criminal Justice 139 at 143.

9 In Australia in 2008, the Clarke Inquiry into the arrest and charge of Dr. Mohamed Haneef in relation to terrorism found that the investigation was seriously flawed be-

work can also promote reliance on stereotypes. A decision that a suspect is guilty can be influenced by stereotypes and can lead to both direct police misconduct in the collection of evidence as well as subtle and not so subtle pressure being placed on witnesses.[10]

Tunnel vision and confirmation bias can take on less insidious forms: evidence may be interpreted in a manner that makes the job of investigators who have perhaps focused on the wrong suspect easier. The high volume of cases through our criminal justice systems encourages many within them to take shortcuts.

It is also worth emphasizing that in Britain the standard to be applied in any post-conviction review (and investigators often become involved in re-investigations) is the *current* standard of good investigation or good practice—not the standard that might have prevailed at the time of the trial:

> . . . we judge the conduct of the investigation of the case, the conduct of the trial, the directions to the jury and the reliability of the evidence on which the jury acted in accordance with *the standards that this court now applies* . . . the practices followed and the reliability of evidence thus obtained are to be judged by *present* standards.[11]

One of the most potent checks or balances to an investigator who has allowed commitment or enthusiasm to cloud his or her judgment is the bracing air provided by a prosecutor who declines to prosecute the case because of deficiencies with the evidence.

## B. PROSECUTIONS

As we mentioned in Chapter 2, all three jurisdictions recognize that the prosecutor has special duties to see that justice is done and not to act as a pure adversary.[12] Lack of full disclosure of relevant material in the prosecutor's possession has been an important factor in many wrongful convictions. The im-

---

cause an investigating officer formed a view based on tunnel vision; Matthew Schultz, "Mohamed Haneef Wants Apology, Compensation" *Herald Sun* (23 December 2008). See also Keith A. Findley & Michael Scott, "The Multiple Dimensions of Tunnel Vision in Criminal Cases" (2006) 2 Wis. L. Rev. 291 at 326.

10 Diane L. Martin, "The Police Role in Wrongful Convictions: An International Comparative Study" in Saundra Westervelt & John Humphrys, eds., *Wrongly Convicted: Perspectives on Failed Justice* (New Brunswick, NJ: Rutgers, 2001) at 88*ff.*

11 *R. v. O'Brien & Ors*, [2000] EWCA Crim 3 [emphasis added].

12 *Boucher v. The Queen*, [1955] S.C.R. 16 [*Boucher*]. The criteria set out in this case have also been applied in Britain and Australia.

portance of such disclosure is now recognized by the courts in Canada and by Parliament in Britain and Australia. In 1991, the Supreme Court of Canada in *R. v. Stinchcombe*[13] said:

> The right to make full answer and defence is one of the pillars of criminal justice on which we heavily depend to ensure that the innocent are not convicted. Recent events have demonstrated that the erosion of this right due to non-disclosure was an important factor in the conviction and incarceration of an innocent person. In the *Royal Commission on the Donald Marshall, Jr., Prosecution*, Vol. 1: *Findings and Recommendations* (1989) (the "Marshall Commission Report"), the Commissioners found that prior inconsistent statements were not disclosed to the defence. This was an important contributing factor in the miscarriage of justice which occurred and led the Commission to state that "anything less than complete disclosure by the Crown falls short of decency and fair play" (Vol. 1 at p. 238).[14]

The Supreme Court then went on to set out the broad constitutional right an accused has to disclosure of all relevant information regardless of whether the evidence was classified as exculpatory and regardless of whether it related to a person that the prosecutor proposed to call as witness.

In Britain, the courts also articulated broad disclosure rights in response to some notorious miscarriages of justice.[15] Parliament enacted the *Criminal Procedure and Investigations Act 1996*[16] which codified but somewhat restricted disclosure requirements. The *Criminal Justice Act 2003*[17] made clear that the prosecution had continuing requirements to disclose material that might reasonably be capable of undermining the prosecution's case, but unfortunately this continuing disclosure ends with a conviction. In the Canadian case of Donald Marshall Jr., a critical piece of exculpatory information was given to the police shortly after Marshall's conviction, but it was not disclosed to Marshall who served eleven years in prison.

In his study of the first ten years of the CCRC, Laurie Elks lists thirty-one cases where non-disclosure was a ground for the CCRC referring the case back to the Court of Appeal.[18] A wide range of material was not disclosed to the

---

13 *R. v. Stinchcombe*, [1991] 3 S.C.R. 326 [*Stinchcombe*].

14 *Ibid.* at 336.

15 *Judith Ward v. The Queen* (1993), 96 Crim. App. R. 1 [*Ward*].

16 (U.K.), 1996, c. 25, s. 3.

17 (U.K.), 2003, c. 44, s. 37.

18 Laurie Elks, *Righting Miscarriages of Justice? Ten Years of the Criminal Cases Review Commission* (London: Justice, 2008) at 309–11 [Elks].

accused in these cases, including information relevant to the credibility of witnesses, the presence of alternative suspects, medical reports, and confidential material that was the subject of a public interest immunity order. Elks notes that the CCRC can have access to undisclosed material held by public authorities, but also warns that it cannot review such material in all cases.[19] Clearly, it is best for there to be proper disclosure in the first place.

## C. THE BRITISH EXPERIENCE

While individual murders and atrocities are bad enough, the terrorist bombings by the Irish Republican Army (IRA) in mainland Britain, in the 1970s, gave rise to great alarm. Fuelled by public concern and resulting pressure on investigators to get those responsible, the police investigation swung into action. The following IRA bombing cases illustrate how police misconduct can give rise to false confessions and the effect that tunnel vision can have on investigators, prosecutors, and forensic scientists in failing to make full disclosure.

### 1) IRA Bombing—The Birmingham Six

In 1974 two bombs exploded at public houses in Birmingham, killing twenty-one people and injuring 162 others.[20] The previous week, a person called McDade had been killed when a bomb he was planting at the Coventry telephone exchange went off accidentally. Six people (McIlkenny, Callaghan, Hill, Hunter, Walker, and Power) who subsequently became known as the "Birmingham Six" had decided to attend the McDade funeral in Belfast. All except Hill had arranged to meet at the railway station in Birmingham, get the train to Heysham, and then take the night ferry to Belfast. As it turned out, five of them (including Hill) travelled on the train together, playing cards.

At 8:18 p.m. the first bomb exploded at the Mulberry Bush pub near the station. A few minutes later the other bomb went off at The Tavern in the Town 300 yards (about 274 m) away. A third bomb, at Barclays Bank, failed to explode. The pub bombs were similar to that at the bank.

The men arrived at Heysham at 10:45 p.m. The police picked them up and took them to the police station for forensic testing and questioning. They were handed over to the West Midlands police force. All six men were charged and subsequently convicted of twenty-one counts of murder. All claimed they

19 *Ibid.* at 306–7.
20 This discussion is taken from *R. v. McIlkenny & Ors* (1991), 93 Cr. App. R. 287.

had been beaten into making confessions by police officers during the interrogations, and they showed signs of bruising during one of their earlier court appearances. They were convicted on the basis of their confessions (which the trial judge ruled were voluntary), forensic evidence suggesting they had handled explosives, and circumstantial evidence linking them to other IRA members, including McDade.

An appeal to the Court of Appeal was unsuccessful. The six then launched civil proceedings against the police, alleging assault during their interrogations. That action, too, was dismissed by the Court of Appeal, as an abuse of process and a collateral attack on the criminal verdict.[21] Lord Denning said:

> Just consider the course of events if this action were to proceed to trial . . . If the six men failed it would mean that much time and money and worry would have been expended by many people to no good purpose. If the six men win, it would mean that the police were guilty of perjury; that they were guilty of violence and threats; that the confessions were involuntary and improperly admitted in evidence; and that the convictions were erroneous. That would mean that the Home Secretary would have either to recommend that they be pardoned or he would have to remit the case to the Court of Appeal under section 17 of the *Criminal Appeal Act 1968*. This is such an appalling vista that every sensible person in the land would say: It cannot be right that these actions should go any further . . . . This case shows what a civilized country we are. Here are six men who have been proved guilty of the most wicked murder of twenty-one innocent people.[22]

Matters would have been left there had it not been for the publication of a book by investigative journalist Chris Mullen in 1986.[23] Partly because of the widespread concern the book had generated about the safety of the convictions, the Home Secretary referred the case to the Court of Appeal in 1987 on the basis of fresh scientific evidence on two issues. First, had the six been subject to police abuse at the time of making their confessions? Second, was the

21 *Hunter v. Chief Constable of the West Midlands Police*, [1982] A.C. 529. In *Treadaway v. Chief Constable of Police for the West Midlands* (25 October 1994) (Q.B.) [*Treadaway* Q.B.], Treadaway was awarded £50,000 for assault by the police. His conviction was not overturned until 1996: see *R. v. Treadaway*, [1996] EWCA Crim 1457 [*Treadaway* C.A.].

22 *McIlkenny v. Chief Constable of the West Midlands*, [1980] 1 Q.B. 283 at 323, aff'd [1982] A.C. 529 (H.L.).

23 Chris Mullins, *Error of Judgement: The Birmingham Bombings* (London: Chatto & Windus, 1986).

scientific evidence linking them with the explosives reliable? Their convictions were upheld after a lengthy hearing in 1988.

On a further reference by the Home Secretary to the Court of Appeal in 1991, their appeals were allowed and their convictions were set aside. The Court of Appeal found two aspects of the evidence led against them at the trial to be unsafe: first, scientific evidence suggesting they had handled the bombs (this will be discussed in the next chapter); second, the way police interviews were conducted to extract confessions, making that evidence unreliable.

## 2) IRA Bombing—The Guildford Four

In October 1975, four people (Hill, Conlon, Armstrong, and Richardson) were convicted of explosives offences and five murders that had occurred in 1974 (five weeks prior to the Birmingham bombs) relating to bombings at the Horse and Groom and the Seven Stars public houses in Guildford.[24] Seven people died, and many more were seriously injured. Armstrong and Hill were also convicted of two murders in relation to the bombing of the Kings Arms in Woolwich. After their arrest, all four were said to have confessed to the bombings. Their first and second appeals were unsuccessful.

In January 1989, the case was referred by the Home Secretary to the Court of Appeal after a detective looking at the case found heavily edited typed notes from Armstrong's police interviews. Deletions and additions had been made, and the notes had been rearranged in a way that suggested the police had manipulated the notes to fit with the case they wanted to present. The court said that the police had lied, and the conclusion was that if they had lied about this, then maybe their entire evidence was unreliable. It quashed the convictions in October 1989.

## 3) IRA Bombing—The Maguire Seven

In 1976 six family members and a family friend were convicted of possessing explosives found during investigations into the Guildford Four bombings.[25] One of them (Giuseppe Conlon) was the father of Gerard Conlon, who was one of the Guildford Four. Important prosecution evidence was that traces of nitroglycerine had been found on their hands and gloves which, the prosecu-

24 This discussion is taken from *R. v. Richardson, Conlon, Armstrong & Hill* (20 October 1989) (C.A. Crim.).

25 This discussion is taken from *R. v. Maguire & Ors* (1991), 94 Cr. App. R. 133.

tion said, was unequivocal evidence that they had been handling explosives. In the wake of quashing the Guildford Four's convictions and the call for the review of the Birmingham Six's convictions, the Home Secretary then set up an inquiry by Sir John May, a former Court of Appeal judge, into the circumstances of the Guildford Four and the related Maguire Seven convictions.[26] The inquiry arranged for tests to be carried out by Prof. Thornburn Burns, an analytical chemist. The tests revealed the possibility of innocent contamination in the handling of the scientific evidence as well as the fact that not all notes made by the scientists giving evidence at the trials had been disclosed to the defence. In 1991 the Home Secretary decided to refer the case back to the Court of Appeal. The court held that their convictions were unsafe on the basis of unreliable scientific evidence (as explained in Chapter 8).

## 4) IRA Bombing—Judith Ward

In 1974, Judith Ward was convicted of twelve counts of murder and three counts of causing an explosion.[27] The explosions occurred at Euston Station in London, in a bus carrying British soldiers and their families, on the M62 motorway (killing twelve people), and at the National Defence College in Buckinghamshire.

The prosecution was based on confessions Ward had made to the police and scientific evidence that traces of explosives were found on her. In 1991, following new evidence revealed at the May Inquiry and because scientific evidence given in her case was by the same scientists as those in the Birmingham Six and Maguire Seven cases, the Home Secretary referred her case to the Court of Appeal. In 1992, in overturning her conviction, the court found that the police and prosecution had deliberately failed to disclose evidence favourable to the defence and that the prosecution expert witnesses had deliberately misled the court. The court also held Ward's confession to be unreliable because of her mental instability at the time.[28]

---

26 UK, HC, *Report of the Inquiry into the Circumstances Surrounding the Convictions Arising out of the Bomb Attacks in Guildford and Woolwich in 1994*, Final Report (London: H.M.S.O., 1994) 499 [May Inquiry].

27 This discussion is taken from *Ward*, above note 15.

28 *Ibid.* at 50. See also Gisli Gudjonsson & James MacKeith, "Disputed Confessions and the Criminal Justice System" (Maudsley Discussion Paper No. 2) (London: Institute of Psychiatry, 1997).

### 5) The Runciman Royal Commission on Criminal Justice's Response to Miscarriages of Justice

As a result of the publicity generated by these cases, the British government set up a royal commission headed by Viscount Runciman "to undertake a review of the criminal justice system in England and Wales."[29] The commission not only examined the dangers of miscarriages of justice but also took on board crime control measures that were designed to facilitate the conviction of the guilty.[30] With respect to the dangers of convicting the innocent, the commission treated its task as twofold:

1. To recommend ways to improve the criminal justice system so that miscarriages of justice will be less likely to occur in the future; and
2. To address procedures for identifying and correcting the errors in human judgment that still slip through the criminal justice system.

The Runciman commission's main recommendation with respect to miscarriages of justice gave rise to the establishment of the Criminal Cases Review Commission (CCRC). The commission also suggested that the Court of Appeal should take a more liberal approach towards considering fresh evidence and reverse convictions because of concerns about their safety. In addition, it made recommendations for external audit and quality control in the forensic sciences. While we look at the faulty science in Chapter 8, it is worth making the

---

29 Runciman Report, above note 6.

30 There were dissents within the commission against its proposals to require increased defence disclosure and to limit the ability of appellate courts to overturn convictions on the basis of due process violations by the police and prosecutor that were not related to the safety of the verdict. See *ibid.* at 221–35 (Michael Zander, dissenting). Prof. Michael Zander, a member of the commission, dissented on the basis that

> nine of my ten colleagues believe that if there is sufficient sound evidence, even the most serious misconduct by the prosecution should not result in the conviction being quashed. I cannot agree. The moral foundation of the criminal justice system requires that if the prosecution has employed foul means the defendant must go free even though he is plainly guilty.

*Ibid.* at 234, paras. 67–68. This dissent provides some support for the idea that the commission's focus on efficient and accurate determinations of factual guilt was in some tension with a focus on the due process rights of the accused. On the relation between innocence protection, crime control, and due process, see, generally, Keith A. Findley, "Toward a New Paradigm of Criminal Justice: How the Innocence Movement Merges Crime Control and Due Process" (2008) 41 Tex. Tech L. Rev. 133. For a collection of essays highly critical of the royal commission's non-CCRC proposals for their focus on efficient determinations of guilt, see Mike McConville & Lee Bridges, eds., *Criminal Justice in Crisis* (Aldershot, UK: E. Elgar, 1994).

point that sometimes the "scientific" errors are so pronounced that thoughtful and reasonable investigators and prosecutors ought not to have used them to prop up an otherwise weak or deficient case.

The following are some of the cases dealing with faulty police and prosecution matters subsequently referred by the CCRC to the Court of Appeal. Laurie Elks has set out sixteen separate cases referred by the CCRC stemming from police misconduct from the West Midlands and one police station in North East London. Convictions were quashed in all but two of the cases with the courts expressing concerns about false and "verballed," or made-up, confessions, police perjury, and the planting of evidence.[31]

## 6) Police Torture and Assault—The Case of Keith Twitchell

In 1982 at Birmingham Crown Court, Twitchell was convicted of the manslaughter of George Smith and of robbery. An appeal against conviction and sentence was refused by the Court of Appeal in 1983. Ten years later the Home Secretary refused to refer the case back to the Court of Appeal; however, the following year he decided to refer it in the light of Treadaway's successful civil action against the police (we discuss this next). Twitchell was released from prison in 1993, but the convictions for manslaughter and robbery stood until they were overturned by the Court of Appeal in 1999 following upon a referral by the CCRC.[32]

In opening his judgment in *Twitchell*, the judge said, "there is before the Court yet another appeal arising from the lamentable history of the now disbanded West Midlands Serious Crime Squad."[33] He said that during the 1980s a significant number of police officers in that squad (some of whom rose to very senior rank) behaved outrageously and, in particular, extracted confessions by grossly improper means, amounting, in some cases, to torture. He said that during the 1990s, it had been the melancholy task of the court to examine the safety of many convictions recorded during that period and approximately thirty had been quashed. Twitchell alleged that he had been tortured into making a confession by having a plastic bag placed over his head by the police.

At the trial it was alleged that Twitchell had been involved in an armed robbery in which a security guard had been shot at point-blank range by a sawn-off shotgun. The guard died almost immediately. At Twitchell's flat the

31 Elks, above note 18 at 247–52.

32 This discussion is taken from *R. v. Keith Twitchell*, [2000] 1 Cr. App. R. 373 (C.A.) [*Twitchell*].

33 *Ibid.* at 374, Rose L.J.

police said they found a cloth cap, a pair of gloves, and a rucksack. A single fibre matching the carpet of the stolen van was found on each of those items. Most damaging to Twitchell was the content of his interviews and his admissions, orally and in writing. He insisted that the notes about the initial interview had been fabricated—he had made no admissions.

Twitchell said that the police had told him they wanted a statement. Twitchell said he was naked, his clothes having been removed for forensic examination. The police had screamed at him and threatened him. He said that eight police officers had handcuffed him to a chair and placed a plastic bag over his head while he was naked. He quickly signed the statement. The next day he signed another statement. He said he was like a zombie—totally numbed by what had happened to him. In effect, he had given up and just signed whatever he was asked to sign. Only after he had signed things was he allowed to see a solicitor. A couple of days later, he said the police had given him a beer and said, "that bag's great. It doesn't leave any marks."

The court said that the case depended crucially on a direct choice between the credibility of the police officers and the accused. In making their choice, the jury did not know of matters that threw severe doubt on the honesty and professional integrity of those officers. If those issues had been put to the officers, they would have been driven to make admissions that should have caused the jury to entertain doubts. If the judge had allowed the case to go to the jury, he would have been bound to warn in strong terms of the danger of relying on the evidence of officers whose veracity had been so severely questioned. The court said that where there had been an acquittal in one case, which indicated that the jury must have entirely rejected the evidence of the police officer, that officer can be cross-examined about that in a subsequent case.

The judge said that the findings in Treadaway's appeal[34] could be relied upon in Twitchell's appeal. The officers involved in Treadaway's case had been found guilty of various disciplinary offences: they included creating a false set of interview notes with the intention of using them to persuade a suspect to make admissions; wrongfully arresting a person; refusing access to a solicitor; assault; forcing a person to sign blank pages of interview notes; and fabricating admissions by him. The prosecution agreed: "It would be facile to suggest that cross-examination of [the officers] with the material, to which reference has been made, would have been anything less than potentially devastating."[35] In view of that, the court allowed Twitchell's appeal.

---

34 *Treadaway* C.A., above note 21.

35 *Twitchell*, above note 32 at 385.

## 7) Police Torture and Assault — The Case of Derek Treadaway

Derek Treadaway spent thirteen years in jail after being convicted in 1983 of robbery and conspiracy to rob. He maintained that his confession had been extracted through torture by the police. In 1996 his conviction was overturned by the Court of Appeal.[36] Two years before that, in 1994, he had been awarded £50,000 damages for assault in a civil action against the Chief Constable of West Midlands.[37] Treadaway, like the Birmingham Six, turned to the civil courts as a last resort. Unlike in the Birmingham Six case, the civil courts considered his claim. In the unlikely setting of the civil case for damages, Treadaway, as the judge in the case said, was a person whose credibility was easy to attack — he had admitted that he was a fraudster and he had many previous convictions. Treadaway agreed that he would often tell lies if it suited him. Yet he persisted in his allegations over many years that he had been a victim of police brutality. He said that during his questioning, police officers had handcuffed his hands behind his back and then put plastic bags over his head which nearly suffocated him. As the judge said, why would he choose to invent an allegation which would be met with derision because it was so unbelievable?

However, when examined in detail, Treadaway's account of what had happened to him had what the judge called "core consistency."[38] He told his story to his wife and his solicitor at the first opportunity and within hours of the alleged assault. As the judge said, if he had made up an account about the five officers being involved in his assault, he could not have known that those who claimed to be elsewhere just happened to have no written verification of their presence at those other locations. The judge said that if Treadaway had invented his complaints, he was indeed a talented fabricator; yet his underplaying to a remarkable extent of the physical and mental consequences of his ordeal was not the approach of a fabricator.

On the other hand, the early record of interview disclosed every sign of a pattern of the crude insertion of developing partial admissions by the police. The economy of language and the lack of detail gave the statement under caution all the hallmarks of a dubious confession. The judge thought that the specific benefit of the lack of detail was to facilitate subsequent scope to shift the account as more facts became available. One senior officer claimed to have been elsewhere, interviewing another suspect, who had already confessed and to whom the officer was not allocated. The judge said that this account, in pref-

36 This discussion is taken from *Treadaway* C.A., above note 21.

37 *Treadaway* Q.B., above note 21.

38 *Treadaway* C.A., above note 21.

erence to attending at the interview of the suspect to whom he was allocated, in circumstances where he might well confess to his involvement in the matter, did not ring true. As the judge said, this officer was clearly prepared to cover up the misdoings of others — he was a fixer and a survivor.

The judge said that having observed the officer over a prolonged period, his account was simply an invention — nothing less than a plain and simple lie. He said that he was impressed by the way in which Treadaway gave his evidence. He regarded him throughout with considerable circumspection having regard to his history of criminal convictions for dishonesty, his criminal convictions for serious violence against the police, and his admissions that he was, in effect, "a practised liar."[39] However, the judge said he was (unlike the police officers in the case) "an unpractised witness."[40]

In the hearing of the criminal appeal, the judge called one of the senior police officers "a most unsatisfactory witness"[41] and said that the officer's stock in trade was ambiguity and he simply did not tell the truth. It did not escape the attention of the judge that the officer concerned was not in attendance at the court on the appeal in response to the witness summons which had been issued to him. It appeared that the officer concerned had left the country for Egypt. The judge referred to a number of other cases in which scientific evidence showed that admissions and records of interviews had been fabricated by the police. The court noted, for example, that in *R. v. Gall and Gall* an accomplice who had been an impressive witness against the accused before the jury had subsequently suffered a collapse in integrity. It was ascertained that he could not have been involved in some 203 offences in which he claimed to have been involved.[42] He had, in fact, been in prison at the relevant times, a matter which the police should have considered in evaluating his claims.

### 8) Intimidation and False Confessions — The Case of Trevor Campbell

In June 1984, Ethel Cawood, a widow who was eighty-four years old, was brutally murdered in her home.[43] On the following day an unsuccessful attempt was made to set fire to her house, where her body was. Two people were tried for her murder: Trevor Campbell, then aged nineteen, and his fifteen-

39 *Treadaway* Q.B., above note 21 at 25.

40 *Ibid.*

41 *Ibid.*

42 *R. v. Gall and Gall* (21 October 1991), transcript (E.W.C.A.).

43 This discussion is taken from *R. v. Trevor Anthony Campbell* (14 October 1999), No. 99/0642/W5 (E.W.C.A.) [*Campbell*].

year-old girlfriend, Christine. Both were convicted. Both tried to appeal without success.

The admissions Campbell was said to have made were the basis of the case against him. The judge explained that Campbell alleged that he had been the subject of physical assault, intimidation, and threats and that he painted a picture of police misconduct. He said that in the light of the material now available to undermine the credibility of the three police officers on whom the prosecution case crucially depended, the court could not regard his conviction as other than unsafe. He said the submission rested on a body of material tending to the serious discredit of three of the four officers involved in the final series of interviews during which admissions were made. In 1999 Campbell's conviction was quashed by the Court of Appeal because of what Lord Bingham described as "the bedrock of the case against him."[44] It was a confession Campbell had made after he had been threatened by members of the now infamous West Midlands Serious Crime Squad.

The court looked to the case of *R. v. Lewis*[45] where Lewis claimed that he had signed in blank a number of sheets of paper, having been threatened with unpleasant consequences if he failed to do so. The sheets were later the subject of electro-static document analysis (ESDA). The analysis showed that the sheets had not been signed sequentially but that the signatures had been put on the pieces of paper in an order quite different from that which the pieces of paper bore when incorporated into the statement. In due course, Lewis brought a civil action against the chief constable of the West Midlands Police which was settled in his favour on entry of judgment for £200,000 and costs, and the reading of a statement in open court in which the chief constable acknowledged, and expressed his regret for, the miscarriage of justice that had occurred.

The court was also asked to look at *R. v. Hickey & Ors* (1997).[46] In the course of that investigation, an officer Perkins made a statement in which he admitted preparing in the case of a defendant named Elwell what were described as "a set of fictitious notes . . . to assist in the duping of persons who had been arrested by myself and other officers." This he described as "an unorthodox method."[47] The judge observed:

> We are satisfied that DC Perkins was an officer who was prepared to resort to deceit to obtain evidence; that that is probably what occurred in the present

---

44 *Ibid.* at 3.

45 This case is without reference in the court judgment of *Campbell.*

46 Unreported (E.W.C.A.).

47 *Campbell*, above note 43 at 6.

> case with regard to the interview and the written statement of Patrick Molloy and that consequently those confessions were obtained by oppression and were inadmissible as evidence in a court of law.[48]

The court observed that it would have directed that the papers be sent to the Director of Public Prosecutions had that not already been done. Ultimately, said the court, in making their choice on credibility, the jury did not know of matters that threw severe doubt on the honesty and professional integrity of those officers. The court could not speculate on what the jury might have done if the case had been presented differently.

### 9) Informer Identification Not Disclosed—The Case of Murphy, McMahon, and Cooper

Wrongdoing by police officers was also a factor in undermining the convictions of those involved in the Luton Post Office shooting in September 1969.[49] Stevens, the sub-postmaster of a post office in Luton, was getting into his car which was parked in the car park of a bank close to his post office, when he was shot with a sawn-off shotgun at point-blank range. There had been a public outcry about the incident. In March 1970 Patrick Murphy, Michael McMahon, and David Cooper were convicted of the murder. In 1971 applications for leave to appeal were dismissed. In 1973 Murphy's appeal was allowed. The appeals of Cooper and McMahon were dismissed in 1973 as they were again in 1978. After the publication of *Wicked Beyond Belief* by Ludovic Kennedy, in July 1980, they were released from prison by order of the Secretary of State, and the remainder of their sentences was remitted because of the widely felt sense of unease about the safety of their convictions. Cooper died in 1995 and McMahon in 1999.

In setting aside the convictions in 2003, the court said that it had become increasingly apparent that there were serious grounds for concern about the way in which the police investigated the matter and put the prosecution case together. It said that the subsequent conviction of Detective Chief Superintendent Drury, the officer in charge of the investigation, on charges of corruption added to the sense of unease. The court said Drury had come to the conclusion that in order to convict Murphy, McMahon, and Cooper it would be necessary to rely on the evidence of a Mr. Mathews. So, in a report to his commander dated November 1969 (and which was submitted to the Director of Public Prosecutions [DPP]), Drury said that Mathews was an essential

48 *Ibid.*

49 This discussion is taken from *R. v. Cooper & Anor*, [2003] EWCA Crim 2257.

witness and that "almost everything he has said is corroborated somewhere or another by a completely independent and impartial witness."[50] As the Court of Appeal acknowledged, that was not correct. The DPP had agreed that proceedings against Mathews should be discontinued, and he then became the principal prosecution witness.

In Murphy's appeal the court said that the vital issue on which clearly the jury believed Mathews was that he had identified the three men who were with him. The others had said that Mathews was lying about their involvement with him, and they had nothing to do with it. There had been an allegation that Drury had "leant" on Mathews. But why would police point the finger at innocent people?

Michael Good had a minor role as a witness at the trial. As it turned out, he had previously owned the gun involved in the shooting; however, what was not known at the time of the trial was that Good had also been a police informant. It appears that on the day of the murder, or possibly on the next day, Good telephoned his police handler and told him he was aware that his gun had been used in the shooting and that he was concerned he would be implicated. He then met with his handler and Drury, identified the gun as his after it was recovered, and then pointed the finger in the direction of the accused.

As the court said, it is clear that the police officers involved had not brought to the attention of the defence other statements previously made by Mathews which might have brought into question his later version of events. They also did not disclose others' statements that might have suggested that Mathews might have been involved in the shooting. So, instead of being impartial and objective investigators, some of the police may have become players in protecting their own interests.

### 10) Police Notebooks Not Correct—The Case of Maynard, Dudley, Bailey, and Clarke

Maynard, Dudley, Bailey, and Clarke were convicted of murder and conspiracy.[51] In July 1998 their solicitors made representations to the Criminal Cases Review Commission (CCRC). The solicitors included a request that the CCRC arrange for scientific testing of the police notebooks. The CCRC instructed a leading forensic document examiner to examine the speeds of writing of the handwritten records of a number of disputed interviews.

---

50 *Ibid.* at para. 7.

51 This discussion is taken from *R. v. Maynard & Ors*, [2002] EWCA Crim 1942.

The Court of Appeal said it would not be unfair to observe that most of the principal personalities concerned in the events that gave rise to the charges were either convicted criminals or members of the families or friends of convicted criminals. Many of them had been involved in serious crime. There was also no doubt that the deaths were of the most brutal kind. Body parts were washed up at separate locations on the Thames foreshore in Essex. A post-mortem revealed the deceased had been tied up and tortured before being killed; his body had been dismembered when he was either dead or (possibly) unconscious. Another body had been shot in the head at close range.

The trial had lasted over seven months, the longest murder trial, the court said, ever to have taken place in England. The summing-up took twelve days. It was described in the earlier appeal as "a masterpiece of clarity."[52]

Nonetheless, police notebooks raised issues. The record of an interview recorded in the police notebook stated 4:28 p.m. as the start of the interview. The finishing time of the interview was recorded as 5:18 p.m. At trial, the officer who had conducted the interview and the officer who claimed to have written the contemporary record in the hard-backed book, each gave oral evidence that the interview began at 4:28 p.m. and ended at 5:18 p.m.—a total of fifty minutes. The document examiner considered that to be a physical impossibility. As the record contained 11,325 properly formed characters, it would mean that the writer would have had to achieve a speed of between 222 characters per minute in forty-nine minutes and 231 characters per minute in fifty-one minutes. In controlled experiments, the fastest speed recorded by the document examiner had been 158 characters per minute. The fastest speed he had ever encountered had been below 170 characters per minute. The fastest speed he regarded as possible of achievement by anyone, allowing a considerable margin, was 190 characters per minute. He said that 222 to 231 characters per minute were far in excess of that which was possible.

The court took the view that the integrity of the interviews was vital to the prosecution case. If the jury had cause to think that the record in the notebooks on any one occasion had been fabricated, it is at least likely that they would have come to doubt the integrity of all of the interviews regardless of whether they had been conducted by the same officers. As a result, the court found that the other convictions were also unsafe and allowed the appeals. This "knock-on effect,"[53] as the court called it, shows the high price that investigators must pay for proven misconduct.

---

52 *Ibid.* at para. 31.

53 *Ibid.* at para. 57.

## 11) An Odd Fellow—and Little Evidence—The Case of Barry George

This case depended upon an over-evaluation of evidence against an "odd" person.[54] In 2001 George was convicted for the shooting murder of the well-known television personality Jill Dando outside her home. His appeal against the conviction was dismissed by the Court of Appeal in 2002. Upon referral by the CCRC, the Court of Appeal in 2007 quashed his conviction. He was retried in 2008 and acquitted by the jury.

While much about George warranted suspicion and inquiry, the emphasis placed by the investigators on a single particle of firearm discharge residue found about a year after the murder in Barry George's overcoat was thought to be inappropriate. The prosecution called expert witnesses at the trial whose evidence suggested that the particle of residue likely came from a gun fired by Barry George rather than from some other source. Various witnesses from the Forensic Science Service told the Court of Appeal that this was not the right conclusion to draw. It was, in fact, no more likely that the particle had come from a gun fired by George than that it had come from some other source.

Of course, one might wonder about what other source might have given rise to a speck of gunpowder in the pocket of an innocent person. The answer is simple; it could have been unwittingly transferred by a police officer who had searched George or searched his belongings, if that officer had either handled a gun or been in contact with someone who had. It could even have got onto the trousers when they were being handled at the forensic science laboratory.[55]

It was said that George's counsel accused the Metropolitan Police of abandoning objectivity and "closing their minds" to other suspects and that the detectives were "livid" at the criticism levelled at them.[56] However, the Court of Appeal concluded that, if this evidence had been given to the jury at the trial, there is no certainty that they would have found George guilty.

---

54 This discussion is taken from *George v. R.*, [2007] EWCA Crim 2722 [*George*].

55 One of the few pieces of forensic evidence once linking Domenic Perre to the National Crime Authority (NCA) bombing in South Australia resulted from a laboratory contamination. The evidence, a microscopic piece of primer from a bullet, labelled DP17, was found on a swab from the pants of a bombing victim, NCA lawyer Peter Wallis. State Forensic Science Centre director Dr. Hilton Kobus said the sample was likely to have been contaminated when evidence from the two locations came into contact with each other. He described the incident as resulting from contamination, error, bad practice, or bad luck; Mark Steene, "The NCA Bombing Inquest—Perre Evidence 'Contaminated'" *The Advertiser* (1 July 1999).

56 Andrew Alderson & Patrick Sawyer, "Jill Dando Murder: Feud Erupts over Verdict" *The Telegraph* (2 August 2008).

As the court explained, the most significant evidence it received owed its origin to the initiative of Dr. Ian Evett who, from 1996 to 2002, worked for the Forensic Science Service. Dr. Evett's role there included assisting scientists to present evidence to the court in a manner that was logical, transparent, and robust. Part of the technique he advocated involved analysing the evidence by reference to the extent to which it supported one or other of two rival propositions. Typically, one proposition would be that an event that formed part of the prosecution case occurred; the rival proposition would be that this event did not occur. The method was referred to as "Case Assessment and Interpretation" (CAI). The object was to clarify *before* evidence is examined and analysed the likelihood of the examination achieving particular results on the two different hypotheses or propositions. The technique facilitates the drawing of appropriate conclusions from results obtained.

The forensic officer who did the examination in this case (Keeley) applied this technique to the likelihood of his finding trace firearms residue on George or his clothing. His conclusions related to the two different propositions: (1) that George was the man who shot Jill Dando; (2) that George was not the man who shot Jill Dando. Keeley estimated that the likelihood of his finding no FDR particle had been 99 in 100 *on either proposition*, the likelihood of his finding one or a few particles as 1 in 100 *on either proposition* and the likelihood of his finding lots of particles as 1 in 10,000 (these figures being intended simply to signify "remote in the extreme") *on either proposition.* The significance of this was that, in Keeley's opinion, the finding that he made of a single particle had been "neutral." It was no more likely to have come from the gun that killed Dando than from some extraneous source.[57]

For this reason George's conviction had to be quashed even though there was other circumstantial evidence and the Court of Appeal was not clear on what effect the impugned evidence had on the jury's verdict. At George's second trial in 2007, the prosecution was unable to produce any scientific evidence linking him to the murder; instead, it relied on his past conduct of being highly obsessive, lacking in social skills, and being a danger to women. He was acquitted.

## D. THE CANADIAN EXPERIENCE

Much of the evidence about police and prosecutorial misconduct in Canada comes from a series of public inquiries held into wrongful convictions in that

57 *George*, above note 54 at paras. 14–18, Phillips C.J.

country. There have been seven major public inquiries into wrongful convictions, details of which are discussed below.[58] In Australia and Britain, the practice has been that inquiries or royal commissions were held to resolve questions about the guilt or innocence of someone who had been convicted of a serious crime; however, each of the Canadian inquiries was held after a conviction was overturned. This means that the various investigators and scientific witnesses already knew that errors had occurred in the trial process when they gave evidence to the inquiries. The Canadian inquiries provide evidence that there have been departures from the rhetoric of impartial investigation and prosecution, and of the reality of miscarriages of justice.

### 1) Tunnel Vision, Police Misconduct, and Inadequate Disclosure—The Case of Donald Marshall, Jr.

In 1971, Donald Marshall, Jr., a seventeen-year-old Aboriginal, was convicted of the murder of a black man, Sandy Seale, in Nova Scotia.[59] They had met by chance and were walking through the park when they came across two other men, Roy Ebsary and Jimmy MacNeil. Following a short conversation, Ebsary fatally stabbed Seale in the stomach. The police investigation, however, led to the prosecution of Marshall. Marshall had been in some trouble with the law

---

58 *Royal Commission on the Donald Marshall, Jr., Prosecution* (Halifax: Royal Commission on the Donald Marshall, Jr., Prosecution, 1989) [Marshall Inquiry]; *Report of the Kaufman Commission on Proceedings Involving Guy Paul Morin* (Toronto: Ontario Ministry of the Attorney General, 1998) [Morin Inquiry]; *The Inquiry Regarding Thomas Sophonow* (Winnipeg: Manitoba Justice, 2000) [Sophonow Inquiry]; *Commission of Inquiry Pertaining to the Cases of Ronald Dalton, Gregory Parsons and Randy Druken* (St. John's, NL: Department of Justice, 2006) [Lamer Inquiry]; *Report of the Commission of Inquiry into Certain Aspects of the Trial and Conviction of James Driskell* (Winnipeg: Manitoba Justice, 2007) [Driskell Inquiry]; *Report of the Commission of Inquiry into the Wrongful Conviction of David Milgaard* (Saskatoon: The Commission, 2008) [Milgaard Inquiry]; *Report of the Inquiry into Pediatric Forensic Pathology* (Toronto: Ministry of the Attorney General, 2008) [Goudge Inquiry]. For an overview of the significance of the Marshall, Sophonow, and Morin inquiries, in particular, see the Department of Justice, FPT Heads of Prosecutions Committee, *Report on the Prevention of Miscarriages of Justice* (Ottawa: Department of Justice, 2004) which also deals extensively with tunnel vision and the recommendations needed to protect against it. The "International Comparisons" section of this report and the footnote references, particularly to the experience in the United States, are most useful, as is the report's summary of the Canadian experience.

59 This discussion is taken from Nova Scotia, *Royal Commission on the Donald Marshall, Jr., Prosecution: Digest of Findings and Recommendations* (Halifax: The Commission, 1989) [Marshall Inquiry, *Digest*].

and was known to and disliked by the police.[60] He was convicted of Seale's murder and sentenced to life imprisonment. He spent eleven years in prison before being acquitted by the Nova Scotia Court of Appeal in 1983. Ebsary was subsequently convicted of that crime.[61] The first paragraph of the inquiry's report bears quotation:

> The criminal justice system failed Donald Marshall Jr. at virtually every turn from his arrest and wrongful conviction for murder in 1971 up to, and even beyond, his acquittal in the Court of Appeal in 1983. The tragedy of the failure is compounded by evidence that his miscarriage of justice could—and should—have been prevented, or at least corrected quickly, if those involved in the system had carried out their duties in a professional and/or competent matter. That they did not is due, at least in part, to the fact that Donald Marshall Jr. is a Native.[62]

In 1986, a royal commission with three judges was set up to review Marshall's wrongful conviction. After hearing 113 witnesses in ninety-three days of public hearings, the commission reported in December 1989 and was highly critical of the roles played by the police, prosecutors, and judges. It found that the investigating officers had acted unprofessionally, inadequately, and incompetently and that their investigation was designed to seek evidence supportive only of their theory about the killing; the officers had discounted all other evidence that challenged it. It was found that the police had used oppressive tactics in obtaining perjured evidence implicating Marshall from witnesses and that the prosecution counsel had failed to disclose statements given by witnesses that were inconsistent with their evidence at trial. It also found that Marshall's trial defence counsel failed to provide him with adequate legal presentation.[63]

It appeared that serious problems continued even after Marshall's conviction. Ten days after he was convicted, Ebsary's companion, MacNeil, told the police that Ebsary, not Marshall had been involved in Seale's death. This critical information was not however disclosed to the defence or prosecution. When hearing Marshall's first appeal, the court of appeal failed to identify fundamental mistakes of law made by the trial judge.

---

60 Dawn Anderson & Barrie Anderson, *Manufacturing Guilt: Wrongful Convictions in Canada*, 2d ed. (Black Point, NS: Fernwood, 2009) at 29.

61 *R. v. Ebsary* (1986), 27 C.C.C. (3d) 488 (N.S.S.C.A.D.).

62 Marshall Inquiry, *Digest*, above note 59 at 1.

63 *Ibid.* at 21–23.

When the case was later referred back to the court of appeal by the Minister of Justice, one of the judges hearing the appeal did not disqualify himself on the basis of a possible conflict of interest. He had been the Attorney General of Nova Scotia at the time of the trial and first appeal.[64] This time the court quashed Marshall's conviction. In doing so, however, it laid the blame squarely on Marshall for being involved in other criminal activities (for which he was never charged) and for not telling the truth at his trial (which was not substantiated by evidence). As the subsequent inquiry found, these observations made by the court were not proper and adversely affected Marshall's later negotiations with the government for compensation.[65]

The inquiry made wide-ranging systemic recommendations, including these:

- that an independent review mechanism be set up to investigate alleged miscarriages of justice—in effect, that a CCRC approach to re-investigations be taken;
- that, where a wrongful conviction has occurred, an independent judicial inquiry should be set up to consider compensation;
- that all the parties involved in the criminal justice system, including government officials, lawyers, judges, police officers and law students, take appropriate steps to show sensitivity to minority concerns and, in particular, to the systematic discrimination against black and Native Canadians;
- that an independent statutory Office of the Director of Public Prosecutions be set up with similar duties and responsibilities, and security to that in England;
- that the law be amended to set out comprehensively the prosecution's duties to make full and complete disclosure of evidence to the defence in a timely manner;[66] and
- that police interviews of suspects and witnesses in serious crimes be recorded electronically.

The federal Parliament did not act on these recommendations, but the province did create a Director of Public Prosecutions. Most important, the Supreme Court relied on the inquiry's recommendations when, in 1991, it recognized that the accused had a broad and continuing constitutional right to disclosure of all relevant and non-privileged material.[67] Under this new rule,

64 *Ibid.* at 4–6.

65 *Ibid.* at 7.

66 *Ibid.* at 34–35.

67 *Stinchcombe*, above note 13.

had his lawyers requested disclosure, Marshall would have received the prior inconsistent witness statements as well as the admission made by the real perpetrator's companion shortly after Marshall's wrongful conviction.

### 2) Tunnel Vision and Jailhouse Informants— The Case of Guy Paul Morin

In 1992 Guy Morin was convicted of the murder of nine-year-old Christine Jessop who had been abducted from Queensville, Ontario, in 1984.[68] Morin, aged twenty-five, was Christine's next-door neighbour when charged with her murder. The investigators thought him to be a little "odd" which caused them to focus upon him in the absence of any more likely suspect. He was tried twice, the first trial resulting in an acquittal. After a successful appeal by the prosecution, that finding was quashed and a retrial ordered. Morin was convicted at his second trial. He successfully appealed in 1995 on the basis of fresh DNA evidence tendered jointly by the prosecution and the defence showing that the semen found on Christine did not come from him.

In 1996, a judicial commission of inquiry was set up, to inquire into the conduct of the investigation and prosecution of this case, and to make recommendations to prevent such cases from occurring again.[69] The commission held public hearings for 146 days during which time evidence from 120 witnesses was heard. Two years later, in releasing a two-volume report, the commissioner, Fred Kaufman (a former judge of the Quebec Court of Appeal), stated:

> The criminal proceedings against Morin represent a tragedy not only for Morin and his family, but also for the community at large: the system failed him —- a system for which we, the community, must bear responsibility. An innocent man was arrested, stigmatized, imprisoned and convicted. The real killer has never been found. The trail grows colder with each passing year. For Christine Jessop's family there is no closure.[70]

Commissioner Kaufman found that a significant cause of Morin's wrongful conviction included the tunnel vision shown by the investigators and prosecu-

---

68 This discussion is taken from the Morin Inquiry, above note 58.

69 *Ibid.*

70 *Ibid.* at 1. It should be noted that Nigel Hadgkiss, southern region general manager of the Australian Federal Police, and Dr. James Robertson, director of forensic services, Australian Federal Police, gave evidence to the Morin Inquiry as did Dr. William Tilstone, executive director of the National Forensic Science Technology Center, Florida, and former director of the Forensic Science Centre in Adelaide, South Australia.

tion in their inappropriate reliance on jailhouse informants. (The other main cause, the misuse of scientific evidence, will be discussed in Chapter 8.)

The commissioner emphasized that tunnel vision was

> . . . the single minded and overly narrow focus on an investigation or prosecutorial theory so as to unreasonably colour the evaluation of information received and one's conduct in response to the information.[71]

He said tunnel vision and its perverse by-product, "noble cause corruption," is the antithesis of the proper roles of the police and prosecutors.[72] He found that the prosecutors at Morin's second trial had not objectively assessed the reliability of the two jailhouse informants, something that was coloured by their genuine view that Morin was guilty. As a result, evidence undermining the informants was discarded and inconsequential evidence became confirmatory. The commissioner found that despite the exonerating DNA evidence, the police officers involved in the investigation still preferred the evidence of the informants. The commissioner found that the lead prosecutor in Morin's second trial had demonstrated "tunnel vision in the most staggering proportion" both during the trial and in his testimony before the inquiry.[73]

The commissioner found the wrongful conviction in Morin's case not to be an aberration but the result of "systemic" problems:

> The causes of Mr Morin's convictions are rooted in systemic problems, as well as the failings of individuals. It is no coincidence that the same systemic problems are those identified in wrongful convictions in other jurisdictions worldwide. It is these systemic issues that must be addressed in the future. As to individual failings, it is hoped that they can be prevented by the revelation of what happened in Guy Paul Morin's case and by education as to the causes of wrongful convictions.[74]

The commissioner made extensive recommendations for police and Crown education on the topic, including fostering a culture within policing that values honest and fair investigation.[75] He also recommended that consideration be

71 *Ibid.* at 1134.

72 This covers a range of inappropriate investigative conduct masquerading as legitimate because it provides a means to achieve the laudable end, namely, justice; see Edwin Delattre, *Character and Cops: Ethics in Policing*, 5th ed. (Washington, DC: AEI Press, 2006).

73 Morin Inquiry, above note 58 at 489.

74 *Ibid.* at 488.

75 *Ibid.*, Recommendations at 91–115.

given to a change in the powers afforded to the Court of Appeal, so as to enable the court to set aside a conviction where there exists a lurking doubt as to guilt of an accused.[76] He further recommended the creation of an independent statutory body to replace or supplement the powers given to the federal Minister of Justice of referring suspected cases of miscarriages of justice to the court of appeal. Crown counsel and the Attorney General for Ottawa apologized to Morin for his ten-year ordeal. He received $1.25 million in compensation.

### 3) Use of Science in Investigations, Eyewitness Evidence — The Case of Thomas Sophonow

Eyewitness misidentifications have been recognized as a common cause of wrongful convictions.[77] An example of improper procedural and evidentiary safeguards in gathering identification evidence is clearly evidenced in the case of Thomas Sophonow.

Thomas Sophonow was tried in the 1980s (on three occasions) for the murder of sixteen-year-old Barbara Stoppel who worked in a doughnut shop in Winnipeg, Manitoba.[78] There was intense media pressure on the police to solve the crime. Sophonow, who was known to the police, came to their attention because he resembled a composite photo. Several witnesses had claimed that they had seen Sophonow walking away from the shop where the victim was found strangled to death. At first, the witnesses gave tentative identifications of Sophonow in live lineups and photo lineups — but those identifications firmed up with repeated interviews and when one of the witnesses was placed in a holding cell with Sophonow.

At one interview with Sophonow, the police conveyed to him how the door of the doughnut shop was locked. When this same information came from Sophonow later in the investigation, it was used to suggest evidence of his guilt. The police investigated but discounted Sophonow's alibi that he was in another part of town at the time of the murder. Sophonow's lawyers were also reluctant to disclose all aspects of his alibi defence because of a distrust of

---

76 *Ibid.* at 87.

77 R. Huff, A. Rattner, & E. Sagarin, "Guilty until Proven Innocent" (1986) 32 Crime and Delinquency 518.

78 In the Australian case involving Earl Heatley, the NSW DPP issued a statement saying that after five trials without a conviction or acquittal, he had decided it was not in the public interest to pursue a further trial. His explanation involved the curious fact that one of the prosecution witnesses subsequently thought he was a race horse, and adverse findings had been made about some of the police officers in police integrity hearings; Statement by the Director of Public Prosecutions (8 April 2004).

the police. The rhetoric of impartial investigation would suggest that the police would impartially and fully investigate alibis because they have no interest in charging an innocent person especially when, as in Sophonow's case, doing this may allow the guilty perpetrator to escape justice. The reality, or at least the perception, may unfortunately be otherwise, and police that are subject to tunnel vision may fail to thoroughly or impartially investigate alibis and alternative suspects.

Sophonow's first trial ended in a mistrial as the jury was unable to reach a unanimous verdict, but Sophonow was convicted at the end of each of the second and third trials. At the third trial, the trial judge refused to allow an expert witness, Dr. Elizabeth Loftus, to be called by the defence to testify about the frailties of eyewitness identifications; he allowed evidence that a jailhouse informer provided to be read into trial even though the witness was not available; he dismissed a juror who apparently thought she had special psychic powers; and he allowed the Crown for the first time to allege that a sexual assault had occurred. The Court of Appeal overturned the convictions after the second and third trials.

In 1998 the Winnipeg Police Service undertook a re-investigation of the murder. In June 2000 it announced that Sophonow was not responsible and that another suspect had been identified. On that same day, the Manitoba government issued a public apology to Sophonow for his having endured three trials and two appeals, and for having spent forty-five months in jail for an offence he did not commit. Shortly after that the Manitoba government appointed former Supreme Court justice Peter Cory to inquire into the conduct of the investigation and the circumstances surrounding the resulting criminal proceedings.[79] The commissioner was also given the mandate to make any findings about the practices or systemic issues that may have contributed to or influenced either the police investigation or the resulting prosecution. He was asked to advise on whether financial compensation was appropriate and if so, how much.

Commissioner Cory reported in September 2001. He found that the causes of the wrongful conviction were multi-dimensional and included faulty eyewitness identification; unreliable jailhouse informants; inadequate disclosure by the prosecution; misleading scientific evidence; and tunnel vision on the part of the prosecution and police. He said that tunnel vision can give rise to

---

79 *The Inquiry Regarding Thomas Sophonow: The Investigation, Prosecution and Consideration of Entitlement to Compensation* (Winnipeg: Attorney General, 2001) [Sophonow Inquiry].

tragic consequences with the investigator becoming so focused on one person that other suspects who should be investigated are eliminated.

The issue of eyewitness identification was particularly significant to this inquiry. Evidence uncovered by the inquiry revealed that Sophonow resembled a composite drawing of the perpetrator and that he also fitted the description of a tall, dark-haired man wearing a cowboy hat near the doughnut shop. Highly questionable police interviews were conducted. Four eyewitnesses were shown a photo lineup in which Sophonow appeared standing a foot taller than all of the other participants in the lineup. Witnesses who expressed uncertainty were cued by the police as to who was the correct selection. Three of the four eyewitnesses could not identify the suspect in the photo array, but they still testified at trial that Sophonow was the man they saw leaving the crime scene. None of this information was disclosed to the defence lawyers. Nor was the fact revealed to the defence that there were witnesses who could support Sophonow's alibi.

Prosecutors also relied on the testimony of three jailhouse informants who claimed that Sophonow had confessed to the murder. The inquiry revealed that the Crown had approached eleven potential informants to testify against Sophonow. The three who did testify against him had charges dropped or received other rewards. Commissioner Cory subsequently recommended that jailhouse informants should, as a general rule, be prohibited from testifying. At most, only one such informants should be allowed to testify and only if he or she revealed unique information about the crime that was subsequently confirmed by the police.

In hearing expert evidence from psychologist Elizabeth Loftus[80] on the frailties of eyewitness evidence, Commissioner Cory recommended that "trial judges consider favourably and readily admit properly qualified expert evidence pertaining to eyewitness identification." Canadian courts, however, have been reluctant to admit such evidence.[81]

Commissioner Cory recommended that police officers conducting a photo lineup should have no knowledge of the case or whether the suspect is in the lineup so that they could not inadvertently advise or cue any witnesses. He said that other participants in lineups (known as "fillers") should match the description given by the eyewitnesses and that the photographs in photographic lineups should be disclosed sequentially and not concurrently.[82] In addition,

---

80 Professor of Psychology at the University of Washington.

81 *R. v. McIntosh* (1997), 117 C.C.C. (3d) 385 (Ont. C.A.), but see *R. v. Henderson*, [2009] M.J. No. 145 (Q.B.).

82 This recommendation means that the photographs should be shown to the witness one after the other, rather than being provided simultaneously.

identification procedures should be recorded, and police officers should not be able to provide witnesses with feedback about their identification.

The commissioner also found problems in the way that the police interrogated Sophonow. For example, they took only selective notes and subjected him to an unnecessary strip search. The commissioner recommended videotaping or at least audiotaping of interviews. Under his proposals, unrecorded interviews would generally be inadmissible.

The commissioner also found numerous problems with lack of disclosure of relevant information to Sophonow, such as prior inconsistent statements and other information inconsistent with the Crown's theory of the case. He concluded that if the Supreme Court's decision in *Stinchcombe* and new police procedures created after it were followed "there should never again be a repetition of the numerous and serious failures to disclose which occurred in the Thomas Sophonow case. The damage caused to Thomas Sophonow's case by these failures was irreparable."[83]

In line with the Marshall Inquiry recommendation, Commissioner Cory recommended that there should be a completely independent entity established to efficiently and quickly review cases in which wrongful convictions are alleged. He said that in the United Kingdom, an excellent model (the CCRC) exists for such an institution and he hoped that steps would be taken to consider the establishment of a similar institution in Canada. He made this recommendation in the course of considering whether Sophonow should be compensated. Both his recommendation for compensation and for the creation of "a completely independent entity which can effectively, efficiently and quickly review cases in which wrongful conviction is alleged" were motivated by a sense that "if the State commits significant errors in the course of the investigation and prosecution, it should accept the responsibility for the sad consequences which will inevitably flow from them."[84] In light of Commissioner Cory's careful examination of the great range of pecuniary and non-pecuniary harms caused to Sophonow by his wrongful conviction, including loss of liberty, privacy, the continuing effects of imprisonment, and loss of reputation, Sophonow was awarded $2.6 million by the Manitoba government.

83 Sophonow Inquiry, above note 79 at 83.

84 *Ibid.* at 101.

## 4) Tunnel Vision — The Cases of Gregory Parsons, Randy Druken, and Ronald Dalton

Retired Chief Justice Lamer was asked by the Newfoundland and Labrador government to inquire into the convictions of Ronald Dalton, Gregory Parsons, and Randy Druken.[85]

In 1994 Gregory Parsons had been found guilty of the second-degree murder of his mother Catherine Carroll and sentenced to life with a non-parole period of fifteen years. In 1996 the Newfoundland and Labrador Court of Appeal overturned the conviction and ordered a new trial. In the meantime, tests showed that the DNA found at the crime scene was not that of Parsons. In 1998 he was acquitted. The Attorney General publicly apologized to him and his family and said that he had no involvement in the murder. Retired Judge Nathaniel Noel was appointed to investigate the circumstances of Parson's arrest and prosecution. In 1999 Parsons commenced civil action against the government and Noel J. suspended his investigation. Parsons has since been awarded $1.3 million by the Newfoundland and Labrador government. Brian Doyle was subsequently convicted of the murder.

In 1995 Randy Druken was convicted of the murder of his girlfriend, Brenda Young. He had a criminal record and been violent towards her in the past. In 1999 the Newfoundland and Labrador Court of Appeal overturned the conviction and ordered a new trial. Subsequently the Crown stayed the proceedings. No further charges were laid against anyone else. In 2002 Druken commenced civil proceedings against the government and he was subsequently awarded $2.1 million for the six years he was in jail. In his report the commissioner said that the police had not cordoned off the crime scene, with many people trampling through it, and exhibits found at the scene were not adequately documented or forensically examined. For example, a cigarette butt found at the crime scene had another suspect's DNA on it. However, the commissioner found that the investigators were interested in collecting evidence incriminating Druken only and that they re-interviewed vulnerable witnesses, including a nine-year-old girl, in a suggestive manner.[86] He recommended the electronic recording of all police interviews in major crime cases in part in order to detect suggestive police interviewing.[87] The police and prosecution had also relied upon a jailhouse

---

85 Lamer Inquiry, above note 58.

86 *Ibid.* at 210: "The deliberate tactics of continually re-interviewing the witnesses, telling them what the police wanted to hear and attempting to intimidate them was particularly egregious."

87 *Ibid.* at 109.

informant whose evidence on other matters had proved to be unreliable. The prosecutor failed to disclose relevant wiretap material to the accused.

In 1989 Ronald Dalton was convicted of the second-degree murder of his wife, Brenda. In 1998 the Newfoundland and Labrador Court of Appeal overturned the conviction and ordered a new trial that resulted in him being acquitted. In 2001 Dalton commenced civil proceedings against Charles Hutton (the pathologist) and his employer, the government.

The commissioner's mandate in the first two cases was in relation to the investigation and prosecution. In the third case it was in relation to the eight-year delay in hearing the appeal.

In referring to the earlier Morin and Sophonow inquiries, Lamer C.J. said that the reports and other literature identified a number of recurring features in wrongful conviction cases. These included a crime that is horrible and alarming, giving it a high profile in the community and creating public pressure to find and convict the perpetrator immediately. They also included cases where there was an absence of direct evidence, leading to reliance upon "circumstances" that are subjectively interpreted to draw inferences of guilt. He said that frequently such inferences are logically weak and are, occasionally, "far-fetched." He also pointed to reliance upon highly questionable evidence, such as jailhouse informants; the demonizing of a suspect, who may be a "loner," "outsider," or member of a minority group; and the exaggeration of the adversarial roles on the part of the police and prosecutors leading to noble cause corruption. This, he said, involves the self-justification of improper professional practices in order to achieve the perceived correct result which might include the "planting" of evidence or "verbals" which amounted to the fabrication of incriminating statements or confessions.[88]

Chief Justice Lamer said that any or all of these features may contribute to tunnel vision. He said that tunnel vision was rarely the result of malice on the part of individuals but most often a product of a police and prosecutorial culture that has allowed the subconscious mind to rationalize a biased approach to the evidence. In the Parsons and Druken cases, he criticized the prosecutors for not questioning the case as constructed by the police. Moreover, he said, tunnel vision provides mutual reinforcement among police officers, among prosecutors, and in the interaction of these groups of professionals—it may even affect judges.

Chief Justice Lamer said that once the officers are "locked in" to the theory of their case, it is not difficult to understand how some of them, with "noble"

88 *Ibid.* at 71.

motivation, may move from the mere interpretation of the evidence to more malignant practices. "I agree with the submission of the Association in Defence of the Wrongfully Convicted (AIDWYC)," he said, "that the causes of wrongful convictions are fundamentally systemic."[89]

Parsons was identified as the suspect within twenty-four hours of his mother's death. The police did not seriously examine alternative explanations, they ignored or minimalized evidence that was inconsistent with his guilt, they questioned witnesses in a manner that was skewed towards Parsons's guilt, they exaggerated the importance of evidence consistent with his guilt, and they interpreted irrelevant evidence as consistent with his guilt. As Commissioner Lamer put it: "In sum, the investigators were securely ensconced in the tunnel."[90] He also found that the conduct of both the police and the prosecutors "were fuelled by the sense of noble cause"[91] and that the prosecutor had engaged in inflammatory and overreaching advocacy that had demonized the accused.[92] Tunnel vision and noble cause corruption need not in all cases go hand in hand, but when they do, they provide a recipe for miscarriages of justice.

Commissioner Lamer noted that "the forensic officer first assigned to the scene testified that he felt totally inadequate." He added, that in respect of the police, at trial, the officers testified with great confidence about the way the investigation ran smoothly, without error and that nothing was overlooked. However, he noted, in retrospect, many of them realized how dysfunctional the investigation had been. He pointed out that the murder scene was not cordoned off and that some eighteen people had entered the house, with twelve to fifteen of them entering the blood-coated bathroom. In the Druken case, a critical piece of evidence, a cigarette butt with an alternative suspect's DNA, was overlooked.

Commissioner Lamer criticized the prosecutors in both the Parsons and Druken cases for failing to live up to the ideal expressed in *Boucher*[93] that the Crown should be interested in the truth as opposed to winning. In both cases, he found prosecutors had overreached in their advocacy. Even more fundamentally, they failed to challenge or question the police. The prosecutors accepted "the police focus on one individual as the perpetrator, to the exclusion of all other reasonable possibilities . . . they marshalled all of their skills as advocates

89 *Ibid.* at 72.
90 *Ibid.* at 78–79.
91 *Ibid.* at 146.
92 *Ibid.* at 153.
93 Above note 12; discussed above in Chapter 2.

to "shore up a weak case" and secure a conviction."[94] The problem, in Commissioner Lamer's view, was not that individual prosecutors acted in bad faith, but that they were part of a prosecutorial culture motivated by a noble cause and affected by tunnel vision.

In the end, Commissioner Lamer, noting that he was the Chief Justice of Canada at the time of Parsons's trial, offered an apology:

> I wish to indulge in this opportunity to extend my apology to all of those who may have suffered injustice in our legal system while I held this role. Since the ultimate problem is inevitably systemic, those of us who form that system cannot simply say that any particular injustice has nothing to do with me.[95]

His important conclusion was that a society that treats its administration of criminal justice as a low priority eventually pays the price. The personal cost of such a tragedy to Gregory Parsons, his family, and friends, the financial cost of compensation to him, and the financial cost of the inquiry all constitute examples of the price to be paid for taking shortcuts in the administration of justice.

### 5) Credibility of Police Witnesses and Non-disclosure—The Case of James Driskell

In 1990, Perry Harder's body was discovered in a shallow grave near some railways tracks. He had been shot several times in the chest. Driskell was sent to trial without a committal hearing. He was convicted of the murder and sentenced to life imprisonment with no eligibility to be paroled for twenty-five years. The prosecution relied heavily on incriminating statements of associates who claimed Driskell had discussed killing Harder to prevent him from testifying against him in relation to property offences. It also relied on three hairs found in Driskell's van that were said to be similar to the victim's.[96] After thirteen years in prison, Driskell was released pending a review of his conviction. That review led to his conviction being set aside and a new trial directed. In 2005, the Manitoba Attorney General directed a stay of proceedings.

In 2005 Patrick Lesage, a former chief justice of the Ontario Superior Court of Justice, was appointed to inquire into aspects of the trial and the

---

94 Lamer Inquiry, above note 58 at 303.
95 *Ibid.* at 101.
96 The forensic aspect of this case will be discussed in Chapter 8.

conviction.[97] It was said that the prosecution and police had failed to disclose information relating to the credibility of the witnesses, including that they had received considerable sums of money from the state; the police had negotiated a protection agreement for one witness which was never revealed to the jury; the other was going to be charged with arson and the police made a secret promise to him that he would not be prosecuted for that.

The commissioner noted that police policies specifically stated that detailed notes were to be taken and that all information relating to any prosecution was to be passed to the Crown Attorney, especially where it related to the credibility of a prosecution witness. In addition, he added, overriding the right to a preliminary inquiry, when that right is available in the *Criminal Code* should be used only in the rarest cases as it allows the Crown and defence to test issues such as the credibility of the Crown witnesses. The commissioner said that there should be regular meetings between representatives of judges, prosecutors, defence lawyers, police, and correctional authorities. Such meetings would open channels of communication between these branches of the justice system and allow them to address the issues that constantly arise. He referred to the Sophonow Inquiry report about the important role that Crown counsel plays:

> The role of Crown Counsel is of great importance to the administration of justice and to the welfare of the community. The Crown prosecutor must proceed with the case against the accused fairly and courageously . . . Crown Counsel must be of absolute integrity and above all suspicion of favouritism or unfair compromise. Crown Counsel must be a symbol of fairness, prompt to make all reasonable disclosure. As well, they must be scrupulous in the attention given to the welfare and safety of witnesses. They enjoy the respect of all the judiciary. The community looks upon the Crown prosecutor as a symbol of fairness, of authority and as a spokesman for the community.[98]

The commissioner also referred to the Lamer Inquiry report where it was said that the role of a Crown attorney requires not only professional skill and judgment, but also courage. Often the working conditions include difficult time pressures and limited resources. It may be particularly difficult for less experienced Crown attorneys to exercise "contrarian" thinking. Commissioner Lamer had said that experienced Crown attorneys, in leadership roles, must

---

97 Driskell Inquiry, above note 58, online: www.driskellinquiry.ca/pdf/final_report_jan2007.pdf.

98 *Ibid.* at 117.

foster critical thinking and independence in their younger counterparts. A Crown attorney, like a judge, must not only exercise good judgment but must also be willing to make unpopular decisions. Commissioner LeSage said, "I concur with and strongly support these views."[99]

He noted that in recent years, non-disclosure issues had arisen in three homicide cases prosecuted by the Driskell prosecutor (Sophonow, Driskell, and Ostrowski). In addition, in two other homicide cases (Unger and Sanderson), hair microscopy evidence given at trial had since been refuted by DNA evidence. The commissioner said he recommended that if there were similar cases of that prosecutor in which people had claimed wrongful conviction, the Manitoba Justice department should direct an independent and external review of them. Manitoba has conducted audits of cases involving hair microscopy evidence.

In relation to post-conviction disclosures, Commissioner Lesage stated that an Ontario Attorney General's Advisory Committee had said:

> The need to disclose extends into appeal periods following conviction. The factual findings of the Marshall Commission demonstrate clearly the need to disclose evidence that Crown counsel realizes raises a doubt about the guilt of someone who has already been convicted, no matter when such evidence comes to Crown counsel's attention . . . . While the obligation to disclose extends throughout any appellate litigation that follows a conviction, it is not tied to the currency of any appeal periods. In a number of recent cases, the disclosure of evidence, whether fresh or otherwise, sometimes even years after all appeal routes had been exhausted and convictions upheld, has led to new trials being ordered, or convictions quashed outright.[100]

The commissioner said it appeared that Manitoba did not have a policy to deal with post-conviction disclosure. He recommended that the pretrial disclosure policy be extended to include post-trial disclosure. He said there must also be a procedure by which the Department of Justice receives this information from the police and then discloses it to the accused or counsel.

Commissioner Lesage also devoted a large section of his report to the difficult issue of how to help innocent people regain their standing in the community. He strongly discouraged the approach taken in Driskell's case of staying the proceedings because it drapes the innocent with a residual taint.

---

99 *Ibid.*
100 *Ibid.* at 118.

In relation to "unsavoury" witnesses he recommended that the policies be revised to specifically provide that all benefits requested, discussed, or provided or intended to be provided at any time in relation to any "central" witness be recorded and disclosed.

Commissioner Lesage noted that the Sophonow Inquiry report had stated that there should be a completely independent entity established to effectively, efficiently, and quickly review cases in which a wrongful conviction is alleged. He concurred in this recommendation. If there was an independent inquisitorial body, such as the CCRC in Britain, it could have obtained access to the results of a police re-investigation of the case that the police refused to disclose. Commissioner Lesage noted that Driskell was in a "catch 22 position" of being unable to support an application to the federal Minister of Justice to obtain a new trial or a new appeal without such material, but also having no way to gain access to the undisclosed material.[101] In this way, information that is unavailable to the applicant because of inability to compel disclosure would be available to the independent agency to allow it to make a better determination of whether a miscarriage of justice had occurred.

Finally, Commissioner Lesage was asked to make findings whether the police and prosecutors who worked on the case fell below existing professional standards and should be referred for discipline. He found that the pervasive failures of disclosure fell below *Stinchcombe* disclosure requirements. Nevertheless, he did not refer the cases to discipline because all of the police officers had retired or resigned, and only the most junior prosecutor still practised law in Manitoba and as such was subject to the law society's jurisdiction. He also decided that there was no reasonable prospect of a criminal conviction against the officials.[102]

### 6) Witnesses Pressured by Police — The Case of David Milgaard

In 1969, David Milgaard, then aged sixteen, a petty thief and habitual drug-user, and his two friends Ron Wilson and Nichol John took a road trip across the Canadian prairies. They stopped briefly in Saskatoon to pick up another friend, Albert Cadrain, whose family had rented part of their house to Larry Fisher and his wife. On that day, the body of a twenty-year-old Saskatoon nursing aid, Gail Miller, was found partly clothed face-down in a snowbank. She had been sexually assaulted and stabbed more than two dozen times. Police originally thought the killer might be the man who had sexually assaulted three

101 *Ibid.* at 121.
102 *Ibid.* at 110–12.

other women in previous months (Larry Fisher); however, interest in those cases diminished when Milgaard was identified as a suspect and could not be linked to the other assaults. The police were tipped off by Cadrain who admitted being interested in the financial reward offered. He gave evidence that he had seen Milgaard return the night of Miller's death in bloodstained clothes. Wilson and John also gave evidence against him. They had initially told the police they had been with Milgaard that whole day, but later changed their story.

In 1970, Milgaard was convicted and sentenced to life imprisonment for the rape and murder of Gail Miller. He unsuccessfully appealed against his conviction. As in the Donald Marshall case, the Court of Appeal upheld a procedure that allowed a witness who was reluctant to testify and might have recanted to be confronted with prior sworn testimony—testimony that was subsequently proven to be false. As a result, Milgaard spent twenty-three years in prison.

In 1988, Milgaard applied to the federal Minister of Justice for a review of his conviction pursuant to section 690 of the *Criminal Code* alleging the scientific evidence used to convict him at trial was exculpatory and that other evidence used at trial had been fabricated. In 1990, Justice McIntyre, a former judge of the Supreme Court of Canada, was retained by the Department of Justice to review and to provide advice to the federal minister on the application for mercy. After receiving the advice but not disclosing it to Milgaard, the minister dismissed the application.

Six months later, Milgaard filed another application, this time focusing on the issue of Larry Fisher as an alternative suspect. After Milgaard's mother had a highly publicized meeting with the prime minister, the minister of Justice referred the matter to the Supreme Court of Canada for a hearing. The Milgaard Inquiry outlined how in their respective memoirs, the prime minister and the minister of Justice gave inconsistent accounts of who ordered the case to be referred back to the court. This finding reveals the lack of transparency and the risk of politicization in processes that require petitions to the executive to reopen cases.

In 1992, the Supreme Court determined that Milgaard had failed to establish his innocence. The Court decided, however, that the conviction was no longer safe given that some of the original witnesses had recanted and there was evidence of an alternative suspect.[103] On the Court's recommendation, the min-

103 *Reference re Milgaard*, [1992] 1 S.C.R. 866. The Court indicated at para. 19 that the fresh evidence that it had considered "could well affect a jury's assessment of the guilt or innocence of Milgaard. The continued conviction of Milgaard would amount to a miscarriage of justice if an opportunity was not provided for a jury to consider the fresh evidence."

ister directed a new trial. However, instead of a further trial, the Crown entered a stay of proceedings. The Attorney General of Saskatchewan stated that the provincial government would not order an inquiry or compensate Milgaard.

In 1997, a DNA report confirmed that semen found on Miller's body did not come from Milgaard, and he received $10 million in compensation. Larry Fisher was later charged and convicted of the murder. In 2004 the Saskatchewan government appointed a royal commission headed by Justice MacCallum to investigate Milgaard's wrongful conviction. In 2008 the findings were released.[104]

The commissioner found that the police reasonably focused on Milgaard and that "tunnel vision, negligence and misconduct have been alleged but not shown."[105] He did find that Saskatoon police had brought in Roberts, a senior detective of the Calgary police, to conduct polygraphs on Milgaard's travelling companions (Ron Wilson and Nichol John), believing Milgaard was the killer, but lacking evidence to charge him. He said that Roberts had pressured them to tell him what Roberts thought to be the truth: "But for the questioning of John and Wilson by Roberts, Milgaard would not have been charged and tried for the crime of murder."[106] The commissioner recommended that interviews be recorded, though he did suggest that unrecorded utterances outside of the formal interview can still be made and should be admissible.[107] He also found that while the disclosure was adequate given the standards of the time, it was not adequate under the broad *Stinchcombe* rule and that it might have given Milgaard's lawyer material that would have led to other suspects.

Commissioner MacCallum found no fault in the way that officials within the federal Justice department investigated Milgaard's two applications to reopen the case. Nevertheless, he found that the investigation simply followed the grounds advanced by Milgaard and was delayed as Milgaard attempted to collect evidence. The findings of the investigation conducted for the minister, as well as advice given by a former Supreme Court justice to the minister, were not disclosed to Milgaard. The commissioner was critical of Milgaard's family and lawyers' extensive use of the media with respect to these two applications. At the same time, however, the commissioner found that the second application was granted by the minister not because of new evidence about Larry Fisher but for "public policy reasons."[108] This finding raises the question of whether Milgaard's media campaign was both effective and necessary.

---

104 Milgaard Inquiry, above note 58.

105 *Ibid.* at 304.

106 *Ibid.* at 303.

107 *Ibid.* at 318.

108 *Ibid.* at 309.

Commissioner MacCallum found that the Saskatoon police did not follow up on a 1980 complaint from Larry Fisher's wife that Fisher was responsible for Gail Miller's murder. He recommended that every complaint to police calling into question the safety of a conviction should be passed to the Director of Public Prosecutions. He added that prosecutors should avoid the impression that they are heavily committed to a case on a personal level. He said that in all homicide cases, all trial exhibits capable of yielding forensic samples should be preserved for a minimum of ten years and that convicted persons should be given notice after ten years of the impending destruction of exhibits relating to their trials, allowing applications for extensions. He also said that in all indictable offence cases, documentary exhibits be scanned and indefinitely stored.

Commissioner MacCallum said that officers' notebooks can be important in claims of wrongful convictions, and should be treated as police files and preserved as such.[109] He said that all police and prosecution files in serious cases should be retained in their original form for a year, then scanned and entered into a database where a permanent and secure electronic record can be kept. He thought that the concept of factual innocence, as the sole criterion for paying compensation, was unduly restrictive and that where a miscarriage of justice has resulted from an obvious breach of good faith in the application of standards expected of police, prosecution, or the courts, the door to compensation should not be closed for lack of proof of factual innocence. He also approved the CCRC model, where cases are referred back to the courts not only because of concerns about innocence, but also on grounds related to unfair trials or the discovery of new evidence that may have affected the verdict.

Commissioner MacCallum recommended that claims of wrongful conviction should be investigated by a review agency independent of government, similar to the British CCRC and not by officials responsible to the federal minister of Justice. He recognized that, at present, the investigative file prepared for the minister is shared with the applicant which was not the case when Milgaard applied to the minister of Justice. Nevertheless, the commissioner found the current process wanting because the ultimate decision is made by an elected official subject to political pressure and associated with prosecutions. In addition, the process "remains reactive in nature and assumes an inquisitorial role only on the basis of the grounds advanced by the applicant. Most applicants are without resources that would allow them to advance their best case."[110]

109 As we saw in the previous section, this proved to be the case in a number of the British cases as well.

110 *Ibid.* at 321.

## E. THE AUSTRALIAN EXPERIENCE

### 1) Police Behaving Badly—Commissions and Inquiries

Over many years police forces in Australia have had investigations and inquiries that have disclosed serious and systemic corruption. For example, Operation Florida, which was reported to the NSW Parliament in 2004, arose from a joint NSW Crime Commission/NSW Police investigation code-named "Mascot," which commenced early in 1999:

> The Police Integrity Commission joined the investigation in July 2000, by which time a substantial body of evidence of serious police corruption had been gathered by the officers from the NSW Crime Commission and the NSW Police Special Crime Unit . . . in October 2001 the investigation was revealed in a public hearing at the Police Integrity Commission . . . [The] hearings continued over the next 14 months . . . The conduct in question was committed by officers attached to a number of different commands within NSW Police.[111]

Juliette Langdon and Paul Wilson summed up the Australian experience of police corruption when they stated:

> . . . there have been a number of inquiries into police corruption in various Australian states. The Fitzgerald inquiry in Queensland found that police corruption was "widespread" . . . and that verbal confessions were "a feature of Queensland criminal trials" . . . In Western Australia, Kennedy . . . concluded police corruption was prevalent, whilst in Victoria, the Ombudsman has been heading investigations regarding allegations of drug-related police corruption with possible links to the underworld . . . Investigations have so far "revealed that mediocrity, rather than professionalism, has been the norm in some areas of Victoria Police" . . . The Wood Royal Commission described the state of police corruption in NSW as "systemic and entrenched" . . . with practices including the fabrication of and tampering with evidence. Interestingly, though victims of police corruption may have been wrongfully convicted because of unethical and criminal police practices, the NSW Royal Commission gave little attention to correcting such miscarriages of justice . . .[112]

---

111 New South Wales, Police Integrity Commission, *Report to Parliament: Operation Florida* (Sydney: Police Integrity Commission, 2004).

112 Juliette Langdon & Paul Wilson, "When Justice Fails: A Follow-up Examination of Serious Criminal Cases since 1985" (2005) 17 Current Issues in Criminal Justice 179 referring to Queensland, Commission of Inquiry into Possible Illegal Activities and

In the New South Wales case involving allegations that Roseanne Catt had assaulted and attempted to murder her former husband, the Court of Appeal said of the police officer in charge of the investigation:

> . . . the letters which Det. Sgt. Thomas wrote making the various allegations were an indication of "his propensity to improperly use his office to damage Ms Catt irrespective of the risk of gratuitous collateral damage to others." . . . "it indicates a lack of objectivity having descended into malice and abuse of power."[113]

Queensland and Victoria have also had major inquiries into police corruption, and some, particularly in Victoria, are still ongoing.

In 1994 the New South Wales government set up a royal commission headed by Wood J., a serving Supreme Court judge, to investigate the existence and extent of corruption in the police service. In its report in 1996, the commission, in setting out examples of serious systemic corruption, recommended wide-ranging reforms, including the establishment of a permanent Police Integrity Commission to investigate serious police misconduct. The integrity commission came into effect in January 1997.

The Fitzgerald Judicial Inquiry was set up in 1987 by the Queensland government in response to widespread allegations of high-level police corruption. When Commissioner Tony Fitzgerald issued his report in 1989, charges were laid against a number of high-profile police officers and politicians, including the premier (charged with perjury for evidence given at the inquiry) and the police commissioner (charged with corruption).[114]

---

Associated Police Misconduct, *Report of a Commission of Inquiry Pursuant to Orders in Council* (Brisbane: The Commission, 1989) at 357 and 206 [Fitzgerald Report]; Western Australia, *Royal Commission into Whether There Has Been Corrupt or Criminal Conduct by Any Western Australian Police Officer* (Perth, WA: Police Royal Commission, 2004) [Kennedy Report]; Victoria, Ombudsman, *Ceja Task Force Drug Related Corruption: Second Interim Report of Ombudsman Victoria* (Melbourne: Government Printer, 2004) at 13; New South Wales, *Royal Commission into the New South Wales Police Service: Final Report* (Sydney, NSW: The Commission, 1997) at 20 [Wood Royal Commission Report]; David Dixon "Reform, Regression and the Royal Commission into the NSW Police Service" in David Dixon, ed., *A Culture of Corruption* (Leichhardt, NSW: Hawkins Press, 1999) at 138–170. See also Paul Wilson, "When Justice Fails: A Preliminary Examination of Serious Criminal Cases in Australia" (1989) 24 Australian Journal of Social Issues 3. The two "When Justice Fails" reports provide an excellent overview of miscarriage of justice cases in Australia.

113 *R. v. Catt*, [2005] NSWCCA 279.

114 Fitzgerald Report, above note 112. This resulted in the setting up of the Crime and Misconduct Commission in Queensland: Wood Royal Commission Report, above note 112.

## 2) Intimidation by Police—The Case of Rupert Maxwell Stuart

In 1959, Max Stuart, an illiterate Aboriginal man, was convicted of the rape and murder of nine-year-old Mary Hattam in the South Australian country town of Ceduna. At that time, Stuart, twenty-seven years old, was travelling with the Funfair Carnival. It appears that after a lengthy interrogation he had signed a "confession" in the presence of six police officers, which he said was obtained under extreme duress when he feared for his life. The police swore the confession was in the "exact words" dictated by Stuart. However, Stuart spoke pidgin Aranda-English, yet the confession was typed in precise and educated English. Following his confession, Stuart was brought to trial in 1959. At his trial he said:

> I cannot read or write. Never been to school. I did not see the little girl. I did not kill her. Police hit me. Choked me. Make me say these words. They say I killed her. That is what I want to say.[115]

The law society had assigned to him a relatively inexperienced lawyer, David O'Sullivan, to represent him without payment. There was little forensic evidence linking Stuart to the young girl, and O'Sullivan had unsuccessfully argued that owing to Stuart's poor command of English, police had coerced Stuart into confessing. Stuart was convicted and sentenced to death. There were two unsuccessful appeals and a further one to the Privy Council in London.

In response to widespread media agitation, a royal commission (made up of three judges—two of whom had prior judicial involvement in the case) was set up in 1959. The commission upheld Stuart's conviction. The South Australian government, however, commuted his death sentence to one of life imprisonment. Stuart was released on parole in 1973. Although the case has come to be regarded as a classic miscarriage of justice case, there has been no further formal review of the conviction.

## 3) Police Pressure to Obtain False Confession—The Case of John Button

In 1963, nineteen-year-old Button was convicted of the manslaughter of his girlfriend, Rosemary Anderson, by running her down with his car. His account was that he had come across her lying at the side of the road. But the police noticed some damage to the nearside front of his car, and through an interro-

---

115 Justice Michael Kirby, "Black and White Lessons for the Australian Judiciary" (2002) 23 Adel. L.R. 195.

gation lasting through the night, he eventually "confessed" at about 4 a.m. Remarkably, the real villain, notorious serial-killer Edgar Cooke, confessed to the killing as he stood on the gallows at his execution some time later.[116] Subsequent appeals to the courts as well as petitions for ministerial interventions were unsuccessful.

Finally in 2002, the Western Australian Court of Appeal, in overturning Button's conviction, noted that new scientific evidence showed clearly that the damage to his car could not have been caused by hitting a person.[117] The court also said that a major part of Button's case was that evidence not given at his trial or on appeal suggested that Cooke was responsible for the death of Rosemary Anderson. That evidence included confessions by Cooke to police and others that he was the person responsible for running down Rosemary rather than John. One confession that Cooke made was to Reverend Jenkins at Fremantle Prison, and a further "gallows" confession was made at the prison approximately fifteen minutes before Cooke's execution. There was also a confession witnessed by I.J. Thorpe, J.P., the deputy superintendent at Fremantle Prison. The confessions had been rejected in 1964 as "utterly worthless" by the Chief Justice at the time.

### 4) Faulty Reasoning by Police—The Case of Edward Splatt

In 1978 Splatt was convicted in South Australia of the murder of Mrs. Simper, an Adelaide woman of seventy-seven years who had been badly beaten, sexually assaulted, and strangled in her bedroom. As we will see in Chapter 8, the only evidence leading to the identification of Splatt in this case was "scientific evidence." No one had ever seen Splatt with the victim or in her house. However, the police investigator had collected trace evidence (bird seed, wood particles, and tiny particles of paint) from the scene, particularly that which was collected from around the window where entry was gained and from the bed on which the victim was found. The hunt was on for someone who had that particular combination of forensic factors about their home or person.

---

116 For the background to this remarkable story, see the transcripts of the ABC Australian Story programs "Murder He Wrote," Part 1 (29 July 2002) and Part 2 (5 August 2002). See also Estelle Blackburn, *Broken Lives* (Perth: Stellar Publishing, 2005); also Estelle Blackburn, *The End of Innocence* (Victoria: Hardie Grant Books, 2007). In this case the media played an important role. Bret Christian of Post Newspapers in Perth provided financial and other support to retain appropriate experts and to assist with the publication of Blackburn's book.

117 *Button v. The Queen*, [2002] WASCA 35.

Splatt lived nearby, and it was noticed that he had an aviary in his back garden. When it was found out that he also worked as a spray painter at a nearby factory, the police investigators became committed to the idea that Splatt was the perpetrator. Splatt protested that incriminating materials found at his home had been taken from the turnups of his trousers which, he said, he had been unable to get into for several years because he had put on so much weight. The investigators were not deterred, although as Splatt said, it wouldn't have taken much for them to ask him to try them on.

A royal commission took place some years later and sat for 196 hearing days. The commissioner, in finding Splatt's conviction to be unsafe, criticized all aspects of the scientific evidence. He was particularly critical of the role of the police officer who headed the investigation.[118] He said that the role of the investigator must not be confused with that of a forensic scientist. Here, he said, the police investigator appeared to have had a dual role, part investigator and part scientist.[119]

The commissioner said that this sort of confusion could happen only in a system which was "an incorrect one with serious defects." He said that some of the original evidence that had been given by the expert witnesses involved completely non-scientific statements that were more like police investigatory suggestions, for example, the statement that the paint particles could have arrived at the crime scene only by being carried there by the perpetrator and that they could not have been airborne as something like "Typhoon Tracey" would have been needed to carry them from the factory to the residence.[120]

The commissioner said that during the conduct of a trial, there is a serious obligation on the lawyers conducting the trial. Their critical responsibility is to ask such detailed and probing questions of the scientists as are most likely to elicit the proper information. Following the commission's findings, Splatt was released from prison and paid $300,000 compensation.

### 5) Fabricated Evidence—The Case of the Mickelberg Brothers

In 1983, brothers Ray, Peter, and Brian Mickelberg were convicted of stealing over $600,000 in gold bars from the Perth Mint in Western Australia. The police investigation focused on the Mickelbergs who were said to have used forged cheques to deceive the mint into handing over the gold. The brothers

118 Carl R. Shannon, *Royal Commission Report Concerning the Conviction of Edward Charles Splatt* (Adelaide: Government Printer, 1984) at 43–52 [Splatt Royal Commission].

119 *Ibid.* at 31.

120 *Ibid.* at 32.

embarked on a series of appeals on the grounds that police had fabricated the evidence on which their convictions were based.[121]

In 2002, during a Western Australian royal commission into police corruption, a retired police officer who was present at the interviews of the brothers and whose evidence was central to the prosecution case against them, confessed that both he and another officer (who went on to head the state's criminal investigation bureau) had fabricated evidence to frame the brothers for the offence.[122] In 2004 this confession resulted in the West Australian Court of Appeal quashing the brothers' conviction and the state government paying them $1.5 million as compensation.

## 6) Discredited Informer Evidence—The Case of Tim Anderson

In 1978 a bomb went off outside the Hilton Hotel in Sydney, New South Wales, the venue for the Commonwealth Heads of Government meeting.[123] Three people were killed. Police identified as suspects three local members of Ananda Marga, a spiritual group whose members had protested against the visit of the Indian prime minister to that meeting.

Police had recruited an informer to infiltrate the group and on the basis of his evidence, Anderson and two others were arrested, not for the bombing, but on charges they had conspired to murder a prominent member of a neo-Nazi group. They were tried, convicted, and sentenced to sixteen years of imprisonment. The prosecution was allowed to introduce evidence regarding the bombing even though they were never charged with that offence. Appeals to the Court of Appeal and the High Court were unsuccessful.

---

121 Avon Lovell, in his book *The Mickelberg Stitch* (Perth, AU: Creative Research, 1985), describes the questionable investigative practices used by the West Australian police force in this case.

122 Kennedy Report, above note 112, vol. 1, Executive Summary at 1–2:

> the full range of corrupt or criminal conduct from stealing to assaults, perjury, drug dealing and the improper disclosure of confidential information have been examined. [The Western Australian Police force] has been ineffective in monitoring those events and modifying its procedures to deal with that conduct and to prevent its repetition . . . . The fact that there remain in WAPS a number of officers who participated in this conduct, and who not only refused to admit it, but also uniformly denied it with vehemence, is a matter of concern.

123 See Tim Anderson, *Take Two: The Criminal Justice System Revisited* (Sydney: Bantam Books, 1992) and Kerry Carrington *et al.*, eds., *Travesty! Miscarriages of Justice* (Leichardt, NSW: Pluto Press, 1991); and Tom Molomby, *Spies, Bombs & The Path of Bliss: Ananda Marga and the Hilton Bombing* (Australia: Potoroo Press, 1986).

After some concerted public campaigning, a judicial commission headed by Wood J. was set up to examine the circumstances leading to the conviction. It recommended quashing the convictions as they were said to have been based on the evidence of the now discredited informer. It exonerated the police of any wrongdoing. In 1985 the three men were freed from prison.

In 1989, Anderson was again arrested and this time charged with murder arising out of the Hilton Bombing. He was charged on the basis of an alleged confession he had made to a fellow inmate while in prison. This inmate later received an indemnity for other offences, in part, for giving evidence against Anderson. Shortly after Anderson's arrest, a former member of Ananda Marga, Evan Pederick, confessed to the police that he and Anderson had planted the bomb. Pederick's evidence was central to Anderson's conviction despite flaws emerging in his story during the trial. Pederick's reasons for making the false confession were never clear, but the police and the prosecution appear to have accepted his story because it fitted their preconceived notions of Anderson's involvement in the bombing. They did not verify parts of Pederick's story that could have been checked, and they ignored other aspects of it that did not fit their preferred version of the events.

Certain journalists were granted privileged access to Crown witnesses and returned the favour by giving an uncritical report of the trial. The prosecutor also unsuccessfully applied to have bail conditions imposed on Anderson which would have prevented him from making public comment or encouraging others to disseminate their views or materials about the case. In 1991 the New South Wales Court of Appeal overturned Anderson's conviction largely owing to prosecutorial errors and unfairness in presenting Pederick's evidence at the trial.

## 7) Manipulation of Mentally Fragile Person, Inadequate Disclosure — The Case of Andrew Mallard

In 1995 Andrew Mallard was convicted of the murder of Pamela Lawrence. She had been alone in her shop in Perth when she was violently assaulted with a heavy instrument which was never found.[124] Mallard had previously been

---

124 *Mallard v. The Queen*, [2005] HCA 68 [*Mallard*]; Gummow, Hayne, Callinan, Kirby, and Heydon JJ. agreed the appeal should be allowed. See also Corruption and Crime Commission, *Report on the Inquiry into Alleged Misconduct by Public Officers in Connection with the Investigation of the Murder of Mrs Pamela Lawrence, the Prosecution and Appeals of Mr Andrew Mark Mallard and Other Related Matters* (Perth: Corruption and Crime Commission, 2008) [Corruption and Crime Commission, *Mallard*]. The

in the shop. He was a user of marijuana. Earlier, on the day of the assault, he had briefly been in the custody of police officers. Following the death he was repeatedly interviewed by police officers, both while he was in hospital and elsewhere, for the treatment of a mental illness. Only one of the interviews was recorded. During the interviews he made some highly fanciful, indeed incredible, assertions and claims, as well as apparently inculpatory, confessional statements. It later became apparent that a good deal of information which had been in the possession of investigating police before and during the trial had not been disclosed to Mallard or his lawyers.

It is clear that, because of his psychiatric condition, Mallard thought he was being used as some sort of consultant by the police to help them to figure out what had happened. Entering into the spirit of things, Mallard suggested, supposed, and theorized about how the crime might have occurred. Subsequently, the police claimed that Mallard's various notes and suppositions were confessions by him to his having committed the crime.

Mallard denied that he had told the police that Lawrence had been killed with a wrench. He said that his sketch of the weapon used in the assault was

> . . . a sketch of a supposed weapon that we were talking about in our theory which I said was a gas wrench to be used on acetylene equipment. I have no idea what a gas wrench looks like. That is what I assumed it would look like in my theory.[125]

Mallard's conviction was upheld by the Western Australian Court of Criminal Appeal in 1996.

It was later revealed that investigators had conducted experiments with a crescent-shaped wrench of the kind said to be the murder weapon. They included striking with a copper anode (of the kind kept in Lawrence's workshop) and a wrench on a pig's head in an attempt, unsuccessfully, to replicate Lawrence's wounds. Although they revealed that such an item was unlikely to be the cause of the injuries, the prosecutor had still suggested to the jury that the weapon sketched by Mallard might have been that which was used in the assault.

In 2005 the High Court quashed Mallard's conviction on the basis of this new evidence. As the Court said, "some, at least, of that evidence, the respond-

---

case came before the West Australian Court of Criminal Appeal on a reference by the Attorney General in *Mallard v. The Queen*, [2003] WASCA 296 when Parker, Wheeler, and Roberts-Smith JJ. all refused the appeal.

125 *Mallard v. The Queen*, *ibid.* at para. 83 (WASCA).

ent concedes should have been disclosed pursuant to clauses 57–60 of the Statement of Prosecution Policy and Guidelines."[126] In an application for leave to appeal in another case, Kirby J. said, "and we know from the *Mallard* case that it was largely because a media organisation pursued Mr Mallard's claim to innocence that ultimately the truth was unravelled and discovered."[127]

In 2006 a cold-case review by the police concluded that another man was the likely suspect.[128] Subsequently, in 2008, the police investigators and the prosecutor were the subject of adverse findings by a Corruption and Crime Commission inquiry for either withholding information about the experiments or for misrepresenting the significance of the possible weapon.[129]

Among the recommendations made by the commission were these:

> Consideration be given by the Commissioner of Police to making special provision for the interviewing by investigating police of mentally ill suspects.
>
> Whenever there is legislation, fresh authoritative case law, or DPP guidelines which relate to the conduct of criminal investigation or the admissibility of evidence in such cases, senior police officers affected by such matters be required to attend formal seminar or meetings at which they can be made familiar with such matters.
>
> Mallard consider making complaint with the legal practitioners' complaints committee regarding the conduct of the prosecutor.
>
> Police Commissioner consider taking disciplinary action against the offending police officers.[130]

As we pointed out in Chapter 5, Mallard subsequently sued for compensation.

---

126 *Mallard*, above note 124 at para. 16.

127 *Manock v. Channel Seven Adelaide Pty. Ltd.*, [2007] HCATrans 414 (7 August 2007), appellant argument. He also added:

> On the other hand, we have got to keep in mind the importance of disclosing and exploring cases of miscarriage of justice. I am not saying that is this case, but Mallard is an instance where it was in a sense persistence of those who were complaining that ultimately brought the matter to a resolution, so that it is important that that entitlement of citizens and of the media to be protected.

*Ibid.*, respondent argument.

128 Simon Rochford was serving a sentence for murdering his girlfriend seven weeks after Lawrence's death. He committed suicide in prison after being named as the suspect in the Lawrence case. Jo Prichard, "Police at Fault in Rochford's Suicide" *Perth Now* (13 October 2008).

129 Corruption and Crime Commission, *Mallard*, above note 124.

130 *Ibid.* at 165.

## F. CONCLUSION: INDIVIDUAL OR SHARED FAILURES?

While in theory, there may seem to be a clear dividing line between the police who investigate, the scientists who collect the evidence, and the prosecutor who takes the case before the criminal courts, our research shows that there is often some confusion between those undertaking these activities as to where the dividing line should be drawn. The only sensible explanation of, for example, the Splatt case in Australia, the IRA bombing cases in Britain, or the Morin and Driskell cases in Canada is that the scientists somehow lost their objectivity and felt that they had some responsibility to assist the prosecution in their pursuit of particular outcomes. Dr. Charles Smith in Canada said just this in his evidence to the Goudge Inquiry.[131]

Inadequate investigations should be identified by prosecutors before laying charges or putting the matter before the courts. Such a role follows from the ideal of prosecutors as interested in the truth. Nevertheless, in many of the cases examined in this chapter, prosecutors failed to provide such a check on police investigations.

This chapter has also revealed how the police have contributed to wrongful convictions either through deliberate misconduct or through tunnel vision, where evidence is interpreted in a manner consistent with a suspect's guilt and other evidence and alternative interpretations or suspects are discounted. Sometimes, witnesses are continually re-interviewed and even harassed until they provide evidence consistent with the police's case.

In Chapter 8, we consider the role of the scientists who, like the police, have a duty to be fair and even-handed.

---

131 Above note 58.

CHAPTER 8

# Forensic Science Issues

Probably more than any other person involved in the interaction between the state and the citizen, the scientist epitomizes neutrality and independence. Clear observations, interpreted according to properly tested scientific principles—how could things go wrong?

In Chapter 11, we will go into more detail about the report prepared by the National Academy of Sciences (NAS) in the United States.[1] For now, it is sufficient to mention that this report takes the view that often, there is simply not enough science behind forensic science and that many items are reported to the courts in ways that are misleading. For example, fingerprint experts will refer to a "match" between prints without explaining the subjective nature of the comparisons involved. The *NAS Report* also notes that there is frequent overstating of the reliability or accuracy of test results, and insufficient attention paid to error rates. It points out that sometimes, presumptive test results are reported as conclusive of the issues involved. It states that there are inherent problems of bias arising from the fact that forensic scientists are often closely associated with police and prosecutors.

The findings of the *NAS Report* will not have come as any surprise to those familiar with these issues. In 1993 Judy Bourke said that scientific test evidence

1 Committee on Identifying the Needs of the Forensic Sciences Community, National Research Council, *Strengthening Forensic Science in the United States: A Path Forward* (Washington, DC: National Academies Press, 2009) [*NAS Report*]. The report can be found online: www.ncjrs.gov/pdffiles1/nij/grants/228091.pdf.

was frequently misused in criminal trials because of its unreliability. She pointed out that there were two dimensions to the issue of unreliability.[2]

First, scientific test evidence may be unreliable because the scientific tests used in reaching that opinion are inaccurate or inappropriate. For example, the tests are based on unreliable underlying scientific principles, processes, or interpretation or a combination of all three. Bourke also pointed to the misuse of presumptive tests, as had occurred in the Chamberlain case in Australia. She mentioned that often not enough attention is paid to the error rates. More fundamentally, she emphasized that scientific testing "should be a search for dissimilarities, not for similarities."[3] It is a scientific principle that tests be "designed to disprove the original assumption" of the accuser's guilt, that is, to exclude the suspect. The Australian Splatt Royal Commission referred to this risk of confirmation bias as "unconscious bias."[4] In some respects, it is the scientific equivalent of the tunnel vision that was applied to much of the police and prosecutorial conduct discussed in Chapter 7.

The second dimension is that irrespective of the accuracy of the tests, scientific test evidence may be unreliable because an aura of scientific infallibility surrounds the evidence in illusory certainty. This aura of certainty may cause judges, lawyers, and the jury to operate under a shroud of assumed scientific omnipotence. Sometimes, observed facts are expressed by experts as "consistent with" the hypothesis of the guilt of an accused person. However, the jury is not told that when experts talk about things being "consistent with" something, they really mean that they "have not eliminated" the connection as a possibility. That is not the same as asserting a positive or causal relationship between them.[5] In addition, the public often wrongly assumes that science is a process that produces infallible truths. The public, including some lawyers and judges, may be unaware of the many controversies in many scientific fields, and of the evolving and dynamic nature of scientific knowledge.

As we pointed out in Chapter 2, Prof. William Tilstone has said that the basic obligation of the forensic scientist is to "gather evidence" of what has been observed.[6] Having done that, the scientist can use it as the basis for any

---

2 Judy Bourke, "Misapplied Science: Unreliability in Scientific Test Evidence" (1993) 10 Austl. Bar Rev. 123 [Bourke].

3 *Ibid.*, citing Carl R. Shannon, *Royal Commission Report Concerning the Conviction of Edward Charles Splatt* (Adelaide: Government Printer, 1984) at 48 [Splatt Royal Commission].

4 Splatt Royal Commission, *ibid.* at 48 and 100.

5 Bourke, above note 2 at 126.

6 William Tilstone, "Where Now for Forensic Science?" in (1986) 4 Proceedings of the Australian Forensic Science Society at 12 [Tilstone]. He is of particular interest to our

inferences to be made. However, in the context of forensic investigations, Professor Tilstone said, there is an enormous gap between "not eliminating" and "positively implicating"[7]—a point emphasized in the Morin Inquiry in Canada. Professor Tilstone referred to the Scottish case of *Preece*[8] in 1981 which involved the rape and murder of Mrs. Wills. In that case, the appeal judges took the view that evidence of fibres and stains, supposedly indicating that Wills had been in a lorry with Preece, would have proved nothing. They said that the merely associative evidence linking Wills to Preece would have been inadequate to convict him. Dr. Alan Clift, who had done the scientific work on the case, had used a test, but had not published or explained his method of doing this so that it could be assessed by other experts. As Professor Tilstone said: "Not only were none of the experts called by each side prepared to accept his [Dr. Clift's] conclusions, he [Dr. Clift] received considerable criticism from the Appeal Court judges who said that, if in fact it had been such a wonderful test, why didn't he publish it?"[9] Professor Tilstone went on to say: "His [Dr. Clift's] response to all of this was that the information was there at trial but nobody asked him about any of the points which subsequently were said to be shortcomings."[10]

Dr. Clift was particularly criticized because he had not divulged all the tests and results in his court report. The appeal court was not impressed by the idea that he had used a novel and unpublished technique. They felt it should have been published to permit peer assessment and to benefit other forensic scientists, if it had withstood critical appraisal.

In this chapter, we examine cases where the scientific evidence of experts has been found to be unreliable. In Chapter 9, we will examine the work of forensic pathologists, medically qualified people who choose to work on legal cases. Forensic scientists, by contrast, give evidence as experts, but not as medically qualified experts.[11]

---

work on these issues as he originally worked in Scotland, then in South Australia, and then in the United States. He has given evidence on proper forensic procedures to several Canadian inquiries.

7 *Ibid.* at 14.

8 *Preece v. Her Majesty's Advocate*, [1981] Crim. L.R. 783.

9 Tilstone, above note 6 at 16.

10 *Ibid.*

11 As to the development of the appreciation of the role of "misleading scientific evidence" and the similarities between the Canadian and the UK cases, see Sir Thomas Thorp, *Miscarriages of Justice* (Auckland, NZ: Legal Research Foundation, 2005) at 23. Thorp pointed out that it had been said (incorrectly) in the United Kingdom, Canada, and Australia that such erroneous cases as had been found were aberrations.

## A. THE BRITISH EXPERIENCE

In the IRA bombing cases discussed in Chapter 7 above, it was revealed that the problems with expert witnesses were greater than had been previously recognized. The cases showed serious deficiencies with the expert evidence given by the forensic scientists. As we will see, the judges referred to the conduct of some of the expert witnesses as "analogous to fraud."[12] They had put forward the results of presumptive tests as if they were conclusive of the issues and had failed to properly articulate the reasoning processes involved.

### 1) Preliminary Test Misrepresented—The Case of the Birmingham Six

At the trial, key evidence, relied upon by the prosecution, was that of a Home Office forensic scientist, Dr. Skuse.[13] He said that his analysis of swabs taken from hands, fingernails, and some belongings had tested positive for traces of nitroglycerine, a pale yellow, heavy, oily substance which explodes with great force when subjected to a shock or detonation. Dr. Skuse had used the Griess test to detect nitrate, which is not present as such in nitroglycerine: caustic soda is used to convert nitroglycerine to nitrite and the level of concentration of that is crucial to the result.

The Court of Appeal held that this test should be used only as a preliminary test and that it must be supported by more sensitive follow-up tests undertaken in a laboratory. Fresh evidence introduced at the appeal showed that

a) if Dr. Skuse had used a weak solution (as he stated at the trial), then the test could have reacted positively only if the appellants' hands had been "dripping with nitroglycerine," which was "an absurdity"; alternatively,
b) if Dr. Skuse had used a stronger solution, then the test could react positively to a number of chemicals, not just nitroglycerine.[14]

Fresh evidence also indicated that the positive results which Dr. Skuse said he had obtained using "gas chromatography spectrometry" may have arisen

---

12 In the context of the discussion of the work of the scientists Elliot and Higgs in *R. v. Maguire & Ors*, [1992] 2 All E.R. 433 (C.A.) [*Maguire*], Stuart-Smith L.J. said that "The cases have been recently reviewed in *R. v. Bolton Justices, ex p Scully* [1991] 2 All ER 619, [1991] 1 QB 537 and are based upon the unfairness of a conviction obtained by conduct which is analogous to fraud."

13 The discussion on the Birmingham Six here is from *R. v. McIlkenny & Ors* (1991), 93 Cr. App. R. 287 [*McIlkenny*]. See also Gary Edmond, "Constructing Miscarriages of Justice: Misunderstanding Scientific Evidence in High Profile Criminal Appeals" (2002) 22 Oxford J. Legal Stud. 53.

14 *McIlkenny*, *ibid.* at 297–98.

from contamination with everyday chemicals, including laboratory detergents that could have been used to wash the test containers. The test procedure could also have been reacting to the nitrite found in some soaps or the nitrocellulose polymer used in the manufacture of playing cards. The Court of Appeal concluded that Dr. Skuse's conclusions were "wrong, demonstrably wrong, judged even by the state of forensic science in 1974."[15]

## 2) Fraudulent Scientific Evidence — The Case of the Maguire Seven

Following the quashing of the Guildford Four convictions (on grounds of police misconduct in obtaining the confessions[16]), the Home Secretary in 1991 set up a public inquiry to identify potential problems in the handling of scientific evidence in the related case of the Maguire Seven.[17] The scientists giving evidence at their trial in 1976 had suggested that the accused people had handled explosives. However, in 1982, one of them jointly wrote an article confirming that innocent contamination can lead to the presence of nitroglycerine under the fingernails.[18] The public inquiry headed by Sir John May appointed Prof. Thorburn Burns, a forensic analytical chemist, to review the literature and undertake experiments in this area.[19]

Professor Burns's research was relied upon by both the May Inquiry and then the Court of Appeal when the *Maguire* case was referred back to it by the Home Secretary. In quashing the convictions, the court held that the two scientists who gave evidence at the trial had lied and suppressed evidence there.[20] They had been selective about the experimental data they produced, choosing material that supported their case and discarding that which did not. Thin layer chromatography (TLC) was done to test for traces of nitroglycerine. At trial the court was told that the TLC test was specific for nitroglycerine. A report on the files at the forensic laboratory, however, stated that the test could not distinguish between nitroglycerine and another type of explosive. This meant that the expert witnesses had either misled the court or lied to it. It was accepted

---

15 *Ibid.* at 318.

16 *R. v. Richardson, Conlon, Armstrong, & Hill* (20 October 1989), (E.W.C.A. Crim.).

17 *Maguire*, above note 12. *Report on the Inquiry into the Circumstances Surrounding the Convictions Arising out of the Bomb Attacks in Guildford and Woolwich in 1994, Final Report* by Sir John May (London: H.M.S.O., 1994) at 449 [May Inquiry].

18 J.D. Twibell *et al.*, "Transfer of Nitroglycerine to the Hands during Contact with Commercial Explosives" (1982) 27 Journal of Forensic Science 783.

19 U.K., H.C. *Interim Report on the Maguire Case* by Sir John May (London: H.M.S.O., 1990) at 556.

20 The scientists were Elliot and Higgs.

that the Crown was unaware of the deficiencies of the tests, the omission and fault having been that of the scientists.

The May Inquiry also obtained fresh evidence (through the tests conducted by Professor Burns) to show that traces of nitroglycerine can be innocently transferred through using hand towels (such as those in the washroom at the public house that the suspects frequented) if they had been contaminated with it. The Court of Appeal said that such a possibility was never excluded at trial.

The Court of Appeal stated that a forensic scientist who is an adviser to the prosecuting authority is under a duty to disclose material which is known and which may have some bearing on the offence charged and the surrounding circumstances of the case. It said the disclosure must be to the authority that retains the expert which must, in turn, inform the defence. However, the court also said that from the point of view of the defence, there was no reason to distinguish between members of the prosecuting authority and those advising it in the capacity of forensic scientists.

### 3) The Fraud Continued, Independence of Scientists—The Case of Judith Ward

Following the May Inquiry and the quashing of the Maguire Seven convictions, in September 1991 the Home Secretary also referred Judith Ward's case to the Court of Appeal.[21] Judith Ward's conviction was quashed by the Court of Appeal in 1992. Like the *Maguire* case, expert scientific evidence was a major feature of the trial. Dr. Skuse had said that swabs taken from Ward using the Griess test had shown traces of nitroglycerine variously described as either "faint" or "definitely positive."[22] It was said that there would not have been any real risk of accidental contamination. Because some of the traces were said to have been found under Ward's fingernails, it was said that this meant that she had been handling the explosives involved in making the bomb.

Investigations that had led to the successful appeal in the *Birmingham Six* case had cast serious doubt upon the opinions expressed by Dr. Skuse. The Court of Appeal now said that his disclosure of scientific evidence had been "woefully deficient."[23] An impressive body of evidence showed that Dr. Skuse's tests, despite his confident assertions to the contrary, were of no value in establishing contact between Ward and explosives in 1974. The court accepted that

21 *Judith Ward v. The Queen* (1993), 96 Cr. App. R. 1 [*Ward*]; the discussion below is taken from this.

22 *Ibid.* at 45–50.

23 *Ibid.* at 51.

the Griess test was no more than an initial step; it was not evidence of the existence of nitroglycerine. Dr. Skuse had relied upon one thin-layer chromatography (TLC) test spot, and his conclusion in relation to that was wrong. The court said he was the most important scientific witness called by the prosecution and the only scientist who claimed to have found nitroglycerine under Ward's fingernails. That enabled the other two scientists (Elliot and Higgs) to say that Ward must have handled the explosives. The court said that both had allowed their objectivity to become clouded by partisanship.

The court said that it was persuaded that the scientific case against Ward was unsupportable: at the trial the scientists had presented a "false and distorted scientific picture."[24] It said the senior scientists had taken the law into their own hands and concealed from the prosecution, defence, and the court matters that might have changed the results of the trials. It said that whether the test for non-disclosure was the here-and-now test or the test of what would have been applicable in 1974 did not really matter in this case because even by 1974 standards, there were clear failures of disclosure.

The court said further that an aspect of the right to a fair trial is a right to timely disclosure by the prosecution of all material matters that affect the scientific case relied on by the prosecution. This duty exists whether or not a specific request for disclosure of details of scientific evidence is made by the defence — the duty is continuous. It applies in the pretrial period and throughout the trial. On the scientific case deployed against her, Ward did not have a fair trial.

The appeal court further said that it must be made clear that if the expert witness has carried out *any* tests that may cast doubt upon the opinion being expressed, the party calling the witness must disclose all such results. It said the expert witness has the duty to bring to the attention of those instructing them the results of all such experiments or tests so that they can be brought to the attention of the other parties. No doubt, the court suggested, the process can be simplified by the experts for both sides working together.

The court made this comment on why it was important to consider why the scientists acted as they did:

> For lawyers, jurors and judges a forensic scientist conjures up the image of a [person] in a white coat working in a laboratory, approaching [their] task with cold neutrality, and dedicated only to the pursuit of scientific truth. It is a sombre thought that the reality is sometimes different.[25]

24 *Ibid.*
25 *Ibid.* at 52.

Forensic scientists may become partisan. The very fact that the police seek their assistance may create a relationship between the police and the forensic scientists. The adversarial character of the proceedings may tend to promote this process. Forensic scientists employed by the government may come to see their function as helping the police. They may lose their objectivity—the appeal court said that this is what must have happened in this case.

One of the scientists, Higgs, said that the policy they followed at the time was to answer questions, not to proffer information. He said they gave the police assistance in investigating what the police wanted—the scientists did not necessarily say what *they* had found out. As he put it, "we were careful about what we said."[26]

The court said the surest way of preventing the misuse of scientific evidence is by ensuring that there is a proper understanding of the nature and scope of the prosecution's duty of disclosure. The prosecution's duty exists irrespective of any request by the defence. It is not limited to the documentation on which the opinion or findings of an expert is based. It extends to anything that might arguably assist the defence. A positive duty, it obliges the prosecution to make full and proper inquiries from forensic scientists in order to learn whether there is discoverable material. Given the undoubted inequality between the prosecution and the defence in access to forensic scientists, the court said it was of paramount importance that those who prosecute and defend in criminal cases appreciate the duty of disclosure. If difficulties arise in a particular case, the court must be the final judge.

### 4) Recommendations of the Runciman Royal Commission on Criminal Justice

The overturning of all these cases caused quite a stir in Britain. The accused had been transformed from "mass murderers" to victims of the justice system. Those who had been guilty of these crimes had escaped undetected. The scientists and police involved, instead of being protectors of the public, had been exposed as going way beyond their proper role in a criminal investigation and prosecution. As a result of the widespread public concern, the government set up the royal commission headed by Viscount Runciman to make recommendations about how these matters could be better dealt with in the future. The Runciman Royal Commission on Criminal Justice eventually led to the establishment of the Criminal Cases Review Commission (CCRC). In its 1993 report the Runciman

26 *Ibid.* at 51.

commission devoted a chapter to the reform of the forensic sciences. It stressed the importance of disclosure of scientific tests and material for testing to the defence.[27] It also recommended that public sector facilities should be willing to do work for the defence as well as for the prosecution. It recognized that "the world of forensic science is a relatively closed one in which in many cases the leading experts are employed by the public sector laboratories themselves" but stressed the need for "external audit."[28] To this end, it recommended the creation of a forensic science advisory council that would create codes of practices for forensic scientists that would cover professional ethics and duties of disclosure. The new council would also encourage the development of centres of expertise in forensic science in the universities and elsewhere.[29] The commission noted the defence often did not have the expertise or necessary funding to challenge or call scientific evidence. The new council should "keep under review the extent to which the interests of the defendant are being properly looked after by the various providers of forensic science services singly and in combination."[30]

Unfortunately, the government did not then create a forensic science advisory council, and it was left to the individual bodies to make voluntary efforts to better regulate the forensic sciences.[31] Subsequent reviews affirmed the call for better regulation of the forensic sciences and in 2008, a Forensic Science Regulator was appointed. The regulator, advised by the Forensic Science Advisory Council,[32] has issued a manual of regulations designed to provide quality standards for the provision of forensic science to the police and other parts of the criminal justice system. In recognition of the challenging diversity of the forensic sciences, the regulator has formed specialist groups, including those in forensic pathology, digital forensics, DNA, and quality standards.[33]

---

27 The Runciman Royal Commission stressed that the *Ward* and *Maguire* cases had demonstrated "the serious risk of a miscarriage of justice if the fullest possible disclosure of scientific evidence is not made by the prosecution to the defence" including when necessary, materials beyond the final report, such as notes made of the tests. *Royal Commission on Criminal Justice Report*, Cmnd 2263 (London: H.M.S.O., 1993) at 154 [Runciman Report].

28 *Ibid.* at 150.

29 *Ibid.* at 151.

30 *Ibid.* at 213.

31 See, generally, Kathryn Campbell & Clive Walker, "Medical Mistakes and Miscarriages of Justice: Perspectives on the Experiences in England and Wales" in Inquiry into Pediatric Forensic Pathology in Ontario, *Independent Research Studies: Pediatric Forensic Pathology and the Justice System*, ed. by Kent Roach, vol. 2 (Toronto: Ontario Ministry of the Attorney General, 2008) at 354–59 [Goudge Inquiry Research Papers].

32 One of the CCRC Commissioners, Julie Goulding, is a council member.

33 Forensic Science Regulator, *Report* (December 2009), online: www.homeoffice.gov.uk/publications/police/790604/FSR-annual-report.pdf?view=Binary.

## 5) Non-disclosure of Test Results—The Case of Sally Clark

In the last ten years, a number of high-profile convictions of women for the murders of their children were quashed by the Court of Appeal: these include the cases of Sally Clark, Angela Cannings, and Donna Anthony. In each appeal, the court was faced with evidence that suggested expert testimony given by, among others, Prof. Sir Roy Meadow was unreliable. Professor Meadow, a consultant pediatrician, was well respected for his work on the now controversial Munchausen Syndrome by Proxy (MSbP) involving parents who were said to wilfully harm their children.[34]

In 1999, Sally Clark was convicted of the murder of her two sons. The first one died within a few weeks of his birth in 1996 and the second in similar circumstances in 1998. After the death of her second child, Clark was tried for the murder of both sons. Although she was convicted, her prosecution was controversial, in part, due to statistical evidence presented by Professor Meadow. Professor Meadow testified that the chances of two children from an affluent, non-smoking family (like the Clarks) suffering Sudden Infant Death Syndrome (also known as crib, or cot death) was 1 in 73 million. The Royal Statistical Society later issued a public statement expressing its concern at the "misuse of statistics in the courts" and arguing that there was "no statistical basis" for Professor Meadow's claim.[35] He had said that the probability of an infant dying in such circumstances was 1:8,543. This figure came from the Confidential Enquiry for Stillbirths and Deaths in Infancy Report (CESDI).[36] He deduced that as there were two children, then the chances of them both dying were 8,543 times 8,543. However, this figure would be valid only for separate and unconnected events, which did not apply where the infants were part of the same family—Professor Meadow had not considered the possibility of genetic or other familial circumstances affecting the probabilities. Despite this, in 2000 the Court of Appeal upheld the conviction.

Later the defence discovered that an expert witness for the prosecution (Dr. Alan Williams, the forensic pathologist who conducted the autopsies on

34 Munchausen Syndrome by Proxy is a recent and controversial "diagnosis" to describe a parent who purportedly induces or exaggerates illness in a child to gain attention from the medical profession.

35 Royal Statistical Society, News Release (23 October 2001).

36 Peter Fleming *et al.*, eds., *Sudden Unexpected Deaths in Infancy: The CESDI SUDI Studies, 1993–96* (London: Stationery Office, 2000). In the paper, the authors had estimated the chance of a random baby dying of crib death was 1:1,303; however, if the child was from an affluent, non-smoking family, with mother over the age of twenty-six, then the chance was 1:8,543.

both children) had failed to disclose microbiological reports that suggested one of Clark's sons may have died of natural causes caused by bacterial infection.[37]

In view of this, Sally Clark's case was referred back to the Court of Appeal by the CCRC in 2003. Although the central reasons for the Clark appeal's success had nothing to do with Professor Meadow, the discredited statistics were revisited in the hearing. In their ruling, the judges stated that "if this matter had been fully argued before us we would, in all probability, have considered that the statistical evidence provided a quite distinct basis upon which the appeal had to be allowed."[38]

## 6) Misuse of Probabilities—The Case of Angela Cannings

In 2002, Angela Cannings was convicted of the murder of her two sons.[39] A third child had also died in infancy. The prosecution relied heavily on the expert evidence given by Prof. Sir Roy Meadow that in view of the babies dying in similar circumstances, Cannings was an MSbP sufferer. Although he did not offer mathematical probabilities, the jury was told that the babies could not have been genuine crib death victims because they were fit and healthy right up until the time of death. He took the firm view that in a family, one sudden infant death is a tragedy, two are suspicious, and three are murder, until proved otherwise.[40]

In quashing her conviction in 2003, the Court of Appeal said that if each was an unexplained death, then the fact of reoccurrence did not lead to the inexorable conclusion that the deaths must have resulted from the deliberate infliction of harm. Fresh evidence was also produced to suggest the possibility of a family history of genetic problems, making the conviction unsafe.

The court was at pains to express the values underlining its approach:

> . . . where a full investigation into two or more sudden unexplained infant deaths in the same family is followed by a serious disagreement between reputable experts about the cause of death, and a body of such expert opinion concludes that natural causes, whether explained or unexplained, cannot be excluded as a reasonable (and not a fanciful) possibility, the prosecution of a

---

37 We discussed his work in Chapter 2 and will discuss it further in the context of pathology in Chapter 9.

38 *R. v. Clark (No. 2)*, [2003] EWCA Crim 1020 at para. 180 [*Clark*]. See also Adam Wilson, "Expert Testimony in the Dock" (2005) 69 J. Crim. L. 330.

39 *R. v. Cannings*, [2004] EWCA Crim 1 [*Cannings*].

40 *Ibid.* at para. 150. This expression not only reverses the burden of proof in a criminal case, but it also reflects the "think dirty" approach favoured by Dr. Charles Smith in Canada and roundly condemned by Goudge J. in his report on pediatric forensic pathology.

> parent or parents for murder should not be started, or continued, unless there is additional cogent evidence, extraneous to the expert evidence, which tends to support the conclusion that the infant, or where there is more than one death, one of the infants, was deliberately harmed. In cases like the present, if the outcome of the trial depends exclusively or almost exclusively on a serious disagreement between distinguished and reputable experts, it will often be unwise, and therefore unsafe, to proceed.
>
> . . .
>
> In a criminal case, it is simply not enough to be able to establish even a high probability of guilt. Unless we are sure of guilt the dreadful possibility always remains that a mother, already brutally scarred by the unexplained death or deaths of her babies, may find herself in prison for life for killing them when she should not be there at all. In our community, and in any civilized community, that is abhorrent.[41]

As we noted in Chapter 2, there was some retreat from the *Cannings* principle (that any difference in opinion between differing schools of reputable experts would make a conviction unsafe) in *R. v. Kai-Whitewind* and some application of it in *R. v. Harris, Rock, Cherry and Faulder*.[42]

## 7) Professor Meadow's Discredited Evidence—The Case of Donna Anthony

Donna Anthony was convicted of two counts of murder, one relating to her infant son and the second to her infant daughter who had died a year earlier.[43] At the trial it was suggested that she had smothered her children in order to get sympathy from her estranged husband. She unsuccessfully appealed her conviction. After the overturning of the Clark and Cannings convictions, the CCRC referred Anthony's case back to the Court of Appeal where her conviction was deemed unsafe on the basis of Professor Meadow's now discredited evidence given at trial.

In 2005 Professor Meadow was struck off the medical register by the UK General Medical Council for serious professional misconduct, but he was reinstated in 2006 after he successfully appealed.[44] On a further appeal by the

---

41 *Ibid.* at paras. 178–79.

42 *R. v. Kai-Whitewind*, [2005] EWCA Crim 1092; *R. v. Harris & Ors*, [2005] EWCA Crim 1980. For further discussion, see Goudge Inquiry Research Papers, above note 31.

43 *Anthony v. R.*, [2005] EWCA Crim 952.

44 *Meadow v. General Medical Council*, [2006] EWHC 146 (Admin).

General Medical Council, the court was split 2:1 on the issue of serious professional misconduct. The dissenting judge, Sir Anthony Clarke, concluded that Professor Meadow was guilty of serious professional misconduct and provided detailed reasons for his conclusion. One of the other two judges, Auld L.J., said that Professor Meadow "was undoubtedly guilty of some professional misconduct" but that it "fell far short of serious professional misconduct."[45]

### 8) Misreading of Bloodstain Pattern Analysis — The Case of Stephen Downing

In 1974 Stephen Downing was convicted of the murder of Wendy Sewell, a typist thirty-two years old, at a cemetery in a small Derbyshire town, and sentenced to life imprisonment. Downing was then a seventeen-year-old gardener working at the cemetery. At his trial the prosecution relied on expert forensic evidence to suggest that the bloodstain pattern on his clothes could be explained only by him being the killer.[46] Downing said he had come into contact with the victim only after she had been seriously injured by someone else.

The prosecution also relied on his confession in a police interview lasting eight hours during which he had not been informed he was under arrest. Downing was denied access to a solicitor — even though he had the reading age of an eleven-year-old at the time. His appeal to the Court of Appeal was dismissed, and he was denied parole as he refused to admit his guilt.

With the help of a local newspaper editor, a concerted media campaign was waged, raising doubts about Downing's conviction.[47] In 2000, the CCRC referred his case to the Court of Appeal. It had commissioned independent forensic reports which suggested that bloodstaining on his clothes was consistent with his account that he had contact with the deceased only after she had been seriously injured. Before his appeal was heard, Downing was released from prison, having served twenty-seven years.

In 2002, the Court of Appeal quashed his conviction on the basis that the forensic evidence given at his trial about the bloodstain pattern analysis was

45 *General Medical Council v. Meadow*, [2007] 1 All E.R. 1.

46 In his report, the forensic scientist, Mr. Lee, had said that the bloodstaining on the appellant's clothing, "might well be described as a textbook example of the pattern of blood staining which might be expected on the clothing of the assailant in a wounding such as that which Wendy Sewell suffered." See *R. v. Downing*, [2002] EWCA Crim 263 at para. 9 [*Downing*].

47 See Don Hale, *Town without Pity: The Fight to Clear Stephen Downing of the Bakewell Murder* (London: Century, 2002).

found to be unreliable—and because the alleged confession he made involved substantial and significant breaches of police rules on questioning of suspects.[48] He was paid £750,000 compensation.

## 9) Poor Scientific Methodology—The Case of Craig McCreight

The case of *McCreight v. Her Majesty's Advocate* is instructive.[49] It involved a person found dead with traces of chloroform in her body. It was said that she had been rendered unconscious by having a cloth soaked in the substance put over her nose and mouth and when unconscious, she was then dumped in the place where she died. At trial, the quantification of the amount in her body was overstated by 1,000 times. The tissues for testing were placed in a container which was porous to the material being tested for and so the quantification some time later would have been totally unreliable. The methods by which the substances could have entered the body were incorrectly stated. Each stage of the process was vitiated by basic errors of process or of understanding.

## 10) New Forms of Scientific Evidence

Miscarriages of justice have been recognized in a number of cases involving novel scientific techniques. In *R. v. Bacchus*,[50] the Crown conceded that a robbery conviction was unsafe because evidence given by a facial mapping expert who compared images from CCTV cameras was not reliable. In *R. v. O'Doherty*[51] a conviction based on an expert's voice recognition was overturned with the Northern Ireland Court of Appeal concluding that the state of the science indicated that no prosecution should be based on auditory recognition alone. Although ear-print evidence has been accepted as admissible, a conviction was quashed in *R. v. Kempster*[52] on the basis that the expert had been over-confident in her conclusions.

---

48 *Downing*, above note 46.

49 *McCreight v. Her Majesty's Advocate*, [2009] HCJAC 69 (Scot.).

50 [2004] EWCA Crim 1756.

51 [2002] NICA B51.

52 [2008] EWCA Crim 975 at para. 28: finding that

> the ear-print at the scene is consistent with having been left by the appellant. But having examined the comparisons of the gross features, it is also apparent to us that they do not provide a precise match. The differences may well be explicable by differences in pressure, or movement, but the extent of the mismatch is such as to lead us to the conclusion that it could not be relied on by itself as justifying a verdict of guilty.

## B. THE CANADIAN EXPERIENCE

In Canada, the public inquiries that have taken place have been severely critical of the approach taken by forensic scientists where they have allowed their findings to be apparently misunderstood or misapplied. Unlike the Australian royal commissions that led to the overturning of convictions, the Canadian public inquiries took place after the convictions had already been set aside by other means. Consequently, the forensic scientists were required to explain to the inquiries their activities when they already knew the outcome of the criminal proceedings in which they had been involved. It is not surprising that, when compared with the clarity and confidence of their evidence at the trials, the scientists were more willing to moderate the expression of their views in the Canadian inquiries.

### 1) Misuse of Scientific Evidence (Hairs and Fibres) — The Case of Guy Paul Morin

In his Commission of Inquiry report into the wrongful conviction of Guy Paul Morin, Commissioner Kaufman discussed the misuse of expert scientific evidence. It was made clear at the inquiry that the scientists at trial had made incorrect use of a report which had been published in Britain. At both trials, the prosecution had relied upon hair and fibre evidence to demonstrate that there had been physical contact between nine-year-old Christine Jessop and Guy Morin and that Christine had been taken in Morin's Honda car to the scene of her sexual assault and murder.[53] It was said that this contradicted Morin's evidence that Christine had never been in his car.

Upon discovery of the young girl's body, a single dark hair was found embedded in skin tissue adhering to her necklace. The hair was not Christine's but was said, by scientific witnesses, to have been microscopically similar to Morin's hair and therefore "could have" come from him. Between the two trials further inquiries revealed that two of Christine's classmates also had hair that was microscopically similar. Also, three hairs found in Morin's car were dissimilar to his hairs and were similar to Christine's hair and also could have come from her.

Commissioner Kaufman said:

> Hair and fibre evidence elevated Guy Paul Morin to prime suspect status, formed the justification in large measure, for his arrest and for the searches of

53 *Report of the Kaufman Commission on Proceedings Involving Guy Paul Morin* (Toronto: Ministry of the Attorney General, 1998) [Morin Inquiry].

> his car and home; was cited by the Crown to support his detention pending trial; was cited by the Ontario Court of Appeal and the Supreme Court of Canada as evidence relevant to their consideration of whether his acquittal should be overturned; formed a substantial part of the case against Guy Paul Morin in his first and second trials and undoubtedly was relied upon by the jury at his second trial to convict him.[54]

The commissioner went on to say that when properly understood, the hair comparison had little or no probative value. He said that generally, it should be understood that such hair comparison evidence, without DNA analysis, is unlikely to have sufficient value to enable it to be received as circumstantial evidence of guilt in a criminal trial.

Commissioner Kaufman also found that the forensic scientist had not adequately or accurately communicated the limitations on her findings to either the police or prosecutors before the second trial. He said that in the early stages, she had done a preliminary comparison of the necklace hair with Morin's hair and in his view, her opinion was overstated and left an impression that it somehow implicated Morin. The initial evidence of the detectives at the bail hearing in relation to this was inadequate, but resulted from the inadequate communications from the scientist. The commissioner thought that the hair comparison evidence was misused in prosecution counsel's closing address.

As to fibre evidence, fibres were collected from Christine's clothing and recorder bag at the scene and from Morin's vehicle and residence. Many thousands of fibres were examined and "several" became significant. The scientists gave evidence that several of the fibres from the Morin locations were similar to those from the crime scene and "could have" come from the same source. The commissioner said that even if such similarities existed, they proved nothing. He said the fibre evidence was contaminated in the Centre of Forensic Sciences and as a result, no inferences could be drawn from *any* alleged similarities.

Commissioner Kaufman said the scientists knew of the problem with the contamination, but withheld their concerns from the police, the prosecution, the defence, and the court. He said they may have done that to save themselves from personal embarrassment. The scientists had no real interest in documenting the contamination, how it occurred, and whether it affected other cases at the centre. However, the existence of in-house contamination was known within the biology section of the Ontario Centre of Forensic Sciences. Further examination of the fibres prior to the second trial yielded potentially

54 *Ibid.*, Executive Summary at 8.

exculpatory evidence not communicated to either the prosecution or the defence. The fibre similarities could have been explained by random occurrence or by environmental contamination.

The scientists had used a published study on fibre transference by two British forensic scientists about the likelihood of random occurrence of different colours and types of fibres to support the conclusion that the fibre evidence indicated contact between the accused and the victim. When Commissioner Kaufman called the authors of that published study, they testified that their research had no relevance to this case and should not have been introduced in it. This finding is a reminder that while more research needs to be done into the forensic sciences, the research itself introduces possible sources for misinterpretation and error.

Commissioner Kaufman found that because the scientists had misunderstood the study and had failed to explain its limited relevance to the prosecutors, not surprisingly the fibre evidence and the study were misused by the prosecution in its closing address. The commissioner commented on the fact that terms such as "match" and "consistent with" were used by the expert witnesses in an inconsistent and potentially misleading manner, and had the capacity to overstate the strength of the opinions expressed.

The commissioner made thirty-four recommendations on the issues of forensic evidence. One recommendation was that there be a comprehensive set of guidelines drawn up for writing forensic reports. These would include an account to establish the integrity of items, including the chain of continuity, the identification of tests conducted, items examined, reasons where items are not examined or tests not done, results of examination and testing, the conclusions that can reasonably be drawn, and any limitations on such conclusions.[55]

## 2) Discredited Hair and Fibre Evidence—The Case of James Driskell

As discussed in Chapter 7, in 1990, James Driskell was convicted of the murder of Perry Harder. The prosecution case was based, in part, on the microscopic hair comparison of three hairs found in a van owned by Driskell. He was finally released after thirteen years in prison when new DNA tests, conducted in 2002, discredited the scientific hair evidence used to convict him.

---

55 The entire list of recommendations is included in Department of Justice, FPT Heads of Prosecutions Committee, *Report of the Working Group on the Prevention of Miscarriages of Justice* (Ottawa: Department of Justice, 2004) at Appendix A.

At the trial, a police hair and fibre expert had given evidence that the three hair samples found in the van belonged to the victim, the prosecution having said that Driskell had killed Harder in his van. The subsequent DNA examinations conducted by the Forensic Science Service in England concluded that not only did the three hair samples not belong to the victim but that they belonged to three different people. The conviction was quashed in 2005. The Manitoba government decided not to order a new trial and then entered a stay of proceedings.

As discussed in Chapter 7, the government appointed a public inquiry to look into certain aspects of the trial and conviction. The commissioner was the former chief justice of the Supreme Court of Ontario, Patrick Lesage. He reviewed how the analyst at Driskell's trial had testified that the hairs found in Driskell's van "were consistent" with those of the victim even though Justice Kaufman had recommended that such terminology not be used because it was misleading.[56] On the basis of an expert report and a panel of experts, Commissioner Lesage criticized the RCMP for not having peer review of hair comparisons in place despite having five qualified people in their Winnipeg lab.[57] He also criticized the lab for not conducting blind reviews of the hair samples given the "insidious danger of 'confirmation bias'."[58] He revealed the dangers of relying on hair microscopy evidence by noting that hairs previously found "to be consistent with those of the accused" in four Manitoba murder cases, including Driskell's, were all established not to be matches by subsequent DNA analysis of the hairs.[59] He concluded that hair microscopy evidence should be received only with great caution and with warnings to the jury.[60]

### 3) Misleading Serology — and DNA — The Case of David Milgaard

David Milgaard was convicted of the raping and stabbing murder of Saskatoon nursing aide Gail Miller.[61] At the trial, the prosecution placed great importance on the scientific evidence linking Milgaard to the victim. Some frozen seminal fluid was found at the scene of the crime, and tests carried out by a serologist

56 *Report of the Commission of Inquiry into Certain Aspects of the Trial and Conviction of James Driskell* (Winnipeg: The Commission, 2007) at 151–52 [Driskell Inquiry].

57 *Ibid.* at 161.

58 *Ibid.* at 163.

59 *Ibid.* at 172.

60 *Ibid.* at 182.

61 *Report of the Commission of Inquiry into the Wrongful Conviction of David Milgaard* (Saskatoon, SK: Queen's Printer, 2008) [Milgaard Inquiry].

at the police crime detection laboratory indicated that the semen came from a type-A secretor. Secretors are people who secrete detectable levels of their ABO blood group substances in their bodily fluids, such as saliva, semen, or vaginal secretions, and this allows their blood group to be identified.[62] Milgaard was found to have type-A blood but was a non-secretor.

The serologist said that one of the tests he carried out led him to suspect that blood type-A might be present and give a positive antigen reading regardless of whether the person was a secretor or a non-secretor. The argument put forward by the prosecution was that Milgaard's blood had contaminated the sample found in the snow, thus rendering his non-secretor status irrelevant. Here, the prosecution seemed to be straining to make the scientific evidence fit the case. All parties at the inquiry agreed that the evidence as presented at trial should have helped Milgaard. In any event, the jury convicted Milgaard despite a generally favourable instruction from the trial judge. It was later shown that the science presented at trial was wrong: Milgaard was a secretor after all.

In 1997 the results of DNA testing conducted by the Forensic Science Service in the United Kingdom indicated that the semen found on Gail Miller's clothes could not have originated from Milgaard—and that it matched Larry Fisher. Eventually, the Department of Justice stated that the results of DNA testing made it clear that a terrible wrong was done to Milgaard by his wrongful conviction.

Subsequently, Fisher was arrested and charged with the rape and murder. In 1999 a settlement was reached with Milgaard and his family, and compensation was awarded of $10 million. Fisher was convicted of the murder. Science can, of course, both contribute to miscarriages of justice and help reveal them.

## 4) The Nature of Systemic Error

In the Morin Inquiry Commissioner Kaufman stated that such circumstances as the report outlined can best be described as "systemic" error, where the practice within or between organizations failed to conform to the declared standards said to govern them. It was shown that the forensic scientists had made statements about "matches" between hairs and fibres which sent the police off in the wrong direction. This situation implied at least two serious systemic errors. First of all, the procedures within the forensic science centre should have

62 The ABO blood group substances are the determinants that define the ABO group of the blood (A, B, AB, or O). About 80 percent of the population secrete their blood group substances in their bodily fluids, such as semen and saliva. These people are known as "secretors."

picked up on this error before it was transmitted to the police. We remember, for example, Dr. Tilstone stating that all opinions from forensic experts should be put in writing. The internal processes at the forensic science centre should have enabled the quality control or compliance manager to have detected that error right away. Second, the police should know enough about these issues to realize that visual similarities between hairs and fibres do not indicate anything about common origin or causal connection.

Similar things could be said about the internal procedures within the police and prosecution services and to the corresponding relationships between them. What this means is that when it is stated that "new guidelines were drawn up," we should know that such action, by itself, will do nothing to resolve the systemic error which produced that action. If the systemic error is failure to follow proper procedures, then rewriting the procedures will not resolve the problem.

## C. THE AUSTRALIAN EXPERIENCE

As previously explained, there have been far fewer formal inquiries in Australia compared to those of Canada and Britain, and those that have occurred took place many years ago. In this section we focus on those inquiries. In recent years, however, there has been public concern about a significant number of other cases that have not yet been the subject of formal inquiries.[63]

### 1) Multiple Scientific Errors — The Case of Edward Splatt

As discussed in Chapter 7, the murder and sexual assault of the elderly Mrs. Simper in her bedroom at her home was a rare case in that the *only* evidence leading to the identification of the accused was the scientific evidence.[64] The prosecution case relied on the cumulative effect of similarities of trace materials between the crime scene and Splatt's home and working environment. Scientific tests were conducted to detect the presence and relative proportions of trace materials, such as paint particles, metal particles, wool fibres, cotton fibres, cotton and artificial fibres, carpet fibres, spicules of foam, seed fragments, wood particles, and human hair all found on the victim's bed.

63 See, for example, those discussed by Robert N. Moles, *A State of Injustice* (South Melbourne: Lothian, 2004).

64 Discussion of this case is taken from the Splatt Royal Commission, above note 3.

The prosecution had said that there were four essential steps in linking Splatt to the crime:

a) First, it was necessary to determine that the trace materials came from where they were said to have come from.
b) Second, it had to establish similarities between the trace materials from the victim's environment and those associated with Splatt, and the absence of any relevant dissimilarities, so that it can be said that the various sets of trace materials *could have* originated from the same source.
c) Third, it had to determine that the trace materials originated from the same source.
d) The final step was to say that Splatt was so closely in contact with the victim as to have been her attacker.
    - Paint particles: At the trial, the presence and ratio of metal to paint fragments, and the ratio of orange to any other colour in the paint particles were the most important aspects of the scientific evidence that seemed to link Splatt to the crime scene. Opposite the victim's home was a factory where spray painting and metal operations were conducted, and it was found that it used similar types of paint and metal to those found in the house. As it happened, Splatt was a spray painter at the factory. Of all the employees at the factory, Splatt had more similar percentages of paint and metal on his clothing than any other of the employees and so too in his car and his house. To prove that those particles were not windblown through the victim's bedroom window, Vaseline-coated slides were left at the crime scene for an extended time. At the trial the jury was told that the particles found on the slides were smaller than those found at the crime scene and therefore those found at the crime scene were too big to have been blown from the factory. So, given that the particles were foreign to the scene and could not be windblown, they must have arrived there on the person or clothing of the assailant.[65]
    - Seed particles: Splatt had an aviary in his back garden. The particles found on the victim's bed were confirmed as seeds by their positive reaction to Iodine (to identify starch) and Sudan IV (to identify oil). The jury was told that the seeds were brought in by Splatt as they matched those found at his aviary; also, the seeds found on the bed were uncooked and

65 *Ibid.* at 23.

were therefore not from biscuits, bread, or toasted muesli—the starch grains had not lost their bipolarized character.[66]

- Other trace material: Splatt also owned a car coat which had been frayed in several places and the lining of which had degenerated and released foam spicules which were said to have matched those found in the victim's bedroom. The jury was also told that the wool fibres on the victim's bed sheet matched those from Splatt's trousers. Eight months after the murder, when the bedroom was being re-examined, Sergeant Cocks found a sweet on the bedroom carpet which had attached to it cotton and artificial fibres that also matched those from one of Splatt's shirts. It was never explained how the earlier detailed forensic examination of the scene had missed something as obvious as the sweet on the carpet. Wood particles from the windowsill were also found on the bedsheet and on items of Splatt's clothing. A hair found on the victim had paint particles attached to it, and the hair and particles were said to have matched hairs taken from Splatt's arm.[67]

At the subsequent royal commission into Splatt's conviction, Commissioner Shannon was highly critical of the conduct of the trial, especially the conduct of the expert witnesses. He found each aspect of the evidence of the scientific evidence unreliable.

In relation to paint particles he said:

> The Vaseline coated slides test incorrectly excluded "windblown" as a source of paint and metal fragments at the crime scene. Evidence presented at the Commission inquiry by experts in atmospheric physics, meteorology and aeronautical engineering showed that size of a material is not the sole determinant of whether something could have been airborne.
>
> The metal-to-paint ratios lose their significance if the crime scene and other sources are affected by wind blown fragments.
>
> The appearance of precision in the ratio was deceiving because the electron microscope analysis is only semi-quantitative.[68]

He found the reliability of the scientific tests regarding seeds dubious in three ways:

66 *Ibid.*
67 *Ibid.*
68 See Splatt Royal Commission, above note 3.

> The Iodine and Sudan IV tests were preliminary as they do not confirm samples found on the victim's bed as being seeds beyond being starch or oily.
>
> The comparisons between the type of seed grains found at the crime scene and those in connection with Splatt was a search for similarities—ie they merely confirmed the hypothesis that he was guilty and did nothing to try and exclude him.
>
> There are other means by which starch grains can lose their bipolarization and not just through heating. Therefore, the grains may have been cooked and thus not be bird seeds.[69]

The commissioner said that some of the scientists involved in the original case appeared to have had a dual role. When analysing what they said and what they did, it was difficult to determine whether they were acting in an investigative role (like the police) or as objective observers (like scientists). The commissioner pointed out that this sort of confusion could happen only in a system which was "an incorrect one with serious defects" and could easily lead to "unconscious bias."[70] He said that some of the original evidence given by the expert witnesses involved completely non-scientific statements that were more like police investigatory suggestions. He also emphasized that a system which did not distinguish between scientific observations and deductions by police in their investigatory capacity was "a defective and therefore a non-acceptable forensic system," and he further said that "in each instance the dual roles are, in my opinion, incompatible."[71]

Commissioner Shannon made special mention of Sergeant Cocks, describing him as "the dominant figure."[72] Cocks was in charge of the scientific section of the police which quickly took over all the inquiries. He did the initial microscopic examinations of the vacuuming and tape lifts. He identified the items to go for further forensic testing. The commissioner said: "Those two roles which Sergeant Cocks fulfilled were, in my view, incompatible."[73] He explained that at the trial, Cocks had described in detail his microscopic examinations and he explained the fact that the materials found at the scene could not have arrived there by atmospheric pollution from the factory. He propounded the sequence of opinions and theories that composed the core of the case against Splatt. In the Crown's final address, his evidence and theories confirmed his dominance

---

69 *Ibid.* at 134.
70 *Ibid.* at 51.
71 *Ibid.*
72 *Ibid.* at 31.
73 *Ibid.*

in the roll-call of witnesses. Chief among them was his evidence that "you would need something like Typhoon Tracy to carry particles of that size from the factory."[74]

The commissioner said Cocks could not have spoken of such things as an investigating police officer; but using scientific concepts in a scientific context, he was placing himself squarely in the arena as a forensic expert. The commissioner said that at trial there was virtually no debate concerning the validity of the sergeant's scientific deductions, subsequently found to be wrong.

> I do not understand how it was that Sergeant Cocks was invited or allowed to express in the course of his Trial evidence 'opinions' or 'theories' . . . several of [which] clearly amounted to a categorical assertion that beyond question the prisoner was the guilty man . . . . I find myself bemused that such could have occurred.[75]

Commissioner Shannon said there should be a clear delineation between the collection of items at the crime scene by the examiner and the subsequent scientific examination of those materials.[76]

The commissioner also said the jury were asked to determine if they thought that there were so many similarities between the trace materials associated with the deceased and Splatt that they could be satisfied that they came from the same source. The various witnesses had used the expressions "were not inconsistent with" or "were consistent with." As the commissioner noted, while those words may have a precise meaning in their scientific context, they were being used for the benefit of the jury which may not have appreciated all the nuances of their meaning. In addition, they were used before the jury in the context of determining whether they came "from the same source."[77]

The jury had been told that they had to rely upon the scientific evidence to find similarities and the absence of dissimilarities—and then *they* had to determine if the items had a common origin. The use of terms such as "similar in all respects" and "no dissimilarities at all" was dangerous. The jury had to move from similarities to common origin, on the basis of the multiplicity of similarities to avoid accident or coincidence. When the scientists referred to things being consistent with coming from the same source, they were using

---

74 *Ibid.* at 22.

75 *Ibid.* at 36. This is similar to the finding by the commissioner in the Lindy Chamberlain case that the evidence of Professor Cameron would not have been admitted if it had been challenged as inadmissible; see below.

76 *Ibid.* at 51.

77 *Ibid.* at 36.

expressions that went beyond what their scientific testing could establish; however, they conveniently provided the step for the jury to move from similarities to common origin.

One expert witness even said that all of the trace materials were consistent with contact transfer between the deceased and the Splatt sources—something that went completely beyond the expression of a valid scientific opinion based upon similarities. As Commissioner Shannon commented, the probable impact of such a statement upon the minds of the jury "can scarcely be exaggerated."[78]

The commissioner said that the jury was told that, in a circumstantial case, they had to have regard to the combined effect of all of the pieces of evidence, like the weak rays of light which combine to create a bright light. But, he said, sometimes an accumulation of weak lights produces only a weak light. The jury was told that they had to determine if the number of similarities was too great to be attributed to coincidence or chance. This idea gives rise to a logical dilemma, though: there is no logical step from a series of similarities to the establishment of a common source. The jury was told that the *number* would provide them with the link, but what number would be sufficient? The judge told the jury, "I think that's a thing you have got to decide for yourselves." As Commissioner Shannon noted: "But how could the jury work out the implications of a scientific principle 'for themselves'?"[79]

The commissioner said he had no doubt that, if the jury had been subjected to the detailed submissions made at the commission, their task would have been impossible. He assessed that if the jury system is to be maintained, then the means by which jurors are to be assisted needs much improvement.[80]

In conclusion, Commissioner Shannon stated that the additional scientific evidence presented to the commission cast doubt upon the validity of the jury's verdict as a whole. It would therefore be unjust and dangerous to allow the verdict of guilty to stand. Edward Splatt was released.

In his report, the commissioner put forward several principles concerning the way in which lawyers and expert witnesses should work. He adopted the recommendations from the scientific experts that had been called from the United Kingdom, about how things should be done for the future. He said:

---

78 *Ibid.* at 53.

79 *Ibid.* at 54.

80 *Ibid.* at 57.

(1) Every scientific operation or observation must be documented on the case-notes and documented in such a manner that they would still be comprehensible perhaps even years later.[81]

(2) All major observations must be checked by an independent observer, who must indicate, by initialling the notes, that the proper checks had been made.[82]

(3) Scientific testing should be a search for dissimilarities, not for similarities.[83]

(4) It is the vital obligation of the scientific expert witnesses to spell out to the jury in non-ambiguous and precisely clear terms, the degree of weight and significance that ought to be attached to the scientific tests conducted and in particular what their limitations are.[84]

(5) It was not acceptable for the scientific expert witnesses to say that it was no fault of theirs if the court was left with the wrong impression of their evidence because they were not asked the right questions by the lawyers; *they* had a responsibility to ensure that their evidence was not misused in any way.[85]

(6) During the conduct of a trial there is a serious obligation on the lawyers to ask such detailed and probing questions of the scientists as are most likely to elicit the proper information.[86]

As the commissioner said, the case presented against Splatt at trial must have appeared to the jury to be overwhelming. He said that this trial represented a formidable encounter between the disciplines of law and science, and from which neither escapes unscathed.[87]

At the commission hearing, Mr. Fish, a forensic scientist from England, had described this case as "unique" in his experience. He said:

> Scientific evidence can often be extremely valuable in corroborating other evidence . . . but I have never had a case such as this one, where science led to a suspect and science, only science, connected him with the scene of the crime.[88]

---

81 *Ibid.* at 51.
82 *Ibid.*
83 *Ibid.*
84 *Ibid.* at 52.
85 *Ibid.*
86 *Ibid.*
87 *Ibid.* at 29.
88 *Ibid.* at 30.

Fish said that this situation placed a much greater emphasis upon the scientists to make sure that they got their evidence right.

### 2) Scientific Tests False and Confusing—The Case of Lindy Chamberlain

In August 1980, Michael and Lindy Chamberlain went for a camping holiday in Central Australia with their two young sons and nine-week-old daughter, Azaria.[89] They arrived at Ayers Rock on the evening of 16 August and pitched their tent in the camping area.

Shortly before 8 p.m. the following evening, the Chamberlains were preparing the barbecue for their meal. Lindy was looking after Azaria and chatting in a relaxed manner with other campers nearby. She then left to put Azaria to bed. She said she tucked the baby into the bassinet at the back of the tent. One of their sons said he was hungry, so Lindy got a tin of beans from the car and took him back to the barbecue area. An estimate of the time Lindy was said to have been away from the barbecue area was five to ten minutes. Shortly afterwards Lindy went to check on Azaria after hearing a baby's cry. It was then, she said, she discovered the baby was missing and she was heard to cry out about the missing baby. The Chamberlains maintained that a dingo (wild dog) had taken their baby. The baby's body was never found but a week after her disappearance, her jumpsuit, singlet, booties, and nappy were found. Scientific examinations of her clothing and the family car became crucial to the prosecution case.

There were two inquests into the baby's disappearance. The first found that she was probably killed by a dingo. The second found a case for the Chamberlains to answer. Lindy was charged with the murder of her baby, and Michael was charged with being an accessory after fact. At the trial, the Crown's case was based entirely upon circumstantial evidence, the major component of which was scientific. It was said that during the absence of the five to ten minutes, Lindy had taken Azaria to the front seat of the car and cut her throat, leaving the body in the car (possibly in a vinyl camera bag), and later that evening burying it in the area.

In support of that theory, the prosecution produced evidence from a number of expert witnesses, including the following.

---

89 This discussion is taken from Australia, Royal Commission of Inquiry into Chamberlain Convictions, *Report of the Commissioner the Hon. Mr. Justice T.R. Morling, Royal Commission of Inquiry into Chamberlain Convictions* (Canberra: Government Printer, 1987) [Chamberlain Royal Commission]. See also John Bryson, *Evil Angels: The Case of Lindy Chamberlain* (Ringwood, Vic.:Viking, 1985).

- Joy Kuhl, a forensic biologist with the New South Wales Health Commission, said her tests indicated that traces of fetal blood (of a child under six months) were found inside the front passenger side of the car as well on the baby's clothes. The Ortho-tolidine test was said to prove the presence of blood, and the "cross-over electrophoresis" test was said to prove that it was fetal blood. Kuhl also said fetal blood was present on a camera bag, a towel found in the spare wheel well, a pair of nail scissors in the pocket of the console between the front seats, and on the carpet in front of the driver's seat. She acted under the supervision of Dr. Baxter, then the senior forensic biologist. He said he agreed with her conclusions.
- Professor Chaikin, from the University of New South Wales' School of Textile Technology, said that damage to the baby's jumpsuit had not been caused by a dingo. In his opinion, "dingoes do not produce tufts when they sever fabric with their teeth" and the presence of such tufts was "the strongest evidence" that it had been cut, probably by very sharp scissors.[90]
- Prof. James Cameron, a forensic pathologist from England, said that the ultraviolet photographs taken of the jumpsuit at his laboratory showed the existence of an incised wound around the neck, suggesting the baby's throat had been cut with a sharp instrument, more consistent with scissors. He told the jury that the clothing showed a bloodied imprint of the hand of a small adult.

In October 1982 after a trial which lasted thirty-five days, Lindy was convicted of murder and sentenced to life imprisonment. Michael was convicted of being an accessory after the fact and received an eighteen-month suspended sentence.

Further appeals, including an appeal to the High Court, were unsuccessful. The Chamberlains always maintained their innocence. The media coverage of this case was sensational with the community divided on the innocence or guilt of the Chamberlains.[91] Michael was the pastor of the Seventh Day Adventist Church, and there was suspicion in the community about their activities.

Over the succeeding years, there was much public disquiet about the case, and eventually the Northern Territory government set up a royal commission

---

90 Chamberlain Royal Commission, *ibid.* at 329.

91 In the media, much was made about the Chamberlains being members of the Seventh Day Adventist Church with rumours that "Azaria" meant sacrifice in the wilderness.

in 1986.[92] Commissioner Morling released his report in 1987, five years after the convictions. He concluded that virtually every piece of scientific evidence in the prosecution case was flawed, misreported, or otherwise without value, and that there was no evidence whatsoever of human involvement in the baby's disappearance and apparent death.

### a) Kuhl's Evidence about Blood

A spray pattern was noticed under the dash next to the glovebox compartment of the front passenger seat of the Chamberlains' car, and Kuhl had taken samples from that area and items around it. She told the jury that she conducted the ortho-tolidine test to prove the presence of blood. However, the commission heard that this was only a preliminary test to detect the presence or absence of blood as it can also give positive reactions to other substances; for example, the sandy dust in Central Australia where the Chamberlains lived also reacted positively to the ortho-tolidine test due to the presence of copper in it.

Commissioner Morling said:

> . . . the ortho-tolidine results obtained from [the car] did not establish the presence of blood. Even if the reactions observed were the product of blood, it could have been of such a small amount that its presence there would not justify the drawing of any inference adverse to the Chamberlains.[93]

Kuhl had told the jury that she then subjected some of the samples from the car to further testing to identify them as fetal blood—on the assumption it was blood. They were told that the "cross-over electrophoresis test" was used to confirm the presence of fetal blood. Kuhl said twenty-two samples gave positive reactions. As the prosecutor had told the jury at the trial, Kuhl got twenty-two positive results showing the blood of a child under six months; Baxter had checked it and agreed twenty-two times; Mr. Culliford (deputy director of the UK Metropolitan Police Laboratory) also checked it and agreed twenty-two times. The idea that they had all got it wrong seemed self-evidently preposterous.

The commissioner said these results were unreliable for these reasons:

1) The cross-over electrophoresis test was merely a preliminary test as it lacked specificity to fetal blood. The Ouchterlony test would have been more reliable but had not been used in this case.[94]

---

92 Chamberlain Royal Commission, above note 89.

93 *Ibid.* at 147.

94 *Ibid.* at 71–74.

2) The actual samples were taken more than a year after Azaria's disappearance during which time the interior of the car would have reached 80°C on several days raising "doubts as to the reliability of the immuno-chemical results and, in particular, those depending upon the use of the anti-foetal haemoglobin anti-serum."[95]
3) The record-keeping procedure was defective. Kuhl had used a number of plates and gels that were destroyed soon after the tests were completed. Only her laboratory notebook was kept as a record of her results—this was the Health Commission's practice at the time. Culliford said he had approved of her methods and conclusions. However, he, in common with the experts for the defence, was unable to see the plates or gels that Kuhl had used in her tests. The interpretation of her results was in doubt as no visible evidence of the tests was kept.

As to the spray pattern evidence, Commissioner Morling concluded that he did not consider that the presence of baby's blood or of any blood had been established on the area under the dashboard. The strong probability was that samples lifted out of the spray pattern on the metal plate were traces of sound-deadening compound originating from under the wheel arches and which contained no blood at all. The commissioner noted that Kuhl did not have available to her the services of an analytical chemist to identify the bituminous compound in the samples.

As the commissioner said:

> The fact that she could come to such a conclusion upon something which was, very probably, sound deadener casts doubt upon the efficacy of her testing generally and upon the accuracy of her other results.[96]

He added, "the evidence as to the alleged arterial blood spray under the dash may have had a considerable impact on the jury."[97]

Commissioner Morling found that in relation to these tests, the recording of the results in the laboratory results book was unsatisfactory. The book disclosed twelve occasions where the results in relation to these tests were crossed out or changed. In contrast, he said, it was unusual to find results crossed out or changed in the rest of the book. A question mark in the book in relation to a sample had been crossed out. The explanation for these changes, he said, was speculative.

---

95 *Ibid.* at 69.
96 *Ibid.* at 106.
97 *Ibid.*

It appeared at the time that the police were pressing for results. Kuhl said that she always allowed twenty-four hours for the plates to be washed before reading them. However, Senior Constable Metcalfe said he delivered the samples to her at the laboratory about 9:30 a.m. and she told him to expect the results by 2 p.m. that day. When he rang at 3:45 p.m. Kuhl told him that she had found the presence of fetal blood. The commissioner said:

> . . . given the written records, I accept that Mrs Kuhl did read and report on the results on these tests before washing the plates. She agreed that if she had done this it would have been improper as she would be committing herself to a result before she could have been scientifically satisfied of that result . . . the fact that [she] was prepared to do this in response to a request by police is a matter of concern.[98]

Similar problems were found with all of the other traces of blood. There was a lack of proper controls, failures to keep the plates or even photographs of them, and failures to follow proper test procedures.

### b) Professor Cameron's Evidence

Professor Cameron had told the jury that what he saw on the baby's clothing indicated that the baby's throat had been cut by an instrument used by human hand. The commissioner said it was "doubtful whether Professor Cameron would have been permitted to give this evidence at trial, had objection been taken."

Commissioner Morling further said:

> Professor Cameron, a pathologist of great experience in London, could only suggest one other occasion on which he was asked to express an opinion about the cause of staining on clothing in the absence of a body, and this was in respect of the Shroud of Turin.
>
> He had no experience of the way in which a dingo or other wild animal would treat a clothed baby as prey and except for his efforts with the Shroud of Turin, he had no experience in ascertaining the cause of death where only blood stained clothing of the deceased is available.[99]

The commissioner said Professor Cameron was not justified in taking the view that he did not require experimental evidence to support his findings.[100]

---

98 *Ibid.* at 104.
99 *Ibid.* at 192.
100 *Ibid.* at 189.

Professor Cameron had also told the jury that on the baby's jumpsuit he saw patterns that looked like the blood-stained hands of a small adult. The Chamberlain Royal Commission was informed that much of the material Professor Cameron thought was blood was, in fact, red sand. The commissioner said it was unsatisfactory that "opinion was placed before the jury with the weight of his great experience behind it, without adequate verification of the assumption on which it was based."[101]

### c) Professor Chaikin and Sergeant Cocks

Professor Chaikin had given evidence to the jury about the cuts to the clothing being by a sharp instrument and not tears by dingo teeth. The commissioner said that this was an "erroneous assumption made by Professor Chaikin that dingoes cannot cut fabric with their teeth and produce tufts [and] was not based on any research work, or any scientific writing."[102]

At the trial, Sergeant Cocks of the South Australian police (the same who had played a prominent role in the Splatt case) had demonstrated to the jury how he thought the severance of the left arm of the jumpsuit was produced by the use of scissors. As the commissioner said, this evidence was "too speculative to be of much value, particularly having regard to the contrary evidence given by other witnesses."[103]

Commissioner Morling noted that the Northern Territory Police Department did not have any extensive scientific expertise or equipment. Its practice was to depend upon services made available to it by laboratories in other states. Kuhl's laboratory had not laid down criteria to determine whether a result was sufficiently certain to use as a basis for evidence. The commissioner said that some of the test results were so uncertain that they should not have been relied upon:

> In criminal cases, where the standard of proof is beyond reasonable doubt, it is highly desirable that complex scientific evidence called by the prosecution should be so carefully prepared and expressed that the necessity for the defence to challenge it is reduced as much as possible . . . . This was especially . . . because of the complexity and novelty of so many scientific questions which arose for the jury's consideration.[104]

He added:

---

101 *Ibid.* at 200.

102 *Ibid.* at 316.

103 *Ibid.* at 218.

104 *Ibid.* at 311.

> Mrs Kuhl was called upon to perform an extremely difficult task in a scientific area where controversy between experts was, to say the least, likely. Yet, it appears that her laboratory had not laid down any criteria for determining whether a particular result was sufficiently certain to be used as a basis for giving evidence.[105]

It is important that, in common with some of the Canadian cases, Commissioner Morling said, "before the Commission, no witness would take responsibility for what was put to the jury."[106]

### d) Summary by the Commissioner

Commissioner Morling summed up the case by saying that the error appeared to be a lack of expertise by some experts, and a lack of proper equipment and lack of consultation between all the experts involved in this important part of the Crown case. For example, the hairs found on the jumpsuit were identified as probably cat hairs whereas they were, in fact, dog hairs. This alleged absence of dingo hairs was relied upon as disproving the dingo story, but the presence of dog hairs on the clothing and in the tent tended to support it.[107] The commissioner made this important statement:

> . . . there should be closer links between forensic science centres and universities and other appropriate institutions so as to ensure that the former have the advantage of the research conducted by the latter.[108]

The commissioner said that individual forensic science centres, such as those in Melbourne and Adelaide, cannot be expected to have a full range of experts in every field of forensic science; they will frequently need to consult outside experts. A central forensic science institute would assist in meeting this need.[109] Eventually, a national institute was established in Australia, but rather than being independent, it has been set up and is administered by the police.

Closer links between forensic science centres, universities, and other institutions so that they might have the advantage of research being conducted by them was also suggested, and (as we have seen) the commissioner agreed.[110] He said the

---

105 *Ibid.* at 312.

106 *Ibid.* at 314.

107 *Ibid.*

108 *Ibid.* at 318. This recommendation is similar to the later one by the Goudge Inquiry in Canada and the National Academy of Sciences in the United States. For more on this, see Chapter 11.

109 *Ibid.* at 316.

110 *Ibid.* at 318.

laying down of appropriate standards in forensic science would not be easy. The evidence he had heard made it clear that there were differences of opinion as to what standards should be adopted. A national forensic institute could address and resolve this type of problem so as to establish a uniform and reliable practice throughout Australia.

The commissioner said that such an institute might also be a centre for the exchange of information and the location of suitable experts in unusual fields of expertise. It might also reduce the need to retain experts from overseas. He noted that as a result of the Splatt case, some changes were made to forensic science procedures in South Australia. He said the fact that two such inquiries had been held pointed to the desirability of further consideration to set up a national institute. The risk of injustice, he said, would be diminished if an accused person, in common with the Crown, had access to a national forensic science institute and its staff of experts.[111]

Commissioner Morling said there were obviously doubts as to the Chamberlains' guilt. He did not think that any jury could have properly convicted them on the basis of the evidence as it stood as almost every facet of the case was beset with serious difficulties:

> The question may well be asked how it came about that the evidence at the trial differed in such important respects from the evidence before the Commission . . . with the benefit of hindsight it can be seen that some experts who gave evidence at the trial were over-confident of their ability to form reliable opinions on matters that lay on the outer margins of their fields of expertise. Some of their opinions were based on unreliable or inadequate data . . . other evidence was given at the trial by experts who did not have the experience, facilities or resources necessary to enable them to express reliable opinions on some of the novel and complex scientific issues that arose for consideration.[112]

Not until further research was done were the opinions found to be of doubtful validity or judged wrong. Some gave evidence without the appropriate experience or resources to enable them to deal with the novel or complex issues that arose. The failure of the defence to put in issue certain items of evidence may have been due, in part, to the lack of the necessary expert witnesses to assist them.[113]

---

111 *Ibid.* at 319.
112 *Ibid.* at 341.
113 *Ibid.* at 320.

In the commissioner's opinion, if the evidence before his commission had been given at the trial, the trial judge would have been obliged to direct the jury to acquit the Chamberlains on the ground that the evidence could not justify their conviction.[114]

On 15 September 1988, the Northern Territory Court of Criminal Appeal unanimously overturned all convictions against Lindy and Michael Chamberlain.[115] The Chamberlains were awarded more than $1 million in compensation.

### 3) Bloodstain Pattern Analysis—The Case of Alexander McLeod-Lindsay

In 1965 Alexander McLeod-Lindsay was sentenced to eighteen years of imprisonment for seriously wounding his wife with the intent to murder her. At about 9:30 p.m. on 14 September 1964, someone had entered the family home via an unlocked door. Mrs. Lindsay woke up and was moving towards the noise when she was attacked and savagely beaten with a metal spike belonging to Lindsay and normally used to prop open a garage workshop door.

Lindsay said that he arrived home from work after midnight and found the house in darkness. This surprised him as the porch light was normally left on. The light switch did not work, and the fuse box had been interfered with. He grabbed a torch and found his wife in a corner of the bedroom covered in blood. He said that when he tried to pick her up, he felt blood strike his face and he leaned her back. She had extensive injuries. He rushed to the neighbour's house for help. His wife survived, but she was brain damaged and lost the sight of her right eye. The police immediately focused their attention on Lindsay. Some staining on his jacket resembled the bloodstain pattern on the wall.

The prosecution case was that he slipped away from his job during a break (he lived only a few minutes away), attacked his wife and child, and then went back to work. As with the Splatt and Chamberlain cases, no evidence supported the investigatory hypothesis that seemed to be based solely upon the absence of any other plausible suspect. Lindsay's appeal against his conviction failed, and four years later, following a petition he made, an inquiry was held—the jury's verdict was confirmed. He was released on parole in 1974 after almost nine years in custody.

---

114 *Ibid.* at 340.

115 *Re reference under s. 433A of the Criminal Code by the AG for the Northern Territory of Australia of Convictions of Alice Lynne Chamberlain and Michael Leigh Chamberlain,* Supreme Court of Northern Territory, No CA2 of 1988, [1988] NTSC 64.

A second inquiry was held in 1991, and this time the commissioner found that new developments in forensic science (bloodstain pattern analysis) had cast serious doubts on crucial Crown evidence, making the conviction unsafe.[116] Lindsay was subsequently paid an undisclosed sum of money in a settlement with the state government.

## 4) Unreliable Scientific Evidence — Douglas Harry Rendell

In 1980 Douglas Rendell was charged and tried for the shooting murder of his *de facto* wife, Yvonne Kendal. As there were no witnesses, the prosecution relied on circumstantial evidence to prove Rendell's guilt. The scenario established was that Kendal was shot while lying down and that the rifle involved in the death (which belonged to Rendell) was not prone to accidental discharge. A police ballistics expert and a scientific officer produced evidence to support that view. Rendell had said that Kendal was shot while standing up and that the rifle had discharged accidentally.

Evidence was put to the jury that Rendell had attempted to cover up his involvement in the death because blood was found around the wash basin in the bathroom. Scientific tests were conducted by a scientist (Joy Kuhl) to establish the presence of blood around the basin.[117] The jury was also told that the rifle had smear marks and no fingerprints were visible, indicating it had been wiped by Rendell. What the jury was not told was that the rifle had previously been handled several times by the police before it was sent for testing and that any wiping took place after this handling.

Rendell was convicted and sentenced to life imprisonment. His appeal was denied. He petitioned twice to the state governor for a review of his case, but the applications were rejected on both occasions. Finally, after further investigations by interested parties suggested that Rendell may have been wrongly convicted, an application was made to the Supreme Court, which resulted in the case being referred to Justice Hunt. In 1987 (seven years into Rendell's sen-

116 R.F. Loveday, *Report of the Inquiry Held under Section 475 of the Crimes Act 1900 into the Conviction of Alexander Lindsay (Formerly Alexander McLeod-Lindsay) at Central Criminal Court Sydney on 5 March 1965* (Sydney: Supreme Court of New South Wales, 1991). See also Anita Y. Wonder, *Bloodstain Pattern Evidence, Objective Approaches and Case Applications* (London: Elsevier Academic Press, 2007) c. 6, "The Alexander Lindsay Second Inquiry." For a similar issue on another case, see Paul Wilson & Dianne McInnes, *Five Drops of Blood: Murder in the Cat Protection Society* (Chatswood, NSW: New Holland, 2008).

117 As seen above, Joy Kuhl was the forensic scientist in the Lindy Chamberlain case.

tence), Hunt J. appointed Arthur Riedel, a magistrate, to conduct an inquiry and report back to him.

In 1989, Hunt J. reported that he was satisfied that Rendell's conviction was "unsafe and unsatisfactory" owing to the unreliability of the prosecution evidence.[118] Rendell was finally granted a pardon. Initially, parts of the Riedel report and Hunt J.'s report were not released for political reasons.

At the inquiry, the scientist acknowledged that the sample of what appeared to be blood on the wash basin was no more than only probably blood. She was also unable to say whether it was human or animal blood. The Hunt report said that virtually no weight should be attached to this evidence.

Expert evidence was also presented at the inquiry to show that the rifle could have discharged accidentally. The inquiry found that police had withheld evidence from the defence and the court that may well have affected the outcome of the trial.

## D. THE DNA EXPERIENCE

One topic of great importance to all jurisdictions is that of DNA.

Probably the United States has the most developed experience in this area. As of 2010, there have been more than 254 post-conviction DNA exonerations in the United States. The first DNA exoneration took place in 1989. Exonerations have been won in thirty-four states; since 2000, there have been 188 exonerations. Seventeen of the 254 people exonerated through DNA served time on death row.[119] In the United States, only four states do not have laws governing the right to access and test DNA as part of post-conviction reviews.

As the law currently stands, there is no statutory obligation on law enforcement agencies in Australia to retain crime scene exhibits after the conclusion of the appeals process. The Australian Law Reform Commission in 2003 recommended that the federal government should amend the *Crimes Act 1914* (Cth.) to require the long-term retention of forensic material found at the scene of serious crimes to facilitate post-conviction analysis. It also recommended the establishment of a national process to review post-conviction applications on DNA evidence, hence limiting it to factual innocence. No action has been taken to date on either recommendation.

---

118 *Report of the Inquiry pursuant to s. 475 of the Crimes Act 1900 into the Guilt of Douglas Harry Rendell*, presented by Justice D. Hunt and conducted by A.M. Riedel (Sydney: Government Printer, 1989).

119 See online: www.innocenceproject.org/Content/351.php.

While DNA has been of considerable value in obtaining exonerations, it has also become a significant tool in obtaining convictions. Most jurisdictions now have a national DNA database which contains the DNA profiles of those who have been convicted or charged with serious offences. Matching the profiles from that database to DNA found at crime scenes either with current or cold-case investigations has proved to be most valuable in detecting offenders.

Of course, if our experience of the use of scientific methods in other areas is anything to go by, we can expect there to be claims in the future about the ways in which DNA evidence has been used to gain those convictions. In the case of *R. v. Dean*, it was found that the DNA used to convict Mr. Dean should have been destroyed prior to him being identified as a possible perpetrator of a crime.[120] The report of the auditor-general stated:

> It is important in matters of this type to be reminded of the comments by Mr Justice Brandeis in *Olmstead v. United States* (1928) 277 US 438. "Decency, security and liberty alike demand that government officials shall be subjected to the same rules of conduct that are commands to the citizen. In a government of laws, existence of the government will be imperilled if it fails to observe the law scrupulously. Our Government is the potent, the omnipresent teacher. For good or for ill, it teaches the whole people by its example. Crime is contagious. If the Government becomes a lawbreaker, it breeds contempt for law; it invites every man to become a law unto himself; it invites anarchy. To declare that in the administration of the criminal law the end justifies the means -- to declare that the Government may commit crimes in order to secure the conviction of a private criminal -- would bring terrible retribution. Against that pernicious doctrine this Court should resolutely set its face."[121]

Clearly, DNA issues give rise to the most basic considerations concerning issues of due process.

### 1) Tunnel Vision — Frank Button: First DNA Exoneration Case in Australia

Frank Button, an indigenous Australian, aged thirty-two, served ten months of a seven-year sentence for the rape of a thirteen-year-old girl in a small indigen-

120 *R. v. Dean*, [2006] SACD 54.

121 Supplementary Report of the Auditor-General South Australia — Matters Arising from the Further Audit Examination of the Administration of the *Criminal Law (Forensic Procedures) Act 1998* and Other Matters; Audit Comments on Further Audit Examination of the Administration of the *Criminal Law (Forensic Procedures) Act 1998*.

ous community before DNA evidence proved that he could not have been the perpetrator of the crime.[122]

In 1999 the girl claimed she had been sexually assaulted during a party at her home. She provided a description of her assailant to the police, but said she would not know the person if she saw him again. Button had been asleep at the girl's house when police arrived to investigate. He became the prime suspect because he had been wearing a shirt similar to the one the girl had described to the police. He denied being involved but was charged with the crime and remanded in custody. The vaginal swabs taken from the young girl revealed semen that resulted in a DNA profile of the victim; however, no male DNA was obtained. The bedsheet and pillowcase from the crime scene were also sent to the forensic science laboratory, but for some reason they were not tested for any DNA evidence.

The absence of incriminating scientific evidence caused the police to collect other evidence to fill the gaps. When a second statement was taken from the girl, she had radically altered her version of events and named Frank Button as her attacker. Police also took a statement from Button's nephew, who claimed Button had confessed to him while they were in a park shortly after Button had been charged. The nephew's statement was later discredited when it was revealed that Button went straight to jail after he was charged, and the confession in the park could not have occurred.

The case against Button relied heavily on the testimony of the young girl, his alleged confession, and his presence at the house at the time of the offence. Button was convicted and sentenced to seven years of imprisonment.

When preparing for his appeal, Button's lawyer raised the issue of the absence of scientific evidence in the case. In response, for the first time the scientists at the laboratory tested the bedsheet and discovered a semen stain that yielded a DNA profile which did not match Button's. The scientists then retested the vaginal swab taken from the young girl and this time they found a male DNA profile which matched the one found on the bedsheet. That profile was run through the Queensland Convicted Offenders database and matched that of a convicted rapist from the girl's community.

At the appeal, the prosecution's explanation as to why these tests were not carried out before the trial was that "it would not [have been] of material assistance in identifying the appellant as the perpetrator of the crime." On 12 April 2001 the Queensland Court of Appeal immediately ordered Button's release from prison.

---

122 This discussion is taken from *R. v. Button*, [2001] QCA 133 at para. 1.

The court started its judgment with this comment:

> Today is a black day in the history of the administration of criminal justice. What is of major concern to this court is the fact that that evidence was not available at the trial. This court can do little so far as compensation to the appellant for the fact that he has had to suffer the ignominy of a conviction for rape which now proves to be entirely false.[123]

The inability to restore an unblemished reputation to someone convicted of a crime is a perennial problem with miscarriage of justice cases. Even after convictions have been overturned, some will say that it was set aside on a "technicality." Certainly the following case raises that very issue in the starkest of circumstances.

### 2) "Low-Copy Number" DNA—The Case of Sean Hoey, Northern Ireland

The method known as "low-copy number" DNA (LCN DNA) has been the subject of some controversy. Its use was challenged in the Northern Ireland case of Sean Hoey, and the work of the Forensic Institute in Scotland has been particularly significant.[124] While the British Forensic Regulator quickly produced a report to suggest that the scientific work on LCN DNA was better or more reliable that might be supposed, the Forensic Institute in Glasgow quickly issued a media release to dispute that claim.[125] "Low-copy number" DNA was developed by British Forensic Science Service in 1999: a tiny amount of DNA (1,000 times smaller than a grain of salt) is recovered for analysis. Because many more cycles of replication are necessary, and contaminants will also be replicated, this process creates a greater risk of inaccurate results. For example, a microscopic sample of sweat or skin cells is taken from a scene and DNA is extracted. A special "Taq" enzyme is then used to amplify the DNA in thirty-four cycles—normal DNA testing uses twenty-eight cycles. A gel is used to separate DNA fragments, and fluorescently tagged dyes help to differentiate the DNA components. The results are then compared with known samples to find a "match." One study noted that the failure rates for low-copy number DNA analysis are high, with one police force estimating the success rate in

123 *Ibid.* at paras. 1 and 3.

124 *R. v. Hoey*, [2007] NICC 49 [*Hoey*].

125 "DNA Technique 'Fit for Purpose'" *BBC News* (11 April 2008) ["DNA Technique"]; Forensic Institute, Glasgow, Press Release, "Regarding the Caddy Review of Low Template DNA" (15 April 2008).

achieving a full profile at about 6 percent.[126] With such tiny samples, explanations about how the sample got to where it was found are intensely problematic as also are the issues of possible contamination.

Sean Hoey was charged with fifty-eight counts related to offences of murder, conspiracy to murder, causing explosions, conspiracy to cause explosions, and possession of explosive substances with intent to endanger life or cause serious damage to property.[127] The incidents arose from thirteen bomb and mortar attacks, attempts at such attacks, and the finding of unexploded devices. They included the devastating car bomb explosion that destroyed much of the shopping centre of Omagh on the afternoon of Saturday, 15 August 1998, with twenty-nine killed and hundreds of others injured. The evidence against Hoey was said to have been common factors related to the construction of the timer power units (TPUs) which showed a common origin, or "authorship." Fibres were recovered from the melted glue used to secure components within the TPUs which were alleged to be consistent with fibre samples recovered from the home of the accused. Four fibres found on one device were said to be indistinguishable from five fibres recovered from the home of the accused. Also, "low-copy number" DNA was said to have shown a connection between the accused and the explosive devices.

In his judgment, Weir J. set out some important principles that relate to the general scientific issues we discussed in Chapter 2. He said:

> The Defence submit, correctly in my judgment, that it is for the prosecution to establish the integrity and freedom from possible contamination of each item throughout the entirety of the period between seizure and any examination relied upon. They contend, and I accept the contention, that the court must be satisfied by the prosecution witnesses and supporting documents that all dealings with each relevant exhibit have been satisfactorily accounted for from the moment of its seizure until the moment when any evidential sample relied upon by the prosecution is taken from it and that by a method and in conditions that are shown to have been reliable. This means that each person who has dealt with the item in the intervening period must be ascertainable and be able to demonstrate by reference to some proper system of bagging, labelling, and recording that the item has been preserved at every stage free from the suspicion of interference or contamination. For this purpose they must be able to demonstrate how and when and under what condi-

126 "DNA Technique," *ibid.*

127 This discussion is taken from *Hoey*, above note 124. See also "Doubt over DNA Conviction Tool" *The West Australian* (24 December 2007).

> tions and with what object and by what means and in whose presence he or she examined the item.[128]

After describing numerous shortcomings with regard to the processing of individual items, the judge concluded:

> My subsequent description of some of the evidence concerning the actual regime that prevailed both within the police and NIFS [Northern Ireland Forensic Services] during the relevant period demonstrates how far short of surmounting that high hurdle the prosecution has fallen in this case. It is not my function to criticise the seemingly thoughtless and slapdash approach of police and SOCO officers to the collection, storage and transmission of what must obviously have been potential exhibits in a possible future criminal trial but it is difficult to avoid some expression of surprise that in an era in which the potential for fibre, if not DNA, contamination was well known to the police such items were so widely and routinely handled with cavalier disregard for their integrity.[129]

The judge also referred to "mendacious attempts to retrospectively alter the . . . evidence so as to falsely make it appear that appropriate DNA protective precautions had been taken at that scene."[130] He referred to false statements by scientific officers that they wore protective clothing at the scene, when photographs subsequently revealed that not to have been the case. He also referred to the "beefing up" of statements and to the "deliberate and calculated deception" by prosecution witnesses. The judge made interesting comments about the lack of proper validation procedures and concluded:

> I am not satisfied that the publishing of two journal articles describing a process invented by the authors can be regarded without more as having "validated" that process for the purpose of its being confidently used for evidential purposes.[131]

He also made the important distinction between findings that might be of assistance in the development of "intelligence" in a case and that which might be used as evidence in a court of law. He added:

> But I also bear firmly in mind the cardinal principle of the criminal law which, in delivering the judgment of the Court of Appeal in *R. v Steenson and*

128 *Hoey, ibid.*, at para. 46.
129 *Ibid.* at para. 59.
130 *Ibid.* at para. 60.
131 *Ibid.* at para. 64.

> *others* [1986] NIJB17 at page 36, Lord Lowry LCJ re-emphasised in his concluding observations: "Justice 'according to law' demands proper evidence. By that we mean not merely evidence which might be true and to a considerable extent probably is true, but, as the learned trial judge put it, 'evidence which is so convincing in truth and manifestly reliable that it reaches the standard of proof beyond reasonable doubt.'"[132]

The problems experienced in relation to DNA techniques might yet cause us to question our standards of scientific validation in other areas. We will return to this issue in our final chapter.

## E. CONCLUSION

It is clear that scientists, like their police and prosecutorial colleagues, can be knocked off balance when involved with investigations into serious crimes. Sometimes, they have engaged in serious misconduct, but more often, the failure to follow proper procedures means that they have unfairly focused attention on the wrong person. While sometimes the underlying methodology may be sound, the misapplication or misinterpretation of otherwise reliable techniques can be the cause of error. It will be interesting to see to what extent the reliability of DNA techniques will give rise to its own miscarriages of justice by the introduction of errors, such as contamination and misinterpretation.

In Chapter 9, we will extend our analysis to those who have been trained as doctors and who are called upon to assist the forensic process, often in the context of post-mortem examinations.

---

132 *Ibid.* at para. 65.

CHAPTER 9

# Forensic Pathology Issues

Forensic pathologists are doctors who are also expected to follow appropriate scientific procedures and to provide testimony that can be understood and used in the legal process. They make observations about the cause of death, preserve relevant evidence of what they have seen, and then identify appropriate conclusions in accordance with established scientific principles. However, in this particular area of science one frequently encounters discussions of the "arrogant" or overbearing expert witness. One warning sign should be a witness who frequently refers to "my experience" as the basis for a conclusion about the cause of death. It should be noted that *experience*, unaided by scientific study or support, has never been a proper basis for the drawing of inferences about a cause of death. It is difficult, if not impossible, to understand or question the basis of an opinion about cause of death simply based on the experience and expertise of the forensic pathologist.[1] Yet, from Dr. Bernard Spilsbury in Britain in the early 1900s to Dr. Charles Smith in Canada more recently, unsubstantiated and unchallenged confidence in causes and outcomes has led to serious miscarriages of justice.

Many of the cases involving flawed forensic pathology in Britain and Canada have been discovered only as a result of discrediting doctors who were previously seen as expert and dominant in their fields. Particularly in cases involving the deaths of children, the testimony of a forensic pathologist may be virtually conclusive of guilt. The obvious question that should be answered is why weren't those witnesses challenged at the time of trial to produce their

1 See the discussion in Chapter 2 on the role of the expert witness and the caselaw referred to there.

published materials or to explain the scientific principles that were supposed to support their conclusions?

In Britain, Canada, and Australia, recent concerns about the causes of pediatric deaths have led to either unwarranted convictions or failure to prosecute based upon unreliable evidence and opinions. Going beyond one's expertise, expressing opinions without clear evidence to support them, and misinterpreting have all emerged in these cases as potent sources of error. In some cases, such as those of Sally Clark in Britain and William Mullins-Johnson in Canada, people have gone to prison for "crimes" that had not occurred. In others, such as the baby deaths in South Australia and the Jenna Waudby case in Canada, pathology errors have led to failure to investigate those who may have been responsible. There is a public interest in accurate and reliable forensic pathology for both those accused and those who are victims.

Forensic pathology is the application of anatomical pathology techniques in areas that might be of assistance to the police and in court proceedings. Pathologists must first qualify as medical practitioners before going on to specialize in forensic pathology. Theirs is an evolving science with certain areas of controversies, such as the indicia of shaken baby syndrome or whether children can die from short falls. Forensic pathology also depends on the ability of the pathologist to interpret the meaning of results found at autopsies, including artefacts of death or the of autopsy itself. In child death cases, the whole case can hinge on forensic pathology evidence. Finally, forensic pathologists must be able to communicate their findings to a lay audience in court. In criminal cases, the prosecution must establish guilt beyond a reasonable doubt; however, the science of pathology may not allow for such levels of certainty.[2]

In most jurisdictions, where a person is found to be dead in circumstances where a general practitioner is unable to issue a death certificate, the case comes within the jurisdiction of the coroner to determine the cause of death. Usually, the coroner will direct that an autopsy be conducted. An autopsy will involve an external and internal examination of the body by the forensic pathologist. Therefore, a forensic pathologist focuses on the interpretation of post-mortem findings in legal proceedings, whether in a criminal trial or in a coronial inquest into the cause and manner of death. While the pathologist's principal focus is the body itself, it is clear that relevant context and circumstances can be taken into account. As we will see from some of the cases, though, the patholo-

---

2 For a general description of forensic pathology, see *Report of the Inquiry into Pediatric Forensic Pathology in Ontario* (Toronto: Ministry of the Attorney General, 2008) c. 6 [Goudge Inquiry].

gist should not feel encouraged to express opinions on matters that go beyond his or her expertise and training.[3]

As we will also see, a worrying number of medical experts who have confidently given their expert opinions at trials were years later heavily criticized, if not totally discredited. The flawed evidence they gave at trial contributed to the wrongful convictions of innocent people. Flawed pathology evidence can also allow the real perpetrators of criminal activities to escape detection.

## A. THE BRITISH EXPERIENCE

Perhaps some of the most tragic cases of recent years have been those in which women were accused, charged, and convicted for being complicit in the murder of their own children, only for the allegations later to be shown without foundation. The British Attorney General pointed to this series of cases as one of the most significant factors that have had an impact on public confidence in expert testimony.[4] He said:

> As you will know, I became very much engaged in the debate as a result particularly of those cases which of course concerned convictions and trials for the deaths of infants. Following the decision of the Court of Appeal in the appeal of Angela Cannings on 9 January 2004 I launched a thorough review of all cases in the previous 10 years in which a parent or carer had been convicted of the unlawful killing of a baby or infant under the age of two. The specific impetus was the finding of the Court of Appeal in *Cannings*, which showed that, in relation to unexplained infant deaths, where the outcome depends exclusively, or almost exclusively, on a serious disagreement between distinguished and reputable experts and natural causes cannot be excluded as a cause of death, it will often be unsafe to proceed.[5]

---

3 For a general description of an autopsy procedure, see Robert N. Moles, *A State of Injustice* (South Melbourne: Lothian, 2004) c. 3 [Moles, *State of Injustice*]. See also the case of *Straker* referred to in Chapter 2 which states that speculation, particularly by pathologists, is to be avoided.

4 The cases of Sally Clark and Angela Cannings prompted a major public debate about the role of experts in general and the standing of certain medical experts, including Dr. Alan Williams and Prof. Sir Roy Meadow, in particular. These cases, mentioned in Chapter 8, are discussed further in this chapter.

5 This part of the discussion is from Lord Goldsmith, "Expert Evidence—The Problem or the Solution?" (John Bolton Memorial Lecture, presented to Academy of Expert Witnesses, 25 January 2007) [unpublished].

Almost 300 baby death cases were reviewed as a result of the audit ordered by the Attorney General. In Chapter 12, we will suggest that proactive audits of cases with suspect or controversial forms of evidence, such as those initiated by Attorney General Goldsmith, can be a positive response to the dangers of miscarriage of justice.

Although audits can be helpful, much will depend on the attitude of the appellate courts. When quashing Angela Cannings's convictions for murder of two of her children, the Court of Appeal indicated that given the present state of knowledge a prosecution should not be brought in cases if there was "a serious disagreement between reputable experts about the cause of death, and a body of such expert opinion concludes that natural causes, whether explained or unexplained, cannot be excluded as a reasonable (and not a fanciful) possibility."[6] The Court of Appeal seemed to be aware of the implications of such a stringent approach and recognized that

> justice may not be done in a small number of cases where in truth a mother has deliberately killed her baby without leaving any identifiable evidence of the crime. That is an undesirable result, which however avoids a worse one. If murder cannot be proved, the conviction cannot be safe. In a criminal case, it is simply not enough to be able to establish even a high probability of guilt. Unless we are sure of guilt the dreadful possibility always remains that a mother, already brutally scarred by the unexplained death or deaths of her babies, may find herself in prison for life for killing them when she should not be there at all. In our community, and in any civilised community, that is abhorrent.[7]

The very next year, however, the Court of Appeal seemed to retreat from or at least qualify the above statements. In the course of upholding a murder conviction in a baby death case, it stated that its decision in *Cannings* did not mean that disagreements among experts about the existence or timing of a fracture in a baby death case should be withdrawn from the jury.[8]

---

6 *R. v. Cannings*, [2004] EWCA Crim 1 at para. 178 [*Cannings*].

7 *Ibid.* at para. 179.

8 *R. v. Kai-Whitewind*, [2005] EWCA Crim 1092. There was, however, some application of the *Cannings* principle in *R. v. Harris & Ors*, [2005] EWCA Crim 1980 [*Harris*]. *Harris* points out at para. 4 [citations omitted] that "following the judgment of this Court in *R. v. Cannings* . . . , the Law Officers set up an Interdepartmental Group to review convictions of defendants in alleged 'battered babies' cases," which had led to those appeals.

For further discussion, see Kathryn Campbell & Clive Walker, "Medical Mistakes and Miscarriages of Justice: Perspectives on the Experiences in England and Wales"

The Court of Appeal's struggle with the proper approach to forensic pathology evidence in child death cases is perhaps understandable. The stakes are incredibly high in such cases. At one end—and candidly recognized in *Cannings*—is the danger that intentional killings of the most vulnerable will go undetected. At the other end is the danger of wrongful conviction of caregivers for what may be tragic and undetermined deaths. Although the stakes on both sides are high, it would be an error to equate the risk of wrongful convictions with the risk of wrongful acquittals. The criminal justice system, with its commitment to the presumption of innocence and proof of guilt beyond a reasonable doubt, accepts that the latter risk is to be preferred to the former.

### 1) Failure to Disclose Test Results—The Case of Sally Clark

In Chapter 2 when we were dealing with the general principles applicable to expert witnesses, we discussed some aspects of the professional conduct proceedings involving Dr. Alan Williams. Here, we are concerned with the aspects of his pathology work.

In this case, pathological evidence was used to establish that the two babies had been killed by their mother and had not suffered accidental cot deaths. Sally Clark was a solicitor who was convicted of the murder of her two children.[9] In December 1996 Christopher, who was Sally Clark's first child, died aged fifteen months. Dr. Williams, a consultant forensic pathologist, carried out a post-mortem examination and concluded that the cause of Christopher's death was lower respiratory tract infection. In January 1998 Sally Clark's second child, Harry, who had been born in November 1997, also died. Dr. Williams carried out a post-mortem examination and concluded that Harry had not died of natural causes but of shaken baby syndrome. This conclusion was derived, in particular, from an examination of Harry's spine, eyes, and brain.

As part of his investigation into Harry's death, Dr. Williams collected samples at the post-mortem examination for microbiological examination. Samples were taken of blood, of cerebrospinal fluid (CSF), and from the stomach (tissue and fluid), both bronchi, both lungs, throat, feces, and the trachea.

---

in Inquiry into Pediatric Forensic Pathology in Ontario, *Independent Research Studies: Pediatric Forensic Pathology and the Justice System*, ed. by Kent Roach, vol. 2 (Toronto: Ontario Ministry of the Attorney General, 2008) [Goudge Inquiry Research Papers].

9 This discussion is based upon *R. v. Clark (No. 2)*, [2003] EWCA Crim 1020 [*Clark (No. 2)*]; see also John Batt, *Stolen Innocence: The Authorised Story of Sally Clark—A Mother's Fight for Justice* (London: Ebury, 2004); UK Policy Advisory Board for Forensic Pathology, Dr. A.R. Williams Mb. Chb. Frc. Path., Judgment (28 March 2006).

The sample of CSF was reported by the laboratory at the Macclesfield District Hospital as "staphylococcus aureus isolated." The microbiological results were considered by Dr. Wills, a consultant microbiologist at the Macclesfield Hospital, who commissioned further tests. In his post-mortem report Dr. Williams did not make any express reference to the microbiological reports on the samples taken by him at autopsy, to the results themselves, or to the further tests commissioned by Dr. Wills. Indeed, in his report he did not state that he had even taken samples at autopsy for microbiological testing. Dr. Williams also reconsidered his conclusion that Christopher had died of natural causes and reported "there is evidence suggestive that he died from an asphyxial mechanism such as smothering."

At the trial, no reference was made to these microbiological results and no evidence was given about them by Dr. Williams, who gave evidence for the prosecution. Neither did any of the other expert witnesses who gave evidence for the prosecution or the defence. Dr. Williams did, however, make a passing reference to his general practice of taking samples for microbiology. In 1999 Sally Clark was found guilty of murdering both children and was sentenced to life imprisonment.

Only one hard copy of each of the microbiological results had been printed, and those copies, having been sent to Dr. Williams, remained in his own file until they were misfiled, during the course of the trial, among the prosecution papers. The results had, however, been electronically stored on the Macclesfield Hospital pathology laboratory computer. In November 2001 the microbiological results came to light when they were sent by Macclesfield Hospital to Stephen Clark (Christopher and Harry's father) in response to his request for legible copies of other results.

In July 2002 the Criminal Cases Review Commission (CCRC) referred Sally Clark's case back to the Court of Appeal. There had been an earlier unsuccessful appeal before the microbiological results had become known.[10] In January 2003 the Court of Appeal concluded that the convictions were unsafe and should be set aside, and Sally Clark was immediately released from prison. The main ground for concluding that the convictions were unsafe was that the microbiological results had not been disclosed by Dr. Williams to the prosecution, defence, expert medical witnesses, or the court. The Court of Appeal expressed extreme concern about the competence of Dr. Williams. It set out guidelines for pathologists on how to approach a post-mortem examination. The guidelines stressed the need to be fully informed about the back-

10 *R. v. Clark*, [2000] EWCA Crim 54.

ground circumstances of the case, to fully record all that is observed, to be open to alternative explanations and not to jump to conclusions too early in the examination.[11]

At the appeal hearing, there was substantial criticism of Dr. Williams by his professional colleagues both for the prosecution and the defence. Dr. Williams had declined to avail himself of the opportunity offered to him by the Court of Appeal to explain himself. The only response the court received was contained in a statement dated 5 September 2002 in which Dr. Williams said: "It is not my practice to refer to additional results in my post mortem unless they are relevant to the cause of death, as the specimens were referred to another consultant." The Court of Appeal found that statement to be wholly unacceptable.[12]

In October 2003 the Quality Assurance and Scientific Standards Board (QASSB) of the Pathology Advisory Board for Forensic Pathology referred a complaint to the Disciplinary Tribunal of the General Medical Council (GMC). Their findings, which were adverse to Dr. Williams, were discussed in Chapter 2.

Subsequently, the findings of the tribunal were the subject of an appeal by Dr. Williams. In upholding the tribunal's decision, the High Court referred to the Home Office Forensic Pathology Practice Guidelines which stated that "comprehensive contemporaneous notes were essential and should be taken of every procedure undertaken."[13] It said that such notes must be retained, as should all tapes, and probably kept until any sentence has been completed; that conclusions must have a proper scientific basis. The High Court said that the potential consequences of an act or omission are part of the context and can bear on the extent of the obligation undertaken.

The High Court said that in the context of a murder trial, possibilities are potentially crucial. Dr. Williams, with all his experience, must be taken in general terms to have known that an incident of a right to a fair trial is a right to timely disclosure by the prosecution of all material matters that affect the scientific case relied on by the prosecution. That is so whether such matters strengthen or weaken the prosecution case, or assist the defence case. This duty exists whether or not a specific request for disclosure of details of scientific evidence is made by the defence. Moreover, this duty is continuous. As the Court said, Dr. Williams should have known that much, even if he did not know specifically that the principle derived from the IRA bombing case of *R. v.*

---

11 *Clark (No. 2)*, above note 9. See also Moles, *A State of Injustice*, above note 3.

12 *Ibid.* at para. 166.

13 *Williams v. General Medical Council*, [2007] EWHC 2603 (Admin) at para. 18.

*Ward*.[14] The High Court said that the doctor's conduct in the *Clark* case represented a catalogue of uncorrected and "formidable" errors of observation and judgment over a three-year period; it concluded that the potential for serious consequences could not be disregarded. Dr. Williams had accepted the "highest level" of forensic responsibility and had put himself in a position where he might have a "pivotal role" in a criminal trial. The fact that he had a previously unblemished career could not detract from the seriousness of the error.

Another medical practitioner connected to the *Clark* case also turned out to be a cause of concern. Although not a pathologist, Dr. David Southall was professor of pediatrics at the University of Keele and a consultant pediatrician at the North Staffordshire Hospital. He had been contacted by local authority social workers who had concerns about the welfare of a child, not one of the Clark family. He was told that there were similarities between current events in the child's life (including apparent suicide threats) and events in the life of his elder brother who, in June 1996, when aged ten, had died by hanging. Dr. Southall gave the social workers certain advice. The child was removed from his parents' care.

Dr. Southall had accused the mother of drugging the older child and then killing him by hanging. The Fitness to Practise Panel found that his action in accusing the mother of killing the boy was inappropriate and an abuse of his professional position. It found that the manner in which he conducted the interview, questioned, and directly accused the mother was incompatible with his position as a doctor. It further said it regarded his behaviour towards her as a serious instance of misconduct.[15]

Dr. Southall became involved in the case of Sally Clark. He had suggested that Clark's husband had been involved in the death of the children. He made the claim having watched a television program about the case. The program, broadcast in April 2000, featured an interview with Clark's husband. After watching it, Dr. Southall claimed that it was "beyond reasonable doubt" that Mr. Clark had killed the babies. Dr. Southall was subsequently banned from child protection work by the GMC.[16] That decision was upheld by the High Court in 2009.[17] In child death cases, there is a danger that clinical and advocacy concerns about the protection of children will overwhelm the need for an evidence-based and forensic approach.

---

14 [1993] 1 W.L.R. 619.

15 Fitness to Practise Panel — Dr David Southall, Determination on Serious Professional Misconduct and Sanction, London (4 December 2007).

16 "GMC Judgment on David Southall" [containing full text of the GMC judgment] *The Guardian* (6 August 2004).

17 *Southall v. General Medical Council*, [2009] EWHC 1155 (Admin).

In 2008 the GMC revoked the earlier restrictions on Dr. Southall's practice. The chairman of the GMC's Fitness to Practise Panel said the doctor had expressed regret and remorse for his actions and demonstrated "considerable insight" into his failings.[18] Dr. Southall told the panel he still thought he had been correct in raising the alarm over Mr. Clark, but admitted that the language he had used in the accusation had been "injudicious."

As mentioned, Sally Clark was cleared by the Court of Appeal and released from prison in January 2003. She never recovered from the trauma. She died accidentally as a result of acute alcohol intoxication in March 2007. She was forty-two.[19]

### 2) Autopsy Findings Inadequate and Misleading—The Case of Patrick Nicholls

In 1975 Patrick Nicholls was convicted of the murder and robbery of an elderly woman and sentenced to life for the murder with eight years for the robbery. His appeal was refused in 1977, and his application for review was rejected in 1996. His conviction was eventually overturned by the Court of Appeal in 1998 after he had spent twenty-three years in prison.[20]

In 1975 Nicholls used to go to a pub where he would meet Gladys Heath, a woman of seventy-four years. They would sometimes have a drink together. In April 1975, shortly after a drink one day, she was found dead at her home at the foot of the stairs. A Dr. Johnson was called to the scene, and following his post-mortem examination, he concluded that death was not attributable to natural causes. He said that Heath had died as a result of a shock of some sort, which had triggered a heart attack. That opinion was agreed to by an eminent pathologist, Dr. Cameron, who had not carried out a post-mortem on the body and had merely examined specimens and slides. This same Dr. Cameron gave evidence in the trial of Lindy Chamberlain in Australia in 1982 (discussed in Chapter 8).

Dr. Cameron said that from the examination of the photographs, he could see that the body had been "dumped" at the foot of the stairs. In his opinion the body could have ended up in that position only if it had been placed there. He said he could discern from the fact that the chair in the living room had been disturbed, yet the jigsaw had not been, that Heath had been assaulted

18 "David Southall, Specialist in Sally Clark Case, Given Another Chance" *The Times* (22 September 2008).

19 "Sally Clark, A Mother Wronged to Death" *Sunday Times* (18 March 2007).

20 This discussion is taken from *R. v. Patrick Nicholls*, [1998] EWCA Crim 1918. This case is discussed in Chapter 3.

while in the chair and that the body had been moved from that chair. He also said he could see from the photographs that there had been a degree of asphyxia before death which suggested that the mouth had been covered by compression from a hand.

Dr. Cameron said that when examining the heart under the microscope, he had seen evidence of an acute incident resulting from shock that could have been precipitated by an assault with an asphyxial element. He agreed with Dr. Johnson that a coronary blockage arising from a degenerative change in the vessels was the immediate cause of death, but his view was that this had been precipitated by shock and asphyxia.

On a request from the CCRC in 1997, the case was reviewed by Professor Crane, the state pathologist from Northern Ireland. After receiving his report, the CCRC referred the case to the Court of Appeal. Professor Crane said the autopsy findings were inadequate, inappropriate, and misleading, and that the cause of death was incorrectly stated. He said that if a coronary defect was the underlying factor causing death, then it should not have been confused with contributory factors unrelated to the cause of death. He was also critical of Dr. Cameron's report. He said the conclusion that the heart showed evidence of shock and an asphyxial element did not make sense. In his view, the idea that the absence of changes in the heart tissues suggested assault or asphyxiation had no scientific basis. He regarded this as inappropriate speculation on the part of the pathologist.[21]

Professor Crane noted that Dr. Cameron had said that as seen in the histology slides, the over-distension of the lungs indicated asphyxia—in his opinion, this conclusion was not correct; over-distension of the air spaces was more related to chronic obstructive airways disease and was not a diagnostic feature of asphyxia. In his opinion the injuries to Heath were trivial and not typical of an assault; on their own they would not have caused or even contributed to the death. It is possible that they were caused as she collapsed.

Professor Crane pointed out that suffocation by obstruction to the mouth and nose is not associated with any obvious signs detectable at post-mortem. While that possibility could not be excluded, no evidence indicated that it had occurred. So, there was an elderly woman with severe coronary artery disease and almost total obstruction of the right main coronary artery, which could have caused a fatal heart attack, at any time. Of course, emotional and physical stresses can exacerbate the condition, but there was no evidence of them. He

21 This issue arises later in the Goudge Inquiry in Canada concerning Dr. Charles Smith. Justice Goudge concludes that the way in which pathologists make claims about asphyxia needs to be dealt with more carefully.

said the use of the term "shock" was misleading since it is not a pathological entity that can be detected at a post-mortem examination. To include it in this way in an autopsy report was inappropriate.[22]

As the court pointed out, once it had been accepted that this was a case of homicide and not death due to natural causes, the circumstantial case against Nicholls, based on his conduct both during that afternoon and later in an interview with the police, was strong. It could not have been effectively disputed by defence counsel that Heath had been unlawfully killed. Things looked very different, however, once it was shown that natural causes could not be excluded. As a result of what the court accepted to be flawed pathological evidence, Nicholls was wrongly convicted.

### 3) Inappropriate Diagnosis of Forcible Asphyxia—The Cases of Kenneth Fraser and Steven Puaca

These two cases were in relation to the suspicious deaths of Mary Moore and Jacqueline Tindsley and the criminal proceedings arising from them.[23] Mary Moore, aged fifty-six, had been living with Kenneth Fraser. Jacqueline Tindsley, aged fifty-five, had been living with Steven Puaca. Both had been found dead in suspicious circumstances. In both cases, Dr. Michael Heath had conducted the autopsies. It is interesting that concerns were first raised about his work by other medical experts who had been consulted in relation to these cases. The other experts in connection with the Fraser trial were Professors Milroy, Crane, and Whitwell. The other experts in connection with the Puaca trial were Dr. Cary, Dr. White, and Professor Crane. The written complaints of these experts led to proceedings that brought Dr. Heath before the disciplinary tribunal in relation to these two cases.[24]

Fraser and Puaca both said that they discovered their respective partners, and both contacted the emergency services. In both cases, there was a history of domestic violence. The men were the only persons present in the house when the deaths occurred. Having conducted the autopsies, Dr. Heath concluded that each woman had been unlawfully killed. Both men were charged with murder and stood trial.

---

22 This assertion is similar to that by Dr. Manock in South Australia that certain baby deaths had been caused by "bronchospasm." (We discuss those cases below.) Any such spasm is a physiological response to immediate stimuli and could not have been seen at post-mortem; Moles, *State of Injustice*, above note 3, c. 10.

23 This discussion is taken from *R. v. Puaca*, [2005] EWCA Crim 3001 [*Puaca*].

24 Disciplinary Tribunal—June–July 2006: John McGuinness QC (Chairman), Peter Ackerley QPM, BA (Hons), Dr. Bob Bramley CBE, BSc, PhD, CChem, FRSC, Prof. Thomas Krompecher MD.

Later independent reviews of each case concluded that the deaths had not resulted from unlawful killing. Fraser had been acquitted of murder. Puaca had been convicted of murder and sentenced to life imprisonment. In his case, the Court of Appeal quashed the murder conviction but did not order a retrial. It is therefore through the report of the judgment in the Court of Appeal in Puaca's case that we get to understand the inadequacy of the forensic pathology.[25]

Puaca's flatmate, Tindsley, had used prescription drugs and alcohol, and the post-mortem toxicological evidence showed that she had ingested alcohol and a number of drugs. The prosecution said that Puaca had smothered her by pressing her face into the bedclothes. Puaca said that he had gone to sleep, had woken briefly to go to the toilet, noticed she was asleep, and then found her dead in the morning. Dr. Heath had concluded (without having had access to the report of the forensic toxicologist or general practitioner, or other medical records) that the death had been caused by asphyxia due to upper airway obstruction. He stated that "tearing and haemorrhaging within the muscles of the scapulae were consistent with having been caused during forceful movement of the upper limbs during upper airway obstruction."[26] He said the muscle damage resulted when Tindsley had tried to push up. He also said that various findings were "consistent with" or were "signs of" asphyxia.[27] He acknowledged that the findings were also consistent with an overdose of drugs or alcohol.

The defence were critical of the failure to refer to the significance of the toxicological findings; the failure also to refer to the absence of the expected positive findings, including bleeding of the vessels in the face and eyelids; also, the absence of pathological indicators of a violent struggle, other than the muscle damage.

The Court of Appeal said that the opinion of the pathologist had to be "objectively reached" and have "scientific validity."[28] It said it was wrong for a pathologist to expect a defence pathologist to set out a contrary argument. The court said the expert witness should clearly state the facts (or assumptions) on which the opinion was based and should not omit to consider material facts that would detract from the concluded opinion. It noted that in certain cases there was also a need to refer to ante-mortem records.

The court said that this unusual case had called for a properly reasoned post-mortem report. The use of the word "asphyxia" was a cause for concern. Its medical meaning was very broad. *Black's Medical Dictionary* defined it as

---

25 *Puaca*, above note 23.
26 *Ibid.* at para. 24.
27 *Ibid.* at para. 41.
28 *Ibid.* para. 32.

"absence of pulse," but the name is given to the whole series of symptoms that follow stoppage of breathing and the heart's action. However, in common usage it indicated the deprivation of oxygen to the lungs by external means, such as smothering, exhaust gases in a car, and so on. It was important that a medical witness should make clear the sense in which the word was being used. In this case, there was a real risk that the jury would have understood the prosecution expert's evidence as "consistent with asphyxia by upper airway obstruction." As will be seen, Dr. Charles Smith's frequent reference to the vague word "asphyxia" also caused many problems in Canada, and the Goudge Inquiry recommended that pathologists no longer use the term as a cause of death.

An important observation by the Court of Appeal was that while "inconsistency" was often probative, the fact of *consistency* was quite often not probative at all. In this case, it said, the evidence of consistency had no probative value. The court said there was a real danger in putting evidence to a jury of matters that were "consistent" with a conclusion, unless it was made clear to them that such matters did not help them to reach the conclusion.

There are other cases involving Dr. Heath. In *R. v. Boreman and Byrne*,[29] the accused were convicted of murder on the basis of Dr. Heath's evidence that they died of injuries and not from a fire. The Court of Appeal held that in light of new pathology evidence it was appropriate to substitute assault for murder convictions. The CCRC has conducted reviews of applications involving Dr. Heath, but there has been criticism both of the CCRC for not having a forensic pathologist conduct the reviews and of the Attorney General for not ordering a review of all of Dr. Heath's cases regardless of whether applications had been made to the CCRC.[30]

### 4) Misinterpretation of Time of Death — The Case of Trevor Wickens

In February 1991 Trevor Wickens was convicted of the murder of a woman of eighty-nine years and sentenced to life imprisonment.[31] After a reference from the CCRC, his conviction was overturned in 2003.

It was said that Mrs. Crandell, who had been living alone in Herne Bay, was murdered in her home. Her body was discovered at about 5 a.m. when fire

29 [2006] ECWA Crim 2265.

30 Satish Sekar, "The Failure of the Review of Possible Wrongful Convictions Caused by Michael Heath" in Michael Naughton, ed., *The Criminal Cases Review Commission: Hope for the Innocent?* (Basingstoke, UK: Palgrave Macmillan, 2009).

31 This discussion is taken from *R. v. Wickens*, [2003] EWCA Crim 2196 [*Wickens*]. This case is also discussed in Chapter 3.

officers were called to a fire at her bungalow. The cause of her death was said to have been multiple facial and neck injuries. Professor Vanezis, the Home Office pathologist, said that the most likely cause of the injuries was stamping on the face and neck with a shod foot. In the absence of a suspect, there was no second post-mortem—procedures requiring an independent, second post-mortem in those circumstances were not yet in place. No independent pathological evidence was obtained at the time to consider and review the findings of Professor Vanezis.

Two ex-wives of Wickens first directed investigators to pay attention to him. They said that about the time of Mrs. Crandell's death, Wickens had been saying he was responsible for it. He had apparently told them that he had assaulted her, causing her death during a robbery at her home. He had then gone to get gasoline and set the house on fire. A key issue in the case was the time of death.

The Court of Appeal expressed surprise that at the time of the trial, there had been no attempt by the defence to provide an independent assessment as to the time of death. It said that almost inevitably, if Wickens or anyone else had been charged with murder at that time, the defence would have instructed their own pathologist. As it was, timing of death was based upon some general observations about rigor mortis and the idea that the "normal situation" was that it was "fully established after 12 hours" and "should be worn off after 24 hours."[32]

Wickens had said that this assault occurred late at night, but other evidence about Mrs. Crandell's clothing and a meal she was preparing suggested that it had taken place during the day. The court noted that although there were additional notes about what Professor Vanezis could say about the time of death, they were not disclosed to the defence and the professor was not called to give that evidence at the trial. Now it appeared that the further evidence available from Professor Vanezis, and to a limited extent from another pathologist, cast doubt upon the safety of the conviction. As it turned out, Professor Vanezis was giving time limits for the death wholly inconsistent with the alleged confession and, therefore, the prosecution case.

In the Court of Appeal, Professor Crane also gave evidence in support of Professor Vanezis to the effect that it was most unlikely that the death had occurred late in the day. The court said that if the jury had heard the later evidence from Professor Vanezis, the evidence would have given the jury an additional cause for concern about the matter over and above the other matters to which the judge had referred in his summing up. The court said it would

32 *Ibid.* at para. 26.

be impossible to say whether the outcome would have been the same or not. Applying the test as emphasized by the House of Lords in *R. v. Pendleton*,[33] it could not view the resulting conviction as safe when this important professional judgment of the Crown's pathologist was never available to the jury. The appeal was allowed.

## B. THE CANADIAN EXPERIENCE

Two Canadian inquiries have examined issues of forensic pathology. One was an inquiry by Justice Kaufman in relation to Stephen Truscott's successful application to have the federal Minister of Justice refer his murder conviction back to the Ontario Court of Appeal. The other inquiry was the Goudge Inquiry that in the wake of concerns about the work of Dr. Charles Smith looked at issues of pathology evidence in criminal cases and made extensive recommendations.

### 1) Stomach Contents and Time of Death — The Case of Steven Truscott

In 1959, at the age of fourteen, Steven Truscott was convicted and sentenced to death for the murder and sexual assault of twelve-year-old Lynne Harper near Clinton, Ontario. Truscott and Harper were classmates and on the evening of 9 June 1959, Truscott had given her a ride on the crossbar of his bicycle. He said he dropped her off at the intersection of the county road and Highway 8, and when he looked back toward the intersection, he noticed that a car had stopped and that Harper was entering it. Harper's body was found two days later in a wooded area, known as Lawson's Bush, beside the county road.

The prosecution alleged that Truscott had taken Harper to the wooded area where he raped and strangled her. The case, entirely circumstantial, had centred largely on placing Harper's death within a narrow time frame which implicated Truscott. Dr. John Penistan, the pathologist who had conducted the autopsy, told the court that her death had occurred between 7:00 and 7:45 p.m. which roughly coincided with the time Truscott was seen with Harper. By 8 p.m. Truscott had returned to the school, and evidence supported that. Dr. Penistan based his opinion on his observations of the stomach contents of the deceased, the degree to which rigor mortis affecting the body had subsided, and the extent to which the body had decomposed.

Truscott was unsuccessful in his appeal to the Ontario Court of Appeal; however, the government commuted his death sentence to life imprisonment.

---

33 [2001] UKHL 66.

In 1966, the federal Minister of Justice referred the conviction to the Supreme Court of Canada for its consideration.[34] The Supreme Court heard competing forensic pathology testimony, including that from two leading forensic pathologists in England about the critical time of death issue. An eight-member majority of that court upheld the conviction.[35] In 1969 Truscott was released on parole. Thereafter he changed his name, got married, raised three children, and led a quiet life.

In 2001, Truscott filed an application with the Minister of Justice to have his case reopened.[36] The government appointed retired judge Fred Kaufman to review the case. He undertook extensive investigation of all the available evidence, including fresh evidence, and concluded that a reasonable basis existed for concluding that a miscarriage of justice had occurred.[37] He found that a memo that Dr. Penistan had written and described as an "agonizing reap-

---

34 This referral resulted from public concern expressed about the safety of the conviction after the publication of a book by Isabel LeBourdais, *The Trial of Steven Truscott* (Philadelphia, J.B. Lippincott, 1966).

35 *Reference re Truscott*, [1967] S.C.R 309. The majority concluded at 363 and 367:

> On the question of the contents of the stomach and the state of digestion as indicating the time of death, there was diversity of opinion. Doctors Sharpe, Simpson, Helpern and Gerber supported Dr. Penistan's opinion that death occurred prior to 7:45 p.m. Dr. Petty, Dr. Jaffe and Dr. Camps rejected any possibility of such precise definition . . . . The effect of the sum total of the testimony of the expert witnesses is, in our opinion, to add strength to the opinion expressed by Dr. Penistan at the trial that the murdered girl was dead by 7:45 p.m.

The dissent was based not on acceptance of the pathologists called by the defence at the reference, but because the trial judge had instructed the jury as follows: "*It will be for you to say whether you accept Doctor Penistan's theory, an Attorney-General's Pathologist of many years' standing, or do you accept Doctor Brown's evidence.*" Justice Hall stated in his dissent at 374:

> The jury should have been told that as between Dr. Penistan and Dr. Brown, if the evidence of Dr. Brown left a reasonable doubt in their minds as to the time of death, they must acquit. No jury can be told that they have to accept the evidence of one witness or that of another. The burden is on the Crown to satisfy the jury on every material aspect of the case beyond a reasonable doubt. I do not find it necessary to go in detail into the medical evidence given on the reference in this Court. This has been done in the majority opinion and is seen to be contradictory in the extreme. This much must, however, be said that it tends strongly to increase the doubt a juryman may honestly have had as to the time of death, if properly charged.

36 This event coincided with the publication of the book by Julian Sher, *Until You Are Dead: Steven Truscott's Long Ride into History* (Toronto: A.A. Knopf Canada, 2001).

37 *Report to Minister of Justice in the Matter of an Application by Steven Murray Truscott Pursuant to Section 690 of the Criminal Code* by the Honourable Fred Kaufman (Ottawa: Department of Justice, 2004).

praisal" of the evidence given at trial had not been disclosed to the defence. The memo suggested that Dr. Penistan recognized that Lynne Harper's stomach contents and degree of rigor mortis were consistent with a later death that would have precluded Stephen Truscott's involvement.[38] Justice Kaufman held that had it been disclosed, this memo "could have been effectively used by the defence at the Reference."[39] He concluded that, when considered with the fresh evidence on the difficulty of determining the time of death, there was a reasonable basis to conclude that a miscarriage of justice occurred.[40]

In 2004, in response to the recommendations made in Kaufman's detailed investigative report, the Minister of Justice directed a reference pursuant to section 693.3(a)(ii) of the *Criminal Code* to the Ontario Court of Appeal. The court was asked to review whether new evidence would have changed the 1959 verdict.

A special five-judge panel of the Ontario Court of Appeal heard extensive new evidence from various experts in the fields of forensic pathology, gastroenterology, and entomology who cast doubt on Dr. Penistan's expert evidence given at trial about the victim's time of death. UK pathologist Dr. Bernard Knight said that Penistan's use of stomach contents to determine when Harper died was "so inaccurate it is hardly worth doing." Ontario's chief pathologist, Dr. Michael Pollanen, testified that there wasn't enough evidence to pinpoint the time of Harper's death and that she could have died as much as a day later than the original finding. The court also considered additional contemporaneous documents not made available to the defence at the trial or during the reference to the Supreme Court. These documents included various versions of Dr. Penistan's autopsy report which varied widely in the estimation of the time of death. In handing down its decision in 2007, the court held that this fresh evidence significantly undermined the medical evidence relied on by the prosecution to establish that Lynne Harper died before 8 p.m. on 9 June

---

38 *Ibid.* at para. 1120.

39 *Ibid.* at para. 1130.

40 He defined miscarriage of justice quite broadly stating:

> It follows that while the continued conviction of a person shown to be factually innocent is the most obvious 'miscarriage of justice', the existence of new evidence which could reasonably have been expected to have affected the verdict may also provide a reasonable basis for concluding that a miscarriage of justice likely has occurred, not because the accused is likely innocent, but because it would be *unfair* to maintain the accused's conviction without an opportunity for the trier of fact to consider the new evidence.

*Ibid.* at para. 163.

1959.[41] The court concluded that, if a new trial were held, Dr. Penistan's opinion would likely be rejected by the jury:

> . . . the defence could have established that Dr. Penistan's opinion had ranged from an initial assessment placing the time of death at 12:45 a.m. on June 10, to a second estimate placing the time of death at least some four hours later on June 10, and finally, to a third opinion placing the time of death at between 7:15 and 7:45 p.m. on June 9, several hours earlier than either of his prior estimates. Absent some plausible explanation for these variations, it seems unlikely that Dr. Penistan's opinion could be accepted as reliable by a reasonable trier of fact. Indeed, the nature of the changes in his opinion leaves Dr. Penistan's evidence reasonably open to the allegation that his opinion shifted to coincide with the Crown's case against the appellant.[42]

The court also disregarded the expert opinion evidence of Crown witness Dr. Spitz who supported Penistan's calculation of time of death. The court said although Dr. Spitz had fifty years of experience as a forensic pathologist, "the only basis for Dr. Spitz's opinion was his own experience in conducting autopsies and his belief arising from this experience that if stomach contents are readily identifiable at autopsy, then death must have occurred within two hours of the last meal."[43] Because of the unreliability of the assessments as to the time of death, the court determined that Truscott's conviction could not stand.[44]

After forty-eight years of living life as a convicted murderer, in 2007 Truscott finally had his conviction quashed. Although the Court of Appeal was unable to rule that Truscott was factually innocent of the crime—there was no longer enough DNA evidence available to do that—it nonetheless decided that the appropriate remedy would be to enter an acquittal rather than order a retrial. In reaching that conclusion, the court said it was more probable than

41 *R. v. Truscott*, 2007 ONCA 575.

42 *Ibid.* at para. 233.

43 The Court of Appeal elaborated:

> Dr. Spitz was unable to cite any recent scientific literature that would support this view. He refused to acknowledge obvious shortcomings in his opinion when these were pointed out to him in cross-examination. He refused to concede that his opinion rested on faulty assumptions and misperceptions of the available primary evidence in this case. These shortcomings could well explain why the Crown does not ask us to rely on his evidence other than in a few very minor respects. In the result, we have not placed any reliance on his evidence and we give it no further mention.

*Ibid.* at para. 166.

44 The court went on to consider the remaining pillars of the prosecution case and ruled that they too were unreliable.

not that a hypothetical new trial would result in an acquittal. It also noted the difficulty of having a retrial fifty years later. In July 2008, the Ontario government announced it would pay Truscott $6.5 million as compensation.[45]

### 2) Pediatric Cases — The Work of Dr. Charles Smith

In the area of forensic pathology, the outstanding issue in recent years has been the unravelling of the experience of Dr. Charles Smith as the former head of pediatric forensic pathology in Toronto. He had been appointed as the director of the Paediatric Forensic Pathology Unit at the Hospital for Sick Children in Ontario.[46] However, he was a pediatric pathologist and had not been properly trained or certified in forensic pathology. Forensic pathology was not a popular area for medical practitioners to move into, and Canada did not even offer certification in forensic pathology until recently. Dr. Smith was the only pathologist who had the time or inclination to take on the role he was given, and his lack of training in forensic pathology contributed to the errors he made in autopsies and when preparing reports and testifying in court.[47] During the 1990s, Dr. Smith's reputation and influence grew — but so, too, did serious doubts about his work. As the Goudge Inquiry pointed out, those responsible for the oversight of his work could have picked up on his errors much sooner if they had been alert to all these warning signs, but regrettably they, too, failed to do their jobs properly.[48]

Finally in 2005, the chief coroner for Ontario set up an independent review team to look at forty-four of Dr. Smith's cases. The team was comprised of Dr. Butt from Vancouver, Dr. Crane from Northern Ireland, Drs. Milroy and Whitwell from England, and Dr. Saukko from Finland. The review panel subsequently concluded that in twenty of the cases, the report or evidence of Dr. Smith was problematic. Team members were concerned about Dr. Smith's lack of training in forensic pathology, his unscientific opinions, and his failure to ensure the chain of evidence in the cases. In response, in 2007 the Goudge Inquiry was established to examine the systemic issues that had led to this sorry state of affairs. The following are some of Dr. Smith's cases discussed by Justice Goudge in his report.[49]

---

45 This decision resulted from the recommendation made by Robins J. in his report to the government on the issue of compensation in March 2008.

46 Goudge Inquiry, above note 2. Our discussion of Dr. Smith and his cases is taken from that four-volume report.

47 *Ibid.*, c. 8.

48 *Ibid.*, vol. 2 at 7.

49 *Ibid.*, c. 2.

### a) "No Possibility of a Fall" — The Case of Amber

In July 1988, Amber, aged sixteen months, was in the care of a twelve-year-old babysitter when she was taken to the hospital in a semi-conscious state. The babysitter said that Amber had fallen down a few carpeted stairs at home. Amber had bruising to the head and swelling of the brain. She died soon afterwards. At first, it was accepted that she had died as a result of the accidental fall, and no autopsy was conducted; however, a month of so after the funeral, concerns were raised, the body was exhumed, and Dr. Smith conducted a post-mortem examination. He determined that she had a subdural hemorrhage, bilateral retinal hemorrhages, and general swelling to the brain. He also said he found bruising to the girl's forehead, to her right cheek, and to her hip and legs. He concluded that she had been shaken to death and that the fall at home as described was not consistent with her injuries.

In December 1988 the babysitter was charged with manslaughter. Her family sold their home and cashed in their retirement savings to get the money for her defence. At the trial, Dr. Smith had said there was "no possibility what-so-ever"[50] that a fall down five, carpeted steps could cause such injuries. He suggested that someone would have to drop children from three storeys in order to kill them like that. Yet the defence experts agreed that in rare circumstances, low-level falls could cause serious injury or even death.

In July 1991, the trial judge acquitted the babysitter of manslaughter. In doing so, he rejected Dr. Smith's evidence in the clearest of terms. He said that Dr. Smith lacked objectivity, that he had failed to investigate thoroughly, and that he failed to keep adequate records. The judge said that the doctor lacked familiarity with the relevant scientific literature and did not understand the science of shaken baby syndrome.[51]

Despite the trial judge's serious criticisms of Dr. Smith, neither the Office of Chief Coroner nor the College of Physicians and Surgeons of Ontario made any serious attempt to investigate his work. Justice Goudge found that Dr. Smith subsequently made false and misleading statements that the judge had privately told Dr. Smith that if he had understood the evidence, he would have convicted the accused and these comments had helped thwart the attempt to investigate the matter properly.[52]

---

50 *Ibid.* at 12.

51 *R. v. M(S)*, 1991 WL 1139467 (Ont. Prov. Div.).

52 Goudge Inquiry, above note 2, vol. 2 at 13.

### b) "99 Percent Certain of Non-accidental Injuries"—The Case of Nicholas

In November 1995, Nicholas, aged eleven months, was taken to hospital by ambulance where he was pronounced dead. His mother, Lianne Gagnon, said he had crawled under her sewing table and had fallen from a standing to a sitting position before losing consciousness. She assumed that he had hit his head on the underside of the sewing machine. She said he cried and then stopped breathing almost immediately. The pathologist conducting the autopsy concluded that the cause of death was undetermined and the findings were consistent with SIDS, provided all other aspects of the investigation were negative.

A year after the death, the matter was referred to Dr. Smith for review. In June 1997, Nicholas's body was exhumed. Dr. Smith conducted the second autopsy and concluded that in the absence of an alternative explanation, the death had been caused by a blunt trauma head injury. Despite some of his findings being questioned, Dr. Smith went on to say that he was 99 percent certain that Nicholas had died from non-accidental injuries. In 1998 the Children's Aid Society commenced an application against Lianne Gagnon for the wardship of the child she was now expecting.

The Gagnon family drained their retirement savings to fund a defence for their daughter. Dr. Halliday, a neuropathologist, said that Dr. Smith's opinion went "far beyond the boundaries that can be supported by the presenting scientific and forensic facts." He said that the cause of death was undetermined. Dr. Cairns, the deputy chief coroner in Toronto, then swore an affidavit to say that he wholly agreed with Dr. Smith's findings despite the fact that he had little pathology training or expertise. Justice Goudge said that the deputy chief coroner's affidavit then misled others into believing that Dr. Smith's opinion was correct.[53] Finally, in 1999, after a further expert review, all findings against Lianne Gagnon were set aside.

Lianne Gagnon's father persisted with complaints about Dr. Smith and Dr. Cairns to the auditor-general and to the ombudsman of Ontario. As Goudge J. said in his report, the complaints were well researched and well reasoned; as it turned out, he found that many of the concerns raised about Dr. Smith were legitimate. Unfortunately, he said, those in senior positions either misunderstood or were misled by Dr. Smith as to the true position, and regrettably, another opportunity for a proper assessment of him was lost.[54]

---

53 *Ibid.* at 16.

54 *Ibid.* at 17.

### c) "Sexual Assault by Babysitter"—The Case of Jenna

In January 1997, Jenna, just under two years old, was left in the care of a fourteen-year-old boy by her mother, Brenda Waudby. Shortly after midnight, the babysitter said he realized that the baby had stopped breathing and raised the alarm. The baby was taken to the hospital where she died soon after. The examining physician saw some signs of a possible sexual assault. Dr. Smith did the autopsy but failed to do a full sexual assault examination. He found a foreign hair in the girl's genital area but did not submit it for forensic examination. The police understood Dr. Smith's opinion to be that the injuries which caused her death would have occurred some twenty-four hours before her death. As a result, the police arrested and charged Waudby with the murder of her daughter. During subsequent discussions with the police, Dr. Smith said nothing about the hair he had found.

In April 1999, after a number of discussions with Dr. Ein (who was consulted by Waudby's lawyers on the timing of Jenna's fatal injuries), Dr. Smith agreed that the injuries to the child must have occurred when she was in the care of the babysitter. The charges against the mother were dropped. In 2001, after the hair found on Jenna was located in Dr. Smith's office, further investigations were undertaken. They resulted in the babysitter pleading guilty to Jenna's manslaughter in 2006. A subsequent investigation found that Dr. Smith's conclusion about the timing was wrong. As Goudge J. stated, "Dr. Smith's decision to seize the hair but not to submit it for analysis directly affected the forensic significance of the evidence." The mother complained about Dr. Smith to the authorities, and again, as Goudge J. stated, Dr. Smith's replies to the inquiries "lacked candour. He made false or misleading statements."[55]

### d) "Stabbed Eighty Times"—The Case of Sharon

In June 1997, seven-year-old Sharon was found dead in the basement of her home. She had dozens of penetrating wounds to her body, and part of her scalp had been excised. Animal urine and excrement was at the scene. A pit bull terrier had been seen in the area at the time of the incident. Dr. Smith performed the autopsy and concluded that Sharon had died from injuries caused by multiple stab wounds and that neither a domestic nor a wild animal could have caused them. Sharon's mother, Louise, was charged with second-degree murder. In 1998, at the committal hearing, Dr. Smith suggested that the stab wounds may have been caused by scissors. Prejudicially, he stated, "as absurd

55 *Ibid.* at 21.

as it is to think that a polar bear attacked Sharon, so is it equally absurd that it's a dog wound."[56]

Subsequently, four distinguished experts disagreed with Dr. Smith and concluded that the injuries may well have resulted from a dog attack. Again, it was necessary for the body to be exhumed as part of the inquiry. Eventually, even Dr. Smith concluded that the other experts may have been correct. In 2001, the charge of second-degree murder against Louise was withdrawn. Justice Goudge stated that Dr. Smith's errors were "basic," and the results were "catastrophic."[57] The cause was his own lack of training and his failure to consult with others. At this time, Dr. Smith's errors began to attract significant media attention which resulted in an article in *Maclean's* magazine titled "Dead Wrong" in May 2001.[58]

#### e) "Rape and Murder of Four-Year-Old Niece"—The Case of Valin

In Valin's case, although the initial events had occurred a decade earlier, their effect was not to be seen until 2003. In June 1993, four-year-old Valin had been left in the care of her uncle, William Mullins-Johnson, after which she was found dead in her bed. Following autopsy findings, Valin's death was declared to be a homicide. Dr. Smith added his support to the view that Valin had been sexually assaulted and had died from asphyxiation. Mullins-Johnson was convicted by a jury of first-degree murder in 1994. He was cross-examined on his prior psychiatric and anger management issues but with no limiting instructions for the trial judge. Four pathologists, including two from the defence, testified, but only Dr. Smith testified as to recent sexual assault, something that was required to be proved beyond a reasonable doubt to establish first-degree murder. Mullins-Johnson's appeal to both the Ontario Court of Appeal[59] and the Supreme Court of Canada[60] was unsuccessful.

In 2003, the Association in Defence of the Wrongly Convicted (AIDWYC) retained Dr. Bernard Knight from the United Kingdom to review the case. Dr.

56 *Ibid.* at 23.

57 *Ibid.* at 25.

58 *Ibid.*

59 *R. v. Mullins-Johnson* (1996), 112 C.C.C. (3d) 117 (Ont. C.A.). The majority of the Court of Appeal concluded that, "although the evidence in this case was not overwhelming, there was sufficient evidence to support the verdict and we do not agree that the verdict is unreasonable." *Ibid.* at para. 6. Justice Borins dissented on the basis that the trial judge had not adequately summed up the defence's case to the jury, namely, that he had not killed or sexually assaulted his niece and that no direct evidence supported the Crown's theory.

60 *R. v. Mullins-Johnson* (1998), 124 C.C.C. (3d) 381 (S.C.C.).

Smith denied that he had materials from the autopsy and it took from June 2003 to November 2004 for slides from Valin's autopsy to be found in his office. In January, 2005, Dr. Pollanen, an Ontario pathologist, concluded that the slides of tissue taken for examination had been misinterpreted and that there was no evidence of sexual assault. He said that Dr. Smith had mistaken post-mortem artefacts for ante-mortem injuries. In 2005, Dr. Knight was able to complete his report on the matter. He agreed with Dr. Pollanen that there was nothing in the histology to support a conclusion of sexual assault. In 2005 Mullins-Johnson was granted bail pending a review of his case.

Three eminent international experts were then asked to review the matter. They all concluded that Dr. Smith had misinterpreted post-mortem changes for ante-mortem injuries. They agreed that the cause of Valin's death was undetermined, and they also agreed that there was no evidence of sexual abuse. In 2007 the federal Minister of Justice referred the case to the Ontario Court of Appeal which quashed the conviction for murder and entered an acquittal. The Crown supported the quashing of the conviction, and the court unanimously said that flawed pathological evidence was at the heart of this terrible miscarriage of justice.[61]

At the subsequent Goudge Inquiry, Dr. Smith apologized to Mullins-Johnson for the role he had played in his wrongful conviction. Mullins-Johnson replied that Dr. Smith had put him in an environment (prison) where he could have been killed any day for something that never happened. He said that his brother and his remaining niece and nephew now hated him because of what Smith had done to him. He said, "I'll never forget that, but for my own healing, I must forgive you."[62]

Justice Goudge found that although Dr. Smith had training in pediatric pathology, he had no training in forensic pathology. Because of his strong interest in autopsies, he had found he was able to move into an area others did not find attractive. Dr. Smith thus had no training in how to approach criminally suspicious cases and no training in preparation for court. Yet, within a few years he was lecturing others on how to do these things. Another notable feature was that he tended to work in isolation. This combination of factors meant that his work became a manifestation of what he saw as common sense, but which was not necessarily scientific. Often, his conclusions were not supported by an elaboration of his reasoning process or references to the scientific literature.

---

61 *R. v. Mullins-Johnson*, [2007] ONCA 720 at para. 6. The Court of Appeal held it had no jurisdiction to determine whether Mullins-Johnson was factually innocent.

62 Goudge Inquiry, above note 2, vol. 2 at 5.

His opinions were often speculative and unsubstantiated. For example, in two cases he listed the cause of death as "asphyxia (infanticide)" and "asphyxia (filicidal)," thus making speculative legal conclusions not in his area of expertise.[63] He offered the police theories about the profiles of mothers and fathers who kill babies, another matter outside of his expertise.[64] He frequently used vague terms like "asphyxia" as the cause of death.[65] He often engaged in "default diagnosis" that assumed non-accidental injury in the absence of other explanations.[66] It was also accepted that pathologists in Ontario did not begin to list the cause of death as unascertained or undetermined until the late 1990s.[67]

Dr. Smith's work was characterized by inexplicable delays, failure to document all the evidence and consultations with others, hasty and dogmatic opinions, and a belief that his role was to support the prosecution, rather than to ensure that they had the benefit of his unbiased scientific opinion. He failed to explain controversies in the field or to admit limits to his own expertise. When his views were challenged, he would respond in a manner which Goudge J. described as "unprofessional, arrogant and unjustified."[68] He disparaged one defence pathologist as a "paid mouth." In some cases, he made false and misleading statements to the court.[69] The report pointed out that those responsible for oversight of the various proceedings, including the Crown, the defence, and the court, had also failed in their duty.[70]

It was also pointed out that sometimes Dr. Smith had acted so as to frustrate meaningful oversight of his work. In this connection, Goudge J. stated, "Dr. Smith was adamant that his failings were never intentional. I simply cannot accept such a sweeping attempt to escape moral responsibility . . . . His attempts to mislead spanned his entire career as director."[71]

---

63 *Ibid.* at 163. At the inquiry Dr. Smith explained that he had been taught to put information he could not prove or verify in parentheses.

64 *Ibid.* at 177–78 and 186–87.

65 *Ibid.* at 148*ff.*

66 *Ibid.* at 156*ff.* Kathy Gruspier has attributed such default diagnoses to a "think dirty" approach which assumes non-accidental causes of death and argues that "a forensically trained expert should assume that an undetermined cause of death is not suspicious unless there is definite evidence that it is." Kathy Gruspier, "Pediatric Forensic Pathology as Forensic Science: The Role of Science and the Justice System" in Goudge Inquiry Research Papers, above note 8 at 175.

67 Goudge Inquiry, above note 2, vol. 2 at 151.

68 *Ibid.* at 185.

69 *Ibid.* at 189.

70 Goudge Inquiry, above note 2, vol. 1, *Executive Summary* at 16–19.

71 *Ibid.* at 119.

Justice Goudge acknowledged that some people in positions of authority should have acted sooner and seemed more concerned about protecting the reputation of the Coroner's Office than ensuring the integrity of the system. The Goudge Inquiry noted that the errors were not necessarily related to pediatric pathology, but to forensic pathology as a whole. Justice Goudge also found that a 1995 infant death protocol that urged coroners and pathologists to "THINK DIRTY" and "actively investigate each case as potential child abuse" was inappropriate in the forensic context.[72] Legitimate clinical and advocacy concerns about child abuse should not influence forensic judgments offered to the court that feed into determinations of criminal liability.

### f) Recommendations by Justice Goudge

Justice Goudge recommended a renewed commitment to education, training, and certification in forensic pathology; a commitment to recruitment and retention of properly qualified forensic pathologists; and adequate and sustainable funding to grow the profession. He pointed out that training in this area must include specific education about the justice system and of the role of the forensic pathologist within that system. Hitherto, it seemed, the medical profession had not covered this aspect of training, and the court system assumed that if a person presented as an expert, then that person must know about legal responsibilities. This belief was clearly misplaced.

Justice Goudge also stated that there must be more clearly stated principles to govern good practice in this area. He said that the pathologist was obliged to "think truth" rather than to "think dirty." Doing this means taking an independent, evidence-based approach grounded in objective and accurate reporting. There must be sufficient safeguards against what he described as "confirmation bias."[73]

Further, Goudge J. said it is important that the pathologist's work be transparent and independently reviewable. Meeting this goal depends upon careful recording and preservation of evidence and a consideration of the full context, including the pre-autopsy history. In addition, the record must be understandable to the criminal justice system so that all processes and findings can be understood by non-medical people. Pathologists "should clearly state not just the opinion but the facts on which the opinion is based, the reasoning used to reach it, the limitations of the opinion, and the strength or degree of con-

72 Goudge Inquiry, above note 2, vol. 2 at 111–12. See also Kristen Kramar, "Coroners' Interested Advocacy: Understanding Wrongful Accusations and Convictions" (2006) 48 Canadian Journal of Criminology and Criminal Justice 803.

73 Goudge Inquiry, above note 2, vol. 3 at 390.

fidence that the pathologist has in the opinion expressed."[74] They should consider alternative diagnoses, communicate areas of controversy, and place their opinion in the context of those controversies. They should not use vague terms such as "asphyxia" as a cause of death[75] or use potentially misleading language, such as "consistent with."[76] They should recognize the limits of their expertise. To guard against isolation, teamwork must be recognized as an integral component of the process. The "team" must involve those within the medical profession who check and validate the work as well as those responsible for legal scrutiny and for critically evaluating the work before it is presented in court.

Justice Goudge placed great emphasis upon the interplay of language and medical and legal cultures. He said greater attention should be given to such issues as the way in which someone expresses confidence in findings so as not to be misleading. There must be greater clarity about the extent to which non-medical factors or the reasons or opinions of others might have influenced findings.

Justice Goudge emphasized that much more must be done to ensure that legal people, such as prosecutors, defence lawyers, and judges, are sufficiently skilled in the scientific and medical disciplines involved so that they can engage in proper scrutiny and critical evaluation of the evidence. In particular, they need to ensure that expert witnesses do not go beyond their expertise, that proper scientific principles support their findings, that they particularize tests, and that they fairly disclose any contrary views or findings which might cause doubt to be cast upon their opinions.

Justice Goudge pointed out that the difficulties were even greater when considering these issues in the context of First Nations and remote communities. In common with Australia, Canada has significant difficulties in providing adequate levels of services to more remote communities with higher levels of Aboriginal people. The broader systemic issues of inadequate medical care, higher mortality rates, lack of funding, and inadequate engagement with cultural and spiritual matters are exacerbated in the context of specialist forensic pathology and legal services. In this context, the removal of a body to a faraway city for specialist examination shortly after death may create additional levels of complexity and tensions. This situation calls for greater levels of care to be given to issues of communication and consultation.

Indeed, in concluding his report, Goudge J. stated that suspicious deaths, especially where children are involved, require things to be done within the

---

74 *Ibid.* at 408.
75 *Ibid.* at 410.
76 *Ibid.* at 435.

context of grief, suspicion, and possibly hostility. Effective outcomes require the collective input of all involved in both the family and the broader social context. He pointed out that especially in child protection cases, the need to keep everyone informed while ensuring best outcomes will undoubtedly require adequate legal representation.

Even before the Goudge Report was released, important changes in forensic pathology took place in Ontario. The "think dirty" approach was abandoned, and new autopsy guidelines were implemented. Autopsies in suspicious child death cases were centralized, and peer review and quality assurance programs were introduced. More emphasis was placed on the impartial role of pathologist expert witnesses.[77]

The *Coroners Amendment Act, 2009*[78] has been enacted as a direct response to the legislative changes recommended by the Goudge Commission. The Act establishes a framework to strengthen the death investigation system in Ontario. Provisions of the new legislation include these:

- the establishment of an oversight council for Ontario's death investigation system;
- an improved complaints system under the oversight council;
- the establishment of an Ontario Forensic Pathology Service headed by the Chief Forensic Pathologist;
- a registry of pathologists authorized to conduct coroner's autopsies in Ontario;
- improved death investigation services to northern and First Nations communities.

The Act should allow the Chief Forensic Pathologist to provide effective oversight of the work of forensic pathologists, something that was not possible before when the work of pathologists such as Dr. Smith was subject to review by coroners not trained in forensic pathology. Ontario has also created a committee chaired by a retired judge and including the Chief Forensic Pathologist, a senior prosecutor, and a defence lawyer to review all criminal convictions involving shaken baby evidence.[79] Few points arising from the Goudge Inquiry could not be taken up with equal enthusiasm in both Britain and Australia. Indeed, it might seem to manifest common sense for such guidelines and proto-

---

77 Goudge Inquiry, above note 2, vol. 2 at 267–75.

78 S.O. 2009, c. 15.

79 Ontario, Ministry of the Attorney General, News Release, "Ministry of the Attorney General Ontario Acts on Two Goudge Commission Recommendations" (2 December 2008), online: www.attorneygeneral.jus.gov.on.ca/english/news/2008/20081202-goudge-nr.asp.

cols as are developed in each of the jurisdictions to be undertaken with full awareness of those in other countries.

## C. THE AUSTRALIAN EXPERIENCE

As mentioned previously, in Australia there has been great difficulty in having cases reopened, just as there was in Britain before the advent of the CCRC. The most notable cases that royal commissions overturned were those of Lindy Chamberlain and Edward Splatt, which primarily concerned unreliable scientific evidence.

There is one case that has not as yet been re-examined by the court system and therefore does not meet our criteria for being a miscarriage of justice.[80] However, because the facts of the case are, in important respects, similar to those of the *Truscott* case, we thought the case worth mentioning here.

### 1) Frits Van Beelen

This case involved the sexual assault and death of a young girl at the beach in the early 1970s.[81] At the time this was the longest criminal trial in the history of South Australia. The time of death was pivotal, and the case is notable from the pathology point of view because the determination of this time was, and still is, unscientific. The method used to determine time of death was the same as that used in the case of Steven Truscott in Canada—timing based upon the examination of stomach contents. Truscott has had his conviction overturned; Van Beelen has still had no review of his case.

The young girl, Deborah, went missing after school, and her body was found the following morning on a nearby beach. Van Beelen, an unemployed carpenter, was near the beach between 4:00 and 4:30 p.m. on the day Deborah disappeared. The pathologist arrived at the scene soon after Deborah's body was found. He examined the body but did not take the body temperature. Dr. Pocock, a pathologist called by the defence, made this comment:

> The body temperature and air and water temperature should always be taken when arriving at the scene and Dr. Manock did not do that. The only exception is when the body is decomposed. A thermometer is quite cheap to buy.[82]

80 See our discussion of this matter in Chapter 1.

81 This case is discussed in Moles, *State of Injustice*, above note 3, c. 5.

82 *The Queen v. Van Beelen* (1973) Supreme Court of South Australia Trial Transcript at 2532 [*Van Beelen* Transcript].

Dr. Manock said at the trial that in view of the seaweed and cold wind, the body temperature would not have been a reliable indicator. He also stated that because it was possibly a case of sexual assault, he did not want to take a temperature from the rectum. If this were so, it would mean that an important diagnostic feature in determining the cause of death (temperature) would be unavailable in all cases where sexual assault is a possibility.

Dr. Manock conducted the autopsy and concluded on diatom evidence (tiny microscopic organisms found in the lungs) that Deborah had died by drowning in seawater. Dr. Pocock said:

> With regard to the diatoms, Dr. Manock should have checked for their presence in the liver, kidney and bone marrow, not just in the lungs, as they can get there without drowning.[83]

Although there were no signs of bruising, Dr. Manock determined that someone had intercourse with Deborah's body *after* her death as there was a small triangular tear in her vagina but no bleeding or bruising. Dr. Manock also found that rigor mortis was present, as was lividity. He said that the skin would not blanch under pressure, which meant that the lividity had become fixed. In other words, she had probably been dead for at least six hours. The prosecution, on advice from Dr. Manock, claimed that this evidence was consistent with death occurring between 3:30 and 4:30 p.m. the previous day. However, Dr. Pocock explained that the evidence about rigor mortis was also consistent with death having occurred up until around 11:00 p.m. that night.

The timing of the death was crucial. Deborah had last been seen alive by a witness at 4:00 p.m., and Van Beelen had an alibi from just after 4:30 p.m. If he was to be found guilty of murder, then it would be essential to the prosecution's case to establish that Deborah was dead by 4:30 p.m. The most contentious of the evidence was the way Dr. Manock fixed the time of Deborah's death. He said he was able to fix it as having occurred between 3:30 p.m. and 4:30 p.m. He did this by relying on an analysis of Deborah's stomach contents. Dr. Manock gave evidence to say it was "virtually certain" that Deborah was dead by 4:30 p.m., most probably around 4:15 p.m. His calculation was based on the rate at which a stomach is emptied of its contents. Some of Deborah's school friends spoke of the time at which Deborah had eaten her lunch, and of what it consisted. Deborah had apparently eaten a pie or pasty, some chips, and a carton of milk around midday. Dr. Manock then "calculated" the time that would be necessary for the stomach to process the food and to pass it through the system.

83 *Ibid.* at 2529.

He asserted that by examining the contents of the girl's stomach, he could be certain that her death had occurred by 4:30 p.m., *and no later.*

In a scientific article subsequently published by Dr. Derrick Pounder, now professor of Forensic Pathology at Dundee University, the method used by Dr. Manock in this case was reviewed and evaluated. Professor Pounder concluded that the most that could be said about this approach to the timing of death was that it could narrow the possibilities down to "a range of some hours." He stated that any suggestion that this method could be exact to "within a half an hour as given in . . . the *Van Beelen* case in Australia would seem to be scientifically unsound."[84]

Dr. Manock has never explained how he was able to calculate the time of death in this way based on the observations he said he made. As we have seen from Chapter 2, the intellectual basis of any such calculations should always be explained if they are to be of any value to the court. In 1984, under cross-examination in another case, Dr. Manock was questioned on Dr. Pounder's statement about the *Van Beelen* case. "I did see that comment, yes," he replied.

> Counsel: And would you agree that estimates of time of death on the basis of stomach contents are *very unreliable.*
>
> Dr. Manock: I do agree with that.[85]

In relation to the *O.J. Simpson* case, Jessica Snyder Sachs said:

> . . . both experts had to admit that the quantity and quality of stomach contents had long ago been dismissed as the most unreliable of all post-mortem time scales. Such grasping at straws would continue to be part of medical expert testimony when all else failed.[86]

Dr. Bernard Knight is quoted by Sachs as stating:

> Unfortunately, it is often the least experienced medical witness who tends to offer the most accurate estimates, not having seen enough cases to appreciate the many pitfalls and fallacies in the process.[87]

---

84 M. Horowitz & Derrick J. Pounder, "Gastric Emptying—Forensic Implications of Current Concepts" (1985) 25 Medicine, Science and the Law 201.

85 *Van Beelen* Transcript, above note 82 at 829 [emphasis added]: Cross-examination at the trial concerning the death of Mrs. Cooke (arising from an autopsy conducted 14 April 1984).

86 Jessica Snyder Sachs, *Corpse: Nature, Forensics, and the Struggle to Pinpoint the Time of Death* (Cambridge, MA: Perseus, 2001) at 45.

87 *Ibid.* at 27; from Claus Henssge *et al.*, *The Estimation of the Time since Death in the Early Postmortem Period* (London: Edward Arnold, 1995).

Unfortunately, the concession by Dr. Manock has been of no assistance to Van Beelen.

Dr. Pocock also made the following comments upon Dr. Manock's evidence:

- Dr. Manock was incorrect when he said that salt water makes the lungs contract. There is no evidence for this in the textbooks.[88]
- The protein fluid in the lungs could have been caused by heart failure; therefore Dr. Manock should have tested for drugs as a cause of death, which he did not do. If sea water had been there, the protein would not have been.[89]
- The stomach contents had been frozen before detailed examination by Dr. Manock, and this would have affected their composition.[90]
- Dr. Manock said that hypostasis showed that the body had not been moved, but it could have been moved before the hypostasis became established, which can take up to one to two hours after death, not 30 minutes as Dr. Manock said.[91]
- Dr. Manock said he had examined the internal organs microscopically, and had excluded other causes of death, but I don't see how he could exclude epilepsy, for example.[92]

Although there were two trials and numerous appeals, including an appeal to the Privy Council in London, Van Beelen's conviction for the murder was upheld. He had been sentenced to death, but it was the practice at that time to commute a death sentence to life imprisonment. The case, however, refused to go away. In 1974, the Adelaide *Advertiser* reported that a juror at the second trial claimed that the stress of circumstances and pressure in the jury room influenced the juror's vote. "It was a moment of weakness which I have lived

88 *Van Beelen* Transcript, above note 82 at 2530.

89 *Ibid.* at 2530.

90 *Ibid.* at 2540.

91 *Ibid.* at 2542. Hypostasis, also known as *livor mortis* or lividity, concerns the way in which the blood settles in the body after death. If a body lies undisturbed for some time after death, the blood, without the heart to pump it around the system, settles at the lowest parts of the body, producing areas of discolouration under the skin. These areas, which can be seen through the skin, turn red and then purplish as the blood pools and changes colour. Those parts of the body that are in contact with the ground will show white patches (blanching) because the pressure of the body on the ground stops the blood from settling in those areas. So, if a body is discovered some time after death, the pattern of discolouration and blanching can help the pathologist to understand fairly accurately the way in which the body was lying after death.

92 *Ibid.* at 2554.

to regret," the juror said. After much thought and counselling, the juror felt compelled to "speak out about it."[93]

Throughout the years since his arrest, Van Beelen has continually asserted his innocence. Because he would not show contrition for the offence for which he was convicted, the Parole Board would not release him on parole until he had served more than seventeen years—at that time, it was quite common for those sentenced to life imprisonment to be released after eight or nine years. Van Beelen was a model prisoner. He continued to be a keen jogger and was from time to time was allowed day-release from prison to compete in races. He frequently competed alongside judges and senior lawyers. He now lives in Adelaide and has been gainfully employed since his release from prison. He still says that he didn't commit the crime.

## 2) The South Australian Baby Deaths

Here, the miscarriage of justice is more in the nature of a failure to prosecute, rather than the bringing about of a wrongful conviction. Between 1994 and 1995, the coroner in South Australia held an inquest into the deaths of three babies who had died in separate incidents.[94] One baby was three months old; the other two, nine months. Dr. Manock had determined that each of the babies had died from bronchopneumonia. The police, aware of various injuries to each of the babies, were treating the deaths as possible homicides. When Dr. Manock's diagnoses were disclosed, it had the effect of terminating the police inquiries. Because of concerns expressed by both doctors and police over those findings, the matter was investigated by the coroner who called for an independent review of the pathology findings. The conclusion of the independent pathologist was that the deaths had not resulted from bronchopneumonia but possibly from non-accidental injuries.

The children involved were Storm Deane, aged three months, who died on 16 October 1992, at the Adelaide Children's Hospital; William (Billy) Barnard, aged nine months, who died on 31 July 1993, at the Adelaide Children's Hospital; and Joshua Nottle, aged nine months, who died on 17 August 1993, at the Modbury Hospital, Adelaide.

---

93 "Juror Claims 'Pressure'" *The Advertiser* (18 February 1974).

94 These cases were the subject of an expert report to the Goudge Inquiry. See Robert N. Moles & Bibi Sangha, "Comparative Experience with Pediatric Pathology and Miscarriages of Justice: South Australia" in Goudge Inquiry Research Papers, above note 8. See also Moles, *State of Injustice*, above note 3, c. 10.

Storm Deane was born on 18 July 1992, to Craig and Heather. Craig said that on 15 October 1992, while he and Heather were both at home, he took Storm from the baby bouncer by grabbing hold of his jumpsuit and without supporting his head. He then "flipped" him onto the waterbed. As he said, "I picked him up by the scruff of his clothes and carried him like a little carrying bag and then I flipped him. He went about two feet forward and then landed on the bed." After this, he and Heather went outside to fix his motor bike. Heather later went to check on Storm and found him looking pale and not moving. Craig tried mouth-to-mouth resuscitation, but without success. Heather called an ambulance, which was despatched at 10:42 a.m.

When the ambulance arrived, Craig was said to have run out of the house with the baby and to have fallen over; Storm, however, did not hit the ground. The ambulance officers connected Storm to an electrocardiograph to measure his heart activity. They said that he was cold and grey, without a heartbeat, and not breathing. He was rushed to the Lyell McEwin Hospital and then from there to the Adelaide Children's Hospital. The following morning it was agreed that Storm's life support would be terminated, and Storm was pronounced dead at 9:50 a.m. One of the doctors reported that at the time the life support was terminated, Craig had placed his thumb on the baby's throat, saying that he did not like to see him gasping. The doctor said that while he was disturbed by this action, it did not (in his view) contribute to the baby's death.

Storm's body was sent to the Adelaide Forensic Science Centre for the autopsy, which was done by Dr. Manock without any other doctor being present. Dr. Manock concluded that the cause of death was bronchopneumonia. He said that there was also a heart defect, although he did not undertake any microscopical examination of the heart tissues. He noted that a circular mark on the buttock was consistent with a burn; however, he said it was probably a healing area of diaper rash. In his view, the microscopical examination of the tissues confirmed the diagnosis of bronchopneumonia.

Dr. Thomas, an associate professor in anatomical pathology at the Flinders Medical Centre in Adelaide, was commissioned by the coroner as an independent expert. He prepared a report on all of the matters related to Storm's death. In his report and evidence during the inquest, Dr. Thomas stated that there were many areas where microscopical examination and weighing of organs (which would have been essential) were not done. He said that even the body was not weighed or measured. Some of these practices were described by Dr. Thomas as "time honoured." In his view, it was clear that bronchopneumonia was not the cause of death and that the injuries were not related to birth trauma—they were "non-accidental."

In relation to the case of Storm Deane, the coroner took the view that as Dr. Manock had been the senior director of Forensic Pathology in South Australia since 1968, his understanding of the criminal process, and his obligation to provide lines of inquiry to investigators, would have been second nature to him. Yet he had fundamentally failed to do that in Storm's case. The coroner said it was "extraordinary" that Dr. Manock did not conduct further inquiries to exclude the possibility of non-accidental injuries. Dr. Manock's explanation to the coroner was that "it was his view, [that] a pathologist should be careful not to influence the investigation and suggest suspicion which is unwarranted."[95]

The coroner, at the conclusion of his examination of Storm's case, said, "the post-mortem examination achieved the opposite of what should have been its purpose — it closed off lines of investigation rather than opening them up."[96] The cause of death would have to be recorded as "undetermined." It was his view that while a proper examination of the issues had not occurred in this case, it was then too late to go back and put things right.

William (Billy) Barnard was born on 29 October 1992 to Cherry and David. He lived with his parents and an older sister aged three. Another sister had died when she had been only three weeks old. On the evening of 30 July 1993, Cherry was in a sleeping bag with Billy. At about 8:00 a.m., she said she found him "not breathing." She called for an ambulance, and the baby was taken to the Adelaide Children's Hospital. Billy was pronounced dead shortly after arrival. One ambulance officer said he had remembered attending at that address before when the other child had died. The ambulance officers noted that Cherry seemed "detached," "nonchalant," "unconcerned" — much the same as on the other occasion. The ambulance officer conveyed his suspicions to the medical authorities upon arrival at the hospital. Dr. Manock conducted the autopsy. Again, no other doctor was present. Dr. Manock's diagnosis was that Billy, too, had died of bronchopneumonia. When talking about Billy, Cherry admitted to having "cracked and snapped his arm."[97] Billy's sister had also died while sleeping with her mother in a sleeping bag.

During the inquest, Dr. Manock said he could not recall why he did not weigh the lungs. He now agreed that bronchopneumonia was unlikely to have caused the death. He could not recall what he saw in the slides which had led

95 Wayne Chivell, Coroner for South Australia, *Finding of Inquest into the Deaths of Storm Don Ernie Deane, William Anthony Barnard, Joshua Clive Nottle* (11 February 1994) at 26.

96 *Ibid.* at 27.

97 *Ibid.* at 35.

him to his first conclusion. Dr. Manock said he did not send the brain for examination because he was waiting for something from the detectives, so that he could tell the specialist what to look for. The coroner said:

> As Coroner I am perplexed at this statement. Dr. Blumbergs [the specialist] is perfectly capable of examining the brain without being told what to look for . . . .
>
> I am quite unable to accept Dr. Manock's explanation as to why he did not offer this further information to the investigators immediately after the post-mortem examination concluded. It is *spurious*, in my opinion, to suggest that he did not offer these alternative explanations because he was waiting for further information from the detectives. Unlike Dr. Blumbergs, who did not need to be told what to look for, the detectives should have received all the assistance possible so that their investigations could focus on particular issues. With a diagnosis of bronchopneumonia the investigation had no focus.[98]

Dr. Tony Thomas again evaluated the pathology evidence in this case. He said that there was no evidence of the weight of the body organs, but that lung weights would have been invaluable. No temperature of the body was taken, which again he described as a "time-honoured" practice. He also noted that there was no list to identify the origin of the tissues taken for examination. The absence of this made interpretation of those tissue samples difficult.

In relation to Barnard, the coroner took the view that the bronchopneumonia explanation had caused the death to be viewed as a "natural" death. He said that the investigation was basically cut off before it began. As in the previous case, the coroner concluded that the autopsy in this case achieved the opposite of its proper purpose. Dr. Manock's report had "closed off" lines of investigation rather than opening them up. He said that the lack of a thorough investigation was disturbing, particularly as this was the second such death in this family, in strikingly similar circumstances.

Joshua Clive Nottle was born on 27 November 1992 to Julieanne and Sean. On 17 August 1993, at 8:45 a.m., Joshua was found dead in his cot. He was taken to Modbury Hospital, where he was declared dead just after 9:00 a.m. Bruising and rib fractures were noted. Two detectives from Holden Hill CIB (Criminal Investigation Bureau) attended. After an interview, Sean was arrested and charged with Joshua's murder. The charge was then reduced to intention-

98 *Ibid.* at 50 and 52 [emphasis added]. Spurious: "not genuine"; "not being what it pretends to be"; "illegitimate" — *The Oxford English Dictionary.* "Not genuine or true"; "counterfeit"; "not from the reputed, pretended or right source"; "not authentic" — *The Macquarie Dictionary.*

ally causing grievous bodily harm when the results of the autopsy were known. Dr. Manock conducted the autopsy the same day. Again, no other doctor was present during the examination. Yet again, the death was described as bronchopneumonia, this time associated with multiple rib fractures.

As with the previous two cases, the independent report by Dr. Thomas was critical of Dr. Manock's autopsy. It showed that no height or weights were given. There appeared to have been no microscopical examination of the bruises. Organs, other than the lungs, were not weighed. The rib fractures were noted, but not the fractures of the clavicles, which were easily detected on the X-rays. Dr. Thomas took the view that a full skeletal survey, as well as further dissection and microscopical examination, was "essential." He stated clearly that further dissection and exploration of the spinal fracture would have been "mandatory." Contrary to Dr. Manock's view, Dr. Thomas thought that bronchopneumonia was not the likely cause of death. Dr. Thomas said that there should have been microscopical examination of the eyes and of the brain. He noted that the "time-honoured" practice of taking the temperature was overlooked. Again, there was no list in relation to the tissues taken, making microscopical interpretation of those sections extremely difficult.

The coroner concluded that, of the three deaths, that of Joshua Nottle was the most serious, with non-accidental injuries most evident. He said that Dr. Manock's diagnosis prevented the establishment of a causative link between the non-accidental injuries and the death. In the coroner's view, what should have been a homicide investigation became one only of serious assault. He said:

> Dr. Manock's investigation, and his subsequent report, provided innocent explanations for the most serious injuries found on Joshua's body, explanations that I am now satisfied were incorrect. In those circumstances, and in common with the other two cases, the post-mortem examination basically achieved the opposite of its proper purpose in that it closed off lines of investigation rather than opening them up.
>
> I consider Dr. Manock's explanation that he was waiting for further information from the police to be spurious. In my view, it was incumbent upon him to provide the detectives with information so that they would know what to look for.[99]

The coroner said that he had no hesitation in accepting the opinion of the independent pathologist, Dr. Thomas, that there was no evidence that Joshua was suffering from bronchopneumonia to any degree sufficient to cause death.

---

99 *Ibid.* at 82.

The cause of his very serious physical injuries remained undetermined. The uncertainties that now surrounded his death were most disturbing, but although there were grounds for grave suspicion, nothing could be proved on the basis of the evidence as it then stood.

Since the revelations about the baby death cases, further research into a number of Dr. Manock's other cases has revealed the possibility of other questionable cases. The details of those have been set out in the books *A State of Injustice* and *Losing Their Grip — The Case of Henry Keogh*.[100]

## D. CONCLUSION

It is clear from our study that forensic pathologists have been among the most unreliable and misleading witnesses in many of the recognized miscarriage of justice cases. This chapter has documented cases where forensic pathologists testified beyond their range of expertise and speculated about the cause of death. At times, controversies within forensic pathology on issues such as shaken baby syndrome or whether children can die from short falls were not explained to the judge and jury. In some cases, the science behind these issues remains controversial and continues to evolve. This chapter has also documented an alarming number of cases where there were clear failures to follow proper procedures.

It may well be because of their status as doctors and as professors that forensic pathologists engender confidence in lawyers, judges, and juries. They not only embody the scientist in the white coat, but overlay this image with that of the doctor, the healer, the wise and trustworthy adviser. They often seem to appear in cases that embody the worst of our fears — the unexplained deaths of young children. In any other context, the suggestion that mothers were suffocating their babies and childminders were bashing them to death would seem implausible. On the other hand, it seems that such eminent and wise people would hardly be allowed to come to court and tell such stories if there wasn't a proper basis to them, would they? If the judge and lawyers are listening to such stories with calm detachment and much interest, then how can ordinary jury members say it is not right? Do we expect too much of juries? Should judges take some time prior to trial to test the evidence and examine if it really does have a scientific basis? To these issues we will return in the final chapters.

---

100 Moles, *State of Injustice*, above note 3; Robert N. Moles, *Losing Their Grip — The Case of Henry Keogh* (Adelaide: Elvis Press, 2006).

PART THREE

# Responses to Miscarriages of Justice

CHAPTER 10

# Error Correction and Systemic Reform

Having looked in Part One at the governing principles relating to miscarriages of justice, and in Part Two at the non-compliant cases, we now move the discussion to a consideration of the broader organizational and institutional responses to miscarriages of justice. The goal here is to discuss how miscarriages of justice may be corrected and prevented in the future.

In this chapter, we will look at what might be called "back-end," or legal system, responses to possible miscarriages of justice. We will focus on the important role of the CCRC (Criminal Cases Review Commission) in Britain. We will also examine the contributions that public inquiries and volunteer innocence projects can make towards the discovery and prevention of wrongful convictions.

In Chapter 11, we will look at what might be called "front-end" responses that are found in the forensic sciences and the way they are used in criminal trials. Front-end responses include improvements in forensic science, such as research to provide a sounder foundation for the developing scientific principles and better means of quality control. They also can include a greater gatekeeping role for the judge, to better identify reliable scientific evidence that can be used in trials and the more speculative, unreliable science that should be filtered out.

The CCRC clearly has an error correction role. It is an independent, non-departmental government body with responsibility for investigating alleged miscarriages of justice, and where appropriate, for sending them back to the appeal courts for a fresh look. In order to send cases back to the appeal court, the CCRC generally needs evidence not available at the time of the trial or appeal. The legal criterion for both the CCRC and the appeal court is the safety of the conviction, *not* factual innocence. Specifically, the CCRC refers if there is a "real possibility" that the conviction would be quashed (or a sentence reduced) if a reference was made to the Court of Appeal. The Court of Appeal will quash the conviction if it is unsafe. Before the establishment of the CCRC, the process was that of petitioning the executive in Britain (a department of the government known as "C3").

The CCRC, however, also has a systemic role of feeding back to the wider criminal justice system matters of concern and common emerging themes gleaned from its experience with error correction. To date, the CCRC has not fully developed this role because of a lack of resources, including an easily accessible and searchable database of its many cases. On another front, we will examine the systemic reform that the Canadian public inquiries, in particular, have achieved and address the need to balance the demands of both error correction and systemic reform.

Given the work of the CCRC in exposing errors in convictions, often in important or notorious cases, it might be argued that one effect would be to undermine confidence in the British legal system. Yet, the opposite seems to be the case. The CCRC regularly receives visitors from all around the world, keen to see how it works and to speak with the people involved in investigations and decision making. It is plain from our discussion so far that its work has featured in the recommendations of many of the Canadian inquiries, and various proposals for the adoption of such a model are being developed in other countries, most notably Australia.

## A. THE MOVE TO ESTABLISH THE CRIMINAL CASE REVIEW COMMISSION

When the setting up of the CCRC was first proposed, it was a bold strategy to deal with a developing crisis of confidence in the criminal justice system. As we saw in Chapter 7, Lord Denning had made it clear that if those convicted of bombing and murder were to be exonerated, then

> . . . it would mean that the police were guilty of perjury; that they were guilty of violence and threats; that the confessions were involuntary and improperly admitted in evidence; and that the convictions were erroneous . . . This is such an appalling vista that every sensible person in the land would say: It cannot be right that these actions should go any further . . . . This case shows what a civilized country we are. Here are six men who have been proved guilty of the most wicked murder of twenty-one innocent people.[1]

1 *McIlkenny v. Chief Constable of the West Midlands*, [1980] Q.B. 283 at 323.

The "appalling vista" was the possibility of establishing that the police had used violence and threats which had led to involuntary confessions resulting in wrongful convictions. The civilized response would have been to examine the challenge and not to ignore it. Britain subsequently took up the challenge by putting the re-examination of questionable cases into the hands of those independent from the police, the courts, and the government.

One might have imagined that if the "appalling vista" was to be substantiated and police were proven to have used violence and intimidation to secure convictions, then the legitimacy of the British criminal justice system would be at an all-time low. As we have seen, the nightmare did become the new reality. Police were found to have used torture to extract confessions.[2] Yet, the response to adversity has led to the suggestion that other jurisdictions, such as Canada and Australia, should adopt the British model. Perhaps the "appalling vista" is not so much in the occurrence of wrongdoing, but in the failure to respond properly to it where it is alleged to have occurred.

Without the CCRC, Britain had great difficulty in reopening cases of suspected miscarriages of justice; Australia and Canada still do. Although in the earlier chapters we have set out at some length the laws relating to appeals and miscarriages of justice, these laws have value only if a case can be brought to the courts to ensure their application. If, as in Australia, the appeal courts cannot reopen appeals, the High Court cannot receive fresh evidence, and attorneys general do not refer cases back to the court for review, then frustration and dissatisfaction with the legal system grows, as happened with the IRA bombing cases in Britain. A CCRC-type body could act almost as a safety valve to dissipate the frustration that occurs when the legal rhetoric and the legal reality are in such evident contradiction.

Until 31 March 1997, when a convicted person had exhausted avenues of appeal (or occasionally when he or she had not appealed or sought leave to appeal), applications for review of alleged miscarriages of justice were made either to the Home Secretary in Britain[3] or to the Secretary of State for Northern Ireland.[4] They had the power to refer cases back to the Court of Appeal. In practice, this power was rarely exercised.

The powers of the Home Secretary and the Secretary of State in Northern Ireland were limited to cases tried on indictment. On average, only four to five cases were referred each year.[5] There appeared to be a reactive and restrictive

2 See the discussion of the *Twitchell* and *Treadaway* cases in Chapter 7.

3 *Criminal Appeal Act 1968*, (U.K.), 1968, c. 19, s. 17 [*CAA* 1968].

4 *Criminal Appeal (Northern Ireland) Act 1980* (U.K.), 1980, c. 47, s. 14.

5 This average is based on the figures for 1981 to 1988.

view of the cases. Rather than commencing their own investigations, departmental officials often appeared to be trying to pick holes in the arguments put forward by the applicants and their representatives. That inference can be drawn from a memo published by the Home Office in 1987 in support of its decision not to refer the cases of the Guildford Four and the Maguire Seven to the Court of Appeal.[6] The reasoning contained within the memo was tortuous and designed to persuade the then Home Secretary (Douglas Hurd) not to reopen the cases. The memo had the desired effect. Perhaps, unsurprisingly, there was grave concern over the independence of the Home Office department known as C3, which had the responsibility for reviewing such cases.

As explained in the earlier chapters, the background to the establishment of the CCRC was the plethora of wrongful convictions in the UK bombing cases. The gross miscarriages of justice that ruined peoples' lives and the lives of their families, close friends, and supporters resulted in a lack of public confidence in the criminal justice system. In addition to the exposed miscarriages of justice, it was becoming clear that C3 was not working effectively to prevent further errors occurring or to take steps to correct those cases where it appeared that justice had miscarried.

In 1989 a committee of the advocacy group JUSTICE, which had been chaired by Sir George Waller, a retired Court of Appeal judge, published a report titled *Miscarriages of Justice*. The report identified the top five causes of miscarriages of justice as wrongful identification; false confessions; perjury by a co-accused or other witness; police misconduct, either by "verbals" or planting evidence; and bad trial tactics by lawyers. It reported that JUSTICE was the only advocacy group then investigating alleged miscarriages of justice. It recommended that C3 be replaced by an independent review body that could investigate and, if necessary, hold hearings into suspected miscarriages of justice and then make recommendations to the Home Secretary about whether cases should be referred back to the courts. The report contemplated:

> The kind of inquiry conducted by the body would probably be very detailed and time-consuming and so we think that an applicant would have to make out a good case before it would embark on an investigation . . . . We anticipate that the sort of cases it would deal with would involve forensic evidence, witnesses who retract their evidence, third-party confessions and new evidence. We do not think that this body should consist solely of lawyers, but it should always be chaired by a lawyer. Such a body would be able to operate along inquisitorial lines, examining the petitioner, his lawyers, the police and

6 Home Office, Press Release (20 January 1987).

> the prosecution as well as any of the witnesses and transcripts and should thus be in a far better position than the Secretary of State, the Court of Appeal or the High Court of Justiciary to get at the truth of the matter.[7]

Given current critiques of the CCRC, it is also worth bearing in mind that JUSTICE accepted "that such a review body will not be infallible and will not satisfy everyone; we doubt whether this will ever be possible whatever system is devised."[8]

JUSTICE issued a subsequent report in 1994. It again called for creation of an independent body this time with the power to make referrals to the Court of Appeal. It recommended that the new body should investigate in cases where some new evidence, issue, or consideration was susceptible to further investigation and would cast doubt on the safety of the conviction.[9] It elaborated that "we do not consider that it would be either right or sensible that the CCRA [the proposed new body that would become the CCRC] should be under a duty to review a case which is the exact re-run of the evidence heard at appeal."[10] It proposed that the new body should be able to refer cases to the Court of Appeal if there was an arguable case that there had been a wrongful conviction, a standard more favourable to the accused than applied by the Court of Appeal. The body should also have the same powers as police to seize material held by a third party. There should be a general rule of full and ongoing disclosure of the investigation to the applicant, and legal aid should be available to assist the applicants.

On 14 March 1991, the Home Secretary announced the establishment of the Royal Commission on Criminal Justice to be chaired by Viscount Runciman of Oxford. The royal commission was charged with examining the effectiveness of the criminal justice system in securing the conviction of the guilty and the acquittal of the innocent. Meanwhile, Lord May, who served on the Runciman Royal Commission on Criminal Justice, made his second report on the *Maguire* case in 1992. He recommended that new independent machinery be established by statute to have the power and resources to investigate cases of suspected miscarriages and refer them to the Court of Appeal. He had criticized the Home Secretary for taking a reactive approach that responded to the grounds raised on behalf of the accused and for not conducting its own investigation.[11]

---

7 Sir George Waller, *Miscarriages of Justice* (London: Justice, 1989) at 5.23 [Waller].

8 *Ibid.* at 5.24.

9 JUSTICE, *Remedying Miscarriages of Justice* (London: Justice, 1994) at vii.

10 *Ibid.* at 30.

11 U.K., H.C., *Return to an Address of the Honourable the House of Commons Dated 3 December 1992 for a Report of the Inquiry into the Circumstances surrounding the Convictions*

The Runciman Royal Commission presented its report to Parliament in July 1993.[12] It recommended the establishment of a body independent of both the courts and the executive to consider suspected miscarriages of justice, to arrange for their investigation where appropriate, and to refer cases to the Court of Appeal where the investigation revealed matters that ought to be considered further by the courts. The royal commission had concluded that the Home Secretary's role was "incompatible with the constitutional separation of powers as between the courts and the executive."[13] It said it was wrong for the Home Secretary to be investigating miscarriages of justice while having responsibility for law and order and the police. It took the view that there should be a new body to deal with alleged miscarriages of justice.

The royal commission recommended that the new body be composed of both lawyers and lay people and that it "be supported by a staff of lawyers and administrators and have access to specialist advisers, such as forensic scientists, as necessary."[14] In addition to its powers with respect to the investigation and referral of individual cases, the new body in its annual reports should draw attention "to general features of the criminal justice system which it had found unsatisfactory in the course of its work, and to make recommendations for changes it thinks fit."[15] The new body would be able to call on the police to conduct new investigations when necessary. It would disclose new evidence it discovered to the applicants.[16] In some cases, the applicants would be assisted by legal aid.[17]

Almost everyone who gave evidence at the Runciman Royal Commission supported what transpired to be its key innovation: that the Home Secretary no longer decide whether suspected miscarriages of justice should be referred to the Court of Appeal and that the decision be taken instead by a new independent tribunal. Even the Home Office appeared keen to give up its responsibilities.[18] The government had been opposed to such a change ten years earlier before the inadequacies of the previous arrangements were laid bare.[19]

---

*arising out of the Bomb Attacks in Guildford and Woolwich in 1974: Second Report on the Maguire Case by Sir John Douglas May* (London: H.M.S.O., 1992) 296 at 12.25.

12 U.K., Royal Commission on Criminal Justice, *The Royal Commission on Criminal Justice Report*, Cm 2263 (London: H.M.S.O., 1993) [Runciman Report].

13 *Ibid.* at 182.

14 *Ibid.* at 185.

15 *Ibid.*

16 *Ibid.* at 187.

17 *Ibid.*

18 Three people who had acted as Home Secretaries—Douglas Hurd, Kenneth Clarke, and Kenneth Baker—supported the change.

19 In 1983 it rejected the idea of an independent review body to advise the Home Secretary on the prerogative of mercy (U.K., H.C., "Government Reply to the 6th Report from

The royal commission did not view the creation of the CCRC in isolation. It observed and approved of an increased willingness of the Court of Appeal to allow appeals from convictions even in cases where there was no fresh evidence or the trial judge had not made legal errors. It stated that the Court of Appeal should quash convictions if it "has a serious doubt" after reading the transcript and hearing the argument. "We do not think that quashing the jury's verdict where the court believes it is unsafe undermines the system of jury trial."[20] It also urged the Court of Appeal to "take a broad, rather than a narrow, approach" to the admission of fresh evidence that "may exonerate the appellant or at least throw serious doubt on the conviction."[21] It urged the Court of Appeal to take a tougher approach to errors by lawyers that may have caused miscarriages of justice.[22] It expressed a hope that rules of evidence would be relaxed or reformed because "it is undesirable for the courts to be deprived of powers to quash a conviction where the evidence, whatever its status, seems clearly to show that the appellant is innocent."[23] As will be discussed in Chapter 11, the Runciman Royal Commission on Criminal Justice also proposed important changes in the forensic sciences, including an independent audit.

## B. THE CRIMINAL CASES REVIEW COMMISSION

The *Criminal Appeal Act 1995* provided for the establishment of the CCRC as an independent, non-departmental public body on 1 January 1997.[24] The CCRC was established to be independent of the courts and the executive. The chairman and the commissioners of whom there must be at least eleven are ap-

---

the Home Affairs Committee Session 1981–82" Cmnd 8856 (1983) at 421.

20 Runciman Report, above note 12 at 171.

21 *Ibid.* at 173.

22 It criticized a Court of Appeal decision that required flagrantly incompetent advocacy to contribute to a miscarriage of justice on this basis:

> It cannot possibly be right that there should be defendants serving prison sentences for no other reason than that their lawyers made a decision which later turns out to have been mistaken. What matters is not the degree to which the lawyers were at fault but whether the particular decision, whether reasonable or unreasonable, caused a miscarriage of justice.

*Ibid.* at 174.

23 *Ibid.* at 184.

24 (U.K.), 1995, c. 35 [*CAA*]. There is a growing literature on the CCRC: see David Kyle, "Correcting Miscarriages of Justice: The Role of the Criminal Cases Review Commission" (2004) 52 Drake L. Rev. 657; Graham Zellick, "Facing Up to Miscarriages of Justice" (2006) 31 Manitoba L.J. 555; Laurie Elks, *Righting Miscarriages of Justice: Ten Years of the Criminal Cases Review Commission* (London: Justice, 2008) [Elks].

pointed by the Queen on the recommendation of the Prime Minister. They are a mixture of both legally qualified and other appropriately qualified and highly experienced individuals of some distinction in their own fields. One-third will be lawyers with ten years' experience and two-thirds with knowledge or experience of the justice system.[25] One such non-legally qualified commissioner is David Jessel, the former investigative journalist who presented *Trial and Error*—a major television documentary series which exposed many miscarriages of justice.[26] No person shall hold office for more than a continuous ten-year period.[27]

Various sections of the *Criminal Appeal Act 1995* outline CCRC powers and responsibilities. Section 13 directs that the CCRC, consisting of a quorum of three members, shall refer a conviction if there is a "real possibility" that the conviction would not be upheld on appeal. The CCRC is to consider either evidence or argument not made at trial or on appeal in the case, but it can also make a reference if there "are exceptional circumstances which justify making it."[28] Section 17 enables the CCRC to obtain relevant documents from public bodies. Section 19 allows the CCRC to appoint investigating officers that it desires, including from a police force that was not involved in the case. Section 21 allows the CCRC to undertake or make arrangements for others to make inquiries or obtain statements, opinions, and reports, including opinions and reports from forensic scientists. Section 23 prevents disclosure of information obtained by the CCRC in the exercise of its functions except for various purposes, such as for the exercise of the commission's functions, to assist in an application for compensation for a miscarriage of justice, or for the purpose of criminal, disciplinary, or civil proceedings.

The CCRC started handling casework from 1 April 1997, some ten years after the Home Secretary decided to refer the Birmingham Six case to the Court of Appeal. That year, 1997, saw a major shift in attitudes towards miscar-

---

25 *CAA*, *ibid.*, s. 8.

26 The following cases are discussed in David Jessel, *Trial and Error* (London: Headline Books, 1994): Mary Druhan, who was convicted of murder because no jury could ever have imagined the chaotic and intoxicated world of the witnesses who gave evidence—*R. v. Druhan*, [1999] EWCA Crim 2011; Mark Cleary was convicted of murder on the psychopathic "say-so" of the real killer; Peter Fell was convicted of murder because of his statements to the police, but all he really wanted was some attention—*R. v. Fell*, [2001] EWCA Crim 696; Gary Mills and Tony Poole were convicted of a murder when all of the evidence was corrupted, untrue, and distorted—*R. v. Poole & Anor*, [2003] EWCA Crim 1753.

27 *CAA*, above note 24, Sch. 1, s. 2(5).

28 *Ibid.*, s. 13(2).

riages of justice and the need for fairness within the criminal justice system. Here is a point worth emphasizing:

> This court is not concerned with guilt or innocence of the appellants, but only with the safety of their convictions. This may, at first sight, appear an unsatisfactory state of affairs, until it is remembered that the integrity of the criminal process is the most important consideration for the courts which have to hear appeals against conviction. Both the innocent and the guilty are entitled to fair trials. If the trial process is not fair, if it is distracted by deceit or by material breaches of the rules of evidence or procedure, then the liberties of all are threatened.[29]

The current chair of the CCRC, Richard Foster, elaborated on this approach in the 2008/2009 annual report. He stated, "It is absolutely right that the Commission concerns itself with safety, not only because it is the standard applied by the appeal courts, but also because it is a far sterner test of the integrity of the justice system than innocence alone would be." He argued that the criticism that the CCRC is not concerned enough with innocence is "misguided" because if there was "compelling evidence of innocence . . . it would, of necessity, also be compelling evidence that the conviction was unsafe."[30]

In 1999 the Lord Chief Justice stated, "the exercise of the power to refer . . . depends on the judgment of the Commission, and it cannot be too strongly emphasized that this is a judgment entrusted to the Commission and no one else."[31] The CCRC was established not to make decisions in respect of an applicant's guilt or innocence, but to decide whether to refer a case back to the Court of Appeal based on the *real possibility* that a conviction would be quashed or a sentence reduced if the matter was so referred. This decision may be based upon some "argument or evidence" not raised in the proceedings or appeals.[32]

The CCRC receives about 1,000 cases a year. Applications involve issues ranging from motoring convictions, drug offences, organized crime, and gangland crime to murder. Both summary and indictable convictions are considered. A conviction may be very old or recent, and a review may take days or years to undertake. Of those 1,000 cases, there are several common grounds of application, such as unreliable confessions; mistaken identifications; new witnesses

29 *R. v. Hickey & Ors* (1997), unreported (30 July 1997); otherwise known as the Carl Bridgewater case.

30 CCRC, *Annual Report and Accounts 2008/09* at 5 [CCRC].

31 *R. v. CCRC ex parte Pearson*, [1999] 3 All E.R. 498, Bingham L.C.J.

32 *CAA*, above note 24, s. 13(b)(i). This Act does not refer to the issue of "miscarriage of justice" unlike the Act which sets up the Scottish CCRC—see Elks, above note 24 at 17–18.

or new expert evidence; prosecution failures to disclose relevant evidence; retractions of evidence previously thought to be reliable; advances in forensic evidence and forensic science; breaches of legal safeguards (e.g., those under the *Police and Criminal Evidence Act*[33]); police malpractice; deficiencies in the conduct of the trial; changes in the common law; and new legal arguments.

The application profile to the CCRC is as follows. It receives four or five applications per day; 33 percent involve no previous appeal; 67 percent involve an unsuccessful appeal; 74 percent of applicants are in custody; 26 percent are at liberty; 86 percent of applications involve the conviction; and 14 percent relate to the sentence.[34]

It is important to bear in mind that when a case is referred to the Court of Appeal by the CCRC, the court is obliged to hear the matter. In some circumstances, as we will see shortly with "change of law" cases, this can be the cause of some tension. There might be a feeling that the CCRC is being used to bypass the strictures that the court would normally place upon the hearing of appeals. Otherwise, the process provides public confidence in appreciating that there is an independent arbiter to determine which cases will be heard again by the courts.

The independence of the commissioners has been fundamental to the continued success of the CCRC. The commissioners work with a team of support, investigative, advisory, and case review staff. They include administrative, clerical, and technical personnel; two legal advisers; two investigations advisers; and case reviewers. The case review personnel include people from a wide range of backgrounds and skills. Some are legally trained, but others are police officers, public servants, or people with a range of different skills. In March 2009, the equivalent of 40.8 full-time individual workers served as case review managers, down from 46.75 full-time case workers in March 2007; there were eleven commissioners, or the statutory minimum, down from a previous complement of sixteen commissioners.[35]

### 1) The Review Process

The CCRC's principal role is to review applications from those who believe they have been wrongly convicted or wrongly sentenced. When an application form is received by the commission, it is acknowledged by the front-of-house

33 *Police and Criminal Evidence Act 1984* (U.K.), 1984, c. 60.

34 Figures supplied by CCRC.

35 CCRC, above note 30 at 17.

administrative staff. Cases will not be accepted if an appeal is pending, if the applicant is asking the commission to review a civil case, or if the matter is otherwise outside the commission's jurisdiction.

The application is assessed for eligibility and passed on to a commissioner to be screened. Every application is, therefore, seen and considered by a commissioner shortly after it is received by the CCRC. This important quality assurance mechanism ensures that every applicant has the benefit of being considered by a commissioner right from the start.

Cases are received, screened by a commissioner, categorized, and assigned to pathways with clear milestones leading to a decision. Before undertaking a full review of a case, the commissioner will need to decide whether there are, *prima facie*, any reviewable grounds. Usually, this process involves identifying some prospect of discovering in reviews of convictions an argument on a point of law, some evidence not raised in earlier proceedings, or some exceptional circumstances that justify referring the case without fresh argument or evidence. In reviews of sentences, one would look for a legal argument or information not raised earlier in the proceedings. Sometimes, the commissioner is able to reach a decision at the conclusion of the screening process based on the information given in the application form, other correspondence, and fundamental core documents, which may include the indictment, summing up, advice and grounds of appeal, Criminal Appeal office summary, single judge ruling, and full court judgment. The commissioner may also request various files, such as defence files, CPS (Crown Prosecution Service) files, and additional court files.

Once the screening is finished, the commissioner will decide to issue a letter either setting out the reasons for declining to take the case further or indicating that some matters require review. If the matter is not to be taken further, the commissioner will issue a reasoned provisional view in the form of a comprehensive letter. The applicant will have twenty-eight days to provide any further submissions. If no further submissions are received—or they do not alter the commissioner's opinion—the commissioner will close the case.

### a) Ways to Assess Possible Cases for Review

The commissioner will consider the following issues when assessing cases for review and will respond accordingly.

*"No appeal" cases:* A normal requirement for review by the commission is that the applicant has exhausted all avenues of appeal. A "no appeal" application is, therefore, normally rejected, *unless* exceptional circumstances apply. If the CCRC had to use its statutory powers to obtain information that an applicant

would ordinarily be unable to access or find, that would be an example of exceptional circumstances. In practice, it is usually only possible to identify the presence of exceptional circumstances when a committee of three members decides there is a real possibility that the conviction would be quashed or the sentence reduced if a reference was made to the Court of Appeal.

Most "no appeal" applications are rejected after the one commissioner's assessment. At this stage, the commissioner will set out the reasons in a letter and give the applicant the opportunity to provide any further information that may assist their application. In respect of a "no appeal" application, not only would it be necessary to decide that the conviction might be quashed if a reference was made to the Court of Appeal, but it would also be necessary to show that, in light of there not being a previous appeal or application for leave to appeal, there were exceptional circumstances for making a reference now. If their cases are rejected at this stage, applicants are advised that they can reapply to the CCRC if, in the future, they do identify something new; however, they cannot reapply to the commission with their rejected grounds of appeal.

*Reapplications:* An application to the CCRC may follow upon a previously unsuccessful application to the commission. Being able to reapply is an important safeguard against the possibility of error by the commission, which rejects the vast majority of applications it receives. It also allows an applicant to bring new considerations and evidence to the commission's attention. In the event of a reapplication, a commissioner with no previous involvement in the case will determine whether or not anything is new. Where this application is clearly a repeat of the previous one, the applicant will be advised that there will be no new review. If, however, the applicant has raised something new that justifies a review, then the application will be accepted and categorized in the normal way.

A large proportion of reapplications are rejected and a further review declined at the one commissioner stage. If, on reapplication, new evidence or information is contained within the submissions, then the case will be sent for a further review and categorized by a commissioner (as described below); if the applicant has raised nothing new since the previous application and the commissioner cannot identify any investigative steps that may assist the applicant, then the applicant will be advised that no new review will occur. The applicant can reapply should some new evidence or information be discovered.

*Cases without reviewable or plausible grounds:* In the majority of these cases, the applicant has previously had an unsuccessful appeal to the Court of Appeal. If, after careful analysis of the submissions, the commissioner is satisfied that no reviewable grounds exist, then the commissioner will issue a provisional statement of reasons in the form of a comprehensive letter, allowing twenty-eight days for any further submissions to be made for consideration. This letter is followed by a final Statement of Reasons, also in letter form.

### b) Ways to Categorize Cases for Review

Once a commissioner has screened the case and determined it is acceptable for review, it will be categorized according to length of time and complexity, and sent to a case review manager to undertake the review. Categories are A, B, C, and D. The case review manager follows a similar process for each category of cases.

*Category A:* These cases are typically straightforward or raise issues that can be addressed thoroughly on available case papers. The case manager normally reviews and passes them on to either a decision-making committee of three commissioners or to a single commissioner.

The case review manager will choose the committee option if the case should be considered for a possible reference to the Court of Appeal—a referral must be made by at least three commissioners. The committee, or DMC, will decide whether it believes there is a real possibility that the conviction would be quashed or the sentence reduced if the reference is made. It will then either set out comprehensive grounds for the referral in a provisional Statement of Reasons (pSOR), prepared largely by the case review manager, or issue a Statement of Reasons (SOR) to applicants, explaining it does not see any real possibility that the conviction would be quashed or the sentence reduced.

The case review manager's other option is to give cases to a single commissioner who can decide not to refer the case to the Court of Appeal and will then issue a pSOR, prepared by the case review manager. The pSOR sets out in considerable detail why the commission has determined that there is no real possibility that the conviction would be quashed or the sentence reduced if a reference was made to the Court of Appeal; the applicant is then given the opportunity (twenty-eight days, which can be extended for good reason) to challenge the statement, correct any factual errors, and provide further information that will assist the commissioner in deciding either to issue the final Statement of Reasons and close the case or to send the case to a decision-making committee. The commissioner will make the latter choice if there seems to be a real possibility of a successful referral or if the case seems complex or finely nuanced enough that it should be considered by three commissioners.

The case review manager prepares the case either for a single commissioner or for a DMC, providing valuable input into the decision-making process. Category A cases are usually finalized within eight weeks of allocation, for either a provisional decision to be made by a single commissioner or for consideration by a DMC. As a built-in safeguard, if concern arises when a case is being considered by a single commissioner, then the case review manager can request that a case under review by a single commissioner be directed to a committee of three members.

*Category B:* These cases are more involved and typically raise issues of some complexity, possibly with extensive material to review often from another agency. They should be ready to go to the decision-making stage within twenty-two weeks of allocation. Either a single commissioner will make a provisional decision not to refer the case to the Court of Appeal or a DMC will make a decision based on the "real possibility" test to refer the case to the Court of Appeal or to issue a pSOR, where the committee decides the test is not satisfied.

*Category C:* These cases are likely to require a more extensive and time-consuming review, where issues are complex, possibly requiring wide-ranging off-site inquiries or the input of other agencies. A commissioner is assigned to each category C case at allocation to assist the case reviewer in planning and executing the review in a timely manner. For each of these cases, there will be a case-planning committee which involves an investigations adviser and a second commissioner. The case-planning committee will agree on actions and investigations and set a target date for completion of the review, which can take months—and, in some cases, even years.

Once the review is completed, the case will go either to a DMC for a possible referral to the Court of Appeal or to a single commissioner who will issue first a provisional and then a final SOR, where it is determined there is no real possibility of either the conviction being quashed or the sentence being reduced if a reference was made.

*Category D:* These exceptional cases, known as section 19 cases, may be very large and extremely complex. Under the *Criminal Appeal Act 1995*, the CCRC can appoint an investigating officer (to date, always a senior police officer) if an investigation is complex or likely to involve looking into other alleged crimes, such as perjury. The investigating officer's report is submitted to the CCRC, where it is considered as part of the review.[36] There may also be groups of cases that share a single issue and that may benefit from being reviewed by the same case review team, with the support of the same commissioner(s), to ensure consistency of approach as well as the more obvious economies of scale.

---

36 *CAA*, above note 24, s. 19.

Once the review is completed, a section 19 case will either go to a DMC or to a single commissioner who can decide not to make a reference to the Court of Appeal.

## 2) Case Review Personnel

Critical to the undertaking of a comprehensive review are the case review personnel. Case review managers come from a range of backgrounds and bring with them a diverse skill set. Some of them have a legal background, some were formerly police officers, and others were involved in professions that had directly transferable skills, such as high-level investigative and analytical skills. Case review managers can call upon the commissioners, the legal advisers, and the investigations advisers when they need advice or wish to discuss the direction of the review. The case review manager identifies the priorities for action against a timeline to ensure that the investigation is focused. The pooling of collective skills, knowledge, and experience is an essential precondition to ensuring that a thorough and independent review is undertaken.

The investigative process can take many forms. It can involve interviewing witnesses; searching for and analysing fresh evidence; instructing experts and analysing expert evidence; commissioning further scientific analysis, such as DNA techniques that may not have been available at the time of the trial or the appeal; visiting applicants in prison; considering and analysing highly sensitive material, for example, from informant files; interviewing informants; analysing TV footage or covert surveillance materials; considering fresh legal arguments and points of law; and analysing volumes of documents, court files, witness statements, non-disclosed material, expert evidence, and any other materials that may be relevant to the case.

If the case depends upon materials held by a public body, the CCRC can instruct it to keep the materials safe or forward them to the commission to allow for inspection.[37] Where there are large numbers of records or files, such as revenue and customs files, social services files, or hospital records, then the case reviewer may go off-site to inspect them. The power does not apply to private organizations or individuals.[38]

The CCRC also has powers to check criminal records and to access the Police National Computer (PNC). These checks are an important part of the

---

37 *Ibid.*, s. 17.

38 The CCRC recognized that this limitation can inhibit its work; submission to the House of Commons Justice Committee (10 March 2009).

commission's investigative processes. Where issues possibly involving the commission of a crime are involved, the power under section 19 of the *Criminal Appeal Act 1995* allows the CCRC to appoint a police officer from a force independent of the issues being investigated. This ability can be most valuable where there are allegations of police malpractice or a need to interview witnesses under caution.

### 3) Fresh Evidence

If new evidence is identified, the CCRC has to determine whether there is a real possibility that the Court of Appeal would receive it. Under the *Criminal Appeal Act 1968*, section 23 provides that the Court of Appeal may receive evidence if it finds that the interests of justice make it necessary or expedient to do so. In applying this, section 23 goes on to state that the Court of Appeal must have regard, in particular, to the following:

A) The evidence appears to the court to be capable of belief;
B) It appears to the court the evidence may afford any ground for allowing the appeal;
C) The evidence would have been admissible in the proceedings from which the appeal lies on an issue subject of the appeal; and
D) There is a reasonable explanation for the failure to adduce evidence in those proceedings.[39]

In practice, in every case where there appears to be fresh evidence, new information, or an argument on a point of law, the statutory test for the CCRC is as follows: if a reference was made to the Court of Appeal, would there be a real possibility that the conviction would be quashed or the sentence reduced?

Any new argument or evidence identified by the CCRC's investigation will, upon referral, be evaluated by the Court of Appeal. The question then is whether the court will be prepared to receive it, taking into account its practices.[40] It is self-evident that whatever view the CCRC reaches on an individual

---

39 *CAA* 1968, above note 3.

40 There has been some criticism that the CCRC has been reluctant to refer cases where the Court of Appeal may accept only fresh evidence on residual interest of justice grounds. Campbell Malone, "Only the Freshest Will Do" in Michael Naughton, ed., *The Criminal Cases Review Commission: Hope for the Innocent?* (Basingstoke, UK: Palgrave Macmillan, 2009) [Naughton, *Hope*]. Laurie Elks, a former commissioner, has expressed awareness of the controversy over fresh evidence cases. He notes that the Court of Appeal "obviously hopes to influence the Commission against too 'liberal' an approach in new evidence cases and, a senior appeal judge has [in an extra-judicial

case, its determination must always address the question of whether the arguments and evidence available are enough to give rise to the real possibility that the Court of Appeal will quash the conviction.

### 4) Deciding Whether to Refer

Once the investigations have been completed, a decision not to make a reference to the Court of Appeal may be made by a single commissioner. As noted earlier, a decision to refer a matter to the Court of Appeal must be made by three commissioners sitting together.

In the case of a referral, a Statement of Reasons (SOR), with all of the appropriate disclosure material, will be sent to the Court of Appeal and to the applicant. The appellate court will determine the case based solely on the grounds submitted by the CCRC. Originally, the accused was able to raise any ground of appeal once the CCRC had referred a case back to the courts, but now appeals are allowed only on grounds certified by the CCRC or on other grounds where the Court of Appeal has granted leave.[41]

Where a decision is taken not to refer a case to the Court of Appeal, the provisional Statement of Reasons (pSOR) will make full disclosure of all evidence and documents acquired through the course of the review. The applicant is then given the opportunity to respond to that statement before a final Statement of Reasons is issued. If the position remains unchanged after the consideration of any further submissions, the case is then closed.

After an unsuccessful application, applicants may apply to the CCRC again, if some new evidence or information has come to light since the previous review of the case. This ability is an important safeguard against the possibility that the CCRC will make errors or that new evidence casting doubt on the safety of the conviction may emerge.

It is an offence for the CCRC to disclose information that it has collected except in relation to its own statutory functions or for the purposes of criminal, civil, or disciplinary proceedings.[42] The CCRC's Statement of Reasons is *not* made public. Statements often contain sensitive information in respect of witnesses, victims, and even informants.

---

letter to Graham Zellick, then chair of the CCRC] counseled against 'undue' citation of *Pendleton*. I am not personally aware, however, of any case where the Commission has drawn back from referral in consequence of this guidance." Elks, above note 24 at 346.

41 *CAA*, above note 24, s. 14, amended by *Criminal Justice Act 2003* (U.K.), 2003, c. 44, s. 315.

42 *CAA*, *ibid.*, ss. 23–24.

### 5) Judicial Review of Commission Decisions

When advised that no referral will be made to the Court of Appeal, a few dissatisfied applicants take action to judicially review the CCRC's decision. Judicial reviews can be expensive in terms of the commission's resources and time consuming in terms of the commission's resources.

In the first judicial review of the CCRC, the Court of Appeal dismissed the challenge of the decision not to refer the case. It concluded:

> Had the Commission decided to refer this case to the Court of Appeal, that would (if based upon a proper direction and reasoning) have been a reasonable and lawful decision. The decision not to refer was in our view equally reasonable and lawful. The question lay fairly and squarely within the area of judgment entrusted to the Commission. If this court were to hold that a decision one way or the other was objectively right or objectively wrong, it would be exceeding its function.[43]

This conclusion sets a relatively deferential standard of review. The courts have upheld the CCRC's decision not to refer the 1950 murder conviction of Timothy Evans to the Court of Appeal. The executed man had received a free pardon and the Court of Appeal was unlikely to declare him innocent even though there was a reasonable basis that it would overturn the conviction in the infamous 10 Rillington Place murders.[44] At the same time, decisions by the CCRC have been quashed on judicial review if based on a clear misdirection in the law.[45]

In *Boyle v. Criminal Cases Review Commission*, the applicant had complained that the CCRC had delayed in providing its decision to him and that the decision not to refer his application was affected by bias.[46] This case reveals significant information about how the CCRC goes about investigating an application—written reasons for the rejection of the application amounted to 248 pages. The CCRC had also appointed independent forensic experts and an investigating officer to help with inquiries, indicating that rejected applications can take up considerable resources at the CCRC. The application for judicial review was refused with the court finding that the CCRC was neither biased nor failed to keep an open mind.

---

43 *Pearson v. Criminal Cases Review Commission*, [1999] EWHC Admin 452 at para. 59.

44 *Westlake v. Criminal Cases Review Commission*, [2004] EWHC Admin 2779 at paras. 34 and 36.

45 *Farnell v. Criminal Cases Review Commission*, [2003] EWHC Admin 835 (misdirection on applicable law governing provocation).

46 [2007] EWHC 8 (Admin).

*Dowsett v. Criminal Cases Review Commission* involved a conviction for murder, an appeal, and proceedings before the European Court of Human Rights at Strasbourg.[47] The court pointed to the "real possibility" test and the fact that the judgment was entrusted to the CCRC "and no one else." The application for judicial review of the commission's decision was refused.

In *Boston and Anor v. Criminal Cases Review Commission*, the application had involved the CCRC in three years of investigations before it declined to refer the matter to the court. The decision was upheld by the court in this application for review.[48]

The possibility of judicial review, like the possibility for reapplications, provides safeguards that the CCRC may inadvertently deny a meritorious application. Judicial review is obviously not an option when an applicant's case is rejected by a volunteer innocence project.

## 6) References to and from the CCRC

The Court of Appeal may direct the CCRC to assist in investigating and advising on an issue which it needs to resolve before it can decide whether to grant leave to appeal or how to proceed with a case. A number of such requests involve interviewing jurors, but not about the content of their deliberations. In 2007 the Court of Appeal issued fifteen directions to the commission in respect of section 15 investigations.[49] This capability again demonstrates how proactive investigations can assist in the investigation of possible miscarriages of justice.

The CCRC has a role to play in royal pardons. The Home Secretary can ask the CCRC for advice when considering whether to advise Her Majesty to issue a royal pardon. The CCRC can also refer cases to the Home Secretary where it feels that a royal pardon should be considered.

## 7) The CCRC as "Last Resort"

The CCRC is a last resort. It cannot normally consider any case until it has gone through the appeal system. This role means that applicants to it should have already filled in a notice of appeal. If that appeal fails, or if leave to appeal is refused, the applicant is then free to apply to the commission. In exceptional circumstances, the CCRC can refer an application where there has not been

47 [2007] EWHC 1923 (Admin).
48 [2006] EWHC 1966 (Admin).
49 *CAA*, above note 24.

any appeal or application for leave to appeal. Exceptional circumstances may arise for a variety of reasons, but one recurrent reason is where the commission has had to use its powers to gain access to information that the applicant or the applicant's legal representative would be unable to.[50]

### 8) Facts and Figures

Over the first eleven years with a budget of about £7 million, the CCRC received an average of 1,000 applications per year. As at 30 June 2010, the appeal courts, including the Supreme Court (House of Lords), had determined a total of 422 referrals since the commission's inception, quashing 299 convictions (71 percent of those referred) and upholding 123 (29 percent). Since its inception in 1997, the CCRC has reviewed more than 12,745 cases and referred 456 cases.[51]

Most of the quashed convictions involved murder (93), but significant numbers have involved robbery (32), drug offences (30), rape/indecent assault (30), assault (24), and fraud (14). Although the work of the CCRC is primarily focused on individual cases, one of its key functions is to contribute to the development of legal principles and to share its "intellectual property" with the wider criminal justice system. We discuss the possible expansion of this role later in this chapter.

## C. THE RECEPTION OF REFERRALS FROM THE CCRC IN THE COURTS

The nature of the CCRC's mandate means that it must pay close attention to the evolving jurisprudence in the Court of Appeal. Concerns have been raised that the CCRC may be too captive to the Court of Appeal,[52] but these have been meet with arguments by Graham Zellick and others that the Court of Appeal refuses to reverse convictions referred by the CCRC in about 30 percent of all cases.[53] Professors Nobles and Schiff have recently recognized that "even without a statutory duty to refer only where there is a 'real possibility' of success, the CCRC would not be acting responsibly if it failed to consider the likely outcome when choosing what case to refer."[54]

---

50 For example, social service files or Criminal Injury Compensation Authority files.

51 See online: www.ccrc.gov.uk/case_44.htm.

52 Richard Nobles & David Schiff, "The CCRC: Establishing a Workable Relationship with the Court of Appeal" [2005] Crim. L. Rev. 173.

53 Graham Zellick, "The Criminal Cases Review Commission and the Court of Appeal: The Commission's Perspective" [2005] Crim. L. Rev. 937.

54 Richard Nobles & David Schiff, "After Ten Years: An Investment in Justice" in Naughton, *Hope*, above note 40 at 157–58.

### 1) Differing Court Judgments

At the same time, it would be wrong to assume that referrals of cases from the CCRC have not caused controversy. One of the commission's references that caused some controversy raised the question of whether a woman had to have an intention to kill or seriously injure her baby before she could be guilty of infanticide. In a controversial judgment, critical of the CCRC, the Court of Appeal held that infanticide was not a sub-category of murder. In other words, one could be guilty of the offence (infanticide) as a result of any deliberate act or omission, however well intended it may have been, if the baby died as a consequence.[55]

Sometimes, referrals by the CCRC are dealt with differently by the Court of Appeal and the House of Lords. In *R. v. Clarke & Anor*, the Court of Appeal upheld a conviction referred by the CCRC for want of a signature on the indictment.[56] Although a technicality, the House of Lords reversed the Court of Appeal and quashed the conviction.[57] In another case, the House of Lords reversed a conviction referred by the CCRC but upheld by the Court of Appeal. In this case and others, the CCRC was faced with divergent authorities in the Court of Appeal. The cases gave different outcomes in cases where an appellant had assisted someone to inject drugs, from which the user had died. One view held the appellant liable for "unlawful Act" manslaughter. The House of Lords preferred the other authority, however, and in so doing, reversed the Court of Appeal. It held that the user's own act of injecting himself with the drug had broken the chain of causation which legally linked the appellant to the death.[58]

In respect of the issue of an alternative lesser offence, the CCRC contributed two references to a group of four appeals, heard together in order to clarify when judges should allow juries to consider the possibility of convicting defendants of some less serious offence than the one for which they were standing trial.[59]

### 2) "Change of Law" Cases

The CCRC also, on occasion, unwittingly causes controversy, as it did in respect of what are known as "change of law" cases. These cases arise when the common

55 *R. v. Gore (Deceased)*, [2007] EWCA Crim 2789.
56 *R. v. Clarke & Anor*, [2006] EWCA Crim 1196.
57 [2008] UKHL 8.
58 *R. v. Kennedy*, [2007] UKHL 38.
59 *R. v. Foster & Ors*, [2007] EWCA Crim 2869, considering *R. v. Coutts*, [2006] UKHL 39.

law changes after the date of conviction and appeal, and the commission and the courts must further consider the cases by applying what has become the law.

For example, the CCRC had referred several convictions following the House of Lords decision in the money-laundering case of *Saik*.[60] The Divisional Court was then asked by the prosecutor in judicial review proceedings to rule that the commission should refer cases only if the Court of Appeal would have granted leave to appeal out of time. The Divisional Court held that the commission was under no such obligation.[61] This meant that where an applicant thought that the Court of Appeal might not grant leave to appeal because the application was out of time, the applicant could turn to commission to gain a referral to the Court of Appeal. Once the CCRC refers a case to the Court of Appeal, the court is obliged to hear the appeal.

The Court of Appeal subsequently expressed the view that the CCRC should have regard to the court's practice not to allow an extension of time based on a change of law unless some substantial injustice had occurred.[62] What particularly caused the court concern was that, once such a case had been referred, the court had to apply the new law and if it rendered the conviction unsafe, it had to quash the conviction—even if it was a case in which it would not have granted leave to appeal. The problem has now been resolved by the *Criminal Justice and Immigration Act 2008*.[63] In section 42, the Act gives the Court of Appeal the power to dismiss an appeal in such circumstances.

Massive publicity and media attention was focused on the CCRC with its decision to refer the case of Barry George to the Court of Appeal. As we saw in Chapter 7, he had been convicted of murdering the television presenter Jill Dando. George's conviction for the murder was quashed in November 2007 and a retrial was ordered. Because of refinements in the way that the Forensic Science Service expressed the significance of microscopic traces of firearms residue, George was acquitted on the retrial.[64]

In practice, there can, at times, be a "healthy tension" between the CCRC and the Court of Appeal, which is only to be expected given their respective roles. A confident commission that presents fully reasoned arguments can afford to be principled and challenging. Over the years there have been a number of conflicts, not only between the CCRC and the Court of Appeal, but within the Court of Appeal, and between the Court of Appeal and the House of Lords.

---

60 *R. v. Saik*, [2006] UKHL 18.

61 *R. (Director of Revenue and Customs Prosecution) v. CCRC*, [2007] 1 Cr. App. R. 384.

62 *R. v. Cottrell*, [2007] EWCA Crim 2016.

63 *Criminal Justice and Immigration Act 2008* (U.K.), 2008, c. 4.

64 *R. v. George*, [2007] EWCA Crim 2722.

## D. THE CCRC COMPARED WITH THE SCOTTISH CRIMINAL CASES REVIEW COMMISSION

There is a separate criminal cases review commission for Scotland, which has its own legal system. The Scottish Criminal Cases Review Commission (SCCRC) is a smaller body than the CCRC, but it has similar appointment procedures and qualifications and similar restrictions on disclosure of information. The SCCRC may refer on the basis that a miscarriage of justice may have occurred and that a referral is in the interests of justice.[65] The Scottish commission also has broader investigative powers than the CCRC: it can obtain a judicial order to examine any person with relevant information under oath as well as to require production of relevant material from any person — not just public bodies, as is the case for the CCRC.[66]

As of March 2010, the Scottish commission had referred 97 of 1,136 completed applications since it began its work in April 1999. The commission's most famous referral was its 2007 decision to refer a conviction in the Lockerbie terrorist bombing trial on the basis of new evidence indicative of frailties in eyewitness identification. This referral was made in the form of an 800-page decision after a three-year investigation costing £1.1 million.[67] Subsequently, the matter was resolved by an executive act of clemency on the compassionate grounds that the prisoner was dying of cancer and the release of Abdelbaset Ali al-Megrahi to return to Libya in August 2009.

## E. REVIEW OF CCRC PRACTICES

In his evidence to a House of Commons committee in March 2009, CCRC Chair Richard Foster said he was mindful that the CCRC does not have a structured database to deal with the analysis of its results, but noted that the CCRC was working with the Ministry of Justice to establish one. He said that the database's purpose would be to examine two key issues: first, to determine what the data would reveal about the systemic causes of miscarriages; and second, to determine whether there was any way the CCRC could use that data to provide some form of external assurance about the reliability of its decisions.

---

65 *Crime and Punishment (Scotland) Act 1997* (U.K.), 1997, c. 48, s. 25.

66 The Scottish commission can interview jurors but not about the actual deliberations; *Re Scottish Criminal Cases Review Commission* (25 July 2001), (High Court of Judiciary).

67 Scottish Criminal Cases Review Commission, News Release (28 June 2007). Scottish Criminal Cases Review Commission, *Annual Report 2009–2010* (Glasgow: Scottish Criminal Cases Review Commission, 2010) at 9.

He noted that the CCRC can determine from the decisions of the Court of Appeal what happens with the cases that the CCRC refers to the courts.

> What we do not have is any process to give us independent assurance as regards the cases that we do not refer, because we are not inspected externally, there is no other external Q and A process. So that is the other area I am hoping, working with the Ministry of Justice, we can do something about.[68]

Critics of the CCRC have recommended that random audits of cases considered by three commissioners, but not referred to the Court of Appeal should be reviewed by a leading counsel or retired judge.[69] As suggested above, a person who has his or her application rejected by the CCRC can either reapply or seek judicial review of that decision. There are, however, only a handful of judicial review cases that have been taken against the CCRC. In 2009, the CCRC implemented an internal quality assurance system.

There is some evidence that applicants who are represented by lawyers are more likely to have their cases referred by the commission, though this is only a correlation that does not necessarily infer causation.[70] In addition, innocence projects have developed in the United Kingdom, and they can help in the preparation of applications to the CCRC.[71] Although one virtue of the CCRC is its ability to investigate cases, representation of applicants through counsel or innocence projects can help ensure that the CCRC does not overlook important issues. It would be ironic to think that the CCRC would be immune from error or tunnel vision just because it is concerned with miscarriages of justice.

The developing critical literature on the work of the CCRC is to be welcomed.[72] Insofar as it raises questions about increasing the importance and funding available to challenge questionable cases, there is much to be said for it. The CCRC could benefit from broader investigative powers that would allow it, like the SCCRC and the Canadian Minister of Justice, to obtain rel-

---

68 House of Commons Justice Committee, "The Work of the Criminal Cases Review Commission" examination of witnesses (10 March 2009).

69 Campbell Malone, "Only the Freshest Will Do" in Naughton, *Hope*, above note 40 at 116–17.

70 Jacqueline Hodgson & Juliet Horne, *The Extent and Impact of Legal Representation on Applications to the Criminal Cases Review Commission (CCRC)* (Working Paper Series, 2009), online: http://ssrn.com/abstract=1483721. Of applicants from 2001 to 2007, 29 percent had legal representation, but 63.5 percent of applicants whose cases were referred during that time had legal representation. *Ibid.* at 4.

71 Stephanie Roberts & Lynne Weathered, "Assisting the Factually Innocent: The Contradictions and Compatibility of Innocence Projects and the Criminal Cases Review Commission" (2009) 29 Oxford J. Legal Stud. 43 [Roberts & Weathered].

72 Naughton, *Hope*, above note 40.

evant information from reluctant private parties. Random external audits of the vast majority of applications that the CCRC rejects could also be helpful if only in strengthening public confidence in the CCRC's work. There may also be a case for increased transparency in the CCRC's work through publications of its reasons for decisions, subject to the significant safeguards that would be required to protect individuals.

At the same time, critiques of the CCRC that propose the creation of a second independent commission with a mandate to inquire into factual innocence seem to us ill advised.[73] An error correction commission limited to claims of factual innocence will be discussed below when we examine the work of the North Carolina Innocence Inquiry Commission.

Some of the criticisms directed at the CCRC are more appropriately directed at the Court of Appeal.[74] The CCRC's performance in "lurking doubt" cases, where there may not be new evidence, undoubtedly reflects the Court of Appeal's reluctance to allow appeals on the basis of a lurking doubt. Similarly, part of the CCRC's perceived hesitancy to refer cases on new evidence may also reflect some reluctance of the Court of Appeal on such matters. To be sure, the CCRC should not hesitate to make warranted referrals, but it may be more constructive to address the procedures used by the Court of Appeal. Perhaps the Court of Appeal needs more resources or should make even greater use of the CCRC's ability to investigate matters for it. Many European jurisdictions allow appeals that are essentially new trials. As discussed in Chapter 6, there may be cases where appeal courts should reconsider a decision in the absence of a referral from the CCRC or the executive in order to prevent a fraud on the court. There are, of course, limits to how much appellate courts can do consistent with their appellate role, but appeal courts should be as flexible as possible and aware of the possibility of miscarriages of justice.[75]

It would not be overly helpful to create a new innocence commission in either the public or the voluntary sector if the Court of Appeal was resistant to innocence claims not packaged in the established legal avenues for appeals. Referring such cases to the Home Secretary for a pardon through the royal prerogative of mercy has been suggested.[76] Doing so, however, would be a step backwards; it would return to the time when claims for justice were decided by elected officials and through the language of mercy and pardons. In our

73 Michael Naughton, "Conclusion" in *ibid.* at 225–26.

74 Michael Zander, "Foreword" in *ibid.* at xvii.

75 Kent Roach, "Wrongful Convictions: Adversarial and Inquisitorial Themes" (2010) 35 N.C.J. Int'l L. & Com. Reg. 385.

76 Michael Naughton, "Conclusion," in Naughton, *Hope*, above note 40 at 226.

view, reformers should use institutions such as the CCRC to their advantage and work on expanding the parameters for successful appeals and admission of fresh evidence. The chair of the CCRC has expressed his firm belief that any case where there was evidence of innocence would also qualify as a case that the commission could refer to the Court of Appeal on safety grounds.[77]

Equally off target are criticisms of the CCRC based upon successful appeals following CCRC referrals as "technicalities."[78] The role of the CCRC can be compared to that of an auditor — the CCRC's function is to monitor cases that have been dealt with by the Court of Appeal and to refer cases back to the court which, in the opinion of the CCRC, have not been dealt with properly by that court. Cases where convictions are overturned because of unfairness in the application of the law also send a signal about the need for police investigations and trials to be conducted properly. CCRC referral of cases back to the Court of Appeal could also lead to improved performance by the Court of Appeal. Such improvements might lead to having smaller numbers of cases referred by the CCRC, but that would indicate a successful outcome of the CCRC's work, not (as its critics suggest) a less relevant role for the CCRC. After all, an auditor's success has (or should have) an *inverse* relationship to the number of fraud cases discovered.

Some of the criticisms appear to be based upon cases where evidence of innocence (or the safety of the conviction) may not be considered by the Court of Appeal to be either "fresh" or "new" according to the terms of the statute. As we saw in Chapter 3, this problem has been dealt with by the court's willingness to not apply those criteria so strictly in the face of compelling claims of innocence based upon material not used (or not used to its full strength) at the earlier trial or appeal.

It is also relevant that several commentators from Australia, Canada, and the United States, who appear well aware of the potential limits and flaws of the CCRC, still wish to see an independent state institution created in their jurisdictions to replace systems of reliance on petitions to a self-interested executive for clemency or referrals to the court.[79]

---

77 CCRC, above note 30 at 5 — Richard Foster has written:

> The fact is that we have never come across, and cannot conceive of, a situation where we would not refer a case where there was compelling evidence of innocence. If there were such evidence of innocence, it would, necessarily, also be compelling evidence that the conviction was unsafe.

78 Michael Naughton, "Introduction" in Naughton, *Hope*, above note 40 at 2.

79 Clive Walker & Kathryn Campbell, "The CCRC Option for Canada: Forwards or Backwards?" and Richard Schehr, "A View from the United States" in *ibid.*; Lynne

## F. AN ERROR CORRECTION COMMISSION LIMITED TO CLAIMS OF FACTUAL INNOCENCE: THE NCIIC[80]

Some critics of the CCRC have suggested that a new innocence commission be created by legislation "to help alleged innocent victims of wrongful convictions that, unlike the CCRC, is not bound to the criteria of appeal courts."[81] They have looked to the American experience even though it has been dominated by volunteer innocence projects. In this section, we will examine the only North American commission that has been created by legislation and appointed by the state — the North Carolina Innocence Inquiry Commission (NCIIC). As will be seen, its mandate is much narrower than the CCRC's and the evidence to date suggests that it will not refer nearly as many cases back to the courts for review. As such, in our view, it should not serve as the model for error correction commissions in Australia or Canada.

In 2002, Barry Scheck and Peter Neufeld, co-founders of the Innocence Project at Cardozo Law School, called for the creation in the United States of independent reviews of officially acknowledged wrongful convictions in the style of Canadian public inquiries and the work of the National Transportation Safety Board. They discussed the alternative of the CCRC but concluded that "proposals based on a CCRC model could be too easily, albeit unfairly, attacked as requiring large government bureaucracies based on un-American notions of an inquisitorial justice system that would squander precious law enforcement funds on prisoners making frivolous claims."[82] To be sure, the CCRC does have some inquisitorial features because it devotes state resources to investigations and does not rely on adversarial presentation of the evidence. Nevertheless, the inquisitorial features of the CCRC should not be taken as a criticism of the institution but rather as a response to the abundant failures of the adversarial system in producing miscarriages of justice, particularly in cases where the accused is overwhelmed by the superior resources and expertise of the state and its forensic witnesses.

---

Weathered, "Does Australia Need a Specific Institution to Correct Wrongful Convictions?" (2007) 40 Austl. & N.Z J. Crim. 179.

80 This part of the chapter draws on Kent Roach, "The Role of Innocence Commissions: Error Correction, Systemic Reform or Both?" (2010) 85 Chicago-Kent L. Rev. 89.

81 Michael Naughton, "Conclusion" in Naughton, *Hope*, above note 40 at 225.

82 Barry Scheck & Peter Neufeld, "Towards the Formation of 'Innocence Commissions' in America" (2002) 86 Judicature 98 at 101. For contemporaneous arguments that American jurisdictions should establish CCRCs to hear claims of wrongful convictions in individual cases, see Lissa Griffin, "The Correction of Wrongful Convictions — A Comparative Perspective" (2001) 16 Am. U. Int'l L. Rev. 1241; Ronald Huff, "Wrongful Conviction and Public Policy" (2002) 40 Criminology 1.

The first CCRC-type body created in North America—that is, a state-appointed, independent body with an error correction function—was the NCIIC. The 2006 legislation[83] creating the NCIIC grew out of recommendations made by another body, the North Carolina Actual Innocence Commission, a self-appointed body chaired by Lake C.J. of the North Carolina Supreme Court. The fact that the NCIIC emerged out of the work and recommendations of a systemic reform commission underlines the symbiotic relationship between systemic reform and error correction in the wrongful conviction field.

The NCIIC is composed of eight voting members appointed by the Chief Justices of the North Carolina Supreme Court and Court of Appeals. Although judicial appointment of commission members may provide some independence from the government, by statute, the membership of the NCIIC must include a superior court judge, a prosecuting attorney, a victim advocate, a defence attorney, a sheriff, a person who is not an attorney or employed by the judiciary, and two others.[84] The NCIIC thus has a composition that represents the major actors in the justice system. Like the British and Scottish commissions, the NCIIC also has some lay representation, but the commission members receive no salary for their services.[85] The absence of remuneration may be appropriate for those such as judges, sheriffs, and prosecutors already employed by the state, but could cause hardship for those not so employed. In the United Kingdom, the CCRC prohibits its commissioners from holding certain appointments, such as judicial appointments within the criminal justice system, because of the potential for conflicts of interest.

The entire legislation establishing the NCIIC is subject to a four-year sunset unless renewed by the legislature. The initial budget appropriation for the NCIIC was $210,000,[86] which has been increased to $372,879 a year. In addition, the NCIIC has received a federal grant of $566,980 from the National Institute for Justice to facilitate DNA testing of claims in the years 2010 and 2011.[87] The commission has five staff members: the executive director, who is a lawyer and a former prosecutor; a staff attorney, who is also a former police officer and prosecutor; an investigator, who is a lawyer and who has worked in innocence projects; an administrative officer, who is a paralegal and who acts

83 N.C. Gen. Stat. § 15A-1460-75 (Supp. 2006) [N.C.G.S.].

84 *Ibid.*, § 15A-1463.

85 *Ibid.*, § 15A-1464(b).

86 Jerome M. Maiatico, "All Eyes on Us: A Comparative Critique of the North Carolina Innocence Inquiry Commission" (2007) 56 Duke L.J. 1345 at 1374 [Maiatico].

87 North Carolina Innocence Inquiry Commission (NCIIC), News Release, "Innocence Inquiry Commission Receives Federal Grant" (30 September 2009).

as a case manager; and an administrative assistant.[88] The commission is also available to offer policy advice to the legislature, if requested, on matters relating to wrongful convictions, such as legislation and other requirements for the preservation of physical evidence. It uses *pro bono* work, including work by law students at various North Carolina law schools.

Unlike the British or Scottish commission, the NCIIC is limited to claims of factual innocence, defined as

> a claim on behalf of a living person convicted of a felony in the General Court of Justice of the State of North Carolina, asserting the complete innocence of any criminal responsibility for the felony for which the person was convicted and for any other reduced level of criminal responsibility relating to the crime, and for which there is some credible, verifiable evidence of innocence that has not previously been presented at trial or considered at a hearing granted through postconviction relief.[89]

Although claims that an offender is guilty of a lesser offence are made in about 15 percent of all applications to the NCIIC, they, like claims of self-defence or diminished responsibility, are rejected because they are inconsistent with the statutory requirement and definition of factual innocence.[90] Indeed, the absence of complete factual innocence accounts for 23 percent of the cases rejected by the NCIIC, with another 18 percent of cases being rejected because there is no way to prove innocence.[91] Claims relating to procedural unfairness and claims that would otherwise be accepted by appellate courts but fall short of factual innocence would, however, be considered by either the CCRC or the SCCRC. Another difference is that the NCIIC is precluded by statute from considering applications on the behalf of deceased persons,[92] whereas the CCRC and the Scottish commission can consider such claims. In short, because it is restricted to factual innocence, the NCIIC has a much more limited mandate than other error correction commissions.

Claims made to the NCIIC are initially evaluated to determine if they satisfy the statutory criteria of actual innocence. If they qualify, a preliminary review,

---

88 See NCIIC, Commission Members, online: www.innocencecommission-nc.gov/commissioners.htm.

89 N.C.G.S., above note 83, § 15A-1460.

90 NCIIC, *Report to the 2009–2010 Long Session of the General Assembly of North Carolina* (12 March 2009) at iii, online: www.innocencecommission-nc.gov/Report2009.htm [NCIIC Report].

91 NCIIC, Case Statistics (31 December 2008), online: www.innocencecommission-nc.gov/statistics.htm.

92 N.C.G.S., above note 83, § 14-1467(a).

its purpose to gather information about the innocence claim, is conducted. The review includes compiling the documents on the case. If the case is moved into investigation, then the applicant is required to enter into a signed agreement to waive procedural rights and privileges relating to the innocence claim and to co-operate and provide full disclosure to the commission. This agreement is signed with the applicant's lawyer present, and the commission chair can appoint counsel for an indigent person. State laws relating to discovery and disclosure apply. The investigation phase is described by the NCIIC as "a detailed and lengthy process that involves interviewing witnesses, obtaining affidavits, seeking court orders for evidence, testing of physical evidence, and compiling of documentation. The entire case is comprehensively investigated with every lead followed and every fact rechecked."[93] The law also provides that

> [e]vidence of criminal acts, professional misconduct, or other wrongdoing disclosed through formal inquiry or Commission proceedings shall be referred to the appropriate authority. Evidence favorable to the convicted person disclosed through formal inquiry or Commission proceedings shall be disclosed to the convicted person and the convicted person's counsel, if the convicted person has counsel.[94]

Disclosure by the commission to the applicant is thus governed by statute, whereas disclosure by the CCRC is governed by the common law.

Since the NCIIC has the power to issue subpoenas and compel the attendance of witnesses,[95] it therefore has somewhat broader investigative powers than the CCRC. The NCIIC can refer a case to the courts for review by a majority vote on the basis that there is "sufficient evidence of factual innocence to merit judicial review."[96] This standard is narrower than that used by the CCRC or the SCCRC, which can refer cases on the basis that they will be overturned on any existing legal standard for appeals, including miscarriages of justice not related to factual innocence.[97] The NCIIC has discretion whether to hold public hearings and there is a requirement for victim notification (as with the CCRC).

Cases will be referred to a three-judge panel with no previous involvement in the case. The judicial panel can dismiss all charges on the basis of a unani-

---

93 NCIIC Report, above note 90 at 3.

94 N.C.G.S., above note 83, § 15A-1468(d).

95 *Ibid.*, §§ 15A-1467(d)–(f).

96 *Ibid.*, § 15A-1468: A unanimous decision is required if the person pled guilty, and such claims will not be considered for the first two years. This was one of the few changes the General Assembly made to the proposal by the North Carolina Actual Innocence Commission. Maiatico, above note 86 at 1345 and 1358, n. 89.

97 *CAA*, above note 24, s. 13; *Crime and Punishment (Scotland) Act*, above note 65, s. 25.

mous decision that there is a clear and convincing case of innocence.[98] In this way, there is symmetry between the grounds used by the NCIIC and the court on referral as there is with the CCRC and the SCCRC. The grounds are, of course, different with the English appeal court applying the broader standard based on safety and the Scottish court applying a miscarriage of justice standard. Both the decisions of the NCIIC and the three-judge panel are deemed to be final and not subject to appeal or judicial review.[99] In contrast, and as has been seen, decisions by the UK Court of Appeal can be appealed to the Supreme Court, formerly the House of Lords (but only on a point of law and where it is in the general interest of the public).

As of May 2010, the NCIIC had received 756 applications, rejected 532 of them while having only four cases in investigation, five cases in formal inquiry, and three cases that went to a formal hearing before the entire commission.[100]

The first case that went to a full hearing by the commission was referred to a three-judge panel. At the hearing, the defence presented evidence that the crime—sexual abuse of the applicant's then six-year-old daughter—did not take place and that the victim had been coached by her grandmother. The convicted person also testified to his innocence. The special panel found that the applicant had failed to prove by clear and convincing evidence that he was innocent of sexually abusing his daughter.[101] The accused continues to seek redress through other means as there is no appeal from the special hearing.

In the second case, in which the NCIIC held a formal hearing, the commission decided that there was not sufficient evidence of innocence. In that case, a man convicted of robbery argued that hair found in a cap at the scene should have been preserved for DNA testing, but the commission stressed the strength of the identification evidence used to convict the man in the case.[102]

In the third hearing, a special three-judge panel found clear and convincing evidence that a man convicted of a 1991 murder was innocent. Gregory Taylor had been convicted on the basis of faulty tests for blood in his car, scent detection by an untrained dog, and the testimony of a jailhouse informant.[103]

---

98 N.C.G.S., above note 83, § 15A-1469(h).

99 *Ibid.*, § 15A-1470(a).

100 NCIIC, Case Statistics, above note 91.

101 *Ibid.*; NCIIC, News Release, "Man's Conviction Upheld in Innocence Hearing" (3 September 2008), online: www.innocencecommission-nc.gov/inthenews.htm [NCIIC, inthenews].

102 NCIIC, inthenews, *ibid.*, "Hearing Concludes without Finding of Innocence" (16 January 2009).

103 "Taylor Declared Innocent after Years in Prison" *ABC* (17 February 2010), online: http://abclocal.go.com/wtvd/story?serction=news/local&id=7282220.

The NCIIC, while an interesting development, has a mandate that is much narrower than that of the CCRC or its Scottish equivalent because it is limited to claims of factual innocence. As noted above, the commission has had only three hearings on factual innocence. It is better than nothing and deserves credit for taking on non-DNA cases, but given its high factual innocence requirements, it investigates and refers a lower percentage of its cases than either the CCRC or the SCCRC. The NCIIC subjects few of its cases to full investigations or formal inquiries. The evidence to date suggests that an innocence commission such as North Carolina's is likely to affect far fewer cases than the CCRC and perhaps even fewer than were referred by the Home Secretary under the old C3 system or by the Canadian Minister of Justice.

## G. INNOCENCE PROJECTS AND THE INVESTIGATIVE MEDIA

Innocence projects are distinct from state-appointed and funded commissions, such as the CCRC or the NCIIC, because they are volunteer projects often located in law schools. In the United States, innocence projects have had significant success in their use of DNA to achieve exonerations of prisoners, many of whom had been on death row for significant periods of time. In response to the American experience, a number of university-based innocence projects have been established in many jurisdictions. In Canada, AIDWYC has achieved some notable successes. There are also some university-based innocence projects in Australia that rely mainly on DNA.[104] Stephanie Roberts and Lynne Weathered have observed that "typically Innocence Projects are under-funded and under-resourced and struggle to the meet the demands of the many calls for assistance that they receive."[105]

With the recent emphasis on innocence projects dealing with DNA, it might be tempting to overlook the work of other organizations that have worked on civil liberties and miscarriages of justice for many years. For example, in Britain, Liberty, also known as the National Council for Civil Liberties, was founded in 1934 and has been a broadly based organization dealing

104 In Australia, there are two innocence projects: the UTS Innocence Project, at the Law School of the University of Technology, Sydney; and the Australian Innocence Project, based at Griffith University, Queensland. The Griffith University project deals principally with cases where the DNA evidence relied on at trial was questionable or where there was no DNA evidence at the trial and its use could bring about a fresh evidence point. See, generally, Lynne Weathered, "The Emerging Role of Innocence Projects in the Correction of Wrongful Convictions in Australia" (2003) 12 Griffith L.R. 64.

105 Roberts & Weathered, above note 71 at 44.

with fundamental rights and freedoms in England and Wales. JUSTICE was founded in 1957 following the visit of a group of British lawyers to observe treason trials in South Africa and Hungary. The British section of the International Commission of Jurists, it was set up to promote the rule of law and to assist the fair administration of justice. Its influential reports helped establish the Ombudsman system, influenced the development of tribunals, and promoted legislation on the rehabilitation of offenders and compensation for victims of crime. It developed expertise in miscarriage of justice casework and worked with the BBC's *Rough Justice* and Channel Four's *Trial and Error* programs, which secured the release of many prisoners who had been wrongly imprisoned. With the establishment of the CCRC, it wound down its casework. There are many more organizations in the United Kingdom dealing with all aspects of miscarriages of justice. Nonetheless, since the creation of the CCRC, some serious concerns have been expressed about the British media taking less of an interest in investigating claims of wrongful convictions.[106]

Some controversy has arisen about the relationship between innocence projects and CCRC-type bodies. Hannah Quirk has expressed concerns that volunteer innocence projects could compromise, contaminate, or delay investigations by the CCRC.[107] In contrast, Stephanie Roberts and Lynne Weathered argue that innocence projects can complement the work of the CCRC. They can help to discover evidence of innocence by providing legal advice for applicants to the CCRC who may not have access to adequate legal aid and can advocate for law reform to prevent wrongful convictions.[108] As discussed above, the CCRC has recently signalled that "compelling evidence of innocence" would be most helpful and would result in referrals on the CCRC's statutory grounds that there is a real possibility of the conviction being quashed because it is not safe.[109]

## H. STRIKING THE APPROPRIATE BALANCE BETWEEN CORRECTION AND PREVENTION OF MISCARRIAGES OF JUSTICE

The skills and resources required to review and correct errors in individual cases may be different from those required to advocate remedies for the systemic

106 Paul Mason, "Press and Release: UK News Coverage of the CCRC since 1996" in Naughton, *Hope*, above note 40.

107 Hannah Quirk, "Identifying Miscarriages of Justice: Why Innocence Is Not the Answer" (2007) 70 Mod. L. Rev. 759.

108 Roberts & Weathered, above note 71 at 43.

109 CCRC, above note 30 at 5.

causes of wrongful convictions. Case-review systems are focused upon mobilizing materials and arguments in relation to discrete outcomes in particular cases. The Canadian public and Australian judicial inquiries, while focusing upon individual cases, have made many recommendations designed to reduce the risk of miscarriages of justice in the future. However, there is little evidence that many of those recommendations have been implemented.

Most jurisdictions have a law commission or law reform commission to consider systemic reforms. Indeed, the Australian Law Reform Commission has considered alternatives to royal commissions and *ad hoc* commissions of inquiry, and the Australian Human Rights Commission has considered the extent to which human rights are adequately protected by existing institutional arrangements. The UK Law Commission has considered the extent to which the rules on the admissibility of expert evidence are adequate or adequately enforced (we will address specific issues about science and admissibility in the next chapter). The Law Reform Commission of Canada called for reforms such as disclosure and proper identification procedures before it was abolished by the government.

It is clear from the experiences of Britain, Canada, and Australia that some permanent body is necessary both to recommend systemic reforms to prevent wrongful convictions and to check how they are implemented. As will be seen, without a body to supervise progress and implementation, many of the most valuable lessons to be learned from expensive royal commissions and judicial and public inquiries will wither on the vine.

## I. THE LIMITS OF ERROR CORRECTION COMMISSIONS IN ACHIEVING SYSTEMIC REFORM

Writing in 2002, Keith Findley recognized that the British CCRC model was oriented more to error correction in individual cases than to systemic reform, but he nevertheless predicted that its work could

> . . . help in the systemic reform enterprise as it could continue to highlight patterns in wrongful conviction cases, draw attention to these issues, and perhaps create a climate of enhanced reception to reform. Indeed, such a commission could also be specifically charged to monitor the errors it identifies in the system and to issue reports with recommendations for reform.[110]

110 Keith Findley, "Learning from Our Mistakes: A Criminal Justice Commission to Study Wrongful Convictions" (2002) 38 Cal. W.L. Rev. 333 at 348 [Findley].

This optimistic account is attractive and is consistent with the hopes expressed by the Runciman Royal Commission on Criminal Justice that the CCRC should draw attention "to general features of the criminal justice system which it has found unsatisfactory in the course of its work."[111] With one exception to be discussed below, the CCRC has not yet been able to fulfill this function because it has focused its limited resources on reviewing individual cases. It also lacks the necessary technology to enable it to identify patterns emerging or features of the criminal justice system that it has found unsatisfactory in the course of its work.

British law has some important safeguards with respect to wrongful convictions — legislated standards for identification procedures and the taking of statements — but most of these predate the work of the CCRC. The last decade has instead seen the government pursue an aggressive tough-on-crime approach with some of the most important "reforms" being restrictions on rights against double jeopardy and the availability of disclosure, allowing more "bad-character" evidence and prosecutorial appeals, adverse inferences from silence, and most recently, the use of anonymous witnesses.[112]

There is a danger of a false sense of security that the CCRC will catch miscarriages of justice that fall through the cracks even while the legislature widens the cracks by enacting legislation that increases the risk of wrongful convictions.[113] This observation is not an argument against the introduction of a CCRC; rather, it is a cautionary tale that suggests that error correction in individual cases should be supplemented by systemic reform efforts and the ability to monitor and critique legislative developments that will increase the risk of wrongful convictions.

Although the Runciman Royal Commission on Criminal Justice had contemplated that the CCRC would "draw attention . . . to general features of the criminal justice system which it had found unsatisfactory in the course of

---

111 Runciman Report, above note 12 at 185.

112 *Criminal Evidence (Witness Anonymity) Act 2008* (U.K.), 2008, c. 15. The legislation was enacted within a month of the House of Lords decision in *R. v. Davis*, [2008] UKHL 36, overturning a murder conviction on the basis that the accused did not have an opportunity to know the identities of three eyewitnesses and confront them.

113 For arguments that wrongful convictions create a crisis of confidence in the justice system and that the justice system will respond in a manner that affirms its legitimacy, see Richard Nobles & David Schiff, *Understanding Miscarriages of Justice: Law, the Media and the Inevitability of Crisis* (Oxford: Oxford University Press, 2000); Richard Nobles & David Schiff, "The Criminal Cases Review Commission: Reporting Success?" (2001) 64 Mod. L. Rev. 280; Robert Schehr, "The Criminal Cases Review Commission as a State Strategic Selection Mechanism" (2005) 42 Am. Crim. L. Rev. 1289.

its work, and to make any recommendations for changes it thinks fit,"[114] the CCRC's annual reports have instead focused on describing the case review process and budgetary matters.[115] When the CCRC has discussed systemic matters, it has focused on how cases it has referred to the Court of Appeal have clarified matters of law.[116]

Laurie Elks, a former CCRC commissioner, has in his helpful study of the first ten years of the CCRC, admitted that the CCRC's contribution on systemic issues has "often been insubstantial and muted."[117] He has added:

> This shortfall in the contribution of the Commission may to some extent reflect limitations on its own internal deliberations. There has been very limited debate within the Commission about directions of criminal justice policy and meetings of the Commission members have been predominantly concerned with internal and organizational issues. The fact that the Commission has not had more to say may reflect this lack of internal deliberation. It is a matter which the Commission might reflect upon for the future.[118]

Commissions, such as the CCRC, that have the extraordinary power to open up convictions may face significant pressures to adopt an impartial and quasi-judicial stance that focuses on the facts of the individual cases they examine.

The CCRC does participate appropriately with colleagues from the wider criminal justice system and the UK Law Commission to influence developments of the law in the future, responding to formal consultation processes, taking part in working groups, and providing feedback on both a formal and informal basis.[119] Nevertheless, the CCRC has not been a vocal advocate of systemic reforms designed to reduce the risk of wrongful convictions in the future. The reticence of the CCRC in this regard can perhaps be explained by the quasi-judicial role it plays with respect to referrals of cases to the court system.

That said, the CCRC made an interesting foray into systemic issues in a twenty-page response to a 2006 government consultation on appeal rights. The government document essentially proposed to abolish the Court of Appeal's ability to allow an appeal on abuse of process grounds in cases where the court was convinced that the accused was nevertheless guilty of the offence. In

114 Runciman Report, above note 12 at 185, para. 22.

115 See, for example, CCRC, *Annual Report and Accounts 2007/08* (2008), online: www.ccrc.gov.uk/CCRC_Uploads/Annual%20Report%202007%20-%202008.PDF.

116 See, for example, CCRC, *Annual Report 2002–2003* (2003) §§ 5.1-5.4; CCRC, *Annual Report 2003-2004* (2004) at 31-53.

117 Elks, above note 24 at 348.

118 *Ibid.*

119 CCRC, above note 30 at 35–36.

a submission that represented the unanimous views of its members, the CCRC responded that reform was not needed: the Court of Appeal was already cautious in allowing appeals in cases where the accused was thought to be otherwise guilty. The CCRC did not approach the issue through the narrow lens of factual innocence that its American counterpart, the NCIIC, is required to take. Rather, the CCRC argued rather strongly that procedural rules relating to interrogation and disclosure

> . . . have been established to prevent miscarriages of justice. If the legislation was to enshrine the principle that any irregularity could be overlooked—provided that those convicted are deemed plainly guilty—this would inevitably cause collateral damage to the criminal justice process by which innocent defendants would be more likely to be convicted.[120]

In short, respect for due process rights even in a case where the accused may not be factually innocent was, in the CCRC's view, important to reduce the risk of wrongful convictions in future cases. The CCRC added that the removal of appeals on abuse of power grounds would not only eliminate its ability to refer cases on those grounds to the Court of Appeal but "would represent a gross violation of the present constitutional settlement for the separation of powers."[121] The CCRC was joined by members of the senior judiciary and various bar groups and legal experts in opposing the government's proposals, now abandoned for the time being.[122]

This episode suggests that it would be wrong to conclude that the CCRC is incapable of engaging with systemic issues that will affect its future work; however, such intervention has been rare and limited to grounds of appeal that directly affect the CCRC's work.

## J. SYSTEMIC REFORM MODELS

A number of bodies have been given a mandate to make recommendations about systemic reforms in order to prevent wrongful convictions or miscarriages of justice in future cases. Such commissions include judicial and public inquiries appointed to examine well-publicized miscarriages of justice and to make recommendations to prevent them in the future. They also include

---

120 *CCRC Response to Quashing Convictions* Consultation Paper (11 December 2006) at para. 36, online: www.ccrc.gov.uk/CCRC_Uploads/QUASHING_CONVICTIONS_RESPONSE_FOR_WEBSITE.pdf.

121 *Ibid.* at para. 65.

122 *Criminal Justice and Immigration Act 2008*, above note 63, Sch. 8.

government-appointed commissions with a mandate to examine systemic issues, such as capital punishment in the United States, and self-appointed projects that examine systemic issues, sometimes in conjunction with examining specific cases of proven or suspected wrongful convictions. Although these commissions may examine specific cases of wrongful convictions, they all have a mandate to make systemic reform recommendations.

### 1) The Canadian Public Inquiries

The pioneer and gold standard of the systemic reform model are the public inquiries appointed by Canadian governments to investigate individual cases of wrongful convictions.[123] Since 1989, there have been seven such inquiries appointed by provincial governments in Canada, and all have been conducted by either sitting or retired judges. The appointment of such inquiries, which is at the discretion of the provincial cabinet, is generally reserved for the most notorious cases. The inquiries typically have multi-million-dollar budgets that are used to conduct extensive investigations and hearings into the causes of the particular wrongful convictions. They can also commission research into the systemic causes of wrongful convictions. They issue detailed reports that make extensive factual findings about the particular case as well as policy recommendations intended to prevent a reoccurrence of similar miscarriages of justice. Canadian public inquiries are temporary institutions, and their mandate is completed with the issue of a public report. Governments are not required to follow their recommendations.

The first Canadian public inquiry to examine a wrongful conviction was conducted in Nova Scotia between 1986 and 1989. The inquiry investigated the wrongful conviction of Donald Marshall Jr., a young Aboriginal man, wrongfully convicted of murder.[124] It was headed by three sitting judges taken from outside the province in order to provide independence. The judges unsuccessfully sought to subpoena some of the judges who had sat on Marshall's case (despite conflicts of interest) and who had essentially blamed Marshall for his

123 Australia and Britain have also appointed royal commissions into specific wrongful convictions: the Splatt and Chamberlain commissions in Australia and the May Inquiry in the United Kingdom. See Kathryn Campbell, "Policy Reponses to Wrongful Convictions" (2005) 41 Criminal Law Bulletin 4; Kent Roach, "Inquiring into the Causes of Wrongful Convictions" (1999) 35 Criminal Law Bulletin 152; Richard Wolson & Aaron London, "The Structure, Operation and Impact of Wrongful Conviction Inquiries" (2004) 52 Drake L. Rev. 677.

124 *Royal Commission on the Donald Marshall, Jr., Prosecution* (Halifax, NS: The Commission, 1989) [Marshall Inquiry].

own wrongful conviction.[125] The Marshall Inquiry made factual findings that helped exonerate Marshall in respect of claims made by the Court of Appeal that he was engaged in a robbery at the time that another person killed his companion. It also made sweeping reform recommendations for the justice system, including greater independence for prosecutors from political pressures and a provision that would have required pretrial disclosure of relevant information held by prosecutors.

Two Ontario inquiries and one in Manitoba have focused on the frailties of forensic evidence: two on hair and fibre analysis and the other on pediatric forensic pathology.[126] The Ontario inquiries recommended multiple reforms with respect to the organization of forensic services in the province. Many of the reforms have been implemented or are in the course of being implemented. These inquiries examined flaws in specific cases, but made recommendations designed to help prevent those and other flaws in future cases.

While investigating specific wrongful convictions, Canadian inquiries have provided in-depth analysis of a number of subjects. These include the use of jailhouse informants; the phenomenon of tunnel vision, where the police and prosecutor discount other possible suspects; proper identification procedures; the adequacy of defence representation; and disclosure issues, including those relating to DNA. They have also looked at the process through which a convicted person applies to the federal Minister of Justice to reopen a case on grounds of a suspected miscarriage of justice once the accused's appeals have been exhausted.

There is a need for a systemic audit of the degree to which the many policy recommendations of the Canadian public inquiries have (or have not) been implemented. The inquiries were conducted by the provinces, and their impact in other provinces is uncertain.

No inquiry has led the federal Parliament, which has exclusive jurisdiction over criminal law, to amend the *Criminal Code* of Canada. One rather spectacular failure has been the federal government's rejection of a CCRC model. In 2002, it reformed its procedures for dealing with applications to the Minister of Justice to reopen criminal convictions, despite the fact that three

---

125 *Hickman v. Mackeigan*, [1989] 2 S.C.R. 796.

126 *Report of the Kaufman Commission on Proceedings involving Guy Paul Morin* (Toronto: Ministry of the Attorney General, 1998) [Morin Inquiry]; *Report of the Commission of Inquiry into Certain Aspects of the Trial and Conviction of James Driskell* (Winnipeg: The Commission, 2007) [Driskell Inquiry]; *Report of the Inquiry into Pediatric Forensic Pathology in Ontario* (Toronto: Ministry of the Attorney General, 2008) [Goudge Inquiry].

inquiries had by that time recommended a CCRC-type commission.[127] Subsequent inquiries also included a similar recommendation. Recommendations with respect to police procedures, such as the use of double-blind procedures, sequential photo lineups, and videotaping of interrogations, have not been implemented in the Canadian *Criminal Code* although they are used in some jurisdictions.

Other reforms proposed by Canadian inquiries have been implemented. Although it was only tangentially related to the specific wrongful conviction reviewed, Nova Scotia introduced the *Public Prosecutions Statute*[128] to create the position of Director of Public Prosecutions following the recommendation of the 1989 Marshall Inquiry. Reforms were initiated in Ontario's Centre of Forensic Sciences in response to the Morin Inquiry's recommendations.[129] Ontario's *Coroners Amendment Act*[130] was amended to create a registry of forensic pathologists and make other reforms in the wake of the Goudge Inquiry on pediatric forensic pathology. The new legislation assigns responsibility to the chief forensic pathologist with respect to the maintenance of a registry of qualified forensic pathologists and any complaints that may be made about forensic pathologists.[131] The chief forensic pathologist, along with the chief coroner, will be subject to oversight by a Death Investigation Oversight Council.[132]

An important feature of the Canadian inquiries is that some of their reform recommendations are addressed, or can be implemented, by the unelected judiciary. The most important reform stemming from a Canadian public inquiry has been the Supreme Court of Canada's recognition of a broad constitutional requirement that the prosecutor disclose all relevant information to the accused, regardless of whether it could be classified as incriminatory or exculpatory.[133] The 1991 decision was in large part based on the 1989 recommendations of the Marshall Inquiry that the *Criminal Code* be amended to require pretrial disclosure by the prosecutor. The Canadian public inquiries, combined with

---

127 *Criminal Code*, R.S.C. 1985, c. C-46, ss. 696.1–696.6, as amended S.C. 2002, c. 13, s. 71.

128 *Public Prosecutions Act* (N.S.), S.N.S. 1990, c. 21.

129 See Jeffrey R. Manishen, "Wrongful Convictions, Lessons Learned: The Canadian Experience" (2006) 13 Journal of Clinical Forensic Medicine 296 at 297–98 (detailing post-inquiry reforms, including DNA testing of hair, recording of preliminary reports, increased training, new protocols for reports and complaints, documentation of contamination, monitoring of courtroom testimony, and creation of an advisory board and a quality assurance unit).

130 S.O. 2009, c. 15.

131 *Ibid.*, ss. 7 & 7.1.

132 *Ibid.*, ss. 8 & 8.1.

133 *R. v. Stinchcombe*, [1991] 3 S.C.R. 326.

the work of the CCRC in Britain and DNA exonerations in the United States, also helped convince the Supreme Court of Canada to reverse its position and refuse to allow the extradition of fugitives without the assurance that the death penalty would not be applied.[134]

Just as error correction commissions can make limited forays into systemic reforms, so, too, may systemic reform commissions be involved in error correction. Canadian public inquiries have typically been appointed after a conviction has been reversed by the courts, but at times, they have played a role in more fully correcting the errors in the case. For example, Canada's first wrongful conviction inquiry exonerated Donald Marshall Jr. of wrongdoing in his wrongful conviction in the wake of a Court of Appeal decision that had blamed Marshall for his wrongful conviction. Similarly, the Sophonow Inquiry played a role in Thomas Sophonow's exoneration in a non-DNA case in which proceedings were stayed after three trials.[135] A recent Canadian inquiry has also called for reviews of other cases involving evidence of shaken baby syndrome,[136] and six of the Canadian public inquiries have called for the creation of a CCRC-type body to hear and investigate claims of wrongful convictions in other cases.[137] Thus, systemic reform commissions can contribute to error correction in notorious cases; however, no jurisdiction will call a public inquiry into every alleged miscarriage of justice. Such cases will be dealt with through a petition procedure directed towards an Attorney General as in Australia and Canada, or by an application to a CCRC-type body.

One limitation on the ability of systemic reform institutions to advance the cause of error correction is that systemic reform commissions are likely to focus on the more notorious wrongful convictions. In Canada and Australia, all the public inquiries called by the government have been into high-profile homicide cases. There have been no public inquiries into less notorious wrongful convictions, including a number in sexual assault cases. The focus of systemic reform institutions on the most well-publicized cases of wrongful convictions might be a weakness in its own right. This is especially so, given recent arguments that the innocence movement should expand beyond concerns about the conviction of the innocent as well as criticisms that innocence scholarship

---

134 *United States of America v. Burns and Rafay*, [2001] 1 S.C.R. 283.

135 *The Inquiry regarding Thomas Sophonow* (Winnipeg: Manitoba Justice, 2001) [Sophonow Inquiry].

136 Goudge Inquiry, above note 126.

137 The Australian royal commissions into both the Chamberlain and Splatt cases were even more directly involved in error correction because, unlike the Canadian inquiries, they were conducted before the convictions in those cases were reversed.

is impoverished by not using controls, such as studies of the rightfully acquitted and convicted.[138] Indeed, a broader based systemic reform commission could evolve into a permanent law reform commission able to conduct studies of the operation of the criminal justice system and make recommendations about a wide range of issues.[139]

## K. CONCLUSION

The revelation of many wrongful convictions in Canada and Australia affirms the urgent need for better and more accessible remedies for the innocent who have been convicted as well as systemic reforms designed to reduce the number of miscarriages of justice in the future. It may be unrealistic to expect that there will be uniform approaches to the role of commissions because "each jurisdiction differs; no one model fits all."[140] That said, however, commissions may fail if unrealistic hopes are pinned on them.

If CCRC-type bodies are to be established in Australia or Canada or if the CCRC in Britain is to remain a credible, permanent, independent, and objective part of the wider criminal justice systems, policy makers and the public should have a clearer understanding of their precise roles, as well as the limits of those roles. The available evidence suggests that however good an error correction commission may be in investigating cases and referring cases of concern back to the courts, it may not have the resources or the personnel either to develop proposals for systemic reform or to advocate for such changes. A CCRC-type commission will also be dependent on the approach taken by the appellate courts to questions such as lurking doubt and fresh evidence.

Systemic reform commissions can build on individual cases of wrongful convictions, but they, too, will be dependent on political will to implement their recommendations. They will have an incentive to focus on notorious wrongful convictions and not to investigate new cases that may not present a good vehicle for systemic reform recommendations. Systemic reform institutions may also have an incentive to win support for their recommendations by stressing that wrongful convictions allow the guilty to go free. The Runciman

---

138 Richard Leo, "Rethinking the Study of Miscarriages of Justice" (2005) 21 Journal of Contemporary Criminal Justice 201.

139 In Canada, a federal law commission was recently abolished, and in the United Kingdom, the Law Commission has focused on matters of statutory reform of the criminal law. A 2009 project was set up to examine the role of expert witnesses, including their possible contribution to wrongful convictions. (We will discuss this further in Chapter 11.)

140 Findley, above note 110 at 339.

Royal Commission on Criminal Justice is best remembered today for making the recommendation that led to the creation of the CCRC, but it was criticized at the time of its 1993 release for its crime control recommendations on matters such as the right to silence and defence disclosure.

The criminal justice systems in Australia, Britain, and Canada (and elsewhere, we suspect) still experience miscarriages of justice. Those countries need to address this problem in a comprehensive manner that includes both error correction of past miscarriages of justice and the prevention of future miscarriages of justice. Bodies such as the CCRC need not only correct errors but also make available to policy makers the information that will help prevent future miscarriages of justice. If they do not directly advocate for systemic reform, they need to provide information that will allow others to evaluate criminal justice and forensic science policies from a perspective of their likely effects on miscarriages of justice. The next chapter, Chapter 11, will deal with some possible improvements to the forensic sciences that may help prevent miscarriages of justice in future cases.

CHAPTER 11

# Improving Forensic Science

The general theme of this book is to compare responses to miscarriages of justice in Britain, Canada, and Australia with a focus on those that have been caused by faulty investigations and faulty forensic evidence. Repeated problems which have occurred in all jurisdictions have arisen from the misuse or misapplication of scientific knowledge. They include the use of preliminary tests as conclusive evidence; failure to identify or disclose procedural errors in the use of scientific methods or tests; misinterpretation or misunderstanding of the significance of findings; and experts going beyond their area of expertise or not explaining their findings or controversies and uncertainties in the science in a clear, impartial manner. To some extent, such matters can be addressed by better quality management systems and better oversight provisions, including the oversight of how forensic scientists prepare their reports and present their evidence in court. There is, however, a deeper issue, one that we address in this chapter.

In this context it is worth bearing in mind the comments of Richard Foster, CCRC chairman, in his evidence to the UK House of Commons:

> The main trend that you see is that the classic historic miscarriage cases—that would be cases arising from improprieties in police procedures, the sort of things that went on pre PACE [*Police and Criminal Evidence Act*]—have largely, if not entirely, disappeared now (the sort of verballing of suspects and so on). What you see a lot more of nowadays is cases that become problematic because of issues around scientific evidence. That is quite a pronounced

> trend. We continue to see a large number of miscarriages that are around non-disclosure of evidence.[1]

The many cases examined in Chapters 8 and 9 concerning forensic science and forensic pathology provide ample evidence of the contributions that science has made to miscarriages of justice.

Apart from problems with the way in which we use, apply, and interpret science, there are difficulties with the very nature of the science. Forensic scientists and forensic pathologists have contributed to miscarriages of justice because in large part lawyers, judges, and juries have deferred to them or been awed by claims to scientific expertise and objectivity. The rhetoric of the system pretends that the scientific expert witness is giving objective, reliable evidence and is above the adversarial fray, but recent reports by the UK Law Commission and the Canadian Goudge Inquiry criticize judges for not ensuring the threshold reliability of expert scientific evidence offered by the state to secure convictions. The Goudge Inquiry also found that pathologist Dr. Charles Smith did not fully appreciate that his role was to provide the court with impartial evidence as opposed to helping the prosecution win its case. In addition, a major report by the National Academy of Sciences (NAS) in the United States suggests that many forensic sciences fail to follow the basic research methods of science. In this chapter, we will first review the work that has been done by the NAS and then relate that report to the recommendations of the other inquiries we have examined in this book, in particular, the recent Goudge Inquiry.

We will then consider in broad terms what reforms might be beneficial. We stress the need for comprehensive reform of forensic sciences that goes beyond the piecemeal approach that has often characterized past reforms. Important reforms followed both the recommendations of the Morin and Goudge inquiries, but they were limited to the specific forensic disciplines that came under review and to the province of Ontario. We note that both the recent *NAS Report* in the United States and the 1993 Runciman Royal Commission on Criminal Justice in the United Kingdom recommended national regulation and audit of all the forensic sciences. A forensic science regulator was recently appointed in the United Kingdom, and he is advised by various forensic sciences advisory committees. Comprehensive regulation of the all forensic sciences that may testify in criminal trials is a key strategy to prevent miscarriages of justice.

Another strategy we will examine is increased judicial regulation, or gatekeeping, before forensic scientists are allowed to testify as experts in court. The

1 House of Commons Justice Committee, "The Work of the Criminal Cases Review Commission" Examination of Witnesses (10 March 2009).

NAS has expressed scepticism about the courts' ability to do this. Its view is based on the American experience of the limited contributions that courts can make to improving the forensic sciences and the reluctance of courts to prevent forensic science experts from testifying. Nevertheless, some developments in Canada and some proposals by the UK Law Commission could allow judges to play a more robust role in ensuring the adequacy and reliability of forensic evidence in criminal trials.

## A. ASSESSMENT OF THE STATE OF THE SCIENCE: THE *NAS REPORT*

The US Congress asked the prestigious National Academy of Sciences (NAS) to investigate the forensic sciences. The committee was chaired by a federal judge and a scientist and included many accomplished scientists, lawyers, and practitioners of forensic science. The chair heard extensive evidence and concluded that a consistent message was that "the forensic science system, encompassing both research and practice, has serious problems that can only be addressed by a national commitment to overhaul the current structure that supports the forensic science community in this country."[2] The report focused on the American experience which is more fragmented at city, county, state, and national levels than those in Australia, Britain, or Canada. Nevertheless, the report's findings about the state of the science behind forensic science transcend national boundaries.

The *NAS Report* points to the danger of giving undue weight to evidence derived from imperfect testing and analysis.[3] It also points to the wide variability across the forensic disciplines with regard to techniques, methodologies, reliability, the types and numbers of potential errors, and the wide variation in the quality of published material. It says the language used to express findings and their reliability is variable and confusing. Many interpretations of findings are also subject to the idiosyncrasies of the researchers or their particular research environment, and may lead to confusion when transferred to other disciplines or geographical areas. Yet, in a criminal trial, a number of experts with different disciplinary backgrounds may be attempting to communicate

---

2 National Research Council, Committee on Identifying the Needs of the Forensic Sciences Community, *Strengthening Forensic Science in the United States: A Path Forward* (Washington, DC: National Academies Press, 2009) at xx [*NAS Report*], online: www.ncjrs.gov/pdffiles1/nij/grants/228091.pdf.

3 *Ibid.* at 4.

with lawyers, judges, and jurors unfamiliar with those disciplines and also the means by which any uncertainties can be identified and expressed.[4]

The *NAS Report* notes that two important questions should be addressed:

1) To what extent is a particular forensic discipline founded on a reliable scientific methodology?
2) To what extent do forensic experts within a particular discipline rely upon methods of interpretation that can avoid being tainted by error, bias or lack of sound operational procedures?[5]

The report points to the *Daubert* case,[6] where it was stated that an important difference exists between the quest for truth in the laboratory and the quest for truth in the courtroom.[7] Nevertheless, the court in that case encouraged judges to pay attention to questions such as the reliability and error rate of scientific evidence before allowing it to be used in court. Lawyers will be familiar with the idea that legal truth is a "negotiated" outcome, with proponents in the adversarial system putting forward competing versions and the untrained jurors then identifying what appears to them to make most sense. It is hardly surprising then that lawyers should look to the "certainty" of the sciences with envy. However, their view may be based upon a misunderstanding. As Judy Bourke put it, "A Solicitor-General for South Australia, J.J. Doyle QC, could not have expressed the point more erroneously: 'The adversarial system adjudicates upon the respective merits of cases. The scientist is concerned with absolute truth or fact'."[8] As Bourke explains, scientists are concerned with *probabilities*, not with conclusive truths. It is important that the law better understand the probabilistic and dynamic nature of science and not equate science with absolute and infallible truths.

## B. SPECIFIC FORENSIC DISCIPLINES REVIEWED BY THE *NAS REPORT*

The *NAS Report*, otherwise known as *Strengthening Forensic Science in the United States: A Path Forward*, critically scrutinized a wide range of forensic disciplines.

---

4 The UK case of *R. v. Harris & Ors*, [2005] EWCA Crim 1980 in the context of injuries and infant deaths is an example.

5 *NAS Report*, above note 2 at 87.

6 *Daubert v. Merrell Dow Pharmaceuticals, Inc.*, 509 U.S. 579 (1993) [*Daubert*].

7 *NAS Report*, above note 2 at 12.

8 Judy Bourke, "Misapplied Science, Unreliability in Scientific Test Evidence" (1993) 10 Austl. Bar Rev. 183 at 191 citing John Doyle, "Admissibility of Opinion Evidence" (1987) 61 Austl. L. J. 688 at 694.

## 1) DNA

The report points out that of all forensic disciplines, DNA is the most stringent with protocols in place for both the laboratories and the processing procedures; however, it also points out that errors are possible in both processing and interpretation.[9] Unlike many other forensic sciences, DNA technology emerged from the universities where it was subject to significant research and peer review. Although DNA has now become the gold standard of the forensic sciences, its use in court was vigorously resisted at first. DNA standards and protocols improved as a response to these challenges.[10] As will be seen, many of the older forensic sciences have received a free ride from the courts, which may have played a role in the failure to engage in adequate research and testing of their underlying premises.

## 2) Controlled Substances

The report suggests that the main issues in this area relate to sampling which can involve a wide range of methods. It also points out that while results are reported, "spectra, chromatograms, and other evidence of the analysis and the chemist's notes are not submitted."[11] Possible sources of error are thus unlikely to be disclosed.

However, a 2009 decision of the US Supreme Court might well have changed things.[12] The 6:3 majority decision states that crime laboratory reports may not be used against criminal defendants at trial unless the analysts responsible for creating them give testimony and subject themselves to cross-examination. The dissenting judges said doing this would subject the criminal justice system to "a crushing burden"[13] and that it means "guilty defendants will go free, on the most technical grounds."[14] Justice Scalia, for the majority, said the requirement "is designed to weed out not only the fraudulent analyst, but the incompetent one as well."[15] He added that the American Constitu-

9 *NAS Report*, above note 2 at 133. Chapter 5 of the report assesses the specific forensic disciplines.

10 Jay Aronson, *Genetic Witness Science, Law and Controversy in the Making of DNA Profiling* (New Brunswick, NJ: Rutgers University Press, 2007). See Chapter 8, Section D, where it deals with DNA cases.

11 *NAS Report*, above note 2 at 135. See also *Daubert*, above note 6.

12 *Melendez-Diaz v. Massachusetts*, 557 U.S. ___ (2009).

13 *Ibid.* at 13.

14 *Ibid.* at 14.

15 *Ibid.* at 13.

tion would require allowing defendants to confront witnesses even if "all analysts always possessed the scientific acumen of Mme. Curie and the veracity of Mother Teresa."[16] This decision underlines the potential for the legal system to contribute to the reliability of science.

The *NAS Report*, however, takes a more pessimistic approach to what the legal system can achieve. It concludes that defence lawyers have been ineffective in challenging forensic evidence presented by the state, even under relatively strict *Daubert* standards.[17] This weakness is undoubtedly related to poor funding because large corporate defendants in civil cases have been able to use *Daubert* to keep unverified science out of civil trials. Instead of relying on increased funding and training for defence lawyers and adverse judicial decisions to reform the forensic sciences, the *NAS Report* focuses on improving the forensic sciences themselves.

### 3) Fingerprints

The *NAS Report* takes the view that comparisons based upon friction ridge analysis share similarities with other experience-based methods of pattern recognition, such as tire impressions, tool marks, and handwriting analysis.[18] Here, the testing facilities may or may not be accredited, training of individuals varies widely, and no auditing of the content of such programs occurs. The initial analysis of the unknown (latent) print depends upon physical characteristics of donor and surface contacted as well as mediating factors, such as sweat, oils, powders, and the dynamics of touch or contact. Methods of characterizing the initial print and comparing it with the known print involve a wide range of subjective judgments. In other words, the process is not repeatable, and not infrequently, the criteria involved are not stated. Results are stated in terms of "match" rather than probability assessments. The report concludes that the methodologies involved cannot be tested, and as the reporting outcomes are likely to be misleading, "experts should exhibit a greater degree of epistemological humility."[19]

---

16 *Ibid.* at 14, n. 6.

17 *NAS Report*, above note 2 at 110.

18 *Ibid.* at 136.

19 *Ibid.* at 142, citing Jennifer L. Mnookin, "The Validity of Latent Fingerprint Identification: Confessions of a Fingerprinting Moderate" (2008) 7 Law, Probability and Risk 127 at 139.

## 4) Other Pattern Evidence

The report states that other evidence relating to tools, tires, footwear, bite marks, and ballistics involves problems similar to those of fingerprints. It states that various training programs do not necessarily require an understanding of the scientific basis of the examinations and do not mandate the use of a validated scientific methodology. It suggests that work in this area is particularly susceptible to biases that can arise in any "experience-based" system without an appropriate feedback mechanism to allow for correction of errors.[20]

In the British case of *Dallagher*, the conviction was based almost entirely on prosecution expert testimony relating to the comparison of an ear-print made by the accused with a latent ear-print found on a window at the scene of a murder.[21] At the trial one prosecution expert said he was "absolutely convinced" that the print was that of the accused, and the second expert said it was only "a remote possibility" that the print had been left by someone else. On appeal, the conviction was quashed, and a retrial ordered because fresh evidence cast doubts on the extent to which ear-print evidence, standing alone, could safely be used to identify the offender. In 2004 at Dallagher's second trial, the prosecution had to drop its case against him because DNA evidence taken from the latent print unequivocally established that it had been left by someone else.[22]

## 5) Reference Image Databases

The report points to a number of databases that deal with issues such as ballistics and footwear and that contain a comprehensive collection of images. It states much useful work could be done with regard to the further development of such databases.[23]

## 6) Hair Evidence

The report points to the inherent variability of samples, even from the same person, and the inherent difficulties of classification of features. It observes that probabilistic assessments have been shown by DNA to be unreliable, and

---

20 *Ibid.* at 149.

21 *Re Dallagher*, [2002] EWCA Crim 1903.

22 Great Britain, Law Commission, *The Admissibility of Expert Evidence in Criminal Proceedings in England and Wales: A New Approach to the Determination of Evidentiary Reliability: 2009* (Consultation Paper No. 190) (Norwich: T.S.O., 2009) at 11, n. 4.

23 *NAS Report*, above note 2 at 153.

significant issues of examiner bias arise.[24] In Canada, public inquiries into the wrongful convictions of Guy Paul Morin and James Driskell showed how analysts overstated their conclusions about similarities of hair samples.[25] In these cases, DNA analysis was able to establish that the so-called matched hairs came from different people; however, DNA analysis cannot or will not be done in every case, and hair and fibre analysis has not been rejected by the courts as evidence. A recent study has found that invalid hair comparisons were a factor in 38 percent of American DNA exonerations.[26]

### 7) Other Issues

The report discusses the comparison of writing, documents, paints and coatings, explosives, fires, bite marks, and bloodstain pattern analysis. The overall assessment is that while each area involves reliable scientific components, such as analytical techniques for identifying inks, blood, and combustion residues, it is difficult for scientists to explain their findings in terms of probabilities that will be meaningful to people who have to assess the probative values in the context of criminal trials.[27]

## C. *NAS REPORT*'S OVERALL ASSESSMENT OF THE USE OF FORENSIC SCIENCE IN THE LEGAL PROCESS

The *NAS Report* states that more research must be conducted to identify appropriate language to express probabilities of results in ways that will be meaningful to the legal process. The report takes up the point that many of the Canadian inquiry reports made about the use of language. Words such as "match," "consistent with," "similar in all respects," and "cannot be excluded as the source of" can have a significant impact at a trial and yet have many variable meanings.

Contextual bias (including expectations and suggestions) is an important issue that requires further research to identify its role in forensic work and

---

24 *Ibid.* at 158.

25 *Report of the Commission of Inquiry into Certain Aspects of the Trial and Conviction of James Driskell* (Winnipeg: The Commission, 2007), online: www.driskellinquiry.ca/pdf/final_report_jan2007.pdf [Driskell Inquiry]; *Report of the Kaufman Commission on Proceedings Involving Guy Paul Morin* (Toronto: Ministry of the Attorney General, 1998), online: www.attorneygeneral.jus.gov.on.ca/english/about/pubs/morin/ [Morin Inquiry].

26 Brandon L. Garrett & Peter J. Neufeld, "Invalid Forensic Science Testimony and Wrongful Convictions" (2009) 95 Va. L. Rev. 1 at 47 [Garrett & Neufeld].

27 *NAS Report*, above note 2 at 163–79.

education to help deal with it.[28] Related to that, the report states that forensic laboratories should be operated independently of (or autonomously within) police and other law enforcement agencies. Laboratories should be able to set their own priorities with respect to cases and expenditures.

The report says that proper scales for developing levels of confidence or certainty have not yet been developed. It notes that all results should indicate the degree of uncertainty in measurements; appropriate research should be conducted to enable the results to be properly quantified. Without proper knowledge of individual variability, it is not possible to determine how many similarities might constitute a match.

The *NAS Report* affirms that laboratory reports must include at least methods, materials, procedures, results, and conclusions along with appropriate indications of uncertainty. It points out that most reports do not meet these standards. Without clear characterization of the nature and scope of uncertainties, such laboratory reports can be misleading.[29]

A major finding of the *NAS Report* was the need for proper research to validate the premises and techniques being used. The report pointed out that few forensic practitioners or academics conduct relevant research—proper funding is lacking. Close involvement with prosecutors and an apprenticeship model of training does not lead to objective methods. Rigorous research and protocols to express the findings are essential and can benefit from research in other areas, such as cognitive psychology. The report said that clearly specifying the question being addressed was crucial and that some techniques cannot identify individuals involved but might be able to exclude people.[30] In most disciplines, studies have not been undertaken to establish uniqueness of marks or features, and yet practitioners make probabilistic claims without statistical foundation. The report said that experience-based probability claims without some statistical expression of experience are virtually meaningless.[31]

The major recommendation of the report was that significant new funding, together with collaborative research, is required to provide a proper scientific basis for many of the forensic disciplines. The *NAS Report* recommended that a new national institute of forensic science should implement and guide these strategies. It said that many concerns can be addressed immediately through studies in which forensic science practitioners are provided with a standardized

---

28 *Ibid.* at 184–85. Chapter 6 of the *NAS Report* addresses improving methods, practice, and performance in forensic science, including the issue of bias.

29 *Ibid.* at 185–86.

30 *Ibid.* at 188.

31 *Ibid.* at 188–89.

set of training materials to explain the complexities of the decision process. It also referred to the extent to which skilled practitioners will reach similar conclusions when presented with materials that lead to disagreements.[32]

## D. STRENGTHENING OVERSIGHT OF FORENSIC PRACTICES

The *NAS Report* stated that with few exceptions, there are no formal requirements to mandate accreditation and enforcement of standards. It pointed to the Houston Police Department Crime Lab which was found to have poor documentation, serious analytical and interpretive errors, inadequate training, use of inaccurate and misleading statistics and even "drylabbing" (the falsification of scientific results). The American Bar Association has recommended accreditation and standardization of procedures.[33]

### 1) Accreditation

Accreditation requires management practices that monitor activity and respond to deviations from standards. It does not ensure that errors will not occur and it does not depend upon self-assessment. It requires some form of external oversight. The *NAS Report* says that some form of national organization is required to mediate the accreditation process. It points out that accreditation is normally part of a process that involves education and training programs. Such assessments cannot prevent intentional deviation from standards, but they can increase the likelihood of detection where they occur.[34]

The report outlines the development of accrediting organizations, especially the American Society of Crime Laboratory Directors (ASCLD) and the DNA Advisory Board (DNAB). Since 2003 there have been moves to implement ISO standards, now available from the International Organization for Standardization, for laboratory accreditation. They involve management and operational procedures, personnel qualifications, and the operation of the physical plant. The complex program requires periodic reviews and surveillance and reporting of errors or concerns. The uptake of accreditation is uneven and, of course, many procedures relevant to criminal investigations take place outside of crime laboratories.[35]

32 *Ibid.* at 189–90.
33 *Ibid.* at 193–94. *NAS Report*, c. 7, addresses strengthening oversight of forensic science practices.
34 *Ibid.* at 195 and 197.
35 *Ibid.* at 197–200.

## 2) Standards and Guidelines

The *NAS Report* points out that the development of standards is an important step in the reduction of bias and individual idiosyncrasies. For example, standards may specify the necessary criteria before something can be referred to as a "match." They allow for replication of procedures and for methodological errors to be distinguished from practitioner errors. They are an essential tool for any accreditation program. The report points out that the American Society of Testing and Materials has developed standards to deal with issues such as document analysis, paint, paper, and fibre analysis. There is also the National Institute of Standards and Technology which engages in research and promotes standards in areas dealing with gunshot residue, trace explosives, and explosive devices. Furthermore, a European Network of Forensic Science Institutes has guidance documentation for laboratories to use in validating techniques used in forensic casework. The FBI has also developed scientific working groups (SWGs) to develop consensus on protocols and policies. These cover areas such as tool marks, document and materials analysis, fingerprints, and tire and shoe impressions.[36]

The *NAS Report* points out that with the proliferation of standards, voluntary membership in standards-setting organizations, and inconsistent application, it is difficult to assess their impact. Without sanctions for non-compliance, measures to identify non-compliance become less effective.[37]

## 3) Proficiency Testing

ASCLD and ISO programs promote proficiency testing as a key tool in the development and monitoring of standards. While some disciplines have had such standards in place for many years, recent court decisions have described the practices as not being sufficiently rigorous. Open and blind testing distinguish whether the person being tested is aware of the assessment. Other procedures may require tests to be conducted by an external laboratory or may involve reanalysis of prior casework. Among laboratories in the United States, most used open testing methods, and about half engaged in random case reanalysis. About 26 percent used blind tests. Most laboratories used externally generated tests which allowed some degree of comparison.[38]

---

36 *Ibid.* at 201–6.

37 *Ibid.* at 203.

38 *Ibid.* at 206–8.

### 4) Individual Certification

The *NAS Report* points out that many professions require certification in order to practise, and it takes the view that the same should apply to forensic science practitioners who give evidence in court. Indeed, the American Bar Association has recommended the use of written examinations, proficiency testing, continuing education, an ethical code, and disciplinary procedures. The report acknowledges that some organizations do provide certification programs, but may lack stringent requirements. Certifying boards exist in areas such as crime-scene investigations, document examination, toxicology, death investigation, and engineering sciences. Certification programs exist in areas of bloodstain pattern analysis, crime-scene investigation, art, photography, fingerprints, trace analysis, firearms and tool marks, odontology (application of the science of dentistry to the field of law), and pathology.[39]

### 5) Linking Funding with Improvements

The *NAS Report* points out that provision of grants may require certain standards as a condition of funding; however, it notes that for the federal Coverdell grants for forensic science improvement in the United States, there had not been effective monitoring and enforcement of the applicable conditions. Although more resources need to be devoted to the forensic sciences, the funding should not be delivered by a blank cheque. Funding should be tied to specific improvements and upgrading of the forensic sciences.[40]

## E. RECOMMENDATIONS RELATED TO EDUCATION AND TRAINING

The report has recommended that proper funding be put in place to mandate development of standards and the certification and accreditation of organizations and individuals. There should be proper testing procedures and quality monitoring of laboratories and individuals along with a national code of ethics. It is important to develop mechanisms for enforcement of serious ethical violations.[41]

39 *Ibid.* at 208–10.
40 *Ibid.* at 210–12.
41 *Ibid.* at 214–15.

## 1) Education and Training

A major thrust of the report was to recommend the move away from apprentice-like training to that based upon sound scientific and educational principles. Being able to replicate the working processes of a mentor is one thing, but it is quite another to understand the relevant intellectual issues, especially regarding the limits of what is involved. Increasing numbers of undergraduate and postgraduate courses deal with forensic issues; however, there is also a need for further and continuing education. Beyond this there is a need to educate consumers of legal services, particularly judges and lawyers, about the issues and limitations involved.[42]

Many laboratories have serious backlogs of work to be done. To attain a turnaround time of thirty days for tests, some areas (such as DNA) would need to increase personnel by as much as 73 percent. As complexity increases, so, too, do the demands for appropriate educational achievements. Many laboratories now demand that analysts have some postgraduate qualifications in addition to their undergraduate degrees in physics, chemistry, or forensic science. The proliferation of programs based upon media popularity in this area has led to a bewildering mix of justice and science programs with a wide variation in standards. General science courses may well be a useful starting point, but they do not cover key forensic issues such as ethics, evidence, and the role of an expert witness. The US National Institute of Justice has undertaken assessments for the minimum educational requirements in these areas. Education and training programs should be linked to the attainment of accreditation requirements.[43]

## 2) Research and Training

The report states that student research and exposure to research is a critical component of forensic science education. Proper development requires more funding for university-based research programs which should be coordinated at a national rather than at a state level. In certain areas, such as those dealing with controlled substances, twelve months of practical training might be sufficient. In other areas, where the analysis is experience based (such as fingerprint, firearms, and tool mark comparisons), up to three years of training may be required before the practitioner can engage in independent casework.[44] Training,

---

42 *Ibid.* at 217–18. *NAS Report*, c. 8, addresses the topic of education and training.

43 *Ibid.* at 219–20.

44 *Ibid.* at 230–32.

like research, can be expensive. Because of evolving legal and scientific issues, continuing education is also essential.[45]

### 3) Education in the Legal System

Specific attention in the report is paid to the issue of training forensic specialists in the need to understand legal terms and procedures; however, it is equally important that lawyers and judges be trained in understanding the scientific issues that confront them. After *Daubert*, the Federal Judicial Center published the *Reference Manual on Scientific Evidence* (latest ed. 2000) to assist judges in identifying relevant scientific issues. Further to that, it has been recommended that specific programs be tailored for judges, prosecutors, and defence lawyers. Specifically funded training programs have been most developed in the area of DNA. The report says that more work needs to be done on jury comprehension of scientific issues and error analysis.[46]

### 4) Issues Pertaining to Death Investigators

There is a wide variation in the ways in which sudden and unexpected deaths are investigated. Some investigators have local and others have state-wide responsibilities. Some are overseen by medically qualified people and others by those with legal qualifications. In the United States the majority are elected: it has 2,342 death investigation jurisdictions.[47] About 500,000 deaths each year require some degree of investigation.[48] In one jurisdiction, a seventeen-year-old high-school senior completed the relevant examination and was appointed a deputy coroner.[49] Referrals of cases to pathologists for reports often depend upon budgetary arrangements.

The *NAS Report* refers to proper training, statutory requirements, and appropriate funding arrangements to enable proper development of these services. The medical determination of cause and manner of death is invariably undertaken by a person with medical training, but that person is not always a qualified forensic pathologist. There are wide variations in the technical support services available, with many lacking in-house support for histology and

---

45 *Ibid.* at 233.

46 *Ibid.* at 234–37.

47 *Ibid.*, c. 9 at 245, citing Randy Hanzlick, "An Overview of Medical Examiner/Coronial Systems in the United States—Development, Current Status, Issues, and Needs" (Presentation to the National Academy of Sciences Committee, 5 June 2007).

48 *Ibid.* at 244.

49 *Ibid.* at 247.

radiology services and some having no dedicated technical support. The National Institute of Justice has provided guidelines for best practice in death investigations, but there is no requirement that they be followed or adopted.[50]

The *NAS Report* recommends the development of standard protocols for computerized records so that data can be shared and analysed properly. It points to the capacity to use radiological scanning and imaging techniques to enable the completion of a "Virtual Autopsy" which can provide much useful information without invasive or destructive procedures. However, to recover evidence such as bullets or bomb fragments, standard autopsy procedures are required.[51]

### a) Shortage of Medical Examiners and Forensic Pathologists

The *NAS Report* observes that a range of people take part in any death investigation process. Their qualifications vary from having general medical skills to extensive training in forensic pathology or specialist areas, such as cardiac and neurological pathology. The report notes that a forensic pathologist usually has several years of general medical training, followed by about three or four years of training in anatomical and clinical pathology, often with sub-specialty training. The United States requires recertification every ten years to maintain practising certificates.[52]

### b) Difficulties in Implementing Standards and Accreditation

The *NAS Report* points out that the underlying structural and jurisdictional problems make implementation of standards and accreditation processes more difficult.[53] It supports national adoption of the criteria for standard performance procedures that the National Institute of Justice (NIJ) developed; these criteria are outlined in the NIJ's *Death Investigation: A Guide for the Scene Investigator*.[54] The report says that professional and continuing education should be mandatory.[55]

### c) Underdevelopment of Forensic Pathology Research

The *NAS Report* says that heavy caseloads and operation independent of university-based medical research programs mean that forensic pathology research is significantly underdeveloped. In particular, little is being done on basic issues

---

50 *Ibid.* at 252.

51 *Ibid.* at 253–54.

52 *Ibid.* at 256–57.

53 *Ibid.* at 258–59.

54 *Ibid.* at 259, citing US Department of Justice, Office of Justice Programs, National Institute of Justice, *Death Investigation: A Guide for the Scene Investigator*, online: www.ncjrs.gov/pdffiles/167568.pdf.

55 *Ibid.* at 259.

such as time of death, injury response, and timing. It seems that most basic research in this area is being done in Scandinavia, Europe, and Japan, largely in response to national funding initiatives. Of the programs available, most are short and do not engage in basic research. There is also a need for improved methods for data collection and analysis.[56]

## F. THE MOVE TO EVIDENCE-BASED AND RESEARCH-BASED FORENSIC SCIENCE[57]

The *NAS Report*, like many other reports, including the Australian, Canadian, and Runciman reports, stresses the importance of building a research base for the forensic sciences (which we take to include forensic pathology) largely through better funding of research and links with the universities and other institutions. One issue to emerge from our study is the way in which "experience" seems to have provided the basis for the evidence used in many cases, despite the fact that the rhetorical pronouncements we reviewed in Part One stress that objective factors must support expert opinion evidence.

The person who attempts to justify a finding based upon "my experience" is likely to become victim of a self-fulfilling prophecy. The principle assumes what it purports to justify. It cannot be validated and is not capable of being falsified. Without proper validated research studies, aimed to falsify hypotheses, there is no proper testing of the assumptions involved. As we have also seen, assumptions tend to provide the impetus for tunnel vision and narrowly focused investigations that exclude much relevant material and focus instead on prejudicial and inaccurate material.

Claims of experience-based expertise thrive when little or no research is done in a particular forensic science. The *NAS Report* noted that pathology departments in American medical schools usually do not conduct research in forensic pathology and that

> a review of the forensic literature for basic research in forensic pathology reveals that significant contributions are largely originating in Europe, Scandinavia, and Japan. In other countries, universities house a department of legal medicine . . . where forensic pathologists have the time, expertise and funding needed to perform basic forensic research.[58]

---

56 *Ibid.* at 261.

57 Parts of this section are adapted from Kent Roach, "Forensic Science and Miscarriages of Justice: Some Lessons from Comparative Experience" (2009) 50 Jurimetrics 67.

58 *NAS Report*, above note 2 at 261.

The *NAS Report* recommended that US Congress should appropriate funds "to support research, education and training in forensic pathology" and to encourage "collaborative research to be conducted by medical examiner officers and medical universities."[59] The Canadian Goudge Inquiry also recommended that teaching and research be seen as an integral part of the work of a forensic pathologist and that funding be provided to that end; it further recommended that funding be made available to establish a centre for forensic medicine and science at the University of Toronto, the most research-intensive university in the province.[60] This centre, now established,[61] is consistent with the goals of the National Academy of Sciences in promoting more integration and common research and best practices among all the forensic sciences.

### 1) Limits of Relying on Published Research: A Cautionary Tale from Canada

Both the *NAS Report* and the Goudge Inquiry recommendations, which appear in *Report of Inquiry on Pediatric Forensic Pathology in Ontario,* support an evidence-based approach to the forensic sciences which makes greater use of published research. The link to research also explains the common focus in both reports on promoting the research base for the forensic sciences and bringing the rigour of the scientific method and peer review to these sciences. As we have seen, this would narrow the gap between the rhetoric and the reality in terms of the admissibility of expert evidence in criminal proceedings.

Although evidence-based forensic science is to be preferred to experience-based forensic science, it is not a panacea, and approaches that place greater reliance on the published research present some dangers. The Ontario-based Morin Inquiry provided an important warning to the effect that published and peer-reviewed studies can be misused in court. In Morin's second trial, a study by two British forensic scientists about the likelihood of the random occurrence of different colours and types of fibres was cited by the prosecution as support for the conclusion that the fibre evidence indicated contact between the accused and the victim. The Morin Inquiry, able to call the authors of the study as witnesses at the inquiry, heard from them that their study had no relevance to Morin's case and should not have been introduced there. This was because their study had:

---

59 *Ibid.* at 267.

60 *Report of the Inquiry into Pediatric Forensic Pathology in Ontario* (Toronto: Ministry of the Attorney General, 2008) [Goudge Inquiry] Recommendation 5.

61 See online: www.forensics.utoronto.ca/site6.aspx.

1) involved only two target fibres while there were 153 to 463 target fibres in the Morin case, yielding much higher likelihood of coincidental "matches";
2) there were more environmental links in the Morin case because the accused and the victim were next door neighbours;
3) their study only examined coincidental matches on the front seats of cars whereas the Morin case involved an examination of the entire car; and
4) their study had relied on a more discriminating test (thin layer chromatography) than had been used in the Morin case.[62]

The inquiry found that the forensic scientists who testified in Morin's case had misunderstood the study and that, not surprisingly, the prosecutors who relied on the study were not in a position to correct such scientific misunderstandings. In the end, the inquiry concluded that "the study, properly understood, did not support the case for the prosecution" and was "seriously misused at Mr. Morin's trial and likely misled the jury."[63] This finding is a warning that the introduction of published research in a trial can introduce another source of error and misinterpretation.

The introduction of "published research" in support of the use of forensic science in a criminal trial can introduce two other possible sources of error and misunderstanding in the trial process. First, it is clear that where research is accurate and substantiated, it is nevertheless capable of being misunderstood. As discussed above, forensic scientists and prosecutors in Ontario misunderstood the published research on fibre analysis and, as a result, misled the jury in the wrongful conviction of Guy Paul Morin. Second, clearly some that is published is simply incorrect or unsubstantiated, and the beneficial effects of peer review of publications can be exaggerated.

Reliance upon published research shifts the onus for validating the hypothesis from the expert appearing in court to some other experts who are not available to the court and therefore cannot be cross-examined. In effect, it amounts to a form of hearsay and may have the tendency to put the real issue in the case beyond effective scrutiny. Research is far from infallible. When articles are put forward for publication, editors may well seek opinions from others about the plausibility of the arguments, but they will not normally conduct a review of the testing procedures or the documentation involved. Sometimes, even substantial research projects can be based upon erroneous assumptions.[64]

---

62 Morin Inquiry, above note 25 at 120–31.

63 *Ibid.* at 119.

64 See, for example, the Imperial College, London, Alvey Project discussed in Robert N. Moles, "Logic Programming—An Assessment of Its Potential for Artificial Intelligence Applications In Law" (1991) 2 Journal of Law & Information Science 1.

Although the *NAS Report* is right that the forensic sciences should be more engaged in research, reliance on published research will not guarantee the accuracy of expert opinions.

### 2) The Role of Proper Methodology and Full Disclosure in Promoting Evidence-Based Forensic Science

An evidence-based approach to forensic science should go beyond reliance on published research. Forensic scientists should try to present the evidence that, in their view, justifies their opinion and not simply assert their final opinion about the cause of death or similarities between various samples. An evidence-based approach to forensic science requires careful and complete documentation of the conduct of all scientific tests performed.

Examination of the British terrorist miscarriages of justice and the Australian Chamberlain and Splatt cases, examined in Chapter 8, reveal problems in the approach to forensic science. The scientific tests were not done properly, were not fully documented, and even when they were documented, not all the relevant documents were disclosed to the accused. In both the Chamberlain case in Australia and the British bombing cases, the scientists expressed confident opinions as to the accuracy and reliability of their results. Only when inquiries were made into the details of the procedures they had followed was it revealed that their results were based only upon "presumptive" tests which were far from accurate. The documentation in support of the findings was also found to be inappropriate or unreliable.

The legal system can support more rigorous, evidence-based forensic science by imposing higher threshold standards on experts to use tested methodologies. The legal system can also, as it did in the Judith Ward case, insist on full disclosure of all relevant material surrounding the tests. Doing so should enable the accused to challenge the tests and methods used by the expert in the particular case as opposed to challenging the expert's experience and credibility, often a difficult task.

## G. THE NEED TO ADOPT A UNIFIED VISION TO REFORMING THE FORENSIC SCIENCES

The most significant contribution of the *NAS Report* is that it offers a unified vision of forensic science, something that contrasts with the fragmented disciplinary and jurisdictional approach that has, so far, characterized the experiences of Britain, Australia, and Canada with controversies and public inquiries into the forensic sciences. In Canada and Australia, as in the United States, federalism aggravates the jurisdictional fragmentation of the forensic sciences.

There is considerable fragmentation among the forensic sciences in terms of research, governance, and common legal issues relating to the admissibility of forensic evidence. In this respect, the unified vision of the *NAS Report* has clear advantages over the approach taken by the public inquiries in Canada: these have much more narrowly focused on the problems created by particular forensic sciences in particular jurisdictions.

Over the years, in response to their findings, inquiries in Australia, Britain, and Canada have all recommended sweeping changes to the forensic sciences. In the 1980s, the Australian reports discussed a wide range of scientific issues related to blood, glass, wood and paint particles, handprints, cutting of fabrics, and the habits and capabilities of dingoes, all of which turned out to be incorrect. In the 1990s in Britain, the scientific evidence in relation to explosives also turned out to be incorrect. In 1998, the Canadian Morin Inquiry concluded that hair, fibre, and blood analysis were overstated and misunderstood by police, prosecutors, and the courts and that contamination problems were not disclosed. The various inquiries have called for better resources, training, quality assurance, research, governance, independence, and monitoring of courtroom testimony. They have also recommended more attention to complaints about forensic scientists, better education of lawyers and judges about forensic sciences, more critical and restrictive approaches to the admissibility of evidence, and attention to language, such as "consistent with," that expert witnesses have used.[65]

Unfortunately, the reforms in Canada and Australia were limited in several ways. They covered the forensic sciences and did not extend to forensic pathology, which was subject to another major inquiry in Ontario (the Goudge[66]) a decade later and is the subject of ongoing concerns in Australia.[67] The inquiries also have limited impact in terms of their geographical and discipline-specific audiences.

The Morin Inquiry provides an excellent example. In 1998, the *Report of the Kaufman Commission on Proceedings Involving Guy Paul Morin* was issued in Ontario after an extensive inquiry relating to a murder conviction proven to be false because of DNA testing. The Morin Inquiry had examined the work of

65 Morin Inquiry, above note 25. Recommendations 1 to 35 all related to forensic science at the Centre of Forensic Sciences and in the courts.

66 Goudge Inquiry, above note 60.

67 See the issues and cases discussed in Robert N. Moles, *A State of Injustice* (South Melbourne: Lothian Books, 2004); Robert N. Moles, *Losing Their Grip: The Case of Henry Keogh* (Adelaide: Elvis Press, 2007) [Moles, *Losing Their Grip*].

the Centre of Forensic Sciences, located in Toronto. It had provided evidence that hair and fibre evidence linked Morin with a nine-year-old girl who was murdered. The inquiry found that the centre's contributions to Morin's wrongful conviction were substantial. The analysts' findings were overstated and misunderstood by police, prosecutors, and the courts. Contamination problems were not disclosed.

As indicated above, the inquiry recommended sweeping changes pertaining to the centre's operation: better resources, training, quality assurance, research, governance, and independence. The inquiry also recommended the following: more attention by the centre to complaints about forensic scientists; monitoring of their courtroom testimony, including the use of misleading language, such as "consistent with"; better education of lawyers and judges about forensic sciences; and more critical and restrictive approaches to the admissibility of forensic evidence.[68]

This inquiry did initiate significant reform in Ontario's Centre of Forensic Sciences,[69] but these reforms were limited in scope. They were limited to the forensic sciences represented at the centre — biological, firearms, handwriting, and toxicology — and did not extend to forensic pathology. It took another major inquiry in Ontario a decade later to recommend similar reforms to forensic pathology in that jurisdiction. This experience underlines the challenges presented by the fragmentation of the forensic sciences.

Forensic sciences are fragmented not only by discipline, but also by jurisdiction. In 2007, an inquiry report from Manitoba, a neighbour province to Ontario, revealed problems with the way that hair and fibre analysis had been conducted in that province.[70] Analysts employed in laboratories of the Royal Canadian Mounted Police (RCMP) resisted some of the reforms proposed — and adopted — in Ontario as a result of the earlier Morin Inquiry.[71]

---

68 See above note 62.

69 See Jeffrey R. Manishen, "Wrongful Convictions, Lessons Learned: The Canadian Experience" (2006) 13 Journal of Clinical Forensic Medicine 296 at 297–98 (detailing post-inquiry reforms, including DNA testing of hair, recording of preliminary reports, increased training, new protocols for reports and complaints, documentation of contamination, monitoring of courtroom testimony, and creation of an advisory board and a quality assurance unit).

70 Driskell Inquiry, above note 25 at 146–85.

71 In this case, an RCMP hair analyst testified in a 1991 trial that three hairs found in the accused's van were "consistent with" those of the victim. *Ibid.* at 149. The analyst defended the use of "consistent with" despite the fact that the term had been specifically criticized by the Morin Inquiry in 1998. *Ibid.* at 151. DNA analysis subsequently determined that the hairs could not have come from the victim and indeed likely came from three different people. *Ibid.* at 155. The inquiry's report criticized the RCMP lab for not

A decade after the Morin Inquiry issued its two-volume report, another Ontario commission of inquiry, the Goudge, issued a four-volume report on pediatric forensic pathology, *Report of the Inquiry into Pediatric Forensic Pathology in Ontario*.[72] This inquiry was appointed by the Ontario government in the wake of concerns raised by the work and testimony of Dr. Charles Smith. Five international experts reviewed some of Dr. Smith's work and raised concerns about twenty of forty-five cases reviewed, including twelve cases that had resulted in convictions.

Although pediatric forensic pathology is a very different field than hair and fibre comparison analysis, the similarities between the recommendations made following the Morin Inquiry and later, the Goudge Inquiry are striking. The Ontario forensic pathology report called for better resources, training, quality assurance, research, independence, governance, and monitoring of courtroom testimony, just as the Morin Inquiry had a decade earlier. It also called for more attention to complaints, monitoring of courtroom testimony, better education of lawyers and judges about science, and more restrictive and critical attention to the admissibility of scientific expert evidence, including the language used by expert witnesses to express their findings.

The similarities of the findings and recommendations by the two Ontario inquiries underline the real fragmentation between the various forensic science disciplines. A similar fragmentation can be observed in Australia, where reforms to some forensic sciences in light of two public inquiries also did not seem to affect the practice of forensic pathology.[73] Without the type of unifying vision seen in the *NAS Report*, there is a real danger that the hard lessons that the discovery of wrongful convictions reveals about weaknesses in the forensic

---

having another analyst verify the "matches" at the time and for the analyst testifying that the hairs were "consistent with" those of the victim despite the varying interpretations of that phrase. *Ibid.* at 163 and 166. The report also affirmed the conclusions of the Morin Inquiry that hair comparison analysis, because of its significant error rates, should be used only to exclude suspects. *Ibid.* at 169. However, like the Morin Inquiry, the Driskell Inquiry stopped short of recommending a complete ban on hair microscopy evidence in criminal cases. *Ibid.* at 172.

72 Goudge Inquiry, above note 60.

73 For Australian commissions of inquiry critical of forensic sciences, see generally *Royal Commission of Inquiry Concerning the Conviction of Edward Charles Splatt* (Adelaide: Government Printer, 1984) [Splatt Royal Commission] and *Royal Commission into the Chamberlain Convictions* (Canberra: Government Printer, 1987) [Chamberlain Royal Commission]. Moles, *Losing Their Grip*, above note 67 at 251–52: "A great many recommendations were made by the two Commissions. As a consequence, the forensic scientific services in South Australia were given an overhaul and procedures were significantly improved. However, forensic pathology was not seen to have been implicated in either of those cases." Controversy subsequently emerged about forensic pathology in South Australia.

sciences will not be assimilated. The wrongfully convicted cannot afford to have these lessons learned slowly on a discipline-by-discipline and jurisdiction-by-jurisdiction basis.

### 1) Central Regulation of the Forensic Sciences

The Chamberlain Royal Commission in Australia called for central regulation of the forensic sciences. Australia did establish the National Institute of Forensic Science, but it was developed under the auspices of the police, hardly what the Chamberlain Royal Commission had envisaged. It had recommended a national institute that would provide access to and have the respect of defence as well as prosecution, and be able to promote and develop proper standards.

In Britain, in 1993 the Runciman Royal Commission recommended the creation of a forensic science advisory council that would have significant audit responsibilities across the forensic sciences.[74] Unfortunately, the government chose not to implement this recommendation, and the position of Forensic Science Regulator was not created until 2007. This person, assisted by staff and a newly created Forensic Science Advisory Council, is responsible for developing and overseeing quality standards and accreditation for those who provide forensic science for the criminal justice system. The Regulator also hears complaints in relation to quality standards and provides independent advice to the government on forensic science issues.[75] The office has embarked on some interesting approaches, including the publication of a draft manual of regulation[76] and a review of the accreditation of forensic practitioners.[77] Both initiatives place considerable stress on the need for broad consultation. The establishment of the Forensic Science Advisory Council demonstrates an important commitment to improving standards across the forensic sciences.

### 2) Limited Availability of Skilled Persons: The Case of Forensic Pathologists

The *NAS Report*, like the Goudge Inquiry's report, refers to severe shortages of forensic pathologists, which is a global problem. It is, therefore, important to

74 *Royal Commission on Criminal Justice*, Cm 2263 (London: H.M.S.O., 1993) c. 9 [Runciman Report].

75 Julie Goulding, a Commissioner at the CCRC, is on the Forensic Science Advisory Council which provides advice to the Regulator.

76 Forensic Science Regulator, *Manual of Regulation* (London: Home Office, 2008).

77 Forensic Science Regulator, *A Review of the Options for the Accreditation of Forensic Science Practitioners* (January 2009).

develop greater international engagement with those who practise similar forensic disciplines in order to help in the transmission of research, best practice protocols, and exposure to different and perhaps better ways of doing things. Engagement with the global experience also creates connections that can facilitate peer review and quality assurance programs, the recruitment of talent, and the development of a common sense of professionalism that will transcend parochial jurisdictional contexts.

The *NAS Report* and the Goudge Inquiry take different approaches to conducting medico-legal autopsies. The *NAS Report* recommends that federal funds be provided "to establish medical examiner systems, with the goal of replacing and eventually eliminating existing coroners systems."[78] The Goudge Inquiry did not recommend the elimination of coroners' systems, but rather focused on ensuring that trained forensic pathologists would have the necessary resources and independence within coroners' systems to perform medico-legal autopsies and to do quality assurance of their own work. Some might argue that Ontario's system of appointed coroners who are medical doctors is much more benign than American systems of elected coroners without medical training. Nevertheless, the Goudge Inquiry implicitly made a judgment that abolishing a coroner's system was unnecessary in order to achieve the same end as that recommended by the NAS, namely, that "all medicolegal autopsies be performed or supervised by a board certified forensic pathologist."[79] Sometimes, incremental reforms are better than no reform, and some of the NAS's recommendations about medical examiners seem unrealistic, especially given the failure to implement similar recommendations made in 1928.[80]

There are real questions about how realistic it is to have all medico-legal autopsies done by board-certified forensic pathologists in any jurisdiction. The *NAS Report* provides important, but alarming data that only about 400 to 500 forensic pathologists practise full time in the United States, even though the estimated need for them is 1,000. Only about seventy residencies and seventy new positions for forensic pathologists are available each year, and 30 percent of these positions go unfilled.[81] Serious considerations for people considering a career in forensic pathology are that they will regularly have their work subjected

78 *NAS Report*, above note 2 at 267.

79 *Ibid.* at 268.

80 Another example would be the recommendation of accreditation of medical examiners; only fifty-four systems now are accredited by the National Association of Medical Examiners (NAME), *ibid.* at 258. The Ontario inquiry considered, but did not recommend that the rigorous NAME standards be implemented.

81 *Ibid.* at 257.

to adversarial challenge in court, they will have to cope with inadequate work facilities, and they will make substantially less financially than regular hospital pathologists.[82] With significant debts after qualifying, there is significant pressure to avoid forensic work in favour of better paying alternatives—loan forgiveness might be a significant incentive.

The Goudge Inquiry also recognized the shortage of trained forensic pathologists as a fundamental restraint on any reforms to forensic pathology. To that end, it recommended adequate and sustainable funding for fellowships in forensic pathology; an increased emphasis on forensic pathology in the medical schools; and in the meantime, sufficient resources to allow Ontario to recruit appropriately credentialled forensic pathologists from abroad.[83] Both the *NAS Report* and the Goudge Inquiry saw the shortage of forensic pathologists and the neglect of forensic pathology in North American medical schools as a key limitation on the ability to reform death investigations.

The Goudge Inquiry recommended a triage principle for pediatric deaths in criminally suspicious cases. It also recommended that autopsies be conducted at centralized locations and be undertaken only by certified forensic pathologists with pediatric forensic experience.[84] Clearly, this issue is of some significance, given the controversies over shaken baby syndrome and other forms of pediatric deaths in many countries, including the United States, Britain, and Australia.[85]

### 3) Forensic Science Centres and the Issue of Independence

The *NAS Report*'s approach to forensic sciences is focused on increasing the reliability of forensic sciences and services supplied in state institutions. One NAS recommendation is that federal incentive funds be used to remove facilities from the control of law enforcement agencies and prosecutors.[86]

---

82 *Ibid.* at 257–58. To this end, the US National Research Council recommends the funding of student loan forgiveness and fellowship support, but does not recommend the salary gap that may send pathologists who initially pursue careers in forensic pathology to higher paying and less stressful jobs in hospitals. The Ontario inquiry recommended that forensic pathologists be included in the Laboratory Medicine Funding Framework to ensure that they are paid on a similar scale as hospital pathologists; Goudge Inquiry, above note 60 at 305.

83 Goudge Inquiry, *ibid.*, at 301 and 306.

84 *Ibid.* at 307.

85 See the discussion of pediatric cases in Chapter 9.

86 *NAS Report*, above note 2 at 190–91 (Recommendation 4).

This recommendation may be another example of the perfect remedy being the enemy of good, more incremental reforms. It runs counter to Manitoba's Driskell Inquiry which rejected proposals that the RCMP's crime laboratories be separated from the RCMP's policing operations in part because the laboratory had admitted its mistakes, co-operated with the inquiry, and formed its own external advisory group. Commissioner LeSage noted that "the forensic science panelists generally agreed that in their experience, formal affiliations between a forensic laboratory and a police force are not always a cause of concern."[87] The *NAS Report* recommendations about the need for increased awareness and further research on human observer bias are more important than its perhaps unrealistic recommendation that police laboratories be abolished.[88]

As mentioned earlier, the Chamberlain Royal Commission in Australia recommended the creation of the National Institute of Forensic Science, but when established, it became a public relations exercise for the police; it awards annual prizes to those employed or retained by the respective police services, for example. It is not the type of organization that can exercise supervision over state-based forensic science centres and is not seen as a potential source of independent expertise or advice for the defence in criminal cases.

## H. THE ROLE OF THE DEFENCE IN CHALLENGING FORENSIC SCIENCE PRESENTED BY THE STATE

Little is said in the *NAS Report* about the role of defence experts as a check on flawed forensic science. This omission reflects the poor legal aid funding in the United States as well as the reluctance of courts to exclude forensic science evidence offered by the prosecution. Courts sometimes include such evidence even in cases where the relevant laboratories are not properly accredited, the witness has not been properly trained, and the science has not been validated.

Although it is difficult to question the conclusions reached by the NAS in the American context that courts—and by implication, defence lawyers—

87 Driskell Inquiry, above note 25 at 185. A report prepared by a forensic science expert for the inquiry put the point even more strongly, concluding that there was nothing in the case under review that suggested the forensic opinion was influenced by the lab's relation to the police and that the Morin Inquiry revealed that independent labs could also produce flawed opinions. He noted that regardless of its relation to the state, most forensic labs would work for police and prosecutors, and the ultimate issue was the objectivity and impartiality of the laboratory regardless of its affiliation. Douglas Lucas, "Report in Forensic Science Matters to the Commission of Inquiry re James Driskell" in Driskell Inquiry, Appendix G at 29–30.

88 *NAS Report*, above note 2 at 191 (Recommendation 5).

could do little to challenge and improve the forensic sciences, there may be more grounds for optimism in other jurisdictions where lawyers are better funded.

The Goudge Inquiry recommended increased legal aid funding and training for defence lawyers in matters involving forensic pathology.[89] In making these recommendations, it was likely influenced by its study of a 1991 case in which Dr. Charles Smith's testimony that the cause of a child's death was non-accidental was effectively rebutted by ten defence experts. The defence experts had been retained when the family of the accused twelve-year-old babysitter sold their family home and cashed in their retirement savings to defend their daughter.[90] The more general lesson of this case is that the defence needs to be adequately trained and funded to deal with and, if necessary, challenge other complex forms of forensic science.

## I. HOW SHOULD UNCERTAINTY IN THE FORENSIC SCIENCES BE EXPRESSED?

As mentioned above, there is a danger that juries and judges may see science as revealing absolute truths that cannot be challenged or questioned. Given this, it is critical that forensic scientists be able to articulate for the court any uncertainty in their evidence. To this end, the *NAS Report* recommended that all forensic sciences establish quantifiable measures of reliability and accuracy of forensic analyses and "quantifiable measures of uncertainty in the conclusions of forensic analysis."[91] To the extent that quantifiable standards can be developed, there is the problem of whether jurors will properly understand them given the NAS's observations about the difficulties jurors have with statistical evidence.[92] Moreover, the difficulties in articulating the degree of certainty with which scientific opinions are held should not be underestimated. During the Goudge Inquiry, the commissioner closely questioned many forensic pathologists about how they would quantify and express the degree of certainty behind their opinions about the cause of death. In the end, Goudge J. concluded:

---

89 Goudge Inquiry, above note 60 at 460–63.

90 *Ibid.*, vol. 2 at 12.

91 *NAS Report*, above note 2 at 190 (Recommendation 3).

92 *Ibid.* at 237. For an interesting discussion as to how medical practitioners (and others) get confused when calculating probabilities, see Gerd Gigerenzer, *Reckoning with Risk* (London: Penguin Books, 2002); also published as *How to Know When Numbers Deceive You: Calculated Risks* (New York: Simon and Schuster, 2002).

> During the Inquiry, I had the benefit of hearing from a number of eminent forensic pathologists from around the world. Through their participation, it became apparent that there is no common understanding of how forensic pathologists think about their level of confidence or certainty in their opinions; how they articulate this level, if at all, when communicating their opinion . . . .[93]

The inquiry assessed that the legal standard of proof beyond a reasonable doubt "has no correlation with science or medicine."[94] It recommended that multidisciplinary work should be done to help forensic pathologists better understand and express the level of certainty with which they hold an opinion.[95] These conclusions were reached after considerable probing by the inquiry.

The Runciman Royal Commission on Criminal Justice in Britain heard evidence from forensic scientists that, in their experience "the trial process was ill-suited to the objective presentation of evidence."[96] The forensic scientists also complained that prosecutors and defence lawyers did not always understand the underlying science. Although the commission affirmed the importance of adversarial challenge to expert evidence and stopped short of recommending the use of court-appointed experts, it recommended that trial judges ask expert witnesses at the end of challenged evidence if they have more to say. This recommendation recognizes that an accurate account of the science may not always emerge from the adversarial process of evidence in chief and cross-examination. In addition, the commission recommended that expert witnesses should inform counsel and then the court if they had second thoughts or wanted to clarify their testimony.[97]

## J. THE ADMISSIBILITY OF EXPERT EVIDENCE: THE JUDICIAL GATEKEEPING ROLE

The *NAS Report* devoted a chapter to the admissibility of forensic science evidence in litigation. This chapter discussed whether judges as gatekeepers can help protect the court from the flawed forensic science that contributes to wrongful convictions. The report recognizes that courts have a role to play both with respect to whether a particular discipline has a reliable scientific

93 Goudge Inquiry, above note 60 at 410.
94 *Ibid.* at 414.
95 *Ibid.* at 413.
96 Runciman Report, above note 74 at 159.
97 *Ibid.* at 160.

methodology and "the extent to which practitioners in a particular forensic discipline rely on human interpretation that could be tainted by error, the threat of bias, or the absence of sound operational procedure and robust performance measures."[98]

Despite its recognition of the potential for increased judicial gatekeeping, the report is pessimistic about the contributions that judges can make. It comments, "*Daubert* has done little to improve the use of forensic science evidence in criminal cases."[99] Given the evidence that the report cites, this comment does not seem unreasonable. It refers to the deference that appeal courts apply to a trial judge's determinations about the admissibility of expert evidence, the courts' continued acceptance of fingerprint evidence,[100] and the danger that more rigorous standards for the admissibility of scientific evidence will work to the detriment of the accused or require a research base that does not exist. The report assesses that "much forensic evidence — including, for example, bite marks and firearm and toolmark identification — is introduced in criminal trials without any meaningful scientific validation, determination of error rates or reliability testing to determine the limits of the discipline."[101]

Although the NAS's approach may be sound in the American context, judicial gatekeeping may have a greater potential, especially in those jurisdictions that are willing to spend more on legal aid than the United States. The Goudge Inquiry recommended that "trial judges should be vigilant in exercising their gatekeeping role" with respect to the admissibility of scientific evidence and exclude such evidence if it "does not satisfy standards of threshold reliability . . . whether or not the science is classified as novel or not."[102] Threshold reliability requires an assessment of the reliability of the proposed witness, the field of science, and the opinion offered in the particular case.[103] Attention must be paid to the limits of the proposed witness's expertise and the language used to express the opinion. The Goudge Inquiry stressed that judges needed to examine the details of the proposed expert evidence. The decision about admissibility is not all or nothing. Judges have the ability to allow some parts of the expert's proposed opinion but not other parts.[104]

---

98 *NAS Report*, above note 2 at 87.
99 *Ibid*. at 106.
100 *United States v. Crisp*, 324 F.3d 261 (4th Cir. 2003).
101 *NAS Report*, above note 2 at 107–8.
102 Goudge Inquiry, above note 60 at 620 (Recommendation 130).
103 *Ibid*. (Recommendation 131).
104 *Ibid*. (Recommendation 133).

The Ontario inquiry's optimism about the contribution that judges could make to the reliability of expert forensic science evidence finds some support in the evolution of Canadian law on the subject of expert evidence. As in the United States, the Canadian courts have moved away from tests that focused on general acceptance of the proposed testimony and the expert having special knowledge through education or experience to more rigorous tests. These tests require that the expert opinion evidence be necessary in assisting the trier of fact, that it be given by a properly qualified expert, and that it not be excluded by an exclusionary rule, such as the general rule that the prejudicial effect of the evidence should not outweigh its probative value.

### 1) Varying Use of the *Daubert* Standards

In 1994, the Supreme Court of Canada warned about the "danger that expert evidence will be misused and will distort the fact-finding process. Dressed up in scientific evidence which the jury does not easily understand and submitted through a witness of impressive antecedents, this evidence is apt to be accepted by the jury as being virtually infallible and as having more weight than it deserves."[105] The Court subsequently recognized the relevance of the *Daubert* factors relating to whether the theory behind the testimony had been tested, subjected to peer review, or established its known or potential error rate.[106] The Supreme Court of Canada has repeatedly stressed that science that might be accepted in a clinical setting to treat a patient may have too high an error rate to justify its use as forensic evidence in criminal proceedings.[107]

The *NAS Report* notes that the *Daubert* rule has been amended in the United States to make clear that a person's experience alone and past acceptance of similar expertise are not precluded as a means to qualify the person as an expert witness. This development explains some of the difficulties courts have encountered holding forensic science "to the more demanding standards of the traditional sciences."[108] The *NAS Report* also notes that when applied in criminal cases, *Daubert* has often been used to exclude expert testimony offered by the accused.[109] These conclusions, however, reflect American law and American practices of poorly funding defence counsel.[110] There is a possibility that

105 *R. v. Mohan*, [1994] 2 S.C.R. 9 at para. 19.
106 *Daubert*, above note 6.
107 *R. v. J.-L.J.*, [2000] 2 S.C.R. 600 [*J.-L.J.*].
108 *NAS Report*, above note 2 at 95.
109 *Ibid.* at 96–97 and 107.
110 Paul C. Giannelli, "*Ake v. Oklahoma:* The Right to Expert Assistance in a Post-*Daubert*, Post-DNA World" (2004) 89 Cornell L. Rev. 1305 at 1338–42; Garrett & Neufeld, above

judges in Australia, Britain, and Canada, assisted by adequately funded defence counsel, could play a more active gatekeeping role with respect to forensic science offered by the prosecution.

Until recently, Canadian law on the admissibility of expert witnesses could easily have been subject to much the same critique as the NAS had made of the *Daubert* standards. In 1993, the Supreme Court of Canada demonstrated the deference to the trial judge (that the NAS stresses) when it refused to strike testimony given beyond the range of a witness's expertise in a child abuse case. In that case, an expert on burns was allowed to provide opinion evidence about the characteristics of abused children, while an expert on child abuse was allowed to provide opinion evidence about the child's burns.[111] In subsequent years, the Canadian courts placed greater reliance on the *Daubert* factors, but these factors were generally applied only to "novel science" and were used in leading cases to exclude expert evidence presented by the accused.[112] The courts' refusal to admit evidence called by the defence relating to the frailties of eyewitness identifications[113] and false confessions[114] underlined the idea that the accused would often not benefit from stricter standards for the admissibility of expert evidence. This story would have been familiar to students of the American experience under *Daubert*.

Recent Canadian experience, however, demonstrates that courts are capable of using *Daubert* tools, combined with the experience of wrongful convictions, to take a much harder look at the reliability of evidence, including that offered by the prosecution. In 2007, the Supreme Court, in a 4:3 decision in *R. v. Trochym*,[115] excluded the post-hypnosis testimony of a witness who purported to provide eyewitness identification. The majority stressed the importance of determining the threshold reliability of the evidence and began its judgment by noting:

> In recent years, a number of public inquiries have highlighted the importance of safeguarding the criminal justice system — and protecting the accused who

---

note 26 at 89 (defence expert evidence presented in only nineteen of 137 trials of subsequent DNA exonerations).

111 *R. v. Marquard*, [1993] 4 S.C.R. 223.

112 *J.-L.J.*, above note 107 (exclusion of results of a penile plethysmograph offered by a person accused of sexual assault). Note, however, that another leading case decided the same year held that expert evidence offered by a psychologist called by the prosecutor about child abuse accommodation syndrome should not be admitted. *R. v. D.D.*, [2000] 2 S.C.R. 275.

113 *R. v. McIntosh* (1997), 117 C.C.C. (3d) 385 (Ont. C.A.).

114 *R. v. Osmar* (2007), 217 C.C.C. (3d) 174 (Ont. C.A.).

115 [2007] 1 S.C.R. 239.

> are tried under it — from the possibility of wrongful conviction. As this Court has previously noted, "[t]he names of Marshall, Milgaard, Morin, Sophonow and Parsons signal prudence and caution in a murder case": *United States v. Burns*, [2001] 1 S.C.R. 283, 2001 SCC 7, at para. 1. In the case at bar, we consider once again the need to carefully scrutinize evidence presented against an accused for reliability and prejudicial effect, and to ensure the basic fairness of the criminal process. More specifically, the decisions at trial to admit post-hypnosis evidence and similar fact evidence in this case constitute errors of law that are neither harmless nor negligible.[116]

In deciding that post-hypnosis testimony should be excluded, the Court was not deterred by the fact that it had been accepted in previous cases and might not be characterized as novel science. It noted that "the admissibility of scientific evidence is not frozen in time."[117] The Court stressed that what was "most troubling" about post-hypnosis evidence was "the potential rate of error in the additional information obtained through hypnosis when it is used for forensic purposes. At the present time, there is no way of knowing whether such information will be accurate or inaccurate. Such uncertainty is unacceptable in a court of law."[118]

Alan D. Gold, a Canadian lawyer with expertise in scientific issues, has stated that "it is hoped that the Court's concern with reliability will diffuse from the novel scientific evidence context to that of prosecution evidence generally" [119] Prof. David Paciocco has observed that developments such as *Trochym*, combined with the Goudge Inquiry's recommendations, have the potential to impose stricter standards on all expert evidence.[120] He proposes that courts should examine

1) whether the theory or technique and its application by the expert is reliable,
2) whether the expert is not biased and keeps an open mind,
3) whether the expert is objective and transparent about all the information used, and
4) whether experts explain the reasoning process that grounds their opinion and are candid about shortcomings and uncertainties.

---

116 *Ibid.* at para. 1.

117 *Ibid.* at para. 31.

118 *Ibid.* at para. 55.

119 Alan D. Gold, *Expert Evidence in Criminal Law: The Scientific Approach*, 2d ed. (Toronto: Irwin Law, 2009) at 54, n. 20.

120 David Paciocco, "Taking a 'Goudge' out of Bluster and Blarney: An 'Evidence-Based' Approach to Expert Evidence" (2009) 13 Can. Crim. L. Rev. 135.

There appears to be a new emphasis in both the legal and forensic science communities in Canada on evidence-based as opposed to experience-based, expert scientific opinion.

In the 2007 Stephen Truscott appeal, for example, the Ontario Court of Appeal disregarded opinions offered by an expert forensic pathologist and an entomology expert about the time of death. Both opinions were based only on the (admittedly considerable) experience of the Crown's experts and did not engage with the scientific literature or other attempts to test the experience of the expert witness.[121] This case demonstrates that courts can encourage the development of a more evidence-based approach in the forensic sciences.

A more recent Ontario Court of Appeal case affirms the judge's gatekeeper role with respect to expert evidence, but also holds that a trial judge erred in excluding expert sociology evidence on the basis that it did not have a known error rate.[122] The Court of Appeal warned that it was inappropriate to apply *Daubert* standards that require scientific methodology and the calculation of error rates to sociological evidence.[123] It relied on *Kumho Tire Co. v. Carmichael*[124] to justify a more flexible approach that does not require the application of *Daubert* criteria to non-scientific evidence based on the experience of the expert.[125] This decision has the potential to allow much forensic science offered by the state's experts to continue to be admitted without regard to its use of scientific methodology or attempts to determine its error rate. If this happens, the *NAS Report*'s pessimism about *Daubert* will be validated in another jurisdiction.

Nevertheless, the Ontario Court of Appeal's decision has some potential to limit the damage of faulty or overbroad forensic science expert testimony. It suggests that trial judges should be careful to limit the scope and language of an expert's opinion, particularly in cases where the testimony may relate to the ultimate issue of guilt.[126] It also follows the recommendations of the Goudge Inquiry in stressing that trial judges are not limited to the remedy of excluding expert evidence. In other words, trial judges can, in their gatekeeping role, place restrictions on the language used by the expert witness in order to reflect uncertainty and controversies in the science and the limits of the witness's expertise.[127] It remains to be seen whether the trend in Canada for courts to apply

---

121 *R. v. Truscott*, 2007 ONCA 575 at paras. 165–69, 313–14.
122 *R. v. Abbey*, 2009 ONCA 624 [*Abbey*].
123 *Ibid.* at paras. 104–17.
124 526 U.S. 137 (1999).
125 *Abbey*, above note 122 at paras. 110–12.
126 *Ibid.* at para. 103.
127 *Ibid.* at para. 64.

*Daubert* standards which require that prosecution evidence meet standards of threshold reliability will continue.

## K. CONCLUSION

Faulty forensic science and forensic pathology have clearly contributed to miscarriages of justice. In Chapters 8 and 9, we discussed how they contributed to several miscarriages of justice in Australia, Britain, and Canada. A similar story could be told in the United States where flawed forensic science, especially hair and blood analysis, has figured prominently in DNA exonerations.[128] If these experiences were not enough, the 2009 *NAS Report* on the forensic sciences convincingly makes clear that improvements in the forensic sciences are required.

The courts can encourage needed reforms in several ways. There is need to move beyond the slow process of reforms being undertaken on a discipline-by-discipline and jurisdiction-by-jurisdiction basis after miscarriages of justice and serious scandals have occurred. There is also a need to move from an experienced-based approach to the forensic sciences, where witnesses are allowed to testify as experts simply because of the positions that they hold in crime labs, to an evidence-based approach where experts must explain and justify the reasons that support their opinions. The courts can require full disclosure of scientific tests. They can also require experts to demonstrate that they have used tested methodologies and that they do not stray from their areas of expertise.

Judges bear some responsibility for allowing unreliable forensic science to be used as evidence and for the resulting miscarriages of justice. That said, the *NAS Report* is correct when it says that stricter judicial screening will not in itself solve the problems of the forensic sciences and forensic pathology. To that end, front-end reforms of forensic science, including better training, quality assurance, and more centralized regulation and audit, are necessary to increase the reliability of forensic evidence and to prevent miscarriages of justice.

128 Garrett & Neufeld, above note 26 at 8–11.

CHAPTER 12

# Recommendations to Bring the Reality Closer to the Rhetoric

We hope that the previous chapters have established that there is a large gap between the rhetoric of impartial forensic science and prosecutions that seek the truth and the realities of flawed forensic science and prosecutions that have been marred by established miscarriages of justice. In this final chapter, we propose some specific reforms that are designed to reduce the troubling gap that has emerged between the aspirations and practice of forensic science and the criminal justice system.

As suggested in Chapters 10 and 11, reforms must be pursued both at the front end by the forensic science community and at the back end by the legal community. Indeed, each of these communities needs to better understand the values, methodologies, and limits of the other. We do not pretend that the recommendations offered below are the only possible ones or that they are a panacea. Nevertheless, they are a start.

## A. RESEARCH AND REVIEW DEVELOPMENTS IN FORENSIC SCIENCE

The *NAS Report*[1] and other reports identify certain problem areas that need further research. One area that has caused particular concern in all the jurisdictions examined is that of sudden infant deaths and, in particular, shaken baby

1 National Research Council, Committee on Identifying the Needs of the Forensic Sciences Community, *Strengthening Forensic Science in the United States: A Path Forward* (Washington, DC: National Academies Press, 2009) [*NAS Report*]. The report can be found online: www.ncjrs.gov/pdffiles1/nij/grants/228091.pdf.

syndrome. The *Harris* case on shaken baby syndrome is a good example of a legal system assessing a controversial form of forensic evidence.[2] The Goudge Inquiry in Canada also found many problems in this area.[3] The scientific community needs to devote more research to these and other issues of controversy frequently encountered in court. This research may not necessarily result in a consensus, but it should reveal areas of controversy and uncertainty. It is vital that lawyers, judges, and juries be made aware of areas of controversy and uncertainty so that they can apply the reasonable doubt standard and be aware of the need for new evidence to be introduced on appeal. Science evolves and is often controversial—the legal system must try to keep up to the evolving nature of the science it uses.

It would be sensible for each jurisdiction to have a forum for the independent review of contentious, emerging, and new issues in forensic science. At various times there will emerge certain principles, propounded by expert witnesses, which appear questionable in the forensic context. With ongoing scientific developments, it is clear that there will be challenges not only to existing areas of forensic science, but also to emerging areas, such as facial and body mapping, voice recognition, and further challenges to DNA evidence that will need to be assessed. There is need to establish standards for such evidence before it is found to have contributed to miscarriages of justice in individual cases.

Some broader review function of forensic issues should be ongoing in each jurisdiction. To counteract the marginalization of most forensic sciences within the larger scientific community, forensic scientists should work with the legal profession and the judiciary to help improve funding and review of the forensic sciences that the courts frequently rely upon. Such reviews may be especially beneficial if they bring scientists together with prosecutors and defence lawyers. Many issues relating to the adequacy of forensic evidence are not suitable for determination and evaluation in the context of a particular criminal trial. If questions about the adequacy of scientific techniques for the detection of explosive residues arise, the time to resolve them is before and not after the bomb goes off. Expert panels, with the assistance of the judiciary and the bar, can help establish standards for new types of forensic evidence. The point of this exercise is not only to ensure adherence to best practices, but to promote better understanding about areas of controversy and uncertainty within various forensic sciences.

---

2 *R. v. Harris & Ors*, [2005] EWCA Crim 1980 [*Harris*].

3 *Report of the Inquiry into Pediatric Forensic Pathology in Ontario* (Toronto: Ministry of the Attorney General, 2008) [Goudge Inquiry].

## B. AUDIT CASES INVOLVING SUSPECT FORMS OF EVIDENCE

Scientific research into areas of controversy, as well as individual cases of miscarriages of justice, can identify classes of cases where there are concerns about suspect forms of evidence, including controversial or evolving forms of forensic evidence. Both CCRC-type bodies and the petition procedure generally rely on individuals to seek redress, but for many reasons, individuals may not always be able or willing to bring miscarriages of justice to the attention of authorities. In non-homicide cases, victims of miscarriages of justice may have already served their sentences and want to focus on getting their lives back together. Especially in Australia and Canada, where reliance on petitions to the executive remains, victims of miscarriages of justice may have trouble in obtaining legal and scientific assistance in presenting their cases.

There is a need to bridge the gap between error correction in individual cases and broader approaches to the discovery and prevention of wrongful convictions. One promising method is to conduct audits of cases that have relied on suspect forms of evidence. If a forensic scientist or forensic pathologist has presented unreliable or misleading evidence in one case, he or she has likely made mistakes in other cases. In some cases, whole classes of evidence—for example, involving sudden infant death or shaken baby syndrome or hair microscopy evidence—may be suspect in light of evolving research and science. In such instances, proactive audits of cases should be taken.

James Driskell and the Association In Defence of the Wrongfully Convicted asked Manitoba's Driskell Inquiry to recommend a national audit of criminal cases, where hair microscopy evidence was used to obtain convictions. The province of Manitoba had already initiated an audit process for such cases, but the flawed evidence in Driskell's case came from a laboratory run by the Royal Canadian Mounted Police (RCMP), the national police force. Commissioner Lesage expressed concerns "that the problems identified relating to hair microscopy evidence in Driskell's case are not unique to his case or unique to Manitoba."[4] He did not however make a formal recommendation for such a national audit or of a review of the forensic laboratories of the RCMP.[5] As suggested above, national leadership is needed on many issues relating to forensic science even in those jurisdictions that follow a federal structure.

---

4 *Report of the Commission of Inquiry into Certain Aspects of the Trial and Conviction of James Driskell* (Winnipeg: The Commission, 2007) at 192.

5 *Ibid.* at 192–94.

In 2005, Ontario's chief coroner announced a review of forty-five homicide or suspicious death cases since 1991, where Dr. Charles Smith had performed an autopsy or provided an opinion. In twenty of the forty-five cases, the reviewers had some issue with the opinions of Dr. Smith that appeared in a written report, or testimony in court, or both. The results from this review led to the Goudge Inquiry, and the Goudge Inquiry, in turn, recommended an audit of more pediatric cases.

There also needs to be systemic reporting of problems associated with particular expert witnesses. Many of the inquiries that have focused on the work of one particular expert have detailed many warning signs about the expert that were all too commonly ignored.

In Britain, various audits of cases were conducted in the wake of the publicity generated by the Sally Clark appeal, controversies over sudden infant deaths, and the performance of certain forensic scientists and expert witnesses. These reviews have not always led to the overturning of many convictions, but they remain worthwhile exercises that can help restore public confidence in the criminal justice system. Moreover, audits have a potential to discover miscarriages of justice that would not otherwise have been discovered. They also can help raise awareness in the scientific and legal communities about certain problems of evidence or practices that fall below professional standards.

## C. ESTABLISH CCRC-TYPE BODIES

In our view, in Canada and in Australia there is a significant need to establish bodies equivalent to the British CCRC (Criminal Cases Review Commission) or its Scottish counterpart. The Canadian inquiries have explicitly recommended it, and even commentators in Australia, Canada, and the United States who have reservations about the CCRC acknowledge that they would like to see a CCRC-type body in their jurisdiction.[6] Volunteer innocence projects can

6 Clive Walker and Kathryn Campbell conclude that "the establishment of the CCRC has secured gains over executive-based review such as the CCRG (in Canada), though the failure to resource it generously or to reform the CACD (Court of Appeal) undermine its delivery." Clive Walker & Kathryn Campbell, "The CCRC as an Option for Canada: Forwards or Backwards?" in Michael Naughton, ed., *The Criminal Cases Review Commission: Hope for the Innocent?* (Basingstoke, UK: Palgrave Macmillan, 2009) at 204 [Naughton, *CCRC: Hope*]. In Naughton, *CCRC: Hope* at 217, Robert Schehr has written that the North Carolina approach, which includes a state-funded error commission, albeit limited to factual innocence claims, is "the most promising and holistic approach to the problem of wrongful and unlawful commissions." Stephanie Roberts and Lynne Weathered go even further. They suggest that innocence projects should

make important contributions by providing legal representation in individual cases and advocating systemic reforms, but the systemic nature of wrongful convictions in all jurisdictions is now so well established that the state should assume responsibility for investigating and providing remedies for miscarriages of justice. This point was expressed with great eloquence by Cory J. in the Canadian Sophonow Inquiry when he recommended that a "completely independent entity" such as the CCRC be established to "effectively, efficiently and quickly review cases in which wrongful conviction is alleged . . . . if the State commits significant errors in the course of the investigation and prosecution, it should accept the responsibility for the sad consequences which will inevitably flow from them."[7]

We must also remember that the victims of miscarriages of justice are perhaps the most vulnerable of people in our societies. The available evidence suggests that victims of miscarriages of justice come disproportionately from disadvantaged groups — indigenous populations in Australia and Canada, African-Americans in the United States, and the poor and mentally disadvantaged in all countries. In addition to these disadvantages, victims of miscarriages of justice have been convicted of serious and often brutal crimes. The acknowledged victims of miscarriages of justice may now be recognized as innocent, but once they were convicted killers and child abusers. In such circumstances, it is important that independent, state-funded bodies have adequate resources and powers to investigate claims of wrongful convictions and if necessary, to refer them back to the courts. The criminal justice system is a state institution, and the state has an obligation to deal fairly and efficiently with the inevitable failure of a justice system that relies on fallible humans — including, we would add, expert witnesses, scientists, and doctors.

The need for CCRC-type bodies in Australia and Canada does not mean that the practices and procedures of the CCRC in the United Kingdom cannot be improved. There are concerns about the CCRC's decreased resources and its lack of powers to compel information from non-public bodies. There may also be a case for external audit of its work as well as the internal quality assurance program now in use. There may be value in encouraging legal representation of

---

not downgrade broader fairness claims considered by the CCRC and that a test based on innocence "would be unworkable in practice." Stephanie Roberts & Lynne Weathered, *Assisting the Factually Innocent: The Contradictions and Compatibility of Innocence Projects and the Criminal Cases Review Commission* (2009) 29 Oxford J. Legal Stud. 43 at 58 [Roberts & Weathered].

7 Manitoba, Commission of Inquiry Regarding Thomas Sophonow, *The Inquiry Regarding Thomas Sophonow* (Winnipeg: Manitoba Justice, 2001) at 101.

applicants before the CCRC. A good percentage of applicants to the CCRC, including a higher percentage of those whose cases are referred to the Court of Appeal, are already legally represented.[8] As a comparison, the Norwegian Criminal Cases Review Commission has the ability to appoint lawyers to represent applicants in its most difficult cases.[9]

The CCRC should have adequate legal powers of investigation. At present, the Canadian Minister of Justice, the Scottish Criminal Cases Review Commission, and the North Carolina Innocence Inquiry Commission have broader legal powers than the CCRC to obtain information from private bodies. The CCRC might also play a more active role with respect to audits of cases involving suspect forms of evidence. As suggested above, a case where there is a problem with a particular type of evidence or a particular forensic scientist may reveal more problems under the surface. The CCRC has the ability to expand its investigations and even make references to the Court of Appeal in the absence of a formal application.[10]

Perhaps in conjunction with the courts and other regulatory bodies, the CCRC could undertake a review and assessment of potential controversies in relation to forensic science issues. The issue that arose for consideration in relation to cases concerning shaken baby syndrome or non-accidental head injury is the type of controversy the CCRC had to evaluate in the context of *R. v. Harris & Ors.*[11] It was plainly an issue that would require systematic evaluation and analysis by the courts at some time. The CCRC could act proactively and make

8 See Jacqueline Hodgson & Juliet Horne, "The Extent and Impact of Legal Representation on Applications to the Criminal Cases Review Commission (CCRC)" (May 2008) at 4 [unpublished], online: http://papers.ssrn.com/sol3/papers.cfm?abstract_id=1483721 (explaining that "[o]f the 219 cases referred back to the Court of Appeal during 01–07, 63.5% were legally represented. Of the 2,248 cases rejected as ineligible or having no reviewable grounds, 29% were legally represented." Even though these findings describe only correlation between legal representation and referral as opposed to causation, they also identify cases where legal representation plays a critical role for applicants, for example, with respect to applications that the CCRC initially rejects, but then reconsiders. This was the case in eleven of seventy-four cases referred by the CCRC to the courts between 2005 and 2007.)

9 The Norwegian Criminal Cases Review Commission appointed counsel to assist in 38 of 137 petitions it decided in 2009, 26 of 143 petitions it decided in 2008, and in 51 of 196 petitions it decided on the merits in 2007. See Norwegian Criminal Cases Review Commission, *Annual Report 2009* (Oslo: Review Commission, 2010), online: www.gjenopptakelse.no/fileadmin/download/Aarsberetning_2009_engelsk.pdf; Norwegian Criminal Cases Review Commission, *Annual Report 2007* (Oslo: Review Commission, 2007), online: www.gjenopptakelse.no/fileadmin/download/NCCRC_Annual2007.pdf.

10 *Criminal Appeal Act 1995* (U.K.), 1995, c. 35, s. 14(1) [*CAA* 1995].

11 *Harris*, above note 2.

assessments beyond the context of a particular complaint. Whether a CCRC-type body conducts such proactive audits of its own volition or upon a request from the Attorney General, the Forensic Regulator, members of the judiciary, or medical or forensic organizations can be determined in due course.

It should be noted that the CCRC has already reconsidered whole groups of cases of its own volition. For example, it has chosen to reconsider groups of cases where the prosecution witness has since been discredited (pathologist Dr. Heath) and after the Omagh bombing judgment, DNA cases, where LCN DNA ("low-copy number" DNA) was relied upon. More recently, in response to changes to the Royal College of Paediatrics and Child Health guidelines, it has re-examined child abuse cases (2009/10) where, under the previous guidelines, certain signs and symptoms were regarded as indicative of abuse. In the revised guidelines of 2008, the same signs and symptoms can be regarded at best as "neutral" findings. At the time of writing, it is too early to say what, if anything, will be uncovered as a result of this "trawl." The recent judgment in *R. v. PF*[12] is an example of a conviction being quashed by the Court of Appeal (Criminal Division) following a reference from the CCRC made, in large part, as a result of the changes to the guidelines. The wider issues raised in respect of other potential cases led the CCRC to commence its own audit of cases in its system, in addition to which, in accordance with its usual practice, it informed the Crown Prosecution Service (CPS) so that it, too, could take all appropriate steps. The CCRC has an ability to respond to changes in the underlying forensic sciences; changes that may not always be fully appreciated by potential applicants to reopen their convictions.

Thought needs to be given as to how a CCRC will best interact with the forensic science community in cases involving forensic science. Laurie Elks devotes a helpful chapter to this topic in his recent study of the CCRC. He makes the important point that the CCRC "is not financially constrained to the same extent as legally-aided defendants in selecting experts and commissioning forensic work." The CCRC, like the Crown Prosecution Service, is a player with access to "a database of leading experts" and is "generally able to call upon the most experienced experts. This luxury is not always available to defence lawyers."[13] Elks also demonstrates how the CCRC's many referrals in forensic science cases have revealed patterns of problems. Such patterns are

---

12 [2009] EWCA Crim 1086.

13 Laurie Elks, *Righting Miscarriages of Justice? Ten Years of the Criminal Cases Review Commission* (London: Justice, 2008) at 77. Justice Goudge made a similar point when he stated "a structure like the CCRC may make it easier to find the necessary expertise because the institution, not the individual, is retaining the requisite expertise." Goudge Inquiry, above note 3 at 540.

often found with experts offered by the prosecution who present "their hypotheses with excessive certainty"[14] and who leave "it to the defence expert—and the adversarial process—to point out the opposite view."[15] He makes the case for better regulation of forensic disciplines as well as the study of difficulties that juries may have in cases with conflicting experts. There has been some controversy over the CCRC and the Court of Appeal's treatment of new expert evidence, as well as some concern in the Court of Appeal that accepting new expert evidence may open the proverbial floodgates of appeal. Such concerns also underline our point about the importance of focusing not just on the CCRC, but on the ability of the Court of Appeal to deal with controversial and evolving forensic science. Laurie Elks submits, correctly in our view, "that the Commission should not hesitate to refer cases where it considers that the defence expert case was 'muffed' for reasons outside the control of the defendant and to the detriment of the fairness of the trial."[16]

One danger is that the focus of limited reform energies will be devoted to the creation of the CCRC-type body without enough attention to whether the appellate courts have adequate resources and tools to deal with cases then referred to them. As suggested in Chapter 10, many of the criticisms directed at the CCRC on matters such as lurking doubt and fresh evidence might be better directed at the Court of Appeal.

It is important that CCRC-type bodies not be considered in isolation. The Runciman Royal Commission on Criminal Justice, which recommended the creation of the CCRC in 1993, also made perhaps less well-known recommendations to increase independent audits of forensic science providers, to ensure that the defence had adequate disclosure and means to conduct its own scientific tests, and to encourage the Court of Appeal to be receptive to new evidence and claims of lurking doubt. Although CCRC-type bodies are necessary, they cannot solve all the problems related to miscarriages of justice. Broader systemic reforms are needed.

In Chapter 10, we discussed the need for both attention to correction of miscarriages of justice in past cases and systemic reform to prevent miscarriages of justice in future cases. Thought should be given to how the CCRC and bodies like it can make better contributions to systemic reform issues. Bear in mind the view expressed by the former chairman of the CCRC, Graham Zellick, when giving evidence to the Home Affairs Select Committee:

---

14 *Ibid.* at 97.

15 *Ibid.* at 98.

16 *Ibid.* at 103.

> We have no funds available for supporting research. We did make inquiries. We approached the Home Office Research and Statistics Unit but they made it plain they did not have the funds to support work of this kind. We are also quite keen that it is work that should be carried independently of us.[17]

The academic community is a critical resource that can and should be better used. Volunteer innocence projects, other researchers in the universities, and the forensic science community should be encouraged to focus on the systemic issues raised by individual cases of miscarriages of justices. Such an approach could help strengthen the ties between the legal, forensic, and academic communities as advocated by many, including the Runciman Royal Commission on Criminal Justice, the Goudge Inquiry, and the National Academy of Sciences. In addition, governments might also ask a CCRC-type body to conduct inquiries somewhat along the lines of the Canadian public inquiries or to issue reports that identify patterns in its cases. A CCRC-type body would have considerable expertise. It might be able to conduct such inquiries more efficiently than a judicial inquiry that comes to the issue without any prior experience in the area. CCRC-type bodies have the potential to contribute to systemic study and reforms to prevent miscarriages of justice, but this potential generally remains largely untapped.

## D. OBTAIN BETTER JUDICIAL CONTROL OVER EXPERT EVIDENCE

The judiciary needs to take a creative approach to forensic science. The question-and-answer format of adversarial proceedings conducted by lawyers who may incompletely understand the issues is ineffective in distinguishing reliable from unreliable evidence. One way to respond to the danger that the adversary system will not prevent the introduction of unreliable forensic science is to conduct pretrial inquiries into the scientific reliability of opinions being propounded by expert witnesses. Such inquiries could take place before the swearing of the jury in a criminal matter. Better preparation of expert reports and even, in some cases, meetings between opposing experts can assist the court. There is no reason why such an inquiry should be adversarial and every reason why it should be inquisitorial. In addition, there may be sound policy reasons why the inquiry should be chaired by a judge other than the trial judge. Doing so would avoid any suggestion of influence from the pretrial inquiry affecting the subsequent assessment

17 Roberts & Weathered, above note 6 at 68, citing U.K., H.C., Home Affairs Committee, The Work of the Criminal Cases Review Commission 1703 (2005–2006) at question 79.

of the evidence given by the experts at the trial. The inquiry should focus on the adequacy of the scientific principles involved and whether they are capable of producing reliable conclusions. It should go well beyond the routine summary of the expert's credentials and experiences: it should get into the substance of the proposed expert evidence. Judges might even specialize in the vetting of scientific evidence and be assisted by scientific advisers. That said, we would caution that there are no guarantees. Now discredited experts, including Dr. Charles Smith and Professor Roy Meadow, would at one time have been the very kinds of scientific advisers used in such a screening process.

Another device that should be considered to promote better review and understanding of forensic science evidence is the online publication and wider sharing of pretrial expert reports. Such a practice would encourage openness and peer review, and the exposure of error or controversy. The separation of the scientific issues from the plethora of other issues raised in criminal cases would increase the likelihood that other specialists in the area will consider them. It could also encourage scientists and doctors to devote more attention to forensic issues presented in court. Online availability of such reports would ensure that anyone thinking of engaging the expert can consider his or her work, irrespective of where the evidence was given. Public scrutiny in this context could become more significant and current than whether the material has been published in peer-reviewed journals. The use of computer technology also means that quality assurance work can be globalized efficiently and cost effectively—a person in Australia can peer-review the work of an expert in Canada in real time.

As we pointed out in Chapter 3, appellate judges in Australia, Britain, and Canada all have powers in some instances to appoint special commissioners to investigate any scientific or other issues that could not be examined in court and to report back. In Britain, this power is limited to requesting the CCRC to undertake further investigation or to make inquiries, not usually of a scientific nature: the CCRC can do so under its section 15 powers.[18] The South Australian provision states that where any question arising on the appeal involves prolonged examination of any scientific investigation which cannot conveniently be conducted before the court, then it can be referred for inquiry and report to a special commissioner appointed by the court.[19] Perhaps such provisions could

18 *CAA* 1995, above note 10.

19 *Criminal Law Consolidation Act (South Australia) 1935*, s. 359(d). For similar powers in Canada, see the *Criminal Code*, R.S.C. 1985, c. C-46, s.683(1)(e). For an American case where a court appointed a forensic scientist to examine the work of another forensic scientist, see *In re Investigation of the West Virginia State Police Crime Lab, Serology Div.*, 438 S.E.2d 501 (W. Va. 1993). For further discussion, see Kent Roach, "Wrongful Con-

be more widely used to enable the court, of its own volition, to examine and assess scientific principles being propounded by expert witnesses. The appeal courts should not hesitate to set out guideline judgments in areas of controversial forensic science and send clear messages to lawyers and forensic scientists about the expectations of the judiciary.

## E. IMPOSE A NEW STANDARD OF DEMONSTRABLE RELIABILITY

Prof. Gary Edmond has argued that a higher standard of demonstrable reliability should be applied to prosecution evidence because the state has the ability to fund the type of research and verification procedure that can affirm the reliability of the evidence that it presents in criminal cases.[20] Although the Goudge Inquiry in Ontario adopted many of Professor Edmond's recommendations about the importance of determining threshold reliability and guidelines that judges could use to accomplish this task, the inquiry did not accept his proposal that the forensic science the prosecutor sought to introduce should be held to a higher standard of demonstrable reliability than would be applied to defence evidence. The UK Law Commission also seems to have dismissed the idea that asymmetrical standards for the admissibility of expert evidence can be applied, even though the prosecutor has an obligation to prove guilt beyond a reasonable doubt.

The imposition of standards that forensic evidence offered by the state be demonstrably reliable before it is admitted in court could help prevent miscarriages of justice; it could also encourage the state to invest in improving the forensic sciences. It has the potential to square the circle in the sense of providing perhaps the strongest incentives for the government to reform, fund, and regulate the forensic sciences to increase their reliability. Finally, it recognizes the special responsibility of judges not to allow people to be convicted on the basis of evidence that is neither reliable nor of unknown reliability. As suggested throughout this text, much work needs to be done by both forensic scientists and the legal community before the reality more closely matches the rhetoric of an impartial and reliable search for the truth.

---

victions: Adversarial and Inquisitorial Themes" (2010) 35 N.C.J. Int'l L. & Com. Reg. 387 at 429–32.

20 Gary Edmond, "Pathological Science? Demonstrable Reliability and Expert Forensic Pathology Evidence" in Inquiry into Pediatric Forensic Pathology in Ontario, *Independent Research Studies: Pediatric Forensic Pathology and the Justice System*, ed. by Kent Roach, vol. 2 (Toronto: Ontario Ministry of the Attorney General, 2008) at 116–20.

# Table of Cases


Ah Yick v. Lehmert (1905), 2 C.L.R. 593, [1905] HCA 22 .......... 143
Ainsworth v. Criminal Justice Commission (1992), 175 C.L.R. 564 .......... 176
Anthony v. R., [2005] EWCA Crim 952 .......... 252
Antoun v. The Queen, [2006] HCA 2 .......... 161
Associated Provincial Picture Houses v. Wednesbury Corporation, [1948] 1 K.B. 223 (C.A.) .......... 172

B. (A Minor) (Care: Expert Witnesses), Re, [1996] 1 F.L.R. 667 .......... 37
Bahri Kural v. The Queen (1987), 162 C.L.R. 502 .......... 143
Beamish v. The Queen, [2005] WASCA 62 .......... 155
Bell v. F.S. & U. Industrial Benefit Society Ltd. (9 September 1987) (Supreme Court of New South Wales) .......... 39
Benedetto v. R., [2003] UKPC 27 .......... 163
Berger v. United States, 295 U.S. 78 (1935) .......... 29, 162
Bilodeau v. Minister of Justice, 2008 QCCS 1036, aff'd (sub nom. Bilodeau v. Canada (Ministre de la Justice)), 2009 QCCA 746 .......... 117
Bonamy v. Canada (Minister of Justice) (2001), 156 C.C.C. (3d) 110, 2001 FCT 798 .......... 117
Boston and Anor v. Criminal Cases Review Commission, [2006] EWHC 1966 (Admin) .......... 343
Boucher v. The Queen (1954), [1955] S.C.R. 16, [1954] S.C.J. No. 54 .......... 5, 29–30, 114, 126, 163, 195
Bounds v. The Queen, [2006] HCA 39 .......... 137
Boyle v. Criminal Cases Review Commission, [2007] EWHC 8 (Admin) .......... 342
Bradshaw v. The Queen (13 May 1997), Library No 970228 (WASC CCA) .......... 158–59, 160
Bugg v. Day, [1949] HCA 59 .......... 38
Burrell v. The Queen (2008), 238 C.L.R. 218, [2008] HCA 34 .......... 20, 139, 164, 165, 170–71
Burt v. Governor-General, [1992] 3 N.Z.L.R. 672 (C.A.) .......... 142

Button v. The Queen, [2002] WASCA 35 .......... 159, 160, 233–34

Cabassi v. Vila (1940), 64 C.L.R. 130 .......... 173
Cesan and Rivadavia v. DPP (Cth.), [2007] NSWCCA 273 .......... 166
Cesan and Rivadia v. The Queen, [2008] HCATrans 320 (3 September 2008) .......... 166
Cesan v. The Queen; Mas Rivadavia v. The Queen, [2008] HCA 52 .......... 68, 150, 155, 166
Chamberlain v. The Queen (1983), 46 A.L.R. 493, [1983] FCA 78 .......... 156
Chamberlain v. The Queen (No 2) (1984), 153 C.L.R. 521, [1984] HCA 7 .......... 136–37, 148, 152, 153, 158
Chidiac v. The Queen (1991), 171 C.L.R. 432, [1991] HCA 4 .......... 153, 158
Christie v. The Queen, [2005] WASCA 55 .......... 156–57, 158
Clarkson v. DPP, [1990] V.R. 745 .......... 159
Coffin, Re (1955), 116 C.C.C. 215, [1955] S.C.J. No. 76 .......... 118
Collins v. The Queen, [1975] HCA 60 .......... 193
Connelly v. Director of Public Prosecutions, [1964] A.C. 1254 .......... 169
Cooley v. The State of Western Australia, [2005] WASCA 160 .......... 157–59, 160, 180
Craig v. South Australia (1995), 184 C.L.R. 163 (H.C.A.) .......... 174

D'Orta-Ekenaike v. Victoria Legal Aid, [2005] HCA 12, 223 C.L.R. 1 .......... 170–71
Dallagher, Re, [2002] EWCA Crim 1903 .......... 375
Daoulov v. Attorney General (Canada), 2008 FC 544 .......... 117
Darkan, Deemal-Hall and McIvor v. The Queen, [2006] HCA 34 .......... 149
Daubert v. Merrell Dow Pharmaceuticals, Inc., 509 U.S. 579 (1993) .......... 34, 48, 49, 129, 372, 373, 374, 382, 397, 398, 399, 401–2
Davern v. Messel (1984), 155 C.L.R. 21 (H.C.A.) .......... 175
Davie v. The Lord Provost, Magistrates and Councillors of the City of Edinburgh, [1953] S.C. 34 .......... 36, 37
Davies and Cody v. The King (1937), 57 C.L.R. 170, [1937] HCA 27 .......... 137, 154
De Jesus v. The Queen (1986), 61 A.L.J.R. 1, [1986] HCA 65 .......... 143
DJL v. The Central Authority, [2000] HCA 17 .......... 139, 171
Dowsett v. Criminal Cases Review Commission, [2007] EWHC 1923 (Admin) .......... 343
DPP (Nauru) v. Fowler (1984), 154 C.L.R. 627 .......... 151
DPP v. Ryan, [2002] VSCA 176 .......... 151
Dr. Alan Williams v. General Medical Council, [2007] EWHC 2603 (Admin) .......... 18, 44, 250–51, 287, 289
Dyers v. The Queen (2002), 210 C.L.R. 285 .......... 152

Eastman v. Director of Public Prosecutions (ACT), [2003] HCA 28 .......... 139, 146
Eastman v. The Queen (2009), 184 A. Crim. R. 1, .......... xx
Eastman v. The Queen, [2000] HCA 29 .......... xx, 238, 241
Edwards v. R. (1993), 178 C.L.R. 193 .......... 151
Evans v. The Queen, [2007] HCA 59 .......... 154

Farley (Aust.) Pty. Ltd. v. J.R. Alexander & Sons (Q) Pty. Ltd. (1946), 75 C.L.R. 487 .......... 172–73
Farnell v. Criminal Cases Review Commission, [2003] EWHC Admin 835 .......... 342

Fingleton v. The Queen (2005), 216 A.L.R. 474, [2005] HCA 34 .................... 151
Freitas v. Benny, [1976] A.C. 239 (J.C.P.C.) .................... 116
Frye v. United States, 293 F. 1013 (D.C. Cir. 1923) .................... 33–34, 48

Gallagher v. The Queen, [1986] HCA 26 .................... 137, 156, 157
General Medical Council v. Meadow (2006), [2006] EWCA Civ 1390, [2007] 1 All E.R. 1 .................... 18, 253
George v. R., [2007] EWCA Crim 2722 .................... 210–11
Gipp v. The Queen, [1998] HCA 21 .................... 136, 137, 143, 144, 154, 158, 165
Grey v. The Queen, [2001] HCA 65 .................... 149, 150, 155, 158, 160, 162
Grierson v. The King (1938) NSW CCA .................... 138
Grierson v. The King (1938), 60 C.L.R. 431, [1938] HCA 45 .................... 20, 138

H.G. v. The Queen (1999), 197 C.L.R. 414 .................... 37
Hargan v. The King (1919), 27 C.L.R. 13 .................... 137
Hayes v. The Queen (1973), 47 A.L.J.R. 603 .................... 144
Heron v. The Queen, [2003] HCA 17 .................... 184
Hickman v. Mackeigan, [1989] 2 S.C.R. 796, [1989] S.C.J. No. 99 .................... 363
Holtman v. Sampson, [1985] 2 Qd. R. 472 .................... 39
Horowitz v. Connor (1908), 6 C.L.R. 38 (H.C.A.) .................... 142
Hunter v. Chief Constable of the West Midlands Police, [1982] A.C. 529 .................... 198

Idoport Pty Ltd v. National Australia Bank Ltd, [2001] NSWSC 123 .................... 37, 43
Investigation of the West Virginia State Police Crime Lab, Serology Div., In re, 438 S.E.2d 501 (W. Va. 1993) .................... 412

Jones v. The Queen (1997), 72 A.L.J.R. 78 .................... 153, 158
Jonesco v. Beard, [1930] A.C. 298 .................... 173
*Judith Ward v. The Queen. See R. v. Ward*

KBT v. The Queen (1997), 72 A.L.J.R. 116 .................... 143
Kelleher v. Parole Board (NSW), [1984] HCA 77 .................... 146
Keogh v. The Queen, [2007] HCA Trans 693 (16 November 2007) .................... 142
Kindler v. Canada (Minister of Justice), [1991] 2 S.C.R. 779, [1991] S.C.J. No. 63 .................... 93
Kumho Tire Co. v. Carmichael, 526 U.S. 137 (1999) .................... 401

Lazarus Estates Ltd. v. Beasley, [1956] 1 Q.B. 702 .................... 173
Lewis v. R. (1987), 88 F.L.R. 104 .................... 39–40
Libke v. The Queen, [2007] HCA 30 .................... 5, 30
Lysaght v. Police, [1965] N.Z.L.R. 405 .................... 37

M. v. The Queen, [1994] HCA 63, 181 C.L.R. 487 .................... 136, 147, 153
Maguire & Others (1992), 94 Cr. App. R. 133 .................... 45
Makita (Australia) Pty. Ltd. v. Sprowles, [2001] NSWCA 305 .................... 28, 35, 36, 37, 38, 39, 40, 41–42
Mallard v. The Queen (2003), 28 W.A.R. 1, [2003] WASCA 296 .................... 165, 237–38

Mallard v. The Queen (2005), 224 C.L.R. 125, [2005]
HCA 68 ................. xviii, 138, 144, 145, 152, 153, 158, 160, 161, 162–63, 166, 237, 238–39
Manock v. Channel Seven Adelaide Pty. Ltd., [2007] HCATrans 414
(7 August 2007) ........................................................................................ 239
McCreight v. Her Majesty's Advocate, [2009] HCJAC 69 (Scot.) ............................... 254
McDonald v. McDonald (1965), 113 C.L.R. 529, [1965] HCA 45 ...................................173
McIlkenny v. Chief Constable of the West Midlands, [1980] 1 Q.B. 283,
aff'd [1982] A.C. 529 (H.L.) ............................................................... 198, 326
Meadow v. General Medical Council, [2006] EWHC 146 (Admin) ............................252
Melendez-Diaz v. Massachusetts, 129 S. Ct. 2527, 557 U.S. ___ (2009) ...................373–74
Miazga v. Kvello Estate, [2009] 3 S.C.R. 339, [2009] SCC 51 .........................................94
Mickelberg v. The Queen (1989), 167 C.L.R. 259, [1989] HCA 35 ............... xx, 138, 139–41
Milat v. The Queen, [2004] HCA 17 ................................................................................139
Milgaard, Reference re, [1992] 1 S.C.R. 866, [1992] S.C.J. No. 35 .....................111, 118, 228
Minister for Immigration and Multicultural and Indigenous Affairs v.
SGLB (2004), 78 A.L.J.R. 992, 207 A.L.R. 12 .....................................................174
Mraz v. The Queen (1955), 93 C.L.R. 493 ..............................................................154, 155
*Mullins-Johnson, Re. See R. v. Mullins-Johnson*

National Justice Compania Naviera S.A. v. Prudential Assurance Co. Ltd.
("The Ikarian Reefer"), [1993] 2 Lloyd's Rep. 68 .............................................40–41
Nelles v. Ontario, [1989] 2 S.C.R. 170, [1989] S.C.J. No. 86 ..........................................94
Ng Extradition (Canada), Re, [1991] 2 S.C.R. 858, [1991] S.C.J. No. 64 .........................93
Nudd v. The Queen (2006), 80 A.L.J.R. 614, [2006]
HCA 9 ............................................................ 19, 137, 150, 154, 155, 162, 163, 164

O'Kelly Holdings Pty. Ltd. v. Dalrymple Holdings Pty Ltd (1993),
45 F.C.R. 145 ................................................................................................... 37
Ocean Marine Mutual Insurance Association (Europe) O.V. v. Jetopay Pty. Ltd.,
[2000] FCA 1463 ................................................................................................ 43
Osland v. The Queen, [1998] HCA 75 ............................................................................ 153
Owens Bank Ltd v. Bracco, [1992] 2 A.C. 443 (H.L.) .....................................................173

Pearson v. Criminal Cases Review Commission, [1999] EWHC Admin 452 .............. 342
Phillion, Re, 2009 ONCA 202 ................................................................................109, 121
Postiglione v. The Queen, [1997] HCA 26 .....................................................................139
Preece v. Her Majesty's Advocate, [1981] Crim. L.R. 783 ............................................. 243
Proulx v. Quebec (Attorney General), [2001] 3 S.C.R. 9, 2001 SCC 66 ........................94

R. (Burns) v. County Court Judge of Tyrone, [1961] N.I. 167 .................. 175, 176, 178, 181
R. (Director of Revenue and Customs Prosecution) v. CCRC, [2007]
1 Cr. App. R. 384 ...............................................................................................346
R. v. Abbey, 2009 ONCA 624 ...............................................................................49, 130, 401
R. v. Apostolides (1984), 154 C.L.R. 563 .......................................................................159
R. v. Appleton (2001), 55 O.R. (3d) 321, [2001] O.J. No. 3338 (C.A.) ............................ 113
R. v. Bacchus, [2004] EWCA Crim 1756 ........................................................................ 254

R. v. Beaudry, [2007] 1 S.C.R. 190, 2007 SCC 5 ....................102–3
R. v. Bentley (Deceased), [1998] EWCA Crim 2516.................... 12, 66, 76, 78, 85, 88
R. v. Bevan, [1993] 2 S.C.R. 599, [1993] S.C.J. No. 69 ....................105
R. v. Bey, [1993] 3 All E.R. 253....................63
R. v. Biniaris, [2000] 1 S.C.R. 381, 2000 SCC 15.................... 103, 104
R. v. Birks (1990), 19 N.S.W.L.R. 677 ....................163, 164
R. v. Birmingham Crown Court; Ex parte Ricketts, Unreported (8 June 1990)....................182
R. v. Bolton Justices; Ex parte Scally and Ors, [1991] 1 Q.B. 537 ....... 172, 178, 182, 183, 184
R. v. Bonython (1984), 38 S.A.S.R. 45 ....................28, 33
R. v. Boreman & Ors, [2006] EWCA Crim 2265 ....................297
R. v. Brooks, [2000] 1 S.C.R. 237, 2000 SCC 11....................94
R. v. Brown (Winston), [1998] A.C. 367 (H.L.)....................159
R. v. Burke, [1996] 1 S.C.R. 474, [1996] S.C.J. No. 27 .................... 101–2
R. v. Button, [2001] QCA 133.................... xx, 279
R. v. Campbell, [1999] EWCA Crim 2264 .................... 79–74, 87
R. v. Cannings, [2004] EWCA Crim 1 ....................18, 251, 288–89
R. v. Catt, [2005] NSWCCA 279.................... 166, 232
R. v. Causley, [2003] EWCA Crim 1840 .................... 85, 88–89
R. v. CCRC ex parte Pearson, [1999] 3 All E.R. 498....................333
R. v. Clark (No. 2), [2003] EWCA Crim 1020 ....................45, 46–47, 251, 289–90, 291
R. v. Clarke & Anor, [2006] EWCA Crim 1196, rev'd [2008] UKHL 8....................345
R. v. Cooper & Anor, [2003] EWCA Crim 2257....................75, 85, 86, 166, 207
R. v. Cooper, [1969] 1 Q.B. 267 (C.A.) ....................147–48
R. v. Corbett (1973), [1975] 2 S.C.R. 275, [1973] S.C.J. No. 157 .................... 100
R. v. Cosgrove, [1948] Tas. S.R. 99....................145, 146
R. v. Cottrell, [2007] EWCA Crim 2016....................346
R. v. Coutts, [2006] UKHL 39 ....................345
R. v. Crown Court at Knightsbridge; Ex parte Goonatilleke, [1985] 2 All E.R. 498.................... 179–80, 181, 182
R. v. D. and J., [1996] 1 Cr. App. R. 455....................69
R. v. D.D., [2000] 2 S.C.R. 275, 2000 SCC 43....................48, 399
R. v. Davis & Ors, [2000] EWCA Crim 109.................... 67, 68, 69
R. v. Davis, [2008] UKHL 36 ....................359
R. v. Day, [2003] EWCA Crim 1060.................... 82
R. v. Dean, [2006] SACD 54.................... 278
R. v. Treadaway, [1996] EWCA Crim 1457.................... 198, 203, 204, 327
R. v. Dixon, [1998] 1 S.C.R. 244, [1998] S.C.J. No. 17 .................... 126
R. v. Downing, [2002] EWCA Crim 263....................80, 253, 254
R. v. Driskell, 2004 MBQB 3.................... 121
R. v. Druhan, [1999] EWCA Crim 2011....................332
R. v. Ebsary (1986), 27 C.C.C. (3d) 488, [1986] N.S.J. No. 199 (S.C.A.D.) ....................213
R. v. Edwards (No. 2), [1931] SASR 376....................138
R. v. Ensor, [1989] 1 W.L.R. 497....................163
R. v. Fanjoy, [1985] 2 S.C.R. 233, [1985] S.C.J. No. 55....................105
R. v. Fell, [2001] EWCA Crim 696 .................... 71, 332

R. v. Forbes; Ex parte Bevan, [1972] HCA 34 ... 186
R. v. Foster & Ors, [2007] EWCA Crim 2869 ... 345
R. v. Foster, [1985] Q.B. 115 ... 145–46
R. v. Fowler (1985), 39 S.A.S.R. 440 ... 39
R. v. François, [1994] 2 S.C.R. 827, [1994] S.C.J. No. 66 ... 102
R. v. Friend, [2004] EWCA Crim 2661 ... 71
R. v. Fulham, Hammersmith and Kensington Rent Tribunal; Ex parte Gormly, [1951] 2 All E.R. 1030 ... 176
R. v. G.D.B., [2000] 1 S.C.R. 520, 2000 SCC 22 ... 112, 128, 164
R. v. Gall and Gall (21 October 1991), transcript (E.W.C.A.) ... 205
R. v. George, [2007] EWCA Crim 2722 ... 210, 211, 346
R. v. Gilfillan, [1998] EWCA Crim 3466 ... 70, 71
R. v. Gilfoyle (No. 2) (2000), [2001] 2 Cr. App. R. 57, [2000] EWCA Crim 81 ... 37
R. v. Gillyard (1848), 12 Q.B. 527 ... 175, 178, 180, 181
R. v. Gore (Deceased), [2007] EWCA Crim 2789 ... 345
R. v. Graveline, [2006] 1 S.C.R. 609, 2006 SCC 16 ... 112
R. v. Green, [2002] NICA 14 ... 71
R. v. Grey (2000), 111 A. Crim. R. 314, [2000] NSWCCA 46 ... 158
R. v. Guyatt (1997), 119 C.C.C. (3d) 304, [1997] B.C.J. No. 2185 (C.A.) ... 103
R. v. Haddon, [2003] EWCA Crim 284 ... 71
R. v. Hanemaayer, [2008] ONCA 580 ... 127
R. v. Hanratty, [2002] EWCA Crim 1141 ... 68, 72, 76, 77
R. v. Hanson and Ettridge, [2003] QCA 488 ... 151
R. v. Harris & Ors, [2005] EWCA Crim 1980 ... 252, 288, 372, 404, 408
R. v. Henderson, [2009] M.J. No. 145, 2009 MBQB 101 ... 219
R. v. Hibbert, [2002] 2 S.C.R. 445, 2002 SCC 39 ... 94
R. v. Hickey & Ors (30 July 1997), (E.W.C.A.) ... 206, 333
R. v. Hinse, [1997] 1 S.C.R. 3, [1997] S.C.J. No. 1 ... 107
R. v. Hoey, [2007] NICC 49 ... 280–82
R. v. J.-L.J., [2000] 2 S.C.R. 600, 2000 SCC 51 ... 48, 129, 398, 399
R. v. James, [1998] EWCA Crim 2521 ... 71, 78, 83
R. v. Jenkins; ex parte Morrison, [1949] V.L.R. 277 ... 37
R. v. Jetté (1999), 141 C.C.C. (3d) 52, [1999] J.Q. no 4641 (C.A.) ... 99
R. v. Jewitt, [1985] 2 S.C.R. 128, [1985] S.C.J. No. 53 ... 169
R. v. Kai-Whitewind, [2005] EWCA Crim 1092 ... 18, 252, 288
R. v. Kamara, [2000] EWCA Crim 37 ... 84
R. v. Keane, [1994] 2 All E.R. 478 (C.A.) ... 159
R. v. Keith Twitchell (26 October 1999), (E.W.C.A. Crim.) ... 12
R. v. Keith Twitchell, [2000] 1 Cr. App. R. 373 (C.A.) ... 202, 203, 327
R. v. Kelly & Anor, [2003] EWCA Crim 2957 ... 71, 79, 89
R. v. Kelly, [2001] 1 S.C.R. 741, 2001 SCC 25 ... 118
R. v. Kempster, [2008] EWCA Crim 975 ... 254
R. v. Kennedy, [2007] UKHL 38 ... 345
R. v. Kent Justices; Ex parte Ashford (No. 2), [1956] 1 Q.B. 167 ... 181
R. v. Keogh, [2007] SASC 226 ... 138

R. v. Khan, [2001] 3 S.C.R. 823, 2001 SCC 86 .......... 105
R. v. Kingston-upon-Thames Justices; Ex parte Khanna, [1986] R.T.R. 364 .......... 182, 183
R. v. La, [1997] 2 S.C.R. 680, [1997] S.C.J. No. 30 .......... 126
R. v. Lewis (E.W.C.A.) .......... 206
R. v. Leyland Justices; Ex parte Hawthorn, [1979] 1 Q.B. 283 .......... 179, 182, 183
R. v. Lifchus, [1997] 3 S.C.R. 320, [1997] S.C.J. No. 77 .......... 114
R. v. Liverpool Crown Court; Ex parte Roberts, [1986] Crim. L.R. 622 .......... 182
R. v. Lohrer, [2004] 3 S.C.R. 732, 2004 SCC 80 .......... 105
R. v. M(S), 1991 WL 1139467 (Ont. Prov. Div.) .......... 304
R. v. M.F., [2003] EWCA Crim 1173 .......... 71
R. v. Maguire & Ors (1992), 94 Cr. App. R. 133, [1992] 2 All E.R. 433 (C.A.) .......... 45, 199, 244, 245
R. v. Maguire & Ors (26 June 1991), (E.W.C.A. Crim.) .......... 15
R. v. Malcolm (1993), 81 C.C.C. (3d) 196, [1993] O.J. No. 967 (C.A.) .......... 103
R. v. Marquard, [1993] 4 S.C.R. 223, [1993] S.C.J. No. 119 .......... 399
R. v. Marshall (1983), 57 N.S.R. (2d) 286, [1983] N.S.J. No. 322 (S.C.A.D.) .......... 114
R. v. Mattan (Deceased), [1998] EWCA Crim 676 .......... 12, 66, 81, 88, 89
R. v. Maynard & Ors, [2002] EWCA Crim 1942 .......... 66, 74, 75, 81, 87, 165, 208
R. v. McIlkenny & Ors (1991), 93 Cr. App. R. 287 (E.W.C.A. Crim.) .......... 15, 197, 244
R. v. McIntee (1985), 38 S.A.S.R. 432 .......... 157
R. v. McIntosh (1997), 117 C.C.C. (3d) 385, [1997] O.J. No. 3172 (C.A.) .......... 219, 399
R. v. McNeil, 2009 SCC 3 .......... 126, 127
R. v. Mezzo, [1986] 1 S.C.R. 802, [1986] S.C.J. No. 40 .......... 94
R. v. Mohan, [1994] 2 S.C.R. 9, [1994] S.C.J. No. 36 .......... 47, 48, 129, 398
R. v. Morin, [1988] 2 S.C.R. 345, [1988] S.C.J. No. 80 .......... 111
R. v. Morin, [1992] 3 S.C.R. 286, [1992] S.C.J. No. 7 .......... 111
R. v. Mullins-Johnson (1996), 112 C.C.C. (3d) 117, [1996] O.J. No. 4459 (C.A.), aff'd [1998] 1 S.C.R. 977, 124 C.C.C. (3d) 381 .......... 307
R. v. Mullins-Johnson, [2007] ONCA 720 .......... 109, 114, 123, 308
R. v. Murphy & Anor, [2002] EWCA Crim 120 .......... 75, 85
R. v. Nicholls, [1998] EWCA Crim 1918 .......... 86, 293
R. v. Nicholls, [1998] EWCA Crim 727 .......... 70
R. v. O'Brien & Ors, [2000] EWCA Crim 3 .......... 71, 76, 195
R. v. O'Doherty, [2002] NICA B51 .......... 254
R. v. Oickle, [2000] 2 S.C.R. 3, 2000 SCC 38 .......... 94
R. v. Osmar (2007), 217 C.C.C. (3d) 174, 2007 ONCA 50 .......... 399
R. v. Palmer (1979), [1980] 1 S.C.R. 259, [1979] S.C.J. No. 126 .......... 112, 123
R. v. Pan, [2001] 2 S.C.R. 344, 2001 SCC 42 .......... 98
R. v. Pantoja, [1998] NSWCA 565 .......... 154
R. v. Parks, [1961] 1 W.L.R. 1484 .......... 70
R. v. Patrick Nicholls, [1998] EWCA Crim 1918 .......... 293
R. v. Patton (1995), 80 A. Crim. R. 595 .......... 151
R. v. Pendleton, [2001] UKHL 66 .......... 55, 58, 60, 61, 62, 67, 69, 70, 71, 75, 90, 341
R. v. PF, [2009] EWCA Crim 1086 .......... 409
R. v. Phillion, [2003] O.J. No. 3422 (S.C.J.) .......... 121

R. v. Phillion, 2009 ONCA 202 .......... 71, 109
R. v. Phillion, 2010 ONSC 1604 .......... 109
R. v. Pinfold & Anor, [2003] EWCA Crim 3643 .......... 69, 86
R. v. Poole & Anor, [2003] EWCA Crim 1753 .......... 84, 332
R. v. Puaca, [2005] EWCA Crim 3001 .......... 295–96
R. v. Reardon (No. 2) (2004), 60 N.S.W.L.R. 454 .......... 159
R. v. Recorder of Leicester, Ex parte Wood, [1947] K.B. 726, [1947] 1 All E.R. 928 .......... 175, 178, 181
R. v. Richardson, Conlon, Armstrong, & Hill (20 October 1989) (E.W.C.A. Crim.) .......... 15, 199, 245
R. v. Robinson (1989), 51 C.C.C. (3d) 452, [1989] A.J. No. 950 (C.A.) .......... 95, 96
R. v. S.(P.L.), [1991] 1 S.C.R. 909, [1991] S.C.J. No. 37 .......... 105
R. v. Saik, [2006] UKHL 18 .......... 346
*R. v. Sally Clark. See R. v. Clark (No. 2)*
R. v. Samra, [2004] EWCA Crim 1797 .......... 71, 80
R. v. Sarson, [1996] 2 S.C.R. 223, [1996] S.C.J. No. 63 .......... 113
R. v. Secretary of State for the Home Department, Ex parte Mullen, [2004] UKHL 18 .......... 2, 9
R. v. Secretary of State for the Home Department, Ex parte Al-Mehdawi, [1990] 1 A.C. 876 (H.L.) .......... 175, 183
R. v. Sheppard, [2002] 1 S.C.R. 869, 2002 SCC 26 .......... 98
R. v. Sherret-Robinson, 2009 ONCA 886 .......... 114, 127
R. v. Shirley, [2003] EWCA Crim 1976 .......... 79
R. v. Smith & Ors, [1999] EWCA Crim 1525 .......... 60
R. v. Smith, [2002] EWCA Crim 2671 .......... 80
R. v. Smith, [2002] EWCA Crim 840 .......... 71, 83
R. v. Smith, [2004] 1 S.C.R. 385, 2004 SCC 14 .......... 99
R. v. Sophonow (1985), 38 Man. R. (2d) 198, [1985] M.J. No. 10 (C.A.) .......... 107
R. v. Stafford, [2009] QCA 407 .......... 30, 137, 152, 155, 193
R. v. Starr, [2000] 2 S.C.R. 144, 2000 SCC 40 .......... 114
R. v. Steel, [2003] EWCA Crim 1640 .......... 71
R. v. Stinchcombe, [1991] 3 S.C.R. 326, [1991] S.C.J. No. 83 .......... 32, 93, 124, 196, 214, 364
R. v. Storey (1978), 140 C.L.R. 364, [1978] HCA 39 .......... 150
R. v. Sunbeam Corp. (1968), [1969] S.C.R. 221, [1968] S.C.J. No. 94 .......... 111
R. v. Tallifer and Duguay, [2003] 3 S.C.R. 307, 2003 SCC 70 .......... 126
R. v. The Justices at Biloela, Ex parte Marlow (No. 2), [1983] 1 Q.R. 552 .......... 176
R. v. Theodosi, [1993] R.T.R. 179 .......... 63
R. v. Thomas (No. 4), [2008] VSCA 107 .......... 151
R. v. Trevor Anthony Campbell (14 October 1999), No. 99/0642/W5 (E.W.C.A.) .......... 205, 206
R. v. Trochym, [2007] 1 S.C.R. 239, 2007 SCC 6 .......... 94, 130, 399
R. v. Trotta (2004), 23 C.R. (6th) 261, [2004] O.J. No. 2439 (C.A.) .......... 97
R. v. Trotta, [2007] 3 S.C.R. 453, 2007 SCC 49, rev'g (2004), 190 C.C.C. (3d) 199, [2004] O.J. No. 4366 .......... 97
R. v. Truscott, 2007 ONCA 575 .......... 19, 106, 107, 113, 119, 130, 148, 302, 401

R. v. Turner, [1975] Q.B. 834 (C.A.) ........ 35, 39
R. v. Unger, 2005 MBQB 238 ........ 121
R. v. Ward, [1993] 1 W.L.R. 619, [1993] 2 All E.R. 577, 96 Cr. App. R. 1 (C.A.) ........ 14, 15, 45, 71, 159, 160, 196, 200, 246–48, 291–92
R. v. Weir, The Times (16 June 2000) ........ 68
R. v. West Sussex Quarter Sessions; Ex parte Albert and Maud Johnson Trust Ltd., [1973] 3 All E.R. 289 ........ 177–79, 183
R. v. Wickens, [2003] EWCA Crim 2196 ........ 75, 86–87, 297–98
R. v. Wildman, [1984] 2 S.C.R. 311, [1984] S.C.J. No. 43 ........ 105
R. v. Wolverhampton Crown Court; Ex parte Crofts, [1983] 1 W.L.R. 204 ........ 174–75
R. v. Yebes, [1987] 2 S.C.R. 168, [1987] S.C.J. No. 51 ........ 100–1, 104
Ramsay v. Watson (1961), 108 C.L.R. 642 ........ 38
Randall v. R. (Cayman Islands), [2002] UKPC 19 ........ 68, 163
Randall v. The Queen, [2002] 2 Cr. App. R. 17 ........ 5, 30
Ratten v. R. (1974), 131 C.L.R. 510, [1974] HCA 35 ........ 148, 150, 154, 156
Raymond McKenzie Gilmour v. Her Majesty's Advocate, [2007] HC HCJAC 48 (Scot.) ........ 71
Reddaway v. Banham, [1896] A.C. 199 (H.L.) ........ 172
Reference under s. 433A of the Criminal Code by the AG for the Northern Territory of Australia of Convictions of Alice Lynne Chamberlain and Michael Leigh Chamberlain, Re, Supreme Court of Northern Territory, No CA2 of 1988, [1988] NTSC 64 ........ 275
Reid v. R., [1980] A.C. 343 (P.C.) ........ 63
Richardson v. The Queen (1974), 131 C.L.R. 116 ........ 30
Robert Adams v. The Queen, [2006] NICA 6 ........ 71
Robinson v. The Queen (1991), 180 C.L.R. 531 ........ 143
Royal Commission on Thomas Case, Re, [1980] 1 N.Z.L.R. 602 ........ 145

Scottish Criminal Cases Review Commission, Re (25 July 2001) (High Court of Judiciary) ........ 347
Shin Kobe Maru v. Empire Shipping Co. Inc., [1994] HCA 5, 181 C.L.R. 404 ........ 140
Sinanovic's Application (2001), 180 A.L.R. 448, [2001] HCA 40 ........ 141–42
Southall v. General Medical Council, [2009] EWHC 1155 (Admin), aff'g General Medical Council v. Southall, The Guardian (6 August 2004) ........ 292
Stafford v. DPP, [1974] A.C. 878 ........ 148
Stirland v. Director of Public Prosecutions, [1944] A.C. 315 ........ 143
Straker v. The Queen (1977), 15 A.L.R. 103 ........ 43–44, 287
Strickland v. Washington, 466 U.S. 668 (1984) ........ 163–64
SZFDE v. Minister for Immigration and Citizenship (2006), 154 F.C.R. 365, [2006] FCAFC 14 ........ 177
SZFDE v. Minister for Immigration and Citizenship, [2007] HCA 35 ........ 171, 173, 174, 175, 176, 177

Taylor v. Lawrence, [2002] EWCA Civ 90 ........ 171
Thatcher v. Canada (1996), [1997] 1 F.C. 289, [1996] F.C.J. No. 1261 (T.D.) ........ 117

The Colonial Bank of Australasia v. Willan (1874), L.R. 5 P.C. 417 ....................174
The Queen v. Robert Farquarson, [2009] VSCA 307 ....................35
The Queen v. Van Beelen (1973) Supreme Court of South Australia
Trial Transcript ....................313–16
Therrien, Re, [2001] 2 S.C.R. 3, 2001 SCC 35 .................... 111
TKWJ v. The Queen, [2002] HCA 46 .................... 155
Treadaway v. Chief Constable of Police for the West Midlands
(25 October 1994) (Q.B.) .................... 198, 204, 205
*Truscott Reference (2007). See R. v. Truscott*
*Truscott, Re. See R. v. Truscott*
Truscott, Reference re, [1967] S.C.R. 309, [1967] S.C.J. No. 26 .................... 19, 118, 300

United States of America v. Burns and Rafay, [2001] 1 S.C.R. 283,
2001 SCC 7 .................... 93, 365
United States v. Crisp, 324 F.3d 261 (4th Cir. 2003) .................... 397

Victorian Stevedoring and General Contracting Co. Pty. Ltd. and
Meakes v. Dignan (1931), 46 C.L.R. 73, [1931] HCA 34 .................... 140
Von Einem v. Griffin and Anor (1998), 72 S.A.S.R. 110 .................... 142

W.R. v. Canada (Minister of Justice), [1999] F.C.J. No. 1059 (T.D.) .................... 117
Walsh, Re, 2008 NBCA 33 .................... 108, 114, 123, 127
Wati v. Minister for Immigration and Ethnic Affairs (1996), 71 F.C.R. 103 .................... 177
Weiss v. The Queen (2005), 224 C.L.R. 300, [2005] HCA 81 .................... 19, 148, 149, 150
Werribee v. The Queen (1928), 42 C.L.R. 1, [1928] HCA 41 .................... 140
Westlake v. Criminal Cases Review Commission, [2004] EWHC Admin 2779 .................... 342
Wilde v. The Queen, [1988] HCA 6 .................... 155
Williams v. General Medical Council, [2007] EWHC 2603 (Admin) .................... 18, 291
Woolmington v. D.P.P., [1935] A.C. 462 .................... 59

# Index


Abuse of process, 169n
Accreditation, forensic science, 378
  American Society of Crime Laboratory Directors (ASCLD), 378
  DNA Advisory Board (DNAB), 378
  implementation difficulties, 383
  International Organization for Standardization, 378
Acquittal, defined, 106
American Society of Crime Laboratory Directors (ASCLD), 378, 379
American Society of Testing and Materials, 379
Anderson, Tim, case of, 236–37
Anthony, Donna, case of, 250, 252–53
Appeals
  acquittal vs. retrial: appellate discretion
    Australia, in, 151–52
    Britain, in, 62–63
    Canada, in, 106–9
  contemporary appeal provisions
    Australia, in, 134–38
      priviso, the, 136, 145
    Britain, in, 59–60
      priviso, the, 60
    Canada, in, 96–98
      priviso, the, 96
  Crown
    Australia, in, 152
    Britain, in, 63
    Canada, in, 110–12
    concessions, Canada, in, 114
  dead, by the, Canada, in, 99
  deference to jury
    Australia, in, 152–54
    Britain, in, 72–75
    Canada, in, 103–4
  disclosure, need for, Canada, in, 131
  error of law and procedural error, Australia, in, 154–56
  exhausted appeals, options for
    Britain, in, 64–65
    Canada, in
      petition procedure, 114–22
        *Canadian Charter of Rights and Freedoms*, 116–17
        *Criminal Code* of Canada, 115, 116, 117, 118–20
        royal prerogative of mercy, 115, 116, 118
  expert witnesses, Canada, in, 128–31
  fragmented appellate structure, Australia, in, 165–67
  fresh evidence on
    Australia, in, 133, 134, 139–40, 144, 156–58
    Britain, in, 69–72
    Canada, in, 96–97, 99, 106, 112–13, 120, 122, 123n, 131, 132
      *Criminal Code* of Canada, 112
      test for, 112
  general

Australia, in, 133–34
*Commonwealth of Australia Constitution Act 1900*, 134n
*Criminal Appeal Act 1907*, 135, 136
*Criminal Law Consolidation Act 1935 (S.A.)*, 135n
Britain, in, 55–56
*Criminal Appeal Act 1907*, 56n, 57, 58
Canada, in, 91–94
*Canadian Charter of Rights and Freedoms*, 95, 98
*Criminal Code* of Canada, 97–98
grounds for
Canada, in, 99–106
*Criminal Code* of Canada, 99–101, 103–4
trial by judge vs. trial by judge and jury, 102–4
guilt beyond reasonable doubt, defined, 113–14
Australia, in, 147–48, 149, 150n
Britain, in, 77–82
Canada, in, 113–14
hearing of vs. new trial, Canada, in, 122–23
history of
Britain, in, 56–59
case-stated procedure, 57
writ of error procedure, 57
Canada, in, 94–96
*Criminal Code* of Canada, 94, 95–96
royal pardon, 95
trial by judge vs. trial by judge and jury, 98
writs, common law, 94–95
incompetent trial representation and
Australia, in, 163–65
Britain, in, 82–84
Canada, in, 127–28
investigative techniques, proper and duty to disclose, Britain, in, 85–88
pardons, Canada, in, 110–11
procedural error: fair trial right, Britain, in, 65–69
process of, Britain, in, 60–62
prosecutor, role of and duty to disclose
Australia, in, 158–60
Canada, in, 123–27
police and others, 160–61
prosecutorial concessions, Britain, in, 88–90
proviso and
Australia, in, 145, 147–50
Britain, in, 60, 136
Canada, in, 96
reopening of
Australia, in, 138–47, 156, 167, 170, 313, 327
*Criminal Law Consolidation Act 1935* (S.A.), 138n, 145n
pardon insufficient, 145–46
petition procedure, 141–45
royal prerogative of mercy, 142, 145–46
royal commissions, 146–47
fraud, criminal proceedings, in and, 171–72
standards, contemporary
Britain, in, 76–77
Canada, in, 113
stay of proceedings, prosecutorial, Canada, in, 106, 109–10
*Criminal Code* of Canada, 109, 110
trial process, public confidence in
Australia, in, 161–63
Association In Defence of the Wrongly Convicted (AIDWYC), 8, 223, 307, 356, 405
Audits
miscarriage of justice cases, of, 406, 408–9
proactive, 288
Australia
baby deaths: failure to prosecute cases, 317–22
expert witnesses
admissibility of in, 33–35
reliability of, assessment of, 35–43
forensic pathology issues in, 20, 313–22
Fritz Van Beelen, case of, 19, 20, 313–17
forensic science issues in, 16–17
bloodstain pattern analysis
Alexander McLeod-Lindsay, case of, 275–76
scientific errors, multiple
Edward Splatt, case of, 16, 260–67. *See also* Splatt, Edward, case of

Splatt Royal Commission, 260n, 262–67. *See also* Splatt Royal Commission
scientific evidence, unreliable
Douglas Henry Rendell, case of, 276–77
scientific tests, false and confusing
Lindy Chamberlain, case of, 16, 267–75. *See also* Chamberlain, Lindy, case of
Chamberlain Royal Commission, 267n, 268–75. *See also* Chamberlain Royal Commission
Kuhl's bloodspray evidence re, 269–71
Prof. Cameron's evidence re, 271–72
Prof. Chaikin's and Sergeant Cocks' evidence re, 272–73
tunnel vision, DNA evidence and case of Frank Button, 278–80
general, 133–34
investigations and prosecutions, 13–14, 231–39
discredited informer evidence
Tim Anderson, case of, 236–37
mentally fragile suspects, manipulation of and inadequate disclosure
Andrew Mallard, case of, 14, 237–39
police and fabricated evidence, case of Mickelberg Brothers, 235–36
police, faulty reasoning by
Edward Splatt, case of, 13, 234–35. *See also* Splatt, Edward, case of
Splatt Royal Commission, 235. *See also* Splatt Royal Commission
police, intimidation by
Rupert Maxwell Stuart, case of, 233
police, poor behaviour of
commissions and inquiries, 231–32
police, pressure by and false confessions
John Button, case of, 233–34
miscarriage of justice, law on, 8–9, 133–68
appeals
acquittal vs. retrial: appellate discretion, 151–52
contemporary provisions, 134–38
Crown, 152
deference to jury, 152–54
error of law and procedural error, 154–56
fragmented appellate structure, 165–67
fresh evidence on, 156–58
incompetent trial representation, 163–65
prosecutor, role of and duty to disclose, 158–60
police and others included in, 160–61
proviso and, 147–50
reopening of, 138–47, 156, 167, 170, 313, 327
pardon insufficient, 145–46
petition procedure, 141–45
royal commissions, 146–47
general, 133–34
trial process, public confidence in, 161–63
Australian and British cases, links to fraudulent, 172–76, 187
Australian Innocence Project, 356n
Autopsies, medico-legal, recommendations for conducting, 392–93

Bailey, Kathleen, case of, 74, 208–9
Birmingham Six, 11, 15n, 197–99, 200, 202, 204, 244–45, 246, 332
Bloodstain pattern analysis, 253–54, 269–71, 275–76, 376, 380
cross-over electrophoresis test, 269
Ouchterlony test, 269
Britain
Criminal Cases Review Commission (CCRC), 3, 7, 8, 9, 11–12, 20–21, 22–23, 55, 59, 62, 64, 65, 66, 68, 73, 76, 80, 90, 92, 93n, 115, 119, 120, 121, 122, 131, 134, 142, 144, 167, 169, 196–97, 201, 202, 208, 210, 214, 220, 227, 230, 248, 251, 252, 253, 290, 294, 297, 313, 325, 326–50, 351, 352, 353, 354, 355, 356, 357, 358, 359, 360, 361, 363–64, 365, 366, 367, 369, 405, 406–11, 412
expert witnesses
admissibility of in, 33–35
reliability of, assessment of, 35–43

forensic pathology issues in, 17–19, 287–99
autopsy findings inadequate and misleading
Patrick Nicholls, case of, 293–295
diagnoses inappropriate
Kenneth Fraser and Steven Puaca, cases of, 295–97
disclosure of test results, lack of
Sally Clark, case of, 289–93. *See also* Clark, Sally, case of
time of death, misinterpretation of
Trevor Wickens, case of, 297–99. *See also* Wickens, Trevor, case of
forensic science issues in, 15, 244–54
bloodstain pattern analysis, misreading of
Stephen Downing, case of, 253–54
discredited evidence, Prof. Meadow's
Donna Anthony, case of, 252–53
Irish Republican Army (IRA) bombing cases, 15, 244–48. *See also* Irish Republican Army (IRA) bombing cases
fraudulent scientific evidence
Maguire Seven, case of, 245–46
May Inquiry, 245–46
preliminary test misrepresented
Birmingham Six, case of, 244–45
scientist independence and fraudulent scientific evidence
Judith Ward (M62 bombings), case of, 247–48
poor methodology
Craig McCreight, case of, 254
probabilities, misuse of
Angela Cannings, case of, 15, 18–19 251–52. *See also* Cannings, Angela, case of
Runciman Royal Commission on Criminal Justice, recommendations of, 248–49. *See also* Runciman Royal Commission of Justice
Criminal Cases Review Commission (CCRC), establishment of, 248
undisclosed test results
Sally Clark, case of, 15, 17–18, 250–51. *See also* Clark, Sally, case of
investigations and prosecutions, in, 11–12, 197–211
informer identification, undisclosed
Patrick Murphy, Michael McMahon, and David Cooper, cases of, 207–8
Irish Republican Army (IRA) bombing cases, 197–211. *See also* Irish Republican Army (IRA) bombing cases
Birmingham Six, 11, 15n, 197–99, 200, 204
Guildford Four, 11, 199, 200
Judith Ward (M62), 11, 200
Maguire Seven, 11, 199–200
over-evaluating evidence and stereotyping
Barry George, case of, 210–11
police
intimidation by and false confessions
Trevor Campbell, case of, 205–7
notebooks of, incorrect
Robert Maynard, Reginald Dudley, Kathleen Bailey, and Charles Clarke, cases of, 208–9
torture and assault by, 202–5
Derek Treadaway, case of, 203–5
Keith Twitchell, case of, 202–3
Runciman Royal Commission on Criminal Justice on, 201–2
miscarriage of justice, law on, 7, 55–90
appeals
acquittal vs. retrial: appellate discretion, 62–63
contemporary provisions, 59–60
Crown, 63
deference of to jury, 59, 61, 67, 72–75
disclosure, need for, 85–88
exhausted, 64–65
fresh evidence on, 69–72
history of, 56–59
investigations, proper, 85–88
procedural error: fair trial right, 65–69
process of, 60–62

prosecutorial concessions, 88–90
reopening of, 156, 313, 327
beyond reasonable doubt, defined, 77–82
contemporary standards, trial, 75–77
general, 55–56
incompetent trial representation, 82–84
Button, Frank, case of, 278–80
Button, John, case of, 233–34

C3 department, petitioning, 326, 327, 356, 405
Campbell, Trevor, case of, 73–74, 87, 205–7
Canada
forensic pathology issues in, 19–20, 299–313
pediatric cases: Dr. Charles Smith, 19–20, 303–13. *See also* Smith, Dr. Charles
Goudge Inquiry, 303, 304, 305, 306, 307, 308, 309, 310. *See also* Goudge Inquiry
recommendations of, 310–13
work of
"fall, no possibility of": Amber, case of, 304–5
"non-accidental injuries, 99 percent certain of": Nicholas, case of, 305
"rape and murder": Valin, case of, 307–10
"sexual assault": Jenna, case of, 306
"stabbing": Sharon, case of, 306–7
stomach contents and time of death
Steven Truscott, case of, 19, 20, 299–303. *See also* Truscott, Steven, case of
forensic science issues in, 15–16, 255–60
hair and fibre evidence
discredited
James Driskell, case of, 15, 257–58. *See also* Driskell, James, case of
Driskell Inquiry, 258
misuse of
Guy Paul Morin, case of, 255–57. *See also* Morin, Guy Paul, case of
Morin Inquiry, 255–57
serology, misleading and DNA evidence
David Milgaard, case of, 16, 258–59. *See also* Milgaard, David, case of
Milgaard Inquiry, 258–59. *See also* Milgaard Inquiry
test methods and results
Thomas Sophonow, case of, 16. *See also* Sophonow, Thomas, case of
investigations and prosecutions in, 13, 211–30
Director of Public Prosecutions, 30n, 31n, 63, 87, 152, 160, 207, 214
police
misconduct and inadequate disclosure
Donald Marshall Jr., case of, 13, 212–15. *See also* Marshall Jr., Donald, case of
Marshall Inquiry, 13, 91n, 124, 125, 127, 212n, 213n, 220. *See also* Marshall Inquiry
witness credibility and non-disclosure
Driskell Inquiry, 224–27. *See also* Driskell Inquiry
James Driskell, case of, 224–27. *See also* Driskell, James, case of
witnesses pressured by police
David Milgaard, case of, 227–30. *See also* Milgaard, David, case of
Milgaard Inquiry, 228–30. *See also* Milgaard Inquiry
public inquiries, 211
royal commissions, 212
science, use of and eyewitness misidentification
Thomas Sophonow, case of, 217–20. *See also* Sophonow, Thomas, case of
Sophonow Inquiry, 13, 218, 219–20. *See also* Sophonow Inquiry
tunnel vision
Gregory Parsons, Randy Druken, and Ronald Dalton, cases of, 221–24

Lamer Inquiry, 221. *See also* Lamer Inquiry
jailhouse informants and
Guy Paul Morin, case of, 13, 215–17. *See also* Morin, Guy Paul, case of
Morin Inquiry, 13, 215–16. *See also* Morin Inquiry
miscarriage of justice, law on, 7–8, 91–132
appeals
acquittal vs. new trial: appellate discretion, 106–9
contemporary provisions, 96–98
Crown, 111–12
dead, by the, 99
deference to jury, 103–4
exhausted: petition procedure, 114–22
fresh evidence on, 112–13
grounds for, 99–106
history of, 94–96
pardons, 110–11
prosecutors and expert witnesses and, 47–52
rehearing of after petition, 122–23
stays of proceedings, prosecutorial use of, 109–10
contemporary standards, trial, 113
Crown concessions, 114
disclosure, duty of full, 123–27
expert witnesses, 128–31
general, 91–94
guilt beyond reasonable doubt, defined, 113–14
incompetent trial representation, 127–28
prosecutor, role of, 123–27
*Canadian Charter of Rights and Freedoms*, 93, 95, 98, 110, 116–17, 128, 161n, 164
Cannings, Angela, case of, 15, 18–19, 250, 251–52, 287, 288, 289
*Cannings* principle, 252
Case Assessment and Interpretation (CAI), 211
Case-stated appeal procedure, 57
Centre of Forensic Sciences, 128, 256, 364, 388n, 389
Certification, individual, forensic science, 380
*Certiorari*, 174, 175–76, 178–80, 181, 182, 184
Chamberlain, Lindy, case of, 13, 16, 17n, 53, 148, 152n, 153n, 156, 158n, 192, 242, 264n, 267–75, 276n, 293, 313, 387
Chamberlain Royal Commission, 146, 267n, 268–75, 362n, 365n, 390n, 391, 394
summary of, 273–75
Change of law cases, 334, 345–47
Circumstantial cases, 79, 86, 265, 295, 299
Clark, Sally, case of, 15, 17–18, 44, 46n, 250–51, 252, 286, 287n, 289–93, 406
Clarke, Charles, case of, 74, 208–9
*Commonwealth of Australia Constitution Act 1900*, 134n, 138n, 139, 140, 141
Confessions, false, 205–7, 222, 233–34
Confirmation bias, 192, 195, 242, 258, 310
defined, 192
Contextual bias, 376–77
Controlled substances, *NAS Report* scrutiny of, 373–74
Convictions, safety of, 32, 59, 60, 61, 62, 68, 69, 70, 72, 73, 74, 75, 76, 78, 80, 81, 82, 84, 87, 89, 90, 93, 97, 98, 100, 101, 103, 130, 131, 136, 137, 144, 147, 148, 152, 154, 167, 198, 199, 200, 201, 202, 206, 207, 217, 228, 230, 235, 251, 252, 254, 265, 276, 277, 288, 290, 298, 299, 300n, 325, 326, 329, 331, 333, 341, 346, 350, 355, 357
Cooper, David, case of, 75n, 85, 86, 207–8
*Crime Scene and Forensic Procedures Manual*, 194
*Criminal Appeal Act 1907*, 56n, 57, 58, 60, 95, 135, 136, 148n
*Criminal Appeal Act 1968*, 60, 61n, 62n, 64n, 69, 70n, 198, 340
*Criminal Appeal Act 1995*, 3n, 331, 332, 338, 340
Criminal Cases Review Commission (CCRC), 3, 7, 8, 9, 11–12, 20–21, 22–23, 55, 59, 62, 64, 65, 66, 68, 73, 76, 80, 90, 92, 93n, 115, 119, 120, 121, 122, 131, 134, 142, 144, 167, 169, 196–97, 201, 202, 208, 210, 214, 220, 227, 230, 248, 251, 252, 253, 290, 294, 297, 313, 325, 326–50, 351, 352, 353, 354, 355, 356, 358, 363–64, 365, 366, 367, 369, 405, 412
application profile to, 333–34
case review personnel, 339–40
*Criminal Appeal Act 1995* and, 331
decision to refer, 341
establishment of, 326–31
facts and figures, 344

focus of, 359–61
fresh evidence, 340–41
*Criminal Appeal Act 1968* and, 340
innocence projects, relationship with, 357
internal and external audits of problem cases, 407, 409
judicial review of decisions of, 342–43
last resort in appeal, 343–44
legal representation of applicants, 408
members of, 331–32, 334
powers and responsibilities of, 332
practices of, review of, 347–50
references to and from the, 343
referrals to courts from, reception of, 344–47
change of law cases, 345–47
court judgments, differing, 345
review process, 334–39
assessing cases for review
no appeal cases, 335–36
no reviewable/plausible grounds, 336–37
reapplications, 336, 343
categorizing cases for review
Category A cases, 337–38
Category B cases, 338
Category C cases, 338
Category D cases, 338–39
Scottish Criminal Cases Review Commission (SCCRC) vs., 347
similar type bodies, establishment of in Canada and Australia, 406–11
systemic reform, ability to bring about, 358–61
appeal rights, 360–61
*Criminal Code* of Canada, 3n, 92n, 94, 95–101, 103–4, 105, 106, 109, 110, 111, 112, 113n, 115, 116, 117, 118–20, 121n, 122n, 123n, 124, 136n, 143n, 164, 225, 228, 300n, 301, 363, 364
*Criminal Law Consolidation Act 1935* (S.A.), 135n, 138n, 142n, 145n, 147n, 151n, 156n, 412n
Criminal proceedings, fraud in, 9–11, 169–87
Cross-over electrophoresis test, 268, 269
Crown
appeals, 63, 111–12, 152
concessions, 114

Dalton, Ronald, case of, 13n, 91n, 212n, 221–24
*Daubert* standards, 34, 48–49, 129n, 372, 373n, 374, 382, 397, 398–402
*Death Investigation: A Guide for the Scene Investigator*, 383
Death Investigators, reliability of, 382–84
National Institute of Justice, 383
Declaration of innocence, 123
Defence lawyers and ineffective counsel
miscarriage of justice, role in, 82–84, 127–28, 163–65
Director of Public Prosecutions, 30n, 31n, 63, 87, 152, 160, 207, 214, 239, 364
Disclosure
duty of, 85–88, 93, 123–27, 363
expert witness', 44–47
forensic pathologists and, 289–93
forensic scientists and, 246, 247–51, 387
jury, to the, 162
prosecutor's, 31–32, 158–60, 162, 195–97, 218
inadequate, 3, 11, 13, 212–15, 220, 222, 224–27, 237–39
DNA Advisory Board (DNAB), 378
DNA evidence, 3, 12, 16, 21, 73, 93, 104, 105, 110, 111, 216, 221, 223, 226, 256, 257–59, 277–83, 302, 339, 356, 363, 375, 376, 382, 388
low-copy number DNA (LCN DNA), 280–83, 409
*NAS Report* scrutiny of, 373
Downing, Stephen, case of, 80, 253–54
Driskell, James, case of, 16, 91n, 121n, 212n, 224–27, 240, 257–58, 363n, 376, 405
Driskell Inquiry, 110n, 123, 224–27, 258, 363, 376, 389n, 390n, 394, 405
Druken, Randy, case of, 13n, 91n, 212n, 221–24
Dudley, Reginald, case of, 74, 208–9
Due administration of justice, fraudulent cases and, 176–77

Ear-print evidence, 254, 375
*NAS Report* scrutiny of, 375
Education and training, forensic science in, 380–84, 402
death investigators, 382–84
*Death Investigation: A Guide for the Scene Investigator*, 383
forensic pathology research, underdevelopment of, 383–84

National Institute of Justice, 383
research and training programs, 381–82
scientific education, legal system's, 382
*Reference Manual on Scientific Evidence*, 382
standards and accreditation, difficulties with, 383
Electro-static document analysis (ESDA), 206
Error correction and system reform, 20–21, 325–67
C3 department, petitioning, 326, 327
Criminal Cases Review Commission (CCRC), 326–50
case review personnel, 339–40
decision to refer, 341
establishment of, 326–31
facts and figures, 344
fresh evidence, 340–41
judicial review of decisions of, 342–43
last resort in appeal, 343–44
practices of, review of, 347–50
references to and from the, 343
referrals to courts from, reception of, 344–47
change of law cases, 345–47
court judgments, differing, 345
review process, 334–39
assessing cases for review
no appeal cases, 335–36
no reviewable/plausible grounds, 336–37
reapplications, 336, 343
categorizing cases for review
Category A cases, 337–38
Category B cases, 338
Category C cases, 338
Category D cases, 338–39
Scottish Criminal Cases Review Commission (SCCRC) vs., 347
factual innocence error correction commission: North Carolina Innocence Inquiry Commission (NCIIC), 349, 351–56
general, 325–26
innocence projects, 21
Association In Defence of the Wrongly Convicted (AIDWYC), 8, 223, 307, 356, 405
Australian Innocence Project, 356n
Criminal Cases Review Commission (CCRC), relationship of with, 357
Griffith University Project, 356n
International Commission of Jurists, 357
investigative media and, 356–57
JUSTICE, 328, 357
National Council for Civil Liberties (Liberty), 356–57
Ombudsman system, 357
UTS Innocence Project, 356n
miscarriage of justice, prevention vs. correction, 358–61
public inquiries, 21
systemic reform
contribution of error correction committees to, 358–61
models of, 361–66
Canadian public inquiries, 362–66
European Network of Forensic Science Institutes, 379
Evidence
DNA. *See* DNA evidence
ear-print, 254, 375
hair and fibre, 255–60
informer, discredited, 236–37, 254
pathology
autopsy findings inadequate and misleading, 293–95, 303
diagnoses inappropriate, 295–97
hypostasis, 316n
*livor mortis*, 316n
stomach contents, 299–303, 313, 314–15, 316
time of death, misinterpretation of, 297–303
unreliable, 287, 322
scientific
contamination of, 256–57
improving, 369–402
new forms of, 254
unreliable, 242, 243, 250, 254, 262, 269, 274, 276–77
serology, 258–59
Expert witnesses, 5–7, 27–28, 29, 31, 114–22, 128–31
admissibility criteria
Australia and Britain, in, 33–35, 41–42

Canada, in, 35n, 47–48, 49
audits of problem cases, 406
challenge of by defence experts, 394–95
codes of conduct for, 50–52
forensic scientists and pathologists, 51–52
disclosure, duty of, 44–47
duties and responsibilities of, 40–41
evidence-based vs. experience-based, 129–30
general principles of, 32–33, 37–38
function of, 32–33
international collaboration between, 53
jury, assisting the, 35
novel science, 48, 49, 131
police and others, 160–61
probative vs. prejudicial value of, 43–44
problems associated with, systemic reporting of, 406
prosecutor's, 200
reliability of, assessment of, 35–43, 48–49
Australian and British positions on, 35–43
Canadian position on, 48–49
*Daubert* standards, 48–49
evidence-based vs. experience-based, 49
threshold reliability, 129, 130, 131
UK Law Commission reforms and, 47
Eyewitness misidentification, 217–20

Factual innocence, 12n, 62n, 67–68, 99, 106, 123, 230, 277, 326, 349, 351–56, 361, 406n
defined, 353
error correction commission: North Carolina Innocence Inquiry Commission (NCIIC), 351–56
Failure to prosecute, Australian cases of, 317–22
Fingerprint experts, 130, 241
evidence of, 21, 193, 397
*NAS Report* scrutiny of, 374, 375, 379, 380, 381
First Nations cases, miscarriages of justice and, 311
Fitzgerald Judicial Inquiry, 232
Forensic investigations and miscarriages of justice
reality of, 4, 10–20, 189–322
forensic pathology issues, 285–322. *See also* Forensic pathology
forensic science issues, 241–83. *See also* Forensic science
investigations and prosecutions, 191–240. *See also* Investigations and prosecutions
responses to, 4, 20–23, 323–413
error correction and system reform, 20–21, 325–67. *See also* Error correction and system reform
forensic science reliability, improvements in, 21–22, 369–402. *See also* Forensic science, improving
impartial vs. flawed forensic science: reforms to close gap, 403–14. *See also* Forensic science, impartial vs. flawed: reforms to close gap
rhetoric: legal proceedings, guiding principles of, 4–10, 25–187
fraud, criminal proceedings, in, 169–87. *See also* Fraud, criminal proceedings, in
miscarriage of justice, law on, 55–168. *See also* Miscarriage of justice, law on
prosecutors and expert witnesses, 27–54. *See also* Prosecutors and expert witnesses
Forensic pathology, 10, 17–20, 285–322
Australian experience, 20, 313–22
baby deaths: failure to prosecute cases, 20, 317–22
Fritz Van Beelen, case of, 19, 20, 313–17
British experience, 17–19, 287–99
autopsy findings inadequate and misleading
Patrick Nicholls, case of, 293–295
baby deaths, wrongly prosecuted
Angela Cannings, case of, 287, 288, 289. *See also* Cannings, Angela, case of
diagnoses inappropriate
Kenneth Fraser and Steven Puaca, cases of, 295–97
disclosure of test results, lack of
Sally Clark, case of, 17–18, 289–93. *See also* Clark, Sally, case of
time of death, misinterpretation of

Trevor Wickens, case of, 297–99. *See also* Wickens, Trevor, case of
Canadian experience, 19–20, 299–313
pediatric cases: Dr. Charles Smith, work of, 19–20, 303–13. *See also* Smith, Dr. Charles
Goudge Inquiry, recommendations of, 310–13. *See also* Goudge Inquiry
work of
"fall, no possibility of": Amber, case of, 304–5
"non-accidental injuries, 99 percent certain of": Nicholas, case of, 305
"rape and murder": Valin, case of, 307–10
"sexual assault": Jenna, case of, 306
"stabbing": Sharon, case of, 306–7
stomach contents and time of death
Steven Truscott, case of, 19, 20, 299–303. *See also* Truscott, Steven, case of
changes in, post-Dr. Charles Smith, 312–13
defined, 286
general, 285–87
pathologists, shortage of, 383, 391–93
Pathology Advisory Board for Forensic Pathology, 291
Quality Assurance and Scientific Standards Board (QASSB), 291
reforms in, 388
research, underdevelopment of, 383–84
Forensic science, 10, 14–17, 241–83
Australian experience, 16–17
bloodstain pattern analysis
Alexander McLeod-Lindsay, case of, 275–76
scientific errors, multiple
Edward Splatt, case of, 16, 260–67. *See also* Splatt, Edward, case of
Splatt Royal Commission, 260n, 262–67
scientific evidence, unreliable
Douglas Henry Rendell, case of, 276–77
scientific tests, false and confusing
Chamberlain Royal Commission, 267n, 268–75
Lindy Chamberlain, case of, 16, 267–75
Kuhl's bloodspray evidence re, 269–71
Prof. Cameron's evidence re, 271–72
Prof. Chaikin's and Sergeant Cocks' evidence re, 272–73
tunnel vision
Frank Button, case of exonerated by DNA evidence, 278–80
British experience, 15, 244–54
bloodstain pattern analysis, misreading of
Stephen Downing, case of, 253–54
discredited evidence, Prof. Meadow's
Donna Anthony, case of, 252–53
Irish Republic Army bombing cases, 15, 244–48. *See also* Irish Republican Army (IRA) bombing cases
fraudulent scientific evidence
Maguire Seven, case of, 245–46
May Inquiry, 245–46
scientist independence and fraudulent scientific evidence
Judith Ward (M62 bombings), case of, 246–48
poor methodology
Craig McCreight, case of, 254
preliminary test misrepresented
Birmingham Six, case of, 244–45
probabilities, misuse of
Angela Cannings, case of, 15, 251–52. *See also* Cannings, Angela, case of
Runciman Royal Commission on Criminal Justice, recommendations of, 248–49. *See also* Runciman Royal Commission on Criminal Justice
Criminal Cases Review Commission (CCRC), establishment of, 248
undisclosed test results
Sally Clark, case of, 15, 250–51. *See also* Clark, Sally, case of

Canadian experience, 15–16, 255–60
hair and fibre evidence, discredited
Driskell Inquiry, 258. *See also* Driskell Inquiry
James Driskell, case of, 16, 257–58. *See also* Driskell, James, case of
misuse of
Guy Paul Morin, case of, 15, 255–57. *See also* Morin, Guy Paul, case of
Morin Inquiry, 255–57. *See also* Morin Inquiry
serology, misleading and DNA evidence
David Milgaard, case of, 16, 258–59. *See also* Milgaard, David, case of
Milgaard Inquiry, 258–59. *See also* Milgaard Inquiry
test methods and results
Thomas Sophonow, case of, 16. *See also* Sophonow, Thomas, case of
communication, scientist's inadequate, 256
contamination, evidence, 256
contextual bias, 376–77
DNA evidence, 277–83
low-copy number DNA (LCN DNA)
Sean Hoey, case of, 280–83
tunnel vision
Frank Button, case of, 280–83
general, 241–43
impartial vs. flawed: reforms to lessen gap, 403–14
Criminal Cases Review Commission (CCRC)-type bodies, establishment of, 406–11
forensic science research and review developments, 403–4
judicial control over expert evidence, obtaining better, 411–12
standard of demonstrable reliability, imposing a new, 413
suspect forms of evidence, audit of cases of, 405–6
improving, 21–22, 325, 369–402
admissibility of expert evidence: judicial gatekeeping, 396–402
*Daubert* standards, 398–402
threshold reliability, 397
education and training programs, 380–84, 402
death investigators, 382–84
*Death Investigation: A Guide for the Scene Investigator*, 383
forensic pathology research, underdevelopment of, 383–84
National Institute of Justice, 383
standards and accreditation, difficulties with, 383
research and training programs, 381–82
scientific education, legal system's, 382
*Reference Manual on Scientific Evidence*, 382
evidence-based and research-based forensic science, move to, 384–87, 400–1, 402
proper methodology and full disclosure, 387
published research, limits to reliance on, 385–87
forensic practices, strengthening oversight of, 378–80
accreditation, 378
certification, individual, 380
funding vs. specific improvements, 380
proficiency testing, 379
American Society of Crime Laboratory Directors (ASCLD), 379
International Organization for Standardization, 379
standards and guidelines, 379
forensic science
challenge of by defence experts, 394–95
uncertainty in, ways to express, 395–96
general, 369–71
*NAS Report*
controlled substances, 373–74
DNA evidence, 373
fingerprints, 374

hair evidence, 375–76
other, 376
pattern evidence, other, 375
reference image databases, 375
state of science, assessment of, 371–72
regulation and audits, 370–71, 402
reliability of, 21–22
unified vision to reform, 387–94
central regulation, 391, 402
Forensic Science Regulator, 249, 370, 391
National Institute of Forensic Science, 391
forensic pathologists, shortage of, 391–93
forensic science centres, independence of, 393–94
laboratory contamination, 210n
reports, recommendations for writing, 257
scientific evidence, new forms of, 254
systemic error, nature of, 259–60
thin layer chromatography (TLC), 245, 247
unconscious bias, 263
unreliability, 200, 202
reasons for, 242
use of in legal process: *NAS Report*, 376–78
Forensic Science Advisory Council, 249, 391
Forensic Science Regulator, 249, 370, 391
Forensic scientists and pathologists
codes of conduct for, 51–52
disclosure, duty of full, 246, 247–48, 251, 289–93, 301, 311
partisanship of, 247–48
Fragmentation, forensic science and, 387–94
central regulation of, 391
National Institute of Forensic Science, 391
Fraser, Kenneth, case of, 295–97
Fraud, criminal proceedings, in, 9–11, 169–87
abuse of process, 169n
appeals, reopening options, 171–72
Australian to British cases, links from, 172–76, 187
*certiorari*, 174, 175–76, 178–80, 181, 182, 184
civil and criminal cases, 170–71
due administration of justice, 176–77
finality principle, 173
forensic scientists and, 245–48
general, 169–70
inherent power, superior court's, 185–86
public law—criminal, 177–85
third party fraud, 175, 176
Fugitive, extradition of, 93, 365
Funding, forensic science, 380

Gatekeeping role, judge's, 48, 49, 128, 193, 325, 396–402
George, Barry, case of, 192, 210–11, 346
Goudge Inquiry, 19, 20, 22, 34–35, 47, 48, 49, 128–29, 240, 294n, 297, 303, 304, 305, 306, 308, 309, 310, 363, 364, 369–71, 385, 388, 391–93, 395, 397, 400, 401, 404, 406, 411, 413
recommendations of, 310–13
*Goudge Report*, 312
*Report of the Inquiry into Pediatric Forensic Pathology in Ontario*, 6n, 34n, 91n, 212n, 286n, 363n, 385n, 390, 404n
Griffith University Project, 356n
Guildford Four, 11, 15, 45, 199–200, 245, 328
Guilt beyond reasonable doubt, 286, 289, 413
Australia, in, 147–48, 149, 150n
Britain, in, 77–82
Canada, in, 92, 113–14

Hair and fibre evidence, 255–58, 259–60, 363, 389
discredited, 257–58
misuse of, 255–57
*NAS Report* scrutiny of, 375–76
Hair microscopy, 405
Hoey, Sean, case of, 280–83
Hypostasis, 316n

Informer identification, undisclosed, 207–8
Inherent power, superior court's, fraud and, 185–86
Innocence projects, 21, 67, 68n, 325, 343, 348, 351, 406–7, 411
Association In Defence of the Wrongly Convicted (AIDWYC), 8, 223, 307, 356, 405
Australian Innocence Project, 356n
Criminal Cases Review Commission (CCRC), relationship with, 357

Griffith University Project, 356n
investigative media and, 356–57
JUSTICE, 357
National Council for Civil Liberties (Liberty), 356–57
UTS Innocence Project, 356n
International Commission of Jurists, 357
International Organization for Standardization, 378
Intimidation, police, by, 205–7
Investigations and prosecutions, 10–14, 191–240
Australian experience, 13–14, 231–39
discredited informer evidence
Tim Anderson, case of, 236–37
mentally fragile suspects, manipulation of and inadequate disclosure
Andrew Mallard, case of, 237–39. *See also* Mallard, Andrew, case of
police
fabricated evidence
Mickelberg Brothers, case of, 235–36
false confessions: police pressure
John Button, case of, 233–34
faulty reasoning of
Edward Splatt, case of, 13, 234–35. *See also* Splatt, Edward, case of
Splatt Royal Commission, 235. *See also* Splatt Royal Commission
intimidation by
Rupert Maxwell Stuart, case of, 233
poor behaviour of
commissions and inquiries, 231–32
Fitzgerald Judicial Inquiry, 232
British experience, 11–12, 197–211
informer identification, undisclosed
Patrick Murphy, Michael McMahon, and David Cooper, cases of, 207–8
Irish Republic Army bombing cases
Birmingham Six, 11, 197–99, 200
Guildford Four, 11, 199, 200
Maguire Seven, 11
Ward, Judith (M62), 11, 200
police
evidence over-evaluation and objectivity lack
Barry George, case of, 210–11
intimidation by causing false confessions
Trevor Campbell case, 205–7
notebooks of, incorrect
Robert Maynard, Reginald Dudley, Kathleen Bailey, and Charles Clarke, cases of, 208–9
torture and assault by
Derek Treadaway, case of, 203–5
Keith Twitchell, case of, 202–3
Runciman Royal Commission on Criminal Justice, 201–2. *See also* Runciman Royal Commission on Criminal Justice
Canadian experience, 13, 207, 211–30
Association In Defence of the Wrongly Convicted (AIDWYC), 8, 223, 307, 356, 405
jailhouse informants and tunnel vision
Guy Paul Morin, case of, 13, 215–17. *See also* Morin, Guy Paul, case of
Morin Inquiry, 215–16. *See also* Morin Inquiry
police
misconduct, inadequate disclosure and tunnel vision
Donald Marshall Jr., case of, 13, 212–15. *See also* Marshall Jr., Donald, case of
Marshall Inquiry, 13. *See also* Marshall Inquiry
witness credibility and non-disclosure
Driskell Inquiry, 224–27. *See also* Driskell Inquiry
James Driskell, case of, 224–27. *See also* Driskell, James, case of
witnesses pressured by
David Milgaard, case of, 227–30. *See also* Milgaard, David, case of

Milgaard Inquiry, 228–30. *See also* Milgaard Inquiry
science, use of and eyewitness misidentification
Thomas Sophonow, case of, 217–20. *See also* Sophonow, Thomas, case of
Sophonow Inquiry, 13, 218, 219–20. *See also* Sophonow Inquiry
tunnel vision
Gregory Parsons, Randy Druken, and Ronald Dalton, cases of, 221–24
Lamer Inquiry, 221–24. *See also* Lamer Inquiry
Case Assessment and Interpretation (CAI), 211
Electro-static document analysis (ESDA), 206
expert witnesses, reliability of, 200
general, 191–93
mental instability, confessions and, 200
police and, 193–95. *See also* Investigations and prosecutions, Australian experience, police; Investigations and prosecutions, British experience, police; Investigations and prosecutions, Canadian experience, police
confirmation bias, 195
credibility of, 203, 207, 209
knock-on effect, 165, 209
*Crime Scene and Forensic Procedures Manual*, 194
stereotyping, 195
predisposing circumstances, miscarriages of justice and, 192
prosecutions, 195–97
Irish Republican Army (IRA) bombing cases, 7, 11, 15, 45, 59, 170, 192, 197, 198, 240, 291–92, 326–27, 328, 387
Birmingham Six, 11, 15n, 197–99, 200, 204, 244–45, 332
forensic science issues and, 244–48
Guildford Four, 11, 15, 45, 199–200, 245, 328
investigations and prosecutions re, 197–211
Judith Ward (M62 bombings), 11, 15n, 45, 196n, 200, 246–48, 291–92, 387
Maguire Seven, 11, 15n, 45n, 199–200, 245–46, 249n, 328, 329

Jailhouse informants, unreliable, 12, 13, 94, 215–16, 221–22
Judicial inquiries, 166, 232, 358, 361, 411
Jury, deference to, 72–75, 152–54, 167
JUSTICE, 328, 357

Knock-on effect, 165, 209

Laboratory contamination, 210n
Lamer Inquiry, 13, 91n, 109–10, 212n, 221, 222–26
Liberty, 356
Lividity, 316n
*Livor mortis*, 316n
Low-copy number DNA (LCN DNA), 280–83, 409
Lurking doubt cases, 62, 97, 100, 103, 131, 147–48, 217, 349, 366, 410

M62 bombings, 11, 15n, 45, 196n, 200, 246–48, 291–92, 387
Maguire Seven, 11, 15n, 45n, 199–200, 245–46, 249n, 328, 329
Mallard, Andrew, case of, 14, 138n, 144–45, 152, 153n, 156, 158, 160, 161n, 162–63, 165, 166n, 237–39
Marshall, Jr., Donald, case of, 13, 93, 114, 124, 130, 192, 196, 212–15, 228, 362, 363, 365, 400
Marshall Inquiry, 13, 124, 125, 127, 212n, 220, 226, 362–63, 364, 365
May Inquiry, 200, 245–46, 329, 362n
Maynard, Robert, case of, 74, 75n, 81, 87, 208–9
McCreight, Craig, case of, 254
McLeod-Lindsay, Alexander, case of, 275–76
McMahon, Michael, case of, 166n, 207–8
Mentally fragile suspects
confessions and, 200
manipulation of, 237–39
Mickelberg Brothers, case of, 138n, 139, 140–41, 235–36
Milgaard, David, case of, 16, 91n, 93n, 109, 110, 111, 130, 212n, 227–30, 258–59, 400
Milgaard Inquiry, 91n, 110n, 115, 117–18, 120, 121n, 212n, 228, 258–59

Miscarriage of justice
correction vs. prevention of, 357–58
defined, 2, 3
Canadian legislation, in, 119
failure to prosecute, 317–22
First Nations cases, in, 311
forensic
pathology issues and, 285–322
science issues and, 241–83
fraud, criminal proceedings, in, 169–87
law on
Australia, in, 8–9, 90, 133–68
appeals
acquittal vs. retrial: appellate discretion, 151–52
contemporary appeal provisions, 134–38
Crown, 152
deference to jury, 152–54
error of law and procedural error, 154–56
fragmented appellate structure, 165–67
fresh evidence on, 133, 134, 139–40, 144, 156–58
police misconduct, 160–61
prosecutor, role of and duty to disclose, 158–60
reopening of, 138–47
general, 133–34
incompetent trial representation and, 163–65
royal commissions, 13–14, 56, 146–47, 212, 255, 313, 358, 362n, 365n
trial process, public confidence in, 161–63
Britain, in, 7, 55–90
appeals
acquittal vs. retrial: appellate discretion, 62–63
appellate system, evolution of, 55, 56–59
contemporary appeal provisions, 59–60
Criminal Cases Review Commission (CCRC), 55, 62, 65, 66, 68, 73, 76, 90. *See also* Criminal Cases Review Commission (CCRC)
Crown, 63
deference to jury, 72–75
exhausted, options for, 64–65
fresh evidence on, 69–72
investigative techniques, proper and duty to disclose, 85–88
procedural error: fair trial right, 65–69
process of, 60–62
prosecutorial concessions, 88–90
standards, contemporary, 76–77
general, 55–56
guilt beyond reasonable doubt, defined, 77–82
incompetent trial representation and, 82–84
Canada, in, 7–8, 91–132
appeals
acquittal vs. retrial: appellate discretion, 106–9
contemporary appeal provisions, 96–98
*Criminal Code* of Canada, 124
Crown, 111–12
Crown concessions, 114
dead, by the, 99
disclosure, need for, 131
exhausted, options for: petition procedure, 114–22
expert witnesses, 128–31
fresh evidence, 96–97, 99, 106, 112–13, 120, 122, 123n, 131, 132
grounds for, 99–106
hearing of vs. new trial, 122–23
history of, 94–96
incompetent trial representation and, 127–28
pardons, 110–11
prosecutors, role of and duty to disclose, 123–27
standards, contemporary, 113
*Canadian Charter of Rights and Freedoms*, 93, 95, 98
general, 91–94
guilt beyond reasonable doubt, defined, 113–14
public inquiries, 7–8, 10, 21, 22, 53, 56, 91–93, 94, 110, 130, 152, 211–30, 243n, 255–60, 299–313, 325, 326, 351, 358, 362–66
reality of, 4, 10–20, 189–322

forensic pathology issues, 191–240. *See also* Investigations and prosecutions
forensic science issues, 241–83. *See also* Forensic science
investigations and prosecutions, 191–240. *See also* Investigations and prosecutions
responses to, 4, 20–23, 322, 323–413
error correction and systemic reform, 20–21, 325–67. *See also* Error correction and system reform
forensic science
reliability, improvements in, 21–22, 369–402. *See also* Forensic science, improving
impartial vs. flawed, reforms to lessen gap, 22–23, 403–14. *See also* Forensic science, impartial vs. flawed: reforms to lessen gap
rhetoric of, 4–10, 25–187
fraud, criminal proceedings, in, 169–87. *See also* Fraud, criminal proceedings, in
miscarriage of justice, law on, 55–168. *See also* Miscarriage of justice, law on
prosecutors and expert witnesses, 27–54. *See also* Prosecutors and expert witnesses
Morin, Guy Paul, case of, 13, 15, 97, 103, 111, 130, 215–17, 240, 255–57, 376, 385–86, 389, 400
Morin Inquiry, 13, 16n, 49–50, 91n, 97n, 102, 111, 128, 212n, 215–16, 222, 243, 255–57, 259–60, 363, 364, 370, 376, 385–86, 388–89, 390, 394n
Munchausen Syndrome by Proxy (MSbP), 17, 250, 251
Murphy, Patrick, case of, 75n, 82, 83, 85, 207–8

Narrative coherence, 79
*NAS Report*, 21, 22, 241, 370, 371–402
admissibility of expert evidence: judicial gatekeeping, 396–402
*Daubert* standards, 398–402
threshold reliability, 397
controlled substances, 373–74
DNA evidence, 373
education and training recommendations, 380–84, 402
death investigators, 382–84
forensic pathology research, underdevelopment of, 383–84
medical examiners and forensic pathologists, shortage of, 383
standards and accreditation, difficulties with, 383
research and training, 381–82
scientific education, legal system's, 382
evidence-based and research-based forensic science, move to, 384–87, 400–401, 402
proper methodology and full disclosure, 387
published research, limits to reliance on, 385–87
fingerprints, 374
forensic practices, strengthening oversight of
accreditation, 378
certification, individual, 380
funding vs. specific improvements, 380
standards and guidelines, 379
forensic science
challenge of by defence experts, 394–95
uncertainty in, ways to express, 395–96
use of in legal process, 376–78
hair evidence, 375–76
other, 376
pattern evidence, other, 375
reference image databases, 375
state of science, assessment of, 371–72
unified vision to reform, 387–94
central regulation, 391, 402
forensic
pathologists, shortage of, 391–93
science centres, independence of, 393–94
National Academy of Sciences (NAS), 21, 241, 273n, 370, 371, 385, 411
National Association of Testing Authorities (NATA), 50
National Council for Civil Liberties, 356–57

National Institute of Forensic Science, 391, 394
National Institute of Justice (NIJ), 381, 383
National Institute of Standards and Technology, 379
Nicholls, Patrick, case of, 70, 86, 293–95
No appeal case, 335–36
No reviewable/plausible grounds cases, 336–37
North Carolina Innocence Inquiry Commission (NCIIC), 349, 351–56
  comparison to CCRC and SCCRC, 353, 354, 356, 361
  description of, 351
  members of, 352–53
Novel science, 48, 49, 131
Nullity, trial, 136n

Objectivity, loss of, 11
Ombudsman system, 357
Ouchterlony test, 269

Pardons, 110–11, 145–46
Parsons, Gregory, case of, 13n, 91n, 130, 212n, 221–24, 400
Pathology Advisory Board for Forensic Pathology, 291
Pattern evidence, *NAS Report* scrutiny of, 375
Pediatric cases: Dr. Charles Smith, work of. *See* Smith, Dr. Charles, work of
Petition procedure after appeal exhaustion, 114–22
Police
  Australia, in,
    fabricated evidence by
      Mickelberg Brothers, case of, 235–36
    false confessions: police pressure
      John Button, case of, 233–34
    faulty reasoning of
      Edward Splatt, case of, 13, 234–35. *See also* Splatt, Edward, case of
      Splatt Royal Commission, 235. *See also* Splatt Royal Commission
    intimidation by
      Rupert Maxwell Stuart, case of, 233
    poor behaviour of
      commissions and inquiries, 231–32
      Fitzgerald Judicial Inquiry, 232
  Britain, in
    evidence over-evaluation and objectivity lack
      Barry George, case of, 210–11
    informer identification, undisclosed
      Patrick Murphy, Michael McMahon, and David Cooper, cases of, 207–8
    intimidation by and false confessions
      Trevor Campbell, case of, 205–7
    notebooks of, incorrect
      Robert Maynard, Reginald Dudley, Kathleen Bailey, and Charles Clarke, cases of, 208–9, 220
    torture and assault by, 220
      Derek Treadaway, case of, 203–5
      Keith Twitchell, case of, 202–3
  Canada, in,
    misconduct, tunnel vision, and non-disclosure
      Donald Marshall Jr., case of, 212–15. *See also* Marshall, Jr., Donald, case of
      Marshall Inquiry, 212n, 213, 214. *See also* Marshall Inquiry
    witness
      credibility of and non-disclosure
        Driskell Inquiry, 224–27. *See also* Driskell Inquiry
        James Driskell, case of, 224–27. *See also* Driskell, James, case of
      pressure of by
        David Milgaard, case of, 227–230. *See also* Milgaard, David, case of
        Milgaard Inquiry, 228. *See also* Milgaard Inquiry
  credibility of, 203, 207
    knock-on effect, 209
  investigations and prosecutions, 193–95
    *Crime Scene and Forensic Procedures Manual*, 194
    investigations, 194–95, 199
      tunnel vision, 194
    prosecutions, 195–97
  misconduct, 13, 14, 73–74, 160–61, 212–15, 219–20, 240, 245
  stereotyping by, 195

suggestive interviewing by, 221, 240
Predisposing circumstances, miscarriages of justice and, 192
Presumptive tests, misuse of, 242, 243
Probabilities, misuse of, 251–52
Procedural errors: fair trial rights, 65–69, 154–56
Professional misconduct, 253
Proficiency testing, 379
American Society of Crime Laboratory Directors (ASCLD), 378, 379
Prosecutions, disclosure, duty of full, 195–97
Prosecutors and expert witnesses, 27–54
codes of conduct, 50–52
Criminal Procedure Rules (British), 50–51
forensic scientists and pathologists, 51–52
expert witnesses, 32–47
Australia and Britain, admissibility of in, 33–35, 41–42
Canada, in, 47–52
disclosure, duty of, 44–47, 218
duties and responsibilities of, 40–41
general principles of, 32–33, 37–38
jury, assisting the, 35
novel science, 48, 49
probative vs. prejudicial value of, 43–44
reliability of, assessment of, 35–43
general, 27–29
international collaboration, 53
prosecutions, 29–32
general principles of, 29–30
guidelines, 30–32
UK Law Commission reforms, 47
Provisional Statement of Reasons (pSOR), 337, 338, 341
Proviso, the
Australia in, 145, 147–50
Britain, in, 60, 136
Canada, in, 96
Puaca, Steven, case of, 295–97
Public inquiries, 7–8, 10, 21, 22, 53, 56, 91–93, 94, 110, 130, 152, 211–30, 243n, 255–60, 299–313, 325, 326, 351, 358, 362–66
CCRC-type commissions, recommendations re, 363–64, 365
Goudge Inquiry, 19, 20, 22, 34–35, 47, 48, 49, 128–29, 240, 294n, 297, 303, 304, 305, 306, 308, 309, 310–13, 363, 364, 369–71, 385, 388, 391–93, 395, 397, 400, 401, 404, 406, 411, 413
Marshall Inquiry, 13, 124, 125, 127, 212n, 220, 226, 362–63, 364, 365
members of, 362
Morin Inquiry, 13, 16n, 49–50, 91n, 97n, 102, 111, 128, 212n, 215–16, 222, 243, 255–57, 259–60, 363, 364, 370, 376, 385–86, 388–89, 390, 394n
Sophonow Inquiry, 4n, 13, 91n, 130, 212n, 218, 219–20, 222, 225, 227, 365, 407
systemic reform of, recommendations on, 362–66
fugitive, extradition of, 365
pretrial prosecutor disclosure, 364

Quality Assurance and Scientific Standards Board (QASSB), 291

Real possibility test, 3, 119, 326, 332, 333, 336, 337, 338, 340, 341, 343, 344, 357
Reality, miscarriages of justice, of, 4, 10–20, 187, 189–322
forensic pathology, 10, 17–20, 285–322
Australia, in, 313–22
Britain, in, 287–99
Canada, in, 299–313
forensic science, 10, 14–17, 241–83
Australia, in, 260–77
Britain, in, 244–54
Canada, in, 255–60
DNA experience, 277–83
investigations and prosecutions, 10–14, 191–240, 285–322
Australia, in, 231–39
Britain, in, 197–211
Canada, in, 211–30
police, 193–95
prosecutions, 195–97
Reapplications, 336
Reasonable doubt, beyond, 7, 12, 38, 77–82, 92, 107, 111, 113–14, 115, 149, 154, 272, 283, 286, 289, 292, 300n, 307, 396, 413
Reference image databases, *NAS Report* scrutiny of, 375
*Reference Manual on Scientific Evidence*, 382

Rendell, Douglas Henry, case of, 276–77
*Report of the Inquiry into Pediatric Forensic Pathology in Ontario*, 6n, 34n, 91n, 212n, 286n, 363n, 385n, 390, 404n
Responses to miscarriages of justice, 4, 20–23, 322, 323–413
error correction and system reform, 20–21, 325–67
Criminal Cases Review Commission (CCRC), 20–21, 326–50. *See also* Criminal Cases Review Commission (CCRC)
establishment of, 326–31
practices of, review of, 347–50
referrals to courts from, reception of, 344–47
Scottish Criminal Cases Review Commission (SCCRC) vs., 347
factual innocence: North Carolina Innocence Inquiry Commission (NCIIC), 350–56
innocence projects, 21
investigative media and, 356–57
miscarriage of justice, prevention vs., 357–58
public inquiries, 21
Runciman Royal Commission on Criminal Justice, 201–2. *See also* Runciman Royal Commission on Criminal Justice
systemic reform
limits of corrections on, 358–61
models of, 361–66
forensic science reliability, improvements in, 21–22, 369–402
admissibility of expert evidence: judicial gatekeeping, 396–402
challenge of evidence by defence experts, 394–95
education and training, 380–84, 402
death investigations, 382–84
research and training, 381–82
scientific education, legal system's, 382
evidence-based and research-based forensic science, move to, 384–87, 400–1, 402
forensic practices, strengthening oversight of, 378–80
accreditation, 378
American Society of Crime Laboratory Directors (ASCLD), 378
DNA Advisory Board (DNAB), 378
International Organization for Standardization, 378
certification, individual, 380
funding vs. specific improvements, 380
proficiency testing, 379
standards and guidelines, 379
National Institute of Standards and Technology, 379
*NAS Report*, 371–78
uncertainty in evidence, ways to express, 395–96
unified vision to reform, 387–94
impartial vs. flawed forensic science: reforms to lessen gap, 22–23, 403–14
Criminal Cases Review Commission (CCRC)-type bodies, establishment of, 406–11
forensic science research and review developments, 403–4
judicial control over expert evidence, obtaining better, 411–12
standard of demonstrable reliability, imposing a new, 413
suspect forms of evidence, audit of cases of, 405–6
Rhetoric: legal proceedings, guiding principles of, 4–10, 25–187
criminal proceedings, fraud in, 9–11, 169–87
appeals, reopening of, 171–72
Australian to British cases, links from, 172–76, 187
civil and criminal cases, 170–71
due administration of justice, 176–77
inherent power, superior court's, 185–86
public law—criminal, 177–85
miscarriage of justice, law on, 55–168
Australia, in, 8–9, 133–68
Britain, in, 7, 55–90
Canada, in, 7–8, 91–132
prosecutors and expert witnesses, 5–7, 27–54

Australia, in, 28, 29, 30, 33–35, 37, 43, 50, 51, 53
Britain, in, 28, 29, 30, 32, 33–35, 37, 44, 50, 53
Canada, in, 47–52, 53
codes of conduct, 50–52
expert witnesses, 32–47
international collaboration, 53
prosecutions, 29–32
UK Law Commission reforms, 47
Rhetoric vs. reality: improving flawed forensic science practices, 403–14
Royal Commission on the Donald Marshall Jr., Prosecution, 122, 124, 126, 196
Royal commissions, 13–14, 56, 146–47, 212, 255, 313, 358, 362n, 365n
miscarriage of justice, correction of
Australia, in, 146–47
Britain, in, 56, 62n, 64n
Canada, in, 91n, 122, 124, 126
Royal pardon, 95, 343, 349
Royal prerogative of mercy, 115, 116, 118, 142, 145–46, 349
Runciman Royal Commission on Criminal Justice, 194, 201–2, 329–30, 331, 359, 366–67, 370, 396, 410, 411
recommendations of, 248–49, 391
disclosure, duty of full, 248–49
external audits, need for, 249
forensic science advisory council, creation of, 249, 391
systemic reform, 359–60
Runciman Report, 11n, 194n, 201n, 248, 249n, 330n, 331n, 359n, 360n, 384, 391n, 396n

Science, use of in investigations, 217–20
Scientific evidence, fraudulent, 245–46
Scottish Criminal Cases Review Commission (SCCRC), 7n, 347, 348, 353, 354, 355, 356
Criminal Cases Review Commission (CCRC) vs., 347, 348
Serology, misleading evidence, 258–59
Shaken baby syndrome, 22, 286, 289, 304, 322, 365, 393, 403–4, 405, 408
Smith, Dr. Charles, 19–20, 97, 114, 240, 251n, 285, 294n, 297, 303–13, 370, 390, 395, 406
errors by, summary of, 309–10
Goudge Inquiry, 19, 20, 22, 34–35, 47, 48, 49, 128–29, 240, 294n, 297, 303, 304, 305, 306, 308, 309, 310, 363, 364, 369–71, 385, 388, 391–93, 392, 395, 397, 400, 401, 404, 406, 411, 413
"think dirty" approach of, 251n, 309, 310, 312
work of
"fall, a, no possibility of": Amber, case of, 304–5
"non-accidental injuries, 99 percent certain of": Nicholas, case of, 305
"rape and murder": Valin, case of, 307–10
"sexual assault": Jenna, case of, 306
"stabbing": Sharon, case of, 306–7
Sophonow, Thomas, case of, 16, 106–7, 130, 217–20, 220, 226, 365, 400
Sophonow Inquiry, 4n, 13, 91n, 130, 212n, 218, 219–20, 222, 225, 227, 365, 407
Splatt, Edward, case of, 13, 16, 234–35, 240, 260–67, 272, 274, 275, 313, 387
Splatt Royal Commission, 21, 53, 146, 235, 242, 260n, 262–67, 362n, 365n, 390n
recommendations of, 266
Standards and guidelines, forensic science
American Society of Testing and Materials, 379
European Network of Forensic Science Institutes, 379
National Institute of Standards and Technology, 379
Statement of Reasons (SOR), 337, 341
Stay of proceedings, prosecutorial, 106, 109–10
Stereotyping, investigations, in, 195
Stomach contents, analysis of, 299–303, 313, 314–15, 316
*Strengthening Forensic Science in the United States: A Path Forward*, 241n, 371n, 372, 403n
Stuart, Rupert Maxwell, case of, 233
Sudden Infant Death Syndrome, 15, 250, 251, 403–4, 405, 406
Systemic reform
error correction commissions, effect of on, 358–61, 365, 367
models of, 361–66
Canadian public inquiries, 362–66. *See also* Public inquiries

Criminal Cases Review Commission (CCRC), 410–11. *See also* Criminal Cases Review Commission (CCRC)

Thin layer chromatography (TLC), 245, 247, 386
"Think dirty" approach, 251n, 309, 310, 312
Threshold reliability, 49, 129, 130, 131, 370, 397, 399, 402, 413
Time of death, assessment of, 297–303
Torture and assault, police, by, 202–5, 220
Treadaway, Derek, case of, 198n, 202, 203–5, 327n
Trial process, public confidence in, 161–63
Truscott, Steven, case of, 19, 20, 109, 113, 114, 119, 122, 123, 127, 129, 148n, 299–303, 313, 401
Tunnel vision, 11, 13, 192, 194, 197, 212–17, 218, 221–24, 240, 242, 278–80, 348, 363
Twitchell, Keith, case of, 12n, 202–3, 327n

UK Law Commission reforms, expert witnesses and, 47
Unconscious bias, 242, 263
UTS Innocence Project, 356n

Van Beelen, Fritz, case of, 19, 20, 313–17
Voluntariness rule, 94

Ward, Judith (M62 bombings), case of, 11, 15n, 45, 196n, 200, 246–48, 291–92, 387
West Midland Serious Crime Squad, 12, 64, 65n, 191, 202, 206
Wickens, Trevor, case of, 84n, 86–87, 297–99
Witness credibility, 11, 73, 79, 80–81, 85, 87, 88, 89, 104, 124, 160, 161, 162, 173, 175, 178, 180, 182, 197, 224–27
Witnesses, expert. *See* Expert witnesses
Witnesses, pressuring of by police, 227–30
Writ of appeal, 95
Writ of error, 57, 95

# About the Authors

**Bibi Sangha** completed her law degree at Middlesex University and her masters degree at the London School of Economics. She is a senior lecturer in law at Flinders University, South Australia and previously taught at the Australian National University. She was called to the Bar at Lincoln's Inn, London and admitted to practice as a barrister in Malaysia and at the High Court of Australia. She is a joint developer of the Networked Knowledge program.

**Kent Roach** is a Professor of Law at the University of Toronto where he holds the Prichard-Wilson Chair in Law and Public Policy. He is a member of the Ontario Bar and a Fellow of the Royal Society of Canada. He served as Director of Research for the Goudge Inquiry on Forensic Pediatric Pathology. His books include *The Unique Challenges of Terrorism Prosecutions* (vol. 4 of Research Studies for the Air India Inquiry) (2010), *Criminal Law* (4th ed., 2009), *September 11: Consequences for Canada* (2003), *The Supreme Court on Trial* (2001), and *Due Process and Victims' Rights* (1999).

**Robert Moles** completed his law degree at Queen's University, Belfast and his Ph.D. at Edinburgh University. He has held academic appointments in law at Queen's University Belfast, the Australian National University, and Adelaide University. He is joint developer of the Networked Knowledge program. His previous books are: *Definition and Rule in Legal Theory* (1987); *Law and Economics* (ed.) (1988); *A State of Injustice* (2004); *Losing Their Grip — The Case of Henry Keogh* (2006).

FSC
www.fsc.org
MIX
Papier | Fördert gute Waldnutzung
FSC® C083411

Kolibri 360 GmbH
Ferdinand-Jühlke-Straße 7
99095 Erfurt, Deutschland
produktsicherheit@kolibri360.de